Juana of Castile

Juana of Castile

History and Myth of the Mad Queen

Edited by

María A. Gómez
Santiago Juan-Navarro,
and Phyllis Zatlin

Lewisburg
Bucknell University Press

Associated University Presses
2010 Eastpark Boulevard
Cranbury, NJ 08512

The paper used in this publication meets the requirements of the American National Standard for Permanence of Paper for Printed Library Materials Z39.48-1984.

Library of Congress Cataloging-in-Publication Data

Juana of Castile : history and myth of the mad queen / edited by María A. Gómez, Santiago Juan-Navarro and Phyllis Zatlin.
    p. cm.
    Includes bibliographical references and index.
    ISBN 978-0-8387-5704-8 (alk. paper)
    1. Spanish literature—History and criticism. 2. Juana, la Loca, Queen of Castile, 1479–1555—In literature. I. Gómez, María A., 1964– II. Juan-Navarro, Santiago, 1960– III. Zatlin, Phyllis, 1938–
    PG6049.J83J84   2008
    860.9′351—dc22

                                                        2007047133

Contents

Acknowledgments   7

Introduction: Juana of Castile: From Romanticism to the
    Twenty-First Century   9
    MARÍA ASUNCIÓN GÓMEZ, SANTIAGO JUAN-NAVARRO,
    AND PHYLLIS ZATLIN

Part I: The Historical Context

Queen Juana: Legend and History   33
    BETHANY ARAM

Juana I of Castile, Catherine of Aragon, and the Failure of
    Feminine Power in the Construction of Empire   47
    ELENA GASCÓN VERA

Part II: Juana of Castile in Spanish Literature

Necrophilia, Madness, and Degeneration in Manuel Tamayo
    y Baus's *La locura de amor* (1855)   61
    DAVID R. GEORGE, JR.

The Historical Truth and Aesthetic Truth of *Santa Juana de
    Castilla* by Benito Pérez Galdós   77
    JOSÉ LUIS MORA GARCÍA

Ramón Gómez de la Serna's Superhistory: An Original
    Approach to the Life of Juana of Castile   92
    MERCEDES TASENDE

Juana the Mad as a Prototype of Federico García Lorca's
    Andalusian Martyr Complex   107
    SALVATORE POETA

Juana of Castile, Reader of Desiderius Erasmus of Rotterdam:
    An Interpretation of Manuel Martínez Mediero's *Juana
    del amor hermoso*   119
    VILMA NAVARRO-DANIELS

Part III: Foreign Representations of the Mad Queen

The Spectacle of the Other: Madness in *Falsa crónica de Juana
    la Loca*   133
BECKY BOLING

Is There a Method to Her Madness?: The Representation of
    Juana of Castile in French Literature   144
TARA FOSTER

Jeanne de Castille at Center Stage: The Spanish Queen in
    Recent French Theater   158
PHYLLIS ZATLIN

Part IV: Juana of Castile in Opera and the Visual Arts

Madness as Nationalistic Spectacle: Juana and the Myths of
    Nineteenth-Century Historical Painting   175
MARÍA ELENA SOLIÑO

Juana la coloratura   198
JAN REINHART

Political Madness: Juan de Orduña's *Locura de amor* as a
    National Allegory   210
SANTIAGO JUAN-NAVARRO

Woman, Nation, and Desire in Juan de Orduña's *Locura de
    Amor* and Vicente Aranda's *Juana la Loca*   228
MARÍA ASUNCIÓN GÓMEZ

Appendix I: Portraits and Paintings   243
PEDRO LÓPEZ GÓMEZ

Appendix II: Juana as a Palimpsest   252

Contributors   256

Index   261

Acknowledgments

THE EDITORS OF THIS ANTHOLOGY WOULD LIKE TO EXPRESS APPRECIA-
tion to the many people in the United States, Spain, and France who
helped in the course of this project from its initial concept to its
fruition. The list, which by no means is limited to those whose essays
or translations appear in this volume, is too long to cite all individuals by name. It includes scholars, who shared insights with us on our
subject or responded to questions about their research; creative writers, who clarified the genesis of their work; university colleagues, who
helped us identify scholars to undertake new studies; and staff at cultural agencies, who assisted us in contacting writers with our questions or in arranging for the use of illustrations in the published
book. Most of all, we would like to thank all contributors for their
involvement in this undertaking and the wonderful exchange of
ideas it produced. Several of the articles in this volume reflect extensive interactions between the editors and the authors over the last two
years. The drive for intellectual excellence of our authors and their
patience with the editorial process underpin this volume's success.

We would like to thank our publishers at Bucknell University and
the Associated University Presses and their staffs for their accessibil-
ity and professionalism in making this book a reality. Their sugges-
tions as well as those of the outside readers enhanced the integrity of
the final project.

Special words of gratitude are due those who provided financial
assistance in the realization of this volume. The editors especially
thank Pedro López Gómez for his generosity in financing the reproduction of several of the paintings.

María Elena Soliño acknowledges with thanks the University of
Houston Small Grants program for financing research trips to the
Biblioteca Nacional in Madrid as well as the cost of reproducing
Pradilla's images of Queen Juana.

Phyllis Zatlin expresses her appreciation to the Office of the Dean
of the School of Arts and Sciences (formerly the Faculty of Arts and
Sciences) at Rutgers, The State University for research grants that

partially supported the translation of essays and the graphics for the cover.

We gratefully acknowledge permission from the following museums for allowing us to reproduce their paintings: Museo del Prado (Madrid), Kunstorisches Museum (Vienna), and Museum voor Oude Kunst (Brussels).

Our thanks also to the editors of *Hispania* for permission to publish an English version of Santiago Juan-Navarro's essay that originally appeared in Vol. 88 No. 1 ("La Patria enajenada: *Locura de Amor,* de Juan de Orduña, como alegoría nacional").

Introduction: Juana of Castile: From Romanticism to the Twenty-First Century

María Asunción Gómez, Santiago Juan-Navarro, and Phyllis Zatlin

JUANA OF CASTILE (1479–1555), KNOWN POPULARLY AS JUANA LA LOCA (Juana the Mad), is one of the most fascinating figures of Renaissance Spain and continues to occupy a realm half way between history and myth. Although Juana was the third offspring of the Catholic Monarchs Isabella and Ferdinand, the deaths of all those relatives who preceded her in line for the throne changed her destiny, making her the heir to a vast empire. However, what could have been a glorious political future was thwarted when she was declared unfit to govern. Her husband, the Archduke Philip of Flanders, otherwise known as Philip the Handsome, her father, and even her son, Emperor Charles V, managed to manipulate Juana and keep her captive from 1509 to 1555 in the castle of Tordesillas, where she endured almost a half-century of loneliness and well-documented physical and psychological abuse. She was a queen who never reigned, but if she had, the history of Spain might have been completely different.

Most modern historians and biographers, such as Ludwig Pfandl, Michael Prawdin, Townsend Miller, and Manuel Fernández Álvarez, present Juana as a woman who was involved in a passionate but self-destructive relationship with her husband. Consumed by jealousy for him at first, and later devastated by his untimely death, she has often been depicted as a feeble-minded woman who soon sank into a mental state that some call melancholia, and others, folly, depression, madness, or schizophrenia. Other more recent studies, especially that of Bethany Aram in *Juana the Mad* (2005), portray a more complex character, victim of a series of court intrigues and betrayals at both the personal and political levels, and not as weak and mentally unstable as other historians have depicted her.

Who was Juana of Castile? What was at stake in her legendary madness? How is it possible that she was forced to endure such a long confinement while holding the titles of queen of Castile and Leon,

9

Aragon, Naples, and Sicily? Who was this person who could have had everything, yet spent most of her life abandoned and neglected, only to die forgotten and alone? After dozens of historical essays, biographies (many of them fictional), and even postmortem clinical analysis, Queen Juana of Castile continues to be an enigmatic figure. Poets and playwrights, novelists and filmmakers have contributed to the creation of a versatile fictional persona, whose ambiguity further obscures (and enriches) the already unfathomable historical character.

Although the dynamic exchange between history and literature is common in the fictionalization of any historical personality or event, the case of Juana is especially remarkable. Instead of fiction mirroring history, here historiography seems to have mirrored fiction. Indeed, many of the supposedly objective historical and psychiatric studies of Juana have proven to be prejudiced by the traditional representation of her in literature and the visual arts, in particular, the popular, romanticized version of a queen whose jealousy drove her mad. This nineteenth-century portrayal of Juana influenced not only later fictional representations of her, but also historical studies.

In the nineteenth century, Queen Juana was rescued from oblivion by Romantic painters and historians. In the twentieth century, she served as a source of inspiration for dozens of fictional works—novels, plays, operas, elegies, and movies—not only in Spain, but also in other European countries and in the Americas. One would think that this theme would have exhausted itself, and yet today its relevance remains unquestionable. *Juana la Loca* (2001), a major film by the well-known Spanish director Vicente Aranda, once again introduced this historical figure to a mass audience. Its triumph at the box office was comparable to that of the enormously successful play *La locura de amor* [The Madness of Love] by Manuel Tamayo y Baus (1829–98) in the nineteenth century, as well as Juan de Orduña's film of that same title produced in the mid-twentieth century. Juana also emerged as the protagonist of an opera, written in 1979 by Gian-Carlo Menotti for soprano Beverly Sills, which has been performed in Europe and the United States. And she continues to fascinate writers and artists on both sides of the Atlantic, as witnessed by the 2004 best-seller *El pergamino de la seducción* [The Parchment of Seduction] by Nicaraguan poet and novelist Gioconda Belli, and by the French plays of Emmanuel Roblès (1984) and Christine Wystup (2003).

THE ENIGMA OF JUANA OF CASTILE (1479–1555)

Before entering into an analysis of the fictional works created around Juana of Castile, it is necessary to explore, however briefly, the historical context that gives rise to the protagonist. In her short biographical account on Juana, included in *Pasiones* [*Passions*] (1999), Spanish writer Rosa Montero summarizes thus the spirit of that epoch: "Europe was living through turbulent times, at once marvelous and terrifying. Grand epic adventures coexisted with the most complex of palace intrigues, dreamers commingled with assassins; superstition thrived despite the scientific momentum of the Renaissance. These were the years of Copernicus, Leonardo da Vinci, Luis Vives and Erasmus of Rotterdam; but it was also the age of the Inquisition and the Borgias" (47–48). On the Iberian Peninsula, the Catholic Monarchs struggled to unify the various kingdoms that would eventually form Spain. Their reign was marked by events that would change the course of human history: the "discovery" of America, the expulsion of the Jews from the peninsula, the establishment of the Tribunal of the Holy Inquisition in Castile and Aragon, and the publication of the first grammar of the Spanish language.

When Juana was born on November 6, 1479, she was third in the line of succession and at that time no one would have thought that she could inherit her parents' kingdoms. She was educated nonetheless with great care in the hope that one day she would become queen in a foreign country, where she could help to promote the Catholic Monarchs' political interests. It is well known that Queen Isabella possessed a stupendous library as well as an extensive collection of art works. She also brought renowned Italian humanists to court and sponsored a musical chapel. Juana had received a well-rounded education by the time she was sent to the Flemish court to marry Philip of Habsburg at the age of sixteen. She could speak and write Latin fluently, knew French, played a number of musical instruments, and danced well.

The Catholic Monarchs arranged a series of strategic marriages between their five offspring and the reigning nobility of the most powerful European countries in order to establish or maintain political alliances. One such arrangement was twofold: Prince Juan would marry Margaret of Austria, daughter of the Holy Roman Emperor Maximilian I; Juana, in turn, would marry Margaret's brother, the Archduke Philip the Handsome. The latter was not only heir to the Hapsburg throne but had been granted control over the Low Countries through his mother, Mary of Burgundy. Ferdinand and Isabella's other offspring were betrothed under similar political considerations: Isabella was engaged to Alfonso of Portugal, and upon his death, to Manuel "the Fortunate." When Isabella died, her sister María of Aragon was then married to Manuel and their youngest daughter Catalina was married to Arthur, the Prince of Wales in of England. (Later she married Henry VIII.)

In mid-August 1496, Princess Juana left Spain for Flanders, where she expected to spend the rest of her life. But a series of tragic deaths altered her fate. On October 4, 1497, Prince Juan died—of unrequited love, according to legend—and his first son was stillborn. A year later Princess Isabel, the firstborn child of the Catholic Monarchs and now married to the king of Portugal, died giving birth to a child that would live only until the age of two. These four sudden deaths seriously threatened the matrimonial politics of the Catholic Monarchs, and transformed Juana into the legitimate heir to the thrones of Castile and Aragon. But these changes in the line of succession were complicated by Juana's alleged unreliability. By 1498, the Catholic Monarchs had already sent to Brussels a secret emissary, the Dominican friar Thomas of Matienzo, to inquire about Juana's supposedly erratic and scandalous behavior. When Juana returned to Spain in 1502 to swear an oath as heir to the throne, there was a serious incident that caused the Catholic Monarchs to confirm their fears. Phillip returned at the end of the year to Flanders and Juana tried to accompany him. However, her parents wished for her to remain in Spain under the pretext that she was seven months pregnant. After the birth of her son Fernando, Juana decided to return to her husband's side. Queen Isabella attempted to stop her, causing her to fall into a deep state of depression. While at the castle at La Mota near Medina del Campo, Juana ordered a return voyage, but nobody obeyed her. She then attempted to leave on her own. The guards prohibited her from escaping on foot, but she refused to return to her lodgings and spent a cold November night in 1503 in the open air. Queen Isabella traveled from Segovia, where she had been convalescing, to convince her daughter to stay. Juana's encounter with her mother was far from peaceful. The queen explains that Juana "spoke to me with such severity and disrespect, so removed from how a daughter should speak to her mother, that had I not seen the disposition in which she found herself, I would not have tolerated her words" (Fernández Álvarez 2000, 87). Although there is a clear ambiguity in the words "the disposition in which she found herself," most historians have interpreted them as a clear realization on Queen Isabella's part of her daughter's demented state, probably inherited from her maternal grandmother who had been considered insane and was confined to the castle at Arévalo for over four decades.

In the following years, Philip decided to spread rumors of Juana's spiritual and mental tribulations, and to promote her insanity: refusal to confess or to receive Holy Communion, poor personal hygiene, mistreating servants, and hatred of other women. When Queen

Isabella died on November 26, 1504, she left a special clause in her final testament in which she stated that should her daughter "be unable or unwilling to govern," then King Ferdinand would do so until Juana's son Charles reached a sufficient age to assume the throne. At first Ferdinand assumed the government of Castile, but the noble classes resented Ferdinand's authoritarianism and opted to support Juana and Philip. They arrived in Spain in 1506 and both Juana and Felipe were sworn in as monarchs of Castile in the Valladolid Cortes.

By this time, Juana had proved herself incapable or unable to defend her own interests. Philip had managed to obtain legal authority to govern Castile, but he barely had time to do so. He died in Burgos on September 25, 1506. Suddenly, with her husband Philip dead and her father Ferdinand in Naples, Juana was handed the opportunity to govern with total legitimacy, but she succumbed to pressure and finally adopted the role of obedient daughter, giving her father all powers. Juana's actions following Philip's death led to beginnings of the legend of her madness. Philip had expressed a desire to be buried at the Royal Chapel in Granada. On December 20, 1506, Juana traveled to the Convent at Miraflores where the body had been interred, ordered the coffin opened, forced some noblemen to identify the rotting corpse, and then began the long trip to Granada in the company of her dead husband. According to eye-witness accounts, the coffin was transported through the night in a carriage led by four horses, accompanied by priests, soldiers, and the entire royal entourage who, as they passed the towns of Castile by torchlight, must have seemed a surreal apparition.

When Ferdinand returned from Naples in August 1507, he was concerned that the nobility that had rejected him and that now accepted him only as the lesser of two evils, would soon withdraw their support. This fear led him to order the confinement of his daughter in the palace at Tordesillas. He placed her under the surveillance of Luis Ferrer, who acted more as a jailor than as a guardian. Nothing that occurred within the palace walls could be known publicly and no one would be allowed access to the queen. Mosén Ferrer complied meticulously with this order, and with Juana locked away, Ferdinand was able to wield complete authority over the Spanish state until his death in 1516.

It is important to keep in mind that Juana was not only queen of Castile, but that upon her father's death she was heir to the throne of Aragon. However, after her father's death, Cardinal Cisneros, who understood that the best thing for Spain was to bring Juana's first-born son Charles to Spain to govern the country, assumed the powers of the regency. Charles arrived in Spain in 1517 with the intention of becoming and acting as king of Castile and Aragon. Although this was technically impossible while the actual queen was alive, he ordered the continuation of his mother's imprisonment at Tordesillas, and placed her under the control of an even more tyrannical jailor, the Marquis of Denia.

On various occasions during the nearly five decades that Juana remained in that place, the town was quarantined due to outbreaks of the plague. The Marquis of Denia wrote to Charles V requesting permission to evacuate the palace, but the emperor refused to allow his mother to leave Tordesillas. Although her life was in grave danger, he was determined to prevent by any means necessary that his mother be seen in public. It is important to note that Charles V spent long periods of time abroad, and that the Comunero uprising of 1520–21 used the figure of the legitimate queen as a symbol of their rebellion against his rule. If the general populace were to have seen Juana traveling through the kingdom, it could have reignited anti-imperialist sentiment and gravely threatened his authority. Padilla and the other rebel leaders had traveled to Tordesillas to place themselves at the service of the forty-one-year-old queen. Though Juana gave her verbal support to the rebels, she refused to sign any documents to that effect, remaining loyal to her son. This lack of a legitimate political backing for their uprising resulted in the failure of the revolutionary movement led by the *Comunidades* of Castile against the centralizing, authoritarian rule of the Emperor Charles V.

Juana lived for forty-seven years locked away in interior chambers without access to natural light. Her jailors were permitted to "give her the strap," which meant perhaps the authority to tie her up or to whip and torture her, and to "use force." The queen died in 1555, paralyzed from the waist down, her legs covered in ulcers and tormented by the agony of gangrene. Juana's physical fortitude, which prolonged her suffering over so many years, could be considered one of the many betrayals that she endured.

BETWEEN FORGOTTEN HISTORY
AND MYTHICAL VINDICATION

Juana I of Castile, queen for over fifty years and mother of six children, all of them monarchs in their own right, was terribly mistreated during her lifetime. Was justice done to her memory after death? All evidence would suggest that, historically speaking, it was not; nonetheless, she has continued to survive through art and literature. Normally artists use history as a source of inspiration. What makes this case so interesting is that artistic representations of Juana seem to have determined the historical approach taken by the majority of scholars, which led to the firmly established myth that Juana was driven mad by jealousy and the death of Philip the Handsome. Starting in the nineteenth century, literary and visual artists have recreated the image of Juana based on what was then considered an historical fact: she had been driven mad by love.

Of all the literary works of art written around this theme, none was better known than Manuel Tamayo y Baus's *Locura de amor* [Madness of Love]. The play premiered in 1855 to great acclaim and soon gained an international audience, having been translated into many languages and produced throughout Europe. This drama in five acts offers a histrionic, melodramatic vision of Juana typical of the decadent, formulaic Romanticism that was already in its waning stages during the mid-1800s. The action begins in the town of Tudela de Duero as Juana is consumed by jealousy; it ends in the city of Burgos with the unexpected death of Philip, which drives Juana over the edge into complete insanity. In the memorable closing scene, the queen proclaims that her husband is not dead, but only sleeping. In this way, Tamayo y Baus accepts and reinforces the myth of insanity that King Ferdinand had used to usurp the throne that his daughter inherited from her mother, Queen Isabella. But perhaps the greatest triumph of Tamayo y Baus's play is the fabrication of a complex web of jealousy and unrequited love: Captain Álvar is secretly in love with Queen Juana; Juana cannot bear living without the Archduke Philip; Philip is in love with the Moor Aldara; and Aldara lusts after Captain Álvar. They are not able to satisfy their desires; all of them suffer greatly and are consumed by jealousy. The reactionary nationalism of the work is clearly expressed in the characterization of the Flemish nobles, who appear manipulative and underhanded, whereas Captain Álvar and the character of the Admiral safeguard the patriotic ideals of the nation. The romance and melodrama of the plot, however, predominate over the political message, and it is undoubtedly the sentimentalism of the play that led to its international success.

The Romantic painters and visual artists of the era recreated the image of Juana based on the legendary figure evoked by Tamayo y Baus. It is easy to see how the story, presented as it was in *Locura de amor*, lent itself to the romantic inclinations of artists who were interested in recreating the historical past in mythical terms. There are dozens of paintings that represent some aspect of Juana's madness. Among these it is worthy to note *Demencia de doña Juana* [Madness of Doña Juana] by Lorenzo Vallés (1830–1910) winner of second prize in the National Exhibition of 1868; or the painting *Juana la Loca frente al cadáver de Felipe el Hermoso* [Juana the Mad before the corpse of Philip the Handsome] by Francisco Pradilla (1848–1921), which would win the gold medal in the same exhibition ten years later. Pradilla's painting captures a moment in which the queen's entourage stops to rest during its macabre journey from Burgos to Granada, where they are headed to bury the dead archduke of Austria. In time, Pradilla's painting would become the most widely known iconographic representation of Juana, and would take its place in the collective national imagination. The success of this painting led its author to portray the mad queen on other occasions, for example, together with her daughters and ladies-in-waiting during her internment in the castle at Tordesillas. Juana was in many ways the ideal representation for the contradictions of the romantic spirit. Juana's personal tragedy, her lack of freedom, and the stifling of her feelings, were placed against the backdrop of political instability and conflicting interests. Juana I of Castile stands at the threshold of modern Spain, occupying the turning point between the nationalistic project of the Catholic Monarchs and the imperialist vision of Charles V.

The series of historical novels known as *National Episodes* written by Benito Pérez Galdós (1845–1920) constitutes what amounts to an historical textbook for generations of Spaniards. However, in *Santa Juana de Castilla* [Saint Juana of Castile] (1918), written near the end of his life, Galdós strays from historical reality, imagining a beatific queen who shortly before her death visits the poor inhabitants of a village near Tordesillas. Above all, *Santa Juana* is a social drama that comments on the collective tragedy of Spaniards. Whereas Tamayo y Baus's Juana centered almost exclusively on the queen's possessive love, Galdós emphasizes an altruistic love that manifests itself in her concern for the dispossessed. In contrast to Tamayo y Baus's play, which deals only with the turbulent end of the relationship between Juana and Philip, Galdós reveals a woman who is resigned to her fate after nearly fifty years of confinement at Tordesillas. The villains in Galdós's play are not the Flemish conspirators, but rather the Spanish nobility, like the Marquis of Denia, who subject the queen to all type of humiliations. Although Tamayo y Baus's text had referred to Juana as an "angel," Galdós sanctifies her on the basis of her heretical insanity: his Juana refuses to conform to traditional Catholicism and finds common ground with the humanistic principles of Erasmus. Galdós had witnessed first hand the Revolution of 1868 and always believed in the possibility of national reconciliation; he felt that he could contribute to a new vision for the future by establishing a dialogue with the past.

The collective nature of this national tragedy as embodied by the alleged madness of Juana is revisited by José Martín Recuerda (1926) in *El engañao* [The Deceived], a drama written in 1976 and produced in 1981. The myth of the "two Spains" is recovered in Recuerda's play, in which Juana symbolizes the dispossessed and those who love liberty but who suffer persecution and imprisonment for their beliefs. As do the other playwrights mentioned in this book, Recuerda bases his play on apocryphal events that serve the ideas he wishes to advance in his text. In this manner, he imagines a physically grotesque Juana who is nevertheless noble of spirit; she escapes from Tordesillas and travels to Granada where she becomes identified with the charitable work of San Juan de Dios. As in the case of Galdós, Recuerda's intention is to demystify official history, in particular the myth of the spiritual greatness of Imperial Spain. There is no historical evidence to suggest any contact between Juana and Juan de Dios, but, as Martha Halsey has conjectured, if Juana did sympathize with the Comunero rebels, she could very well have sympathized with the outcasts to whom Juan de Dios offered assistance, personifying in this way precisely the Christian values that Galdós promoted in her name in *Santa Juana de Castilla* (1978–79, 54).

The Comunero Revolt against the rule of Charles V and his Flemish advisors has always been an attractive subject for historical plays. The relationship between Juana and the uprising led by the *Comunidades* of Castile is the focus of the play *Los Comuneros* (1974) by Ana Diosdado (1938). This expressionistic play offers a powerful portrait of Queen Juana. When the rebels break into the castle at Tordesillas, they encounter a laughing, disheveled Juana who has already suffered a decade of imprisonment and mistreatment. In her mind the present and the past become confused. Her memories of Flanders, in stark contrast to those of Spain, repeat almost verbatim the words of the German biographer Ludwig Pfandl: "In Flanders there is no thyme or rosemary. No lavender or bayberry or cypress. But it is filled with oak groves, and there are huge woods of poplars, pines, and beech trees" (Diosdado 65). "For them [the Spaniards] it was the land where there was not rosemary or lavender or thyme; yews, bayberry, and cypress did not grow there. . . . They were also astonished . . . at the woods of oaks, pines, elms, poplars, and beech trees." (Pfandl, 1945, 45).

The use of such a conservative and old-fashioned historian as Pfandl should be understood in the framework of the strategies of textual appropriation practiced by contemporary theater. Pfandl was one of those who promulgated the myth of Juana as a woman "of limited intelligence" (1945, 60), who even before the death of Philip "had fallen for the rest of her days into a dull state of idiocy" (61). This is one of the images that many recent writers have contested from a revisionist perspective. Although the form in which Diosdado describes the queen evokes the writings of Pfandl, the manner in which she presents her personality is more in tune with the ideological position of playwright Manuel Martínez Mediero. Diosdado's Juana promotes love and despises war: "Should we not replace hatred with love?" she asks, adding that it would have been marvelous to have realized such a goal (1993, 59). She finds no reason for hating the French, considered archenemies by her mother. In this play, Juana promotes an openly pacifist attitude: "No one can claim justice and right when there is war" (60). In this final instance, Juana's madness reveals its quixotic nature, both in the words of one of the Comunero leaders and in her own idealistic declaration: "Do you know who is mad? Those who believe in something that seems impossible, those who are capable of seeing what the others do not" (66).

The image of an idealistic and reform-minded Juana forms the basis of José Martín Elizondo's one-act play *Juana creó la noche* (1998) [Juana Created the Night]. Martín Elizondo, who has lived in France since 1947, has written and directed theatrical works both in Spanish and in French. His plays are often built around historical, artistic, and literary motifs taken from Spanish culture. This text begins with an epitaph taken from the poem "Elegy for Juana the Mad" by Federico García Lorca (1898–1936): "In the lead coffin, inside your skeleton, / you will have a heart broken into a thousand pieces." In fact, it is a brokenhearted Juana who in this play recounts her ordeals (the absent king, the daughter who was taken away, the conspiracies that drove her mad, the execution of the Comunero rebels) to a so-called Unknown One who exists, perhaps, only in her imagination. The queen, withered and barefoot, spends her time writing poetry, and is accused by the Unknown One of purposely faking her insanity. Juana does not deny having created what is in essence her own dark night of madness. She confesses to it in one of her poems: "Juana, as if it were a game, created the night . . . And the heavens then said, 'what pleasure, to go on letting her speak, to have her talk to her shadow' " (1998, 15). Although this play stays much closer to the historical record than that of Martín Recuerda, Martín Elizondo's portrait still constitutes a lament for what could have been, had the queen not fallen victim to the political conflicts and palace intrigues of her day.

Although they pertain to different generations, both Martínez Mediero and Emmanuel Roblès (1914–95) make use of creative anachronisms, humor, and metatheatricality to vindicate the memory of Juana from an ideological point of view. In *Juana del amor her-*

moso [A Love so Beautiful] (1983), Martínez Mediero follows the trajectory of her life from adolescence to old age. The text emphasizes her victimhood in relation to the patriarchal political interests represented by her family, the church and the state. For Martínez Mediero, Juana represents love itself, as embodied both in her relationship to her husband and to the nation. In contrast to her parents, the Catholic Monarchs, Juana champions individual liberties, and is open politically and religiously to the new ideas put forth by Humanism. In the end, however, she is unable to join the Comunero rebellion, which hopes to restore her to the throne, because she does not wish to confront her son. The freedom she discovers resides inside herself and includes the acceptance of her madness: "I want to remain mad, Juan Padilla, forgive me. . . . To do everything you want to do . . . one has to kill and I don't know how to do that." (1995, 143). "When there are feelings in a story, then what happens is what has happened to me. . . . Everything, everything is materialism, and one is either materialistic or one is simply mad." (144).

Although Juana can easily be seen as the tragic heroine of a martyr play, *Juana del amor hermoso* has a marked humoristic streak that is evident both in the inclusion of deliberate anachronisms and in the caricaturistic portrayal of historical characters, such as the Catholic Monarchs and Cardinal Cisneros. Queen Isabella goes so far as to reappear from beyond the grave to express her displeasure at her husband Ferdinand's behavior, in particular his marriage to a French woman and his mistreatment of their daughter Juana. She also informs Juana of the wisdom she has gained in heaven where, she says, "in the afternoons now we're reading Erasmus's *The Praise of Folie*" (1995, 134). In spite of Isabella's religious fanaticism and rigid political vision, Martínez Mediero imagines a strong bond between mother and daughter. Juana remembers her mother with nostalgia (her ghost may very well be the projection of her desire to fill the void left by her absence) and invokes her name to no avail when Ferdinand decides to confine her to Tordesillas.

This suggestion of a tender mother-daughter relationship, as well as the demystification of Isabella, are nowhere to be found in Emmanuel Roblès's *Un Château en novembre* [A Castle in November] (1985). The protagonist of this play suffers from a generational conflict with her mother, whom she accuses of never having loved her. For Roblès's Juana, love is more important than politics or religion. The character's personality is decidedly modern. She renounces the culture and values of her parents in search of her own happiness. In the final scene, which functions as a sort of epilogue, Juana addresses the audience and says, "The truth is that I've lived in a dark century where love was enslaved. And I already belonged to your century, with today's women who assert themselves and live according to their hearts. What risks one runs when one is ahead of her time!" (344). If on the one hand Roblès's Juana is a self-absorbed character concerned with her own happiness, on the other hand, *Un Château en novembre* makes use of the Juana's tragic history as a vehicle for social and political protest. On a superficial level the play shares a similar structure with Tamayo y Baus's *Locura de amor,* but ideologically speaking, it is much closer to contemporary Spanish plays like Concha Romero's *Razón de estado* [Reason of state] (1991) in that it portrays Juana as the victim of a repressive political regime. Although the Juana that Roblès imagines does not create her own dark night as does Elizondo's protagonist, she continues to be seen as a martyr, pushed into the abyss of madness by the representatives of the patriarchy, satirized so explicitly by Mediero in *Juana del amor hermoso.*

Though it is true that Juana of Castile has inspired an abundant and prolific dramatic production, the same cannot be said of her impact on poetry. Other than the obscure book by May Earle titled *Juana of Castile* (1910), only a single poem on the subject by Federico García Lorca is known: "Elegy for Juana the Mad" (1918). García Lorca's elegy revives the stereotyped image of Juana that the Romantics before him had exploited, but he infuses it with his own vital poetic sensibility. One of the recurrent themes in García Lorca's work is the tension and anguish that result from love that is discouraged and repressed by society or by destiny, and that inevitably leads to death. García Lorca sees in the tragic figure of the mad queen a kindred spirit and an ideal instrument for expressing his own ill-fated vision of love. In fifteen stanzas the poet summarizes the sad destiny of a woman dragged into the abyss of madness by an unfaithful husband and an adverse destiny. Like the other great tragic heroines of Spanish literature mentioned in the poem—Isabel de Segura and Melibea—as well as the heroines fashioned in the creative imagination of the poet himself, Juana personifies unbound passion and fatalistic love.

In the field of narrative, Ramón Gómez de la Serna (1888–1963) offers a humorous counterpoint to Lorca's tragic vision. In fact his self-styled "superhistory" *Juana la Loca* (1944) can be interpreted as an attempt to recast the nineteenth-century myth of the mad queen in the absurdist spirit of the High Modernist aesthetic of the period. The object of Gómez de la Serna's analysis is not limited, however, to the historic figure in question, but also explores (and eventually parodies) the historical preconceptions that were used to approach Juana and other characters from the nation's past.

Sixty years later, in *El pergamino de la seducción* (2004), the Nicaraguan writer Gioconda Belli (1948) vindicates the memory of Juana by portraying her as a cultured, courageous, and modern woman who was ahead of her time. In this novel, a historian and a young woman who bears a striking resemblance to Queen Juana of Castile investigate the enigma of the character most commonly known as Juana the Mad. Had she gone insane in the manner portrayed by the history books, or had she been the victim of betrayals and power politics? Belli clearly opts for the latter interpretation in her novel, at once historical and contemporary, in which Juana returns to tell her own version of events.

The shadow cast by this extraordinary historical figure extends far beyond the confines of literature. Her presence has also been felt in the visual arts, as mentioned earlier, in the opera, in choreography, in film, and in popular culture. It is perhaps the cinematic art which has been most responsible for new approaches to the figure of Juana. *Locura de amor* (1948), directed by Juan de Orduña (1900–1974), was at the time one of the most financially successful pictures in the history of Spanish cinema. In addition to being a histrionic melodrama, Orduña's film emerged from the propagandistic movie industry of the time, during which Franco's dictatorship was attempting to project an image of itself as an "organic" democracy. At the beginning of the twenty-first century, Vicente Aranda (1926) reached large audiences with his movie *Juana la Loca* (2001). In contrast to the sanctimoniousness of Orduña's film, Aranda presents a woman who openly embraces her eroticism and challenges the norms of her day. It is nevertheless paradoxical that Aranda's film often repeats the most worn-out clichés of the Juana legend, and that its intertextual references continue to be derived from Tamayo y Baus's play and Orduña's film, against which the director is supposedly rebelling.

A detailed review of all the fictional work created around Juana of Castile would be tedious and practically interminable. What we have just presented is simply a preliminary approach to some of the modern representations of this unusual historical figure. Readers are directed to the appendix at the end of this volume ("Juana as a Palimpsest"), which includes a comprehensive list of fictional versions of the legend, as well as biographies and historical treatises on the period. The metaphor of the palimpsest could not be more appropriate when describing the intertextual phenomenon that is Juana of Castile. Just as in those manuscripts in which the old text is still visible beneath the new, the history of the Mad Queen continues to generate new recreations, new histories that maintain a constant dialogue with the enormous bibliography, and iconography that exists and continues to expand around her memory.

MAPPING THE REINVENTIONS OF A LEGEND

The fifteen chapters that make up *History and Myth of the Mad Queen* are grouped into four categories. The first part establishes the historical framework for understanding Juana of Castile, initially in light of the dynastic tradition of the time, and later in terms of gender relations and in comparison to other historical figures of her age. The second part studies the characterization of Juana in the work of representative Spanish authors. Works by Manuel Tamayo y Baus, Benito Pérez Galdós, Ramón Gómez de la Serna, Federico García Lorca, Manuel Martínez Mediero, Ana Diosdado, Concha Romero, and others are analyzed in this section. The third part is dedicated to characterizations of Juana outside the Iberian Peninsula, with special emphasis placed on literary production in France and Latin America, the two areas that have shown the most interest in revisiting this historical persona. The fourth and final part explores visual and musical appropriations of Juana of Castile. Painting, opera, and cinema are the three media chosen in order to examine modern representations of Juana that go beyond the strictly literary.

In "Queen Juana, Legend and History," Bethany Aram questions traditional views of Juana, which, although rooted in Romantic historiography, remain strong to this day. Aram's article explains how three nineteenth-century historians—G. A. Bergenroth, Louis Prosper Gachard, and Antonio Rodríguez Villa—uncovered the best-known documents and developed the dominant themes around the historical Juana of Castile. The queen's supposed "love madness," heresy and victimization remained central to her twentieth-century biographers, including Ludwig Pfandl, Michael Prawdin, and Manuel Fernández Álvarez. In addition to the debt incurred with their Romantic predecessors, these and other historians have clung to a positivist reading of the primary sources. In contrast, Aram's study attempts to differentiate between facts and representations. She argues that the standard chronicles and political correspondence regarding Juana should be questioned in light of their authors' political interests. New evidence about the queen's dynastic and pious commitments casts a fresh light on many of her actions and should lead more historians to reconsider the accepted historical record.

Drawing on recent studies of Renaissance politics, Elena Gascón Vera also provides the reader with an historical analysis, albeit from a gender perspective. In "Juana I of Castile, Catherine of Aragon, and the Failure of Feminine Power in the Construction of Empire," Gascón Vera analyzes the cultural and historical forces that prevented Juana and her sister Catalina from ascending to the thrones to which they were entitled, and for which they had been trained since childhood. As queen, wife, and mother, Isabella I of Castile wielded great power during her lifetime. Yet she could not prevent the abandonment and humiliation to which her daughters Juana and Catalina were subjected after her death by their husbands, Philip of Habsburg and Henry Tudor. Juana and Catalina, in the absence of their mother, became clear casualties of power in the new imperial project undertaken by their father, Ferdinand of Aragon. His endeavor was based upon the establishment of monarchical absolutism with its inherent patriarchal hegemony.

In "Necrophilia, Madness, and Degeneration in Manuel Tamayo y Baus's *La locura de amor* (1855)" David R. George seeks to understand the relevance of Juana for nineteenth-century audiences by reading Tamayo y Baus's drama against the backdrop of the theories of degeneration that had become increasingly influential in mid-nineteenth-century Europe. George focuses on the tension between the two seemingly contradictory impulses of necrophilia and necrophobia displayed in the final scene of Tamayo y Baus's play as metaphors through which to examine the ways in which Juana's madness spoke to the preoccupations of Spain's emergent bourgeoisie. The article traces the manifestation of these drives through the development of the plot in order to expose how nineteenth-century concerns with disease and social decay are projected onto the historical figure. The resulting nosology and pathology of Juana's mental condition align her story with conservative ideologies of the time that sought to expose the origins of social maladies, in order to stem what they considered to be an insidious cycle of change by memorializing the past and moralizing the present.

José Luis Mora García provides an in-depth analysis of *Santa Juana de Castilla*, a play written in 1918 by Benito Pérez Galdós (1843–1920), one of the most prolific and famous authors of Spanish Realism. The action in Galdós's play starts two days before the death of Queen Juana and reflects on the meaning of the confinement in Tordesillas: a purgatory where Juana paid for her heretical actions and for exercising her freedom of conscience. In contrast to her mother, Isabella the Catholic, Juana demonstrated a tolerant disposition that was apparent in three fundamental aspects of her character: her Erasmian loyalty, her identification with Castile and the Castilian people, and her social sense of property. Galdós presents us with what history could have been but was not, even though he continued to hope that tolerance would eventually prevail in Spain's future. Galdós asks us to transcend the negativity of traditional historiography and opt for a new, balanced interpretation born of common sense and orthodoxy.

Far from the grandiloquence and excess of the Romantic period and the objectivity and restraint of Galdós's Realism, avant-garde writer Ramón Gómez de la Serna (1888–1963) approaches this historical character from an expressionistic and parodic perspective. In "Ramón Gómez de la Serna's Superhistory: An Original Approach to the Life of Juana of Castile" Mercedes Tasende analyzes how Gómez de la Serna undermines historiographic notions of objectivity and impartiality in his *Doña Juana la Loca: Seis novelas superhistóricas* [Juana the Mad: Six Superhistorical Novels]. Drawing on Linda Hutcheon's *A Theory of Parody,* Margaret Rose's *Parody/Metafiction* and Gerard Genette's *Palimpsestes,* Tasende also explores the intertextual relationship between Gómez de la Serna's concept of "superhistory" and Miguel de Unamuno's (1864–1936) "*intrahistoria.*" Tasende argues that Gómez de la Serna's parody of "intrahistory" is done both by mimicking the premises underlying the concept created by Unamuno, and by using similar analogies to explain his own notion of history.

Federico García Lorca published "Elegy for Juana the Mad" a few years after Gómez de la Serna's novel. García Lorca's fascination with this historical figure is well documented and Juana makes sporadic appearances throughout his literary works. Salvatore Poeta's essay explores Juana as the prototype of the "Andalusian (not strictly Castilian) Martyr," whose continued presence becomes one of García Lorca's most prominent motifs throughout his more mature lyrical and dramatic works, starting with *Romancero gitano* [Gypsy Ballads] through *Yerma* and *Doña Rosita la soltera* [Doña Rosita, the Spinster], and ultimately leading to *La casa de Bernarda Alba* [The House of Bernarda Alba].

Vilma Navarro-Daniels's "Juana of Castile, Reader of Desiderius Erasmus of Rotterdam" interprets Manuel Martínez Mediero's *Juana del amor hermoso* as a modern Juana who subscribes to Humanism, and devotes herself to the reading of Desiderius Erasmus's *The Praise of Folly.* This Juana has her Catholicism permanently called into question, and is even accused by her own mother, Queen Isabella, of being Jewish, or of being possessed by the devil. Throughout the play, Juana insists on defending the joy of life, the playful aspects of human existence and the value of fantasy. Martínez Mediero's Juana incorporates Erasmus's words as well as his concept of utopia into her own worldview. Rather than being mad and heretical, Juana is portrayed as a follower of the Stultitia method of self-defense, whereby her madness is revealed as nothing more than a humanistic openness.

In "The Spectacle of the Other" Becky Boling examines the representation of power and national identity through the rewriting of the history of the mad queen by Mexican playwright Miguel Sabido. Staged in Mexico City in the mid-1980s, *Falsa crónica de Juana la Loca* [False Chronicle of Juana the Mad] is simultaneously a drama, poem, chronicle and antihistory. Through its various modes of theatrical representation, which include puppet theater tableaux, choral elements, Brechtian *geste*, and *danse macabre*, the play depicts the story of Juana and her politically motivated relegation to "madness" as a legacy for contemporary Mexican identity. Sabido combines elements of Spanish high art and Mexican popular art in his spectacle in order to dramatize the political and ideological reasons behind Juana's exclusion from the exercise of power and to explore their ideological consequences for Mexican identity. Her "madness" becomes a symbol for the dispossessed within Mexican culture itself in this gendered rereading of the historical period of conquest and colonization of the New World.

From the nineteenth century through the twenty-first, at least twelve texts have been written in French about Jeanne de Castille. Tara Foster's "Is There a Method to Her Madness? The Representation of Juana of Castile in French Literature" examines Juana of Castile in three French works. In her 1843 novel, *Jeanne de Castille,* Clémence Robert accepts the popular sobriquet, presenting her reader with a protagonist whose mental fragility adds to the pathos of her exotic, romantic character. However, the authors of two later texts, Jeanne Champion and Charles Samuel, paint a different picture. The heroine of *Ma fille Marie-Hélène Charles Quint* [My Daughter Marie-Hélène Charles the Fifth] (1974) and *Tordesillas, ou la reine morte* [Tordesillas or the Dead Queen] (1994) is a woman who is labeled as mad by her political enemies. Aware of her role as a pawn, the Juana of these two twentieth-century texts nonetheless resists her persecutors and, in the case of Samuel's *Tordesillas,* uses her reputed madness as a weapon. Foster's article seeks to trace the extent to which later French texts rehabilitate the so-called Mad Queen.

Phyllis Zatlin's "Jeanne de Castille at Center Stage" explores the plays of dramatists in France who have focused on Juana in the past quarter-century: Emmanuel Roblès's *Un Château en novembre* [A Chateau in November] (written 1984), José Martín Elizondo's *Jeanne créa la nuit* [Juana Created the Night] (staged 1995), Eduardo Manet's *Juana la Folle* [Juana the Mad] (forthcoming), and Christine

Wystup's *Jeanne de Castille, ou La Reine qui n'aimait pas Dieu* [Juana of Castile, or The Queen Who Did Not Love God] (2003). Like contemporary historians, these four playwrights tend to see Juana as a political prisoner, an unfortunate pawn held captive by the ambitions of her husband, Philip the Handsome, Archduke of Austria. In their view, the Spanish queen expresses the rebellion and suffering of oppressed minorities of all times and all parts of the world.

Links between nineteenth-century historical painting and Restoration social norms regarding gender form the territory explored by María Elena Soliño in "Madness as Nationalistic Spectacle: Juana and the Myths of Nineteenth-Century Historical Painting." The paintings analyzed here were originally shown at the National Exposition inaugurated by King Alfonso XII as part of the week-long celebration of his marriage to his beloved cousin María de las Mercedes. They represent Romantic depictions of a "mad queen" who publicly expressed blind devotion and obedience. Such representations filled a need to erase the images of unruly female sovereignty left behind by the ousted Isabel II, and to replace them with a visual landscape of female passivity and helplessness more in accordance with the values of the restoration of a Spanish monarchy still firmly rooted in traditional patterns. Historical paintings in general provided a formula for humanizing the sovereigns while evoking past glories and the myth of Spanish unity, and this particular depiction of the infirm queen provided a docile body on which to remap the history of a hegemonic Spain.

The darkly romantic legend of the mad queen of Castile has also provided an ideal subject for opera composers. It was set to music (though without notable success) by French and Spanish composers of the nineteenth century, by the late twentieth-century Italo-American composer Gian Carlo Menotti, and more recently, by two Northern European composers, all with an eye toward exploiting the tale for its possibilities as a vehicle for soprano voice. In his contribution "Juana la Coloratura," Jan Reinhart researches the operatic transpositions of the legend during the last two centuries.

The remaining two essays focus on two films loosely based on Tamayo y Baus's famous play: Juan de Orduña's *Locura de amor* [Madness of Love] (1948), and Vicente Aranda's *Juana la Loca* [Juana de Mad] (2002). In "Political Madness: Juan de Orduña's *Locura de amor* as a National Allegory," Santiago Juan-Navarro analyzes the political subtext underlying Orduña's film as a dramatization of the construction of the "New State" (the term used by Spanish dictator Francisco Franco to refer to the political system that emerged after the Spanish Civil War). The difficulties that Franco's regime encountered in formulating its own ideology led to searching the past, especially moments of crisis, for a mythology that would legitimize its nationalist "Crusade." Orduña's *Locura de amor* reflects the conflicts of a regime that tried to communicate an image of change abroad, while showing an autarchic pride in domestic politics. Produced simultaneously to the passage of the Law of Succession (1948), the film proposes a return to an authoritarian monarchy controlled by the military.

María Asunción Gómez's "Woman, Nation, and Desire" approaches Orduña's film from a gender perspective and compares it to another much more recent box office success, Vicente Aranda's *Juana la Loca*. Both Orduña and Aranda share an interest for violent passions and an unusual fascination with strong and assertive women, but their aesthetic and ideological approach could not be more different. Orduña turns Tamayo y Baus's *Locura de amor* into an allegorical film in which the heroine, virginal but desired, embodies the motherland, harassed and alienated by foreigners whose greed endangers the unity of Spain. Aranda, on the other hand, abandons politics and focuses on the personal obsessions that recur throughout all of his work: jealousy and madness, erotic desire and sexual addiction, pleasure and pain. In Aranda's film it is made clear that constructions of madness are inextricably related to constructions of female sexuality.

Two appendices are included. The first one shows several commented upon portraits and paintings from the fifteenth and the nineteenth centuries. The second is a list of works about Juana of Castile, including plays, novels, poems, operas, choreographies, paintings, films, biographies, and other historical studies.

Focusing on literary, pictorial, operatic, and screen representations of Queen Juana, *History and Myth of the Mad Queen* is the first interdisciplinary book that looks at both sides of the story—history and myth, fact and fiction—that shaped the enigmatic image of this much maligned Spanish queen. Even though the fictional reinvention of Juana of Castile has been the subject of sporadic articles, this is the first time that the reader has access to a book that takes an in-depth look at the full range of literary, pictorial, musical, and cinematic recreations of Queen Juana. Our aim has been to bring together works by authors from different countries (Spain, Mexico, Argentina, Dominican Republic, France) and to include a complete spectrum of literary genres (narrative, poetry, theater, essay) as well as opera and the visual arts (painting and film) in the analysis of this fascinating historical figure. Likewise the points of view included cover a broad array of theoretical approaches: from formal analysis to historiography, from narratology to feminism, from psychoanalysis to historicism. The variety among the articles compiled here affirms the interest this character continues to elicit. Furthermore the interdisciplinary scope of *The Mad Queen* makes this book a resource that should be of great interest not only to literary and film scholars, but to historians of Hispanic and European culture as well.

WORKS CITED

Aram, Bethany. 2005. *Juana the Mad: Sovereignty and Dynasty in Renaissance Europe*. Baltimore: Johns Hopkins University Press.

Diosdado, Ana. 1993. *Los comuneros*. Madrid: Preyson.

Fernández Álvarez, Manuel. 2000. *Juana la Loca: La cautiva de Tordesillas*. Madrid: Espasa Calpe.

Halsey, Martha. 1978–79. "*Juana La Loca* in Three Dramas of Tamayo y Baus, Galdós, and Martín Recuerda." *Modern Language Studies* 9, 1:47–57.

Martín Elizondo, José. 1998. *Juana creó la noche*. *Estreno* 23, 1:12–22.

Martínez Mediero, Manuel. 1995. *A Love Too Beautiful: The Story of Joanna of Castile*. Translated by Hazel Cazorla. University Park, PA: Estreno.

Montero, Rosa. 1999. *Pasiones*. Madrid: Aguilar.

Panfdl, Ludwig. 1945. *Juana "la Loca": Su vida, su tiempo, su culpa*. Translated by Felipe Villaverde. Madrid: Espasa Calpe.

Pérez Galdós, Benito. 1918. *Santa Juana de Castilla: tragicomedia en tres actos*. Madrid: Librería de los sucesores de Hernando.

Roblès, Emmanuel. 1985. *Un Château en novembre*. *Théâtre*. 249–347. Paris: Grasset.

Juana of Castile

I
The Historical Context

Queen Juana: Legend and History

Bethany Aram

FACTS AND FICTIONS ABOUT JUANA OF CASTILE (1479–1555) HAVE BEEN deeply intertwined since her own day. The daughter and successor of Queen Isabella of Castile and King Ferdinand of Aragon remains a problematic figure associated with conflicting interests. She belonged to the divergent courts of Castile and Burgundy, simultaneously representing the Trastámara family of her parents and Habsburg dynasty of her offspring. Living on the threshold from late medieval to early modern times, Queen Juana pertains to literature as well as history and emerges most clearly at the intersection of both disciplines. Rather than conforming to a single category, "Spanish" or "foreign," "pious" or "heretical," "mad" or "sane," Juana defies preconceived and anachronistic ideas.

While resisting classification, the proprietary queen who never ruled Castile or Aragon offers insights into the role of legend in Spanish history. Juana's image—as projected by others and the queen herself—responded to concrete, shifting political ends. This essay will consider the major authors of Juana's legend, including the queen herself, and their motivations. After examining sixteenth-century representations, it will analyze romantic and other agendas cast upon Juana since the late 1800s.

EARLY MODERN FACTS AND FICTION

Ambassadors at different European courts and chroniclers writing for her husband, father, and son penned the earliest literary representations of Juana I. Oftentimes they drew upon the rumors circulated and correspondence generated by the queen's relatives and servants—a tendentious type of primary source. Driven by diverse political aims, such accounts merit analysis in terms of their motivations. However unreliable, these images of Juana provide a point of departure for considering when and how the queen may have attempted to express herself.

33

At sixteen years of age Juana left the port of Laredo on the coast of Asturias and the lands of her parents to meet her fiancée, Philip of Burgundy, in the Low Countries. Juana's parents and the Holy Roman Emperor Maximilian of Austria had arranged a double alliance to bind Juana to Philip, Maximilian's son, and Juana's brother, Juan, to Philip's sister, Marguerite. No one imagined that Juana would inherit her parents' realms. Isabella and Ferdinand did, however, expect their second daughter to uphold their interests and to oppose those of the French monarch at the Burgundian court. Rather than providing Juana with a dowry, however, they agreed that Philip and his lands would support the bride. Such economic dependence, in practice, prevented Juana from countering Philip's Francophile advisors.

Concerned about Juana's inability to defend their position, Isabella and Ferdinand sent a number of ambassadors—most notably the subprior of Santa Cruz, Tomás de Matienzo, and the bishop of Córdoba (later Burgos), Juan Rodríguez de Fonseca—to reorient their daughter. The testimony of these ambassadors illuminates Juana's penury, vulnerability, and isolation in the Burgundian court. Although initially concerned about Juana's religiosity, Matienzo grew increasingly sensitive to her plight.[1] Fonseca, who had organized the fleet of 1496 and would oversee subsequent voyages to the Americas, helped Juana adopt postures more acceptable to her parents when she and Philip went to Spain in 1501–2.[2] By that point three successive deaths had made Juana the heiress apparent to the kingdoms of Castile and Aragon. The events of 1502–4 nevertheless convinced Queen Isabella that her daughter might not be able or willing to rule Castile. In either case Queen Isabella indicated that her husband, Ferdinand (and pointedly not Philip), should govern Castile until the majority of Juana's eldest son, Charles (later Charles V).[3]

All eyes turned to Juana following the death of her mother, Isabella, on November 26, 1504. Yet Juana failed to appear. The Venetian ambassador at the Burgundian court, Vicentio Quirini, solicited an audience with the queen for over five months before receiving a glimpse of her.[4] King Ferdinand reprimanded his own ambassador, Gutierre Gómez de Fuensalida, for conferring with Philip instead of Juana. Yet Fuensalida insisted that Juana cultivated her own solitude.[5] While mourning her mother, the queen may have shunned disloyal company in the Burgundian court, where Fuensalida's companion, Don Juan Manuel, and other servants favored Philip over Ferdinand as ruler of Castile. Their discourse, even when ostensibly about Juana, reflected a struggle between two kings.

From 1504 through 1506 Philip and his allies enforced Juana's silence in order to control Castile. While confiscating the queen's letters and keeping her confined, they laid the foundations of the legend of her great passion for Philip. The case of a missive purportedly from Juana to Philip's ambassador in Castile, Philibert de Veyre, demonstrates that Philip's partisans could dupe (or use) even Fuensalida, who declared himself loyal to Ferdinand. In the propaganda battle with Ferdinand, Philip's supporters drafted a declaration that Juana wanted her husband to rule her kingdoms, due to her "great love" for him. According to Fuensalida, who had reported frequent conflict between Juana and Philip, the queen objected to the word "love" and repeatedly edited the missive, although "in the end, she signed it that way" (Gómez de Fuensalida 1907, *Correspondencia,* 358–59). In contrast to what the ambassador reported, comparison of the signature on the letter to de Veyre with forty-four unedited documents signed by the queen suggests that the former was a falsification (Aram 1998, 331–58). Juana did not sign the letter to de Veyre. Indeed, she supported Ferdinand, rather than Philip, as ruler of Castile until her son, Charles, reached his majority.[6]

Like ambassadors, chroniclers could propagate rumors. A potential distance from events as they wrote and revised, moreover, enabled these early historians to begin elaborating legends. Pedro Mártir de Anglería, a humanist attached to the Castilian court who received certain favors from Philip,[7] declared Juana was "lost in love for her spouse" in letters allegedly written in 1501 but potentially retouched at a later date.[8] Following the death of Philip on September 25, 1506, Mártir de Anglería notes the exclusion of women from the entourage around the king's remains and speculated that Juana suffered from "the same jealousy that tormented her during her husband's life."[9] In fact, Juana simply complied with the rule of the Carthusian monks who prayed for Philip's soul by barring nonroyal women from their presence.[10]

An anonymous Burgundian chronicler of Philip and Juana's second voyage to Castile also highlighted the theme of Juana's postmortem devotion to her spouse. Drawing upon Renaissance views of the passions, the chronicler described Juana as visiting her husband's corpse every day and kissing its feet. According to this author, Philip's "government and governors" had pushed Juana's jealousy "to the point of love madness (la rage d'amours), an excessive and inextinguishable fury, so that in three years the Good Queen had no more profit or repose than a woman damned or deranged."[11] In this characterization, the queen's connubial passion rendered her incompetent.

Such accounts of Juana's eternal attachment to Philip, however degrading to the queen, advanced her main ends. Following the death of her husband, Juana clung to two political ambitions: (1) to avoid a second marriage, which could only complicate her situation and prejudice her children; and (2) to secure the inheritance of her offspring, particularly that of her eldest son in Castile. The queen's legendary devotion to Philip furthered both goals. While refusing to bury Philip's corpse before it reached Granada, where the remains of Queen Isabella lay, Juana managed to fend off eager suitors, including Henry VII of England. By honoring Philip's remains and staging elaborate exequies around them, the queen publicized her husband's status as a legitimate king of Castile. Queen Juana's presence in Castile alongside Philip's remains helped ensure the succession of their son, Charles, following the death of Juana's father on January 23, 1516 (Aram 2005, 97–101).

Beyond a political posture, incapacitating grief for a deceased spouse appeared socially and culturally acceptable in late medieval Castile. The noble poet, Gómez Manrique, and his wife, Juana de Mendoza numbered among the servants who had been attached to Queen Juana's parents. In a recent "search" for Juana de Mendoza, Ronald E. Surtz depicts her as a pious and discreet patron of letters and recipient of her husband's verses. Interestingly enough, Manrique's last will and testament named his spouse its executor unless overwhelming grief incapacitated her (Surtz 2004, 48–70).

Mourning entailed an obligation for royal and noble widows. Notwithstanding the assertions of male relatives and servants, it did not prevent the widows from pursuing their own policies. Hence Queen Juana, while supposedly lost in grief, issued an important document revoking her husband's grants and restoring the royal patrimony that he had alienated on December 18, 1506.[12]

Illness, like mourning, proved acceptable and even advantageous for royal women. As Magdalena S. Sánchez has shown, early modern elites used illness, particularly melancholy, as a political tool. According to Sánchez, maladies recorded in the correspondence of ambassadors and attendants enabled Philip III's female relatives, the Empress María and Queen Margaret of Austria, and even his "favorite," the Duke of Lerma, to assure contact with the monarch and to attract attention to their demands.[13] The "sick" or the "sad" may have fomented rumors (even legends, in the case of Queen Juana) about their conditions. Rather than objective fact or clinical observation, scholars encounter reports produced for strategic ends.

The governor that King Charles appointed for Juana's household, Bernardo de Rojas y Sandoval, Marquis of Denia, and the Count of

Lerma, informed Charles and has informed subsequent historians about Queen Juana's life after 1518. Denia's letters, however, were designed to remind Charles of his importance and the need to reward his family rather than to provide an impartial view of the queen. Further complicating matters, the Marquis of Denia actively assisted the king in creating a fictional world to confine and undermine Juana. By his own admission, the Marquis informed Juana that her father, Ferdinand, and the likewise deceased Emperor Maximilian survived, urging her to write them. In order to maintain Juana's isolation during an outbreak of plague, Charles instructed Denia to inform the queen that the pestilence had depopulated any principal cities and towns that she might wish to visit. To make the story more convincing, the emperor even advised the Marquis to stage mock funeral processions alongside Juana's palace several times each day (Aram 2005, 120–25).

The queen saw and heard another version of events in 1520 when the Comunero rebels against Habsburg rule temporarily freed her from Denia's control. The Comuneros, to Juana's dismay, proved just as self-interested as the Denias had been. They proclaimed Juana "sane" and capable of ruling until she refused to support their program. At that point they set about "curing" the queen. Their tactics became increasingly desperate. When surrounded by troops loyal to Charles, the rebels informed Juana that the emperor would burn Tordesillas and send her to the fortress of Benavente (in central Castile) unless she signed their decrees (Aram 2005, 125–28). Skeptical of such claims, Juana steadfastly refused to act against her son.

The queen's consistent, self-sacrificing support for her offspring emerges as one fact in a sea of fictions, rumors, and legends elaborated around her. Typically contradictory sources as chronicles, letters, and ambassadors' reports tend to agree on this point. The queen acted to secure the succession of her son, Charles, and his descendents following the death of Philip in 1506 and again during the Comunero rebellion of 1520–21. When Charles took Juana's belongings (not to mention her throne), the queen tactfully blamed her servants. She remained particularly attached to her second son, Ferdinand, and her youngest daughter, Catalina, begging visitors for news about them (Aram 2005, 144–45, 151).

The fictions created around and about Juana do not preclude the recovery of certain facts. An unglamorous counterpoint to the queen's legends emerges from itineraries, accounts, and papal grants. In the absence of chronicles written for Juana, her activities, and expenses offer glimpses of an image that the queen may have chosen for herself. These sources reveal devotional activities appropriate for Juana's station and consistent with those of previous duchesses of Burgundy. Like Juana, Isabel of Portugal and Margaret of York, the wives of Philip the Good and Charles the Bold, had been drawn to Franciscanism and the *devotio moderna,* a current of contemplative, interior spirituality, as a refuge from the Burgundian court.[14] As queen of Castile, Juana may have adopted Queen (later Saint) Isabel of Portugal (1271–1336) as another devotional model.

The accounts of daily expenses (*État Journaliers*) conserved in the archives of Lille and Brussels indicate that Juana cultivated ties to female Franciscans in the Low Countries as well as Castile. As duchess of Burgundy, Juana visited the "Gray Sisters" of Brussels, ordering her dinner and supper service transferred to their convent of Bethlehem on at least two occasions in 1499.[15] She also helped the Franciscan sisters obtain a bull authorizing them to adopt the more austere, reformed rule of Saint Clare, which Pope Alexander VI issued in 1501.[16] During that same year, Juana and her female attendants hired seven chariots to visit a cloister of discalced Clares outside of Bruges "several times."[17]

When Juana traveled to Castile as the apparent heiress to her mother's realms she visited the Clarisan convent of Rejas outside Madrid at least four times, spending the night there on three occasions.[18] Juana made these visits in 1502–3, after her confirmation as princess of Asturias in Toledo and before and after her designation as heiress to her father's kingdoms in Zaragoza. Juana went back to Rejas on January 15, 1503, after Philip the Handsome had left Madrid for the Low Countries. Conventional sources—such as Pedro Mártir de Anglería—provide no hint that Juana moved with such apparent autonomy and composure during a time of political unrest. Juana may have even bequeathed the Clares of Rejas certain relics from the eleven thousand virgin martyrs that she received in 1500.[19] As late as 1587, the Monastery of Rejas contained the heads of some of the virgins reputed to have gained martyrdom with Saint Ursula at Cologne.[20] Other relics from this group of saintly martyrs found their way to the convent of Saint Paul outside Burgos, home to Juana's tutor, fray Andrés de Miranda,[21] and to the Cathedral of Santiago in Galicia, which Juana and Philip visited in 1506.[22]

Juana's relations with the female Franciscans of Brussels, Bruges and Rejas, suggest that she may have chosen aspects of her retirement alongside the Clarisan Royal Monastery of Tordesillas after 1509. Not only did she trust the community of Clares to guard Philip's remains, Juana made regular donations to the community. According to her household accounts, Juana personally donated thirty ducats to the

Clares on Holy Friday in 1511; forty ducats in 1512 and again in 1513.[23] During Holy Week, the queen customarily ordered tapestries transferred from her own residence to the monastery and sponsored an annual monument there commemorating Christ's burial and resurrection.[24] Juana also made donations to the Clares on the day of Saint Sebastian[25] and to certain preachers who gave sermons at their convent.[26] Quite typically, the patroness and nuns had their differences. In 1512 the sisters moved an altar and image of Saint Francis, which Juana paid 1,506 maravedíes to restore to its original location.[27] Two years later, the abbess and nuns attempted to replace the same altar with a statue of Santiago, which the queen ordered removed.[28] Juana intervened again when the Clares planned to construct a new chorus in the middle of the main apse, "because it seemed to Her Highness that the said church was shortened." The queen accordingly sent the abbess of Saint Claire money in order to help finance a tribunal above the previous chorus.[29]

Such prosaic details, recorded in royal accounts, point to more than a queen meddling in her neighbors' business. Parallels to the life of Queen Isabel of Portugal—who supposedly passed her nights in vigil and fasted for up to three days (Miranda 1610, 69, 163)—indicate that Juana may have adopted such a spiritual model. The Portuguese queen devoutly nursed her husband, Don Dionis, during his final illness, just as Juana had attended to Philip on his deathbed. Once widowed, Isabel of Portugal established her residence alongside the Clarisan monastery of Coimbra, where she frequently joined the nuns in holy exercises (168) While participating in the life of a Clarisan community, Juana made modest efforts to exercise charity, for which Isabel of Portugal was particularly renowned (Muñoz Fernández 1988, 42–56).

Legends about Queen Isabel of Portugal may have inspired a number of Juana's choices. These decisions, revealed in itineraries and recorded in accounts, received little publicity in the sixteenth century. No chronicler, ambassador, or courtier celebrated them. In the nineteenth century, like the sixteenth, the theme of Juana's "love madness" would prove much more attractive than the queen's pious defense of her offspring.

ROMANTIC AND OTHER AGENDAS

In the second half of the nineteenth century three historians unearthed most of the standard sources about Queen Juana. G. A.

Bergenroth, Louis Prosper Gachard, and Antonio Rodríguez Villa painstakingly began extracting and publishing ambassadors' reports, letters, and chronicles referring to the "Mad Queen." Representing distinct national and religious traditions, they were influenced by different aspects of the romantic movement. In line with these interests, the histories of Bergenroth, Gachard, and Rodríguez Villa tended to foreground the "literary" aspect of their sources.

G. A. Bergenroth first came across references to Queen Juana at the Archivo General de Simancas while collecting material for the *Calendar of Letters, Despatches, and State Papers Relating to the Negotiations Between England and Spain*. In particular, Bergenroth recorded evidence of Henry VII of England's desire to marry Juana after the death of Philip of Burgundy—an initiative that Juana's father claimed to support but seemingly thwarted.[30] Intrigued by a tone of secrecy around the queen, Bergenroth subsequently edited an entire volume of documentation about her. He claimed that Queen Isabella had considered Juana a heretic and that kings Ferdinand and Charles ordered her confined and tortured for the same reason.[31] Although no one could doubt the Catholic fortitude of Juana's sister, Catalina (Catherine of Aragon), the hereditary queen of Castile provided an intriguing foil.

If Bergenroth appeared to romanticize a "black legend" around Queen Juana, Louis Prosper Gachard rushed to defend the queen's Catholic credentials. Gachard took issue with the German scholar's interpretations of archival documents and especially the claim that Juana had been tortured.[32] Whereas Bergenroth had noted that Juana died without receiving extreme unction, Gachard highlighted the queen's exchanges with Francisco de Borja, the third general of the Jesuit order and future saint, at the end of her life (Gachard 1870, 290–323, 389–409). Six years later Gachard published the chronicles of Juana and Philip's voyages to Spain in 1501–2 and 1506 alongside relevant documentation.[33] Fascinated by the subject, the Belgian historian collected extensive information about Juana, including transcriptions from the archives of Lille, Paris, Simancas, Valenciennes, Vienna, and Ypres, which he never published.[34]

Following Bergenroth and Gachard, Antonio Rodríguez Villa devoted seventeen years of research in Spanish libraries and archives to Queen Juana. Like his contemporaries, Rodríguez Villa amassed a plethora of information that went beyond his interpretive framework. Believing that Juana had penned the 1505 letter to Philibert de Veyre, this historian declared her madly devoted to her husband, although not crazy in the "general and proper sense of the word"

(1892, 407, 410). Like Bergenroth and Gachard, Rodríguez Villa placed a romantic twist on inconclusive evidence.

While attributing Juana's "madness" to heresy, jealousy, or love, the queen's nineteenth-century historians bequeathed their successors an invaluable documentary corpus. Those of us who have attempted to extend their research and to nuance their views remain indebted to Gachard, Bergenroth, and Rodríguez Villa. Just as these forerunners were influenced by Romanticism, many of their successors have been drawn by psychobiography. The label of schizophrenia, first applied by Ludwig Pfandl (1943, 107) and Nicomedes Sanz y Ruiz de la Peña (1942, 256), has recently been adopted by art historian Miguel Ángel Zalama (2000, 540–46). Like the nineteenth-century diagnosis of "love madness," the idea of "schizophrenia" accommodates conflicting evidence by allowing rational behavior to be attributed to "moments of lucidity" (Dénnis, 1969). Such verdicts, however reassuring, preclude an understanding of the restrictions on the queen and how she may have maneuvered within them.

Other recent studies highlight the limitations Juana faced, concluding, essentially that she was "driven mad." Isabel Altayó and Paloma Nogues adopted this verdict in their 1985 biography of the queen (1985, 11). A similar approach has informed the bestseller by Manuel Fernández Álvarez, who depicted Juana as a victim of unfortunate circumstances and ruthless political actors. My own approach, while having points in common with the above studies and undoubtedly certain defects, seeks to establish how and why Juana may have acted of her own volition and why and when she may have chosen not to act. Beyond the influence of feminist studies, the so-called linguistic turn in historiography, and specifically the work of Michel Foucault, have informed my analysis of representations of the queen.

Beyond whether or not Juana was really mad, researchers are beginning to consider what the sources can really tell us about her. My own work suggests that a sixteenth-century emphasis on the passions and belief in female debility colored a legend that Juana projected in order to protect her children's inheritance. Overlooking this dynastic strategy, however, nineteenth-century portrayals of Juana emphasized romantic, national, and confessional interests. Since then, the rise of psychiatry has prompted attempts to diagnose the queen. Although celebrated in the sixteenth, nineteenth, and twentieth centuries, Juana appears to be reaching the height of her popularity today. This recent fascination with a queen who never ruled, beyond the scope of most historians, invites the scrutiny of other scholars.

NOTES

1. Archivo General de Simancas (hereafter AGS), Patronato Real (hereafter PR) 52–112, The subprior of Santa Cruz to Queen Isabella, July 31, 1498 and AGS, PR 52–116, The subprior of Santa Cruz to Ferdinand and Isabella, January 15, 1499. Transcribed in Luis Suárez Fernández, *Política Internacional de Isabella la Católica. Política Internacional de Isabel la Católica: Estudio y Documentos* (Valladolid: Universidad de Valladolid, 1972) V: 279–80, 351–56, documents 72 and 100.

2. Louis Prosper Gachard, ed., *Collection des Voyages de Souverains des Pays-Bas* (Brussels: F. Hayez, 1876), 1:132–37. Joseph Chmel, ed., "Reise des Erzherzogs Philipp nach Spanien 1501," in *Die Handschriften der K.K. Hofbibliothek in Wien. Interesse der Geschichte* 1841, 2:568–69. For Fonseca's first assessment of Juana in the Burgundian court, see Real Academia de Historia, Colección de Salazar y Castro (hereafter RAH), A-9, fol. 132, Bishop of Córdoba Juan Rodríguez de Fonseca to Secretary Miguel Pérez de Almazán," August 12, 1501.

3. AGS, PR 56–18, "La carta patente de la reyna," November 23, 1504.

4. Biblioteca Nazionale di San Marco, ms. It. cl. VII, cod. 1129 (7452), Registrum Vincentii Quirino oratoris ad Serm. Philip Ducem Burgundie, 1505–6, fol. 61–61v, partly transcribed in Constantin von Höfler, "Die Depeschen des Venetianischen Botschafters Vincenzo Quirino," *Archiv für Osterreichische Gestchicte* 66 (1885) 150.

5. Gutierre Gómez de Fuensalida, *Correspondencia*, 1907, 307–63; published by the Duke of Berwick and of Alba.

6. Biblioteca Nazionale di San Marco, ms. It. cl. VII, cod. 1129 (7452), Registrum Vincentii Quirino oratoris ad Serm. Philippe Ducem Burgundie, 1505–1506, fol. 112, in Höfler, "Die Depeschen des Venetianischen Botschafters Vincenzo Quirino," 242.

7. Archives du Département du Nord à Lille (hereafter ADN Lille) B 18846 (no. 29611), Pietro Martire to Claude de Cilly, undated [1505].

8. José López de Toro, ed. and trans., *Epistolario de Pedro Mártir de Anglería* (Madrid: Imprenta Góngora, 1953), IX: Epists. 221 and 222. See Bethany Aram, *Juana the Mad: Sovereignty & Dynasty in Renaissance Europe* (Baltimore: Johns Hopkins University Press, 2005), 68–69.

9. *Epistolario de Pedro Mártir de Anglería*, 10: Epistle 324.

10. "Apéndice: Costumbres de la Cartuja," in *Maestro Bruno, padre de monjes* (Madrid: Biblioteca de Autores Cristianos, 1995), 350–51. Bethany Aram, "Juana 'the Mad,' The Clares, and the Carthusians: Revising a Necrophilic Legend in Early Habsburg Spain." *Archiv für Reformationsgeschichte* 93 (2002): 172–91.

11. Gachard, ed., "Deuxième Voyage de Phillipe le Beau en Espagne en 1506," 415, 458–59, 462–63.

12. AGS, Cámara de Castilla, Diversos 1–12, "Revocación de las mercedes que hizo el Rey Don Phelipe I," December 18, 1506, inserted in a provision of July 30, 1507. Real Biblioteca de el Escorial, mss. castellaños Z. II. i, 62a–b, Royal mandate of doña Juana, December 18, 1506, inserted in a letter by the royal council, August 26, 1507.

13. Magdalena S. Sánchez, "Melancholy and Female Illness: Habsburg Women and Politics at the Court of Philip III," *Journal of Women's History* 8, 2 (Summer 1996): 81–102. By the same author, see also *The Empress, The Queen, and the Nun: Women and Power at the Court of Philip III of Spain* (Baltimore: Johns Hopkins University Press, 1998).

14. Wim Blockmans, "The Devotion of a Lonely Duchess," in *Margaret of York, Simon Marmion & the Visions of Tondal* ed. Thomas Kren. (Malibu, CA: Paul Getty Museum, 1992), 29–46. Monique Sommé, *Isabelle de Portugal, Duchesse de Bourgogne.*

Une Femme au Pouvoir au Quinzieme Siècle (Villeneuve d'Ascq: Presses Universitaires du Septentrion, 1998), 451–78.

15. ADN Lille B 3457, nos. 120863 and 120865, Juana's dispense, June 26 and 30, 1499. Aram, "Juana 'the Mad,' The Clares, and the Carthusians," 172–91.

16. Stads Archief Brussel no. 8, fol. 350v–353v, "Copie vander bullen vander clausuren vanden Graubben Zusteren," September 4, 1501 [contemporary copy]. ASV Archivum Arcis, Arm. 1–18, 4173, fol. 138v–142, Alexander VI to the Convent of Bethlehem, September 4, 1501 [seventeenth-century copy].

17. ADN Lille B 3459, no. 121104, Dispense for Juana and her children in Bruges, May 3, 1501. Aram, "Juana 'the Mad,' The Clares, and the Carthusians," 172–91.

18. ADN Lille, B 3460, N. 121326, 121327, 121333, and 121334, Wages and dispense for Juana's household, September, 30, October 1, 6, and 7 1502. ADN Lille, B 3460, N. 121384 and 121385, B 3461, nos. 121456 and 121458, Wages and dispense for Juana's household, December 9, 1502 and January 15–16, 1503.

19. AGS PR 27–58, "Auténtica de las reliquias de los mártires que se trajeron de Roma para la Princesa Doña Juana con facultad para poderlas colocar en iglesias," October 27, 1500.

20. Francesco Gonzaga, *De origine Seraphicae Religionis Franciscanae* (Rome: Dominici Basae, 1587), 640. On Saint Ursula and the 11,000 virgin martyrs, see Jacobus de Voragine, *The Golden Legend*, trans. William Granger Ryan (Princeton: Princeton University Press, 1993), 2:256–60.

21. Lorenzo Galíndez de Carvajal, "Anales Breves del reinado de los Reyes Católicos," *Crónicas de los Reyes de Castilla* ed. Don Cayetano Rosell (Madrid: BAE, 1878), 3:556. BN Madrid ms. 6020, OSORIO DE MOSCOSO, fray Alvaro: "Historia del Príncipe Don Fernando que después fue Emperador," f. 158v.

22. István Szásdi, "El Viaje a Galicia de Felipe el Hermoso y el Hospital Real de Santiago de Compostela," *Jacobus* 9–1 (2000): 324–25. *Relicario de la S. A. M. Iglesia Catedral de Santiago de Compostela: Guía del Visitante* (1960), 5.

23. AGS Casa y Sitios Reales (hereafter CSR) 15–1/34, Mosen Ferrer to Ochoa de Landa, June 5, 1511; CSR 15–1/35, Receipt of ducats for Holy Friday, June 6, 1511. AGS CSR 53–12, Paybills of Mosen Ferrer, May 3, 1512. AGS CSR 15–7/675, Receipt by Mosen Ferrer, May 3, 1512. AGS CSR 53–16 and 15–5/533, Orders and receipt by Mosen Ferrer, April 22, 1513.

24. AGS CSR 53–8 and 17, Payments of Mosen Ferrer, June 6, 1511 and July 17, 1513. AGS CSR 15–1/20, Mosen Ferrer to Ochoa de Landa, June 12, 1511. AGS CSR 96–553, Annual extraordinary expenses, 1512. AGS CSR 15–7/677, "Memorial de lo que se comprase para el monumento," April 15, 1512. AGS CSR 15–6/540, "Memorial de la semana santa," March 29, 1513; 15–5/423, Mosen Ferrer for Diego de Ribera, July 17, 1513; 15–7/652, Mosen Ferrer for don Alonso de Alva, June 29, 1514; and 15–7/693, Mosen Ferrer for the sacristan and Lorenzo, carpintero, June 29, 1514.

25. AGS CSR 15–7/738, Mosen Ferrer to Alonso de Alva, January 29, 1515.

26. AGS CSR 15–8/864, King Ferdinand to Ochoa de Landa, July 11, 1515. AGS CSR 96–36, Nomina of King Ferdinand, November 20, 1515.

27. AGS CSR 7/655 and CSR 53–12, Mosen Ferrer to Ochoa de Landa, August 5, 1512.

28. AGS, CSR 15–7/63, Mosen Ferrrer to Ochoa de Landa, March 9, 1514.

29. AGS CSR 24–46/611, Gracia de Carreño to the principal accountants, July 14, 1523. See Aram, *Juana the Mad*, 105–106.

30. G. A. Bergenroth, *Calendar of Letters, Despatches, and State Papers Relating to the Negotiations Between England and Spain* (Nendeln, Liechtenstein: Kraus-Thomson, 1969, orig. 1862), 403–405, 452–53, 459, 464.

31. G. A. Bergenroth, ed., *Letters, Despatches, and State Papers Relating to the Negotiations Between England and Spain, Supplement to Volumes I and II* (London: Longmans, Green, Reader and Dyer, 1868). Bergenroth, G. A. "Jeanne la Folle." *Revue de Belgique* I (Brussels, 1869), 81–112.

32. Louis Prosper Gachard, "Jeanne la Folle Défendue contre l'imputation d'hérésie," *Académie Royale de Belgique. Extrait des Bulletins,* 2nd series, tome 24, no. 6, 1869. See also Louis Prosper Gachard, "Sur la question de Jeanne la Folle," *Académie Royale de Belgique, Extr. des Bulletins,* 2nd series, tome 27, no. 5 (1869); "Sur Jeanne la folle et la publication de M. Bergenroth," *Académie Royale de Belgique, Extr. des Bulletins,* 2nd series, tome 28, nos. 9 and 10 (1869).

33. Louis Prosper Gachard, ed. *Collection des Voyages de Souverains des Pays-Bas* (Brussels: F. Hayez, 1876).

34. Archives Générales du Royaume à Brussels (hereafter AGRB), Fonds Gachard 611, 612, 614, and 615.

WORKS CITED

Altayó, Isabel, and Paloma Nogués. 1985. *Juana I: La reina cautiva.* Madrid: Silex.

Aram, Bethany. 1998. "Juana 'the Mad's' Signature: The Problem of Invoking Royal Authority, 1505–1507." *The Sixteenth Century Journal* 29, 2:333–61.

———. 2002. "Juana 'the Mad,' The Clares, and the Carthusians: Revising a Necrophilic Legend in Early Habsburg Spain." *Archiv für Reformationsgeschichte* 93:172–191.

———. 2005. *Juana the Mad: Sovereignty & Dynasty in Renaissance Europe.* Baltimore: Johns Hopkins University Press.

Bergenroth, G. A., ed. 1969 [1862]. *Calendar of Letters, Despatches, and State Papers Relating to the Negotiations Between England and Spain.* Nendeln, Liechtenstein: Kraus-Thomson.

———. 1868. *Letters, Despatches, and State Papers Relating to the Negotiations Between England and Spain Preserved in the Archives of Simancas and Elsewhere.* Supplement to volumes 1 and 2. London: Longmans, Green, Reader, and Dyer.

Blockmans, Wim. 1992. "The Devotion of a Lonely Duchess." In *Margaret of York, Simon Marmion, and the Visons of Tondal,* edited by Thomas Kren, 29–46. Malibu, CA: J. Paul Getty Museum.

Chmel, Joseph, ed. 1841. *Die Handschriften der K.K. Hofbibliothek in Wien.* Vienna: Carl Gerold.

Dénnis, Amarie. 1969. *Seek the Darkness: The Story of Juana la Loca.* Madrid: Sucesores de Rivadeneyra.

Fernández Álvarez, Manuel. 1994. *Juana la loca, 1479–1555.* Palencia: Diputación Provincial.

Gachard, Louis Prosper, ed. 1876. *Collection des voyages des souverains des Pays-Bas.* Brussels: F. Hayez.

———. "Les derniers moments de Jeanne la Folle." 1870. Extrait des *Bulletins de l'Académie des sciences,* 2nd series, tome 29. Brussels: M. Hayez.

———. "Jeanne la Folle et Charles Quint," première parte. 1870. Extrait des *Bulletins de l'Académie royale de Belgique,* tome 24, no 6. Brussels: M. Hayez.

———. "Jeanne la Folle et Charles-Quint," deuxième parte. 1872. Extrait des *Bulletins de l'Académie royale de Belgique*, tome 33, no. 1. Brussels: M. Hayez.

———. "Jeanne la Folle défendue contre l'imputation d'hérésie." 1869. Extrait des *Bulletins de l'Académie royale de Belgique*, 2nd series, tome 27, no. 6. Brussels: M. Hayez.

———. "Jeanne al Folle et François de Borja." 1870. Extrait des *Bulletins de l'Académie des sciences*, 2nd series, tome 29. Brussels: M. Hayez.

———. "Sur Jeanne la folle et les documents concernant cette princesse." 1869. Extrait des *Bulletins de l'Académie royale de Belgique*, 2nd series, tome 27, no. 3. Brussels: M. Hayez.

———. "Sur Jeanne la Folle et la publication de M. Bergenroth." 1869. Extrait des *Bulletins de l'Académie royale de Belgique*, 2nd series, tome 28, nos. 9 and 10. Brussels: M. Hayez.

Galíndez de Carvajal, Lorenzo. 1878. "Anales Breves del reinado de los Reyes Católicos." In *Crónicas de los Reyes de Castilla*, edited by Don Cayetano Rosell. Madrid: BAE.

Gómez de Fuensalida, Gutierre. 1907. *Correspondencia*. Madrid: Duque de Berwick y de Alba.

Gonzaga, Francesco. 1587. *De origine Seraphicae Religionis Franciscanae*. Rome: Dominici Basae.

Höfler, Constantin von, ed. 1885. "Die Depeschen des Venetianischen Botschafters Vincenzo Quirino." *Archiv für Österreichische Gestchicte* 66.

López de Toro, José, ed. *Epistolario de Pedro Mártir de Anglería*, Madrid: Imprenta Góngora, 1953.

Mártir de Anglería, Pedro. 1953. *Epistolario*. Edited and translated by José López de Toro. Madrid: Imprenta Góngora.

Miranda, Luis de. 1610. *Vida de la Gloriosa Virgen Sancta Clara con la declaración de su primera y segunda regla y un memorial de las cosas más insignes y memorables que en esta ilustrísima y sagrada religión han sucedido*. Salamanca: La Viuda de Artus Taberniel.

Muñoz Fernández, Ángela. 1988. *Mujer y experiencia religiosa en el marco de la santidad medieval*. Madrid: Asociación Cultural Al-Mudayna.

Pfandl, Ludwig. 1943. *Juana la Loca: Su vida, su tiempo, su culpa*. Translated by Felipe Villaverde. Madrid: Espasa Calipe.

Rodríguez Villa, Antonio. 1874. *Bosquejo Biográfico de la Reina Doña Juana*. Madrid: Aribau.

———. 1892. *La Reina Doña Juana la Loca: Estudio Histórico*. Madrid: Librería de M. Murillo.

Sánchez, Magdalena S. 1998. *The Empress, The Queen, and the Nun: Women and Power at the Court of Philip III of Spain*. Baltimore: Johns Hopkins University Press.

———. 1996. "Melancholy and Female Illness: Habsburg Women and Politics at the Court of Philip III." *Journal of Women's History* 8, 2:81–102.

Sanz y Ruiz de la Peña, Nicomedes. 1942. *Doña Juana I de Castilla, la reina que enloqueció de amor*. Madrid: Biblioteca Nueva.

Sommé, Monique. 1998. *Isabelle de Portugal, duchesse de Bourgogne. Une femme au pouvoir au Quinzieme Siècle*. Villeneuve d'Ascq: Presses Universitaires du Septentrion.

Suárez Fernández, Luis. *Política internacional de Isabel la Católica: Estudio y documentos*. Valladolid: Universidad de Valladolid, 1971–72, vols. 4 (1494–96) and 5 (1497–99).

Surtz, Ronald E. 2004. "In Search of Juana de Mendoza." In *Power and Gender in Renaissance Spain*. Edited by Helen Nader. Urbana: University of Illinois Press.

Szásdi, István. 2000. "El Viaje a Galicia de Felipe el Hermoso y el Hospital Real de Santiago de Compostela." *Jacobus* 9–1:309–43.

Voragine, Jacobus de. 1993. *The Golden Legend*. Translated by William Granger Ryan. Princeton: Princeton University Press.

Zalama, Miguel Ángel. 2000. *Vida Cotidiana y Arte en el Palacio de la Reina Juana I en Tordesillas*. Valladolid: Universidad de Valladolid.

Juana I of Castile, Catherine of Aragon, and the Failure of Feminine Power in the Construction of Empire

Elena Gascón Vera

When I saw her, she looked very well and she spoke
with good sense and discreetly and never loosing
her point of authority; and although her husband
and those who came with him wanting
her to be crazy, I only saw her as sane.
　　　　—Henry VII of England (Gómez de Fuensalida 1506, 151)

But it be determined by judgement that our
marriage was against Goddes law and clerely voyde,
then I shall not onely sorowe the departing
from so good a Lady and lovying companion.
but muche more lament and bewaile my infortunate chaunce
that I haue so long lived in adultry to Goddes great displeasure,
and have no true heyre of my body to inherite this realme.
　　　　—Henry VIII of England (Hall 1533)

As QUEEN, WIFE, AND MOTHER, ISABELLA OF CASTILE (1451–1504) WIELDED GREAT POWER DURING HER LIFE. Yet after her death, she could not prevent the abandonment and humiliation her daughters would be subjected to by their husbands—Philip of Hapsburg and Henry Tudor. Juana (1479–1555) and Catherine (1485–1536), in the absence of their mother, became the clear casualties of power in the new project of empire undertaken by their father Ferdinand, a project based upon the establishment of monarchical absolutism and its inherent hegemony of patriarchy. The mimesis of the Roman Empire, brought about by the Renaissance, changed the conventional approach of individual rule—where the representation of royalty transcended gender—into a more patriarchal concept of political government. The new modernity defined these women as marked exclusively by

47

their gender, which prevented them from exercising their own capacity as rulers, a role for which they had been trained since childhood.

Juana and Catherine were educated to govern, if not an empire—the destiny of Juana—then at least to rule as powerful queens alongside their husbands. Nevertheless neither one of them would be permitted the autonomy or the independence to exercise her power. As Bethany Aram has exhaustively and brilliantly analyzed in *La reina Juana: Gobierno, piedad y dinastía* and *Juana the Mad: Sovereignty and Dynasty in Renaissance Europe* (2001, 2005), the reason for Juana's abdication of her obligation to rule was not only due to her mental derangement but, above all, to the fact that a woman was fated to be queen of an empire that needed wars to uphold itself. With regard to Catherine, the abandonment of her obligation to rule manifested itself in the first case of repudiation and divorce in the Catholic Church, giving rise to schism and the formation of the Anglican Church. (Holmes 1993; Paul 1966).

Ideas about the politics of governing in the Iberian Peninsula had to evolve from a posture of vassalage, where the royal houses of Castile and Aragon had to fight for their legitimacy of governing, as was true in the case of both Catholic Monarchs (Nieto Soria 1993; Ladero Quesada 1999), to where Juana rose to the throne after the death of her mother. Following the absolutism that the Catholic Monarchs had already established, as a necessity for their survival, there were multiple reforms that they also had initiated from the beginning of their reign. These reforms were comprised of changes that were absolute and revolutionary. The first was to achieve territorial unity, realized through marriage and the Conquest of Granada in 1492. This was coupled with religious unity, first initiated by the Inquisition. The Inquisition—which reestablished itself in 1478 and brought together the interests of church and state—eliminated the religious pluralism of Christians, Moors, and Jews (1492) and became an instrument of political repression. The implantation of monolithic territorial and religious entities had as its purpose the establishment of a modern state inspired by political theories of the Renaissance, achieved through an authoritarian monarchy (Villapalos 1997; Simón Tarrés 1996). This modern political stance was accompanied by continued territorial expansion, first in the Mediterranean—which came to an end with the fall of Constantinople in 1453—and later in the Atlantic with arrival in the New World (1492).

The personalities and circumstances of the princesses of Castile who would be queens, who inherited the political and economic expertise of their parents, appear to us, even after five hundred years, as eminently modern. Despite the spectacular success of their mother,

Isabella, both as queen and as a woman—able to forge support for her person among the Spanish nobility (Martín Acosta 2003; Liss 1992)—she was not able to prevent the domestic violence that her daughters would be subjected to by their husbands. The princesses' education, pious and strict, was typical for royal ladies of the Renaissance: instruction in music and Latin, mastery of the enormous codes of protocol befitting a princess (Torre 1956, 256–66).

With regard to moral formation, Juana and Catherine were educated according to ideas set forth in various texts: the treatise entitled *Regimiento de príncipes de Egidio Romano* [Rules for Princes by Egidio Romano] (1344); the more contemporary *El jardín de las nobles doncellas* [Garden for Noble Maidens] (1468), written by Martín de Cordoba for the education of their mother, Isabella; and a text that Juana had in her library, *Carro de las donas/Llibre de les dones* [Book of the Ladies] (1410) written in Catalan by the misogynist Fransesc Eiximenis. These texts emphasize the important role that education played in noble and royal women, exhorting them to govern themselves in a direct and personal way—always controlling their own passions and exercising moderation—in order to be able to govern their palaces and their territories. Nevertheless the treatises relegate discussion to the domestic arena, never venturing into politics. The princesses had also been very well educated in Latin and the humanism of the period under the tutelage of Antonio and Alessandro Geraldino, Italians who composed a treatise on education in honor of their pupils: *De eruditione nobelium puellarum* [On the Education of Well-Born Girls], which emphasized the need for the princesses to be well versed in the most advanced philosophical ideas of the period (Paul 1966, 62–63).

Juana's desire was to become a nun, but the political reality of her parents' international ambitions determined that she would be married to the spoiled and handsome Archduke Philip of Austria (1478–1506), young orphan to Mary of Burgundy and heir of the Emperor Maximilian (Calderón 2001; Pérez-Bustamante and Ortega 1995). Attraction between the two young people was immediate, but after a few months, Philip returned to the dissolute habits of his bachelorhood. Faced with the jealousy of his wife—who knew herself to be abandoned and betrayed—the prince kept her pregnant almost annually—she gave birth to six children in ten years—while abusing her both physically and mentally. During their last two years of marriage, Juana fought against the indifference of her husband in excessive and obsessive ways. She found herself caught between marital jealousies and difficulties of assimilation within the Flemish court. All this finally ended with the unexpected death of her young husband, who had held her obsessively dependent upon his passions and rejections.

The case of Catherine is more complex, based upon the reasons for her divorce and consequent repudiation. Henry VIII wished to father a son to inherit his kingdom and despite the fact that Catherine had many miscarriages and gave birth to various sons, only her daughter, Mary Tudor, survived. (Arteaga 2002; Olaizola 1994). In both instances, the princesses were fully aware that their marriages were, above all, issues of state with international implications.

Nevertheless we must not forget that because they were women, their power, despite their lineage, was based in their capacities of procreation. Everything in them was marked by their sex. Their worth and conduct were valued within interpretations of their biological and social behavior and how the societies of their times reacted to and catalogued them, was also determined by their femaleness. Therefore we must evaluate the activity and conduct of Juana and Catherine in the face of their repudiation and mistreatment, as two different forms of feminine reaction—comparable to a literary polyphony described by Iris Zavala and others (Zavala 1993; Díaz-Diocaretz 1993; Moi 1988). Although their public identity was fixed, first as a political body theoretically based in absolute power, it was also determined by their physical female body, as procreators of political male heirs. Therefore their first identity, legitimate inheritors of their mother's power, was annulled by the second, obfuscating their absolute power and making them dependent upon the physical and sentimental authority of their husbands (Perry and Joyce 2005; Somerville 1995). The personal and political aspirations of these young women, upon their marriages to powerful young men, contrast sharply with historical portraits of Juana and Catherine in their maturity: women marked by madness and repudiation. For Juana and Catherine, their experiences with their husbands framed the cultural articulation of their historical personas even though each reacted in her own fashion. Juana retreated from the world in a self-absorbed derangement, leaving behind her political responsibilities. Catherine boldly fought until death for her right to be legitimate queen consort and for her daughter to inherit the throne of England.

As Bethany Aram has convincingly demonstrated in her exhaustive historical study of Juana I of Castile, the supposed madness of the queen should be questioned. When they married, neither Juana, nor her husband Philip, thought that one day they would become rulers of the rich kingdom of Castile—which, indeed, they inherited from her mother Isabella, upon her death. Juana was but third in the line of succession and she had a brother who was a rightful heir, so upon her marriage to the archduke she was assumed to be yet another second rank pawn serving the political interests and power plays of her husband and her parents. Her difficult stay in the palace of Philip in Flanders, subjected to his infidelities, aggressions and humiliations, and aggravated by his efforts to control and distance her from the influence of her mother, left her in a state of derangement and constant anxiety. Eventually her conduct was deemed out of control, battered between the love and fear she felt for her husband.

It cannot be denied that on many occasions Juana's behavior proved to be excessive in her reactions and her paranoia. Nevertheless if we analyze the situation in which she found herself shortly after meeting her husband, we can better understand the reality of her circumstances.

The journey of Juana to Flanders for her wedding, in which 133 ships and 15,000 men accompanied her, was the most luxurious and extravagant trip that had been undertaken not only in Castile, but also in all of Europe (Suárez Fernández 1971, 569–89). Yet when she arrived, her future husband did not even appear to greet her. Juana's education had not been a political one; nevertheless, her parents had planned for her to help forge an alliance between the Emperor Maximilian and Castile, to the detriment of France. Juana, however, soon learned that the majority of her young husband's advisors were all on the side of France (Aram 2001; 2005). Likewise, the independent and capricious temperament of Philip—leading him to fight against the cities and townships to win favor with the nobility—contrasted acutely with the somber and respectful approach of Juana's parents. They had always favored the cities and jurisdictions in order to limit the power of the noble classes. Furthermore the love-smitten Juana—while finding herself the archduchess of Austria, duchess of Burgundy, and princess of Castile—could not compete with the series of lovers that her husband paraded before her eyes.

Another source of anguish and desperation for Juana during her first stay in Flanders was witnessing the hunger and hardships endured by her Spanish escorts, because her own royal house did not have the necessary funds to sustain them (León Tolosana 1991). This lack of personal funds, with which she might have provided for her servants and exercised dominion over her advisors, is essential to understanding Juana's physical and emotional instability during her years outside Castile. In those early years, during which Juana was learning to rule her house and her future territories, she was completely dependent upon her husband's money and surrounded by Philip's political intrigues, bantered between the interests of Spain and France. Juana was enthroned in isolation. Little by little she had to dismiss her servants and advisors, sending them back to Spain because she could not support them economically in Flanders.

It is possible to argue, as Aram does, that Juana's political body—governance of her household, and later of her kingdoms—was not as appropriately developed as her sexual body—a woman in love and prolific mother. However, it is also possible to argue that the reasons for her failure to exert her legitimate power were due to confusion and conflict compounded by desires, that is to say, reasons more personal and psychological than political. Juana was always torn between her desire for peace and seclusion, and her desire to govern her household and her kingdom in accordance with the teachings of her mother. Neither her spoiled husband nor her father would allow her to bring those desires to fruition. During the painful years as archduchess of Burgundy in Flanders, Juana saw herself exiled and impoverished, without friends and countrymen, and without the protection and help of her parents. The emotional upheavals caused by the ambitions of her husband, and the unexpected reality of her inheritance after her mother's death, brought her to personal and political confusion, which was well exploited by her husband, who started the rumor of her mental incapacity.

Juana alternated between the desire to pursue a normal life—pious and remote from the court—and the obligation to fulfill the exigencies of protocol—ostentatious and exhibitionist—that her royal rank required. Finding herself surrounded by her husband's servants exacerbated her tendencies to hysteria and lack of control. After the death of her mother, despite some doubts, Juana accepted her husband's intention to rule Castile in her name (Rubin 1991, 375).

From that moment, still in Flanders—to which she had escaped from Spain against the wishes of her infirm mother—she vacillated between spiritual retreat and engagement with her royal duties, always trying to maintain and affirm her royal authority and will (Prast 1932, 508–22). Upon her return to Flanders, Juana had found her husband with a lover; she had ordered the woman banished from the court and her hair to be cut off, but relations with her husband continued to deteriorate. This match of wills prompted Juana's erratic behavior, which further marginalized her royal authority. Philip then refined his plan to declare Juana unfit to rule.

Once Philip and Juana returned to Castile, the relations between them worsened. Philip wanted Juana to submit to his authority and give him power to rule in her name, but she refused to sign the letter of submission. Juana called upon her father to protect her from Philip's ambitions, but her father aligned himself with her husband. They would finally forge her signature to the document giving over absolute authority (Aram 1998, 331–58). Despite this seeming alliance between Philip and Ferdinand, the truth is that the actions of Philip and his friends and advisors in Castile were abominable, and his unforeseen death on September 25, 1506 has always been shrouded in the suspicion of a possible poisoning (Dousinague 1947).

The well-known iconography of the enraptured Juana, accompanying the dead body of her husband on the byways of Spain, while it exists, should be examined. Juana could not have been so madly in love with her dead husband when the first thing that she did was try to secure her own rights and those of her children by revoking an edict in which Philip granted lands and favors to his friends. The fact that she insisted that the body of her husband be transported to Granada in order to be buried alongside her mother was born of the desire to comply with Philip's wishes as set forth in his will. This was interpreted as some form of necrophilia, but was more likely inspired by her somewhat erratic desires to assert her own authority and lay claim to her royal rights.

In any case, during this period, Juana continued to vacillate between the urge to seek pious seclusion and her obligation to rule, as her mother had, with autonomy and firmness. But the great difference between them is that Isabella needed to affirm her own precarious legitimacy and she did it with a husband by her side. After the turbulent rule of her brother Henry IV, Isabella was supported by the rebirth of the new Castilian nobility, aspiring to new privileges (Pérez-Bustamante 1998, 569–89). Juana, on the other hand, had had her authority undermined by her foreign husband and had never developed ties to the nobles of Castile. The cultural differences, which were obvious from the beginning between Philip and Juana, became more acute during ten years of marriage. Later those same cultural differences were again revisited in Spain, among her subjects, upon her return. She found herself surrounded by those who distrusted a widowed queen, whom they viewed as a stranger because she had spent her last years in foreign lands. They deemed her incapable of correctly handling the responsibility of international politics in the interest of Castile, and, without her permission, called her father Ferdinand to act as regent until her son Charles came of age (Aram 2001).

The double repudiation of Catherine is less complex, and at the same time more banal and sinister. First, she was widowed before her marriage was even consummated, several months after her betrothal (1501) to Arthur Tudor (1486–1502), heir to the English throne. She remained exiled in England, at the young age of only sixteen, for another eight years before she was married again to the younger brother of her dead husband, Henry VIII (1491–1547). Finally after twenty-four years of marriage and various children, her husband divorced her in 1533 with allusions to the fact that she had not been a virgin when they married. In truth, Catherine was past the age of reproduction and he simply wanted another woman to father a male heir.

The political body of Catherine was more clearly intertwined with her sexual body, because, due to her age, she could not bear more children. Her argument for the support of her daughter, Mary, as future queen of England, was reasoned on the nongendered grounds of the laws of inheritance: female rule was acceptable in countries where it had been established by law or custom or in exceptional circumstances deliberately channeled by God. Although she could not prevent her divorce, her arguments created the possibility of a reign for Mary (1516–58) and her half-sister Elizabeth (1533–1603), who were able to claim the same prerogatives as their male predecessors.

The situation in which these two Spanish sisters found themselves—despite the fact that one was queen of an empire and the other was queen consort—is not really unlike that of any modern woman without her own autonomy who must depend upon a man in order to exert her authority. Although their mother had educated them to be queens, neither one of them—and this is particularly true of Juana—had developed the interior strength that might have led to autonomous power. The great irony with regard to Catherine is that she was repudiated for maintaining that Mary—their legitimate daughter—was, although a woman, the heir to the English throne. Many years later, upon Henry's death, Catherine's prophetic forecast came true: despite years of violence and anger and the five subsequent marriages of her husband, it was two women, Mary and Elizabeth, who would reign over England for the rest of the century. However, with them the dichotomy of women confronting the political against the biological body remains relevant, for neither one of them could exert the prerogative of having children.

One could also argue that the failure to assert authority, in the case of these two Castilian princesses, was due to their education in the very virtues extolled by their male tutors, misogynists all. These tutors reinforced the traditional virtues of Christian womanhood also upheld in the writings of Desiderius Erasmus (1466–1536), friend and teacher of Philip and Juana in Flanders. In his *Moriae Enconium* [In Praise of Folly] (1509), Erasmus accepts that women are the biggest fools, because their whole existence is predicated on the notion of pleasing men (Rummel 1996). Also, Juan Luis Vives (1492–1540), teacher of Catherine of England, wrote for the education of her daughter in his *Institutione Feminae Christianae* [The Instruction of a Christian Woman] (1523). Vives emphasized female chastity and submission to all the desires of men to such an extent that Erasmus was even moved to declare that he hoped Vives treated his own wife better than he instructed in his treatise (Fantazzi 2000).

The heirs of Isabella did not need to prove their legitimacy nor fight for their territories, as their mother did. They did need, however, to assert their authority. According to the doctrinal teachings of theologians from the times of the early Christian Church, authority resided not with the female member of a household, but rather with her closest male relative—be he father, husband, or brother. Despite the fact that Catherine had proven that she could rule in place of her husband—when he absented himself during the wars with France (1511–14) and directed the battles against Scotland (1513)—she was not allowed to affirm that the legitimate Mary was the true queen of England.

Neither one of these sisters could, nor wanted, to become the "ideal woman" proposed by Christine de Pizan (1364–1431) in her allegorical *Livre de la cité des dames* [Book of the City of Ladies] (1405) where female authority could be expressed in the image of a *virago* like the legendary Dido: a woman who behaved with the intellectual and physical characteristics of a man. They sensed that this type of woman could not survive in a society where a male, although weak and fragile, would never be replaced by a woman, although strong and capable (Quilligan 1991).

The militaristic society of the Middle Ages conceived of its queens not as female soldiers, but as wives and mothers. However, this assumption was put in question and annulled by Elizabeth, the Virgin Queen, who maintained her reign for over forty years, without direct male intervention. The two Castilian sisters were caught between opposing desires: the desire to affirm a rightful place on the throne, and the desire to assume the role of "strong, silent women," expressing only unconditional love for their king and their children, never asking anything for themselves. The two sisters fought for their rights as best they could. Catherine never relinquished her title as queen of England, resisting the divorce requested by her husband and taking her case all the way to the pope, paving the way for the Protestant schism. Juana, more acutely mistreated and lacking any years of happiness with her husband, stopped fighting against the handiwork of her father and the nobles of Castile, and retired to Tordesillas until her death, never renouncing her own title as queen of Castile and Leon, Aragon, Naples, and Sicily.

Works Cited

Aram, Bethany. 1998. "Juana 'the Mad' Signature: The Problem of Invoking Royal Authority, 1505–1507." *The Sixteenth Century Journal* 29, 2:331–58.

———, ed. 2001. *La reina Juana: Gobierno, piedad y dinastía*. Madrid: Marcial Pons.

———. 2005. *Juana the Mad: Sovereignty and Dynasty in Renaissance Europe*. Baltimore: Johns Hopkins University Press.

Arteaga, Almudena de. 2002. *Catalina de Aragón: Reina de Inglaterra*. Madrid: La Esfera de los Libros.

Calderón, José Manuel. 2001. *Felipe el Hermoso*. Madrid: Espasa-Calpe.

Díaz-Diocaretz, Myriam. 1993. "La palabra no olvida de dónde vino. Para una poética dialógica de la diferencia." In *Breve historia feminista de la literatura española (en lengua castellana)*, ed. by Myriam Díaz-Diocaretz and Iris M. Zavala. Vol. 1. Barcelona, Anthropos.

Dousinague, José M. 1947. *Un proceso por envenenamiento: La muerte de Felipe el Hermoso* Madrid: Espasa Calpe.

Fantazzi, Charles. 2000. "Introduction." In *The Education of Century Manual Christian Women*. Juan Luis Vives. Chicago: University of Chicago Press.

García de Castrojeriz, Juan. 1947 [1344]. *Glosa castellana del Regimiento de Príncipes*. Edited by Juan Beneyto Pérez. Madrid: Instituto de Estudios Políticos.

Gómez de Fuensalida, 2001. "Correspondencia." In *La reina Juana: Gobierno, piedad y dinastía*. Edited by Bethany Aram. Madrid: Marcial Pons.

Holmes, David Lynn. 1993. *A Brief history of the Episcopal Church: With a Chapter on the Anglican Reformation and an Appendix on the Annulment of Henry VIII*. Valley Forge, PA: Trinity Press Internacional.

Ladero Quesada, M. A. 1999. *La España de los Reyes Católicos*. Madrid: Alianza Editorial.

León Tolosana, Carmelo. 1991. *La imagen del Rey: monarquía, realeza y poder ritual en la Casa de los Austrias*. Madrid: Espasa Calpe.

Liss, Peggy K. 1992. *Isabel the Queen: Life and Times*. New York: Oxford University Press.

Martín Acosta, Emelina. 2003. *Isabel I de Castilla y América: hombres que hicieron posible su* política. Valladolid: Universidad de Valladolid.

Martín de Córdoba, Fray. 1953. *El jardín de las nobles doncellas*. Madrid: Colección Joyas Bi-bliográficas.

Moi, Toril. 1988. *Teoría literaria feminista*. Madrid: Cátedra.

Naccarato, Frank, ed. 1981. *Lo libre de les dones de Francesc Eiximenis*. Barcelona: Curial Edicions Catalanes.

Nieto Soria, José Manuel. 1993. *Ceremonias de la realeza: Propaganda y legitimación en la Castilla Trastámara*. Madrid: Editorial Nerea.

Olaizola, José Luis. 1994. *Catalina de Aragón, mujer legítima de Enrique VIII*. Barcelona: Planeta.

Ortiz, Alonso. 1983. *Diálogo sobre la educación del Príncipe Don Juan, hijo de los Reyes Católicos*. Madrid: Studia Humanitatis.

Paul, John E. 1966. *Catherine of Aragon and Her Friends*. New York: Fordham University Press.

Pérez Bustamante, Rogelio, and J. M. Calderón Ortega. 1995. *Felipe I*. Palencia: Olmeda.

————. 1998. *Enrique IV de Castilla, 1454–1474.* Burgos: Editorial La Olmeda.

Perry, Elizabeth M., and Rosemary A. Joyce. 2005. "Providing a Past for 'Bodies that Matter' " Judith Butler's Impact on the Archeology of Gender." In *Butler Matters: Judith Butler's Impact on Feminist and Queer Studies,* edited by Margaret Sönser Breen and Warren Blumenfeld 111–22. Burlington, VT: Ashgate.

Prast, Antonio. 1932. "El Castillo de la Mota, de Medina del Campo: Intención de *huída* de doña Juan La Loca," *Boletín de la Real Academia de la Historia,* 101.

Quilligan, Maureen. 1991. *The Allegory of Female Authority: Christine de Pizan's Cité des Dames.* Ithaca: Cornell University Press.

Rubin, Nancy. 1991. *Isabella of Castile, the First Renaissance Queen.* New York: St. Martin Press.

Rummel, Erika. 1996. *Erasmus and Women.* Toronto: Toronto University Press.

Simón Tarrés, Antonio. 1996. *La monarquía de los Reyes Católicos: hacia un estado hispánico plural.* Madrid: Historia 16.

Somerville, M. R. 1995. *Sex and Subjection: Attitudes to Women in Early Modern Society.* London: St. Martin Press.

Suárez Fernández, Luis. 1971. *Política internacional de Isabel la Católica: Estudio y documentos.* Valladolid: Universidad de Valladolid.

Torre, Antonio de la. 1956. "Maestros de los hijos de los Reyes Católicos," *Hispania* 63:256–66.

Villapalos, Gustavo. 1997. *Justicia y monarquía: puntos de vista sobre su evolución en el reinado de los Reyes Católicos.* Madrid : Marcial Pons.

Zavala, Iris M. 1993. "Las formas y funciones de una teoría crítica feminista: Feminismo dialógico." In *Breve historia feminista de la literatura española (en lengua castellana),* edited by Myriam Díaz-Diocaretz and Iris M. Zavala 27–76. Vol. I. Barcelona: Anthropos.

II
Juana of Castile
in Spanish Literature

Necrophilia, Madness, and Degeneration in Manuel Tamayo y Baus's *La locura de amor* (1855)

David R. George, Jr.

Queen.	*Where is he? He's here. I'm with him.*
Almirante.	*Now he is only a cadaver.*
Queen.	*Then with his cadaver. His cadaver is mine. Get away! Stand back! Mine, all mine! I will shower him with tears from my eyes; caress him with kisses from my lips. Always by my side! He is dead; I am alive. So what? Together forever! Indeed, implacable Death, I will evade your intentions. Silence. Silence! . . . The King has fallen asleep. Silence! . . . Do not waken him. Sleep my love. Sleep . . . Sleep!*

—1885, 475[1]

THE FINAL SCENE OF MANUEL TAMAYO Y BAUS'S 1855 HISTORICAL DRAMA, *La locura de amor* [The Madness of Love] is an emblematic representation of Juana I of Castile's supposed madness. The dramatization of Philip the Handsome's death at the end of the play culminates with these disturbing declarations of the young queen as she takes possession of his corpse and protects it with distrust from the advances of palace attendants and nobles gathered in the king's chamber. Since its debut, critics have found it irresistible to comment on the famous scene—immortalized in painting and on film—that dramatizes the transformation of Juana's jealous obsession into necrophilic impulse. Obvious to readers and audiences alike is the interpretation of Tamayo's treatment of love and madness, and the resulting macabre sexual desire, as a nineteenth-century exaggeration of the Petrarchan trope of unrequited love. The morbid sentimentalism played out in the final scene, presented as the outcome of Juana's progressively destructive oscillation between feelings of sublime love and the unbearable anguish of an unfulfillable desire, fits neatly into the Romantic aesthetic paradigm through which the play has most often been read. Nevertheless the full implications of the image of

61

Juana jealously protecting Philip's lifeless body as an act of necrophilia have yet to be examined.

Like the rest of Tamayo's theater, *La locura de amor* has received very little attention from literary critics, save the obligatory references to the play in histories of nineteenth-century drama and global studies of the evolution of Spanish theater.[2] Given its enormous popularity at the time of its debut in 1855, the drama merits mention as representative of a transitional period in the history of the Spanish stage during which the emergence of commercial theater companies accompanied a change in aesthetic tastes from Romanticism to Realism and the High Comedy. While *La locura de amor* has been identified with these developments, the play's dramatic content and its treatment of Juana I of Castile still await study in terms of the sociopolitical and culture concerns that defined this context. The present essay seeks to understand the relevance of Juana the Mad for the theatergoing public of the mid-nineteenth century by focusing attention on the ways in which the performance of the queen's madness might have spoken to the preoccupations of Spain's ascendant bourgeoisie. The study focuses attention on the theme of necrophilia, and the necrophilic legend associated with the historical figure, in order to make the argument that *La locura de amor* as historical drama, fulfills an urgent need, perceived by the author and felt by period audiences, to communicate physically with the past.

Manuel Tamayo y Baus's *La locura de amor* debuted at Madrid's Teatro del Príncipe on January 12, 1855. It is the dramatist's most famous play, and is also considered to be among his very best works (second only to his *Un drama nuevo* [A New Drama] [1867]). The action is set in 1506 and takes place as Juana and Philip the Handsome travel through Castile on their way to Burgos. The first and second acts take place in Tudela where the royal entourage has stopped for several days; the three final acts occur in Burgos, in Palacio del Condestable where Philip will accept the crown of Castile. The two settings roughly demarcate the division between the two nuclei around which the plot turns as it is developed. The first orbit corresponds to the psychological drama that unfolds as Juana's suspicions of her husband's infidelity lead her to uncover his affair with Aldara, a Moorish princess. This drama comes to a climax in the final scenes of act 4 when the queen confronts her husband about his relationship with Aldara, who is posing as a handmaiden in the palace at Burgos; and Juana is in turn accused of being unfaithful herself with her childhood friend Don Álvar. The second nucleus centers on the sociopolitical and historical repercussions of Juana's personal situation for the kingdom of Castile. Through references to events at Burgos, and the inclusion of the commentaries made by courtiers and the common people who witness the queen's strange actions, the drama communicates what was perceived to be at stake in the struggle between Juana, Philip, and Ferdinand of Aragon for control of the Castilian throne. The drama concludes with Aldara's conversion to Christianity, and the reconciliation between Juana and Philip moments before his death.

La locura de amor is just one of an entire corpus of nineteenth-century literature and art on the themes of Juana I of Castile's madness and her postmortem devotion to Philip. In order to understand the motivations behind his decision to use such a popular theme, it is necessary to consider the historical and fictional appeal of Juana's story in the context of the theater and the broader cultural milieu of mid-century Spain. The work is representative of this period in terms of its formal characteristics: it combines elements of Romantic theater and the Spanish Golden Age tradition, with the realism and moral content of the bourgeois High Comedy. The blending of these two major currents of nineteenth-century theater are reflective of two salient characteristics that define the period during which Tamayo composed this play, and several other of his historical dramas: 1) the rise of commercialized mass entertainment in all forms; and 2) the collective fascination with all periods of Spanish history among the newly consolidated and politically empowered middle class.

The world of the theater was not impervious to the vast changes wrought by the rise of mass culture in the middle of the nineteenth century. With its direct antecedents in the consolidation of the middle class as a political force, the entertainment industry was transformed by the emergence of new technologies for the distribution of print materials and the promotion of all forms of entertainment. The theater became a venue for the newly moneyed and empowered classes to spend their leisure time and to display their wealth in society. As a result of the commercialization of the theater, which had previously been under state control, the decade of the 1840s witnessed a rise in the demand for new plays. During this period, literally hundreds of playwrights were at work in Madrid feverishly trying to supply impresarios with what were touted as "original" dramas, but which in many cases were adaptations or translations of already staged foreign titles (Gies 1994, 175). At the same time, a relaxing of censorship laws and technological advances in the art of printing sparked a similar boom in the publishing business, flooding the market with cheap translations of foreign novels and new fiction by Spanish authors (Ferreras 1987, 60).

Tamayo, the playwright, was a product of this context. Notwithstanding the fact that he was born into the world of the theater—his parents were successful actors and impresarios—critics agree that he began to write for the theater out of the promise of an easy source of income (Esquer Torres 1965b, 75). It is not surprising then that many of the author's early plays, as Neale Tayler documents, were either direct translations or loose adaptations of already successful foreign works (1959, 111). However, both Tayler and Esquer Torres point out that this does not appear to be the case of *La locura de amor*. His treatment of Juana, according to the latter critic, appears to be entirely original, although the young playwright was most certainly influenced by the works of other European and Spanish authors who had already taken up the figure of Juana in their dramas and historical novels (Esquer Torres 1965a, 92–93).[3] All the same, the financial motivation behind the creation of the work should not be underestimated since the undertaking was almost sure to be a commercial success given the mid-century theatergoer's taste for historical melodrama. In fact this was the case; the play's debut was a resounding success and acclaimed by audience and critics alike (Esquer Torres 1965a, 88).

By the time Tamayo began to work on *La locura de amor*, audiences and readers were already familiar with the story of Juana I of Castile and the necrophilic legend associated with her, through a wide variety of popular and romantic literature, theater, and histories published in the first half of the century. Works like Clémence Robert's 1852 historical novel *Jeanne la Folle* [Juana the Mad] and anonymous pamphlets such as the 1848 *Historia de la célebre Reina de España, Doña Juana, llamada vulgarmente, La Loca* [History of the Famous Queen Juana of Spain, Otherwise Known as The Mad] circulated widely.[4] The theatergoing public would have taken note of the 1848 Paris debut of the opera *Jeanne la Folle*, based on a libretto by Eugène Scribe, since it coincided with the opening of Ramón Fraquelo's historical drama *Doña Juana la Loca* [Juana the Mad] in Madrid. The French translation of American historian William Hickling Prescott's 1838 *History of the Reign of Ferdinand and Isabella the Catholic* and the reedition of Alonso Estanque's *Chronica de los reyes don Fernando y doña Isabel, reyes de Castilla y de Aragón, donde van escritas parte de las vidas de los príncipes don Felipe y doña Juana, condes de Flandes y Tirol* [Chronicle of King Ferdinand and Queen Isabella, Kings of Castile and of Aragon, wherein are also written part of the lives of Prince Philip and Juana, Counts of Flanders and Tirol] offered erudite readers of the 1850s a new vision of Juana's life that reflected the new view of History as a science (Esquer Torres 1965a, 93).

Interest in the Mad Queen in the nineteenth century depended very heavily on the appeal of the necrophilic legend that had overshadowed interpretations of her historical importance since at least the sixteenth century (Aram 2002, 173). With few exceptions, both foreign and Spanish authors tended to focus attention on the episodes in the queen's life story that led up to or that directly represent the well-known tales of her legendary obsession with Philip's corpse in order to confirm allegations of the weakened mental condition that caused the young queen to be called "the Mad." The insistence on this appellation into the nineteenth-century signals— beyond the function of differentiating Juana I from "the Beltraneja" —that there was something more at stake in the diagnosis of the queen's madness confirmed by these necrophilic episodes. During her lifetime, and in the century that followed, speculations about Juana's mental condition provided historians with a case to study, analyze, criticize, and denigrate the political, social, and cultural conditions that explain Spain's emergence as a nation, as the capital of a vast empire, and its decline into decadence. Bethany Aram observes that sixteenth-century Dutch and English historians enthusiastically incorporated tales of Juana's requests to have the coffin opened from time to time so that she could kiss her husband's remains into their "Black Legend" chronicles as further evidence of Spain's Catholic fanaticism (2002, 172). While foreign historians and writers in the sixteenth century found confirmation of their negative images of Spain, Juana's story provided century Spanish historians with a pretext to contest foreign exaggerations of the legend and to offer alternative explanations that reappropriated the story within a nationalist agenda.

La locura de amor appeals to the nationalist sentiments of mid-century audiences by offering an original interpretation of the days preceding the event that supposedly triggered Juana's descent into total madness: the death of Philip. The drama provides a novel psychological study of the character that sheds new light on her biography and offered audiences a new version of the tale, in tune with the aesthetic tastes of the period. By treating a historical figure in this manner, Tamayo's play connects to the revolutionary changes that occurred in the field of historiography in the nineteenth century. A second determinant of the culture in which La locura de amor debuted, therefore, has to do with the historiographical debates of the moment, and the resulting popularization of images and narratives based on episodes from Spain's recent and distant past.

In the middle years of the century the study of history not only emerged as a modern social science, but, consequentially, also became a popular pastime among the bourgeoisie. The phenomenon gave rise to the large-scale history paintings that dominated the national salons of the 1850s and 1860s, and assured the continued success of the historical drama even in the face of Romanticism's waning influence.[5] Nineteenth-century histories tended to deal with the origins and transformations of the nation as a permanent community with intention of offering a narrative that would demonstrate claims of Spain's unity (Álvarez Junco 2001, 196). Historians sought to define and exalt national character through the recreation of emblematic moments and figures from the past that incarnated such essential values as honor, loyalty to king and country, and faith. Juana I of Castile certainly occupied a prominent place in this national pantheon: as the daughter of Isabella and Ferdinand, and the mother of the Emperor Charles V, her biography encapsulates a key transitional period in the life of the nation. The political struggle that provides the background to Tamayo's drama is wedged between the end of the Reconquest of the national territory, and the beginning of the Conquest of empire in Europe and America. The interpretation of Juana's story offered in *La locura de amor* directly incorporates allusions to both processes by linking the queen's tribulations to the Flemish conspiracy to secure the throne for Philip, on the one hand, and the desire for revenge among the vanquished Moors that motivates Aldara to seduce the king, on the other.

In this way, Tamayo's use of the necrophilic legend as the inspiration for his version of Juana's story in *La locura de amor* reflects the intellectual and ideological debates spurred by the national project of constructing a single narrative of Spanish history. Granted the internal political divisions that had divided Spain since the War of Independence (1808–14), two versions of this narrative emerged and competed for acceptance among academics and the growing public of bourgeois readers: one advocated by liberal and moderate historians, and the other propagated by conservative and neo-Catholic writers. Both ideological perspectives largely coincide in their interpretations of events up to and including the reign of Ferdinand and Isabella: the Middle Ages are seen as the Golden Age of "Spanishness," that culminates with the Catholic Monarchs as the absolute expression of national character and values. In the writing of Spain's history in the early modern period, a bifurcation occurs in the presentation of the events following Isabella's death (the short reigns of Juana I and Philip, and the regency of Ferdinand) and the ascension of the Habsburgs to the Spanish throne with Charles V. Following the tradition of Enlightenment historiography, liberal historians almost unanimously tended to interpret the crowning of Charles V as the event marking the beginning of Spain's decline into decadence fueled by religious fanaticism, intolerance, and vain imperial endeavors. Conservative historians, on the other hand, tended to offer a more ambiguous interpretation of the Hapsburgs and the manner in which they took control of the Spanish throne. For the most part, these writers saw in the reign of Charles V (and the "Philips") the culmination of Spain's imperial destiny (in Europe and America) and the ultimate triumph of Catholicism. However, at the same time these writers also saw that the glories of Spain came with a price: the infiltration of foreigners and foreign ideas that would eventually lead to decadence and the degeneration of national character. Conservatives saw a direct link between Renaissance Humanism, Enlightenment thought, and the emergence of Liberalism and the corrosion of the most essential value that defined Spanish national character: the Roman Catholic faith.

The lack of attention given to Tamayo's theater by contemporary literary critics is at least in part based on the writer's association with the most retrograde sectors of Spanish society. Following the 1868 September Revolution, he became actively associated with various neo-Catholic groups and belonged to the Junta Central Tradicionalista, which supported the Carlist movement.[6] In spite of his adherence to these reactionary causes later in life, his treatment of Juana I, and the political consequences of her madness, is not so easily categorized in terms of the version of Spanish history defended by conservative historians. A brief comparison between Tamayo's play and Juan de Orduña's 1948 filmic adaptation *Locura de amor,* is illustrative of this point. The most notable difference between the film and the play is the addition of the frame narrative in which the young Charles V, who has just arrived in Spain to take possession of the throne, listens to his mother's story as told by Álvar. The addition is significant for interpretations of both works, and especially important in situating them within the historiography of the periods in which they were produced. The absence of the figure of Charles in *La locura de amor* positions it squarely within the debates described above, but aligns it more closely with the vision of liberal historians who saw everything after the reign of the Catholic Monarchs as decadent. As a fervent defender of Catholic values over and above anything else, here and in his later works, in *La locura de amor* he is most concerned with the notion that after a certain point in the nation's history things began to go astray. For Tamayo, this moment pivots around the question of Juana's madness and the necrophilic impulse that accompanies it. The author appears to leave the issue unresolved and open to interpretation. In so doing, it can be argued that the drama focuses attention on the problem that the diagnosis of insanity posed for Spain in the sixteenth century, as a way of emphasizing its resonance for the nineteenth century. By contrast, Orduña's frame narrative imposes on viewers the interpretation that Juana's madness was the product of Flemish machinations, and that her necrophilic obsession with the cadaver of Philip was a triumph over these foreign infiltrators since it served to preserve the throne for Charles V. The 1948 film connects the present triumph of Franco's National Movement to the glories of the past achieved under the emperor's reign, while the nineteenth-century playwright looks back to the past, seeking a lesson for solving the problems of Spain's present rather than merely a justification for present actions.

Having located *La locura de amor* within the commercial culture of the 1850s and the historical debates of the period, it is now pertinent to focus on the theme of necrophilia and the relationship between Tamayo's play and the emerging scientific discourses on madness and degeneration of the time. Literature written after 1850 was increasingly influenced by advances in modern science, as writers adopted the language and applied the methods of the scientist to the creative process. Even though the drama in question belongs to a transitional moment, such an awareness of the science of the period is nevertheless apparent. The title, *La locura de amor* sets this interpretation of Juana I of Castile apart from other fictional works of the time in that it alludes not to the person (Juana the Mad), but rather to her condition (madness). Some scholars choose to omit the definite article when citing the play's title, thus creating confusion with the twentieth-century filmic adaptation. Notwithstanding, the drama debuted and was published as *La locura de amor*.[7] The difference between the two is indeed subtle, yet the addition of the definite article is more specific and less poetic, announcing a more generalized description of a particular condition or category of madness associated with love, of which the story of Juana I of Castile offers merely an example. The title has the ring of the many scientific pamphlets and treatises that circulated during the period and through which the public at large was made aware of the vast advances of the modern age.

Throughout the first half of the nineteenth century, understandings of madness, and mental illness in more general terms, were dominated by Etienne Esquirol's concept of monomania. The notion fundamentally redefined the concept of madness by distinguishing between partial delirium limited to a single object or small numbers of objects and complete insanity. The suggestion that such partial insanity might be isolated and cured gave scientists working in the emerging field of psychiatry the recognition of both physicians and of legal professionals who saw in it practical applications for the development of institutions of public health and social reform. That

Esquirol's theory had important implications for the interpretation of Juana's supposed madness among writers and historians is supported by Tamayo's text in the manner in which he clinically redefines her madness as a localized obsession with an unfaithful husband. As monomania, the necrophilic impulse manifested in the final scene of the drama can be written off as an extension of the queen's jealous fixation with Philip beyond his death. At different moments over the course of the drama it is suggested that what had been traditionally interpreted as total madness was nothing more than an unhealthy obsession. For example, at the end of act 3, when Juana cries out "Mad! . . . Mad! If it were only true! And why shouldn't it?" (1947, 448) she contemplates the accusations made by those around her that she has gone mad in an ironic tone, realizing that indeed her plight would be easier if she were truly mad and revealing that she might have adopted this position to further her own political agenda. For mid-century audiences, such an explanation of Juana's madness was plausible from a historical and political perspective, and was supported by a widely accepted understanding of mental illness. Nevertheless the idea, repeated throughout the play, that Juana was not mad but simply obsessed, is complicated by the way in which the queen's actions and statements suggest that madness—feigned or true—is the only means of surviving in a society and a world that has gone mad.

In the decade of the 1850s, Esquirol's notion of the *idée fixe* came to be challenged by new research that emphasized the study of the human body and its function as a single unitary organism. The concept of monomania was displaced by new studies that suggested that even though many mental afflictions appear to affect a single capacity, it is wrong to assume that the rest of the mind is completely healthy (Campos, Martínez, and Huertas 2003, 78–79). The hypothesis that even the most isolated abnormality in behavior was a manifestation of a more profound state of mental degeneration had tremendous resonance for the medical sciences, as well as for almost all fields of social and scientific inquiry. The 1855 debut of *La locura de amor* occurred at a moment of growing concern with the nature of social changes and the consequences of progress for the "health" of European civilization. The notion of *dégénérescence* or degeneration emerged in response to preoccupations with the classification of the whole variety of new social ills that seemed to accompany the processes of rapid industrialization and urbanization, and the triumph of Liberalism (Pick 1989, 7). The theory, which had developed in France in the 1840s in response to what was perceived to be an internal crisis of French society wrought by the contradictions inherent in the ideals of progress, quickly spread across the continent as the mass social upheaval of events like the 1848 Revolution in Paris caused scientists and social thinkers to adopt a profoundly pessimistic view of contemporary society and the state of civilization. For many, the grave social problems associated with growth of the city and the emerging influence of mass political movements like socialism, were signs of a deep moral crisis and irreversible social decline. Such developments seemed to confirm an already growing fear that the human species had reached an impasse and had begun to regress back toward its atavistic roots (Downing 2003, 37). As a corollary to Darwin's theory of evolution, the degenerate condition was understood to be the result of physical and/or moral morbidity transmitted hereditarily (Huertas 1987, 25). Questions of biological reproduction and concerns with hereditary degeneration were juxtaposed with discussions of the historical processes at work in European society. The repetition of events of profound social impact, such as revolutions and war, was described in medical terms as chronic affliction, and the suggestion that history might advance cyclically rather lineally gave rise to "fears about a fundamental [pathological] disorder of national history" (Pick 1989, 40). The language of degeneration, formalized by Benedict Morel in his 1857 *Traité des dégénérescence physiques, intellectuelles et morales de l'espèce humaine* [Treatise on the Physical, Intellectual and Moral Degeneration of the Human Species] offered a convenient and attractive means of "conceptualizing a felt crisis of history" that marked every field of scientific inquiry as well as the visual and literary arts in the second half of the century (Pick 1989, 7).

Through the writings of Morel and others, the concept of degeneration spread throughout Europe in the 1850s. The solutions offered by science and the state to arrest the cycle of decline, characterize it as an essentially conservative discourse. Morel posited that such noxious social symptoms as materialism, madness, crime, and prostitution could only be reversed through the institutionalization of a program of mass moralization (Downing 2003, 37). With a firm grounding in the fundamental teachings of the church, it is not surprising that the writings of French degenerationists found acceptance among Spanish conservatives. The solutions offered for combating the cycle of decline perceived to afflict French society, are reflected in the writings of Juan Donoso Cortés and Jaime Balmes. In his *Ensayo sobre el catolicismo, el liberalismo y el socialismo* [Essay on Catholicism, Liberalism, Socialism], Donoso Cortés (who was Spanish ambassador to Paris during the 1848 uprising) presents an apocalyptic view of modern Spanish society, and concludes that only through a return to traditional Catholic values could such trends be counteracted (Álvarez Junco 2001, 376). In a similar way, Balmes sought to lay the basis for a movement that would "reconstitute" the nation in terms of its traditions and its existing social structure (403).

Turning to Tamayo's theater and his ideas about the role of the theater in society, it is clear that he shared the concerns of Spanish conservative thinkers and neo-Catholic ideologues. Neale Taylor points out that "The perceived gravity of the historical, political, economic and social events of his time shaped Tamayo's conservative ideology, and inspired him to use the stage as a platform to express his concerns" (1959, 18). As an avid reader, proficient in French, he was probably familiar with the discourse of degeneration that had begun to appear in pamphlets and articles on a broad range of topics that reached Spain's middle-class readers in the 1850s. In spite of the fact that the author would not become directly involved in politics until after the 1868 Revolution, very early in his career he explicitly tied his theater to the sort of moralizing project envisioned as necessary by Morel and his predecessors. In the prologue to his play *Ángela* (1852), Tamayo lays out the basic principle that would guide him throughout his career as a dramatist. He held that good drama is built around moral portraits of individuals with all of their deformities, and that through the portrayal of fictional lives as examples, theater could offer valuable lessons for a society trapped in a cycle of decadence (1947, 153–54). Degeneration theorists held that the individual case should be studied, not to provide an individualized cure, but to identify the societal causes of the behavior or affliction, and to propose measures to eradicate them from the larger social body (Pick 1989, 54). Tamayo's 1852 definition of theater echoes this basic tenet of degeneration theory in several ways; most obvious is his proposal to use the study of the individual as a means of providing a lesson for the nation. In general, his characters are not idealized, but rather deformed and less than perfect. The moral portrait he offers audiences in *La locura de amor* is in fact a psychological profile of the individual in a degenerate state. The promise of regeneration is held out not to the individual but to the entire social body, and resides largely in first identifying the affliction or source of degeneration that lies within. The theme of necrophilia introduced at the end of the play becomes the focal point for both exposing the situation of degeneracy and illuminating the path toward regeneration.

Necrophilia was among the many degenerative behaviors identified by social scientists as proof of the dismal moral and physical condition of society at large. In the emerging scientific framework of the period, necrophilia was studied, together with other "perversions" like homosexuality, masturbation, bestiality, and pedophilia, as symptomatic of the morbid biological condition of the individual patient (Downing 2003, 32). The vast catalog of "perverted behaviors" observed and collected by scientists was conceptualized as a single continuum of afflictions, all of which were indicative of an all-encompassing process of physiological and psychological degeneration. Although the word necrophilia was not used until 1861, descriptions of criminal cases involving sexual acts performed on cadavers had already begun to receive special attention from scientists in the fields of sexology and psychiatry in the 1840s, and were also reported with increasing frequency to the general reading public in the scandal driven press of European capitals (31–32).

La locura de amor was written precisely around the same time that necrophilia was first identified as a category of sexual perversion and of criminal behavior. The play depicts the Mad Queen as trapped between two conflicting roles: on the one hand, in her intimate declarations she expresses—in century terms—a deep desire to be a wife; on the other she recognizes the duties imposed on her by birth as queen of Castile. The personal struggle to navigate the exigencies of the roles of wife and queen are symbolized by the two cadavers that haunt and attract her simultaneously. Traditionally the myth of Juana's necrophilic desire was based on her physical obsession with the body of her dead husband, however Tamayo introduces the theme almost from the outset. In her early tribulations Juana is already shown as caught between the living and the dead; the memory of her mother Queen Isabella haunts her as she tries to come to terms with Philip's infidelity. Speaking to Philip in act 1, scene 7 she confesses the following: "The venerated shadow of my mother Isabella often appears before my eyes . . . And I hear . . . [her] voice saying to me: think of your sacred duties, and I think of you; love your people, and I adore you; preserve my legacy, Spain debates new glories and fortunes; and my heart only responds: I love with every heartbeat, and I want to cry like a penitent Queen, and but I can only cry like a woman in love" (1947, 403). Juana finds herself in a moral and emotional impasse: she is caught between the hereditary duties imposed on her by birth and demands that she be a loyal and submissive wife, a political environment that only seeks to steal her power, and a licentious husband who makes her miserable. The queen is locked in a cycle of attraction and repulsion that is reflective of, and a contributing factor in, the degeneration of her mental condition. In this way, Juana is offered to audiences as an allegory of the Spanish nation at a crucial moment in its development: she can either continue along the path laid out by the stoicism of the Catholic

Monarchs (embodied by Isabella), or give in to the appeal of the Renaissance cult of human beauty incarnated in the figure of Philip the Handsome. The situation was easily transferable to the experience of mid-century audiences: seen through the eyes of neo-Catholics like Tamayo, Juana, like Spain, is caught between the pursuit of her true Spanish Catholic nature and unnatural foreign influences of liberalism, democracy, and progress.

The repugnance that accompanies mention of necrophilic desire is based on the designation that there is something wholly unnatural in the attraction to the dead. Likewise, however, there is also something strangely unnatural in the absolute repulsion caused by the sight of a dead loved one. The queen reflects on the natural and unnatural impulses that motivate her (and those around her) in an earlier scene, prior to Philip's death: "People make fun of my love for you? Of course. It's natural for a woman to love a dashing young man, but not her husband for years and years. Illegitimate love, adulterous love, that's love. Legitimate, sacred love, that's not love, that's strangeness, absurdity, madness" (1947, 425). Her reflections in this instance foreshadow her declarations at the end of the play. She finds that there is something terribly wrong and immoral with a society that condemns a wife's eternal devotion to her husband. Juana's comments undermine the romantic ideals of Tamayo's time by contrasting what is accepted by contemporary society as legitimate with her traditional definition of love. She contemplates a world in which the essential values of family and marriage, the cornerstones of the nation, have been turned upside down and deemed signs of madness. Juana is confused by the reversal of what is natural and unnatural; however in her confusion she makes clear that her own madness is but a symptom of a greater process of degeneration at work in Spanish society.

By the middle of the century, as Downing observes, "[t]he degeneration of the individual psychiatric patient and the society as a whole, or the organic body and the body politic, become interchangeable echoes of each other" (2003, 39). The connection between Juana's personal struggle, and its repercussions for the life of the nation, hinges on the queen's mental condition. The two realms, as presented in the play, are echoes of each other. Act 2 opens with a conversation among the common folk that congregate at the rural inn where Philip's illicit relationship with Aldara begins. They discuss the present political state of the nation and all agree with the ironic conclusion expressed by the owner of the establishment: "We'll surely prosper with a mad queen and a scatterbrained king" (1947, 410). The insertion of such observations by common people not only adds local color to the drama, but also makes explicit the relationship between Juana's mental condition, Philip's behavior, and the "progress" of the nation. As the play develops, Juana's supposed madness is progressively revealed to be the product of an essential contradiction in the social and moral fabric of the nation. Near the middle of act 4 Juana is surprised by the reaction of the nobles who have gathered to decide her fate: "They, too, keep quiet? With reason the proverbs says that one mad man makes many madmen. As you can see, gentlemen, it's amazing how the mad abound in Burgos" (1947, 459). The queen's observation late in the play reiterates the essential message that is developed around the historical figure over the course of the drama: if Juana has gone mad, it is only because Spain has also gone mad.

The influence of the discourse of degeneration in *La locura de amor* becomes evident in the way Juana's mental condition is performed in the play and how it exposes the origins of contemporary social maladies in the biography of the Mad Queen. Tamayo aligns his version of the story with conservative ideologies that sought to stem what was considered an insidious cycle of change by memorializing the past and moralizing the present. Downing writes, "Degeneration theory operat[ed] according to a fantasy of necrophobia—a fear of death and the dead body—at the social level" (2003, 39). Returning to the closing scene of the play, Juana's emotions move from an initial attitude of elation at finally being able to possess her husband's body to an unsettling tranquility of denial. She is torn between a necrophilic impulse to possess the cadaver, and a necrophobic rejection of its lifeless state. The paradox of necrophilia is that while such feelings can never be fully reciprocated, physical contact with the dead nevertheless functions as a mechanism for preserving a sense of the relationship between the living and the dead (Roach 1988, 29). As if recognizing that madness offers the only solution to her dilemma, Juana embraces the accusations fully and decides to play the part of the mad queen.

Halfway through her final declarations there is a sudden: "Indeed, implacable Death, I will evade your intentions. Silence. Silence! . . . The King has fallen asleep" (1947, 475). She consciously decides to accept the challenge of the situation presented to her by society and providence; from this point forward she insists that Philip is only sleeping. In the push and pull between the feelings of attraction and repulsion, necrophilia and its concomitant necrophobia, act as conservative forces that stem change and petrify the existing order. The king is not dead and the royal couple has finally reconciled their differences. Yet, Tamayo, like Juana, resists the idea of petrifaction as such, and suggests that out of the contact with the past, and the dead, the health of the Spanish nation might be renewed. In spite of her madness, Juana has to live as Philip himself declares moments before he expires, "Yes, you will live because God orders you to live for a nation that pins all of its hopes on you" (1947, 473). The moralizing message that is woven into the story of Juana I of Castile in *La locura de amor* is a proactive call to action, by embracing madness, to reverse the hereditary cycle of degeneration of which her tragic life is the starting point. If Spain is to regenerate itself it must accept its true nature even if this implies holding onto the Catholic values that nineteenth-century liberals and progressive thinkers—and sixteenth-century Dutch and English historians before them—deemed as mad and degenerate.

NOTES

1. All translations are the author's unless otherwise noted.
2. See David T. Gies, *The Theatre in Nineteenth-Century Spain* (Cambridge: Cambridge University Press, 1994), 238–47; Francisco Ruiz Ramón, *Historia del teatro español (Desde sus orígenes hasta 1900)* (Madrid: Cátedra, 1992), 345–46.
3. Notwithstanding, it should be mentioned that the character Aldara and the plot of *La locura de amor* are similar to Clemence Robert's *Jeanne la folle* (Paris, 1852) even though the setting of the French novel is Toledo and the timeframe is sometime prior to the death of Isabella in 1504.
4. The Bibliothèque National Française lists in its catalog what appears to be an earlier edition titled *Jeanne de Castille: Nouvelle historique* (Paris, 1843).
5. For a study of history painting and its relationship to literature and other arts see Carlos Reyero, *La pintura de historia en España: Esplendor de un género en el siglo XIX* (Madrid: Cátedra, 1989).
6. See Ramón Esquer Torres, "Tamayo y Baus y la política del siglo XIX," *Segismundo* 1 (1965): 71–91.
7. The original program held in the theater archives at the Fundación Juan March, as well as the first published version of the drama from 1855 owned by the Biblioteca Nacional, both carry the title *La locura de amor;* see Manuel Tamayo y Baus *La locura de amor* (Madrid: F. Obieuzo, 1855).

WORKS CITED

Álvarez Junco, José. 2001. *Mater dolorosa: La idea de España en el siglo XIX*. Madrid: Taurus.

Aram, Bethany. 2002. "Juana 'the Mad,' the Clares, and the Carthusians: Revising a Necrophilic Legend in Eary Hapsburg Spain." *Archiv für Reformationsgeschichte* 93:172–91.

Campos Marín, Ricardo, José Martínez Pérez, and Rafael Huertas García-Alejo. 2003. *Los ilegales de la naturaleza: Medicina y degeneracionismo en la España de la Restauración, (1876–1923)*. Madrid: CSIC.

Downing, Lisa. 2003. *Desiring the Dead: Necrophilia and Nineteenth-Century French Literature*. Oxford: Legenda.

Esquer Torres, Ramón. 1965a. *El teatro de Tamayo y Baus*. Madrid: CSIC.

————. 1965b. "Tamayo y la política del siglo XIX." *Segismundo* 1:71–91.

Ferreras, Juan Ignacio. 1987. *La novela española en el siglo XIX (hasta 1868)*. Madrid: Taurus.

Gies, David T. 1994. *The Theatre in Nineteenth-Century Spain*. Cambridge: Cambridge University Press.

Huertas García-Alejo, Rafael. 1987. *Locura y degeneración: Psiquiatría y sociedad en el positivismo francés*. Madrid: CSIC.

Pick, Daniel. 1989. *Faces of Degeneration: A European Disorder, c. 1848–c. 1919*. Cambridge: Cambridge University Press.

Reyero, Carlos. 1989. *La pintura de historia en España: Esplendor de un género en el siglo XIX*. Madrid: Cátedra.

Roach, Joseph. 1998. "History, Memory, Necrophilia." In *The Ends of Performance*, edited by Peggy Phelan and Jill Lane, 23–39. New York: New York University Press.

Ruiz Ramón, Francisco. 1992. *Historia del teatro español (Desde sus orígenes hasta 1900)*. Madrid: Cátedra.

Tamayo y Baus, Manuel. 1947. *La locura de amor*. In *Obras completas*. Madrid: Ediciones FAX.

Taylor, Neale H. 1959. *Las fuentes del teatro de Tamayo y Baus*. Madrid: Gráficas Uguina.

The Historical and Aesthetic Truth of *Santa Juana de Castilla* by Benito Pérez Galdós

José Luis Mora García

Few people in Spanish history have generated as much attention as Queen Juana of Castile. Known as Juana the Mad by the majority of historians, she is nonetheless promoted to the category of saint in *Santa Juana de Castilla: Tragicomedia en tres actos* [Saint Juana of Castile: A Tragicomedy in Three Acts] (1918) by Benito Pérez Galdós (1843–1920). Not even the passage of time has managed to diminish the interest in her that was passionately revived in the second half of the nineteenth century. At that time the romantic undercurrent provided an appropriate environment for the introduction of such a character with a *chiaroscuro* disposition. Juana's character served a historical perspective in which contrasts were amplified both by the grandeur of political acts and by personal tragedies, reasons of state and its manipulations, and even by the repression of individual feelings. Nothing is more human than one's love for an analysis of this type of character in which the essence of Spanishness is made so manifest.

However, political aspects combined with such a complicated life story, filled with jealousy, conspiracy, and sorrow were not enough; European historiography, mainly German, now raised an almost taboo topic within the context of early modernism: the role of religion in relation to politics and present-day knowledge. The moment coincided with European and Spanish events that favored a Manichean mind-set. These were the years of the *Syllabus,* a papal act leading up to the Vatican I debate and the condemnation of liberal Catholicism, when the reign of Isabella the II of Spain was reaching its end. This event made way for the Revolution of 1868, the expulsion and later replacement of the Krausists in their teaching positions, the dawning of a six-year term of reformation, and the Alfonsian restoration. In accord with Article 11 of the 1876 Constitution, it was the Alfonsian restoration that left those religious problems hanging precariously in

the balance. This viewpoint was immediately tested and in truth it did
not fare very well. Benito Pérez Galdós would play a role, surely to his
regret, in some of the most reverberating episodes of this poorly
resolved religious issue from which he could not rescue even Queen
Juana.

In the twentieth century, interest still burned in the embers of this
nineteenth-century controversy of which Galdós's play, *Santa Juana
de Castilla,* was a product. The play premiered in 1918, two years
before the author's death. However, it was almost certainly first conceived around 1892 just after Galdós published *Angel Guerra,* written
a few years before its premiere, and finally presented to the audience
as his intellectual testament. Galdós found Queen Juana of Castile a
key historical character since she represented the beginning of modern Spain. She is positioned between the nationalistic point of view
of her parents, the Catholic Monarchs, and the *universitas christiana,*
a model society made up of Christians, formed by her son, Emperor
Carlos.

If one examines the decline that overpowered the intellectuals of
the generations of 1868, 1898 and 1914, Juana's character is vital in
clarifying the role Castile could have played, yet did not fulfill. Galdós
witnessed the failure of the revolution of September 1868. He was
part of the group that most rallied for change and in the beginning
he was eager for national reconstruction and for Spain's universal-
ization. He went through distinct stages of discussion and adjustment
of his view of history and finally diagnosed the causes of the decline
and proposed a solution. In other words, he thought that what could
have been and was not, might still be possible. Galdós developed a
friendly disagreement between history and literature that culminated
with the representation of this paradoxical protagonist. Galdós
invites his audience to examine Juana's character in order to overcome a negative view of history and to opt for a new interpretation
in tune with reason and orthodoxy. The past cannot be changed but
art, reinterpreting history, can propose a new future.

REALITY: HISTORY AND LITERATURE

Galdós's writings have an internal cohesion that always compels one
to search for the meaning in each work in reference to its role in the
whole. Certain rumors about Galdós's allegedly weak intellectual
training were spread by young writers from the 1898 generation and
have been misleading the public probably due to the lack of good
biographies. Although belatedly, more details are now known about

his substantial training in the classics and about his knowledge of Latin that he acquired from the San Agustin school in his birth town Las Palmas on Gran Canary Island. Equally relevant is his appreciation for the sixteenth century that he gained in school through reading *Compendio de Historia Universal* [Outline of our Universal History] (1842–43) by Alfredo Adolfo Camus (1797–1889). When Galdós arrived in Madrid, Camus was the professor of Latin literature. Little has been said about this scholar, but it is known that in 1868 he offered a course titled *Historical-Critical Studies of Spanish Humanists during the Renaissance* at the Ateneo cultural center of Madrid (Mallo 1990, 161). It would not be surprising to find that Galdós attended that class given his appreciation for Camus. That would support the following statement by Josette Blanquat:

> Among the Renaissance Humanists cited by Benito [Pérez Galdós], one name stands out: Erasmus. One of Erasmus's works left a lasting mark on Galdós: *In Praise of Madness*. In the Las Palmas library, they still have the book with Galdós's pencil marks in the margins. He highlighted the passages that really caught his attention and also wrote the translations of isolated words. This emphasizes Galdós's desire to perfectly understand the Humanist's thinking and to clarify everything while reading the text translated by Gueudeville. . . . From one end to the other in Galdós's play one sees these evangelic truths (contempt for wealth and madness for God) illustrated. However, it cannot be confirmed whether or not the ideas were directly taken from Erasmus. Nevertheless, in his old age, Galdós wrote a short play, *Santa Juana de Castilla*, that premiered May 8, 1918, as a special tribute to this great humanist. (1970, 178)

Influenced by his classic, humanist training, Galdós went about amassing his knowledge of the nineteenth century, which favored the birth of his new novel *La fontana de oro: Novela histórica* [The Golden Fountain Cafe] (1870) and the first two series of *Episodios Nacionales* [National Episodes] (1873–75), before undertaking thesis or contemporary novels. This was an aspect that had gone unnoticed yet was key in understanding Galdós's work and why he was a reformist of realist esthetics who wanted to move away from escapist literature and false historical novels.

Nothing could be written without taking reality into account. Throughout the 1870s the positivist mentality prevailed as a correction of the overindulgence of Krausist idealism, whose limits were made obvious by the 1868 revolution. It will be precisely this event that will shape Galdós's life and the lives of key players of that time period. Therefore it was the rejuvenation of history that impelled the revitalization of the novel as the premier literary genre that could recuperate the splendor that it had not had since Cervantes. Galdós was most concerned with getting to know the truth about things without deceptions, idealizations, or references to supernatural causes; at this point his interests for natural sciences, history, and literature came together. The ideological climate during this time was dominated by the theme of Spain's decline. This aspect ends up being crucial in order to explain the strong initial bond between history and literature in relation to reality and should be explained in order to clarify why Spaniards are the way they are. In blending history and narrative, Galdós's purpose was to teach improvement and change. The construction of this framework was meant to provide the readers lessons in heroism and morality that contrasted with the historical situation they were living, under the leadership of mediocre and egotistical politicians.

Around 1885 Galdós published *Fortunata y Jacinta* [Fortunata and Jacinta], fictional prose that did not deviate from his original style and that revolved around a detailed description of Madrid at the end of the 1870s. After publishing this novel Galdós decided to set aside his analyses of contemporary history to write articles for newspapers. He introduced a more global reflection of Spain's history. This new reflection influenced a new genre to Galdós: theater. He started writing plays in 1892. In 1885 Galdós published an article titled "Religious Sentiment in Spain" and "Its Grandeur and Decline." The article reflected on the history of Spain in general terms and did not express any radical viewpoint. It stated that "the religious sentiment in Spain, a powerful force, a fortitude of our history, a fundamental vigor in happy times, underwent great advances but later declined until it came to a regrettable end" (Shoemaker 1973, 145). For Galdós the peace of Westfalia was a turning point for a period dominated by religious sentiment, and in the seventeenth century "there were fewer luminaries of church and state" (146). Meanwhile it was "the eighteenth century, with its ruthless inquiry, that was the sponge that erased everything from Spain's glorious past" (147). The end of the fifteenth century and the sixteenth century were times of glory for Spain. There were "the Catholic Monarchs' massive endeavors" (148). and individuals with the stature of Juan de la Cruz or Ignacio de Loyola that make us believe that "mysticism is the true Spanish philosophy" (149).

To understand Galdós's theories that will be associated with the decline of the Hapsburgs, three issues need to be clarified. First, his stance was that of a positivist who analyzed history and came to the conclusion that "foreign" solutions were not favorable and that they were the basis for the decline. In other words, he advocated national solutions to the problems of the decline and was convinced of the need for the construction of social values. Secondly, Galdós distanced himself from the neo-Catholic stance considering he rejected intolerance and was in favor of freedom of religion. He supported these ideas even though he held that Protestantism in Spain could not be an alternative to Catholicism. Thirdly, he believed that the causes of the decline were historical and that the solutions should be looked for in the historical context.

For twenty years Galdós embarked on this task: to search history for the inexhaustible impetus that served as the driving force in Spanish society. Aesthetic truth, although not strictly formal, occupied the entire focus, and there was no room for historical facts. Yet, there was room for what he called "true feeling and thought of the people" (1897, 27). But why return to the sixteenth century? Why show that our mystics were capable of being free despite their oppressive environment? Why the parallelism between the mature Galdós and the young writers at the end of the century in this reappraisal? The answer has to do with what is called the *fin de siècle* that affected all of Europe and Spain in an exceptional way. The growing presence of the United States in the global arena and the progressive development of pragmatism as a philosophy that inspired a new epistemology, brought about an in-depth revision of the principles on which European history had been established up until then.

Literature began to interpret or rewrite those parts of human behavior that the positivist method did not incorporate. Unamuno called it intrahistory and Galdós could have named it the scope of conscience, of dreams, or of willpower. He really thought that official Spain was in crisis and with even more fervor he was convinced that Spain had a dynamism that should be awakened. The problem was drowsiness or, equally problematic, a weak will that should have been corrected with vigor. But, where did one find that vigor?

That was the role reserved for literature. It was capable of searching for revisions within history and reality, within that which was desired or possible, and even in the present and the future. The novel was an inadequate way to transmit the social values that were to be learned collectively. As Unamuno noted, theater became the genre that fulfilled that function by not only imparting forms of knowledge, social values, and morals but also by provoking a feeling of exaltation or catharsis.

In 1892, Emilia Pardo Bazán published an article about a queen that never governed. It is precisely at this time when the character Juana of Castile acquired relevance for Galdós. Above all it was a perfectly logical adaptation to the internal cohesion of his own work that was clearly aimed at the construction of national conscience through dialogue about the thoughts and opinions of the time.

It is likely that Galdós was familiar with the plays premiered in the period: *Locura de amor* [Madness of Love] (1855) by Manuel Tamayo y Baus and *Juana la loca: drama histórico dividido en seis cuadros y escrito en verso* [Joan the Mad: A Historical Drama Divided in Six Acts and Written in Verse] (1848) by Ramón Franquelo. Both plays are very different from Galdós's view of Juana's character. Tamayo y Baus is interested in jealousy and Franquelo's play is an epic full of empty effectism. For Galdós, as a humanist and an expert on the sixteenth century, the interpretations that German historiography, and specifically Gustav Bergenroth, began forming of the Spanish queen were much more appealing. Galdós probably read Bergenroth's work in English. As Rodolfo Cardona summarizes, Bergenroth's important points are these:

1. Queen Juana was not mad when the rumors were spread as a result of Philip's death or even before.
2. She was a prisoner in Tordesillas. Her father, Ferdinand the Catholic, and later her son, Charles V, ordered the Marquis of Denia to keep her imprisoned there out of jealousy.
3. Juana could have returned to become queen of Castile when the Council of Comuneros met in Tordesillas, but she refused in order to not harm her son.
4. After this period of freedom, Tordesillas fell into the hands of the nobles again. Allegedly they came to rescue her from the "barbarians," but in reality, it was to reinstate her as a prisoner for an additional thirty-five years.
5. During both periods of her confinement she constantly demonstrated her lack of interest in religion and, specifically, Catholic rites. From the very beginning this made her suspect of heresy. (1977, 466–67)

What Cardona does not say is that Galdós had immediate knowledge about Bergenroth's work through the quotation that Antonio de la Fuente gave the University of Madrid's journal (1870). In that quotation he refers to Bergenroth as a Prussian who died in 1869 and was the author of the text already reviewed.

De la Fuente immediately published *El pensamiento español* [Spanish Thought] (1869) and later *Altar y trono* [Altar and Throne] (1869) that contended with the ideas expressed by Bergenroth and Altmeyer. Their ideas contrasted with those of Gachard, the general archivist of

Belgium, Pichot, and Mignet. With historical sources at his disposal, De la Fuente tried to free Queen Juana from all alleged heresy. He did so by taking into consideration the testimonial of Luis Vives who spoke about her in *De institutiones christianae feminae* [Feminine Christian Institutions] (1524). In contrast to those that said she had been secretly learning French, Vives describes Queen Juana as a woman of talent that knew Latin and had learned it with Beatriz Galindo. Of course, he used the testimonial of Cienfuegos, the author of *Vida de San Francisco de Borja* [The Life of Saint Francis of Borja] (1717), which emphasizes the role of this person whom we will study in Galdós's play. Lastly it is based on the records of the Castilian queen's personal doctor who wrote as her death certificate: "She confessed her sins, and asked God to forgive her sins, knowing that she had offended Him, and died a Catholic" (Coloma 1943, 222). All of this emphatically rejected the idea that she could have been among those Protestants persecuted in the sixteenth century.

Galdós adopted a stance equidistant from both the apologetic approach of Catholic writers and from those that simply convicted her of heresy. Both perspectives interested him but it was precisely this division that he wanted to overcome in order to introduce social aspects overlooked in this controversy. From the onset of the new century until he joined the republican-socialist coalition in 1909, Galdós had become evermore sensitive to these social aspects.

Even though Galdós started writing theatrical pieces in 1892, he did not begin with his play about Juana. It is, however, possible that around this time he could have created the idea for the play but put it aside. Together with his novels from the last decade of the nineteenth century, Galdós developed a policy of reflection that was centered on moral values and their social function in Spanish society but without a concrete historical framework. History provides the basis and literature, the feeling. For Galdós, Juana la Loca's character takes on a historical and symbolic dimension key to what could have been and has not yet happened. As far as history is concerned, it cannot be altered. However, literature can correct it and allow what did not happen to still be possible.

It was very clear to Galdós, at his age and with his life experiences, that the problem was linked to the lack of freedom and tolerance that overshadowed one's will. However, Galdós must have thought two things were missing in order to definitely prove that there was no place for despair or idleness. First, he wanted to demonstrate that reason is powerful and even capable of rationalizing senselessness. There is an inner strength that mankind has that is made up of memories accumulated over the centuries and wisdom passed on through education. One should make good use of this in order to organize historical events. To achieve this, one has to resolutely dream it and cause something like a regenerative cataclysm in individual and collective conscience.

Secondly, Galdós wanted to prove that some key historical figure had already achieved this creative madness. In other words, that someone rescued reason using an apparently irrational method like madness. This is to demonstrate that true reality lies in conscience above everything else. It is the obverse of things and a version *sui generis* of this dual truth.

Without a doubt Galdós thought that this task should be carried out by literature. History contributed the raw materials, and no other character combined so many of the requirements to convey this lesson as the daughter of the Catholic Monarchs. The different versions that, since the middle of the nineteenth century, had been circulating about Juana made her very attractive and turned her into the key for Galdós to conclude his plans. The different versions ranged from the meaning for Spain of her mother, Queen Isabella, to the role of her son, the first foreign monarch. The last lesson should be exhibited in a dramatic way and staged so that it could be shared with the audience and equally so with Spanish society. This should be done so that, just as literature is able to discover, the example of this woman locked up for forty-six years can become a part of the Spanish collective memory in accordance with historical truth, facts, and conscience.

LITERATURE: THE SPACE OF CONSCIOUSNESS

According to several sources, mainly the letters in Galdós's files, the play was written around 1915 or even earlier. Before completing the play and his life (he died in 1920), with a sanctified Juana, Galdós needed time to reflect. He, as philosopher, also needed time to develop his theory about why it is necessary to reconcile reason with everyday life. The unity of principles in the realm of conscience and one's circumstances in life can make the development of reason in history very difficult or even impossible. Reason and senselessness leading toward harmony dissolved the paradox.

Since Galdós was not so much a philosopher as he was a novelist and playwright, he expressed this view in allegory, a hybrid genre between novel and play. It did not have any concrete historical references but had a geographic framework more symbolic than real. Utopia? Could be. Perhaps Galdós did not have any other hope for

Spain's recovery except dreaming it and he had time to create an example from history itself.

In the end Galdós respected history but did not conform to it. He taught that "if time is undone, the more imagination will build." Likewise, Galdós considered literature to be the instrument necessary for unraveling his meaning. This was his intention: to discover the mystery of Tordesillas and leave humankind its legacy so that it would serve as a lesson for all.

Manuel Fernández Álvarez endorsed the traditional idea of the weak mental disposition of Juana that caused her removal from power after the death of her husband around 1506. "No one questioned Juana's emotional condition, which in today's medical terms could have been classified as a severe exogenous depression, but perhaps she could have overcome it." (1994, 193). This last point reinforces the discussions about the right of the government and those that favored her confinement against the popular belief that she was always the legitimate queen. This would explain the episode with the Comuneros and her brief period of freedom that was her last opportunity to complete this urban movement, however unfeasible, with her awkward alliance of peasants. It was a political rebellion to which was added a social rebellion and therefore was unsuccessful. How can one govern without the support of the nobles?

Galdós skillfully and with poetic license creates a meeting between the prisoner of Tordesillas and the peasants. However, he displaces this moment to a memory she has two days before she dies. This allows Galdós to keep the effectiveness of the myth without judging history or Juana's cowardly act: she could have ruled Spain supported by the *comuneros* but chose not to.

Referring to the debate over orthodoxy, Fernández Álvarez maintains the following with regard to reports about Juana's indifference on religious matters: "even her actions and gestures could be attributed to heretical inklings" (1994, 233). This caused the future Philip II to ask the future San Francisco of Borja to visit his grandmother. San Francisco of Borja soon found that the treatment Juana received was inappropriate, and after his human contact she returned to religious practices and even recovered her mental faculties. The panegyrists made the most of the situation and attributed it to the saint as a miracle he performed. Symbolically Juana's death occurred in the early morning on Good Friday in the spring of 1555. Her death was completely orthodox; upon the recommendation of Domingo de Soto, she received extreme unction but not Holy Communion due to the vomiting she experienced. On the other hand, nothing was said about Juana possibly reading Erasmus, being in tune with the Dutch friar's teachings, and this causing her to forego her attendance at mass and other religious rites. This aspect takes on a much more important dimension in Galdós's play.

Manuel Martínez Mediero, whose work *Juana del amor hermoso* [A Love Too Beautiful] (1982) is an assertion in defense of feelings as opposed to the logic of the government, uses history and language in critical terms that Galdós would hardly have discerned except on two points. Galdós would have concurred with a phrase of Padilla's that disagrees with Pfandl's notion: "One would need all the sand from the desert in order to conceal the name Juana of Castile" (Martínez Mediero 1982, 142). The second point refers to the moral of the story spoken by Juana's character: "In history feelings are not possible. What happened to me happens when there are feelings in history . . . everything is materialism. And you are either a materialist or simply crazy" (Pérez Galdós 1963, 124). However, we might ask, could it be that she was a saint? As Erasmus said: "Those that believe that peoples' happiness lies in things [are truly mistaken]. In reality it depends on the opinion one holds about material things. The followers of Plato, the least pretentious among the philosophers, wisely contended that darkness and the variety among human things are so vast that everything cannot be crystal clear for everyone" (1976, 85). According to Galdós, *Elogio de la locura* appeared by the bedside in which Saint Juana of Castile died. On the other side, there was the Jesuit Francisco of Borja, who blessed her and her blessed madness.

And what did this blessed madness consist of? Stanley Finkenthal skillfully responds to this question by asserting that Queen Juana's heresy consisted in carrying out that which her mother was not able to do: using her "freedom of conscience" (1980, 188). That freedom could have been the basis for tolerance and coexistence. Her confinement in Tordesillas was a time for purification. It was her purgatory for having been open-minded on three fundamental concepts: religious tolerance, her nationalism expressed by her unity with the people, and her social sense of property. In these concepts resides her sainthood, in the unity of principles on which humanity rests with true history. As was stated earlier, what could have been and was not. Yet, thanks to theater it is still possible to create a new government. How great if the dream presented on stage could become reality just as Benigna in *Misericordia* [Marcy] said, "Unlucky are the people that do not have a basic, habitual dream. It should be a norm of reality or a milestone placed in the distance along your path!" (Pérez Galdós 1963, 1497). This exclamation used regularly after 1898, is now presented on stage as a radical lesson, a fundamental dream and a norm for reality.

Santa Juana de Castilla is a play in three acts whose action starts two days before the death of Juana. There are three important points in the play. The first refers to Juana's commitment to Erasmus, of which the audience learns through the opinion of her elderly servant Mogica. His words provide an idea about how the queen became familiar with Erasmus's teachings. "I was in Gante at the service of Secretary Conchillos when a Dutch man named Erasmus arrived to visit her Majesty. Erasmus was famous for being a very wise man, the wisest man in those times." He gave to her *Elogio de la locura* that certainly had "to be a very Christian work if Pope Leon X read it and re-read it with delight" (1331). This event is the first focus in the play.

During her entire confinement her behavior corresponded to the principles of the Erasmus reform. "Our Queen has religion in her devout soul. She passionately loves the humble and clean of heart" but she does not appear to attend religious rituals (1332). So Galdós made his version the one in which Queen Juana practices the teachings of Erasmus. Far from the idea that this attitude was heretical, in his version therein lay the true idea of religion.

The second point, focusing on her identification with Castile is conveyed when Juana appears on stage. Her identification with Castile is manifested on three levels. The first is her own conscience and perspective expressed by the following words, "For me there exists no other history than the history of Castile. Everything great that humanity has seen, came from this land." This history with its "far-off glories" is the one occurring right before me "without leaving the slightest trace of my solitary existence" (1334). She ends up confiding this to Mogica as she recognizes that her place is in "silence . . . darkness and oblivion" (1336). The second level has to do with her son, whom she reproaches for this reason: "My son, ignorant of the great virtues of this land, where honest hearts and clear intelligence are abundant, has brought us a Flemish cloud that devours all richness. And when all is said and done, those Flemish will bring complete ruin to Castilian soil" (1337). Lastly the final level refers to the role of Juana's mother: "My mother raised Castile to the highest pinnacles of glory. In doing so she helped that splendid, crazy Christopher Columbus, who earned Castile vast lands called the New World. These facts are imprinted in my mind. I would have wanted to be just as great as my mother, but it is too late now. Now I am worth nothing" (1341). Therefore, "the grandeur would not return" (1336). The social sense of property, which was a very sensitive issue for Galdós, was the third of the core points of the play. This point is visible in the encounter between Juana and the peasants outside of the castle. The scene begins with a show of respect for Juana and her solemn statement, "I am not the greatest Castilian, nor the least. You and I are the same" (1343). The first two scenes of the second act are a constant reaffirmation of these ideas. "The Queen is right," says Peronuño after Juana speaks, "the people should govern themselves in accordance with the Sovereign." To which Juana responds, "Do not separate me from my people" (1340).

Then comes the memory of the scene with the Comuneros a quarter of a century earlier. It would have been the beginning of a different nonabsolutist political and social history if the queen had signed the Comuneros's proposal. But she could not accept the social revolution that it involved, so Galdós, without adhering strictly to history, allows the queen to express her kind-hearted and charitable desires in front of the people of Tordesillas. "Gather what remains of my scarce wealth and distribute it among these unhappy people. Give Poca Misa what she needs to support her children without working and give enough to poor Sanchico so that he may continue studying the art of war with the friar" (1341).

The counterpoint to this triple message is seen in the role of the Marquis of Denia, who puts all his energy into accusing Juana of heresy. "Today I can assure you that, based on recent inquiries from reliable sources, this woman continues her heresy. And for her there are no other beliefs besides the foolish doctrines of that terrible Dutch philosopher, Erasmus" (1344).

With the same resolution he maintains his position on her unbalanced mental condition. He was the voice of official Spain, the representative of the emperor and the reasoning of the government in which absolutism and intolerance were fixed. From there one already knows the results.

Galdós entrusts to a different character of official Spain the task of harmonizing everything and recognizing that Juana embodies a message. First of all, the message was orthodox according to the teachings of the Catholic Church, and secondly it was worthy of not being buried by the sand that buries history. Historiography proves that San Francisco of Borja had been sent by the emperor to attend to his mother in her final moments. Galdós simply tries to attain the maximum meaning from this character given his strong symbolism. He was the great grandson of Pope Alexander VI and of Ferdinand the Catholic. Also, before becoming a Jesuit, as the duke of Gandia, he was an influential nobleman in Charles's court and an ally of the first wife of the emperor.

The last scene is comprised of the dialogue between Juana and Borja until the moment of her death. After reconfirming her beliefs, Borja specifically recognizes them as being from Erasmus. "Erasmus says that we should not be concerned with formulism nor formal rites, but rather with the pureness of our heart and the honesty of our actions." Moreover he emphatically asserts, "You are not a heretic. In Erasmus's book it says nothing contrary to dogma. What it is, is a caustic satire against difficult theologians, insubstantial canon lawyers, hysterical pious women and hostile preachers that have distorted divine simplicity with rhetorical gimmicks. Erasmus celebrated madness and called all the heroes that extolled humanity mad. Heroes like Marcus Aurelius and Trajano from ancient times. Marcelino Menéndez Pelayo, Alfonso the Wise and holy King Ferdinand from old Spain and nowadays our glorious mother, Queen Isabella" (1344).

This specific statement, delivered almost at the end of the play, would guarantee that religious tolerance is possible. There were not any substantial differences between Borja's faith and the queen's. Finally they join together to pray the Creed, and the queen's confessor realizes that he is dealing with a saint. "Holy Queen! Unfortunate woman! You, who have loved so much without anyone loving you; you, who have endured humiliations, rejection and ungratefulness without anyone sweetening the bitterness with the tenderness of your family; you, who have helped the poor and consoled the humble" rest "in the bosom of God the Father" (1346). A saint who should be recognized as a martyr for her beliefs and for the suffering produced by those who confined her.

After the premiere of the play, with the great actress Margarita Xirgu playing Juana's role, the critics acknowledged that Galdós had managed to move the audience to feel "pity and admiration" for this woman in her greatest moments of suffering and anguish. Alejandro Miquis points out that "Juana la Loca was destined to be the Queen of Galdós; however Galdós did not only want to present to us a Castilian queen, but rather the soul of Castile itself. It would be difficult to present us a more complete personification of Castile than the wretched exile of Tordesillas. Nor could there be a more appropriate background than Castilian soil, still humid from the unselfish blood of the *comuneros*, as if the five-year period had not been in vain" (477). Without a doubt it was the poet Manuel Machado in *El Liberal* (May 9,1918) who came closest to the radical meaning of Galdós's play after referring to studies about this character in German historiography. Machado stated that, "Galdós, however, has done more with true guesswork and unquestionably brilliant intuition, to have the daughter of Isabella the Catholic represent all of what was former Spain in the moment of its own genuine rebirth. Spain that was suffocated by the universal ambition of Charles V, destroyed in Villalar and failed in its most noble desires for freedom, democracy and a national life. *And even more so failed in its autonomy of conscience*" (quoted in Berenguer 1988, 480). To conclude Machado said, "I noticed in this somber, powerful play that the hand of genius *opened the doors to the great artistic truth* and the shock of supreme beauty in the play moved my spirit at certain moments."

Manuel Machado's words help to conclude this analysis of how this play concluded Galdós's life work and, as Finkenthal said, it ended at a beginning moment in Spain's history full of possibilities. The play combines historical and literary truths to serve a common purpose. "Vindicate history in these times," said Antonio Muñoz Molina not too long ago, "and that in itself is intellectually daring." To do so using literature without spreading confusion between what is real and fictitious, just as Galdós did, responds to a political and moral feeling that never renounces knowledge of reality. To maintain true knowledge about things is not an easy task nor is it reserved only for learning. In this sense, literature and history come together in Galdós's play as a genuine exercise in humility in order to obtain knowledge of the facts without losing their meaning. In other words, without rejecting shades of gray, one will not know that therein lies the truth. Galdós quickly knew that Juana's character held the key to knowing the authentic truth about Spain.

Translated by Christine Jenack

WORKS CITED

Berenguer, Ángel. 1988. *Los estrenos teatrales de Galdós en la crítica de su tiempo.* Madrid: Consejería de Cultura.

Bergenroth, G. A. 1868. *Supplement to Volume I and Volume II of Letters, despaches, and State Papers, relating to Negotations between England and Spain, Preserved in the Archives of Simancas and Elsewhere. I. Queen Katharine. II. Intended Marriage of King Henry VII with Queen Juana.* Londo: Longmans Green, Reader and Dyer. R. Cardona, "Fuentes históricas de *Santa Juana de Castilla*," *Actas del I Congreso Internacional de Estudios Galdosianos.* Las Palmas: Cabildo Insular, 1977, 466–67.

Blanquat, Josette. 1970–1971. "Lecturas de juventud." *Cuadernos hispanoamericanos* 84. 50–52 (October 1970–January 1971): 161–220.

Calvino, Italo. 1989. *Seis propuestas para el próximo milenio.* Madrid: Siruela.

Camus, Alfredo Adolfo. 1842. *Compendio de Historia Universal.* Madrid: Boix.

Cardona, Rodolfo Cardona. 1977. *Fuentes históricas: Actas del I Congreso Internacional de Estudios Galdosianos.* Las Palmas de Gran Canaria: Cabildo Insular.

Coloma, P. 1943. "La intercession de un santo." O.C., Madrid: Razón y Fe.

Erasmo de Rótterdam, Desiderio. 1976. *Elogio de la locura.* Madrid: Espasa Calpe.

Fernández Álvarez, Manuel. 1994. *Juana la Loca 1479–1555.* Palencia: Diputación Provincial.

Finkenthal, Stanley. 1980. *El teatro de Galdós.* Madrid: Fundamentos.

Heredia, A. 1990. *Actas del VI Seminario de Historia de la Filosofía Española.* Salamanca: Universidad de Salamanca.

Jover, J. M. 1991. *Realidad y mito de la Primera República: Del "Gran Miedo" meridional a la utopía de Galdós.* Madrid: Espasa Calpe.

———. 1997. "Restauración y conciencia histórica." *ESPAÑA. Reflexiones sobre el ser de España.* Madrid: Real Academia de la Historia.

———. 1999. "De la literatura como fuente histórica." *Historiadores españoles de nuestro siglo.* Madrid: Real Academia de la Historia.

———. 1999b. "El siglo XIX en la historiografía española de la época de Franco." *Historiadores españoles de nuestro siglo.* Madrid: Real Academia de la Historia.

Mallo, Tomás. 1990."La filosofía en el Ateneo de Madrid en el siglo XIX." *Actas del VI Seminario de Historia de la Filosofía Española.* Salamanca: Universidad de Salamanca.

Martínez Mediero, Manuel. 1982. *Juana del amor hermoso.* Madrid: Fundamentos.

Miquis, Alejandro. 1988. "Crítica en el *Diario Universal.* In *Los estrenos teatrales de Galdós en la crítica de su tiempo,* edited by A. Berenguer. Madrid: Ediciones de la Comunidad de Madrid.

Muñoz Molina, Antonio. 1996. "El malentendido." *Revista de Occidente.* (April): 84–100.

Nuñez, D. 1975. *La mentalidad positiva en España.* Madrid: Universidad Autónoma de Madrid.

Olaizola, José L. 1998. *La vida y la epoca de Juana la Loca.* Barcelona: Planeta.

Pardo Bazán, Emilia. 1892. "Un drama spicológico en la historia de España: Doña Juana La Loca según los últimos documentos." *Teatro Crítico* 2.14 (February): 67–105.

Pérez Galdós, Benito. 1963. "Santa Juana de Castilla." Edited by Carlos Sainz de Robles. O.C. 6. Madrid: Aguilar.

———. 1968b. "La razón de la sinrazón. Fábula teatral, absolutamente inverosímil." Edited by Por Carlos Sainz de Robles. O.C., 6, Madrid: Aguilar.

———. 1968a. "El caballero encantado. Un cuento real inverosímil." Edited by Carlos Sainz de Robles. *O.C., 6.* Madrid: Aguilar.

Pérez Galdós, B. 1897. "La sociedad presente como material novelable." In *Discursos leídos ante la Real Academia Española,* edited by Menéndez Pelayo-Pereda-Galdós. Madrid: Tip. De la Viuda e Hijos de Tello.

———. 1963 "Soñemos, alma, soñemos." O.C., 6. Madrid: Aguilar.

Pfandl, Ludwig. 1943. *Juana la Loca: su vida, su tiempo, su culpa.* Buenos Aires: Espasa Argentina.

Shoemaker, William H. 1973. *Las cartas desconocidas de Galdós en "La Prensa" de Buenos Aires.* Madrid: Ediciones Cultura Hispánica.

Ramón Gómez de la Serna's Superhistory
An Original Approach
to the Life of Juana of Castile

Mercedes Tasende

Rᴀᴍóɴ ɢóᴍᴇᴢ ᴅᴇ ʟᴀ sᴇʀɴᴀ (1888–1963) ʜᴀs ʙᴇᴇɴ ᴀᴄᴋɴᴏᴡʟᴇᴅɢᴇᴅ ᴀs a prolific and innovative writer whose literary contributions radically changed the perceptions that early twentieth-century readers had of many traditional genres, including the novel. Most critics, however, have concentrated on the revolutionary nature of his early works, and only a few have studied the novels written after the Spanish Civil War; as Nigel Dennis suggests, Gómez de la Serna's "immense prestige before 1936 conflicts alarmingly with the oblivion in which he has subsequently languished" (1988, 7). In addition to *El hombre perdido* [The Lost Man] (1946), *Las tres Gracias* [The Three Graces] (1949), and *Piso bajo* [Basement Flat] (1961), Gómez de la Serna published seven short novels in 1944 under the title *Doña Juana la Loca (y otras) [Doña Juana the Mad (and Others)]*.[1] The texts included deal with a variety of historical and legendary characters, such as Queen Juana of Castile, the Gentleman from Olmedo, Queen Urraca of Castile, Juana La Beltraneja, and the Seven Princes of Lara. The public and private lives of these characters are seen from the unique perspective offered by a new genre that the author half humorously called "super-historical novel" and whose ideological bases and main guidelines are explained in the prologue. Gómez de la Serna manipulates the historical and legendary tales by introducing surprising and humorous elements, such as the transformation of Queen Urraca into a bird, the suggestion that the Gentleman from Olmedo might be a homosexual, or Queen Isabella's plot to get rid of her rival *La Beltraneja* by having her kidnapped by Captain Gofrán and taking her to Granada, where she falls in love with her captor.

As for Juana of Castile's life, Gómez de la Serna chooses to concentrate on certain aspects of the queen's legend that had already become commonplace by the 1940s.[2] He examines Juana's compulsive personality, the stormy relationship with her husband, Philip "the Handsome," his death, the journey through Castile with the king's corpse, her reclusion at the Tordesillas castle, and her death. Like most works written about Juana's life, the superhistorical version portrays the queen as a woman tormented by numerous obsessions, deeply devoted to her husband, and completely consumed by her jealousy of blonde women. Although Eugenio de Nora states there are not many new or surprising elements in Gómez de la Serna's book (1968, 146), a closer look at the novel reveals that its divergences from previous versions of the queen's life are significant.

Unlike his predecessors, Gómez de la Serna invites the reader to consider this historical figure under a different light. First of all, he exploits the humorous potential of the legend, exaggerating certain traits that have been traditionally associated with the queen, such as her erratic behavior, her irrational fears, her superstitious beliefs, and her delusional imaginings; as a result, the novel presents many colorful and amusing incidents that could easily be read as examples of Gómez de la Serna's intranscendent, dehumanized, and playful avant-garde art. The privileged perspective and the access to secret data also allow the superhistorian to: 1) offer a new explanation for the queen's behavior; 2) view more closely the morbid details of the king's death; 3) reveal the reactions experienced by the surrounding objects and animals upon contemplating the monarchs' misfortunes; 4) create a different ending for the story; and 5) develop different aspects of the queen's character that were either ignored or overlooked by previous biographers and historians. Furthermore Gómez de la Serna manipulates the story of the Mad Queen to parody the scientific pretensions of some historians that write about her, to emphasize the lack of objectivity and the mythical component prevailing in most of their works, and, by extension, to challenge the value of all historical reconstructions. The author also elaborates on other ideas that keep recurring in his works, like the unknown angles of reality, particularly the intricacies of the world of objects, the concept of death, which seems to permeate most of his writings, and the absurdity of life, expressed not only by inverting the value of inanimate entities and persons but by transforming the actions of a potentially tragic figure into a source of humor. Therefore the purpose of this chapter is to examine some of Gómez de la Serna's innovations concerning the portrayal of Queen Juana within the context provided by the generic conventions of the superhistorical novel, as well as by the author's general attitude toward reality and life.

Gómez de la Serna defines the superhistorical novel in the prologue of the first edition of *Doña Juana la Loca (y otras),* and he establishes the ideological bases that guide his work as a superhistorian. First, while a professional historian such as Nicomedes Sanz y Ruiz de la Peña claims to use only written testimonies and other materials "within the limits of the strictest scientific norms" (Gómez de la Serna 1949, 5–6), and even includes as evidence of the queen's emotional instability a "scientific opinion" written by a prominent Spanish psychiatrist whose findings are irrefutable and must be accepted by all specialists (261), the superhistorian has neither scientific pretensions nor the desire to present irrefutable truths. In fact, he has no qualms about admitting that superhistory is "a complete fraud, like everything in life," and "a perpetually unfaithful depiction of past events" (10);[3] besides, he declares openly his intention to mix real events with fictional accounts and is prepared to resort to improvisation and subconscious data whenever necessary (9).

Secondly, if the historian usually presents in chronological order a given set of events that have been carefully selected, the superhistorian prefers instead to offer an entanglement of possible facts and times. According to him, the arrangement of historical events based on chronology and causality confuses even more the complicated nature of the past (9). Such disposition of past events does not take into account that there are centuries that last one hundred and thirty-five or one hundred and ninety years, while others only last fifteen or five years (13), or that the personal history of kings and historical figures is always unpredictable. Besides, this notion of the past does not reflect the movement of the river of superhistory, which always flows ahead of us (11), or the fact that we are older than the past and, therefore, the past gets younger because it is already acquainted with a future that we will not be able to experience for a while. In addition, chronological order does not take into consideration that the dead change because they are always older and more modern at the same time; that would explain the coincidences in the same temporal level of historical figures belonging to different times, such as Cleopatra and Isabella, or the possibility that a queen from antiquity is centuries ahead of us and may show up wearing a hat that will be fashionable in future centuries (11–12).

While the traditional historian has to face countless limitations and can only rely on written documents, the superhistorian has secret data in his power that are banned to the historian. He enjoys a privileged perspective from which he has access to "supreme inspiration" and feels at the center of time. From this position, he is able to watch both the depths of history and the uncertainty that man experiences when he dies. Thanks to this demiurgic vision, capable of revealing the most hidden secrets of the universe, the superhistorian can apply new X-rays to history and reveal what it swallowed and what nobody ever suspected it had inside; he can also correct certain errors of history, which was never as historians supposed it to be or as the documents describe it (11). In theory, then, Gómez de la Serna would be capable of revealing details about Juana's life ignored by chroniclers and historians that would clarify and correct many of the inaccuracies about the queen's life.

Finally, in contrast with history, which is dry, affected, and finds itself strangled by the rigidity of limitations and elements that are untransferable and untransformable, superhistory offers great richness, flexibility, and, especially, freedom, allowing the superhistorian to mix historical events and hypothetical situations, to connect animals and kings, and even to find kinship between himself and Queen Doña Urraca of Castile (9–10). While history offers a materialistic, vulgar, and belated version of past events, superhistory presents a "supersubconscious, superidealistic, futuristic and disinterested" interpretation (13). Unlike history, which only exudes death, superhistory represents a song of liberty and an affirmation of life over death. As the author states, "History is being dead, and we are still alive" (12).

The subversive nature of the superhistorical novel is made clear throughout the prologue to *Doña Juana la Loca (y otras)*. Gómez de la Serna's ideas about the new genre reveal that the author's defying attitude has been kept intact over the years. He is still faithful to the "principle of permanent revolution" that characterized his early works (Soldevila-Durante 1988, 33) and still willing to challenge the limits of traditional genres (Nicolás 1988; Rey Briones 1988; Sabugo Abril 1988). Regarding the superhistorical novel, he undertakes the project of demolishing the conventions associated with the writing of history to liberate the genre from the straps that keep it immobilized. Clearly the superhistorical novel represents an attack on the most sacred principles of historiography, on its claimed objectivity, its accuracy, its scientific pretensions, and its alleged faithfulness to the past. By insisting on the need to get rid of the limitations that keep life, literature, and history confined, Gómez de la Serna joins forces with other European intellectuals, such as Nietzsche, Proust, Unamuno, and Ortega y Gasset, who tried to undermine both historical consciousness and the work of traditional historians since the early nineteenth century in an attempt to liberate Western man from the "burden of the past" (White 1973, 27–50).

But the superhistorical novel is more than a new genre or a new vision of past events; like most of Gómez de la Serna's fictional works, it contains autobiographical elements that "reflect his peculiar personality, vision, love of things, and concept of reality" (Mazzetti Gardiol 1974, 42–43) and that weaken the dividing line between fiction and reality (Serrano Ajenjo 1991, 37). The author's deep concern with human existence is evident when the superhistorian states that the history of kings and other historical figures is as uncertain as our own lives (Gómez de la Serna 1949, 9), that both superhistory and life are complete frauds and both are halfway between being and not being (10), and that we all become part of the river of superhistory when we are born. Similarly he points out that superhistory allows him to observe not only how the drama of history unfolds, but also the uncertainty experienced by all human beings upon dying (11). Such statements about life evince the author's dissatisfaction with the world around which, according to Gaspar Gómez de la Serna, generates all his creative experience (1963, 109). They also reveal a deep sense of disillusionment upon confronting the unpredictability of life and death, and the confusion felt by both fictional characters and human beings. Clearly, as Luis Granjel maintains, Gómez de la Serna's vision changed dramatically after the Spanish Civil War, his nihilism became even more profound than before in his portrayal of a chaotic world, and as his personal crisis worsened, he was faced with the crucial and inescapable problem of his own mortality (1963, 83–110).[4] Finally these reflections about human existence expressed in the prologue disrupt the humorous tone of the novels and cast a dark cloud over stories that otherwise would be extremely entertaining.

The feelings of disorientation and disappointment that prevail in the superhistorical novel are deeply connected to Juana's character. Gómez de la Serna associates Juana's erratic behavior with the overwhelming presence of death in such a way that all actions appear to be the result of her obsession with mortality. Thus while some twentieth-century historians like Ludwig Pfandl, Sanz y Ruiz de la Peña, and more recently, Miguel Angel Zalama conclude that, in addition to suffering from a genetic problem that affected several members of the royal family, the queen was schizophrenic, the superhistorian resorts to his superior perspective to refute such diagnoses and explains Juana's erratic behavior as the result of her fixation with death. According to the superhistorical version, the queen's obsessive behavior started during her childhood and would result in the development of superstitious beliefs. The superhistorian mentions, for instance, that when she was little she insisted on talking constantly about death with her teachers (Gómez de la Serna 1949, 18); on one occasion she even told the governess that she wanted to try on her skeleton, and cried when she found out that it was already inside her (17). She also developed a fear of people with small noses because she associated them with death. These convictions would influence her decisions to take preventive measures, such as ordering all doors to be covered with tapestries and preparing hunting expeditions in forests where death might be hiding; she also sought the advice of gypsies, magicians, and witch doctors, who convinced her to fire the male cook and hire a female cook instead (19–20), and suggested that she start wearing her scapulars on her back, to have her shirts made out of wool from unborn lambs, and to order a checker board placed on her bedroom table and zithers hung in every room (18–19).

The superhistorian even associates Juana's jealousy with her obsession with death. In contrast to the traditional versions of the story that follow Pedro Mártir de Anglería's reports and interpret both her ardent desire to seduce her husband and her morbid jealousy as symptoms of emotional instability (Pfandl 1969, 59–67; Miller 1963, 225–29; Prawdin 1939, 76–81), he maintains that death and jealousy are really the same thing and, therefore, that the queen's fear of death was actually fear that the king would fall into the arms of an emaciated woman (Gómez de la Serna 1949, 20). The author resorts to his superhistorical vision to investigate the matter of Juana's jealousy more closely and share new details that most chroniclers probably ignored. The readers find out, for instance, that the problems the Flemish fleet had during the trip to Spain had nothing to do with a storm at sea or excess cargo, as many historians have reported (Pfandl 1969, 63–66; Prawdin 1939, 104–10), but with the queen's "excessive load of black jealousy" (Gómez de la Serna 1949, 21). We also discover that the queen's mistrust of her husband was not as unfounded as many historians want us to believe; according to Gómez de la Serna's superhistorical version, when the boat that transported them to Spain was about to sink, Juana discovered a blonde woman disguised as a page among the crew.[5]

As far as the extreme measures taken by the queen to eliminate her female rivals and capture her husband's affection, we find out that she tries every weapon available in the feminine arsenal: she changes the sleeves and trains in her dresses several times a day, she wears dresses with a thousand slits and she even decides to get rid of all her blonde ladies-in-waiting and keep only brunettes.[6] Nevertheless all these changes are made in vain, for she does not succeed in reforming her unfaithful husband, who always manages to bring a new blonde mistress from his homeland. Desperate, Juana resorts to necromancy once again. Following the advice of a flying witch, she has Philip drink a cup of chocolate with a few drops of his own blood; unfortunately the concoction has no effect on him and the only change that she accomplishes is that Philip switches mistresses (Gómez de la Serna 1949, 21). Juana then decides to try one last

resort: she dyes her hair blond. The queen actually succeeds in rekindling Philip's passion although, sadly, the conjugal harmony and happiness are soon interrupted by her husband's death (21–22). At the
end, Juana's efforts to get rid of her invisible enemy prove to be futile.
The steps taken to keep her female competitors away, the details
about Juana's constant preoccupation with death, and her determination to find and eliminate it once and for all are purposely exaggerated by Gómez de la Serna to create a comic effect. But Gómez de
la Serna was not just an ordinary humorist. As Rodolfo Cardona
points out, for him, humor was at once "a negative antidote composed of the most varied ingredients and a positive affirmation of the
sense of life renewing itself . . . the soundest position one can take
toward the fluctuation of life . . . an unyielding devotion to reason . . .
the perception by the intellect of the grim absurdities of life" (1957,
68–69). Humor is, in Gómez de la Serna's words, "an attitude towards
life" (1948, 650), as well as a manner of literary expression and a
"metaphorical device" (Camón Aznar 1972, 67). Therefore, although
the episodes of Juana's life might seem humorous at first, the overwhelming presence of death in the novel soon takes the reader to a
more transcendent level where fiction and reality seem to converge.
Juana's fears, the absurdity of her quest, and her profound sense of
disappointment are shared by most human beings who struggle uselessly against the passage of time and their own mortality. The humor
we find in the superhistorical version of Juana's life, then, is just a way
of dealing with the tragic nature of the queen's life and, for that matter, of human existence in general. In many of Gómez de la Serna's
works, the writer "brings us its hero as a comic figure, but only in
order to transform his role and finally turn the proceedings into a
tremendous tragedy which at the same time seems grotesque" (Cardona 1957, 69).

As the story progresses, the overwhelming presence of death ends
up relegating the comical effects to the background, especially after
King Philip's death. The humorous episodes are interrupted soon
after the king drinks a glass of contaminated water from the well. The
readers witness how death is slowly taking over the king's body with
each sip of water, as the author examines some particulars of the
infectious process that are outside the reach of the human eye.
Unlike historians who have investigated and speculated the possible
causes of the king's death (Pfandl 1969, 66–70; Miller 1963, 262–65;
Prawdin 1939, 133–35), or the emotional consequences for the
already unstable queen, the superhistorian disregards human emotions and shifts the emphasis to the surrounding world. We learn
about the reaction experienced by everything around Philip after he

requests a glass of water: "everything stopped . . . the corners moved to the center of the field to watch him drink that glass full of water from the well" (Gómez de la Serna 1949, 22), the details pertaining to the slow and lethal process of infection experienced by Philip's body from the moment he started drinking until he has the last sip (22–24), the joy and pride felt by the miasmas, larvae, and microbes, which finally have a chance of causing "a royal fever," and the queen's fears upon hearing the noise made by a lute that had been hit, which for her represented one of the unequivocal signs of death's arrival. As the narrator indicates, neither the precautions taken by the queen to drive death away nor Philip's brave captains could provide him with the necessary cells to fight the infection that was invading his body (23). Death is simply unpredictable and undiscriminating, as proven by the fact that even the most powerful and handsome king can die from drinking a glass of water.

Gómez de la Serna's interest in exploring unusual angles of reality is also present in his recreation of Juana's famous pilgrimage through Castile with Philip's body.[7] Gómez de la Serna uses many of the existing sources to describe the macabre procession led by the queen, the commotion and the atmosphere of expectation prevailing in Castilian towns that she visited with her dead husband, her overnight accommodations in convents and the rituals performed every evening by the sizeable funeral cortege that accompanied her. There are, however, considerable differences between the superhistorical version and the previous accounts of the queen's journey through Castile. Unlike many historians who treat the funeral procession as the culmination of her derangement and the ultimate sign of her devotion to Philip (Prawdin 1939, 144–65; Fernández Álvarez 2000, 141–51; Miller 1963, 267–302), the superhistorian stresses the great historical and historiographical significance of this journey because it not only gave name to a period, "the Juana the Mad and Philip the Handsome period," but it also represents an exception to the "historians' gaunt and dry prose" (Gómez de la Serna 1949, 25). Furthermore Juana's journey gives him the opportunity to take a closer look at some details about the queen's madness that had been overlooked or simply misinterpreted by historians. We learn, for instance, that her inability to cry after Philip's death was the main cause of her mental instability since, according to him, madness comes from being horrified and not being able to cry (24); we find out, too, that she had made up a story about how the throne's lion bit the king and caused his death because "it was humiliating for a king to have died after drinking a glass of water" (29), that she was overwhelmed by boundary and distance stone markers she found on the road that reminded her of tombstones, and that she avoided bridges because she was afraid of jumping from them into history (30).

Another important piece of information revealed by the superhistorian has to do with her decision to avoid convents and other religious institutions run by nuns, which some historians tend to associate with her aversion to women, her jealousy, or her obsessive personality. The superhistorian takes another look at this matter to let us know what really went on at those nunneries and the reason behind Juana's refusal to spend the night in them.[8] We learn, for instance, that while the queen was staying at the Las Huelgas monastery she caught the abbess trying to have a look at Philip's face in the middle of the night, proving that her jealousy was not the product of a sick mind, as many historians want us to believe, and that she had plenty of reasons to suspect women, before and after Philip was dead. He was simply too handsome and too irresistible, and all the precautions the queen took to keep women away from him were not enough. Finally, contrary to many historians who delve into Juana's despair following Philip's death, the superhistorian emphasizes the sense of triumph that she experiences after fighting for so long to win Philip's heart and attention; the unfaithful king was finally hers and could no longer offer resistance.

But Juana's journey also provides the writer with an opportunity to look at other angles of reality and make an incursion into the world of objects, which, as many critics argue, is one of Gómez de la Serna's major interests (Cardona 1957, 113–30; Marías 1966; Gaspar Gómez de la Serna 1963, 108–14; Ynduráin 1969, 192–95; Garrido 1982, 55–57). The writer believed that reality was made up of infinite elements and that everything was equally important, including the most trivial details or those things that have been rejected or forgotten (Gaspar Gómez de la Serna 1963, 111). As Cardona points out, "Ramón conceives a system of a world encompassed by feeling, the movement of feeling is experienced as an objective process in which all things take part, for all things are linked together and communicate through a magic scheme of relatedness" (1957, 117). The author's concept of the world would explain why reality is described in so much detail and why inanimate objects often become the subject of his writings.

In contrast to other writers who allude to the queen's increasing derangement or the upheaval that her journey created among Castilians, the superhistorian is not only interested in Juana's suffering or in the Castilian people's response to the sight of the funeral procession; he is equally concerned with the reaction experienced by animals and objects. Thus, when he describes the members of the funeral cortege, he also mentions Philip's favorite horse, with its "deep mourning eyes," among the group of mourners (Gómez de la Serna 1949, 25). In addition, he notices that all of the elements in nature are deeply moved by the passing of the royal corpse and the widow's suffering: plants and trees writhe when their majesties the king and queen go by, cypresses dress in black, flowers open their eyes as if they were sunflowers, dogs howl, roosters crow at any time of the day to greet their king, the land is tempted to commit suicide and acquires a deadly look, the country goes crazy, the sea appears in the wells trying to have a look at the inconsolable queen, the landscape acquires aristocratic status, and the towns are dignified by the royal presence. Even some churches and statues feel the urge to follow the funeral procession (28–29). In sum, the presence of the dead king and the widow seems to alter the course of the universe. The commotion is such that other widows who were "crazier than Doña Juana" (28) also decided to join the funeral procession, convinced that they were following their dead husbands.

Finally Gómez de la Serna concentrates on another aspect of the queen's life that has fascinated historians, novelists, and dramatists for generations: her reclusion at the Tordesillas castle for more than four decades. Like many writers before him, Gómez de la Serna alludes to the political intrigues that led Ferdinand and Charles V to conclude "Juana's exodus" (27) and lock her up in "numerous castles"; after all, as the narrator explains, "that is the reason why Castile was full of castles, to lock up the intemperate queen, who did not want to stop reigning and traveled the roads with her love slogan" (30). He also refers to the queen's acts of defiance, her refusal to give up her rights, her desperation, her pleas for help during the four decades she spent isolated in a palace, and the popular indignation caused by the injustice that was being done to the queen: "the towns raised their voices with fury around the castles where she was confined, and then she had to be exiled to other deserted places" (31). Yet, although the author acknowledges the magnitude of the queen's personal tragedy and suffering, he seems more interested in exploring the reaction experienced by the objects surrounding the queen.

If previously the superhistorian described how the people, the trees, and the statues of Castile shuddered with sorrow for the widow queen, now the castles echo the desperation and cruelty suffered by Juana at the hands of her jailers for almost fifty years: "The castles remained insane, and the lonely battlements waved their short arms . . . the stones crumbled trying to see the landscape" (31). Gómez de la Serna also comes up with an original ending for the queen's life: instead of dying in Tordesillas, the superhistorian takes her to Torresoles, and more specifically to the church where Philip's body was; there, she is shut away in a room inside a temple that has a little window from where she can see her "trunk of love." When everyone is waiting for her to die, so they can build the king a mausoleum, she decides to jump from the window and lands on the casket of her handsome husband. Thus the superhistorian decides to save Juana years of reclusion and suffering by cutting her life short and allowing her to commit suicide. Juana's superhistory concludes with the narrator's final reflection: Juana's "alleged madness" is now over and history will never be able to add anything else (32). As José Camón Aznar states, the vision of the past, so artificially carved by the centuries, ends with superhistory (1972, 375).

The superhistorical version of Juana's life and death represents a novel alternative to the studies on the Mad Queen published until the 1940s. By that time, the historical figure had been distorted and mythologized to such a degree that most studies on the life of the queen that pretended to be "scientific" and impartial turned out to be almost as fictitious as the dramas or novels published on the same subject. For that reason, Gómez de la Serna's version of Juana's life is as plausible as Pfandl's or Sanz y Ruiz de la Peña's. The superhistorian's operational bases, explained in the prologue to *Doña Juana la Loca (y otras)*, constitute a parody of the conventions used by the historian. Upon declaring openly that superhistory is "a complete fraud and a perpetual infidelity to past events," stating that history was never as documents present it, announcing his intention of mixing up what actually occurred with what did not happen, and resorting to subconscious data when needed, the author is clearly challenging the basic principles of historiography. At the same time, he invites the reader to question the alleged objectivity and scientific nature of the historians' work. After all, the procedures followed by both the historian and the superhistorian are not that different: both select the information they want to present and interpret the data as best suits their needs; both let their personal beliefs, their prejudice, and their feelings toward the queen interfere, consciously or unconsciously, with the presentation of the information selected.[9] In addition, both the historian and the superhistorian resort to assumptions and speculations when trying to fill the gaps, and they use a considerable dose of imagination to reach conclusions regarding the life and madness of Juana, and even her most intimate moments.[10] Some even offer modern diagnostics to the queen's problem based on symptoms described four hundred years earlier. Both, in sum, end up resorting to the same methods employed by writers of fiction and give ample evidence of the numerous parallels existing between historical narrative and fictional narrative (Gossman 1987; Mink 1974; White 1978, 51–80 and 1973, 1–38). If, in addition, we take into consideration that the written testimonies used by biographers and historians for the last four hundred years were produced by men that, most likely, were part of a defamatory campaign organized by the kings to prove the queen's madness at all cost, then we will have to conclude that there is no objectivity or historical fidelity when it comes to Juana's life. Rather there are only sensationalistic versions of it.

Gómez de la Serna's priority, however, is not to offer his readers just another version of Juana's life. Rather his overall objective seems to be to frame Juana's life inside the particular context of his own aesthetics. In this context, objects, animals, and even the landscape acquire as much relevance as the characters and their actions when they become part of a universe deeply affected by the presence of death. Juana's life and demise reach a new dimension when they become part of this constant reflection about life, death, and time that permeates Gómez de la Serna's works. As José Begoña explains, what pervades in Gómez de la Serna's literature is the idea that death is always present in our lives, because when we are born we actually start dying; time and mortality constantly confront the author with the sad reality of his own approaching disappearance (1980, 94–95).

A closer look at Juana the Mad's superhistory will reveal, in fact, that this new version of the queen's life revolves around death: it starts by exploring Juana's obsession with death, goes on to narrate the details of Philip's fatal illness and ends with Juana's suicide. If at first sight Gómez de la Serna's approach appears comical, it soon starts to acquire tragic overtones when death and the temptation of suicide take over the characters and everything around them, including the Castilian land (1949, 28). Clearly this overwhelming concern with mortality is also a reflection of the author's fears since it permeates most of his novels, essays, stories, and *greguerías* [aphorisms] (Cardona 1957, 49–67); this preoccupation is even manifest in his autobiography, which he presents as "the story of how a man has been dying" (Gómez de la Serna 1948, 9). Queen Juana's superhistory, then, surpasses the mere recounting of famous events in the queen's life to explore the essence of reality and human existence and to uncover the absurdity of individual human aspirations, the unpredictability of death, and the anguish produced by the awareness of the passage of time and mortal condition of all human beings.

Notes

1. The first edition of *Doña Juana la Loca* was published in Buenos Aires in 1944 by Editorial Clydoc and it included only six novels. The second edition, published in Madrid in 1949 by Revista de Occidente, included seven.

2. By the time Gómez de la Serna wrote his superhistorical novel, the legend of the Mad Queen had already generated a plethora of novels, plays, operas, paintings, essays, biographies, and other studies (Aram 2001, 13–15); it had also contaminated Spanish history to such a degree that it would no longer be possible to distinguish fact from fiction. Chances are that in addition to being familiar with many of the fictional works on the queen, Gómez de la Serna had also read those written by historians like Sanz y Ruiz de la Peña and Ludwig Pfandl, whose book was published in Spanish in 1937. Judging by the number of editions, particularly of Pfandl's text, one has to assume that these historical studies enjoyed great popularity at the time.

3. All English translations of Gómez de la Serna's *Doña Juana la Loca (y otras)* included in this paper are mine.

4. Undoubtedly, as Miguel González-Gerth demonstrates, the metaphysical preoccupations of the author increase in the last of the four "novels of the nebula," *El hombre perdido* [The Lost Man] (1947), as well as in autobiographical works like *Cartas a mí mismo* [Letters to Myself] (1956) and *Nuevas páginas de mi vida* [New Pages of My Life] (1957), and especially in *Automoribundia* (1948), where life and death simply become indistinguishable.

5. Although this incident might be interpreted as the product of Gómez de la Serna's imagination, there is some truth to this story. When preparations for the 1506 trip to Spain were taking place, Juana insisted that the Flemish court ladies be left behind, as well as "the horde of prostitutes who traditionally accompanied any Habsburg army" (Miller 1963, 246). Although Philip had agreed that they would not be taken along, in the end he decided to have them shipped (Prawdin 1939, 104–5). José Luis Olaizola explains that among the forty vessels that transported Philip, Juana, and their retinue to Spain in 1506, there were several prostitutes traveling in the same vessel as the horses. After three days struggling to stay afloat in the middle of a storm, they decided to put the women in a separate boat and leave them adrift (2004, 93–95).

6. Once again, Gómez de la Serna's description of the queen's morbid jealousy finds its source in Martín de Moxica's diary. According to Moxica, Juana was convinced that her husband's alienation from her had been caused by a love potion; thus, she decided to resort to black magic and sought help from Moorish slaves, who were knowledgeable about counter-charms, love potions, and other sorceries (Prawdin 1939, 80–81; Sanz y Ruiz de la Peña 1942, 257; Miller 1963, 228–29).

7. Interestingly enough, when Juana decided to take Philip's body from Burgos to Granada, she was simply trying to fulfill her husband's will (Miller 1963, 273–74). Two years before, "Isabella's funeral train had traveled . . . nearly as far and almost by the same route. That procession, too, was accompanied by bishops and grandees" (Prawdin 1939, 150).

8. Gómez de la Serna is alluding to an episode recorded by Mártir, which is also the origin of the legend that Juana was led by jealousy to remove Philip's body from a convent that was run by nuns instead of monks (Miller 1963, 227). William H. Prescott maintains that, after Philip died, Juana still retained the same envy of women that she had during Philip's life (1837, 281). Ironically Philip's precious bones would end up under the care of Clarist nuns.

9. The lack of objectivity prevailing in the historical studies about the Mad Queen is especially noticeable in Pfandl's book. This author not only sympathizes with Philip but also presents him as a poor victim of the senseless passion of his wife (1969, 51). He emphasizes Philip's goodwill toward his wife when he tried to seek her participation in the government of his country (1969, 61), maintains that Juana's behavior made Philip's life a living hell and almost drove him to suicide, and understands why Philip had to take extreme measures, such as locking the queen up in her room and firing her Spanish attendants. In addition to showing a complete lack of sympathy for the queen, Pfandl also includes many derogatory comments about women.

10. Miller speculates about what Cisneros must have thought when Charles became king of Spain (306) or how Juana must have received Chievres (1963, 310). He also provides numerous examples of what the first love encounter between Philip and Juana must have been like: "Philip was blond and sturdy; the gunpowder train of Juana's emotions, long and dark and twisting, exploded at last. Philip's eyes must have seen, if nothing else, a girl in virginal flush, a young body of sixteen. He could hardly endure the presentations of the nobles." Miller goes on talking about "their haste and hunger, " how "they tore off their clothes" and how "the union was hotly consummated" (1963, 183). Similarly, when he describes the wedding night, he mentions that "the pair escaped from the revelry and fell once more into bed" and concludes that "it is impossible to overemphasize the carnal in this match: that is all they had, all they were ever to have" (184). Miller even tries to present Juana's passionate behavior as characteristic of the traditional Spanish woman: "smoldering, vehement when aroused, incapable of half measures" (236).

WORKS CITED

Aram, Bethany. 2001. *La reina Juana: Gobierno, piedad y dinastía*. Madrid: Marcial Pons.

Begoña, José. 1980. "Evaluación y contraste dentro de una de las constantes de Ramón Gómez de la Serna." In *Actas del Sexto Congreso Internacional de Hispanistas*, edited by Alan M. Gorsdon and Evelyn Rugg, 94–98. Toronto: University of Toronto Press.

Camón Aznar, José. 1972. *Ramón Gómez de la Serna en sus obras*. Madrid: Espasa-Calpe.

Cardona, Rodolfo. 1957. *Ramón: A Study of Gómez de la Serna and His Works*. New York: Eliseo Torres and Sons.

Dennis, Nigel. 1988, ed. *Studies on Ramón Gómez de la Serna*, Ottawa: Dovehouse.

De Nora, Eugenio. 1968. *La novela española contemporánea (1927–1939)*. Vol. 2. 2nd ed. Madrid: Gredos.

Fernández Álvarez, Manuel. 2000. *Juana la Loca: La Cautiva de Tordesillas*. Madrid: Espasa Calpe.

Garrido, Carlos. 1982. "La vida secreta de las cosas: Cosalogía de Ramón Gómez de la Serna." *Quimera* 24 (October): 55–57.

Gómez de la Serna, Gaspar. 1963. *Ramón*. Madrid: Taurus.

Gómez de la Serna, Ramón. 1948. *Automoribundia (1988–1948)*. Buenos Aires: Editorial Sudamericana.

———. 1949. *Doña Juana la Loca (y otras). (Seis novelas superhistóricas)*. Madrid: Revista de Occidente.

González-Gerth, Miguel. 1986. *A Labyrinth of Imagery: Ramón Gómez de la Serna's Novelas de la Nebulosa*. London: Tamesis.

Gossman, Lionel. 1987. "History and Literature: Reproduction or Signification." In *The Writing of History. Literary Form and Historical Understanding*, edited by Robert H. Canary and Henri Kozicki, 3–39. Madison: University of Wisconsin Press.

Granjel, Luis. 1963. *Retrato de Ramón*. Madrid: Guadarrama.

Marías, Julián. 1966. *Al margen de estos clásicos*. Madrid: Afrodisio Aguado.

Mazzetti Gardiol, Rita. 1974. *Ramón Gómez de la Serna*. New York: Twayne.

Miller, Townsend. 1963. *The Castles and the Crown: Spain: 1451–1555*. New York: Coward-McCann.

Mink, Louis O. 1974. "History and Fiction as Modes of Comprehension." In *New Directions in Literary History*, edited by Ralph Cohen. 107–24. Baltimore: Johns Hopkins University Press.

Nicolás, César. 1988. "Imagen y estilo en Ramón Gómez de la Serna." In *Studies on Ramón Gómez de la Serna*, edited by Nigel Dennis. 129–51. Ottawa: Dovehouse.

Olaizola, José Luis. 2004. *Juana la Loca:* Barcelona: Planeta.

Pfandl, Ludwig. 1969. *Juana la Loca. Su vida, su tiempo, su culpa*. 9th ed. Madrid: Espasa-Calpe.

Prawdin, Michael. 1939. *The Mad Queen of Spain*. Translated by Eden and Cedar Paul. Boston: Houghton Mifflin.

Prescott, William H. 1837. *History of the Reign of Ferdinand and Isabella the Catholic*. Philadelphia: J. B. Lippincott.

Rey Briones, Antonio del. 1988. "Ramón y la novela." *Insula* 502 (October): 17–18.

Sabugo Abril, Amancio. 1988. "Ramón o la nueva literatura." *Cuadernos Hispanoamericanos* 461 (November): 7–27.

Sanz y Ruiz de la Peña, Nicomedes. 1942. *Doña Juana I de Castilla: La Reina que enloqueció de amor*. 2nd ed. Madrid: Biblioteca Nueva, 1942.

Serrano Ajenjo, José Enrique. 1991. "Escritura para el túnel (Acerca de *El hombre perdido* de Ramón Gómez de la Serna)." *España Contemporánea* 4, 1 (Spring): 23–45.

Soldevila-Durante, Ignacio. 1988. "El gato encerrado (Contribución al estudio de la génesis de los procedimientos creadores en la prosa ramoniana)." *Revista de Occidente* 80 (January): 31–62.

White, Hayden. 1973. *Metahistory: The Historical Imagination in Nineteenth Century Europe*. Baltimore: Johns Hopkins University Press.

———. 1978. *Tropics of Discourse: Essays in Cultural Criticism*. Baltimore: Johns Hopkins University Press.

Ynduráin, Francisco. 1969. "Sobre el arte de Ramón." In *Clásicos modernos: Estudios de crítica literaria*, edited by Francisco Ynduráin, 192–201. Madrid: Gredos.

Zalama, Miguel Angel. 2000. *Vida cotidiana y arte en el palacio de la reina Juana I en Tordesillas*. Valladolid: Universidad de Valladolid, Secretariado de Publicaciones e Intercambio Editorial.

Juana the Mad as a Prototype of Federico García Lorca's Andalusian Martyr Complex

Salvatore Poeta

She was a splendid woman, strong, keenly
intelligenced, sardonic, passionate. Little
surprise that it took so many men so long
to bring her down.
Joan Connor, *Juana la Loca*
No one fecundates you. Andalusian martyr,

. . . .

The immense sadness that floats in your eyes
speaks to us of your broken and failed life.
Federico García Lorca, "Elegía"
I have been disowned by our Lord, because
a secret and impossible love hides in my heart
     —Federico García Lorca, "Estado sentimental: La primavera"

IN ATTEMPTING TO GET A SENSE OF JUANA I OF CASTILE'S SO-CALLED madness, the curious reader immediately is thrust into a labyrinth of speculation, open-ended questions, and contradiction. At the heart of this labyrinth resides the beast of material greed and political intrigue. How is one to determine the mental state of any individual, let alone one living between the fifteenth and sixteenth centuries (1479–1555)? Regardless of whether one subscribes to Michael Prawdin's theory, which denies any hint of madness from which Juana may have suffered; Ludwig Pfandl's heredity theory, which traces a direct genetic link between the precocious dementia or schizophrenia suffered by Juana's grandmother, Queen Isabella of Portugal, and passed down to Juana's great grandson, the Prince Don Carlos (1959, 107); or the more balanced position Townsend Miller assumes, which on the one hand does not reject outright an inherited mental condition but on the other considers much more consequential Juana's physical and mental mistreatment by her captors, one fact remains undeniable: Juana's resilience of spirit and steadfastness of moral character, which over time is proving to transcend the purported per-

verseness of the legend. Beyond the many enigmas surrounding
Juana's circumstances, the million dollar questions on whose answer
we can only speculate are: had circumstances been different, what
kind of queen would Juana have been and whether Spain might have
been spared her tragic sociopolitical decline as a nation heading aim-
lessly into the apocalyptic darkness of the seventeenth century. Miller
provides us with his prognostication:

> What kind of Queen Regnant would she have made? . . . For the question,
> no sooner posed, inevitably resolves itself into another: could her reason
> have been preserved? And this one is simpler to answer—by the lights of
> the sixteenth century, assuredly not. . . . If the root of her madness was a
> fear of her being unloved, then clearly Philip was the person who best
> could have saved her. And even after Philip had done his dreadful dam-
> age, perhaps there was still someone else who might have healed the
> wounds and prevented the final wreckage—Fernando. These were, as we
> have suggested, the only two people whose love she really desired, and
> had either one of them been willing, or equipped, to treat her with under-
> standing or even a little kindness, then the tragedy for herself—and by
> extension her country—need never have developed. (1963, 347–48)

It should come as no surprise, moreover, that the speculation surrounding the historical figure would also translate into divergent
artistic portrayals of Juana. In general, however, even a cursory review
of the most notable works reveals a progressive tendency to vindicate
Juana's memory by way of poetic truth without violating the objective
facts. Needless to say, some authors and works are more successful
than others in maintaining this delicate balance between poetic truth
and historic accuracy.[1]

My proposal in this chapter is much more modest than attempting
the daunting task of elucidating the numerous enigmas surrounding
Juana's historical circumstances. Rather I hope to build a bridge of
common ground between Federico García Lorca, as perhaps one of
Juana's greatest admirers, and the Mad Queen. There is no question
that García Lorca saw Juana as a kindred spirit during his adolescence
and apprenticeship phase of his literary production. From a strictly
geohistorical standpoint, the poet and queen remain permanently
associated with Granada as a Moorish/Christian capital. Just as Juana,
upon the death of her husband, is desperate to escape the political
perils and air of stifling religiosity of Castile, Lorca would react with
similar disdain to Castile's taste for the macabre and physical side of
death, which he captures in his first work of prose entitled *Impresiones
y paisajes* [Impressions and Panoramas] (1918). Moreover, in a tragic
twist of fate, the remains of the Castilian queen and those of the poet

from Fuente Vaqueros would find permanent repose in Granada. If the remains of Juana lie peacefully in the Chapel of San Francisco next to those of her husband and parents, Lorca's ashes, in yet another ironic twist of fate, remain in an unmarked grave somewhere in the Grenadine countryside.

From the psychic-emotional perspective, the poet's homosexual predisposition and Juana's unhappy marital status notwithstanding, both personalities remain forever linked through their mutual identification as victims of unrequited and betrayed love. In the case of Lorca, the motif of tragic love, which he termed his "calvario carnal" (martyrdom of the flesh) or "deseo de lo imposible" (desire for the impossible), would become a thematic cornerstone of his entire lyrical, dramatic, and, in many respects, even visual production. (García Lorca 1994, 32–38). Indeed virtually all of Lorca's feminine protagonists strive to transcend conflicting forces that threaten to impede, often with tragic and violent results, their absolute and unhindered self-expression. These determining forces may be internal, biological or psychological, and/or take on sociocultural, geopolitical, religious, or metaphysical manifestations. It is precisely the conspiratorial nature of these forces that ultimately destroy the Lorca protagonist as a natural, divine embodiment of love and life and that serve as the underpinning of the Grenadine poet's tragic sense of life.

In Juana's case we are dealing with an avalanche of sociopolitical, ethical, psychological, emotional, as well as ideological (religious) agendas and intrigues bombarding simultaneously and inexorably a single mind from all conceivable directions and, perhaps, even more tragic, at the hands of the very individuals Juana trusted the most and whom she so desperately looked to for love: "Amid this terrible conflict [her] inner self was now the arena between the husband whom she so ardently loved at the cost of so much anxiety and distress, and the father whom she so deeply revered and to whom she would fain be an obedient daughter" (Prawdin 1938, 94).

Perhaps Juana's severest physical and mental mistreatment came at the hands of the Marquis of Denia, employed by and with the full consent of the queen's son Charles V of the Holy Roman Empire:

Belittlements, incomprehension, the trial of daily vexations—these in themselves were enough to bring any mental cripple close to collapse. But Denia did not stop with that. Far more insidious, far more lethal in its effect on the very foundations of her reason, was his campaign to trap her in a net of lies and conundrums so knotted, so insoluble, that a failure to unravel them would take the last of her mental strength, would sink her forever in a fatal bog of doubts and battlements, would, in sum, annihilate her own confidence in her rational powers and show her, show her herself, that her mind was hopelessly gone and that she might just as well give up. (Miller 1963, 325)

In addition to identifying Juana as a kindred spirit Lorca, the writer, would look to her as an historic model or prototype when creating his feminine protagonists throughout his lyrical and dramatic production.

It has been suggested that in 1492, Juana, seated along with her sister (Isabella) and brother (Juan) on their white mules, witnessed the scene of her parents' victory over the Sultan Boabdil as he was forced to surrender, weeping, the Nirvana on Earth, which he and previous Moorish kings had made of the Alhambra Palace. Angna Enters writes the following in the "Preface Notes" to her dramatic representation entitled *Love Possessed Juana (Queen of Castile)* (1939): "Ferdinand and Isabella could now enjoy its patios with their pink roses, and cool their eyes on the snows crowning the Sierra Nevada, visible everywhere from the new Christian Eden. Yet Juana wept as though she, a Catholic Spanish *Infanta,* and not the now homeless Moorish infidels, were being driven from Spanish soil—proof of her 'madness'" (1939, 10–11).[2]

If this be enough to constitute an individual's madness, then García Lorca would share in the same "madness" since he, too, would interpret with a comparable bittersweet sadness Spain's loss of a rich, exuberant, and mysteriously sensual Moorish culture: "It was a disastrous event, even though they may say the opposite in the schools. An admirable civilization, and a poetry, astronomy, architecture and sensitivity unique in the world—All were lost, to give way to an impoverished, cowed city, a 'misers' paradise" (Gibson 1989, 29).

Even the most casual tourist of the Alhambra would certainly come to a similar conclusion on comparing the breathtaking architectural grandeur of the Moorish palace with the Renaissance austerity and coldness of the structure Juana's son, Charles V, commissioned to be built as a competing "substitute" on the same "hallowed" grounds. Moreover Federico, frolicking in his youth throughout Granada's lush Albaicín region, could not have helped but marvel at the curious twist of fate associated with the remains of Isabella, Ferdinand, Juana, and Philip, entombed in the royal chapel and situated precisely at the feet of the Alhambra palace. Simple pride, therefore, " in his Granada!," as Antonio Machado would lament on the occasion of the poet's nonsensical assassination, would be enough for Lorca to have succumbed to Doña Juana's allure as her spirit reached out to him from across the centuries.

The queen of Castile, however, would make a much more indelible mark in Lorca's artistic production. Indeed she makes her presence known very early in the poet's aforementioned adolescent prose, poetry, and drama, which only recently have been published (1994). However, the Grenadine poet prefers to capture Juana from a slightly different perspective, as compared to her portrayal in the works of the other artists previously mentioned. Lorca presents Juana as a curious combination of spiritual lover and martyr of an unrequited human love, yearning to transcend the empty shell that history and legend continue to feed upon. In Lorca's prose poem "Fray Antonio (poema raro)" (strange poem) (1917), Juana's endless search for true love beyond the grave is identified, curiously, with Saint John of the Cross's mystical journey and ultimate union with the *Amado* (Beloved) or Christ himself: "Saint John of the Cross is inquiring of a rosebush for his Beloved and Juana the Mad has her tragic and dark eyes fixed on an impossible afterlife" (1994, 311).

In a second unedited prose composition entitled "María Elena: Canción" ["Maria Elena: Song"] (1918) Lorca's protagonist is not named Juana nor does she have royal blood flowing through her veins. Nonetheless Maria Elena's story mirrors Juana's since both figures die for an impossible love (1994, 410–12). The reader senses, in addition, a revealing autobiographical sub-theme in this piece. Lorca, himself, identifies with the same desperation shared by these feminine figures and even goes so far as to beseech Maria Elena, in a type of desperate prayer not unlike that of Lope de Vega in the funeral elegy dedicated to his son Carlos Félix, to intervene with the Almighty on his behalf so that he might receive spiritual alleviation from his own torture resulting from a lost and impossible love:

> Oh Maria Elena! . . . Don't sigh, don't sigh for him that left you; or God's sake I beseech you. . . . He wasn't worthy of your love. . . . Don't think about him, he doesn't deserve the doves of your fantasy. . . . The flower of your life is withering . . . even though he perhaps sleeps without a worry. . . . You who suffers with burning passion because of a pair of eyes that caught your fancy. You are virginal! You are magnificent! You are pure! . . . Maria Elena! Maria Elena! Your soul is no longer of this world. . . . Pray for me, since I am a sad case; pray for me, since I am not loved; intercede for me, since I am without life. Don't abandon me. Maria Elena! Maria Elena! (1989, 411)

In what is considered to be perhaps the very first sonnet Lorca wrote, entitled "La mujer lejana (Soneto sensual)" ["The Distant Woman: A Sonnet of Sensuality"] (1989, 96–97), we find, once again, the three-fold connection of an unfulfilled feminine lover, an implicit reference to Juana as archetypal symbol of the Andalusian Martyr and the poet's explicit personal identification with the motif of unrequited love:

> My body is like an amphora made of the dark night which
> spills its essence into you, divine mad woman!
>
> (1994b, 96)

The thematic connection between Lorca's adolescent poetry and his aforementioned *Impresiones y paisajes* becomes quite evident when we turn our attention briefly to the vignette entitled "Sepulcros de Burgos" ["Sepulchers of Burgos"] (1986, II, 58–64). This book, it must be remembered, was the direct result of Lorca's so-called educational tour throughout Castile organized by the poet's professor, Martín Domínguez Berrueta, from the University of Granada and in which he participated with a group of fellow students. The Castilian queen, as would be expected, makes several appearances throughout its pages. In this particular piece our poet portrays the Mad Queen precisely at the moment of the tragic loss of her husband, as she sheds heart-wrenching tears before an empty, albeit finely decorated, tomb, which once contained the remains of Philip the Handsome:

> Almost all of these sepulchers of Burgos that enclose so many magnificent ideas are without an inhabitant . . . and they bear inscriptions with sarcasm written on posters of faded color that speak very solemnly of indulgences and glories of the dead person who no longer exists even in his ashes . . . and one feels very peculiar contemplating the empty sepulchers in the Cartuja monastery which enclosed within an amphora the remains of Philip the Handsome and before which the ideal Juana the Mad, with passion, cried bitterly before the body of his soul as Brunhild before Siegfried in the epic poem *Nibelungenlied* . . . but all we think about is humanity's tremendous vanity, so punished and ridiculed by the leveling centuries. . . . And, above all, to think that all this will end . . . because the world and eternity are but an infinite dream. (1986, III, 64)

Finally, and still rather early in Lorca's literary production—in his *Libro de poemas* [Book of Poems] (1921)—Juana receives "first billing" in "Elegía a Doña Juana la Loca" [Elegy to doña Juana the Mad]. The term "elegía" in the poem's title suggests an ironic twist very reminiscent of the subtitles Lorca was to apply to the last two sections of his elegy entitled *Llanto por Ignacio Sánchez Mejías* [Lament for Ignacio Sánchez Mejía] (1935) "Cuerpo presente" [Presence of the Body], "Alma ausente" [Absence of the Soul]. As mentioned earlier, Lorca's *Impresiones y paisajes* captures Juana's spirit shedding tears before a tomb empty of Philip's body. In contrast "Elegía a doña Juana la Loca" does not lament precisely Juana's physical presence in death, a secondary theme to be sure, rather the continued yearning for the love that was denied her in life. Even in death Juana's unrequited love illuminates the material world from beyond the grave: "Princess in love and whose love was unrequited. A red carnation in a profound and desolate valley. The grave which contains you oozes with your sadness through the eyes that it has opened over the marble" (1986, I, 21–23).

The irony between "Elegía a doña Juana la loca" and "Sepulcros de Burgos" is reconciled completely when we compare the former with another poem contained in *Libro de poemas,* simply entitled "Elegía" . and (*Granada*) as a sort of subtitle (1986, I, 39–41). In fact the two poems are considered by most García Lorca scholars as companion compositions. In the latter piece the particular circumstances of the historic Juana transcend to the archetypal representation of the Andalusian martyr. If "Elegía a doña Juana la Loca," takes as its starting point the queen's unhappy marriage and the untimely death of her husband, "Elegía" redresses the protagonist in the garb of prototype of unfulfilled lover; the Andalusian spinster who goes to the tomb with body and passion intact and who attains through silent suffering "virginal" transcendence beyond the grave:

> No one fecundates you. Andalusian martyr, . . .
> Your body will go to the grave intact of emotions.
> A dawn will sprout from the dark earth.
> Two bloody carnations will spring from your eyes,
> and from your breasts, roses as white as snow.
> But your great sadness will disappear with the stars,
> as another star worthy to wound them and eclipse them.
>
> (1986, I, 40–41)

Notwithstanding its lack of specific historical detail, "Elegía a doña Juana la Loca" is bound to a specific time and place while "Elegía" assumes a more universal and metaphorical perspective, paving the way for a fuller and richer development of the Lorca motif in the poet's more mature works:

> You are the mirror of an Andalusia
> that suffers gigantic passions and is silent,
> passions rocked back and forth by fans
> and by mantillas over the throats
> that contain the quiverings of blood, of snow,
> and the red scratches made by stares.
>
> (1986, I, 40)

The direct references to Juana the Mad throughout Lorca's artistic production are, admittedly, sparse; however, there is no doubt that the Grenadine poet deliberately used Juana as an historical cornerstone on which to build his motif of the Andalusian Martyr. For Lorca, Juana served as a true "flesh and blood" embodiment of "Juliet without her Romeo," as he would characterize virtually all his tragic feminine protagonists (1997, 209). Indeed Juana would be the first of a long succession of anguished women tragically torn between the sweet allure of erotic love as a carnal, natural and divine "rite" and the multiple forces of its prohibition imposed by a hypocritical society (Gibson 1985, 387).

If we accept the premise of Juana the Mad as prototype for Lorca's. motif of the Andalusian martyr, we should be able to trace a clean and uninterrupted association between similar feminine protagonists throughout the Grenadine poet's entire artistic production. We have already confirmed that Juana, as historic prototype in "Elegía a doña Juana la Loca" takes a step forward to archetypal status in its companion piece "Elegía."[3] The thread is not broken. The Andalusian martyr goes on to join hands with "La monja gitana" [The Gypsy Nun], Soledad Montoya of "Romance de la pena negra" [Ballad of the Black Sorrow], and "El martirio de Santa Olalla" [The Martyrdom of Saint Olalla], among others, contained in Lorca's *Romancero Gitano* [Gypsy Ballads] (1928).

The succession continues. Lorca fleshes out the protagonists of his lyrics by recontextualizing the motif in his works of drama. Mariana Pineda as tragic Grenadine heroine shares many qualities with Juana, her historical counterpart.[4] Both women champion the causes of love and liberty in their own way and within their respective circumstances. Both women are betrayed in the end by these very principles they fought to preserve. In fact, Lorca's description of Mariana Pineda as the protagonist of his play of the same name clearly echoes the poet's vision of Juana as Andalusian prototype: "She is a Juliet without Romeo and she is closer to a madrigal than an ode. When she decides to die, she is already dead, and death does not frighten her in the least" (1997, 207–209).

Juana's spirit even travels with Lorca to New York (1929–30) as she inhabits the body of the Novia (fiancée) of *Así que pasen cinco años* [When Five Years Pass] (1931), as well as reuniting with Juliet herself from beyond the grave in *El público* [The Public]:

JULIET: Enough. I don't want to hear you any more. Why do you want to take me away?

It's a lie, the word of love, a broken mirror, a step in water. Afterwards you would leave me in the grave again, as everyone does trying to convince those who listen that true love is impossible. (1986, II, 630)

Juana does not abandon Lorca in New York. She follows him back to Spain to join hands with the Novia in *Bodas de sangre* [Blood Wedding] (1933), Yerma, in the play of the same name (1934), and, ultimately, with Adela, the tragic protagonist of Lorca's last and perhaps greatest drama, *La casa de Bernarda Alba* [The House of Bernarda Alba] (1936). The circle is complete. Indeed when one rereads the verses of Lorca's poem "Elegía" it is not difficult to confirm an early projection of the miserable existence Adela and her four spinster sisters would suffer as Andalusian martyrs forever imprisoned within the thick walls of the Alba house:

> The immense sadness that floats in your eyes
> speaks to us of your broken and failed life,
> the monotony of your poor surroundings
> watching people pass from your window,
> listening to the rain fall on the bitterness
> which the old, provincial street possesses,
> while in the distance sound the clamors,
> blurry and confusing, of bells.
>
> (1986, I, 41)

In conclusion, Juana the Mad serves as Lorca's very first prototype of frustrated love. She initiates an unending succession of feminine protagonists throughout the Grenadine poet's lyrical and dramatic production. Moreover from the perspective of social commentary she serves perhaps as a vehicle through which the poet directs the reader's consciousness to conflicting socioreligious forces, which affected Lorca deeply and constitute the ideological underpinning of his entire artistic production: carnal love versus spiritual redemption, maternal instinct versus sociocultural prohibition, human versus divine love as equally mystical experiences, the taboos of the church and the Old Testament versus Christ as a humanistic symbol of complete and unhindered self-expression and forgiveness through love of nature and humanity. Finally we need to make the ultimate connection between Juana's tragedy as an historical figure and García Lorca's Andalusian martyrdom, which he defines in terms of his personal failures in matters of love and which he endured throughout a life tragically cut short by the sadistic madness of an assassin's bullet. Here is the poet in his own words: "[while I] am made of impossible love. . . . In life, the great problem is spiritual isolation, for men are so cruel that they love to embitter the lives of the only people who think and feel. . . . There are many who scoff at love and at art, and these are the ones who achieve happiness on earth. Those who have a fiery heart and love truly . . . those are the ones who reap only sorrow and the unhappiness of the other life. I am one of them. And I will lean on the shepherd's staff of art, and will advance until my eyes open to the truth."[5]

Many critics have contended, the poet's brother among them, that personal experience and direct observation constituted the true foundation of Federico García Lorca's entire artistic production. Perhaps it is not an exaggeration, therefore, to affirm that the Grenadine poet and dramatist, in succumbing to Juana the Mad's spiritual allure from across the centuries, would discover in the queen of Castile not only a kindred spirit but also the historic prototype of his own Andalusian martyr complex.

NOTES

1. The most notable artistic portrayals of Juana the Mad may be classified, merely for convenience, into four general categories: 1) those authors in whose respective works, mostly prose but not excluding drama, exercise a conscious effort to respect the empirical facts notwithstanding their reasonable application of poetic license (Manuel Tamayo y Baus, Bethany Aram, Aroní Yanko, Julio Rodríguez); 2) those authors whose works continue to maintain an historic accuracy but with a decided "feminist" interpretation of the events (Carmen Barberá, Rosa Montero, Joan Connor); 3) those authors who elevate Juana to "martyr" status (Benito Pérez Galdós, Miguel Sabido, Manuel Rueda); and 4) those authors whose application of poetic license results in a notable distortion or contradiction of the historic events (Ramón Gómez de la Serna, Martínez Mediero, Vicente Aranda).

2. Needless to say, Enters is not speaking literally since she does not believe that Juana was in fact mad; rather the circumstances constituted "political madness." The artistic mission of Enters in the play was to create a political and ideological parallel between events under the Comunero revolts against Charles V and the Republican defense against Franco's troops during the Spanish Civil War.

3. See Rafael Martínez Nadal for this poem as an early projection of the play *Doña Rosita la soltera* [Doña Rosita the Spinster] (1935).

4. See Cedric Busette for Mariana Pineda as religious martyr.

5. From "Estado sentimental: La primavera" ["State of Emotion: Spring." Translation from *Collected Poems*, xxv].

WORKS CITED

Aram, Bethany. 2001. *La reina Juana: Gobierno, piedad y dinastía*. Madrid: Marcial Pons.
Aranda, Vicente. 2003. *Mad Love*. Sony Pictures Classics. Culver City, California.

Barberá, Carmen. 1992. *Juana la Loca: Colección Mujeres Apasionadas/1*. Barcelona: Editorial Planeta.

Boling, Becky. 1989. "The Spectacle of The Other: Madness in *Falsa crónica de Juana la Loca.*" *Gestos* 8: 87–97.

Busette, Cedric. 1984. "Mariana Pineda as Religious Martyr." *Revista de Estudios Hispánicos* 18, 1: 115–21.

Campbell, Roy. 1952. *Lorca: An Appreciation of His Poetry*. New York: Haskell House Publishers, Ltd.

Castro, Eduardo. 1975. *Muerte en Granada: la tragedia de Federico García Lorca*. Madrid: Akal.

Connor, Joan. 2003. "Juana la Loca." In *History Lessons*. Amherst: University of Massachussets Press. 69–94.

Enters, Angna. 1939. *Love Possessed Juana (Queen of Castile)*. New York: Twice a Year Press.

García Lorca, Federico. 1986. *Obras completas*. 3 Vols. Edited by Arturo del Hoyo. Madrid: Aguilar.

———. 1991. *Federico García Lorca: Collected Poems*. Edited by Christopher Maurer. New York: Farrar Straus Giroux.

———. 1994a. *Prosa inédita de juventud*. Edited by Christopher Maurer. Madrid: Cátedra.

———. 1994b. *Poesía inédita de juventud*. Edited by Christian De Paepe. Madrid: Cátedra.

———. 1994c. *Teatro inédito de juventud*. Edited by Andrés Soria Olmedo. Madrid: Cátedra.

———. 1997. *Epistolario complete*. Edited by Andrew Anderson and Christopher Maurer Madrid: Cátedra.

Gardiol, Rita Mazzetti. 1974. *Ramón Gómez de la Serna*. New York: Twayne Publishers, Inc.

Gibson, Ian. 1989. *Federico García Lorca: A Life*. New York: Pantheon Books.

———. 1985. *Federico García Lorca: 1. De Fuente Vaqueros a Nueva York (1898–1929)*. 2nd ed. Barcelona: Grijalbo.

———. 1987. *Federico García Lorca: 2. De Nueva York a Fuente Grande (1929–1936)*. Barcelona: Grijalbo.

Gómez de la Serna, Ramón. 1949. *Doña Juana la Loca (y otras seis novelas superhistóricas)*. Madrid: Revista de Occidente, 2–32.

Halsey, Martha. 1979. "Juana la Loca in Three Dramas of Tamayo y Baus, Galdós, and Martín Recuerda." *Modern Language Studies* 9, 1:47–59.

Machado, Antonio. 1981. *Soledades/Poesías de la guerra*. Madrid: Ediciones Felmar.

Magnarelli, Sharon. 1989. "Dramatic Irony and Lyricism in Historical Theater: *El pobre Franz*, and *Falsa crónica de Juana la Loca.*" *Latin American Theater Review* 22, 2:47–57.

Martínez Mediero, Manuel. 1984. *Juana del amor hermoso/debate histórico sobre figuras*. Madrid: Preyson.

Martínez Nadal, Rafael. 1974. *Federico García Lorca and The Public: A Study of an Unfinished Play and Love and Death in Lorca's Work*. New York: Schocken Books.

Miller, Townsend. 1963. *The Castles and the Crown: Spain 1451–1555*. New York: Coward-McCann, Inc.

Montero, Rosa. 1999. *Amores y desamores que han cambiado la Historia.* Madrid: Alfaguara.

Pérez Galdós, Benito. 1971. *Santa Juana de Castilla: Tragicomedia en tres actos.* In *Cuentos y teatro.* Madrid: Aguilar, 953–69.

◐ Pfandl, Ludwig. 1959. *Juana la Loca.* 8th ed. Madrid: Espasa-Calpe.

Poeta, Salvatore. 1990. *La elegía funeral en memoria de Federico García Lorca (Introducción al género y antología).* Madrid: Editorial Playor.

Pollin, Alice, M., ed. 1975. *A Concordance of the Plays and Poems of Federico García Lorca.* Ithaca, New York: Cornell University Press.

◑Prawdin, Michael. 1938. *The Mad Queen of Spain.* Translated by Eden and Cedar Paul. London: George Allen and Unwin Ltd.

Rodríguez, Julio. 1991. *Satrapia I: El libro de memorias de Doña Juana la Loca.* Caracas: Editora Internacional 7, C. A.

Rodríguez-Fischer, Ana. 1996. "La reina Loca." *Cuadernos Cervantes de la Lengua Española* 10:84–85.

Rodríguez Villa, Antonio. 1892. *La reina doña Juana la Loca.* Madrid: Imprenta de Fortanet.

Rubin, Nancy. 1991. *Isabella of Castile: The First Renaissance Queen.* New York: St. Martin's Press.

Rueda, Manuel. 1996. *Retablo de la pasión y muerte de Juana la Loca en dos jornadas.* Madrid: Ediciones de Cultura Hispánica.

Sabido, Miguel. 1985. *Falsa crónica de Juana la Loca: Obra de teatro original.* Mexico: Editorial Katun.

◑Schoonover, Lawrence. 1959. *The Prisoner of Tordesillas.* Boston: Little, Brown and Company.

Tamayo y Baus, Manuel. 1970. *La locura de amor: Un drama nuevo.* Madrid: Espasa-Calpe.

Taylor Woots, Jeremy. 1999. *Enigmas de la historia.* España: Edimat Libros, S. A.

Walters, Gareth D. "The Queen of Castile and the Andalusian Spinster: Lorca's Elegies for Two Women." In *Lorca: Poet and Playwright. Essays in Honour of J. M. Aguirre,* edited by Mildred Adams Cardiff of Wales Press; New York: St. Martin's Press.

Yanko, Aroní. 2003. *Los silencios de Juana la Loca.* Barcelona: Belaqva.

Juana of Castile, Reader of Desiderius Erasmus of Rotterdam: An Interpretation of Manuel Martínez Mediero's *Juana del amor hermoso*

Vilma Navarro-Daniels

Erasmus is read even in Heaven.

MANUEL MARTÍNEZ MEDIERO'S *JUANA DEL AMOR HERMOSO* [A LOVE TOO Beautiful] (1982) presents an image of Juana of Castile as a modern woman who subscribed to humanism, who devoted herself to the reading of *The Praise of Folly* first published in 1511, the most famous work written by Erasmus of Rotterdam.[1] As we will see, the Juana represented in this play is permanently questioned in relation to her Catholicism; she is even accused by her own mother, Queen Isabella of being Jewish, or being possessed by the devil, as the Marquis of Denia affirms. More than being crazy and heretic, Juana is a close follower of the self-defense of Stultitia, which Erasmus depicts in *The Praise of Folly*. These beliefs brought upon her the title of the "Mad Queen," although indeed this was the reaction of an intolerant Spain that had expelled the Moors from the peninsula and that was trying to create a powerful empire. In Martínez Mediero's work, Juana's madness is quite simply humanist openness.

From the structural point of view, this piece consists of two parts, and opens and closes with Queen Juana "in the autumn of her life" (1995, 7), as indicated in the text.[2] Juana gladly plays and sings in spite of her prolonged confinement in Tordesillas. In the play, Juana is visited by the Marquis of Denia in the beginning of the first part and toward the end of the second part, when the leader of the Comuneros, Juan de Padilla, also visits the queen in order to make available to her the people of Toledo. Between these two moments, the work resorts to a series of flashbacks that transport us to diverse stages of Juana's life and the lives of those who surrounded her and intervened in deciding her fate.

119

Since her first encounter with the Marquis of Denia, Martínez Mediero shows Juana as an expert in the philosophy of Erasmus. When Denia forces Juana to pray and humiliates her by ordering "And now, go to bed. . . . Pray for Spain, for our Emperor, and don't consider the urinating in your petticoat again." (1995, 10). Juana, crying, responds to him reading a paragraph from *The Praise of Folly*, book that she zealously hides between the sheets of her bed:

> If you also ask me where I was born, I will tell you that I do not stem from the vagabond Delos nor from the undulating sea, nor from the deep caverns, but rather from the same Fortunate Islands where everything grows spontaneously and without effort. *(One hears the sweet voices of the chorus of the Benedictine monks.)* There is no work, nor hatred, nor old age, nor illnesses, nor does one see in the fields the mallow or the thorn, but rather wherever it may be, ones eyes and nose are given to the delight of marjoram, sagebrush, lotus flowers, roses, violets and hyacinth like other Garden of Adonis. . . . *(She closes the book and gently sobs.)* Because I didn't begin my life by crying, but upon being born I smiled lovingly at my mother. . . . *(The figure of JUANA vanishes)*. (1995, 10–11)

In this text, which is read by Juana very early in the play, the author sets what will be the ideological controversy of the drama: on the one hand, Juana leans on the ideas of Erasmus of Rotterdam; on the other, Cardinal Cisneros and Queen Isabella worry about the defense of the Catholic religion, to such a degree that the monarch rejects printing, self-teaching, humanism, and, of course, the Reformation.

Erasmus of Rotterdam (1466–1536) lived when Europe was passing from the fifteenth to the sixteenth century. This was a time marked by deep changes at different levels, as Stefan Zweig indicates. It was an era of great discoveries and inventions, when human beings dared to challenge traditionally held beliefs in order to permit themselves to decipher the mysteries of the unknown. To the names of the great explorers such as Bartolomé Díaz, Christopher Columbus, Sebastián Cabot, Pedro Álvares Cabral, and Hernando de Magallanes, we need to add those of Nicholas Copernicus and Johann Gutenberg as well as those of Renaissance and Italian humanists such as Leonardo da Vinci and Giovanni Pico della Mirandola, and thinkers of the stature of Thomas More and Martin Luther. As Zweig notes, their discoveries enlarged the notion of world that man held at the end of the Middle Ages. Once earthly secrets were scrutinized, human beings dared to try to understand the Divine; this intellectual questioning threatened the absolute authority of the Catholic Church.

Humanism was particularly interested in the development of an intimate relationship between man and God, a relationship that perhaps might be able to set aside ecclesiastical mediation (Zweig 1962, 31). This humanist tendency was seen as very similar to illuminism, which, according to Lucien Febvre, is an internalized Christianism that tries to have human beings intensely experience the grace of God in themselves. The illuminati's methods were abstraction and abandonment, and they were against religious formalism, monastic rules, papal bulls of indulgence, excommunications, fast and abstinence, the cult of saints and intermediaries, postulating instead an introspective religiousness (1970, 125). It is not by chance that Martínez Mediero presents Juana's jailer, Luis Ferrer, accusing her of being touched by illuminism, in addition to asserting that she is demoniac, an atheist, and a witch. In fact, in her confinement in Tordesillas, Juana manifests rejection toward formal religion. She is forced by the Marquis of Denia to cross herself and to recite formal prayers aloud. Queen Isabel herself questions the faith of her daughter, her love for Spain, her mental health, and her morality, always blaming Erasmus's teachings, which were in vogue at the Flemish court.

Erasmus enjoyed fame in his day, especially among other humanists. Nevertheless after publishing his edition of the New Testament in 1516 and with the ascent of Martin Luther, Erasmus became a very well known public figure when he involved himself in certain disputes with conservative theologians. As Erika Rummel explains, "Unwilling to commit himself to either party in the religious debate, he was attacked by both. Reformers called him an opportunist, reactionary Catholics a heretic. Thus Erasmus's name stands for both greatness and tragedy" (1990, 3). *The Praise of Folly* was considered to be an antecedent of the Reformation, so much so that Luther himself wanted to count on Erasmus as one of his followers; this designation, however, Erasmus refused. This rebuff brought him problems with Luther in addition to the suspicions that had been raised about him inside the Catholic Church.

In Martínez Mediero's drama, the ideological counterpart of the philosopher of Rotterdam is represented by Francisco Jiménez de Cisneros. Denise M. DiPuccio sees this contrast as the fight between a Spain locked up in obsolete values and another quite different Spain that could have opened its doors to modernity, "to shun Cisnero's religious indoctrination and to embrace Erasmus's humanistic philosophies, to end cultural introversion and to integrate European and New World influences" (1987, 9). In order to be able to have an idea of the amount of power held in the hands of Cardinal Cisneros, it is useful to consider the way Marcel Bataillon describes the prelate: "Confessor of Queen Isabella since 1492, almost immediately afterwards the Provincial of the Franciscans of Castile, Archbishop of Toledo and Primate of the Spains from 1495, General Inquisitor from 1507, Regent of the Kingdom on two occasions, this friar so clearly dominates the Spanish religious life during the twenty years which precede the breaking out of the Reformation, that we cannot avoid going back to him if we want to understand the attitude of Spain towards the Protestant Revolution" (1950, 1–2).

It is the function of Juana, as a follower of Erasmus, to oppose these two figures. Prior to her trip to Flanders, Martínez Mediero presents a scene in which Juana and Isabel engage in a dialogue on the imminent marriage of the princess and her royal responsibilities. The dramatist shows a very young Juana, "full of life" and "radiant" (1995, 12), who hastily enters into the room where her mother awaits her. Juana's joy is so much uncontainable that Philip's letters fall from her hand. Juana comes from the kitchen where she has read these letters to the servants, making very clear that "All the servants were there too, absolutely spellbound, as if they were in church listening to something in Latin from Cardinal Cisneros" (1). Later, she adds that, "All the ladies' maids were going crazy over Philip's portraits" (1). Queen Isabella tries to minimize the Flemish, reducing them to the stereotype of cheese and tulip producers, against which Juana argues that Flemish have also given birth to humanism:

> Joanna: Mother, you musn't forget that Flanders is where Humanism had its beginnings, right there in Rotterdam.
> Isabella: How can you possibly compare a loud-mouth like Erasmus with our own dear Cardinal Cisneros?
> Joanna: The Cardinal's forever saying that we shall all be damned in Hell. . . .
> Isabella: Precisely because the people here in this Court of Castile have lost their holy fear of God. (1995, 1–2)

The comparison between the Flemish and the Castilian courts is a recurrent motif. Mourning and attendance at ten daily masses seem to be the indicators that it is Isabella's opinion to confirm Spain as the defender of Catholicism and orthodoxy. While Juana delights in Philip's beauty, her mother's only concern is "to build an Empire in the name of God" (1995, 3). The explicit intention of giving to Spain a hegemonic place in European culture is, perhaps, the most anti-Erasmian characteristic that Isabella displays in the play. As will be discussed later, Erasmus does not place reason against passion. On the contrary, he considers that both reason and passion are important dimensions of human beings. For Erasmus, as Stefan Zweig has highlighted, fanaticism is the strongest force opposing reason; he sustains that intolerance is the great sin that can be found in the root of all human conflicts (1962, 10). According to Zweig, Erasmus impugned all kind of fanaticism either at the religious or national levels. This position led him to deny the existence of heresies, because what was thus labeled was not more than a dissident opinion born from the independent exercise of critical thinking (11). In addition, Erasmus did not recognize any superiority of one nation over another, a position that caused him be against any type of nationalism (13) and to postulate a supernational and panhuman ideal (17). These ideas to which Juana subscribes collide with the nationalistic mission that Isabella anxiously desires to impose on her daughter: "Your future husband is a Catholic—I've made very sure of that—and *that* is the only kind of beauty that matters. Whatever do you think made us drive the Moslems out of Spain? There are men who are attractive because of their looks, or the perfume on their bodies, or because they know the power of the senses, and they are constantly in pursuit of pleasure and fantasies of the flesh. Trust them no further than you would a pistol-packing saint!" (1995, 3).

Intransigence will take Isabella and Cisneros to the practice of forced conversions in Granada as well as to confiscation and burning of thousands of copies of the Koran, actions that fill with happiness the queen and her advisor. Yet Martínez Mediero twists the queen's narrow point of view when he makes her to appear before Juana as a ghost, defending the ideas of Erasmus, whose works she is reading in heaven. The sovereign also regrets the expulsion of the Moors and Jews as well as forced conversions. Juana makes the Marquis of Denia notice this when he accuses her of being possessed by the devil: "Not one of you understands anything. Erasmus is read even in Heaven; my mother has told me so herself! You can tell the King that his grandmother is sorry now for having burned the Koran, and that the tower of the Cathedral in Seville is Moorish, whether he likes it or not!" (1995, 2).

Unlike Isabella, for Juana there is no contradiction among hedonism, fantasy, and reason. Juana insists on defending the joy of living, the playful aspects of human existence, and the value of imagination, attitudes that show her compenetration with Erasmus's work, particularly when he asserts that life cannot be called life if we take pleasure away from it. In this manner, Juana says that, "The Romans went in for their share of perfume and fantasy, but, even so, they were the ones who invented Roman Law" (1995, 3). As Erasmus does in *The Praise of Folly,* Juana defends delight as a good in itself, as well as diversion, joy and the value of pleasure. Erasmus sustains that delight is the supreme good of human beings, asking, "After all, what is this life

itself—can you even call it life if you take away pleasure?" (1995, 9).
To the aforementioned we must add what Stefan Zweig indicates to
be one of the most prominent characteristics of Erasmism: the search
of the harmonic synthesis of those elements that seem to be contradictory within the human spirit (1962, 12). In this way, irreconcilable
things are so only in appearance. Instead of rejecting the undeniable
dimensions of human beings, Erasmus trusted human capability to
be educated in such a manner that morality can be taught and
learned (Zweig 1962, 14).

Juana wishes to please Philip; for this reason she learns French in
secret. This provokes the immediate rejection of Isabella, because it
is very well known, and the play insists on it, that the marriage
between Juana and Philip had the purpose of asphyxiating and iso-
lating France, by looking for alliances with the rest of the European
countries. For Isabella, the happiness that her daughter can obtain
through her marriage with Philip is totally secondary. The most
important thing for the queen is being realistic, as can be concluded
from the advice she gives to Juana: "Be less happy and keep your feet
on the ground. Spain has a noble task to accomplish through you.
Converting Europe is our sacred destiny. The Empire cannot be
achieved until all Europe prays as one beneath the joint flags of
Castile and Aragon. Once *that* is a reality, then we can look forward
to a new dawn of happiness, and even the Day of Judgment (which
they say is about to happen anyway). We can't be truly happy until we
enjoy the presence of God the Father, in Heaven" (1995, 5).

Oppositions between mother and daughter multiply. As DiPuccio
has noticed, "For every reactionary comment offered by Isabella,
Juana retaliates with a liberal point of view" (1987, 9).[3] To the true
happiness of Isabella, Juana opposes "enjoying the small things that
life offers us" (Martínez Mediero 1995, 5); to the contempt for life
due to its fleeting nature, Juana responds proposing to journey
through existence beautifully loving one another. Isabella indeed
sees in France the negation of all the moral, spiritual, and religious
values of which Spain would be the incarnation, holder, and carrier.
From there the queen asserts that Juana will marry Philip because:

It is in the interests of Spain and most of all because Spain will not be
happy until we have eliminated France. France delights in doing everything possible to give us a bad image. The French are jealous because we
invented the fashion of wearing black, and above all, because we have St.
James the Apostle to protect us. They envy us our other-worldliness, our
martyrs and our saints, while they indulge in earthly pleasures in a society

based on a market economy. And their conscience troubles them. Spain is called to high endeavors, Joanna, and you, my child, are to be our spiritual flag-bearer in the forefront of Europe. (1995, 5)

Yet Juana does not identify herself with this mission assigned by her mother. Boasting of great lucidity, the princess chides Isabella by questioning the resignation and victimization that seem to have marked the queen's life. Juana accepts Isabella's decisions, but before she wants to make it plain that she does love earthly pleasures. Even more, it is possible to say that the uncontrollable love that Juana manifests toward Philip is totally based on Erasmus's notion of voluptuousness, passion, and emotion. Erasmus argues that it is obvious that "emotions all belong to Folly. Thus, the usual distinction between a wiseman and a fool is that the fool is governed by emotion, the wiseman by reason. . . . But actually the emotions not only function as guides to those who are hastening to haven of wisdom, but also, in the whole range of virtuous action, they operate like spurs or goads, as it were, encouraging the performance of good deeds" (1979, 45).

Erasmus attacks the stoic theories that postulate the suppression of emotions. Putting passions aside would be equivalent to eradicating what is human in man. This would transform the human being into some kind of imperturbable and impassible God or, even worse, a statue made of marble with human appearance, but totally insensitive and distant from other people and feelings. From Erasmus's point of view, a man that has managed to ignore any kind of affection in order to permit reason to prevail in him will consider himself to be perfect so that he will believe he is the only wise and free person in the world. Such an attitude will necessarily lead him to condemn and judge others harshly because he has become the standard for other men. The philosopher of Rotterdam does not vacillate in rejecting this model of humanity as incomplete. Erasmus explicitly indicates that such a monstrosity would never be elected as governor in case a nation had the possibility of choosing a leader. Erasmus would prefer a governor who is pleasant to others, who shows his affection, is joyful and gentle, and who fundamentally, "considers nothing human foreign to him" (1979, 46), all of which is part of the humanist philosophy to which the Juana created by Martínez Mediero subscribes.

The dramatist includes the very well known episode of the first encounter between Juana and Philip. As soon as the fiancés see each other, passion seizes and sweeps them so overwhelmingly that Friar Martín de Mogica decides to marry them immediately. Within the

Erasmus philosophy, human passion is a source of joy and happiness. In the life of man, rationality does not have a place greater than passion, which is positive because it reduces the sadness and bitterness of existence. Erasmus follows the model established by Plato when restricting reason to the narrow space of the head, from where it has to face the forces of wrath and concupiscence, "anger, which occupies the citadel and very fountainhead of life, the heart; and passionate desire, which holds wide side over the rest, all way down to the genitals" (1979, 28). Juana succumbs before her passion and, as a disciple of Erasmus, she tries to flee from sadness, conscious that, as Stultitia asserts, "a sad life can hardly be called life at all" (Martínez Mediero 1995, 30). To Juana's apprehensions about what people could think and say in the repressive court of Castile and her fears, which appear to her as a shadow that could stop the expression of her overflowing desire, Philip responds, "Forget about Castile! God is joy and goodness" (8), an idea that is shared by Friar Martín.

The concept of a joyful and good God is reinforced by presenting the report that Cardinal Cisneros offers to Queen Isabella. His information is based on the network of spies that has been installed in Flanders. The royal advisor criticizes what he categorizes as "depravity of customs and liturgy in the Flemish church" and later he adds: "Our clergy have unassailable proof of a new image of God which could do great harm to the consolidation of our Empire. The Flemish God is a permissive God who forgives. . . . This God, this new God whom your daughter Joanna has accepted, is a God who knows no revenge, a weak God who calls for total forgiveness, a God who radiates joy" (11). For Isabella there is no doubt that this god is a false image, which must be destroyed.

Nevertheless Isabella does not question—on the contrary, she seems to approve and stimulate—the use of religion with ideological aims. When Juana and Philip visit Spain, they are received with a religious ceremony in which Cardinal Cisneros, based on the Bible, presents an image of God as the greatest punisher and avenger:

> It is written in Holy Scripture and told by St. John in the book of the Apocalypse, how the Lord God saved His people from Egypt and caused all disbelievers to perish; and how He keeps the fallen angels eternally imprisoned awaiting Judgment Day; and how Sodom and Gomorrah, and neighboring cities which had likewise fornicated and indulged in unnatural vices, were condemned to everlasting fire. In like manner, dearly beloved children, if we fail to follow the precepts of Holy Scripture under the divine mandate of our sovereigns Isabella and Ferdinand, the fire of Vulcan will fall upon Spain and purify her. And what do our sovereigns command? First, to love Spain, after God, above all things, not to betray

her holy name and to pray to God for new saints in this land which has always been prodigal in wild thyme, lavender and saints. (1995, 18)

The appeal to Spain as a country prolific in saints on Cisneros's part has its roots in a very personal ambition. The audience sees the cardinal most interested in the monarchs' support and promotion for his canonization. Martínez Mediero satirizes the cardinal, who keeps a record of the miracles he performs. Frequently he asks the queen and, once she dies, Ferdinand, if they have received news from the pope in relation to his possible beatification in life. It is interesting to see what Cisneros includes within the list of his marvelous feats. Ferdinand requests that the prelate add the return of his sexual power to his list of achievements, miracle that would allow him to beget a son with his new French wife:

> Cisneros: I have to consider what will count toward my beatification. I've already made it rain one afternoon in Villaumbrales, and that was some downpour. And I made the statue of Our Lady cry real tears in Granada, when the Moors refused to go to confession. Then I caused the death of the French Cardinal Besaçon with a serving of poisoned mushrooms when he tried to bring his Erasmian heresies into Spain and I cured the sacristan of Toledo Cathedral of a tumor in his armpit. (1995, 45)

Likely enough, among Erasmus's heresies, Cardinal Cisneros counts the mockery about miracles that the philosopher of Rotterdam puts in the mouth of the Stultitia. In *The Praise of Folly*, the belief in miracles is depicted as one of many forms of stupidity. Erasmus asserts that there are people who are pleased in believing stories relative to prodigious facts, which are more accepted the farther they are from verisimilitude. Erasmus's criticism does not stop there; he lashes clergymen and preachers who use miracles as a means to obtain money. Erasmus does not look with sympathy toward the miracles worked by supposed saints not only because they constitute a delight for the imagination of common people but because they also count on the consent of theologians. Even more serious is the fact that what people ask saints to do as miracles is nothing but a series of nonsense. King Ferdinand begs Cardinal Cisneros to endeavor and skillfully manage to reinstitute his diminished sexual vigor. According to the king, that miracle would be so remarkable, that it would really allow the prelate to shine and thus to reach his so coveted beatification. Martínez Mediero, by doing an Erasmian turn, makes the cardinal assert that he will have to resort to a spell proper of witchcraft in order to produce such a prodigy: "We'll make a brew of bull's testicles and tender cats' eyes, while you stroke the genitals of a she-rabbit" (1995, 45).

Cisneros, like the clergymen condemned by Erasmus, foments superstition, when measuring what this spell, if successful, could mean as
personal gain. Instead of advising Ferdinand about justice, Cisneros
is seduced by the possibility that his intervention can in fact make it
possible for the king to engender a son. In this way, the cardinal
becomes a contributor to the usurpation of the throne of which
Juana is the victim.

Toward the end of the play, Juana receives the visit of Juan de
Padilla, who breaks into Tordesillas in order to meet the one he recognizes to be the queen. If the Marquis of Denia wants to force Juana
to sign a document in support of the governors chosen by King
Charles, Padilla comes to request her to take immediate steps against
the foreign presence in the court and to support the rise of the
Comuneros. Juana, nevertheless, rejects both proposals and consciously prefers to assume the title of "mad," but not the madness that
Erasmus condemns, but the one that the philosopher rescues. Juana
repels violence and, instead, she embraces love: "I'm crazy and the
crazy only know how to love" (97). In fact, Erasmus distinguishes two
kinds of madness:

> one which is sent up from underworld by the avenging Furies whenever
> they dart forth their serpents and inspire in the breasts of mortals a burn-
> ing desire for war, or unquenchable thirst for gold, or disgraceful and
> wicked lust, or parricide, incest, sacrilege, or some other such plague, or
> when they afflict the guilty thoughts of some criminal with the madden-
> ing firebrands of terror. There is another kind far different from the first,
> namely the kind which takes its origin from me and is most desirable. It
> occurs whenever a certain pleasant mental distraction relieves the heart
> from its anxieties and cares and at the same time soothes it with the balm
> of manifold pleasures. (1979, 58)

Martínez Mediero masterfully opposes these two types of folly. As
we have seen, the characters that surround Juana are moved by violence, economic and political ambition, as well as by lust. Nevertheless none of them is considered mentally imbalanced. On the contrary, ironically they believe themselves to be the paradigm of
rationality and mental sanity that tries to measure Juana's lucidity.
Like Erasmus, who gives a voice to the Stultitia to make a mordacious
critic to the powerful people of his time, Martínez Mediero gives a
voice to Juana of Castile, the Mad Queen, to show to those who had
some authority on her and on her people that there is no bigger folly
than that which justifies abuse and fanaticism. If one believes that the
quest for internal and external harmony along with the desire for
unity of all nations, and the rejection of any intolerance and dogma-

tism can be defined as insanity, only then could both Erasmus and Juana be considered "mad."

NOTES

1. *Juana del amor hermoso* was first staged in Madrid, on February 14, 1983, at the Teatro Príncipe.

2. The quotations of the play have mostly been taken from the English translation made by Hazel Cazorla. All other cases will be specifically indicated. Cazorla's translation was made from an edition published in 1982 by Editorial Fundamentos. Martínez Mediero himself in that edition did not include scenes that I discuss from the Preyson edition published in 1984.

3. John P. Gabriele analyzes the divergences between Juana and her mother from a feminist perspective. He considers that an ideology relative to gender and traditional roles of women supports what would be the national and political mission of Juana, defended by her parents. Among the divergences highlighted by Gabriele there is the opposition between the doctrines of Cardinal Cisneros, so appreciated by Isabel, and the humanist ideas of Erasmus, which are crucial to understanding Juana.

WORKS CITED

Bataillon, Marcel. 1950. *Erasmo y España: Estudios sobre la historia espiritual del siglo XVI.* Translated by Antonio Alatorre. Mexico: Fondo de Cultura Económica.

DiPuccio, Denise M. 1987. "*Juana del amor hermoso:* A Struggle For Identity." *Estreno* 13, 1:8–11.

Erasmus, Desiderius. 1979. *The Praise Of Folly.* Translated by Clarence H. Miller. New Haven: Yale University Press.

Febvre, Lucien. 1970. *Erasmo, la Contrarreforma y el espíritu moderno.* Translated by Carlos Piera. Barcelona: Ed. Martínez Roca, S. A.

Gabriele, John P. 2000. *Manuel Martínez Mediero: Deslindes de un teatro de urgencia social.* Madrid: Fundamentos.

Martínez Mediero, Manuel. 1982. *Las bragas perdidas en el tendero: Juana del amor hermoso.* Madrid: Fundamentos. Colección Espiral.

———. 1984. *Juana del amor hermoso.* Madrid: Preyson.

———. 1995. *A Love Too Beautiful.* Translated by Hazel Cazorla. University Park, PA: *Estreno,* Contemporary Plays 8.

Rummel, Erika, ed. 1990. *The Erasmus Reader.* Toronto: University of Toronto Press.

Zweig, Stefan. 1962. *Erasmo de Rotterdam: Triunfo y tragedia.* Translated by Ramón María Tenreiro. Mexico, D. F.: Editorial Diana, S. A.

III
Foreign Representations
of the Mad Queen

The Spectacle of the Other:
Madness in *Falsa crónica de Juana la Loca*

Becky Boling

MARIANA, "A DWARF DRESSED LIKE ONE OF VELÁZQUEZ'S LADIES-IN-waiting," and a Mexican "muerte catrina" (a popular caricature of death as a skeleton dressed in frills and feathers) fashioned on José Guadalupe Posada's prints and the Diego Rivera mural in the Hotel del Prado, are two of Miguel Sabido's central figures in the production of his play, *Falsa crónica de Juana la Loca* [The False Chronicle of Juana the Mad].[1] The story, simultaneously drama, poem, chronicle, and antihistory, is set in sixteenth-century Spain. It presents the political stratagems that deposed the insane and would-be queen of the Spanish Empire, Juana, daughter of Ferdinand and Isabella. In spite of its peninsular setting, Sabido's production juxtaposes "two worlds so contradictory that they could produce Mexico." The playwright-director endeavors to "popularize Spanish elitist art" and at the same time "validate popular Mexican elements" (1985, 7) in order to create a Mexican theater that speaks to national concerns, i.e., the construction of power.

Falsa crónica de Juana la Loca constitutes a return to elements of spectacle present in earlier Spanish and Mexican drama. It is in the popular elements of the spectacle that Sabido finds the basis for a national theater: the music, the puppet shows, the *danse macabre* with Death, the Spanish archetypal figures (the gypsy-witch and the court dwarf Mariana), the choral effect of the secondary characters, and the personification of death as the "muerte catrina" of Mexican popular art achieve a synthesis of cultures and arts, both dramatic and plastic.[2]

Finding correspondences between Spanish high art and popular Mexican art, the production of *Falsa crónica de Juana la Loca* sponsored in Mexico City, March 1986, by UNAM, National Autonomous University of Mexico, Institute of Bibliographic Research, foregrounds the spectacle. Within the system of potential dramatic signs, the performance of this play utilizes the metadiscourse (props, gestures, space, costumes) in a highly conscious, symbolic, and stylized manner. Indeed the play is stamped by the visual image; the scenes are tableaux. The imaginative sources for Sabido's play are a mixture of dramatic and visual arts. The playwright himself describes his play as "a monologue . . . illustrated by monks and grotesquely and lyrically commented upon by the dwarf, daughter of Buñuel's beggars, granddaughter to Valle-Inclán and Goya, perhaps a protagonist in one of "The Dreams" by Quevedo" (1985, 11). The dramatist minimizes the anecdote, eliminates the chronological order, and develops the play by an accumulation of episodes that have the force of medieval and Renaissance emblems. Each scene dramatizes various confrontations between imperialism and national independence, love and manipulation, reason and witchcraft. However, since the play breaks with the conventions of naturalistic drama, the organizing principle is found in its metadiscourse—the props, setting, disposition of the characters on the stage, and the costumes. The image that *Falsa crónica* sketches, through these tableaux, is the battle between Death and Juana—between the politics of death and the reasons or "sinrazones" or absurdities of love—for the privilege of stamping their character upon the New World and, therefore, the future.

Within the "density of signs" that Roland Barthes attributes to theater's "polyphony," Sabido's play privileges the iconic function of the setting and the gesture (1972, 262). As in Brechtian theater, "the priority of the *geste*" creates "a new theatrical (and non-literary) mode of representation" (Elam 1980, 69). Sabido employs the *geste* in several scenes to foreground specific themes. For example, the conquest and its ideological implications are apparent as the auxiliary cast, dressed in black, marches in unison across the stage, carrying Spain's banner and nearly trampling Juana and deafening the audience. Here, as in the Mexican murals of Rivera, Orozco, and Siqueiros, we have a mass of undifferentiated soldiers who massacre the indigenous population. Sabido's portrayal of the conquest undermines the cult of the Conquistador as a heroic individual in search of self-actualization. If there were any doubt as to the meaning of the conquest, Sabido discloses that the Conquistadors are in the service of death, not life. In this scene, Death plays the drum to which the soldiers measure their step.

Similarly, in another scene of the performance, disruptive metadiscursive elements foreground the issues of imperialism, church complicity, and the construction of gender. Juana's confessor, Cisneros, dances with the "muerte catrina." This proximity of death, as well as Cisneros's necromantic cape decorated with chains, aligns religion with the same destructive forces apparent in the scene of the conquest. Indeed in the published text of the play, the roles of Cisneros and Death were to be played by the same actor (Sabido 1985, 13). However, in Sabido's production, Death is not portrayed as a man, but rather as a woman. By using two different actors in the performance, Sabido can have Death present on stage in a greater number of scenes and avoid a simplistic reduction of death to the consequences of a misguided religious fervor. In addition, the bifurcation of the role also subsumes politics, hierarchy, and imperialism, as well as religion, under the hegemony of death. However, more significantly, the modification of the text raises the issue of gender. In scene 4, Sabido visually intensifies the conflict that Juana experiences by having her confront each of her tormentors simultaneously. From the "niches for saints in church" (1985, 15), Ferdinand, Cisneros, and Isabel lecture Juana on her role: "woman owes her husband eternal loyalty and respect" and "we queens have obligations" (62). Like stone statues, their lessons, too, are lifeless (60–63). In Sabido's production, the niches were scaffolding that suggested cubicles, cages, or gallows. When not center stage, Death often occupied one of these cubicles, as main spectator if not imbedded director/author of the action. The dictates and accusations expressed by the occupants of the cubicles are, moreover, not those dealing with life, but rather pronouncements of the dead, epitaphs on tombstones: "Born to maintain the only universal truth: Catholicism" and "Elected by God to be the mother of my grandson, Charles, Emperor of the West Indies, ruler over the entire world" (62). Their intention is to turn Juana, too, into a statue to glorify the ideology of imperialism.

In much the same manner, discourse is often subverted by metadiscursive elements. According to Keir Elam, the contradiction of simultaneous linguistic utterances is "one of the more prominent roles of theatrical gestures" (1980, 78). The prologue begins with the solemn chant of Juana's titles: "Juana the First of Castile./Empress of the West Indies./ . . . /Captain of the Ocean." But, in contrast, Juana, "a pathetic and defenseless figure," appears on stage dragging her husband's coffin behind her (Sabido 1985, 19). Scene 4 begins with the narrator, Mariana, reciting the attributes of a good queen: "The Queen had the good fortune / of being educated well/ . . . / Juana always knew what was good / and what was bad" (1985, 59). In this case, Sabido deftly subverts the discourse by showing, only after Mariana's recitation, Juana in a temper tantrum: "sitting on the floor. Disheveled. She is in a nightdress" (60). In the performance, the narrator Mariana ironically introduces the scene of the marriage arrangements as follows: "King Ferdinand plays with his children" (29). Using children's rhymes, Ferdinand chooses the matches while Death looks on: "Eeny, meeny, miney, mo, Catch a tiger by the toe" (31).[3] The royal sycophants place bets on the side (33) as the puppeteers enact parodies of weddings that perfunctorily turn into funerals. In this way, Sabido creates a carnivalesque setting for the discussion of power. Indeed the irony is that the familial scene of playtime with the children turns into political strategies that assign the children, like pawns, to expedient marriages and ultimately lead to their deaths. The contradiction between linguistic utterance and *geste,* together with this sort of ironic reversal, structures the dramatic movement of *Falsa crónica.*

The metadiscourse does more than create a mood in this play: it defines a symbolic world. Actually all dramatic worlds are hypothetical constructs "recognized by the audience as counterfactual (i.e., non-real) states of affairs . . . embodied as *if* in progress in the actual here and now" (Elam 1980, 102). Sabido's dramatic world is anti-history.[4] However, this hypothetical world is accessible to an audience because it involves the referential world of the spectator, in this case, Mexico. According to Joan Rea Boorman, the ethical consciousness of Brechtian theater has led from what she terms the "theatre of disruption" to a "theatre of reconstruction" (1980, 33). Indeed, Sabido's purpose is ultimately social, integrative, and concerned with present-day Mexico: "For 25 years my professional obsession had been to understand Mexican culture: its roots, its history, its essence" (1985, 7). The world of *Falsa crónica* must resonate within the audience's actual world. As Sabido himself puts the questions that the play addresses: "Would the brutal process of the Conquest have been different if Juana had possessed royal authority? Would corruption within the viceroyalty have been institutionalized as the base of life in the nation if she had truly governed? The possibilities of change in our daily life takes on a vertiginous perspective when we think that Juana would have actually governed New Spain, she who had the right to do so" (1985, 8). The dramatic world created by Sabido examines the hegemony of phallogocentric power, legacy of Renaissance and Counter-Reformation Spain, and speaks to the subsequent anguish of "marginality" that many Mexican writers, such as Octavio Paz and Carlos Fuentes, discern in their culture.

Paz in his landmark essay *The Labyrinth of Solitude* finds this "marginality" expressed in *La Malinche,* the Indian woman who acted as Cortes's translator. Paz explains Mexican solitude in terms of the feminine: "the violated Mother . . . she disappears into nothingness; she *is* Nothingness. And yet she is the cruel incarnation of the feminine condition" (1985, 85–86). *La Malinche,* not Juana la Loca, is associated with the birth of the mestizo "mixed Indigenous and Spanish" and the Mexican state, and this identity, therefore, is the result of betrayal. Fuentes recognizes, furthermore, that such a view of the feminine arises from the paranoia of an exaggerated and defensive *machismo* and must be revised (1978, 63). Miguel Sabido, like Paz and Fuentes, uses gender to discuss alternatives that have been repressed by Mexican history and culture, but he empowers the feminine by recasting it in the image of Juana. Rather than being the cause of "marginality" like *la Malinche,* Juana is its sign. The play asks the audience to identify with the feminine insofar as they experience the "marginality" of being Mexican. Juana exists eccentrically, in a world dominated by phallocracy. And in such a world, woman must be recognized as the Other.

How does Sabido create the Other in his play? Largely it is the result of a production that expresses through the metadiscourse the dialectic between politics of death that historically constituted Spain's colonial world and the ideals of love that necrophilic Spain exiled and buried. Juana brings to center stage her own condition of otherness. The ever present coffin of her husband, whom she refuses to bury, attests to her unwillingness to be forever repressed. The metadiscourse signifies through constant ironic play. The association among the diverse sign systems (costumes, gestures, discourse, props) subverts initial meanings and discloses the mechanisms of repression. A deadly politics parades as life, and life is hidden by the trappings of death.

The play is a constant dialogue between "reasons of state" and Juana's madness, "reasons of love." Sabido lambastes the egotism and inhumanity of politics. Scene 1, which is central to *Falsa crónica*'s message, is organized thematically around the political maneuvers of Ferdinand, who in turn is a model for Machiavelli's *The Prince* (1985, 29). Ferdinand plays several games of chance with the personification of Death. The pawns in the games of marriage and alliances are the royal couple's children and grandchildren. Sabido's stage production has the actors dressed in black, positioning large cardboard puppets attached to poles. Much of the comedy of this scene arises from the mocking actions of the puppeteers with their puppets. The parodic marriages are grotesquely comic as is the rapidity and inevitability of Death's selection of each victim (29–37). Of course following the conventions of puppet theater, the audience need not be conscious of the actors who manipulate the puppets. However, the performance is dealing with exactly this idea: manipulation. As each match is contrived for the political necessity of Spain, all thought of love and human dignity is absent.

The principle of irony in the play is grounded in Juana's madness, the ostensible sign of her otherness. At first, we are to think that it

springs from an exaggerated love for Felipe. In the prologue, she has
chained herself to her husband's coffin. Mariana reports her legendary madness: "Everyone said / the Queen believed / that the King
had not / had not, had not / had not died / and one day would
awake" (22). This is the orthodox version. Sabido offers an alternative. Her madness could well be "a strategic ploy," as he suggests in a
foreword to the printed text (9). There are good reasons in the play
as well to believe this. She acts demented before the monks, but she
reveals herself to the audience: "I know that you're dead / . . . / and
I am also dead / and I will be dead until the blessed day of my death
arrives" (23). And later in the play in her own defense, Juana explains
the political strategy behind her apparent necrophilia: "I was looking
for a way to go south to get the support of the nobles in Andalusia in
order to defend myself from my own father" (79). Indeed, as she
argues, her father had made a similar journey with the body of
Isabella: "Two years earlier my mother's corpse had traveled through
all of Spain . . . and no one accused my father of being crazy for taking her" (79). The drama discloses how and why Juana is forced to
cling to a false madness.

The answer begins with the machinations of Juana's father to gain
world power. Hers is the only voice during the marriage games that
defends the rights of the individual: "And our daughter's happiness,
my Lord?" (32). Each scene brings Juana into confrontation with a
world of power, represented in turn by the men in her life. Her husband uses Juana's otherness to defend his own abusive behavior: "We
men are different from you women" (46). Her father strips her of her
power, and when in despair she cries she would like to die, he answers
with the prudence of his world: "That would ruin everything, Juana.
Maximilian . . . would take advantage in order to name himself regent
in my stead. . . . At this moment it's a luxury we can't afford" (71). Even
her son, Carlos, usurps her power and imprisons her on the pretext of
her madness: "Juana (in a whisper): Carlos . . . I'm not insane. . . ." "Carlos: You are: for reasons of State" (83). That final betrayal, for the sake
of political power, is the real reason for condemning Juana as mad.

Juana's madness is just the name for an ideology that is proscribed.
On the one hand, Juana recognizes a displacement, for it is the court
that suffers from the madness of power: "You are the crazy ones: you
who don't recognize that each one of us is one of God's unique exper-
iments, that each couple is God's unique experiment" (48). And the
metadiscourse often shows the court as an upside-down world. In
this world, love exists only as an aberration, as we understand when
it is represented by the gypsy-witch (51–57). The court associates love
with the peripheral, the other, the dangerous. On the other hand,

Juana's "madness" becomes her downfall only when it threatens the state organization of power. As rightful queen, Juana questions "Ferdinand's dreams of grandeur" (81) and, subsequently, the imperialistic concerns of her son, Carlos. Her program would follow very different criteria, as she advises Carlos: "Be the king of Spain who needs you and be a human being. . . . Let them [the colonists] live in peace. . . . Each country has the right to have its own king and it own way of understanding God's divine works" (81–82). It is at this point that Juana must be imprisoned (83).

There is another reason to define Juana as mad: her gender. Phyllis Chesler in her study, *Women and Madness,* sees a connection between madness and the suppression of women: "Madness and asylums generally function as mirror images of the female experience, as penalties for being 'female,' as well as for desiring *not* to be" (1973, 16). Catherine Clément provides an enlightening account of the hysteric [madwoman] and the sorceress as dominant tropes of femininity in *The Newly Born Woman.* The condition of the hysteric and the sorceress, as well as Juana's, arises from their marginalization: "Societies do not succeed in offering everyone the same way of fitting into the symbolic order; those who are, if one may say so, between symbolic systems, in the interstices, offside, are the ones who are afflicted with a dangerous symbolic mobility. Dangerous for them, because those are the people afflicted with what we call madness, anomaly, perversion" (Cixous and Clément 1986, 7). In *Falsa crónica,* Juana is punished for her otherness. This otherness is constructed in terms of gender. When she confronts Felipe with his infidelity, he defends himself by recourse to his rights as a male to unbridled desire: "we men have needs different from those women have" (Sabido 1985, 46). Their exchange, however, reveals that significant differences from a female's point of view (menstruation and pregnancy) are suppressed in the dominant ideology of the court:[5]

Juana: Of course, if men menstruated every twenty-eight days wars would be different.

Felipe: How dare you speak of things inappropriate to a queen's modesty?

Juana: (Smiling) It seems I speak only of inappropriate things: menstruation, love, God, conjugal respect, absolute values and other inconveniences.

Felipe: Life is not made of absolutes. Life is relative.

Juana: Well, no. I didn't get pregnant six times relatively, nor is the salvation of the soul relative, nor is one's oath relative. I don't swear to you that I half love you, nor do I half swear that I love you. (1985, 46–47)

Faced with Juana's language of difference and desire, Felipe informs us of what are considered legitimate concerns: "I'm talking of real things: political alliances, territorial expansion, the organization of a universal empire ruled over by my son" (47).[6]

Juana's problem is one of desire. Paz describes feminine reserve as the virtue the Mexican most esteems in a woman: "Like almost all other people, the Mexican considers woman to be an instrument, sometimes of masculine desires, sometimes of the ends assigned to her by morality, society and the law. It must be admitted that she has never been asked to consent to these ends and that she participates in their realization only passively, as a 'repository' for certain values" (1985, 35).

It is through her desire that Juana is portrayed as monstrous: "She's a witch, she spends her time performing spells all night long" (Sabido 1985, 43). She is "[c]razy from love, crazy from abandonment, crazy from absence" (44). Her displays of passion are "eruptions from Etna or storms on the dessert" (47). The dominant ideology constructs her desire in this fashion, and in turn this desire, as it is interpreted against the ideology of the court, transforms Juana into the horrific. As desiring subject, she loses herself and, thereby, her sanity: "it is impossible for her to have a personal, private life, for if she were to be herself—if she were to be mistress of her own wishes, passions or whims—she would be unfaithful to herself" (Paz 1985, 33). The gypsy-witch calls her by her new names: "Enamored bitch / Desperate hyena / Passionate sow" (Sabido 1985, 57).[7] Isabel, in contrast, describes the route that Juana, as ruler and woman, should have traveled: "we queens have obligations: to be silent and rule, to smile and die inside" (62). But Juana, unlike Isabel, will not accept the court's view of her role. Her madness is, therefore, defined by two conditions: power and gender.

Through its metadiscursive elements, *Falsa crónica* comments upon the political and ideological foundation of Mexico. The feminine, represented as the passive Virgin of Guadalupe or the traitorous *Malinche,* is denigrated by an ethos that would see itself only in terms of the masculine, leading to a world of "solitude" (Paz 1985). But Sabido criticizes Mexico's adherence to what feminist critic, Jane Gallop, calls "a sexuality of sames, of identities, excluding otherness," i.e., excluding the feminine. This world and, indeed, the world Sabido deconstructs in the play is based upon "an exchange of women between men . . . a mediated form of homosexuality" (Gallop 1982, 84). Hence the feminine is condemned to the realm of madness, anomaly, or perversion. Clément suggests that, in the manifestation of this anomaly, there is a strong component of spectacle: "These women [the sorceress and the hysteric], to escape the misfortune of their economic and familial exploitation, chose to suffer spectacularly before an audience of men: it is an attack of spectacle, a crisis of suffering. And the attack is also a festival, a celebration of their guilt used as a weapon, a story of seduction. All that, within the family" (Cixous and Clément 1986, 10). Within this spectacle, Juana and Death are perhaps the most theatrically dynamic elements. As already stated, Death is portrayed as a women, "la muerte catrina" of the Rivera mural and Posada's prints. Dressed to kill in turn-of-the-century fashion, brandishing her lethal fan, she silently marks her victims with a caress. Does Sabido contradict himself by changing his original printed text to place the conflict between two women? On the contrary, the ultimate irony rests on yet another twist added to the performance text by the author-director himself.

Through the elements of spectacle, Sabido deconstructs the bases of phallocracy and its designation of Juana as "mad." In the last scene, a rejuvenated Juana defeats her true rival, Death. She rips open the scarlet dress to reveal the true visage of death: a man. The alliance between Death and the Spanish rulers has been based on an economy of the masculine in which Juana's otherness guarantees their hegemony. This directorial mark graphically underscores the dialectics of power and gender within the play and polarizes the conflict between the world of the feminine and the world governed by phallocracy. In her section on celebration and madness, Clément associates transvestism and masks with the upside down world of celebration (Cixous and 1986, 22–23). Juana's unmasking of the "female" Death to discover a man inaugurates her own celebration. The world of the court has been seen to be deceptive, an upside-down, distorted world. The reversal, then, implied in the celebration would ironically lead to some measure of the world's truth: "The sorceress and the hysteric manifest the festival in their bodies, do impossible flips, making it possible to see what cannot be represented, figures of inversion" (1986, 23). Juana's last scene of triumph in which she unmasks the destructive power of the phallocracy by unveiling Death, i.e., representing what had been unrepresentable under the phallocratic order, is her way of "outmaneuvering the Symbolic order, overturning it: it is festival" (24). Sabido is not simply taking advantage of the woman as a metaphor for the Other, nor simply using her as a symbol of Mexico's struggle with patriarchal order. Indeed he revises Paz's portrayal of the feminine and redeems woman from society's brand of "madness" and "marginality."

Notes

1. Rivera's mural had to be recovered and removed from the Hotel del Prado, which suffered structural damage during the September 1985 earthquake in Mexico City.

2. The "muerte catrina" was popularized in the satiric prints by José Guadalupe Posada (1852–1913). See Jean Charlot's *Art From the Mayans to Disney* (1969, 85–93) and Justino Fernández's *Mexican Art* (1965, 18). Posada's skeletons (city dandies, distinguished *señoras,* soldiers, vaqueros) represented a wide range of Mexican society and politics. Rivera incorporated many features of popular Mexican art and shared Posada's critical stance toward the government. In the Rivera mural referred to, the skeleton, a lady of the *Porfiriato,* attired in a Victorian dress, enjoys an afternoon in the park.

3. In the performance, the character Death is given no lines. Mariana, instead, introduces the games. The reason for this divergence from the printed text is discussed later. The rhyme, "De tin marín, de don Pingüé, cúcara mácara . . . títere . . . títere," is similar to the rhyme in English used to make a selection. In this case, in the Spanish, the word "títere" becomes literalized on the stage by the use of puppets.

4. The title of the play itself indicates as much. Sabido explains: "And why false chronicle? Because this work doesn't try to be Juana of Castile, Juana the Mad's biography. It attempts to present the world off-course and beyond all limit—like the passions that made their home in that Queen and that I try to divine in the character— . . . It is a false chronicle because it doesn't agree with the traditional interpretations, even if all the facts and elements that are used are perfectly correct" (1985, 8–9).

5. Inscribed in the language of her body (feminine periodicity or menstruation) is a threat of cataclysmic nature. Hélene Cixous and Catherine Clément, in *The Newly Born Woman,* discuss Lévi-Strauss's analysis of the relationship in Amerindian mythic patterns between woman's biology and its consequences for order: "A natural and dangerous order, always open to the possibility of lasting, turning into cataclysm; hence, perceived by culture, by men who take on its value, as disorder. That is why women, who are still savages, still close to childhood, need good manners-conventions that keep them under control. They have to be *taught how to live*" (1986, 29). Sherry Ortner's article, "Is Female to Male as Nature is to Culture?," also finds that women are viewed as somewhere between human society (as producer of signs) and the animal body (as breeder). Ortner traces transcendent archetypes of women, as well as subversive feminine symbols, to the view that women are lower on the scale of transcendence, i.e., closer to nature, than man. *Falsa crónica* exposes, by means of Juana's madness, the way patriarchy has dealt with what is perceived as a threat to its order.

6. Cixous's description of love underscores the same male appropriation of desire that we find in Sabido's play: "And once again upon a time, it is the same story repeating woman's destiny in love across the centuries with the cruel hoax of its plot. And each story, each myth says to her: 'There is no place for your desire in our affairs of State' " (Cixous and Clément 1986, 67).

7. Renaming Juana only hints at the enormity of her exile. Consider Cixous's lament in *The Newly Born Woman:* "She has not been able to live in her 'own' house, her very body. She can be incarcerated, slowed down appallingly and tricked into apartheid for too long a time—but still only for a time. One can teach her, as soon as she begins to speak, at the same time as she is taught her name, that hers is the dark region" (Cixous and Clément 1986, 68). Juana is imprisoned, her desire is denied, and she is rebaptized "Juana the Mad."

WORKS CITED

Barthes, Roland. 1972. "Literature and Signification." *Critical Essays*, translated by Richard Howard, 261–67. Evanston: Northwestern University Press.

Boorman, Joan Rea. 1980. "The Theatre of Disruption and Reconstruction." *Latin American Theater Review* 13, 2:31–35.

Charlot, Jean. 1969. *Art from the Mayans to Disney*. Freeport, NY: Books for Libraries Press.

Chesler, Phyllis. 1973. *Women and Madness*. New York: Avon.

Cixous, Helene, and Catherine Clément. 1986. *The Newly Born Woman*. Translated by Betsy Wing. Minneapolis: University of Minnesota Press.

Elam, Keir. 1980. *The Semiotics of Theatre and Drama*. New York: Methuen.

Falsa crónica de Juana la Loca. 1986. By Miguel Sabido. Directed by Miguel Sabido. Produced by UNAM, Instituto de Investigaciones Bibliográficas. Teatro Independencia, Mexico City. March 16.

Fernández, Justino. 1965. *Mexican Art*. London: Paul Hamlyn.

Fuentes, Carlos. 1978. *Tiempo mexicano*. Mexico: Cuadernos de Joaquín Mortiz.

Gallop, Jane. 1982. *The Daughter's Seduction: Feminism and Psychoanalysis*. Ithaca: Cornell University Press.

Ortner, Sherry. 1974. "Is Female to Male as Nature is to Culture?" In *Women, Culture, and Society*, edited by Michelle Rosaldo and Louise Lamphere. Palo Alto: Stanford University Press.

Paz, Octavio. 1985. *The Labyrinth of Solitude*. Translated by Lysander Kemp, Yara Milos, and Rachel Phillips Belash. New York: Grove Press.

Sabido, Miguel. 1985. *Falsa crónica de Juana la Loca*. Mexico: Editorial Katún.

Is There a Method to Her Madness?: The Representation of Juana of Castile in French Literature

Tara Foster

"SKIMMING THROUGH '*LE GRAND ROBERT*' *DICTIONARY OF PROPER NAMES* and stumbling upon a certain 'Juana' known as 'the Mad' is enough to arouse any author's curiosity, whether he be a playwright or not."[1] Charles Samuel's assertion seems to hold true for a number of French dramatists and novelists from the nineteenth and twentieth centuries, for at least seven plays and five novels penned in French have featured the Spanish queen as a principal character. The plays include Alexandre Parodi's *La reine Juana* [Queen Juana] (1893), Louis-Lucien Vermeil's *Jeanne la Folle* [Juana the Mad] (1895), François Aman-Jean's *Jeanne la Folle* (1949), Frédéric Feusier's *Jeanne la Folle* (1958), Henry de Montherlant's *Le Cardinal d'Espagne* [The Cardinal of Spain] (1960), Emmanuel Roblès's *Un Château en novembre* [A Castle in November] (1984), and Charles Samuel's *Tordesillas ou La Reine Folle* [Tordesillas or the Mad Queen] (1995); the novels include Antoine-Jean-Baptiste Simonnin's *Jeanne la Folle, reine d'Espagne* [Juana the Mad, Queen of Spain] (1825), Clémence Robert's *Jeanne de Castille* [Juana of Castile] (1843), Janina Villars's *La Reine folle d'amour* [The Queen Mad for Love] (1961), Jeanne Champion's *Ma fille Marie-Hélène Charles Quint* [My Daughter Marie-Hélène Charles the Fifth] (1974), and Catherine Hermary-Vieille's *Un Amour fou* [A Mad Love] (1991). Indeed as Phyllis Zatlin points out: "Juana's story lends itself to interpretations at the individual or political levels. At the extremes, she is either a woman whose obsessive love and jealousy degenerate into madness or the hapless victim of the Machiavellian conspiracies of her husband, her father, and her son, all of whom need the myth of her insanity in order to retain their own political power" (1994, 148). In this chapter, I will examine the interpretation of Jeanne's story in the works of Clémence Robert, François Aman-Jean, Jeanne Champion, and Charles Samuel as seen

144

in the position taken by each author with regard to Juana's supposed madness.

In her 1843 novel *Jeanne de Castille*, Clémence Robert presents her reader with a lonely figure whose mental fragility adds to the pathos of her character. Before Jeanne's appearance in the opening chapter, Isabelle expresses her concern for her daughter's well-being to Philippe, explaining that Jeanne's melancholy began at an early age when the young princess would show a "fraternal friendship" for flowers that had been broken by rainstorms, cradling them in her hands. Isabelle recalls that "each time the poor little girl was asked about that strange sadness, she would put her hand on her heart and reply with a single word: 'Premonition' " (1843, 14). As an adult, Jeanne remains doleful, but her reverence for her husband borders on idolatry, and a troubled Isabelle remarks that Philippe has the power of the storm to break the blossom that is Jeanne: "Something tells me that Jeanne's life is fatally linked to this love [that she feels for you], that you hold the key not only to the happiness, but also to the existence of my child" (15). Jeanne's absorption in her unrequited love for Philippe fuels her predisposition toward isolation and madness; it also precludes the possibility of Jeanne fulfilling her political role. When Jeanne shows no interest in acceding to the throne of Castile, Isabelle laments the "extravagant love" that has driven out all other thoughts, chiding, "You don't think of your people whom you must govern, nor of your empire that you must defend, nor of your son whom you must raise as a king" (19–20). Jeanne's inability to subjugate her personal interests to those of the crown render her strikingly different from her formidable mother and from the typical protagonist of the sentimental novel that was so popular in the early nineteenth century. As Margaret Cohen explains, novels written between 1830 and 1850 still bear some of the hallmarks of the sentimental novel in which the hero or heroine must choose between personal happiness and a greater social good (1997, 56–58). Whereas the typical sentimental novel showcases the suffering of an individual who has put the social good before his or her own happiness, Robert's novel features a woman who suffers yet makes the "wrong" choice, which is perhaps a further signal to the reader that Jeanne is mad.

Robert accepts the sobriquet attributed to Juana, initially publishing her novel under the title *Jeanne la Folle*, and in this respect she follows the conventional view of Jeanne at the time. According to Georges Imann-Gigandet, "until 1868, it was accepted without dispute that the Queen of Castile was insane and that the despoiling of which she was a victim and her internment in Tordesillas were dictated by the greater necessity of not leaving an obvious mental patient on the throne" (1947, 149). Furthermore Robert's protagonist accepts the moniker also, recognizing her own mental instability and urging her mother to disinherit her. When Isabelle holds a council to name Jeanne as her successor, Jeanne interrupts the proceedings to announce her incapacity to rule: "At certain moments, night makes itself felt in my mind, and in the middle of this night pass strange phantoms, terrible visions . . . then, everything fades away, and reason returns, but, alas! so feeble, so troubled, that I sense by the quavering of that flame that it is going to fly away forever. . . . Madness is going to take possession of me completely" (1843, 84–85). Jeanne's grave prediction is realized when Philippe flees from her and she knows that she has irrevocably lost him. Wandering in the wilderness and crooning to a lily flower, which has come to represent Philippe in her mind, Jeanne passes into a dream world in which she and Philippe are united in love. As Robert explains, "the terrible evil had just taken possession of her, not to leave her except at rare intervals. Her insanity appeared, for the first time, to the eyes of her subjects; it was the moment when she took, to retain into the most remote posterity, that sad name of *Juana the Mad*" (150).

In the Romantic medieval Spain that Robert has created blaspheming Moors are thrown to the lions in the amphitheater as a public spectacle and passion is the driving force behind the sequence of events. Léon-François Hoffmann shows that the exoticism and passion attributed by Romantic authors to Spain were part of an enduring, if not altogether accurate, French view of Spain and its culture: "the image of Spain that the French made for themselves is a tissue of fallacies and misinterpretations that would make historians, geographers and sociologists cringe," and the Spaniard ruled by his or her passions was a figure that was firmly fixed in the French psyche (1961, 136, 99). Jeanne's initial admission of madness takes place at a moment when she has "come out of the tomb of insanity that had buried her" and has been orchestrated to punish Philippe for his infidelity (Robert 1843, 86). Indeed Jeanne's love for Philippe is rivaled by Philippe's passion for the Moorish slave attendant upon the dying Isabelle, the princess Oléma who was taken as a prize during the defeat of Granada. Jeanne's discovery of Philippe's devotion to the young slave spurs her desire to be disinherited, thereby disinheriting Philippe; she also takes her revenge upon Oléma by denouncing her to the Inquisition, despite Jeanne's own revulsion for that institution. Oléma has a second passionate devotee: Ben-Zagal, another Moorish slave and former prince who makes use of Philippe's power to free Oléma from the Inquisition but avenges himself upon his rival by stabbing Philippe to death during a final uprising of the Spanish Moors. As for Oléma, she reserves her energy and devotion for her dream of a Spain that is once again under the rule of her dispossessed people. When confronted by a jealous Ben-Zagal, Oléma berates him for his pettiness: "You have only a vulgar jealousy, I tell you! You only feel the rivalry of a lover; whereas I, my blood burns from that great rivalry of nation, of family, of gods, of flags that divide the Spanish and the Muslims. . . . In order to accomplish a great project, one must vanquish both one's virtues and one's weaknesses, one must vanquish love itself" (58–59). Upon her discovery that the uprising has failed and that Philippe has been killed, however, she impales herself on the prince's sword, revealing that she had sacrificed her love for the Fleming in hopes of restoring her people to power, all in vain. Here, then, is the true heir of Isabelle's indomitable will and sense of statecraft, the character who fits most closely the profile of the sentimental heroine as studied by Cohen.

Robert published her novel in installments in newspapers because she wanted the opportunity "to preach to the humble [and] to spread principles of ethics in the masses" (Séché 1908, 287). She wrote that the principal aim of literature should be to instruct rather than to please, comparing works that are written purely for the sake of formal esthetics to frivolous entertainments and declaring that "writers who have a sense of the future see that the time for these festivities is over for literature . . . and they charge it to provide a stone to the social edifice" (288). Cohen points out the appeal of the novel for authors as "a medium in which to pass serious social and cultural judgments" (1997, 58), and this view of the novel's social potential may well explain Robert's treatment of the Inquisition in her text. In a narrative aside, she explains its origin and horrific outcome, remarking that from what began as a noble desire to eradicate heresy in Isabelle's lands sprang a bloody and vicious institution that cost Spain many noble families and much of its riches; ultimately, "the number of its victims must have risen to more than three hundred thousand" (1843, 118). It seems likely that Robert is aware of the reestablishment of the Inquisition after Spain regained its independence from Napoleon, for at this point in her narrative, she refers in footnotes to several historical studies of the Inquisition. Furthermore at least one of Robert's characters shows an awareness of the Inquisition's long life: Ben-Zagal makes a deathbed visit to Isabelle and predicts a terrible and enduring legacy of Isabelle's reign. As another victim of the *auto-de-fé* burns at the stake outside, Ben-Zagal tells the queen,

You created the Inquisition in order to be called the Very Catholic Queen, and by that act you have done more evil than the cruelest tyrants on earth. As long as the Inquisitors remain on the globe, you will be responsible for their crimes. The most bloodthirsty princes kill only during their lifetimes, striking only as long as their hand can hold a blade; but you, Isabelle, by unleashing your exterminator-priests on the earth, you are going to massacre, torture, burn your subjects for centuries; your voice will still dictate death sentences, when it will have long since been extinguished; you will spread the venom of superstition and cruelty from the very depths of your tomb. . . . Look at that *auto-de-fe* behind your window . . . your cursed memory, that's your reward! Look at this poor lunatic [Jeanne], she's your posterity! (204–5).

This denouncement of the legacy of cruelty established by Isabelle jibes well with the nineteenth-century French view of Spain as "fundamentally" cruel (Hoffmann 1961, 90), a cruelty that Robert repeatedly holds up to her readers as deplorable.

The Jeanne of François Aman-Jean's 1949 play shares the aversion for the Inquisition felt by Robert's protagonist, but unlike the queen of the nineteenth-century novel, the pathos of this twentieth-century Jeanne stems from her isolated confinement, a woman whose profound capacity for love goes unanswered by her closest family members. In his study of contemporary French theater, Jean-Pierre Thibaudat writes that "the post-war years primarily witnessed the success of authors such as Sartre, Camus and Montherlant, producing works of death and fear where history ponders questions of freedom" (2000, 113–14); Aman-Jean's drama shows many of these same preoccupations. The deadly menace of the Inquisition hangs over the first act of the play, and the thirteen-year-old Jeanne is already keenly aware of her isolation and of her role as a political pawn whose liberty is sharply curbed. Her nursemaid recounts to the court jester that when the *Infante* (or Princess) woke up that morning, she looked out the window and declared "that she wanted to be free, that it wasn't appropriate, that the servants should be commanded to remove the bars that 'imprison the countryside'" (1949, 11). Jeanne's sense of incarceration is echoed in the stage directions that indicate that she "paces up and down . . . furious" (27) and that she "walks around the courtyard, as though in a cage" (41). In this act, Jeanne confronts the limitations of her intellectual and emotional freedom, limitations that are imposed upon her by her distant, indeed absent, parents and by the institution that they founded. Before her daily lesson begins, the grand inquisitor appears to inform her that the king has decreed that her education be overseen by a delegate of the Inquisition, "in order to be assured that all the notions given to Your Highness are fully in keeping with the teaching of Our Holy Church" (20). Jeanne's governess uses the presence of the clerical chaperone to control the spirited princess, threatening her that if she does not stop laughing at the antics of the jester and pay attention, the monk will ring the bell signaling heretical behavior; this threat is greeted with a "mortal silence" (22).

Despite her limited opportunity for revolt, Jeanne provides a potential example of the "humanist models of behavior" championed by Camus and Sartre in their writings by showing "dignity [and] engagement" in her encounters with her oppressors (Evrard 1995, 37). The "question of liberty while in a situation of oppression" that Evrard sees in so many of Sartre's works also plays a crucial role in *Jeanne la Folle* (39). When the astronomer informs Jeanne that despite what the church teaches, the sun does not orbit the Earth, but vice versa, the grand inquisitor sends the astronomer off to face the Inquisition, but Jeanne murmurs that the sun will forevermore be immobile in her heart. She counters the Inquisitor's shock and outrage with the question, "Are you at the helm of my heart and of the sun, Sire?" (Aman-Jean 1949, 40), escaping his wrath thanks to a well-timed diversion staged by the nursemaid and the jester Bosco. These two characters do their best to protect the young princess and she recognizes the exceptional nature of their kindly rapport with her. As she remarks to the nursemaid, "Other than you and Bosco, people oblige me to think differently than I would like. People are all in one faction, against me, and they throw their thoughts at me" (32). The issue of Jeanne's impending engagement shows most clearly the extent to which Jeanne is a pawn in the royal court. After receiving contradictory pleas from two courtiers, Jeanne muses, "Why does that Lord want me to marry this Philippe and that other want me not to marry him? Why am I not left free to decide on my own, about the time and about the boy?" (31) Jeanne does choose a young man herself, the captive Moorish prince Boabdil, but immediately thereafter a messenger arrives bearing the royal edict declaring Jeanne's betrothal to Philippe. The inquisitor tries to quash Jeanne's defiant resistance by telling her, "You belong to Spain and to your religion, just as Christ is attached to his cross" (54–55), but she persists, crying, "I'm being married to this Philippe, as though I were for sale in the name of Christ and of Spain! It's a horror! . . . Christ, make the Inquisitor die and make me free, free, free! Christ in love, who was so betrayed" (55). This desperate yearning for freedom and love will be denied Jeanne throughout the play.

In acts 2 and 3, Jeanne is still a metaphorical captive. She explains to her husband that despite his waning interest in her, she cannot break her intense attachment to him, for he is the wind that carries her along like a cloud; her "cloud of love" makes the power of the wind manifest (82). Philippe, who is "less vibrant and intelligent than the one who loves [him] and whom [he] no longer love[s]," wonders aloud at this comparison whether Jeanne is "a bit mad," to which she replies that she is "simply a prisoner of love" (82, 83). Her profound bond to Philippe survives his death, as she journeys through the countryside with his embalmed corpse, challenged at regular intervals by squadrons of Ferdinand's soldiers. Her entourage recognizes that she is not mad, and they explain to those whom they meet on the road that the queen is overwhelmed by her grief. One particular stop is punctuated by the appearance of two famed characters of Spanish literature: Don Quixote, the mad wanderer on a quest for love, and Don Juan, the incorrigible womanizer. These two characters resemble in some ways Jeanne and Philippe, but their conversations with the heroine serve chiefly to highlight the depth of her feelings, for Don Quixote is pursuing a woman who is a complete stranger to him, and Don Juan is pursuing his latest intended conquest, admitting that he has "never loved" (130). Don Quixote also reiterates the objection to Jeanne's behavior voiced by Ferdinand's envoy, who orders the queen's company to stop and give up the body for burial. The envoy says, "I beseech you to stop the scandal. In the wake of this grief and of this cavalcade, you know quite well that Sacrilege, Revolt and the Plague are stirring!" (110). Jeanne again meets this accusation with defiance: "And in yours, hypocrisy . . . ! For what you call Sacrilege, I proclaim to be Love. What you say is Revolt is my indifference for public matters. As for the plague, it comes from the dying, not from the embalmed dead. You know all this. Get back, Sir Hypocrite, go away!" (110–11). When Jeanne asks Don Quixote why she should be called mad, given that she does not "defy death, but custom," he replies, "that's even more serious" (124). In these encounters, we see Jeanne's dignity, recognized by those who travel with her, and her ongoing struggle to maintain a modicum of freedom in the face of the restraints imposed upon her by others for their own ends.

The final act takes place in 1545 in a Spanish convent built, as Jeanne explains, "to honor the beautiful cadaver that [Philippe] was and to bury the old woman that I am" (140). As was the case in the first act, the windows of Jeanne's room are barred, and she is all too aware of her lost freedom: "My father, King Ferdinand, kept me prisoner here because I was the Queen of Castile. He is dead. Charles, my son, continued under the pretext that I am very strange. In fact, out of distrust, in order to govern Castile himself. I am still in prison, and tired" (140). Jeanne's estrangement from her son redoubles her sense of isolation; when she receives a visit from three commoners asking her to rebel and reclaim her throne, she sadly recognizes that the men could not have entered without the permission of her jailer, who is loyal to the emperor: "Thus compromised in this plot, Emperor Charles V who is scheduled to arrive in just a few minutes, would have a reason to keep me in prison. And I tell you that I am not giving him that reason!" (153). Despite her protests that she will offer no political resistance to his rule, Charles points out that he must keep her confined, leaving her to her solitude and despair. With only Charles's chaplain to comfort her, she cries out for solace and companionship: "I am called mad! I am not! Mad about someone, I was. And here I am. Make me mad, Lord! Mad about You, if You wish it" (176). Amarie Dennis concludes in his history of Juana that "in loneliness the Queen had lived, and in loneliness she died" (1956, 260), and although we do not see Jeanne's death, the closing moments of the play foreshadow the same end for the dramatic heroine. In the moving final scene, Jeanne attempts to rally the spirits of those who once cared for her, then calls out for her husband and her son: "Philippe! No one. Charles! No one. Jeanne! Jeanne the Mad! No one! No one" (Aman-Jean 1949, 180). The poignancy of her last words echoes through the emptiness of her prison cell, filling the stage with a sense of Jeanne's loss.

The protagonist of Jeanne Champion's *Ma fille Marie-Hélène Charles-Quint* also expresses her defiance in the face of her own isolation and the emotional indifference of others, and as the title suggests, Champion conflates her own story with that of the historical Juana. The interweaving of the two stories shows evidence of the "fragmented subjectivity of the writer" that Edmund Smyth finds in postmodern autobiographical fiction (1991, 71–72); this fragmentation requires some work on the part of the reader to determine whether the speaking subject is the fictional/historical Jeanne or the authorial Jeanne. Engrossed in the writing of her novel, we learn that Champion comes to identify with her heroine, acting as a medium through which the Spanish queen at last makes her voice heard. At a dinner party, Champion is asked about her interest in Juana "the Mad" by another guest who asks with an air of bemused condescension whether the author wants to cure the Mad Queen by writing about her; Champion doesn't respond but later wonders, "Why didn't I answer her . . . ? Well yes, *madame*. It is never too late to make reparation" (1974, 16). Champion immediately sets about rehabilitating her heroine, allowing Jeanne to explain the legacy of the intolerable suffering that she endured in her lifetime: "That's why they locked me up. Juana the

Mad, that's how I am known. . . . Does that mean that in order to have the right to a more honorable title, and faced with eternity, I should have had locked up in my place, who knows, had my husband assassinated, then my father, then my son? Philip of Habsburg, Ferdinand of Aragon, Charles V, my three torturers; monsters with human faces gripping the breasts of power. That power of which I wanted no part and that destiny threw on my shoulders to be ironic" (1974, 17). Thus the queen was branded as mad because "History does not forgive those who despised power" (16), because the men around her were too consumed by their ambitions to risk having her as a rival.

This indictment of the lust for political power on the part of Philip, Ferdinand, and Charles and of its destructive consequences for Juana accords in large part with Imann-Gigandet's assessment of the Spanish queen: he states that the madness inherited by Juana from her maternal grandmother could have been kept at bay by "an existence devoid of pain and political intrigue" but was instead "carefully stirred up by all those who saw in the queen's delirium an aid for the realization of their plans" (1947, 12). In the interwoven parallels that she draws between the queen's story and her own, Champion also addresses the question of a familial propensity for madness, for her own grandmother was mad, like Isabel of Portugal. Despite her comments in the opening pages ("Madness and cancer are not hereditary. Isn't that simply marvelous? Thank you, sirs!" [15]), she goes on to write that, as the family feared, her grandmother's madness did become contagious, affecting her uncle as well. Champion's inclusion of conversations with her psychiatrist suggests a struggle with her own sense of psychological well-being and explains the author's connection with her heroine: "Why does one feed on the suffering of others? To avoid one's own" (15). But the process of writing the novel, composed at a time when so many French women writers "focused on the relation between madness, women and social change" (Winston 1997, 237), allows for more than just avoidance of distress. Champion heals herself in writing the story of Juana, and she finds her own recovery as she gives Juana redemption. Whatever role genetics might have played in the mental health of the historical Juana, Champion presents her readers with a protagonist whose mental and emotional state springs primarily from her mistreatment at the hands of those who then exploit her ongoing unhappiness.

Another aspect of the power of Juana's story for Champion apparently resides in the queen's resistance to the Inquisition, for her resistance contrasts with Champion's own experience of World War II and the loss of Jewish friends and neighbors rounded up by German soldiers. In her treatment of the attitudes of the adults around her toward the growing threat of Hitler's regime, Champion seems to want to make amends not only for Juana's sullied reputation but also for the French collaboration with Nazi Germany and for her own inability to comprehend and prevent what was happening to the Jewish friends of her childhood. Champion again calls attention to the similarities between herself and Juana, pointing to the political climate into which each was born: "I was born on June 25, 1931. Hitler, arm outstretched, was climbing to the heavens. . . . I was born Jeanne of Castile. My cradle rests on intolerance. My nursemaid was named torture" (1974, 27–28). Champion emphasizes the endurance of intolerance and torture that belies the words of her smugly hypocritical teacher in 1941: " 'The Inquisition, we couldn't see that again in our days. Man has evolved; today, he fights injustice.' From the mouth of the schoolmaster, the only one never to be mistaken, flowed the honey of calm certitude. Above the old walnut desk . . . there was . . . a portrait of Marshal Pétain, that affable man" (29–30). Furthermore Champion's research into the life of Juana informs her of a particular incident that predates the Inquisition but resonates in her mind, the massacre of eleven thousand Jews in 1391 in Barcelona on the feast day of Nuestra Señora de Las Nieves: "1391/1931, a date seen in a reflection. I learn through the intermediary of a book that I was born under the sign of Our Lady of the Snows, and not under that of Cancer, as I had thought up until now. The year 1931 doesn't exist. One was the reflection of the other. . . . 1391/1931, rise of fascism and of Nazism and of all the isms. Year of my birth" (40–41). Champion's horror for all the "isms" feeds into her desire for reparation: she denounces the atrocities committed under Isabelle, those under Hitler, and the complacency or weakness that allows them free rein.

Jeanne's suffering and isolation is intensified over the course of her marriage and she writes to her mother, "You sold me to a rogue. In my head something is dying . . . and perhaps it's me" (111). Her resistance does not, however, die, for through the words of Champion she continues to proclaim her sanity that dwells beneath her at times debilitating sorrow, exposing the political machinations of her husband and her father, then of her son. When Ferdinand declares, "It would be pleasant for me to no longer hear talk of the eccentricities of my daughter; it seems dangerous to me to grant power to a sick mind," Philippe replies, "Ah now, father-in-law, I'm hearing a language that I am able to understand. On this point, you can count on me" (163). As Jeanne gives in to her despair over Philippe's betrayal, then his unexpected death, followed by her solitary confinement,

Ferdinand stages a scene destined to convince the Cortes at last of
Jeanne's madness. Upon Ferdinand's death, Charles employs a new
jailer charged explicitly with driving his mother into true insanity.
Champion pens Charles's letter of confession and regret: "Your
guardian and your son reduced you to madness, *madame*. 1524 . . .
1525 . . . 1526 . . . And you, more and more overwhelmed, resisting
step by step mockery, vexation, machinations, finally illness, you continued, tirelessly, trying to extort the truth out of your guardians who
lied with effrontery. O mother, how could I? . . . Time has not yet stifled your cries. We were the ones who were mad! . . . Today we know.
Madness is suffering" (216–17). With this final attempt at reparation,
Champion lays her Jeanne to rest.

Charles Samuel's heroine resembles the Jeanne of the other twentieth-century texts discussed here, but she also uses her proclaimed
madness as a subtle weapon, the only one remaining to her. *Tordesillas ou La Reine Folle* takes place in Tordesillas in 1520, and the Jeanne
of the opening scene sits brooding over a portrait of her late husband
while her attendants whisper about the impending arrival of a delegation sent by the emperor Charles. Jeanne's desire to be left alone
("Can't you see that I need to be alone? Must I shout? Scream out my
sorrow, my distress, so that I can finally be understood?" [1995, 9])
abruptly changes when she overhears one of her attendants asking
whether Jeanne is really mad: "I just understood, all of a sudden! I
am called mad, definitively mad, they want to take power away from
me, deprive me of my crown. How can Charles scheme that far,
against his own mother?" (11). In this moment of realization, Jeanne
rouses herself from her melancholy and prepares to meet the delegation, learning who her son has sent to meet her and how she might
best defend herself against each. The queen's awareness of the political ramifications of her interviews with these individuals corresponds to Bethany Aram's findings in her historical study of Juana,
where Aram does not "argue that Juana's contemporaries considered
her 'sane' but rather that they depicted her 'madness' based on shifting political interests" (2005, 167). Indeed Jeanne resolves to meet
with her father's former doctor only in the company of her own doctor, for she is sure that out of allegiance to the emperor the other
"without doubt will go report everywhere that I'm barking mad!"
(Samuel 1995, 12). She likewise resolves that if the inquisitor makes
any mention of burning, "I will finally tell him what I think about it:
that he himself should be burned instead along with all those judges
who believe they have God's mandate!" (14). This rapid change in
the queen startles the attendant who is in fact part of the delegation,

but Jeanne's permanent lady-in-waiting assures her that Jeanne "will never abandon her power" (16), despite the emperor's attempts to exploit his mother's vulnerable isolation.

In the conclusion of her study of Juana, Aram remarks that "Renaissance authors from Desiderius Erasmus to Sebastian Brant to Pietro Martire d'Angleria denied the 'madness' of madness itself—depicting folly as a necessary, pious, and even reasonable escape from social conventions and political responsibilities. Did Juana seek such an escape?" (2005, 168). Samuel explores this possibility in his play, querying in his prologue whether the queen "played mad in order to better isolate and protect herself" (1995, 3). As Miguelito, the court jester, explains to the attendants, Jeanne's supposed madness serves a purpose, and he finds himself in a similar position: "It is her best protection! Just as it is mine. People tolerate from you what would otherwise appear intolerable. So you will understand why I refuse to abandon such a privilege. Jester I am, jester I remain!" (19). Jeanne confirms Miguelito's theory in her meeting with him, for she admits that she is not as mad as people say she is, adding, "It is true that I do nothing to prove the opposite. I have settled into this state, I am comfortable in it. But people shouldn't trust in it! I can scratch or bite if I want to, and I want to quite often" (24). We see the strength of Jeanne's will during her confrontations with the doctor, Rafael Gil, and the inquisitor, Miguel de Morillo. When Gil offers her a number of different remedies, she queries, "Do you expect to offer them to me to treat—let's be clear, and call a spade a spade—my madness? There! The word is out! You didn't dare use it and you did well. You would have immediately regretted it. . . . You didn't come here as a doctor, Senior Gil, you came as a spy!" (53). Gil stammers guiltily that he was indeed asked to report that the queen was mad, and Jeanne repeats her affirmation that she will not give up the throne to Charles any more than she did to Ferdinand, not until the day of her death.

Jeanne dismisses Morillo forcefully as well, taking care to underline how much she despises the atrocities he and his brethren have committed and clearly demonstrating her understanding of the purpose of his visit. She states quite sedately, "You are just a dirty bastard, the sight of whom makes me ill. You are only here to provoke me. . . . What are you hoping for? That I will roll on the ground, drooling, in a hysterical fit? . . . Well, I will not grant you that joy and I will very calmly entreat you to disappear" (62–63). The disgust felt by Jeanne for the malicious and sadistic inquisitors surfaces in the words of most of the other characters as well, confirming Evrard's view that "one of the great vocations of contemporary [French] theater" is "unearthing the cadavers of History, showing them to the collective conscience and memory, exhibiting the traces of past and present abominations" (68); Jeanne declares that "if Hell exists, they will all meet there again, that's for sure" (67). This show of force comes at a price, however, for it fatigues a Jeanne who is used to playing the role of withdrawn madwoman. Alone again with the queen, Miguelito questions her once more about encouraging the rumors of her madness; she replies that she is slightly mad, that the cries of her nightmares pursue her during the day "when ennui overtakes [her]" or "when people that [she] despises talk to [her]": "My madness, as some call it, is in fact my revolt against those who surround me!" (69). Her revolt continues in the final act when she refuses to collaborate with the Comuneros in part because she is unwilling to betray her son as he has betrayed her, but also in part because she sees a parallel between their political maneuvers and those of other intolerant groups, chiefly the Inquisition. She probes their intentions at length, finding that they want to banish foreigners from Spain, do not oppose the desire of a group with which they are collaborating for enforced conversion of Muslim traders, and will rely upon the Inquisition to denounce and destroy other potentially harmful groups. Concluding that the Comuneros "demand . . . liberty for [themselves] no doubt, but not for all" (87), the queen refuses to give them her support and dismisses them. Having finally repelled the hypocrisy that assailed her, Jeanne retreats into the grief that is her only shield.

As we have seen, the authors of the three twentieth-century texts present their readers with a queen who was not definitively mad, but who was deeply affected by despair, isolation, and imprisonment. It is likely that Aman-Jean, Champion, and Samuel would agree with the assessment of Juana proposed by Townsend Miller: "Juana's mind was far more sound than unbalanced during her dealings with Philip and Fernando, and . . . the labeling of her as mad by those two former persecutors was a gross example of political foul play," a tactic required by the political desires of both kings that would bring about Juana's "final commitment to insanity" (1963, 320, 314). Where Robert subscribes in the nineteenth century to what Townsend calls the "pure fantasy" of Juana's utter madness (1963, 320), Aman-Jean, Champion, and Samuel reevaluate the legend and rehabilitate the queen.

NOTE

1. Citation taken from author's Web site. All translations of French texts in this essay are my own unless otherwise noted.

WORKS CITED

Aman-Jean, François. 1949. *Jeanne la Folle.* Paris: Fasquelle.

Aram, Bethany. 2005. *Juana the Mad: Sovereignty and Dynasty in Renaissance Europe.* Baltimore: Johns Hopkins University Press.

Champion, Jeanne. 1974. *Ma fille Marie-Hélène Charles Quint.* Paris: Calmann-Lévy.

Clémence Robert, Antoinette H. 1843. *Jeanne de Castille.* Brussels: Société Belge de Librairie.

Cohen, Margaret. 1997. "Women and Fiction in the Nineteenth Century." In *The Cambridge Companion to the French Novel: From 1800 to the Present,* edited by Timothy Unwin, 54–72. Cambridge: Cambridge University Press.

Dennis, Amarie. 1956. *Seek the Darkness: The Story of Juana la Loca.* Madrid: Sucesores de Rivadeneyra.

Evrard, Franck. 1995. *Le Théâtre français du XXe siècle.* Paris: Ellipses.

Feusier, Frédéric. 1958. *Jeanne la Folle.* Paris: [s.n.].

Hermary-Vieille, Catherine. 1991. *Un Amour fou.* Paris: Olivier Orban.

Hoffmann, Léon-François. 1961. *Romantique Espagne: L'Image de l'Espagne en France entre 1800 et 1850.* Princeton: Département de Langues Romanes.

Imann-Gigandet, Georges. 1947. *Jeanne la Folle: reine, amoureuse, démente.* Paris: Nouvelles Éditions Latines.

Miller, Townsend. 1963. *The Castles and the Crown: Spain: 1451–1555.* New York: Coward-McCann.

Montherlant, Henry de. 1960. *Le Cardinal d'Espagne.* Paris: Gallimard.

Parodi, Alexandre. 1893. *La reine Juana.* Paris: E. Dentu.

Roblès, Emmanuel. 1984. *Un Château en novembre.* Paris: Éditions du Seuil.

Samuel, Charles. 1995. *Tordesillas ou La Reine Folle.* Nice: Imprimix.

———. Liste des oeuvres de Charles Samuel. http://www.charlessamuel-theatre.com/pieces.cgi?type=2&id=7

Séché, Alphonse. 1908. *Les Muses françaises: Anthologie des femmes poètes, 1200 à 1891.* Paris: Louis-Michaud.

Simonnin, Antoine-Jean-Baptiste. 1835. *Jeanne la Folle, reine d'Espagne.* 3 vols. Lugan: Guérin, Lecointe et Durey.

Smyth, Edmund J. 1991. "The Nouveau Roman: Modernity and Postmodernity." In *Postmodernism and Contemporary Fiction,* edited by E. J. Smyth, 54–73. London: Batsford.

Thibaudat, Jean-Pierre. 2000. *Théâtre Français Contemporain.* Translated by Simon Beaver. Paris: ADPF Publications.

Vermeil, Louis-Lucien. 1895. *Jeanne la Folle.* Montreux: [s.n.].

Villars, Janina. 1961. *La Reine folle d'amour.* Paris: Laffont.

Winston, Jane. 1997. "Gender and Sexual Identity in the Modern French Novel." In *The Cambridge Companion to the French Novel: From 1800 to the Present,* edited by Timothy Unwin. Cambridge: Cambridge University Press.

Zatlin, Phyllis. 1994. *Cross-Cultural Approaches to Theatre: The Spanish-French Connection.* Metuchen: Scarecrow Press.

Jeanne de Castille at Center Stage:
The Spanish Queen in Recent French Theater

Phyllis Zatlin

OVER THE CENTURIES, THE FRENCH STAGE HAS OFTEN TURNED TO Spain for inspiration. Among outstanding examples of this tendency are such plays as Pierre Corneille's *Le Cid* (1636), Molière's *Don Juan* (1665), Beaumarchais's *The Barber of Seville* (1775), Victor Hugo's *Hernani* (1830), and Henry de Montherlant's *The Cardinal of Spain* (1960). In this latter historical drama, Montherlant (1896–1972) introduced as a foil to his protagonist the allegedly mad Spanish queen, a tragic figure who continues to capture the imagination of playwrights. Dramatists in France who have focused on Juana of Castile in the past quarter century include Emmanuel Roblès (1914–95), José Martín Elizondo (1922–), Eduardo Manet (1930–), and Christine Wystup (1951–).

Montherlant's Jeanne has been aptly described as a "prisoner of her despair after the death of her husband" (Bersani et al. 1970, 347).[1] Contemporary playwrights, like contemporary historians, are more likely to see Juana of Castile (1479–1555) as a political prisoner, an unfortunate pawn held captive by the ambitions of her husband, Philip the Handsome, Archduke of Austria (1478–1506); her father, Ferdinand the Catholic (1452–1516); and her son, Charles V of the Holy Roman Empire (1500–58). American historian Townsend Miller in *The Castles and the Crown* (1963) suggests that it was the imprisonment itself, lasting more than four decades, that destroyed Juana's reason. It is worth remembering that Ferdinand was the model for Machiavelli's *The Prince,* and Charles was a worthy successor to his grandfather. Martín Elizondo's imprisoned queen astutely observes why her son will never release her: "As long as Juana is mad Charles rules, and Charles has no desire to forsake the scepter" (*Juana* 1997, 14).[2]

There is no doubt that Juana of Castile is a compelling dramatic figure. As one reviewer in Toulouse stated following the French-language premiere of Martín Elizondo's play, the Spanish queen is a "magnificent female character," on a par with Antigone and Camille Claudel as representative of "the tragedy of the feminine spirit broken by masculine law" (C. B. 1995). Juana readily fulfills the definition Herbert Lindenberger has provided for the martyr play, a genre in which women protagonists have predominated. Her function as martyr indeed is highlighted in Roblès's play when she is described as clinging to the castle's iron gates like "a great crucified bird" (1985, 334). Lindenberger observes that there is a natural affinity between conspiracy plays and the role of martyr (1975, 39). Those who conspire against Juana condemn her to perpetual imprisonment; consistent with Lindenberger's discussion, the only freedom Juana can achieve is an inner one.

The character of Juana is multifaceted; her life and the legends that surround her offer many impassioned moments that can provide the vehicle for a stunning theatrical performance. In his opera *Juana, La Loca* (written 1979, revised 1982), Gian Carlo Menotti attempts to recreate her total experience of love, betrayal, jealousy, martyrdom, and madness, dating from her adolescence to her death at age 76. In *Juana del amor hermoso* [A Love Too Beautiful] (1983), through the use of an episodic structure marked by spatial and temporal fluidity, Spanish playwright Manuel Martínez Mediero (1939–) similarly incorporates many of those dramatic moments into the action of a single chronicle play in which the protagonist is portrayed at various stages in her life, ranging from adolescence to middle age. With reference to Hazel Cazorla's English translation, Judy Kelly has characterized *A Love Too Beautiful* as a "surrealistic thriller—filled with mystery and romance, political intrigue, ghosts, torture, buffoonery, and betrayal. Yet, at the center of the action is a very real—and strikingly modern—woman." (1995, vii).

Taking an opposite approach from Martínez Mediero's episodic structure, Roblès in his contemporaneous *Un Château en novembre* [A Chateau in November] (written 1984), and Martín Elizondo in *Jeanne créa la nuit* [Juana Created the Night] (staged 1995), each spotlight a particular point in time.[3] On the other hand, while not attempting to capture all of her protagonist's life, Wystup contrasts widely separated moments. The third and final act of her *Jeanne de Castille, ou La Reine qui n'aimait pas Dieu* [Juana of Castile, or The Queen Who Did Not Love God] (2003), takes place in 1525, eighteen years after the action of the opening act.

Martínez Mediero, in what is to date the most commercially successful Juana play of recent European theater, does not limit himself to one level of reality.[4] Queen Isabella's death does not prevent subsequent conversations with her daughter, to whom she brings advice based on what she has learned in the great beyond. Manet's forth-coming play, *Juana la Folle* (the title is deliberately bilingual), is built on an equally whimsical premise: his Juana has been coming back to Earth once a century for therapy. During her visit in the early twenty-first century, the Spaniard, who spent crucial years of her life in French-speaking Flanders, exchanges roles with a French-Algerian psychoanalyst, who is having her own identity problems (2005).

Montherlant was a well-known novelist long before he turned his attention to the stage. Jean-Louis Vaudoyer, director of the Comédie Française during World War II, invited Montherlant to translate a Spanish drama. Trying not to antagonize the German occupying forces, Vaudoyer had "decided that playwrights of the Spanish Golden Age were right for the times: their plots were well removed from either France or Germany and they had already been successfully per-formed by German companies" (Bradby 1991, 20). Montherlant's first play, *La Reine morte* [Queen After Death] (1942), was thus inspired by Luis Vélez de Guevara's seventeenth-century work, *Reinar después de morir* [To Reign After Death] (1652). But Montherlant's interest in Spain was not new. During his student days he had tried his hand at bullfighting and in fact had killed two bulls in Burgos, Spain (Lanson and Tuffrau 1953, 831). Moreover, he was from a "noble Catalan family" (Académie Française Web site), an ancestry that linked him to the Spanish-French border.

Three of the four more recent authors in France who have dealt with Juana of Castile likewise have strong Hispanic ties. Emmanuel Roblès was born in Oran, Algeria, but was of Spanish descent on both sides of his family. His novels and plays were all written in French, but he spoke fluent Castilian and read widely in Spanish history (1987). As Martha O'Nan, among others, has observed, his works frequently have Spanish or Latin American themes. José Martín Elizondo was born in Guecho, Vizcaya, in the Spanish Basque country; in 1947, he moved to France where he has lived since with the exception of a few years in Madrid in the late 1980s/early 1990s. Like much of his the-ater, his Juana of Castile play has been performed in both French and Spanish. Eduardo Manet was born in Santiago de Cuba in 1930, went to France in 1951 to study, and returned to Revolutionary Cuba for the period 1960–68. He has lived in Europe most of his life, has been a French citizen since 1979, and generally writes his novels and plays in French.[5]

A lifelong knowledge of Spanish history and ready access to Span-ish-language references comprise the background information avail-able to Roblès, Martín Elizondo, and Manet. Wystup's route to Juana of Castile is notably different; it relies on French sources, primarily literary. She discovered the character in a French book about tragic queens, read Catherine Hermary-Vieille's 1991 novel *Un Amour fou* [A Mad Love], and additionally consulted several historical encyclopedias in the library when preparing her own text (2005b). She is also familiar with Roblès's *Un Château en novembre* (2005a).

Les Reines tragiques [The Tragic Queens] (1962), a novel by Juliette Benzoni that has undergone a number of editions over the years, encompasses the biographies of an international array of eighteen tragic queens from varying periods. Le Club, when featuring this best seller on their Web site in 2000, identified Benzoni as "the most translated French author in the world" and a worthy successor to historical novelist Alexandre Dumas, "whom she surpasses in the rigor and accuracy of her sources." On that same Web site, Benzoni affirms that she places her heroines in their relevant periods but clarifies: "I make them react like modern women so that my women readers can identify with them." Given that Wystup bases herself to a large degree on Benzoni, it is not surprising if her character, like Martínez Mediero's, is, as Judy Kelly said, a "strikingly modern woman."

In this respect, Wystup also parallels Roblès, who affirmed that the psychology of his character was deliberately contemporary (1987). Roblès's Jeanne de Castille reflects a generational conflict with her mother when she engages in open rebellion against the very concept of arranged and loveless royal marriages. In an optional epilogue, she directly addresses the audience: "The truth is that I've lived in a dark century where love was enslaved. And I already belonged to your century, with today's women who assert themselves and live according to their hearts. What risks one runs when one is ahead of her time!" (1985, 344).

In *Montserrat* (1948), his best-known stage play, Roblès established his interest in Hispanic themes, his adherence to the structure of classic French tragedy, and, similar to his close friend Albert Camus, his commitment to existentialist philosophy. Roblès's intense drama about the Latin American struggle for independence from Spain has been staged around the world and was revived as recently as 1997 at the Avignon festival (Roblès Web site). It conforms precisely to the Aristotelian three unities and the French rule of *bienséance;* the unified action takes place within twenty-four hours and violence—a series of executions—takes place offstage. *Un Château en novembre* breaks from this classic mold through the introduction of a humorous, anachronistic prologue as well as a slight extension beyond the classic time limit for the main action.

Both *Montserrat* and *Un Château en novembre* exemplify what Georges-Albert Astre has identified as a repeated dramatic formula in Roblès's theater. That formula is based on "a paradox that tackles and destroys all reassuring conformity: it is through the most provoking and quixotic madness that the unacceptable absurdity of social norms and, beyond them, the ontological absurdity of the world are vanquished" (Astre 1987, 72). Roblès's heroes are forced to make existential choices: "Gripped by a passion for life that implies action, problematic heroes par excellence, they question all things, and above all themselves. Sooner or later, they inevitably confront an hour of choice which is also their hour of greatest solitude" (Astre 1983, 13).

The episode from Juana's life that Roblès foregrounds occurs in November 1503. In act 1, the anguished young woman despairs that she has received no word from her husband, who had returned to Flanders without her the previous December. In act 2, she finally receives a letter. With her loyal servants' help, she hastily prepares her own departure only to discover that the devious Bishop Fonseca and the Catholic Monarchs, for their own reasons of church and state, intend to prevent her from leaving Spain and being reunited with Philip and her older children. Finding herself imprisoned in La Mota castle, in the final act the princess feigns calm and thus is able to elude her captors and mount a protest. In offstage action, she clings to the iron bars of the castle gate, remaining out in the cold for days until the ailing Queen Isabella arrives and gives in to her daughter's demand that she be allowed to leave.

Official history has considered that protest to be the first indication of the future queen's madness. Roblès's perspective on Juana is revisionist and he presents her stance in a more favorable light. By play's end, his protagonist may appear on the brink of madness, but the scandalous scene she stages at the gates is Pirandellian: the role she assumes is a deliberate one, intended to force her mother's approval of her departure to avoid dishonoring the royal family name. Roblès's Jeanne is a quixotic figure caught in her time of decision; she chooses to defy authority rather than accept the sacrifice that her royal parents and their absurd world would impose upon her. Although her fight for freedom and happiness appears more self-centered than that of most Roblès heroes, she resembles his other protagonists in perceiving "a single truth: that of the sun and that of death" (Depierris 1967, 167).

In the context of their creation, the protagonists of the Mediero and Roblès plays come into being after American involvement in Vietnam, and both subscribe to that era's "Make love, not war" ideology. Roblès's Jeanne repeatedly equates her husband with the sun and the Spanish royal court with darkness and death: "All my childhood memories are gray and black" (1985, 324). Her mother and the

Bishop symbolize death; thus she lashes out at them: "I am alive, alive, do you hear? And you are killing me!" (1985, 340).[6] The play points out that state and church burned "heretical" Jews and Arabs at the stake; Jeanne, in favoring the sun and freedom of Flanders, is opposed to Spanish religious fanaticism. She maintains a close friendship with Aïcha, a Moorish slave, who is likewise exiled from the sun. They are "sisters in the same prison" (1985, 270). In Roblès's play, the Arab woman is shown to be an admirable character who resists forced conversion to Christianity.

In *Un Château en novembre,* King Ferdinand does not appear and the mother-daughter relationship is emphasized. In *A Love Too Beautiful* Martínez Mediero takes great pains to debunk the official image of Queen Isabella that was nurtured by the Francoist government. In the post-Spanish Civil War period, the regime needed what A. P. Foulkes has termed an "exemplary myth": a national legend that could be used as propaganda to resist opposition or change (1983, 13). For that purpose, those in power turned Queen Isabella into a model wife and mother. Roblès's portrayal of the bishop is thoroughly negative and his attitude toward the queen is critical, but it is not caricaturesque, like that of the Spanish playwright. Having not experienced the exaggerations of Francoist propaganda, Roblès continued to view Queen Isabella as a figure of undisputed grandeur (1987). On the other hand, there is also no hint of a tender, loving relationship between Isabella and Juana in the Roblès play as there is in Martínez Mediero's work.

Roblès reserves his humor in *Un Château en novembre* for his anachronistic prologue, in which a television reporter has come to interview the characters. Admitting that he knows nothing about their story, the reporter invites them to provide him with the same background information that the French audience may need.[7] The metatheatrical frame play thus serves as an entertaining exposition to the main action. The characters, in their eagerness to discuss past events and their interpersonal relationships, recall Pirandello's six characters rather than a theatrical troupe. They speak in contemporary, colloquial language but self-consciously remain in character as Jeanne or Isabelle. The optional epilogue continues this self-reflexive device and further enhances the contemporary reading that may be given to the events just seen on stage.

Martín Elizondo also focuses on the modern aspects of Juana of Castile's character. In comparing the original Toulouse production to Montherlant's *The Cardinal of Spain,* French critic André Camp appropriately found Elizondo's protagonist, as played by Marie-José Ereseo, to be "more human, more touching, in a word, more contemporary" (1995, 43). Created by Théâtre Sans Frontière, a professional French/Spanish bilingual company, *Jeanne créa la nuit* ran for three weeks in Toulouse, was performed at the annual Avignon-Off theatre festival in both 1995 and 1996, and has successfully toured to Bordeaux, Tarbes, and other cities in both France and Spain. This intense analysis of madness and power now ranks among Martín Elizondo's most performed scripts.

Concern for individual freedom and for political history informs many of Martín Elizondo's plays. In 1988 his *Antígona entre muros* [Antigone behind Walls] became the first winner of the international Teatro Romano de Mérida prize. Set in a political prison in Greece at the time of the colonels' military dictatorship, *Antígona entre muros* focuses on a group of women inmates, several of whom are attempting to recreate from memory the roles of Sophocles's tragedy. *Jeanne créa la nuit* is a related text. As María José Ragué notes, this latter play "is not the first time that Martín Elizondo resorts to History to speak to us about the contemporary world" (1995).

Because of its potential political import, one of the most tantalizing episodes in the life of Juana of Castile is the failed effort of the Comuneros to persuade the queen to leave her confinement in Tordesillas and join them in their popular revolt against the imperialist policies of her son and his foreign advisers. Among the questions often associated with this episode are whether Juana was really mad, why she turned down the opportunity to regain her freedom and political power, and how Spanish history would have been altered had Juana said yes to the leaders from the several rebellious communities. *Jeanne créa la nuit* proposes answers to two of these repeated questions; in keeping with the play's tendency toward dialectical propaganda, the audience is left to ponder the third one.[8]

Elizondo's portrait of Juana after sixteen years of imprisonment, deprivation, conspiracy, silence, and fear is a contemporary view of a liberal woman, ahead of her time, who was betrayed and held hostage by those who wished to suppress her ideology and usurp her position of power. Significantly, Elizondo prefaces his text with a line from Lorca's elegy to the queen; his character indeed reveals that she has "el corazón partido en mil pedazos" (her heart broken into a thousand pieces). His Juana passes the time writing poetry and making tapestries.

Elizondo's one-act play is divided into several segments. His stage directions recommend that transitions between segments be facilitated by a revolving stage that may whirl rapidly enough to create the effect of a carousel. The resulting image visualizes the chaos within Juana's mind as well as the external, political forces that prevent her from breaking away and moving forward on a path of her own choice.

Avoiding the difficulties associated with long monologues, Elizondo provides a second character, an Unknown Man. Throughout the first segment, the stranger listens in silence to Juana's rambling speech. His subsequent intervention breaks the pattern of her solitude and gives rise to impassioned dialogue and dramatic interplay between the two characters.

The stranger's identity is never fully clarified. A fictional character (perhaps a construct of the queen's imagination), he represents the people who would carry on the Comuneros' struggle after the execution of the historical leaders—an event to which Juana alludes in her initial lament. Expressing sympathy for the visitor's ideas, Juana proclaims: "The kingdom is ill, like its queen. Like our times, like my son" (*Juana* 1997, 12). Charles V is the cause of the people's ills: "his hunger for power devours us" (16). But she declines the stranger's invitation. She does not wish to "swim in a well of blood" (18), to become part of the bloodbath required to overturn the tyrant.

Striking metaphorical images visualize Juana's sympathies. In the fourth scene, she sets the table for supper, placing upon it glasses that represent those who have caused her martyrdom: her father, her husband, her son, and Cardinal Cisneros. She then deliberately overturns the table and its symbolic contents. She tends to address her visitor as "Hermano" (Brother), and when he is about to depart, she offers him as a remembrance her most prized possession: the clogs she wears to dance and whose sound breaks her solitude. As the Théâtre Sans Frontière press kit for the original production emphasizes, the action gives poignant expression to Juana's democratic spirit, "her mystical alliance with the people."

As was true in *Un Château en novembre*, there is a Pirandellian element in *Jeanne créa la nuit*. The stranger accuses Juana of feigning madness, of playing a role and wearing a disguise in order to avoid joining a just insurrection. Juana, of course, overtly equates that insurrection with more butchery. Thus Martín Elizondo's Juana is a "walking ghost" (1997, 21) who chooses to remain in the psychological night that she has created for herself. Ultimately Juana's commitment to the people contributed to her long imprisonment, and her long imprisonment has made her incapable of joining their cause. As the years of darkness become decades, she is left alone with her poetry and her madness, which (reminiscent of Pirandello's *Enrico IV*) may be feigned or real or both.

Christine Wystup's *Jeanne de Castille, ou La Reine qui n'aimait pas Dieu*, like Martín Elizondo's *Jeanne créa la nuit*, builds upon the comparison of night with solitude and madness. The first line of dialogue makes that point as Jeanne, referring to her deceased husband, says "I love night, because it softens the sorrow of absence" (2003, 7). Like Roblès's protagonist, Wystup's Jeanne accuses the Catholic Monarchs of rejecting love and committing atrocities against those who do not share their religion: "You chased men away from Spain because they did not pray to your God, you exterminated whole peoples so that our regions would be purified of any belief that was not ours. Have you acted like a saintly man and my mother like a saintly woman? I don't know and I don't care. I do not espouse your battles. I would have loved Philippe if he had been a Jew or a Moor" (2003, 14–15). Also like Roblès, Wystup equates the sun with freedom and uses a sun metaphor that, in this case, reinforces the identity question that Manet will raise in his forthcoming play: "I am a stranger, father, I carry within me the pale sun of Flanders, where Philippe took me and loved me" (12). By contrast, Spain has stifled the spirit of Jeanne's people. "Castile used to be vibrant with passion" but now the Inquisition "weighs like a coat of lead on every village" where everyone must "murmur submission to God and the king for fear of being denounced" by their neighbors (20).

While Wystup develops some motifs that are present in the works of Roblès and Martín Elizondo, she deviates from those predecessors in various ways. Structurally her *Jeanne de Castille* bears little resemblance to Roblès's ten-character Aristotelian drama or to Martín Elizondo's one-act play with its limit primarily to one moment in time. Like Martín Elizondo's work, her text calls for a relatively bare stage and incorporates monologue and two-character dialogue. But the characters Wystup chooses to interact with Jeanne are different: her father, King Ferdinand, and her youngest child, Catalina. In choosing to emphasize an encounter with Ferdinand in 1507, after Philip's death, and Catalina's departure from Tordesillas in 1525, Wystup introduces two key episodes that do not appear either in the other plays written in France or in Martínez Mediero's sweeping *A Love Too Beautiful*. The choice of these moments allows Wystup to confront two controversial aspects: Juana's alleged necrophilia and her rejection of her parents' God.

Contemporary historians suggest that Juana's decision to take her husband's remains to Granada for burial could have been an astute political move, but Wystup focuses instead on the macabre explanation of the widow's actions. In her confrontation with Ferdinand in act 1, Jeanne realizes that her father has not joined her in Burgos to comfort her in her sorrow. On the contrary, the king is reacting to rumors of necrophilia and accuses Jeanne of being possessed by the devil. Jeanne's impassioned response contrasts dramatically with the cold, self-righteous tone of the king. The young woman ardently defends her love and the kiss she gives each morning to her husband in his casket. Wystup avoids having the audience perceive Jeanne as hopelessly mad through the character's repeated association between her situation and the general repression of her people. Ferdinand says that the Inquisition has brought power and peace but Jeanne responds that peace means nothing if the people are not happy: "You rule over shadows who tremble as they bow before you" (2003, 21).

Acts 2 and 3 both take place in Jeanne's barren room of the castle at Tordesillas. Stage directions for act 3 in the published version state that eighteen years have passed (32) but that is with reference to the opening act. Although not stated, act 2 would have taken place in 1512, with five years intervening between acts 1 and 2 and an additional thirteen years before the final act's action in 1525.[9]

Act 2 is a monologue in which Jeanne is engaged in a hunger strike. She wants her people to know her plight but her voice cannot be heard outside the castle walls. In her rambling but relatively lucid speech, she asks why her father betrayed her when she gave him the power he wanted, but she refuses to marry Henry VII as he wishes. She finally admits that Philippe mistreated her and concludes that "Philippe and Ferdinand were of the same race. I didn't speak their language, therefore I got in their way" (28). She asks how the people could believe she was crazy merely on her father's word and questions a possible double standard: "Would you have let me lock up Philippe or Ferdinand if I had said that they were crazy? Men and women of Tordesillas, have you never thought to force the gates of this citadel to see for yourselves this queen that they have hidden from you for so many years?" (30). She repeatedly proclaims that she is not insane. She dreams of being outside, in the sunlight. Her only consolations are her guitar and visits with her little daughter.

Jeanne's monologue highlights the issue of religious belief. She recalls rejecting at age fourteen the grand inquisitor's sermon and his denunciation of non-Christians: "I was indifferent to that homage paid to God. . . . Was it really necessary to rid Spain of the Jews and Moors who peopled the country of my childhood, of the bright colors of their garments, the soft, rough sounds of their languages?" (26). Like Roblès, Wystup contrasts the black garments imposed by the Catholic Monarchs in Spain with the bright colors found in other countries and cultures.

Taking Catholic beliefs head on, the set for acts 2 and 3 features an image of Christ on the upstage wall. At the end of her act 2 monologue, Jeanne objects to the reproachful way that Christ looks at her and says that the image frightens her; she refuses to pray and wants the crucifix removed (31). In her final lines of act 3, she repeats the request for its removal (39). If, as Wystup's title affirms, Jeanne did not love God, it is in large part because of the religious intolerance that the Christian God has come to represent.

At the end of act 1, Ferdinand implores Jeanne not to go out again to Philippe's casket for the sake of her baby. At the height of her anguished monologue in act 2, Jeanne calls out for Catalina, the only one of her children that is with her at Tordesillas. For act 3, Wystup chooses the tragic moment when Catalina is being taken away and Jeanne will be left alone. Catalina is being forced by her brother Charles V into marriage with the king of Portugal. In tender, loving tones, she expresses her sorrow at abandoning Jeanne: "What are you going to do, mother dear, what are you going to do in this icy fortress? The only moments when we have escaped from despair we have been together. . . . What will you do with no one to love you, to calm you during your rebellions, to comfort you in your sadness?" (34). Catalina evokes with fondness her mother's singing and her tales of life in Flanders. She would refuse this arranged marriage if she could. At play's end, Catalina has tiptoed away while her mother reminisces, and Jeanne reverts to monologue. A neutral offstage voice informs us that Jeanne's solitary confinement continued for thirty years until her death.

In general terms, the multifaceted character of Juana offers a potential vehicle for a stunning theatrical performance. That is precisely what has occurred for Maria Vaz in the role of Wystup's protagonist.[10] Positive reaction to Vaz's acting skills include this 2004 review: "Tears roll down her face, she vibrates with emotion, going from love to despair and then to revolt, with a truth and violence that paralyzed and captivated me" (Une spectatrice). Vaz's emotional range is underscored by selected music from various periods, reaching its crescendo against Manuel de Falla's "Ritual Fire Dance." Manet does not intend to create a dramatic role on this impassioned level, but he has selected a Juana of Castile theme precisely to spotlight a particular actor's skills.

Manet explains that Christine Cottendy, who has been working primarily in radio of late, asked him to write a stage script for her. Well-known and highly acclaimed both as actor and director, Cottendy includes among her honors a Molière prize in 1987 for best actress based on a production at the Colline National Theatre in Paris. She has previously performed with Manet's wife Fatima, and he finds them both to have a strong emotional and comic range. He has thus conceived a play freely based on the story of Juana of Castile that will give Cottendy some monologues but, like the Martín Elizondo, and Wystup pieces, include two-character dialogues as well. Fatima Manet, who is French-Algerian, will play a psychoanalyst who rejects her Algerian identity. One afternoon, when she believes that she has seen all of that week's clients, another person suddenly appears. The unknown woman is dressed in strange clothing. Frightened, the analyst pulls out a gun and shoots her, but nothing happens. The long-deceased stranger, Juana la Folle, is logically immune to bullets.

Of the four recent French playwrights discussed here, only Manet refers to the historical figure as "folle" (mad). Roblès, Martín Elizondo and Wystup all conscientiously give her the proper name, in French, Jeanne de Castille, or refer to her as Queen Jeanne. To be sure, Manet's more lighthearted approach to Juana of Castile is intended to focus on the mental health problems of both the ghost and the analyst. French audiences are unlikely to be upset. Lindenberger has clarified in some detail that audiences generally accept poetic liberties that dramatists take with historical reality, particularly when the events are distant in time and space (1975).

In her monologues, Juana will provide exposition on the historical figure and on the unsuccessful efforts to regain her sanity in which she has been forced to participate every century. The first dream she recalls occurred when she was eight years old: her parents took her to see a Jew being burned at the stake. Juana also speaks of the similar execution of Arabs. Her treatment after death has included being placed in an insane asylum and, at the end of the nineteenth century, being classified as a hysteric and submitted to cold showers by Jean-Martin Charcot, the French predecessor to Freud. Given her diversified experience with analysis and alienation, it is not surprising that Juana is prepared to turn the tables on the psychoanalyst. She determines to help the analyst accept her Algerian identity and stop being ashamed of her Arab connection. Of course such role reversal is a classic comic device, and Manet will present it for humorous effect. In the afterlife Juana, as viewed by Manet, effectively transcends her role as tragic martyr.

Herbert Lindenberger has affirmed that martyr plays are quickly dated because the "particular mode of idealism for which the martyr is sacrificed" varies from generation to generation (1975, 48–49). The case of Juana of Castile, as portrayed in France in recent years, is an exception. As notes on the characters for Wystup's play point out, her role extends well beyond the sixteenth century: "Jeanne expresses the rebellion and suffering of oppressed minorities of all times and all parts of the world. She is all women who have been crushed by men's power, she is all those who bend under the weight of a religious dictatorship, she is all those who are locked up and called crazy because they think differently" (Le Vieux Balancier press kit). In an ideal world, the struggle of Juana of Castile would no longer be relevant. Unfortunately religious intolerance, false accusations for purposes of political propaganda, imprisonment, and torture of those perceived as a threat to those in power all continue as widespread practices. Thus the existential anguish of Spain's mad queen of the sixteenth century continues to speak directly to audiences today, in France and elsewhere.

NOTES

1. Unless otherwise indicated, all translations are my own.
2. Martín Elizondo originally wrote his Juana of Castile play in Spanish in 1960; the revised version, first staged in 1995, was translated into French by his wife Madeleine Pujol. Citations in this study refer to the published version in Spanish and hence are labeled *Juana*.
3. I have previously discussed *Un Château en novembre* in my book on connections between Spanish and French theater and Martín Elizondo's work in the introductory note to that play in *Estreno*.
4. Starring Lola Herrera as Juana and Emma Penella as Isabella, *Juana del amor hermoso* opened in Madrid's 592–seat Teatro Príncipe in February 1983 and ran for over 200 performances. With a change in cast (Pilar Bardem substituting for Penella), the production subsequently toured throughout Spain.
5. I have dealt extensively with Manet's life and works in my book on this Cuban-French writer. All discussion of Manet's forthcoming play, *Juana la Folle*, is based on our June 2, 2005, interview.
6. As I have previously pointed out, Jeanne's rebellion for freedom and against her mother's repression has a noteworthy parallel in Federico García Lorca's *The House of Bernarda Alba* (written 1936; first staged in Buenos Aires, 1945). See Zatlin 1974, 161–62. Certain motifs here, such as metaphorical references to the sun and to water, also appear in Montherlant's *The Cardinal of Spain* and are echoed in Wystup's recent play.
7. When I was in Paris in late May 2005, I visited the history sections of two large bookstores on the Left Bank near the Sorbonne. I could find no reference at all to Jeanne de Castille in any of the French books related to Spanish history. A clerk who helpfully checked the computer for me discovered several books related to Jeanne d'Arc but none to Jeanne de Castille, about whom he personally knew nothing.
8. George Szanto states that theater is always political, whether the political message is overt (agitation propaganda), covert (integration propaganda), or more subtle and hence thought provoking (dialectical propaganda). The Francoist regime's attempt to turn Queen Isabella into a role model is agitation propaganda because it clearly tells young women how to lead their own lives. Efforts to view Juana of Castile as willingly taking refuge from a sinful world may be seen as integration propaganda because they lead the spectator to set aside any concerns he or she may have had about the queen's imprisonment and torture; the problem ceases to exist and all is well in the patriarchal world. Martín Elizondo's play, like the other works from France considered in this chapter, is intended to have the audience see Juana of Castile in a new, more complex light than before and hence to contemplate the

impact that her life had or could have had on Spain. For this reason, I classify *Jeanne créa la nuit* as dialectical propaganda.

  9. Juana was taken to Tordesillas in 1509. In the opening lines of her act 2 monologue, Wystup's character says that she has been there for three years.

  10. The Vieux Balancier production, directed by the author, premiered in 2003, was performed at the Avignon festival that year, and continues to be staged. Another appearance at Avignon was scheduled in 2005, and in cooperation with the Association CinéQuaNon, the play has also been recorded as a DVD.

Works Cited

Astre, Georges-Albert. 1983. "Le Monde d'Emmanuel Roblès." *Folio* 15 (November): 13–17.

———. 1987. *Emmanuel Roblès ou le risque de vivre*. Paris: Bernard Grasset.

B., C. 1995. Review of *Jeanne créa la nuit*. *Flash* (Toulouse), May 17–23, n.p.

Benzoni, Juliette. 2000. "Le Club reçoit Juliette Benzoni." Interview in "Rencontre avec . . ." March 7. Available online at: http://www.gradlivredumois.fr/static/actu/rencontres/benzoni.htm (accessed June 10, 2005).

Bersani, Jacques, Michel Autrand, Jacques Lecarme, and Bruno Vercier. 1970. *La Littérature en France depuis 1945*. Paris: Bordas.

Bradby, David. 1991. *Modern French Drama 1940–1990*. 2nd ed. Cambridge and New York: Cambridge University Press.

Camp, André. 1995. Review of *Jeanne créa la nuit* in Toulouse. *L'Avant-Scène Théâtre* 974 (July 15): 43.

Depierris, Jean-Louis. 1967. *Entretiens avec Emmanuel Roblès*. Paris: Aux Éditions du Seuil.

Foulkes, A. P. 1983. *Literature and Propaganda*. London and New York: Methuen.

Kelly, Judy. 1995. "A Note on the Play." Preface to Manuel Martínez Mediero's *A Love Too Beautiful*, translated by Hazel Cazorla. University Park, PA: ESTRENO Contemporary Spanish Plays 8, vii.

Lanson, G., and P. Tuffrau. 1953. *Manuel illustré d'histoire de la littérature française*. Paris: Classiques Hachette.

Lindenberger, Herbert. 1975. *Historical Drama: The Relation of Literature and Reality*. Chicago and London: University of Chicago Press.

Manet, Eduardo. 2005. Personal interview. Paris: June 2.

Martín Elizondo, José. 1997. *Juana creó la noche*. *Estreno* 23, 1 (Spring): 12–22.

Miller, Townsend. 1963. *The Castles and the Crown: Spain: 1451–1555*. New York: Coward-McCann.

"Montherlant, Henry de." 2005. In *academie-française*. Available online at: http://www.academie-francaise.fr/immortels/base/academiciens/fiche.asp?param=617 (accessed June 5, 2005).

O'Nan, Martha. 1978. "Emmanuel Roblès: Spanish Themes in a French Writer." In *Papers on Romance Literary Relations*, edited by Olga Ragusa 18–26. New York: Department of Italian, Columbia University.

Ragué, María José. 1995. Review of *Juana creó la noche* at Avignon-Off. *El Mundo* (July 15).

Roblès, Emmanuel. 1985. *Un Château en novembre. Théâtre*. Paris: Grasset, 249–347.

———. 1987. Personal interview. Paris: October 12 and 21.

"Roblès, Emmanuel." 2004. Available online at: http:// emmanuelrobles.online.fr/ (accessed June 5, 2005).

Spectatrice, Une. 2004. Review of *Jeanne de Castille. Journal de Millau*. December 16. n.p.

Szanto, George. 1978. *Theater and Propaganda*. Austin: University of Texas Press.

Théâtre Sans Frontière. 1995. "Présentation de la pièce." From the press kit for *Jeanne créa la nuit*.

Vieux Balancier, Le. 2003. "Étude des personnages." From the press kit for *Jeanne de Castille, ou La Reine qui n'aimait pas Dieu*.

Wystup, Christine. 2003. *Jeanne de Castille, ou La Reine qui n'aimait pas Dieu*. Paris: Editions Art et Comédie.

———. 2005a. Telephone interview. May 30.

———. 2005b. Personal e-mail. June 10.

Zatlin, Phyllis. 1994. "Juana la Loca as Dramatic Figure: *Un Château en novembre* by Emmanuel Roblès." In *Cross-Cultural Approaches to Theatre: The Spanish-French Connection*, 147–62. Metuchen, NJ: The Scarecrow Press.

———. 1997. "Martín Elizondo and his Portrait of Juana de Castilla." *Estreno* 23, 1 (Spring): 9–11.

———. 2000. *The Novels and Plays of Eduardo Manet: An Adventure in Multiculturalism*. University Park, PA: Pennsylvania State University Press.

IV
Juana of Castile in Opera
and the Visual Arts

Madness as Nationalistic Spectacle: Juana and the Myths of Nineteenth-Century History Painting

María Elena Soliño

In fact, historians begin from present determinations. Current events are their real beginning.
—Michel de Certeau, *The Writing of History*

IN THE WINTER OF 1878, FRANCISCO PRADILLA ORTIZ ASTONISHED NOT only the art world of Madrid, but also a broader general public with his depiction of Queen Juana of Castile escorting the casket of Philip the Handsome across the Castilian countryside. The painting presented at the National Exposition of Fine Arts drew huge crowds, willing to wait in the cold and rain to see the latest rendition of the legendary queen who had gone mad for the love of her husband. Pradilla situates Juana in the center of the painting, thoroughly isolated spatially through the distance that separates her from the courtiers, and alienated emotionally as she stares blankly at the coffin, oblivious to all that surrounds her. The viewer is made to feel the bitter cold of a night spent on the road through the movement of the flames that blow in the wind, both on the candles and on the small fires by which one of the ladies-in-waiting attempts to warm her hands. A lone, bare tree trunk in the background echoes the sorrow and hopelessness seen in the posture and expression of the despondent queen, who despite her obvious pregnancy, is anchored in the world of the dead, with no productive future.

For this painting Pradilla was awarded the Medal of Honor, a distinction never before bestowed at a National Exposition in Spain. The prize had originally been conceived as an honor to be granted to a mature artist for a lifetime of achievements. Instead the Medal of Honor was given to Pradilla, who was little more than a student, and for an individual painting with a number of flaws.[1] In concor-

Figure 1. *Juana la Loca frente al cadáver de Felipe el Hermoso* (Juana the Mad Holding Vigil over the Coffin of Her Late Husband, Philip the Handsome) by Francisco Padilla, Image courtesy of the Museo del Prado.

dance with the jury's acclaim, the state immediately purchased the painting for the very high sum of forty thousand pesetas and would later hang it in the Prado, where more than a century later it will now anchor the nineteenth-century section in the newly remodeled Casón del Buen Retiro. Like many of the gifted art students of his time, Pradilla studied for three years on a government scholarship at the Spanish Academy in Rome. At the end of each year, these students were expected to present a major work. Pradilla's final painting from the Spanish Academy needed to be of especially high quality, in part to compensate for the poor showing he had suffered the previous year and also because, in basic terms, this was for him comparable in significance to a final exam. The success of Pradilla's *Juana la Loca* [Juana the Mad] continued outside of Spain where the painting triumphed at that summer's Paris International Exposition, winning Pradilla the Grand Cross of the French Legion of Honor, and the Medal of Honor at the Vienna exposition of 1882. That Pradilla achieved such success with his painting of Queen Juana, whereas others with equal or greater talent attained much more moderate benefits with the same subject, requires some explanation and analysis based on an understanding of the sociopolitical climate of Spain in

1878, especially as it pertains to the role of women in society, and the role of history painting, the genre of painting that depicts famous historical events and key figures, in the century-long project of building a spirit of nationalism that would support Spain's budding constitutional monarchy.

Pradilla's international success with *Juana la Loca* is all the more remarkable since it came long after history painting had lost its status in other European countries. Perhaps as one more example of Spain's problematic relationship to modernity, history painting there remained the most highly praised by the Academy, in part because it supported the project of modernizing the Spanish governmental system in its transformation from an absolutist monarchy. The ideals of the constitutional monarchy required a shift in perspective regarding the role of the average citizen in constituting the nation. For the liberals in power throughout much of the reign of Isabel II, the collective people comprised the state in contradiction to the more conservative view of the monarchy as the defining unit of national cohesion. The nineteenth century thus demanded a new conceptualization of history as an academic discipline, not only in the publication of numerous tomes in the mold of the *Historia general de España* [General History of Spain], but also in the visual arts through paintings that depicted the national heroes and the events that forged the spirit of the hegemonic Spanish nation, and then through the distribution of photographs and prints of the most famous paintings through the popular press. In an attempt to forge a strong sense of collective memory, history was presented as a genealogy of the present with the heroes of the medieval past seen as the direct ancestors of the Spanish people who correspondingly should inherit the nation these ancestral heroes built.

Within this vision, the direct line was truncated with the arrival of the first foreign monarch, Charles V, the first of the Spanish Habsburgs, thus situating Queen Juana of Castile as the last true Spanish monarch, a hinge at a key historical junction, albeit a problematic one, for due primarily to her gender, she was perpetually ruled by others. Juana became for the nineteenth-century historiographers a symbol of the death of an era whose story could capture the popular imagination framed within the tenets of the romantic heroine driven to insanity by her passions. These are the passions so eloquently captured by Pradilla who situates the queen at the crossroads of history, literally as she halts her journey in the middle of a road trapped between the end of an era, represented by Philip's coffin, and birth of the new dynasty, a problematic modernity born of Juana's pregnant body. In what might seem a contradictory move, liberal reform in nineteenth-century Spain was symbolically based on a return to what historians and politicians presented as the less authoritarian monarchies of the middle ages.[2] The word *austracismo* designated Spain's straying from this more democratic path toward the despotism of the Habsburg dynasty that produced Spain's decline in the age of empire, a decline that might have been avoided had Juana been able to rule, and the newly unified nation willing to grant full powers to another powerful female monarch. Instead her story is the swan song of the middle ages, a vision reinforced by paintings such as Pradilla's that portray Juana as isolated not only from politics, but from any aspect of life. She can see nothing but the coffin.[3]

In the nineteenth-century phase of the nation-building enterprise we cannot ignore the links between those who wrote history and those who devised the political project, for they were often the same individuals. A number of the senators had previously headed one of the *Academias,* and many of the top leaders came from the Academy of History. One important example of this is Modesto Lafuente, also known as Fray Gerundio, the very popular author of *artículos de costumbres* (literature of manners) and political satire, who was the representative from León-Astorga to the parliament. It was a government headed by leaders like Lafuente that passed the 1857 Moyano law that made history, and their particular brand of the history of continuities, a required subject at all levels of education, and established the discipline within the university system. Their vision, replete with their own contemporary projections and political agendas, was transferred to the instruments of cultural hegemony, such as school textbooks and the popular media, including the theater and history painting.

Oftentimes ignoring the foreign origins of the current Bourbon monarchy, the key historians, whose works Pradilla studied, directly linked the mythic mother of national unification, Isabella the Catholic, and the current queen, Isabel II. Chief among these was Modesto Lafuente mentioned above, who coupled the transformative effects of the Isabels. With both, "the scene changes, the set is transformed; and we shall attend the magnificent spectacle of a resurrected people, reborn, who rise up, organize, and grow" (Donézar y Díez de Ulzurrun 1999, 315). Overlooking Juana, he states that many centuries would pass before another woman, "Castilian and Spanish" ruled Spain: "generations, dynasties, and centuries would pass before another Isabella appeared" (315). The use here of the word *another,* refers only superficially to the repetition of the name, but more significantly to the revolutionary possibilities of the current reign they hoped would transform the present state of the monarchy and shepherd Spain through the process of modernization. Furthermore

Isabel's ascension to the throne had been so strongly contested that converting her into a direct descendent of the Catholic Monarch lent an additional degree of legitimacy. Isabel II and her handlers collaborated through their patronage of the arts, buying and commissioning a number of works on the various aspects of the reign of the mythic mother of modern Spain. The constant comparisons between the two Isabels were meant to flatter the young queen, but whereas the frivolous Isabel II merely accepted this tribute as that due a monarch, for many the comparisons served as an exhortation to her regime to become a beacon of change.

In both instances, however, the male forgers of the national mythologies were forced to incorporate the femininity of these queens into a narrative structure that rarely accommodated female protagonism. As Barbara Weissberger has shown, a number of Isabella's historians presented the topos of the virile woman, even scripting the queen as a military leader as in the case of Juan de Lucena who in his fifteenth-century *Epístola exhortatoria a las letras* portrays her as "pitching our camps, leading our battles, breaching our sieges; hearing our complaints; informing our moral judgment . . . circling her kingdoms, traveling, traveling, never stopping" (2004, 83). In the case of Lucena and others, Isabella the Catholic controlled her discursive self-fashioning by hiring her official historians, and accordingly the chronicles of her reign are now read through the prism of more modern historians such as Michel de Certeau who portrays official historians mainly as courtiers who present their prince (in this case a woman) as the subject of action whose role it is to make history (1988, 7). Isabella's will and ability to shape historical discourse is strongly felt in the presentation of her uncle, Enrique IV, defamed forever as an effeminate homosexual, and "The Impotent" incapable of having fathered the daughter he would present as his heir, Juana la Beltraneja, claims that would serve to legitimize Isabella's usurpation of the throne of Castile.

The misogynistic discourse that would eventually discredit Juana as monarch was already present in the chronicles produced by her mother's historians, at times reiterating the accusations of gender/sexual disorders and impiety.[4] Thus we read in the *Crónica de Enrique IV* [Chronicle of Henry IV] by Alfonso de Palencia that not only was Enrique an effeminate king unfit to rule, but just as unfit to rule were the women of his court because of "that passion characteristic of the sex that makes them willingly plunge into the promptings of desire, and will the destruction of everything, provided that their desire be satisfied" (Weissberger 2004, 88).[5] Isabella's particular set of circumstances, including an absence of male family members and her own

character, permitted a wider range of gender-role transgressions and
even uxorial usurpation in an attempt to balance the power of the
competing kingdoms. Isabella submitting herself entirely to Ferdinand, as was expected of a wife, was the equivalent of Castile bowing
before Aragon, thus giving Isabella a degree of visible power.

But these privileges of Isabella would not extend to her daughter.
The ability to hire, and thus control, those who wrote her story
eluded Juana, whose gendered body later came to symbolize the disorders of the state. Her history was written by historians hired by others, mainly those who wished to usurp her power, first her husband,
and later both her father and son. Although mainly unacknowledged
and even cloistered, Juana was legally queen of Spain after the death
of her parents, but the portrayal of her as a hyperfeminized vessel of
love toward her husband incapacitated her as a ruler. Following the
notion of the *corpus mysticum,* in the analogy between the kingdom
and the human body, with the monarch as the head, this portrayal of
Juana gone mad for love displaced the head of state to the lower
regions of the passions in a decapitating move, reinforced by the
uncritical transmission of the epithet "the Mad."

Juana's symbolic decapitation continued in the realm of the visual
arts as painters ignored what may have been her actual features as
recorded during her lifetime in the surviving paintings of Juan de
Flandes and Colin de Coter. Instead the nineteenth-century Spanish
history painters invented features that epitomized madness, obscur-
ing any trace of the historical individual.[6] Yet these portrayals were,
and still are, accepted as depictions of true historical events. Even
today, the bestselling biography by Manuel Fernández Álvarez, *Juana
la Loca: La cautiva de Tordesillas* [Juana the Mad: The Captive of Torde-
sillas], is marketed with a close-up of Pradilla's Juana on the cover.[7]
Like the popular historian Fernández Álvarez, Pradilla based his work
on an accredited source, in this case the eyewitness account of Pedro
Mártir de Anglería, which he read filtered through the 1869 edition
of the *Historia general de España* by Modesto Lafuente, the most widely
read historian in Restoration Spain. Anglería's account is worth citing
at length to note the precision of Pradilla's visual interpretation.

They would walk only at night, because an honest woman, she [the Queen]
said, after having lost her husband, who is her sun, should flee the light
of day. They would perform funeral rites in the towns where they rested
during the day, but the Queen would not allow any woman to enter the
temple. The passion of jealousy, the origin of her mental disorder, tortured her even onto the grave of he who had motivated it in life. It is told

that on one of the days of this journey, walking between Torquemada and Hornillos, the Queen ordered that the casket be placed in a convent she thought belonged to friars; but as she later discovered it to be occupied by nuns, she was horrified and immediately ordered that it be removed and taken to the countryside. There she ordered that the entire retinue remain, exposed to the elements, suffering the bracing cold of the season with the wind extinguishing the torches. The retinue was composed of a multitude of prelates, clergymen, nobles, and gentlemen: the Queen wore a long veil in the manner of a cloak that covered her head and shoulders with a thick, black cloth: a large procession composed of people on foot and on horseback followed with lit torches. (Centellas 1999, 56–57)

Key to understanding this passage is the fact that Mártir never gained patronage from Juana, but did from nearly everyone else at the Castilian court, primarily those who wished to prevent Juana from ruling.

Today historians have provided logical explanations for much of Juana's behavior, and have proven that in the eleven months between Philip's death and the return of her father, Ferdinand, she was politically active.[8] As Bethany Aram points out, in this seemingly insane journey, Philip's corpse became a political prop Juana used to preserve the hereditary rights of her eldest son. Against the wishes of her father, who had remarried and was still intent on fathering another heir, Juana tried to bury Philip in the royal mausoleum in Granada, next to her mother. "The queen's four nighttime pilgrimages with her husband's coffin from December 1506 through August 1507, surrounded by torches, presented her people with the image of Philippe as king and father of their future sovereign" (2005, 97). When she defied her father's attempts to bury the body in the north, Ferdinand took his namesake, the younger of his grandsons, away from her, leaving Juana to fight with the only weapons at the disposal of an abandoned, impoverished woman. She refused to eat, sleep, bathe, or attend religious services.

The romantic historiographers, who took these acts of rebellion as madness, preferred to focus on the image of a woman incapable of ruling herself, much less a nation. Many of the illustrations of Juana in nineteenth-century histories label her portrait as "la Loca." The argument that Juana was insane, but insane because of love and not illness, had already been popularized by works such as Tamayo y Baus's 1855 play *Locura de amor* [The Madness of Love], but it gained further strength when in 1874 her biographer Antonio Rodríguez Villa found a letter he claimed was from Juana to Philip's ambassador, Filibert de Veyre, transferring her power to Philip and his offspring, in effect seeming to give up her throne in the name of love.

The letter to de Veyre remained among the papers of the Marquis de Alcañices in the Archive of the Dukes of Albuquerque. Curiously the Marquis de Alcañices sponsored the artistic training of Lorenzo Vallés, who in 1866 had received a second prize at the National Exposition for his painting *La demencia de Juana la Loca* [The Insanity of Juana the Mad]. Here Vallés portrays another of the popular incidents highlighting Juana's madness. She is shown at the bedside of the recently deceased Philip, with her fingers to her lips, begging silence from everyone in the room so as not to awaken her dead husband. This also illustrates one of the climactic scenes from Tamayo y Baus's play. Yet while these two works of superior artistic merit did achieve a certain level of success, they failed to spark the popular imagination, both then and now, in the same way as Pradilla's painting.[9]

According to Carlos Reyero, Spain's leading expert on history painting, one of the most important dimensions of history painting is its ability to mirror the present national consciousness (1989, 109). Consequently, in the transitional period of the reign of Isabel II, a time plagued by continuous civil wars and the rapid disintegration of the overseas Spanish empire, themes that reinforced a sense of national unity and the role of Spain in bringing Christianity to the Americas were among the most popular. In the spirit of building a sense of nationalism, the government commissioned paintings that highlighted these themes. Among the paintings ordered by Isabel II and Francisco de Asís are Francisco de Paula Van Halen's *La Rendición de Granada* [The Surrender of Granada], Francisco de Mendoza's *Isabel la Católica admite las proposiciones de Colón* [Isabella the Catholic Accepting Coulmbus's Proposals], Francisco Cerdá's *Isabel la Católica entrega al hijo de Boabdil* [Isabella the Catholic Delivers Boabdil's Son], José Galofre's *Isabel la Católica firmando las capitulaciones de Santa Fe* [Isabella the Catholic Signing the Capitulations of Santa Fe], and Joaquín Espalter's *El suspiro del moro* [The Moor's Last Sigh], and *La primera entrevista de Colón con los indios* [Columbus's First Meeting with the Indians]. However, Isabel II exhibited so many personal flaws, especially with her scandalous love affairs, that once she had reached adulthood, no amount of comparisons to Isabella the Catholic could polish her image. Toward the end of Isabel II's reign, a decade before Pradilla's triumph, such a graphic image of Juana's love-induced madness would have invited a negative comparison to the contemporary queen, so publicly incapable of loving her husband. To some, Isabel's behavior was abnormal, almost to the point of being labeled a nymphomaniac. Many of the dangers that were thought to accompany female rule were shared by Isabel and Juana. There was an insistence that Isabel marry young, but not a foreigner, to avoid Spain falling prey to the dangers of foreign rule, as had happened in the case of Juana. With both queens there is an insistence that women might rule, but not govern. As one of the French delegates wrote as early as 1840, "The difficulties of the situation in Spain are extreme, and if monarchic ideals are to prevail in Spain, given that it is impossible for a women to carry herself with dignity among revolutionary tendencies, it is absolutely necessary to have a man at the head of the Peninsula's affairs. Isabel's marriage should offer these guarantees" (Burdiel 2004, 252).

Similarly the images of Juana that are popular in the mid-nineteenth century portray Juana as a domestic consort, rather than as someone capable of independent rule. The popular chapbook of 1848, *Historia de la célebre Reina de España, llamada vulgarmente, La Loca* [Story of the Renowned Queen of Spain, Commonly Called, the Mad], highlights women's scarce talents for governance outside the realm of the household. Her hyperfemininity is emphasized through the contrast between the boredom Juana feels when confronted with political duties, and her joy when performing duties befitting a woman: "on the contrary, any task assigned to her appropriate for her sex, she would embrace with boundless joy; thus, at still a young age, she was the marvel of all who heard and observed her amusements" (Anon. 1848, 4). In this version of the story, her father and Cardinal Cisneros are presented as her benign protectors, continuously shielding her from harsh realities. Juana, in turn, is grateful, and willingly plays the role of loving daughter, "for she never minded that they never considered her will in any of the matters of state" (5). The author presents Juana's story as a cautionary tale for all women, "one can see oneself in this monarch, as in the sad mirror of the tragic results of violent passions taken to an extreme, when they are not modified or repressed through logic" (6). There are obvious attempts here at creating a sense of identification between a female reader and Juana in passages such as, "Whoever has loved should pause at this point, and consider the devouring fever that would consume a character as firm and energetic as Doña Juana" (11). The establishment of this type of personal identification was becoming typical of the portrayal of royalty.

In the nineteenth-century constitutional monarchies, royal families, were expected to perform the new bourgeois family values for their subjects. The survival of monarchic institutions relied on the perception that the royals were adapting the old aristocratic culture, based purely on inherited privileges, to conform to the middle-class ideals of morality and merit. In this aspect, as in many others, Isabel II failed dismally. As Isabel Burdiel points out, from the beginning of

her reign, the queen ignored the changes instituted by the new political culture of liberalism and bourgeois moral codes, especially as
they pertained to women. With her scandalous private and public
life, she was the antithesis of the domestic angel that encapsulated
the feminine ideals of the emerging class (2004, 24–26). Her inability to perform her roles came as an enormous disappointment to
those who had once looked to the child Isabel as the symbol of hope
for the future of the constitutional monarchy in Spain. Instead Isabel
II, who was raised in a climate of ignorance and superstition, headed
a royal family so dysfunctional and corrupt that the legitimacy of
her children was in question, and many Spaniards believed that her
own husband, rumored to be homosexual, was implicated in her
assassination attempt the day her oldest child was baptized. Isabel
began her political career at age four as the symbol of the liberalism
that would finally lead Spain toward modernity, and ended her reign,
condemned as the incarnation of absolutism banished by the 1868
revolution.[10]

Part of the task of Alfonso XII and the politicians and generals who
orchestrated the Restoration was to restore the image of the royal
family so tarnished by Isabel II and her consort Francisco de Asís.
Alfonso's marriage to his cousin, María de las Mercedes, did much to
repair the family honor and correct the grave errors of his parents.
In María de las Mercedes, Alfonso found a bride who satisfied all the
demands of his constituencies. Although raised partly in France, this
daughter of Isabel's younger sister, Luisa Fernanda, and the duke of
Montpensier, was accepted as a true Spanish princess through whose
marriage two feuding factions of the Bourbon family were reunited.
The fact that Isabel vehemently opposed her son's wedding only
strengthened the union and served to prove Alfonso's independence
from the ousted monarch. This marriage was portrayed as a union
based on pure love, and María de las Mercedes became the people's
princess.[11] The royal wedding was a lavish public spectacle that lasted
over a week, with parades, concerts, the traditional bullfights, and all
the central parts of Madrid illuminated by electricity. In the issue
released the thirtieth of January 1878, the chronicler for *La Ilustración
Española y Americana,* Peregrín García Cadena, highlights the participation of every element of society: "all work is paralyzed; even the
pots must have stopped boiling on the hearth, because the maids
have also rushed out into the streets" (1878, 58), and emphasizes
their love, "María de las Mercedes entered the temple a princess and
emerged transformed into a queen. The King's countenance showed
the sheer satisfaction of having his ardent desire fulfilled. The Queen's
face was made more beautiful by intimate and profound emotions.

The people watched as the splendid procession of the royal couple passed, and every person of noble sentiments wished that the love of the young monarch be rewarded with many years of matrimonial bliss" (59).

It is precisely as part of these festivities that served to herald in a new era for a Spanish monarchy, one that attempted to redefine and strictly limit the role of women within these structures of power, that the Spanish public was introduced to what instantly became the iconic image of *Juana la Loca*. The king inaugurated that season's National Exposition of Fine Arts with one of the many short speeches he delivered that week, and it is thus as part of the reporting of the royal wedding that the general public received the analysis and reviews of Pradilla's painting. In this same issue, *La Ilustración* declares *Juana la Loca* "a gem" (62) and writing in the Catholic *El Siglo Futuro*, Manuel P. Villamil states, "it has justifiably attracted everyone's eyes, entrancing both the wise and the ignorant" (1878). *La Ilustración* publishes detailed descriptions of the painting side by side with lavish illustrations of the current nuptial chamber, with separate pages for a lavish drawing of the royal bedspread and other gifts received by the couple. The illustrated coverage continues through February 15 in which the prizes awarded at the Exposition are announced in an issue still carrying illustrations of the royal wedding. Both events, the wedding and the Exposition are portrayed by the press as symbols of hope and renewal for Spain, both in the realms of politics and the arts. On the Exposition in general, *La Ilustración* states that "it has managed to inspire hope, if not in an immediate and grandiose regeneration, then in the plausible good results to which this tendency can lead" and positions Pradilla "among those privileged artists from whom we can expect the regeneration of our effeminate painting, empty of thought and orphaned from ideals" (1878, 62). The critic here reveals through his choice of words the devaluation of the feminine in Restoration Spain, for the nation and its arts are now to be saved from being "effeminate," freed from a corrupt queen and delivered into the hands of the virile Alfonso.

To help ease this anxiety of queenship left behind both by the regency of María Cristina in the 1830s, with her continued interference in the 1840s, and Isabel's reign, the female members of the royal family were described in the popular press as suitably conforming to the ideals of the domestic angel. While on his reentry into Spain, accompanied by Martínez Campos, a hero from the African wars as well as Cuba and Catalonia, Alfonso is portrayed with an ultramilitary/masculine image, the coverage of his sister situates her as the loving woman who will set up his household until her place can be filled by a wife. The chronicler of the March 8, 1875, issue of *La Ilus-tración Española y Americana* describes her in terms of the bourgeois angel of the house: "If after many hours of work, filled with the satis-factions that can surround a throne but also its troubles, the monarch needs to deposit his impressions in a loving heart, freed from lowly passions, the Princess of Asturias has arrived to fill that void, at the same time that she fulfills her spirit's most ardent desire: to return to her beloved homeland." When an appropriate bride does enter Spain, her role is likewise described in terms of the archetypal domes-tic angel. In honor of the royal wedding, Dolores Cabrera de Miranda publishes a poem in *El Correo de la Moda* that clearly defines the con-trasting masculine/feminine societal roles: "The throne brings bit-terness that I can guess,/ Shared by you they will be less;/ If the king is crushed by his royal scepter;/ You will lighten its weight with a touch of the hand" (1878, 35).[12] It is clear that these royal women were the necessary, supportive background figures that would correct Isabel's failure to perform the ideals of bourgeois domestic bliss for the Spanish nation, and it was clearer still, that they were never to be seen exercising political power. Faustina Sáez de Melgar, a popular writer at the time, echoes the conventional wisdom in the magazine *La Mujer* (7/8/1871): "the most ridiculous thing into which our sex can be transformed is into a political woman. . . . A woman political! . . . what an unfortunate error, what a horrible deviance! She who should be all tenderness, docility, and love, shoved defenseless, with-out instruction, without guidance, without support, into that deep pit, that abyss of malice they call politics" (Sánchez Llama 2001, 156). By the end of her life, even Isabel II's image had undergone a trans-formation that represented the lewd queen within the strictures of an acceptable, infantilizing femininity. Benito Pérez Galdós, an author adept at depicting the dysfunctions of the angel of the house in so much of his fiction, leaves us this portrait of Isabel: "Isabel II's kindness had much of the domestic. The Nation to her was a family, inherently a large family, that precisely because it is limitless allows one to give and take with familiarity . . ." (1906, 19) "no one denies nor ignores the immense tenderness of that innocent soul, indolent, quick to offer pity, forgiveness, and charity, but incapable of a firm and vigorous resolve. Doña Isabel lived in a perpetual state of child-ishness, and her major misfortune was having been born Queen, and having to conduct the moral path of a people, an obligation too bur-densome for such a tender hand" (33).

In the last years of Isabel's reign there had already been a shift in the representations of Isabella the Catholic to domesticate her image. Whereas previously she had been emphasized as "the highest example of virtues and the ability of a woman to rule on the throne of Spain" (Díez 1992, 78) as part of the effort to justify having a woman on the throne, now as the reign of Isabel II was coming to an end the focus shifted to a more feminized Catholic monarch. Modesto Lafuente offers this image of the curative effects of royal domesticity: "The daughters of the Queen of Castile spun, sewed, embroidered, and did other handicrafts, with which they did nothing but follow the example set by their mother, whose knowledge and practice of such crafts at times gained her an immense popularity, because a flag personally embroidered by her and granted to an army, a cloak, an altar cloth, or a vestment personally sewn and embroidered by her and destined to be used in the temple of a city recently reconquered from the Moors, would incite ardent warriors and ardent religiosity, and gained her the love and enthusiasm of the army and the people" (1922, 74). These themes were carried over to the visual arts. Two of the most popular paintings of 1864 focus on the more feminized Isabella I. The first, Isidoro Lozano's *Isabel la Católica presidiendo la educación de sus hijos* [Isabella the Catholic Supervising the Education of Her Children] seems to be a direct illustration of the scene described above. One of the true masterpieces of this genre is Eduardo Rosales's *Doña Isabel la Católica dictando su testamento* [Doña Isabella the Catholic Dictating her Will], depicting the moribund queen as she dictates a last testament that will one day be used to deprive Juana of her power to rule over the kingdoms that her father will usurp from her. In the painting, a woman draped in black stands beside Ferdinand who is slumped into a chair by the side of his wife's deathbed, overwhelmed by grief. Although it would be a historical inaccuracy to place Juana in Spain at the time of her mother's death, many have read this woman as Juana whose presence at the scene ratifies Ferdinand's future rule over her kingdoms, as well as her person, converting her into an eternal child, who instead of ruling, will be ruled.[13]

In her study of images of women, mainly photographs, in the nineteenth-century popular press, Lou Charnon-Deutsch explains that she refers to these "images as 'fictions' to emphasize that they were a product of an imaginary vision of femininity and that many of them functioned as compressed narratives, signposts for the complex stories that an evolving bourgeois society was propagating about ideal gender arrangements" (2000, 6). We can apply this same structure of analysis to the above cited verbal portraits about the royal women, and most certainly to the ways in which women were portrayed in history painting. In 1866, José García, one of its leading proponents, writes that "the goal of this branch of the arts is to teach, to make virtue agreeable, to raise up the good, to moralize and perfect the people" (Reyero 1989, 35). Artists were instructed to take into account the moral, social, and political values represented in their rendition of a historical event, for as José Casado del Alisal, the most powerful of these painters, expressed in the chambers of the San Fernando Academy of Fine Arts, history painting was "teacher of the masses, whose education it completes and whose spirits it elevates through the representation of the major events and great heroes of the past" (Reyero 1989, 35). It was Casado del Alisal who recommended the subject of Juana to Pradilla for his final, and most crucial, painting submitted at the end of his training at the Spanish Academy in Rome. What lesson was the Spanish public to learn from Juana's tragic journey? As Charnon-Deutsch points out, at the time the conflation of a variety of social "discourses produced graphic images of women's *docile* bodies for a culture enthralled with femininity" (2000, 2).

In the various portrayals of Juana by Pradilla, the queen epitomizes this docile body. Juana's unruliness, her continuous acts of rebellion, is what have traditionally served to define her as insane. Pradilla's original idea for his painting of Juana draws upon one of the first episodes of Juana's personal rebellion that served to define her as mad. A large study still survives of his *Juana la Loca en los adarves del Castillo de la Mota* [Juana the Mad on the Battlements of the Mota Castle], portraying an incident in which Juana was imprisoned in this castle by her parents when after Philip's departure to Belgium she remained in Spain to give birth to her son Ferdinand. When she was prevented from leaving the castle, and Spain, to join her husband, Juana refused to return to her rooms, and instead spent cold nights on the castle's battlements until her mother returned to try to convince her to remain. Like the episode on the road to Granada, this incident was also captured by Anglería's *Epistolario*: "She, nonetheless, like an African lioness, in a fit of rage, spent that night under the stars in the interior esplanade of the fortress; and I am not sure if all the remaining nights until the Queen arrived, who, informed of the matter, came swiftly and endeavored to console her with the promise to immediately prepare a fleet for her crossing" (Rincón 1987, 389). Later historians would even attribute Juana's very lack of docility toward Isabella for upsetting her mother to the extent of accelerating the ailing queen's death, a prime example of the notion that female unruliness threatens the stability of the nation. However, as in his other portrayals of her, the moment captured by Pradilla is that of defeat. Far from being shown as an enraged African lioness, Juana is the humiliated docile female body as she desperately clings to the battlements of the castle, down on her knees. The center of the study is occupied by the figures that loom over her powerless form of a woman marginalized, cast to one side in a struggle for power. The idea for this painting was rejected on the basis that fewer spectators would recognize the story, instant recognition of the event being a crucial component in the success of a history painting.

But the project of painting Juana was not abandoned. With an obvious thought to international success, Casado del Alisal had proposed this topic because "it is viable for Spaniards for being Spanish, and dramatic of the sort they can understand over there" (Reyero 1989, 36). He counseled Pradilla well. At first, few in Spain believed that the painting would live up to the fanfare it had received at its initial showings in Rome. Pradilla's success and elevation to celebrity status was instant: "Daily, a large group stood in front of Pradilla's painting in the Barracón del Indo, the place where the fine arts were exposed on the Paseo de la Castellana. At certain times on certain days, when the light dimmed and wrapped the painting in mystical mystery, the public remained silent in its contemplation, as if overcome by the misfortune of that monarch, whose mind was dominated by that inexplicable jealousy awakened by the imaginary loves of chaste death, not noticing either the inclemency of a cold and rainy night nor the vexation and bother that her mad fears produced among the grand retinue" (Rincón 1987, 27). The grammatical structure of this passage, in which the subject of "not noticing" could be either the public or Juana's mind, creates a strange conflation of emotions in which the awe and wonder of the viewers blends with the suffering of the queen.

This fusion approximates the notions so popular in nineteenth-century art of the Romantic sublime, a form of tragic art that derives pleasure from the feelings of terror that unleash the strongest possible emotions, but always a distanced terror that cannot harm the spectator. Umberto Eco reminds us that crucial elements of the Sublime are the representation of "nonfinite things, difficulty, and aspirations to greater and greater things" (2004, 290). In Juana's case her refusal to relinquish the beloved, the continuation of her love beyond death, converts her into the ideal heroine of a movement that finds beauty in "a gaunt, emaciated face behind which, not overly concealed, peeps Death" (299). Many have compared Pradilla's aesthetic sensibilities to Velázquez (García Loranca and García-Rama 1987, 58), whose work he does approximate in the use of color and the baroque-like crisscrossing diagonal thrusts that create the masterful drama in a painting that could easily have been static. Yet if one were to look for connections within Pradilla's own century, the colors and overall use of nature bear more resemblance to displays of tragic Romanticism such as Caspar David Friedrich's *Abbey in an Oak Wood*.

Pradilla would have been familiar with the style of the German Romantics through one of his study excursions to Germany as part of his training at the Academy. Pradilla's Juana is the personification of the many ruins that appear in romantic painting, included both for the sense of incompleteness, but also as a connection to a common past. In Spain, Juana, a human ruin, encapsulated the symbolism of the tragic sense of life (Reyero 1989, 122), as she embarks on a quixotic quest across the Castilian countryside in a vain attempt to defeat death, not only that of her husband, but of the traditional Spain of the Middle Ages.

Casado del Alisal was also right in recognizing that the spectacle of Juana's madness would attract an international following. Throughout the rest of Europe, Spain was still perceived as the romantic, exotic "other" of Lord Byron, Victor Hugo, and later Gautier and Mérimée. Bizet's triumph with the opera *Carmen* had only begun three years earlier. Pradilla's Juana, with her melancholy beauty, the feeling of being surrounded by ruins, the exalted sense of honor of a widow who retires into darkness, and her intense uncontrollable passions, fed the perceived orientalism of this Spanish "promised land for Romantic expansiveness" so enjoyed by the French (Johnson 1997, 48). The Spanish capitalized on the popularity of this "otherness" as is obvious from the architectural format of the Spanish Pavillion, adorned in imitation of Andalusian palaces, with arabesque plaster designs and Moorish arches.

Tragically, during the Paris Exposition, the world's attention again shifted toward the melodrama of the Spanish royal family. The success of Pradilla's *Juana la Loca* here coincides once again with a crucial moment in the romance between Alfonso and María de las Mercedes. She died that very summer at age eighteen. And thus the images of two monarchs pursuing a love that transcends death commingled in the issues of the illustrated journals. *La Ilustración Española y Americana* publishes within the space of a month reproductions of the docile bodies of two Spanish queens, Juana and María de las Mercedes, offering the Spanish public an opportunity to replace the unacceptable images left behind by Isabel II with those of a more humanized and approachable royal family sharing their grief with the nation. In the issue of *La Ilustración* that follows the coverage of the Parisian triumph of *Juana la Loca*, Alfonso is described as on the verge of madness with grief over his "love, interrupted and ruined in its most thriving, passionate period" (1878, 426). We could apply Alfredo Escobar's statement that "it's a madness that attracts, and not the madness that repels. . . . It's Ophelia remembering her love" to both grieving monarchs (1878, 369–70). Decades later, in 1921, the grief Juana expresses over her lost love is again compared to that of a current monarch, Queen Victoria, the century's most successful ruler in performing the bourgeois ideal for her people. According to *El Mundo,* a reproduction of *Juana la Loca* was purchased by the consul to hang in the summer palace at Nice in which Queen Victoria spent a number of summers. Miguel España reports that "the inconsolable widow of Albert Saxe-Coberg-Gotha, spent hours contemplating the likewise inconsolable Castilian queen. The idolatry that Queen Victoria felt for her audacious Albert was as great as that which, having felt for her handsome Philip, deprived the less hearty spirit of Queen Juana of reason and of life" (1921, 68).

It would be tempting to censure Pradilla for perpetuating the romanticized notions of female fragility and submissiveness. However, if Pradilla trapped Juana into the image of a woman driven insane by love, this image in turn later ensnared him as an artist, tagging him eternally as a history painter, in spite of other interests and obvious talents. Joaquín Sorolla, a disciple of Pradilla who began his own career with *The Second of May,* complained that "In Spain few painters of our generation have been able to free themselves from the dead" (García Loranca and García-Rama 1987, 61) meaning that for success, painters were forced to practice the genre of history painting.[14] One of the stated tasks of the Restoration was to "reestablish Spain's historical continuity," enforcing a policy of "silence and forgetfulness" regarding the failures of Isabelline Spain, and one might add, female sovereignty in general (Peiró 1989, 29). Due to the influence of the Academy and the power of the state as main patron of the arts, painters became the instruments of those in power, as much the courtiers to their rulers as were the chroniclers of the Catholic Monarchs. While still in Italy, Pradilla had shown a marked preference for painting landscapes and scenes of rustic life, some of his compositions becoming clearly impressionist. He was initially a student of Carlos de Haes, Spain's premier landscape painter. These talents and interests peek through in his well-known history paintings. His treatment of the Castilian landscape that surrounds Juana was widely praised as a sign of the modernity of the painting, but only as a secondary issue. While Pradilla never lacked clients for his landscapes and rustic scenes abroad, the Spanish refused to acknowledge this facet of his career, as the Academicians continued to denigrate genre painting.

And thus he returned almost obsessively to the theme of Juana, painting at least twelve images between 1906 and 1912 of her captivity in Tordesillas. In this series, Juana is figured by a large window, in a room in disarray, being watched by two of her ladies. In most, the

Princess Catalina, still a young child, is caught in the act of running
into her mother's arms. Juana's madness is revealed through the
blank stare pointed at the viewer, ignoring the child's upward glance.
The scene is vaguely reminiscent of *Las Meninas,* especially through
Pradilla's inclusion of an open door in the background that adds
depth and dimension to the painting. But here again the main
impact is that of Juana as helpless and infantile. The Meninas here
are not caring for a child, but for an adult woman, driven to madness
by love. In one of the versions, Catalina is missing, leaving Juana in a
similar pose, with her hands still in the same position, but empty, indicating a lack. This variation suggests that Pradilla was painting
another instance of rebellion on the part of Juana. Soon after Charles
arrived in Spain to rule the kingdom after Ferdinand's death, ignoring that his mother was still queen, he arranged for Catalina to be
kidnapped from the castle in Tordesillas. Upon discovering her loss,
Juana staged one of her hunger strikes and reacted so violently, that
Catalina was returned to her. Juana, previously viewed as wife, now
reveals her maternal facet at a moment in which she became the
queen mother to Charles. The paintings are done with an aura of religiosity, perhaps in reaction to those who read Juana's rebellions as
heresy, for she sits next to a window with a frame hung with crucifixes,
holy water fonts, and rosaries, while on the opposite wall there is a
fresco with a Christ-like face. Her seclusion and exclusion from power
are reflected through the inclusion of a child's toy knight on horseback, whose miniature opponent lies defeated on the floor. But this
battle scene rests in a separate segment of a painting with an empty
center that leaves Juana isolated, at the extreme left, and separated
again from the world on the other side of the window.

Less than a year after the debut of *Juana la Loca,* Pradilla was
awarded a coveted commission by the Spanish Parliament. He was to
paint *La Rendición de Granada* [The Surrender of Granada], following the instructions of the Marquis de Barzanallana: "as a representation of Spanish unity: the point of departure for the grand actions
conducted by our grandfathers under the rule of those glorious
monarchs" (1882). Isabella was to figure prominently in the center
of the painting, perhaps to symbolize Castile's superior hold over
the peninsula although, historically, Ferdinand was at the surrender
of Granada, while Isabella waited at a nearby town. For most, in spite
of the historical inaccuracy of placing Isabella at the scene, the painting, completed in 1882, was a success. But for serious critics, not
only of art but of politics, such as Fernanflor (Isidoro Fernández
Flórez), who dedicated five articles in a weekly cycle to Pradilla in *El
Liberal,* "*La Rendición de Granada* is worse than a bad painting: it is a

Figure 2. *Juana la Loca recluida en Tordesillas* (Juana the Mad Secluded in Tordesillas) by Francisco Padilla. Image courtesy of the Museo del Prado.

bad example. . . . Pradilla's latest painting is the synthesis of a decadence" (5/21/1882). In many respects, Pradilla's success with *La Rendición de Granada,* but especially with *Juana la Loca,* signals the decadence of an entire system in which national identity is figured through a gendered ideology in Spain's struggles with modernity at the end of the nineteenth century. Romantic depictions of a "mad queen" publicly expressing blind devotion and obedience filled a need to erase the memories of unruly female sovereignty left behind by the ousted Isabel II, and replace them with a visual landscape of female passivity and helplessness more in accordance with the values of the Restoration of a Spanish monarchy still firmly rooted in traditional patterns. History paintings in general provided a formula for humanizing the sovereigns while evoking past glories and the myths of Spanish unity, and this particular depiction of the infirm queen provided a docile body on which to remap the history of a hegemonic Spain.

NOTES

1. To mention just one, Pradilla was working at great speed and with a limited budget so that it is obvious that he uses the same model for a number of the women who thus have strikingly similar features.

2. The Comuneros revolt was idealized as upholding the medieval tradition threatened by the modern state apparatus of Charles. In 1805, Quintana published a hagio-

graphic poem to their leader, "Oda a Padilla," which was initially censored by the Inquisition. In the theater Martínez de la Rosa triumphs with *Padilla's Widow*. When in 1860 Gisbert's painting *Padilla, Bravo and Maldonado* failed to win the medal of honor at the National Exposition, there was an uproar. In amends, the government hung it in the Hall of the Parliament and there was a subscription set up to present Gisbert with a gold crown to compensate for the medal he was denied. (Álvarez Junco 1999, 44).

3. One of the ways historians eventually integrated Charles was by differentiating him from his father, eliminating Juana's importance altogether, and, ignoring Charles's northern upbringing, linking him to his grandfather, Ferdinand the Catholic. The emphasis on Charles and his Habsburg descendents as protectors of the true Catholic faith in line with the policies of his grandfather, becomes even stronger in the hands of Franco-era historians. In the journal *Razón y Fe* [Reason and Faith] of 1949, J. Ma. Doussinague explains that "In the person of Charles I we see the incarnation of what was the exterior viewpoint of the Catholic King and of the great estate men of that century" (Martínez Millán and Reyero 1999, 29). These readings eliminate all female protagonism in the progression of Spanish history, even that of Isabella.

4. While Isabella's chroniclers manipulated her uncle's image using ideologies of gender to her advantage, she ignored those written to guide her. Fray Martín de Córdoba tried to educate the young Isabella according to the Augustinian notions that women are "both corruptible (by the devil) and corrupting (of Adam), with his *Garden of Noble Maidens*" (Weissberger 2004, 33).

5. Palencia's case is a prime example of Isabella's power to control her chroniclers, who at some level were her servants. After disagreeing with Isabella, about whom he wrote in his *Chronicle*, "she was considered a master of pretense and deception," Palencia was marginalized in favor of the promotion of Fernando del Pulgar who was more willing to submit to royal censorship. (Weissberger 2004, 86–87)

6. Reyero speculates that Pradilla was inspired by the face of Teodora Lamadrid, the well-known actress who portrayed Juana in Tamayo y Baus's *Locura de amor*. (1989, 36)

7. Ironically Aroní Yanko's novel in autobiographical mode, *Los silencios de Juana la Loca* [The Silences of Juana the Mad], has on its cover what is believed to be a realistic portrait of Juana painted in her adolescence by Juan de Flandes, as does Gioconda Belli's *El pergamino de la seducción* [The Scroll of Seduction]. This inverted use of historical sources highlights the instability of the boundaries that separate the narrative strategies of literature, especially in the genre of the historical novel, and history as it is packaged for the general reader in series such as those published by Espasa and marketed to the general reading public.

8. Chief among her activities was an attempt to regain the patrimonial lands and revenues that Philip had illegally distributed among the nobility whose loyalty he had so purchased. Clearly these were orders said aristocracy was not eager to enforce. Instead measures were dispatched without her signature or approval. Soon after the arrival of Ferdinand, Juana became a prisoner in Tordesillas.

9. Tamayo y Baus's play is remembered today mainly because of the two popular films it inspired, the 1948 blockbuster of the same title, directed by Juan de Orduña and Vicente Aranda's 2001 *Mad Love*, both of which include photography based on period paintings. See my article "La iconografía de Juana la Loca: representaciones de la locura femenina en pintura, teatro y cine" (2005) for a detailed study of the use of painting in these films.

10. Near the end of her life, the exiled Isabel defended herself to Benito Pérez Galdós in this fashion, "Put yourselves in my place. Nineteen and trapped in a labyrinth, through which I had to walk feeling the walls, for there was no light to

guide me. If someone turned on a light for me, someone else would come along and shut it off" (1906, 21). "What was I to do, so young, queen at fourteen, with no reins to my will, with all the money at my disposal for my whims and to satisfy my desire to aid those in need, not seeing that the people who surrounded me bent like reeds in the wind, not hearing beyond the flattering voices that overwhelmed me? . . . Put yourselves in my place" (22).

11. In Galdós's novel *Cánovas*, the last of the *Episodios nacionales* [National Episodes], the antimonarchic character Tito describes the "charming Merceditas, who in the theater as at the bulls, in the promenades and everywhere, took all our hearts with her" (1951, 1332). As her illness becomes apparent, "We were concerned for the young monarch as if she were a member of our family, and I believe that same sentiment was felt by all the people of Madrid. Mercedes came to the throne of Spain as a symbol of peace, without hatred on her part, without hesitation on the part of the nation" (1333).

12. The entire poem is a series of contrasts in the male/female roles. "He will make the nations / respect the integrity of our rich land; / Destroying rancor, ambitions,/ He will make industry resume its flight:" vs. "He has in you a heart that understands him; / A soul that will admire and adore him; / A being who will listen to him, yet never bind him: / And who with him will feel, think, enjoy or cry: / A lip that will smile at him and never offend: / An angel who will beseek God for him"

13. Many historical accounts at the time emphasize this image of Juana as an eternal child. According to the popular Padre Mariana, at *Las Cortes de Toro*, where Ferdinand met with Philip to decide who would rule, "It is known that his vice-chancellor, Alonso de Caballería, aimed to establish and even persuade him [Ferdinand] to abandon the title of governor, and take the name of administrator and proxy, as by right befits fathers with the inheritances that their children inherit from their mothers before reaching emancipation; and even then they have a part of the settlement. The queen Doña Juana was not yet emancipated, and when she was, she could be considered a minor, either for her malady, or for being oppressed by her husband, and without freedom" (1867, 1175).

14. Pradilla would have been well aware of the poverty faced by liberal artists unwilling to collaborate with those in power. Early in his career, he had been a friend of the Bécquer brothers, the poet Gustavo and his brother the painter Valeriano, both famously impoverished. Pradilla had collaborated with the Bécquers when they launched their own journal, *La Ilustración de Madrid*. Pradilla was probably among the circle of friends familiar with the pornographic depictions of Isabel II in the *Sem* watercolors now known as *Los Borbones en pelota* [The Naked Bourbons] in which Isabel is shown in a number of sexual positions with her various lovers, especially Carlos Marfori, but also a horse. According to Charnon-Deutsch, "these sketches show a fundamental anxiety about a woman's occupying Spain's most visible place in the public sphere, the queen's body (like the other public menace, the prostitute) can only corrupt the body politic. In nearly every image, a minor detail highlights the fact that Isabel is desecrating the throne" (2000, 119).

WORKS CITED

Anonymous. 1848. *Historia de la célebre Reina de España Doña Juana, llamada vulgarmente, La Loca*. Madrid: Imprenta de José María Marés. Available in facsimile at: www.cervantesvirtual.com.

Anonymous. (La Redacción). 1878. "La Reina ha muerto." *La Ilustración Española y Americana,* June 30: 426.

Álvarez Junco, José. 1999. "La construcción de España." In *El siglo de Carlos V and Felipe II,* edited by Martínez Millán, José y Carlos Reyero, 31–48. Valladulid.

Aram, Bethany. 2005. *Juana the Mad: Sovereignty and Dynasty in Renaissance Europe.* Baltimore: Johns Hopkins University Press.

Belli, Gioconda. 2005. *El pergamino de la seducción.* Barcelona: Seix Barral.

Burdiel, Isabel. 2004. *Isabel II: No se puede reinar inocentemente.* Madrid: Espasa.

Cabrera de Miranda, Dolores. 1878. "A la Serenísima Señora Infanta Doña María de las Mercedes de Orleans y Borbón." *El Correo de la Moda,* February 2: 35.

Centellas, Ricardo. 1999. *Francisco Pradilla: Un pintor de la Restauración.* Zaragoza: Caja de Ahorros de la Inmaculada de Aragón.

Certeau, Michel de. 1988. *The Writing of History.* Translated by Tom Conley. New York: Columbia University Press.

Charnon-Deutsch, Lou. 2000. *Fictions of the Feminine in the Nineteenth-Century Spanish Press.* University Park: Pennsylvania State University Press.

Díez, José Luis. 1992. "Evolución de la pintura española de historia en el siglo XIX." In *La pintura de historia del siglo XIX en España,* edited by José Luis Díez, 69–101. Madrid: Museo del Prado.

Donézar y Díez de Ulzurrun, Javier María. 1999. "El *austracismo* de los historiadores liberales del siglo XIX." In *El siglo de Carlos V and Felipe II,* edited by Martínez Millán and Reyero, 311–41. Valladulid.

Eco, Umberto, ed. 2004. *History of Beauty.* Translated by Alastair McEwen. New York: Rizzoli.

Escobar, Alfredo. 1878. "La Exposición Universal de Paris." *La Ilustración Española y Americana,* June 8, 369–70.

Fernández Álvarez, Manuel. 2000. *Juana la Loca: La cautiva de Tordesillas.* Madrid: Espasa.

Fernández Flórez, Isidro (Fernanflor). 1883. "El Cuadro de Pradilla." *El Liberal,* May 7–June 1: unnumbered.

García Cadena, Peregrín. 1878. "Crónica general." *La Ilustración Española y Americana,* January 30: 58–62.

García Loranca, Ana, and Ramón García-Rama. 1987. *Vida y obra del pintor Francisco Pradilla Ortiz.* Zaragoza: Caja de Ahorros de Zaragoza, Aragón y Rioja.

Johnson, Warren. 1997. "*Carmen* and Exotic Nationalism: *España à la Française.*" *Romance Notes* 38, 1:45–52.

Lafuente, Modesto. 1922. *Historia General de España desde los tiempos primitivos hasta la muerte de Fernando VII por . . . Continuada desde dicha época hasta la muerte de Alfonso XII por Don Juan Valera en colaboración con D. Andrés Borrego, D. Antonio Pirala y D. José Coroleu.* Vol. 7. Barcelona: Montaner y Simón, Editores.

Mariana, Padre Juan de. 1867. *Historia general de España.* Vol. 3. Madrid: M. Rodríguez y Comp. Editores.

Martínez Millán, José y Carlos Reyero, eds. 1999. *El siglo de Carlos V y Felipe II: La construcción de los mitos en el siglo XIX.* Vol 1. Valladolid: Sociedad estatal para la conmemoración de los centenarios de Felipe II y Carlos V.

Peiró Martín, Ignacio. 1995. *Los guardianes de la historia: la historiografía académica de la Restauración.* Zaragoza: Institución Fernando el Católico.

Pérez Galdós, Benito. 1906. *Memoranda*. Madrid: Perlado, Páez y Compañía.

———. 1951. *Cánovas: Obras completas*. Vol. 3. Madrid: Aguilar, 1273–1363.

Reyero, Carlos. 1989. *La pintura de historia en España: Esplendor de un género en el siglo XIX*. Madrid: Cátedra.

Rincón García, Wifredo. 1987. *Francisco Pradilla: 1848–1921*. Madrid: Cipsa.

———. 1997. "Locura de amor: La Reina Juana de Castile en el arte español." In *La mujer en el arte español: VIII jornadas de arte*, edited by Rincón García, 383–400. Madrid: Departamento de Historia del Arte "Diego Velázquez" del Centro de Estudios Históricos C.S.I.C.

Sánchez Llama, Íñigo. 2001. *Antologia de la prensa periódica Isabelina escrita por mujeres (1843–1894)*. Cádiz: Universidad de Cádiz.

Soliño, María Elena. 2005. "La iconografía de Juana la Loca: representaciones de la locura femenina en pintura, teatro y cine." *Lecturas: Imágenes Revista de Poética del Cine*, 4: 247–64.

Una dama española. 1875. "La Condesa de Girgenti." *La Ilustración Española y Americana*, March 8:147.

Weissberger, Barbara F. 2004. *Isabel Rules: Constructing Queenship, Wielding Power*. Minneapolis: University of Minnesota Press.

Yanko, Aroní. 2003. *Los silencios de Juana la Loca*. Barcelona: Belacqva.

Villamil, Manuel P. 1878. "La Exposición Nacional." *El Siglo Futuro*, February 19: unnumbered.

Juana la coloratura

Jan Reinhart

Throughout the Renaissance, music making was a thing done at court. And no court was more musical than that of Philip the Handsome and Juana of Castile. From his father, the Habsburg Holy Roman Emperor Maximilian I, and his mother Marie of Burgundy, Philip had inherited a rich tradition of musical appreciation, as did his Spanish bride from her family. Together in their Flemish and Iberian palaces, they employed a staff of about three dozen composers and musicians, including some of the greatest of the age: Pierre de La Rue, Alexander Agricola, Marbrianus de Orto, Henry Bredemers, and Juan de Anchieta (Van Doorslaer 1934).

Even after Philip's untimely death in 1506 at the age of twenty-eight, many of the musicians continued on for a while in Juana's service. Anchieta remained with Juana until his death in 1523, entertaining the queen during long, sad retirement at the Santa Clara Monastery in Tordesillas. That music continued to lift Juana's spirits—as the chronicler Alonso de Estanques asserted—is demonstrated in the decisions of Ferdinand and then Charles V (Juana's father and son, respectively) to increase by half what Philip paid the choirmaster Anchieta, with Charles doing so over the advice of his councilors (Stevenson 1960).

It might seem then that given the musical richness of Juana and Philip's court and the tragic story of their passionate marriage, some enterprising composer might have found sufficient grounds for a good opera. Music is fired by emotion and no genre needs emotional turmoil more than the lyric stage. Certainly composers have perennially used fits of madness and rage to craft crowd-pleasing vocal acrobatics for singer superstars. And indeed, eight operas have so far been composed about Juana since the mid-nineteenth century (two having debuted in the last three years). The first composers, in the Romantic era, were naturally captivated by the exquisite details of Juana's tumultuous personal life. There was her passionate love for the handsome Philip, frustrated by infidelity and then his early death, the serial betrayals by her family and court, the long years of enforced confinement, and, possibly (or probably), madness. More recently as feminist thought has influenced public discourse, composers have seized on the theme of the brutal marginalization of women in politics that is vividly illustrated by the series of aforementioned outrages perpetrated on the historical Juana of Castile by patriarchal authority. So far, none of these works have captured the public's sustained interest. Juana of Castile remains as stubbornly marginal in the operatic canon as that other unlucky Iberian princess, Inês de Castro. The reasons for that obscurity are as various as the composers who have tried their hand at casting Juana's life in music.

Although Juana lived in the sixteenth century, it took another three-and-a-half centuries for a noted composer to make her celebrated story the center of an opera. As a form, opera was dominated from its beginnings in the early seventeenth century through the Enlightenment by classical mythology—the struggles of Greco-Roman deities and their human protégés—leavened by the occasional ancient history or biblical borrowing.

It was not until the nineteenth century and the arrival of Romanticism that opera composers began mining the rich vein of popular literature based on recent, and preferably exciting, events (that literature having arrived, along with the new middle class, just a few decades earlier). Building on the successes of Gioacchino Rossini (1792–1868) with operas like *Elisabetta, regina d'Inghilterra* and *Donna del Lago,* the Italian composers Vicenzo Bellini (1801–35) and Gaetano Donizetti (1797–1848) established what is commonly called the Bel canto school of opera by systematically converting every hit play and novel they could into passionately graceful vocal pyrotechnics. (Indeed, one and a half centuries later, bel canto is a brand that still sells, as one can see by a casual glance at the current repertoire of any national or regional opera company.) Nobody was better, or more prolific, at providing workable libretti for Bellini and his French contemporaries than the Parisian dramatist Eugène Scribe (1791–1861). He had a knack for crafting stories with sharply contrasting characters whose conflicts neatly resolve into big finales at the end of each act.

In 1838, Scribe did a treatment of the Juana tale for Donizetti that the Italian did not use. As with his other theater works based on historical events, Scribe's libretto for *Jeanne la folle* takes some liberties with the historical record of Juana of Castile to facilitate the onstage action. It is set in 1506 in the former Moorish capital of Granada. When Philip (Phillipe in the opera) is observed cavorting with a Moorish princess, Jeanne stabs him in a fit of jealousy and goes mad. The opera ends with the prince's body being carried to a triumphal coronation scene.

In 1848, a Scribe protégé, Antoine-Louis Clappison, decided to set the rejected libretto to music. Clapisson (1808–66) was the son of a prominent horn player and himself a virtuoso violinist. In the 1830s, he studied composition with the great Czech pedagogue Antoine Reicha and made a name for himself with his chamber songs and comic chansonnettes. His first musical theater success came in 1838 at the Opéra-Comique with *Figurant,* a light opera that used a Scribe libretto. Ten years after that initial collaboration, Clapisson made a stab at grand opera, this time with Scribe's "Jeanne la folle." Beyond the fanciful addition of a band of captive Moors, Scribe had written a story that expanded the characters beyond the historical nucleus of Ferdinand (Fernando), Phillipe and Jeanne (Juana) to include one Don Fabrique, a cousin of Jeanne. Fabrique's function in the libretto was to serve as a contrast to the faithless Phillipe, loving his cousin deeply and chivalrously from a distance while her husband lavishes his affection on other women. In this opera, Phillipe's attentions are riveted on Aïxa, the daughter of the captured Moorish prince Aben-Hassan. The two live with their servants and vassals near the palace of the Catholic Monarchs in Granada. Both Aben-Hassen and his daughter are given considerable chunks of the music to sing, including parts in a Donizetti-style quintet that, as in *Lucia di Lammermoor,* crystallizes the protagonist's romantic dilemma and introduces her ensuing madness. A chorus of Moors also get to sing of their tragic oppression in the newly Catholic Spain.

Jeanne la folle received generally positive notices at the time of its performance. In a lengthy review of the opera for the Revue et Gazette Musicale de Paris, Henri Blanchard favorably compares Aben-Hassan and Aïxa to the characters of Eléazar and his daughter Rachel in *La Juive,* another Scribe libretto whose opera (by Jacques Halévy) survives in the repertoire to this day. But Blanchard's overall evaluation was decidedly mixed. He praises the handiwork of Scribe (whose productivity Blanchard compares to a "perpetual motion machine") in crafting a libretto that handily moves the dramatic action of the play while yielding ample opportunities for music, and in particular the critic praises the heroic and moving character of Don Fabrique. Blanchard also hears much to praise in Clapisson's score, particularly in the orchestration and in various instrumental solos, which the critic compares to "a good symphony" decorated in a warm Iberian style. But he believes Clapisson was not up to the demands of Scribe, that the young composer lacked the high poetry and dramatic precision that Scribe's art needed. And while Blanchard thinks the final scenes of the fourth and fifth acts of *Jeanne la folle* and the ballet for the coronation scene have a compositional richness comparable to the Saint

Bartholomew's Day Massacre scene in Giacomo Meyerbeer's *Les Hugenots,* he faults the composer for being generally unable to unify the music with the drama. Of the vocal writing, most particularly Jeanne's, Blanchard says "the recitative is too songlike, over an orchestra that is too forced, too fraught and the arias are too easily confused with recitative" (Blanchard 1848, 351). The Paris operagoing public apparently agreed with Blanchard. In spite of a powerful performance of the heroine by a Mademoiselle Masson, *Jeanne la folle* closed after an embarrassing eight performances at the the Opéra and was promptly and thoroughly forgotten. Clapisson wisely returned to comic opera and enjoyed a successful career thereafter.

A few years later in 1851 Emanuèle Muzio (1821–90), a student of the great Italian opera composer Giuseppe Verdi, debuted his *Giovanna la Pazza* in Brussels. It was apparently not a success and Muzio's efforts to get a new production in Italy—Opera Central in those days —were also unsuccessful (Cánepa Guzmán 109–10). And that was that for the next four decades.

In the 1890s, two Spanish language operas of the Juana story were composed. The first was by Emilio Serrano (1850–1939), an acclaimed composer who regularly conducted at the Royal Opera in Madrid. According to the music historian José Subirá, Serrano had been "seduced" by a long popular play on the Juana theme by Manuel Tamayo y Baus called *Locura de amor.* Serrano composed his opera, *Doña Juana la Loca* while on a fellowship at the Spanish Academy of Fine Arts in Rome. Based on the Tamayo y Baus play, it mixes Basque and Catalan folk tunes with religious and mystical music material (the "Ave Maria" figures prominently). Subirá reports that the sets and costumes left much to be desired in the March 3, 1890, debut of the opera, but that the performers "made an excellent effort" particularly the diva Teresa Arkel, who sang the lead role and the opera was received "enthusiastically" by the public. Not, however, enthusiastically enough to make it part of the continuing repertoire (Subirá 1953, 418). The historical record notes another Spanish language opera treatment of the Juana story about the same time: that of Chilean Eliodoro Ortiz de Zárate (1865–1952). As part of his graduation from Milan Conservatory in 1889 he composed another *Juana la Loca,* which was staged a year later at Milan's La Scala theater. But there are no reviews or records of future productions. The composer made his modest mark a half decade later with another opera entirely, *La Florista de Lugano* (*The Flower Girl of Lugano*), which debuted in his native country (Cánepa Guzmán 1976, 110–12).

Deserved or not, all of these efforts save Clapisson's have vanished into oblivion. And even in the case of Clapisson, the massive database

OCLC WorldCat can find only two crumbling copies of a miniature score published in 1848. Juana was a failed Romantic heroine, a compelling subject for folktales but not perhaps in an expensive art form dominated by conventional bourgeoise tastes. It is interesting to note that until recently the only composer who used Juana even as a subsidiary character for an opera was the atonalist Ernst Krenek. Unafraid of dissonance, either psychological or musical, he cast Juana as an alto, one of several supporting roles in his 1933 operatic psychodrama of the troubled Holy Roman Emperor Charles V. The opera is highly regarded by musicians and historians but generally unknown outside their circles, no doubt due to the difficulties of appreciating the groundbreaking twelve-tone score. Juana did not appear in another grand opera for four more decades.

As she approached the age of fifty, the diva Beverly Sills had decided it was time to retire. Her soprano voice, whose coloratura virtuosity had catapulted Sills to international fame two decades earlier, was inevitably showing the wear and tear of a long and busy career. She had decided to quit at the top of her game and pursue other options, which in those days could include subbing for Johnny Carson on the *Tonight Show*. To celebrate Sills's birthday, her friend the impresario Tito Copobianco, then director of the San Diego Opera, convinced two wealthy West Coast donors to commission a new opera to the tune of $176,000 that would feature the diva in the role of the protagonist (Rich 1979). To compose this farewell vehicle would be none other than Gian Carlo Menotti (1911), the brilliant Italian auteur who since his time as a close companion to Samuel Barber had fashioned a number of operas to English librettos—also of his own composition—often to critical and public acclaim. In an era of classical music still dominated by the dogmatic disciples of atonalist Arnold Shoenberg, Menotti was a stylish rebel who dared yet to compose accessible and often beautiful music on compellingly romantic themes. He chose the subject of the new opera: Juana la loca, the headstrong daughter of the Spanish monarchs Fernando and Isabel who, according to legend, was driven mad by her love for the handsome but inconstant Philip of Burgundy. To all concerned, it seemed like a triumph in the making—until the debut.

Menotti struggled mightily with the score. Large chunks were yet uncomposed when he flew into San Diego a week before the premiere on June 4, 1979. He was still handing freshly composed pages to the conductor hours before the performance. In fact, he would go on recomposing and finishing the piece for the next few years. Sills, Copobianco, the cast, and conductor did the best job they could under the circumstances—which included a brief interruption in act

2 when a cast member was almost electrocuted backstage. The performance was warmly received by the San Diego audience that night, but less so by the international critics attending that night at the premiere or at the handful of revivals a few years later in Europe.

The opera comprises three acts and seven scenes, beginning with the meeting in Lierre, Flanders, of the lovestruck Juana with her handsome groom-to-be. At Philip's impetuous request, the two dismiss their respective retinues—Juana's includes her giggling ladies-in-waiting, a prudish nurse, and the knight Miguel de Ferrera, who is open about his unrequited passion for the princess, and Philip's includes a gaggle of bodyguards/hunting buddies. The couple sing a rapturous love duet ending on high notes (a stratospheric high D for Juana and an equally altitudinous high A for her baritone lover) followed by a medieval version of the shotgun wedding. Scene 2 sets the tragedy in motion as an increasingly distant and inconstant Philip presses the pregnant Juana to sign over her claim to the Spanish throne, her inheritance from Isabel of Castile. Juana's principled refusal leads to her enforced confinement in the Flemish castle. The next scene occurs at the young Philip's deathbed and includes a bit of nastiness when Juana, coming back from the chapel and catching her friend Doña Manuela tenderly confessing her illicit love for Philip, angrily cuts the hair of the adulteress and slashes her cheeks with the scissors.

In act 2 Juana leads a funeral procession back home to Spain, pausing in a mountainous wasteland to remove the lid of the coffin and address her deceased husband directly. In a somber yet bravura aria she reprimands Philip for his faithlessness and the misery she now feels in spite of it. Scene 4 ends with a reunion of Juana with her father Ferdinand (here Fernando), who greets his bereaved daughter rather coolly. In the next scene, we see why: he is tired of being a prince consort, or worse, a common administrator, first to his wife and then his daughter. Using the pretext of her madness, Fernando has Juana placed in confinement, taking away her young son Carlos when she again refuses to sign over the kingdom.

Fernando's death in act 3 brings no relief, however. Carlos is now the Holy Roman Emperor Charles V and when Juana refuses a last time to sign over her throne, he takes away her daughter Catalina and for good measure boards up the window to her convent cell to prevent further communication with the outside world. The final scene is set near the end of Juana's life, after she has been confined to the same cruel room for more than forty-six years. Covered with sores and crumpled on a filthy straw mat, she once more meets Miguel, now a priest, who tells Juana that "God is an ever waiting bridegroom." "Does he exist?" she asks. "His love exists," Miguel replies. The opera ends quietly with Juana singing twice on descending notes "Do you promise?"

A central conceit of the opera is that the three roles of Philip, Fernando, and Carlos are performed by the same singer—in fact, in the last act Juana says they are "the devil in three disguises." It was more than a sly Menottian nod to the three-in-one baritone villains of Jules Offenbach's "Tales of Hoffman." In an interview with the *New York Times* during a restaging of the opera several years later, Menotti said that he was struck during his research by how Juana was exploited by the three men she loved most. "I've always had this obsession that love is some sort of prison, and that when we fall in love, we abandon our freedom. I made the three men in her life sung by one singer, because she was always in love with the same man. She was in love with love, and the only way she could free herself was to betray the person she loved" (Waleson 1984, H23).

Although Menotti had already composed some previous seventeen musical dramas, Juana was his first stab at grand opera—big orchestra, big chorus, expensive sets, and period costumes—and it was his first based on historical figures. The composer had always been a world-class procrastinator, and in the week before the San Diego premiere Menotti arrived in town with a suitcase full of unfinished music. He was forced to lock himself in his hotel room with an around-the-clock staff of copyists. Meanwhile the cast, conductor, and director rehearsed what they could.

The composer was torn between his fascination with Juana, an historical figure whose story is as colorful as it is curiously ambiguous, and his instincts as a straightforward neo-Romantic composer. "One reason I was so late in delivering the score, was that Juana's life was so full of wonderful anecdotes and dramatic situations," he told the *New York Times* a few months after the premiere. "With *La Loca* I made a number of drafts because I tried to include as much as possible. Only in a few instances did I take liberties with the facts in Juana's life, for I wanted the opera to be as historically accurate as possible. That took time" (Ardoin 1979, D1).

In spite of those difficulties, the opera was warmly received by audiences at its debut in San Diego and then in September at the City Opera (Sills's home base in New York). Critics uniformly praised Sills's valedictory performances, which called upon every vocal and dramatic technique in her considerable arsenal. They were more mixed on the opera itself. They ranged from modest raves to outright pans. Manuela Hoelterhoff of the *Wall Street Journal* blasted the libretto, which she believed should have been composed by a fully qualified poet (Hoelterhoff 1979, 23). And a few critics agreed with the *New York Times*'s Harold Schonberg that Menotti's Italianate tunes were as uninteresting as they were derivative (Schonberg 1979, C13). Even positive reviewers faulted Menotti for his tendency to overuse recitative (the drier sing-song that links arias in traditional opera) to keep the action moving at the expense of his attractive melodies. Still the influential Andrew Porter of the *New Yorker* summed up several reviewers when he wrote that *La Loca* was "perhaps Menotti's best opera" and "a decent and accomplished piece of work, and I imagine it will bear revival" (Porter 1979, 214).

That it did. Menotti, who also considered "La Loca" to be his strongest work to date, was determined to get it restaged under better circumstances (Waleson 1984, H23). Being the director of the prominent Festival of Two Worlds held annually in Charleston, South Carolina, and Spoleto, Italy, he had the means to implement his plans. A slightly revised version was tested in 1981 at the provincial German opera house of Giessen with soprano Pamela Myers replacing the fully retired Sills. Satisfied with the results, Menotti took the production and cast to Spoletto and Charleston three years later. Again the work was warmly greeted by audiences and less so by critics. Since then, *La Loca* has languished, unrecorded and virtually unpublished—a performance copy is available only for rental from the publisher G. Schirmer.

The apparent failure of Menotti's *La Loca* to join the general repertoire has not discouraged other modern composers from trying new operas on the story. In 1983, only a few years after San Diego debut of *La Loca,* the respected Belgian electro-acoustic composer Paul-Baudouin Michel (1930–) created his own *Jeanne la folle.* According to his Web page, Michel considers the opera to be a "psycho-political" work in which the protagonist "is primarily considered as a victim of the 'raison d'état.'" The work was staged in 1993 in Liege.

More recently two young composers have used the Juana story to create strikingly different works. The first to be debuted in the twenty-first century was *Rage d'Amours* by the maverick Dutch composer Robert Zuidam (1964–). Zuidam integrated a handful of historical texts in Latin, Old French, and Old Castilian to tell a stylized version of Juana's tale that emphasizes her passion and madness. It begins and ends in the tower of the Santa Clara monastery in Tordesillas in north central Spain, where the historical Juana of Castile was interned for nearly a half century. The opera then proceeds in a set of flashbacks related by a baritone narrator, Pierchon de Rue (a version of Pierre de La Rue, the famed Franco-Flemish composer of Philip's court), from a nearly disastrous sea voyage the young couple survived through Philip's death—here strongly suggested to be by poisoning—and then Juana's odd peregrination through northern Spain with the unburied corpse of her husband, ending again at Tordesillas and pining madness.

The libretto veers toward the grotesque. For instance, during the storm in scene 2 sailors inflate a leather bladder around Philipe (the composer's spelling) so his body might be found for proper burial after the shipwreck. The orchestra divides into two groups of instruments to pantomime the sound of the air bellows that the sailors are pumping. In the next scene, when the ship has found safe harbor, the crew leave Philip onstage with his leather balloon deflating. The king proceeds to die onstage, singing of his nausea and dizziness as the poison of his father-in-law takes effect. Later in scene 5, the queen sings in paraphrase of the Psalm of Psalms, describing Philipe's lovely features in sensual detail, each stanza alternated by a chorus of monks who explain in Latin how they are removing the king's brains and inner organs for separate burial. Scene 6 consists of an ironic aside from a charwoman, who pauses while scrubbing the floor to explain in slangy, archaic Spanish that the poor queen has gone from raging to almost catatonic, no longer bathing or managing to relieve herself properly. Juana implores her husband to embrace and kiss her, while the monks in her retinue comment on his deteriorating state and dreadful smell. They convince Juana to stop at the Monastery in Tordesillas, which becomes her home/prison for the next forty-six years. Near the end there is a touching duet between the stricken Juana and Philipe, either a figment of her imagination or a ghost, heeding at last her call to "Venid, venid al luz del dia" ("Come, come to the light of day").

In spite of the black comedy implied by the libretto, the work is a somber meditation on passion with soaring vocal lines accompanied by dissonant chordal blocks of shimmering, modernist music. Zuidam has Juana portrayed by three sopranos of varying vocal color. They appear on stage together, sometimes singing in harmony, other times trading solos. The lead Juana sings over an extended range using virtuoso vocal techniques. It was created specifically for soprano Lucy Shelton, a faculty member at Tanglewood and reportedly a friend of the composer. *Boston Globe* critic Richard Dyer, reviewing the opera's premiere at Tanglewood in 2003, praised the unusual tripartite casting of the protagonist because the keening and interlocking vocal lines "depict the obsessive personality of the queen, always turning in on itself" (Dyer 2003b, E1).

Zuidam told the *Globe* that he was initially drawn to Juana's story because of the presence of so many famous composers and musicians in Philip and Juana's Flemish court and he lightly quotes some of that music in the opera's score. But it was the queen's obsession that inspired the composition most. "The relationship of Philip and Juana was strange before he died and even more so after he was dead," (Dyer 2003a, N3) he told Dyer in an interview. "She could not let him go, and he remained an object of her passion for the rest of her life; she didn't listen to the part of the wedding vow that says 'till death do us part!' She had a teenager's crush on him and never outgrew it. She lived out a dream. Most of us have our hearts broken at 17, but we go on with living" (Dyer 2003a, N3).

Rage d'Amours was the second of two one-act operas commissioned by Tanglewood that year; the other was a treatment of Federico García Lorca's *Ainadamar* by the Argentinian composer Osvaldo Golijov. Zuidam's opera received excellent notices after the Tanglewood premiere and again in June 2005 when it was staged in a new production at Amsterdam's Holland Festival. There are plans to bring the production to the Muntschouwburg Royal Opera in Brussels.

If *Rage d'Amours* embraced the love mad Juana of folk tradition, *Juana,* the latest addition to this operatic subgenre, moved it firmly back to the politics of Menotti's *La Loca. Juana* debuted in 2005 as part of the Chamber Opera and New Creations Festival of the Liceu Theater in Barcelona. It was composed by Catalan Enric Palomar (1964–) on a libretto by Rebecca Simpson (1960–), a British playwright and actress living in Barcelona. In three acts the work focuses on an historical development eleven years into Juana's internment at Tordesillas, when she briefly became the focal point of an uprising of the so-called Comuneros (the commoners or townspeople of Castile), which was quickly crushed by Charles V. The opera lays out in detail Juana's precarious political situation and the magnitude of the betrayal by her son and his courtiers, whose disastrous policies had set the revolt in motion. She is no madwoman but rather a victim, in succession, of her beloved husband, father and son, who cruelly isolate her for purposes of political expediency.

In their online notes for the historical background of the opera, the authors wonder aloud what might have happened to Spain if the bourgeois revolt (the first of its kind, preceding the Glorious Revolution in England by more than a century) had somehow succeeded and championed the cause of Juana's claim to the Spanish throne: "Would it have led to a parliamentary government and the establishment of a constitutional monarchy?"

As one might expect from a chamber opera festival, Juana is no grand opera like most of its predecessors. It was composed for a cast of six singers and six accompanying musicians—a string trio, flute, piano, and lute—in a modern classical style with strong traditional Spanish musical references. While most of the Juana operas composed previously sought to capitalize on the virtuoso soprano singing opportunities offered by their unhinged protagonist, this somber politico-historical piece cast Juana as a mezzo soprano, a darker and generally less flashy voice type. The opera debuted in June 2005 in Halle, Germany, opera house and at the time this chapter was written it was scheduled for performance at the Romeu Theater in Barcelona in November 2005.

So if Juana of Castile has not become an operatic character with the same sort of ubiquitous profile as, say, a Figaro, Don Juan, or Electra, it is not for want of trying. While nineteenth-century composers were drawn to the tale of Juana, none of them could transcend the central weirdness of her story in convincing way. Menotti's effort to lash the Romantic heroine elements to a vague politico-historical scaffold has apparently also failed. It is too early to tell if the more self-consciously ambiguous and politically textured musical dramas by Zuidam and Palomar will end up as musical footnotes or find their way into a future operatic canon. But with so much material to draw from, it would not at all be surprising to see a future handful of opera composers take a crack at Juana's story.

WORKS CITED

Special to the New York Times. 1979. "Miss Sills in Premiere of Menotti's 'La Loca.' " *New York Times* (June 5): C7.

Ardoin, John. 1979. "Menotti's New La La Loca, a Triumph for Beverly Sills." *High Fidelity/Musica America* 29 (October): MA 38–39.

———. 1979. "Frantic Nonstop Preparations for a New Menotti Opera." *New York Times* 2 (September 16): D1.

———. 1984. "Charleston." *Opera News* 49 (September): 61–62.

Bellingardi, Luigi. 1982. "Da Spoleto." *Nuova rivista musicale italiana* 16 (October–December): 621–23.

Blanchard, Henri. 1848. "Théâtre de la Nation." *La Revue et Gazette Musicale de Paris* 46 (November 12): 349–52.

Cánepa Guzmán, Mario. 1976. *La opera en Chile 1839–1930.* Santiago, Chile: Editorial Del Pacífico.

Casadevall, G. 2005. "La opera 'Juana' lleva a Alemania la vida trágica de la reina que pasó a la historia como 'la loca.' " *Estrella Digital* (June 27).

Dyer, Richard. 2003a. "The posthumous passion of Juana la Loca." *Boston Globe* (August 3).

———. 2003b. "Well-matched 'Rage' and 'Ainadamar' stir Tanglewood passions." *Boston Globe* (August 12).

Eckert, Thor, Jr. 1979. "City Opera's Loca: Uninspired Menotti." *Christian Science Monitor* (October 10): 18.

Hoelterhoff, Manuela. 1979. "Beverly Sills Retires from Lustrous Career." *Wall Street Journal* (September 28): 23.

Jacobson, Robert. 1979. "New York." *Opera News* 44 (December 8): 26.

Menotti, Gian Carlo. 1979. *La Loca* (opera). New York: G. Schirmer.

Michel, Paul-Baudouin. 2005. In CeBeDem's index of composers available at: http://www.cebedem.be/composers/michel_paul_baudouin/nl.html

Page, Tim. 1984. "Opera: Menotti's 'Juana' Performed at Festival." *New York Times* 1 (June 3): 23.

Palomar, Enric, and Rebecca Simpson. 2005. *Juana* (opera). Available at: http://www .festivaloperabutxaca.org/juanacas.html

Pendle, Karin. 1979. *Eugene Scribe and French Opera of the Nineteenth Century.* Ann Arbor, MI: UMI Research Press.

Porter, Andrew. 1979. "Further Events: Heroine." *New Yorker* 55 (November 19): 212–215.

Rasponi, Lanfranco. 1982. "Spoleto." *Opera News* 47 (October): 42.

Rich, Alan. 1979. "No Reign in Spain." *New York* 12 (June 25): 74–75.

Saal, Hubert. 1979. "San Diego Madness." *Newsweek* 93 (June 18): 90.

Schonberg, Harold C. 1979. "Opera: 'La Loca' Makes a Debut." *New York Times* 3 (September 17): C13.

Scribe, Eugène. 1848. *Jeanne la folle: opéra en cinq actes* (libretto). Paris: Beck.

Smith, Patrick J. 1979. "New York." *Opera* (England) 30 (December): 1175–1176.

———. 1980. "New York: Opera." *Musical Times* 121 (February): 124.

Stevenson, Robert. 1960. *Spanish Music in the Age of Columbus.* The Hague, Netherlands: Martinus Nijhoff.

Storrer, William Allin. 1984. "Spoleto U.S.A.: Variegated Languages." *Opera* (England) 35 (Autumn): 109–10.

Subirá, José. 1949. *Historia y anecdotaria del Teatro Real.* Madrid: Editorial Plus-Ultra.

———. 1953. *Historia de la Música Española e Hispanoamericana.* Barcelona: Salvat Editores, S.A.

Sutcliffe, James Helme. 1981. "Gießen." *Opera* (England) 32 (October): 1053–1054.

Tommasini, Anthony. 2003. "New Operas Remember the Agony of Lovers Left Behind." *New York Times* (August 13): E1.

Van Doorslaer, G. 1934. La Chapelle Musicale de Philippe le Beau." *Revue belge d'archéologie et d'histoire de l'art* 4, 21–57:139–65.

Waleson, Heidi. 1984. "Gian Carlo Menotti: I'm Taking Stock of What I've Done." *New York Times* 1 (June 3): H23.

Zuidam, Robert. 2002–2003. *Rage d'Amours* (opera). Available at http://www.robert zuidam.com/rage-general.htm

Political Madness:
Juan de Orduña's *Locura de amor*
as a National Allegory

Santiago Juan-Navarro

Beginning in the nineteenth century, Juana I of Castile, more generally known as "Juana the Mad," has continuously captivated the imaginations of historians, novelists, playwrights, musicians, poets, painters, and, most recently, filmmakers. Almost entirely forgotten as an historical figure three hundred years after her death, Queen Juana began to acquire near mythical status during the latter half of the 1800s. Spanish Romanticism, which persisted in its most reactionary tendencies in the fields of theater, historiography, and turn-of-the-century painting, saw in Juana not only the embodiment of stereotypical romantic motifs such as uncontrolled passion, alienation, jealousy, and necrophilia, but also, and most importantly, the personification of a purely nationalistic legend, according to which Juana's madness was seen as a consequence of the conspiracies plotted by Flemish courtiers during the period of consolidation of the Spanish Empire. The purpose of this essay is not to explore the formation of this national myth, but rather its appropriation by the dictatorship of Francisco Franco (1939–75) and specifically through the historical films produced by CIFESA, a production company that reached its peak in 1948 with the release of Juan de Orduña's film *Locura de amor* [Madness of Love].

Locura de amor debuted at a critical juncture during the ideological restructuring of Francoism. At the end of the 1940s Spain underwent a cunning political transformation designed to guarantee that Franco would remain in power for several decades. Following the violent collapse of European Fascism in 1945, the Spanish regime found itself in need of a drastic change in image. Though dominated by the Falange, the Fascist paramilitary party, together with other profascist groups, Spain adopted an authoritarian model of government characterized by the continuation of a purely figurehead monarchy, the

210

increasingly dominant presence of National-Catholicism, the promotion of *Hispanidad* (or *Spanishness*) as a cultural ideology designed to satisfy a frustrated imperial desire that was impossible to achieve politically or militarily, and, finally, the adoption of a pseudoconstitutional democracy meant to assist in garnering Spain's reintegration into the international community.

It is important to recall that in May 1945 the United Nations unanimously rejected Spain's request for admission into the world body, a decision that was ratified in February of the following year. The majority of nations participated in a diplomatic blockade of Spain, and withdrew their ambassadors from Madrid. This initial show of unity by the world community swelled the hopes of the republican liberals in exile who awaited the collapse of the Franco dictatorship under foreign pressure, as well as those of the monarchists who dreamt of the restoration of the monarchy under Juan of Bourbon. The hopes of both were shattered with the start of the Cold War in 1947. The democratic nations preferred a right-wing dictatorship they could control to a leftist regime within Moscow's sphere of influence (Tusell 1993, 129). Under the Truman Doctrine and its policy of containing communism, the United States was prompted to stabilize its relationship with the Spanish government in the 1950s. This would later open the door for Great Britain, France, and the remaining Western countries to officially recognize the Franco regime.

Franco reorganized his cabinet in July 1945 in a show of conformity to the new state of affairs in Spain. The secretary general of the Falangist Movement was eliminated from the new government, while the Catholic presence was increased. The Law Charter for Spaniards (*Fuero de los españoles*) was adopted, as was the Referendum Law, which would be applied only twice: to pass the Law of Succession in 1947 and a Spanish Constitutional Law in 1966. The Law of Succession established Spain as a monarchy as well as a representative Catholic state led by the *caudillo* Francisco Franco. Franco's cabinet would undergo a further reorganization in 1951, which, to the detriment of the Falangists, would establish the Catholic Nationalists as the architects of the foreign policy and economic program of the regime. The Concordat between the Spanish government and the Vatican was signed in 1953; two years later, Spain would achieve diplomatic normalization by entry into the United Nations.

Historical cinema produced in Spain during this period can be interpreted as an allegorical chronicle of the regime's political transformation from isolationism in 1945 to international recognition ten years later.[1] However, the subject matter chosen for the films produced during that decade was not taken from Franco's Spain or the still-recent Spanish Civil War; rather, it centered on distant historical eras such as the Middle Ages, Imperial Spain, or the Napoleonic Wars. Of course, this insistence on times past was not accidental; it was in direct response to the desire of the regime to create a tailor-made, legitimizing genealogy for itself. The absence of a defined, stable political plan meant a constant renovation of Francoist ideology based on timeless conceptual constants whose foundation lied in the long history of Spanish reactionary thought. The nation's unity revolved around the hegemony of Castile, resistance to aggression by enemies foreign and domestic, equating the terms "Spanish" and "Catholic," and glorification of the military as the institution responsible for political stability and national peace.

A production company like CIFESA was an ideal conduit for culturally channeling this ideological message. At that time CIFESA seemed to specialize in "period" films that rewrote Spain's history from a nationalist and deeply reactionary point of view; for example, in *La Princesa de los Ursinos* [Princess of the Ursinos] (1947), *Locura de amor* [Madness of Love] (1948), *Agustina de Aragón* [Agustina of Aragon] (1950), *La leona de Castilla* [The Lioness of Castile] (1951), *Alba de América* [The Dawning of America] (1951), and *Lola la Piconera* [Lola, the Coalgirl] (1951). Through the use of an anachronistic, teleological, and providential point of view, the rise of Francoism was not only explained by these films, but explicitly justified as a preordained inevitability (Fanés 1982, 165; Font 1981, 306).[2] All of these films follow the same narrative outline: two tales are superimposed, one a love story and the other a political account, which serve as background for the omnipresent theme of the death or survival of Spain (Fanés 1982, 179). In an effort to provide a greater commercial appeal to the otherwise turgid, propagandistic discourse, these films were usually enhanced with features taken from some of the most popular genres of the time: melodramas, musicals, and adventure films. Of all those films, only *Locura de amor,* based on the eponymous work by Manuel Tamayo y Baus (1829–98), enjoyed a degree of international success (Fanés 1982, 168–69).

Juan de Orduña was given the job of directing a third adaptation of Tamayo y Baus's dramatic work. The first two adaptations had been silent films, one directed by Ricardo Baños in 1909 and the second by Miguel Villar Toldán in 1926. It was Orduña himself who pushed for this third version. The filming of *Locura de amor* started on October 20, 1947, and ended February 14, 1948, although CIFESA had long been interested in the project, having applied for permission to start production on October 11, 1944. The film was going to star Amparo Rivelles or Mary Carrillo as Juana, Armando Calvo as Felipe, and Alfredo Mayo or José Sánchez as Captain Álvar. There had also been talk of Rafael Gil as director, with Rafael Durán in the starring role. The script had been written by Manuel Tamayo y Baus, grandson of the original playwright, in collaboration with Alfredo Echegaray, but it had long since been forgotten, filed away by the Valencian production company four years previous, until at last it was rescued by Orduña.

The Characters Allegory

> Spain is a woman, and a great woman. And women, like Spain, at the height of their charm and fruitfulness, are reserved only for those brave individuals who know how to conquer and inseminate them.
>
> —Ernesto Giménez Caballero

Locura de amor conforms to the allegorical norms of CIFESA's historical cinema. As with other films in that category, the story begins at a moment of crisis: the royal succession after the death of Isabel the Catholic and the insanity of her daughter Juana. This event is narrated and interpreted by means of consecutive flashbacks, which delay resolution until the closing scenes. By means of Captain Álvar de Estúñiga's backward glance through time, the origin of Juana's insanity is explained as a consequence of the jealousy provoked by Felipe, and even more so, of the conspiracies orchestrated by his Flemish advisor, Filberto de Vere.

The character of Juana would serve as the model on which the rest of the female protagonists in the historical films produced by CIFESA would be fashioned. She would therefore be the first woman inducted into that "league of famous, heroic women (queens, heroines, saints, and mothers) who were surrogates for the motherland and exemplars of a woman's responsibility to defend her home and family in times of danger, through the abnegation and self-denial of physical and spiritual love" (Monterde 1995, 236). Whereas Tamayo y Baus's play begins *in medias res* with Juana's fit of jealousy on the eve of her departure for Burgos, *Locura de amor* adopts the characteristic structure of all of Orduña's historical films, which, according to Francisco Llinás, can be best described as a double redundancy. The film starts with the ending—Juana's madness—and by means of several flashbacks, the audience is informed of something that they already knew beforehand, namely the legend, deeply rooted in popular tradition since the nineteenth century, according to which the origin of Juana's madness is to be found in the jealousy provoked by her husband.

Consequently the narration lacks any suspense whatsoever; the audience's interest is maintained through empathy with the protagonist —the queen that went mad over love—and through the film's complex plot made up of a series of unrequited loves: Juana longs for her husband, her husband longs for the Moorish woman Aldara, Aldara longs for Captain Álvar, and Álvar longs in silence for Juana.

Juana's mental instability, her madness, alludes to the biological metaphors that were so in vogue within the long tradition of "regenerationist" discourse concerning "Spain's illness." According to this train of thought, which reached its climax at the end of the nineteenth century, Spain was seen as a sick organism afflicted with a "tumor" and in need of an "iron surgeon" (Richards 1996, 150). There were multiple inconsistent attempts at identifying both the "tumor" and the "surgeon." For José Ortega y Gasset (1883–1955) the illness that plagued "invertebrate Spain" was the lack of a significant bourgeois class that could have championed modernity. Ortega also associates the "tumor" with the Catalan and Basque separatist movements, which he saw as part of the "progressive territorial fragmentation suffered by Spain over three centuries" (1972, 92). The "surgical politics" proposed by the lawyer Joaquín Costa could only be carried out by someone uniquely familiar with the anatomy of the Spanish people. His "iron surgeon" recalled the image of Plato's philosopher-king: a superior individual sent by providence to carry out the regeneration of his homeland. Franco would often be presented as that providential leader even though he did not remotely fit the profile of the cultured, anti-oligarchic politician that Costa envisioned as his messianic hero.

Other proposed remedies for this diagnosis were equally as radical and Franco's political machine never hesitated in appropriating them. They varied from the isolationism proposed by Ángel Ganivet (1865–98) to avoid "infection" from the "virus" of foreign ideas (Blinkhorn 1979, 16–68; Richards 1996, 153–54) to the establishment of a fascist dictatorship by means of a military coup (Primo de Rivera 1930 and 1936). Even though these pseudopositivistic diagnoses were formulated from very different, if not opposed, ideological stances, they were all fair game for the impassioned Francoist rhetoric of legitimation. As far as Franco was concerned the diagnosis was accurate: Spain suffered from an illness spawned by separatism, Masonic conspiracies, international communism, secularization, and political chaos and he was destined to be that iron surgeon who had been called upon to correct the situation. In the meantime, Spain should isolate itself from "negative influences" and remain under the protection of the church and the army, in much the same way as Juana is portrayed during her confinement in Tordesillas in the opening moments of Orduña's film.

While the four flashbacks in *Locura de amor* narrate the events that triggered the queen's madness, the opening image, a painting by Francisco Pradilla, acts as an iconic prolepsis for the film's final moments: it ends with a *tableau vivant* of the same initial painting. As a result of this circular structure, in which the beginning mimics the closing and the story is told backward, the audience finds itself trapped in a temporal loop where history seems to have come to a standstill. Furthermore the allegorical subtext leads the spectator not so much to the origins of the Spanish Empire, but rather to a mystified version as seen from the lens of late Romanticism or, more accurately, the historical present of the film's production, namely the final years of the autarchy. *Locura de amor* ensnares the audience in a circular, recurrent version of history formulated during a period that was devoid of any dialectical counterpoint, and therefore, of any possibility for change (Seguin 1997, 232).

Within this atemporal fantasy beyond history (or historical fantasy lacking any temporal progression), Orduña presents us with a moral and political allegory: Spain has been isolated by the machinations of foreign powers as well as its overpowering, yet repressed, desire for international validation. Every character in this allegory is implicitly associated with aspects of the ideology that was predominant at the time the film was produced. Juana personifies the motherland "justly" driven mad by the infidelity of a king who has been manipulated by foreign agents intending to take power. The way in which the film portrays Felipe the Beautiful is not so different from the farcical perception Franco had of Juan of Bourbon. The depiction of young Carlos, on the other hand, reflects the hope that the Franco regime placed on Juan Carlos, son of the "legitimate" heir to the throne.

In *Locura de amor* Juana's plight is presented as a legitimizing precedent for the paranoid rhetoric of Francoism. During that time the regime found itself besieged by hostile forces that it believed misunderstood what it conceived of as a crusade to create a New Spain. The identity of that New Spain was to undergo numerous changes based on international circumstances and the tension between the political factions that supported the 1936 coup d'état, although its historical constants were to be found almost exclusively in the premodern past (Cano Ballesta 1994, 45–53). After the end of World War II, Franco and his right-hand man on ideological matters, Admiral Carrero Blanco, saw the restoration of a "figurehead monarchy" as the life preserver that would allow Franco to remain in power indefinitely. Juana's madness conveys the regime's own schizophrenia, which simultaneously desired and despised official recognition from the Western democracies, while paradoxically attempting to modernize by returning incessantly to the age of the Catholic Monarchs for validation, which constituted the utopian ideal for their "New" Spain.

If they wanted the new regime to survive, then the restoration of a full monarchy was impossible because it would inherently exclude the military strongman Franco from power. The only feasible option was the implementation of a pseudomonarchy that would be loyal to the new institutional order that had emerged after the Spanish Civil War, destined to regain power only after the death of the dictator. In *Locura de amor,* the elaborate way in which this message is conveyed and justified is evident upon analysis of the characterization of the two individuals that personify the monarchy in the film: Felipe the Beautiful and Carlos V.

Queen Juana embodies the besieged motherland and Captain Álvar de Estúñiga pertains to an extended lineage of great captains that Franco himself admired and with whom he deeply identified. It is Captain Álvar himself who recounts the story of Juana to young Carlos, the future king and protector of the "eternal values" that Captain Álvar defends. In the film, Álvar maintains a strange love-hate relationship with the Moorish woman Aldara, which closely resembles the relationship maintained by the Franco dictatorship and the Arab world for years. Although Captain Álvar is secretly in love with the queen, he knows that theirs is an impossible relationship, just as it was impossible in Franco's lifetime to establish a dynastic succession without destroying the ideological framework of Francoism, in which the institutional legitimation of the dictatorship within the history of Spanish traditionalism was equally impossible. Hence the "soft" or weak personality of Carlos, whose naiveté in the film borders on idiocy. The future emperor is consistently portrayed in accordance with the ideological characterization of Juan of Bourbon's son at the hands of the Franco dictatorship. As Franco's testament makes clear, Juan Carlos represented the continuation of the New Spain after the death of the dictator for the ideologues of the regime, a belief they maintained from the end of the 1940s until Franco's death in 1975.

In Orduña's film the image presented is that of a supervised monarchy, which relies on the unwavering support of a loyal and faithful admiral. The superimposition of Carrero Blanco onto the character of the admiral in *Locura de amor* becomes obvious through the words placed in his mouth and by his role as the main guarantor, along with Captain Álvar, of the Eternal Spain that Francoism purported to defend. As in all allegories the plot is completely Manichean. The forces of good are led by Álvar and the admiral who are faced with the task of foiling the evil plan of the foreign enemy, the satanic Filberto de Vere, together with his domestic allies, the corrupt Don Juan Manuel and the Marquis de Villena, in a plot that brings to mind "the eternal Spanish response with those foreigners who try to tamper with their independence" (Preston 1994, 563).

A FIGUREHEAD MONARCHY

The most well educated Kings were instructed with rigorous discipline alongside erudite men who were completely separated from worldly concerns. They thought only about their service to God, the good of their Country and the opinion that History would hold of the Prince.
—Francisco Franco
(Response to a letter from Juan of Bourbon)

In both its form and content Orduña's film dramatizes in allegorical fashion the ideological project of Franco's New Spain. Structurally the narrative point of view is conveyed through the four flashbacks, which allow Captain Álvar to give an up-to-date evaluation on the state of the kingdom to a young and weak monarch who seeks information and guidance. However, the events that are narrated lie beyond the character's limited scope and so, as with other historical CIFESA films, Orduña once again adopts an omniscient point of view. Consequently many of the events that appear throughout the four flashbacks undermine the narrative's credibility, since the captain could not have been aware of them. But if one chooses to see Álvar's point of view as standing in for the regime's perspective, then the explanation for this lack of discursive coherence becomes evident. Captain Álvar embodies the values that Franco adopted as the guiding principles for his life's work: duty and sacrifice. At all times Captain Álvar shows his absolute loyalty to the queen, to the point of engaging in fights over her, first with Felipe, and later on with the conspirator de Vere. He tolerates Juana's fits of madness, including her threat to kill him during one of her jealous rages. The captain's tense relationship with Aldara, downplayed in the film when compared to the original Tamayo y Baus play, is especially interesting when analyzed in the context of the ambiguous relationship that the Franco dictatorship maintained with the Arab world throughout its existence.[3] Their relationship reaches its climax in the farewell scene between the two characters. After having saved the captain's life in a rather peculiar way, Aldara (played by an inexpressive Sara Montiel) and Álvar seal a pact of eternal friendship. After listening to the captain's words of gratitude, Aldara replies, "When I return to Africa I will also say: My eyes greet this morning's light because Álvar, the greatest captain of Christendom, looks toward the East and thinks of me."

When seen in the context of Orientalist thought, so in vogue at the end of the nineteenth century, the words of the Moorish woman become all the more meaningful: the colonial subject lacks any identity apart from its reflection in the imagination of the mother country (Rivière Gómez 2000, 131). This romanticized view of the subaltern Other is closely associated, as in the most typical displays of Orientalist thinking, with its origins in the imperial past (the subject matter of the film) as well as in its neocolonial present (the allegoric subtext of the film). What makes this message even more interesting is that it is at precisely the height of Spain's imperialistic rhetoric that it loses its last remaining colonies in Africa. It is ironic that Franco felt obligated to emancipate these final colonies of the old empire—Guinea, the protectorate of Morocco, and Sidi Ifni—during his tenure. Additionally it is ironic that the dictator's final days coincided with the Green March that would put an end to Spanish hegemony in the Western Sahara (Fleming 1980, 133–49). Neocolonialist sentiment, therefore, had to limit its activities to the rhetoric of official speeches and the magic of cinema where it would appear through the sentimental filter of nostalgia. Films such as ¡A mí la legión! [Follow the Legion!] (1942), La canción de Aixa [Aixa's Song] (1938), and La llamada de África [The Call of Africa] (1952) are part of a genuine tradition of films centered on Africa that are characterized by a certain "desert mystic" (Zumalde Arregi 1997, 311) inspired by French and Italian colonial cinema.

Captain Álvar de Estúñiga plays a pivotal role in transmitting the film's ideological message. His point of view guides the narrative from beginning to end, and therefore provides a focal point for the propaganda apparatus that underlies the plot. On occasion, the character's access to information is so unbelievable that it borders on the ridiculous: for example, that a lowly captain would be permitted to counsel two monarchs, Felipe and then Carlos; that his wardrobe would be the most sumptuous of all, contrasting grotesquely at times with the simple garments of the emperor who serves as his main interlocutor; or that on his deathbed, Felipe would entrust Don Álvar with the protection of the queen (i.e., the "motherland"). The boundless sublimation that the character undergoes together with his explicit association with military values confirms the projection of Franco's image onto the character of Captain Álvar the entire time. What makes this excessive focus on Captain Álvar even more absurd, something that was lacking in the original play, is that it reveals the difficult relationship that Franco had with the monarchy. Franco's professed devotion to Alfonso XIII and his paternal-filial relationship with the prince Juan Carlos were well known. However, Franco was also aware of the illegitimate and irregular nature of his monopoly on power within the traditions of the Spanish monarchy, a fact that was made apparent by his tense relationship with Juan of Bourbon. The unfulfilled love of Álvar for Queen Juana can be interpreted as an expression of Franco's selfconscious awareness of his own political illegitimacy. His love should be repressed because he knows it to be an impossible. Though he cannot possess Spain, he can defend her from her enemies.

The portrayal of Felipe mirrors the stereotypical image of Juan of Bourbon held by Franco for many years. To Franco and his followers, especially Admiral Carrero Blanco, the potential heir to the Spanish throne was a misguided playboy who had been educated abroad and manipulated by ambitious advisers working for an imagined international conspiracy of Masonic and communist bent (Preston 1994, 568, 579). So it is not surprising that in *Locura de amor* the death of Felipe is presented as an almost divine punishment that allows for the pacification of the country: "It was the will of God. With his death the partisanship in Castile came to an end. Together, the nobility and the common people prayed, alongside your mother, for the king." There is an interesting casuistic inversion of events in the historical process recreated by the film. The continuity of the monarchy is assured by Carlos V, but only after having passed through the hands of a soldier like Álvar who is presented as instrumental in the restoration of nationalist values.

In short, Álvar is a representative of that soldierly class that Francoist cinema highlighted in their productions "in order to remind us that there are ways other than intrigue, slander and corruption to get ahead in the world" (Fanés 1982, 179). But one must not forget that his post as mentor to royalty implies his status as mentor to the audience itself, which, as in the rest of the historical films by CIFESA, is ultimately the final interlocutor of the regime's ideological discourse. As Félix Fanés points out, CIFESA's historical films "maintain an authoritarian, admonishing relationship with the audience" (1982, 179). Álvar's off-camera narration at several points in the film further calls attention to this exemplary element presented through the four flashbacks around which the plot is organized.

Within this story line, the admiral serves as another heroic character with a similar function to that of Captain Álvar as the queen's most faithful servant. During the period when *Locura de amor* was being filmed another admiral, Carrero Blanco, had already taken over the reins of Franco's ideological machine. Carrero served as undersecretary to the president for thirty-two years.[4] His post consisted of being the dictator's main policy advisor, which in practice transformed Carrero into Franco's political alter ego and the *éminence grise* of the dictatorship (Fernández 1984, 8). Generally speaking, he was the most influential person in the regime and the only one to survive its many structural changes. The secret to his political longevity has been ascribed to the fact that he shared Franco's basic values: conservatism, nationalism, authoritarianism, and Catholicism. Also, his modesty and discretion allowed him to remain in the background so as not to overshadow the dictator (Tusell 1993, 168). However, his survival (until his death in a terrorist attack in 1973) was probably due to the fact that Carrero himself had been the real advocate of many of the changes that the Franco dictatorship underwent. More specifically he was the main architect of the authoritarian figurehead monarchy that ultimately displaced the other political alternatives promoted by various governing factions within the regime.

The most overtly political speeches in Orduña's film are reserved for the admiral. On two occasions the passionate reaction of the character to the political crisis of the kingdom leads him to call for a civil war. In response to the counsel of the Castilian nobles, he exclaims: "How can we help the Queen? Conspiring in her favor the way the King's followers conspire!" A frightened noble then shouts, "That would be cause enough for a civil war!" The admiral then paraphrases the legitimizing discourse of Franco's "Crusade" in a speech that is presented as a prophetic foreshadowing of the 1936 coup: "Even though we want to prevent it, it will happen any day now; the people are willing to take their rights by force. Even if war breaks out, we have to act with vigor!" A short time later, during a climactic scene when the court meets at the Cathedral in Burgos, the admiral repeats the same conspiratorial message. When Filberto de Vere invites the king to take the throne, the admiral stops him by saying that no foreigner should give orders in Castile. De Vere reminds him that the majority of the nobles support his appointment, but the admiral warns him that in Andalusia people have already revolted in support of Queen Juana and cautions him once again that "the wickedness or ambition of a few could bring about a civil war!"

Carrero Blanco, just as the admiral in Orduña's film, personified the fundamentalist reactionary thinking of the Franco regime, obsessed with safeguarding traditional values and opposing the perceived infiltration of foreign liberalism, which it associated with licentiousness, atheism, materialism, and freemasonry (Villacañas Berlanga 2004, 188, 195). In Orduña's film the admiral is portrayed as a champion of essential patriotic values and, together with Captain Álvar, provides the only check on the ambitions of the Flemish courtiers. Although there is no proof that Carrero participated directly in Orduña's film project, such a relationship would not be surprising, since the undersecretary to the president was a close personal friend of the chairman of CIFESA, Vincente Casanova, and had a profound interest in history and in revisionist interpretations of it. Furthermore Carrero aided Sánchez Bella in the promotion of *Alba de América* (1951), the film that put an end to the series of historical "megaproductions" made by CIFESA.

THE INTERNATIONAL MASONIC CONSPIRACY AND DOMESTIC ENEMIES

> History offers us numerous examples of conspiracies that . . . courtiers tended to endorse to serve their own interests in order to lead the Prince astray.
> —Francisco Franco
> (responding to a letter from Juan of Bourbon)

The international isolation that Franco's regime was subjected to after World War II affected its political propaganda in two ways. On the one hand, it launched a campaign for domestic consumption that fashioned an image of Spain victimized by dark forces plotting against her. On the other hand, the government was desperately looking for a means of gaining acceptance abroad that would provide it with a façade of normality and lead to the end of the diplomatic blockade. Spanish cinema, which rarely penetrated external markets, reflected the domestic side of this dual propaganda effort. The countries with which Franco hoped to normalize relations—an essential step if he was to remain in power—were portrayed on the screen as the perpetrators of the fictitious international conspiracy that the regime believed existed. Therefore the daring spirit of the Spanish resistance against French occupation in the nineteenth century or the defense of the Alcázar in Toledo during the Spanish Civil War, were common subjects for the cinematographic productions of the period. What is interesting about this case is that the autarchical rhetoric, even as it disappeared from popular culture, lasted well beyond the years of the autarchy (1945–51), and would reappear in political speeches every time there was a national crisis. A few weeks before his death, in his last public appearance at the Plaza de Oriente (October 1, 1975), Franco continued to reference these imagined plots in order to discredit not only the liberal democracies, but even the Vatican, because they had recently denounced the latest acts of repression on the part of the dictatorship (Ferrer Benimeli 2000, 246).

Locura de amor provided a new dramatic version of the timeless crusade that Francoism believed itself to be waging. In opposition to the forces of good personified by Captain Álvar and the admiral, the sinister character of Filberto de Vere, the Flemish advisor to the king whose sole motivation is an unbounded desire for power, manipulates Felipe and the court against Juana and the Castilian nobles. In the film de Vere personifies the political intrigues that Franco and his followers so despised. He also provides a visual paradigm of the ambitious foreigner and usurper who appears physically in an almost diabolical pose. The composition of the shots tends to emphasize the evil nature of the character. The typical frame for scenes of intrigue utilize mid-range shots in which the villain appears behind the other characters, whispering deceitful things in their ears. In some instances the effect is comical, for example, in the scenes with the childlike and perplexed Felipe, who de Vere goads into giving free rein to his lust. The attempt at seriousness on the part of the director—the arrangement of the characters recalls the portrayal of the temptations of Christ or the kiss of Judas in Christian iconography—is often undermined by the histrionic gesturing of Fernando Rey in the role of Felipe the Beautiful, who in turn is portrayed as an absurd caricature of the scatterbrained womanizer that Franco and his court favorites associated with the figure of Juan of Bourbon. The film insists upon establishing an insurmountable dichotomy between the lust of the Flemish and the austere chastity of the Castilians. At the beginning of the film, the court at Flanders, and in particular the scene of Felipe's "hunting" retreat, is presented as nothing more than a brothel, in contrast with the monastic seriousness of the Castilian court. The almost complete absence of any sensuality in what is supposedly a love story is noteworthy. Any trace of eroticism is confined to the representatives of the anti-Spanish faction: the Flemish who embody decadent Europe, and Aldara, who personifies the last remnants of Moorish Spain on the eve of its definitive expulsion from the peninsula.

The fact that the death of the Machiavellian de Vere occurs at the hands of the Moorish princess in a surprising turn of events, and that his death serves, at the same time, to save the life of Captain Álvar, offers an allegoric interpretation that cannot be overlooked. This sequence is especially significant as it constitutes a drastic deviation from the original play by Tamayo y Baus, in which the de Vere character is not assassinated, but slowly recedes from the action until he completely disappears from the text, and Aldara does not return to "her homeland of Africa," but ends up joining a convent instead. The salvation of Captain Álvar, the character meant to embody the *Caudillo* in the film, and in particular the farewell scene between him and Aldara, exemplifies the paradoxical relationship of the regime with the East and the stereotypical orientalist view of the "Moor" within the political imagery of Francoism.

It is well known that relations with the Arab world formed a key part of the "substitution politics" employed by Franco during the diplomatic blockade imposed on his government in 1945. As María Dolores Algora Weber points out, "the Arab world helped to fill the void that the Western world created for Spain" (1995, 303). For the League of Arab States it was also important that Spain stabilize its diplomatic relations with the West in order to consolidate the new territorial order that had emerged as a result of the decolonization process in the Middle East and, more specifically, the end of British rule in Palestine. The symbiotic relationship between Spain and the Arab states is dramatized in *Locura de amor* through the ambiguous relationship between Álvar and Aldara. It is a relationship that culminates with a pact of eternal friendship consummated over the recent corpse of a corrupt Europe personified by Filberto de Vere.

In Orduña's film the importance of de Vere is exaggerated to the point where any connection to the original text that served as its inspiration is almost completely lost. In the play by Tamayo y Baus, the schemes of the Flemish courtier constitute but one of the many factors that trigger Juana's madness. But in *Locura de amor*, de Vere is the main culprit behind all the palace intrigues until the very moment of Juana's death. He is the one who encourages and sometimes arranges Felipe's love affairs; he urges him into ever more lascivious acts by questioning his virility. It is de Vere who bribes and blackmails the Castilian nobility into taking power away from Juana and acknowledging Felipe as the only monarch. It is he who organizes the evil plot around Aldara's letter, a plot that in the eyes of the court seals a general consensus concerning the queen's madness. In short, de Vere is the personification of the vague international conspiracy of which Francoism thought itself the victim, leading it to develop a xenophobic streak that bordered on paranoia.

Filberto de Vere's allies in the Castilian Court are the Marquis de Villena and Don Juan Manuel. Their participation in the Flemish conspiracy in exchange for privileges makes them perfect representatives of those courtiers to whom Franco alludes in the epigraph that opens the present section of this article. The same actors that play these two characters also portray the anti-Spanish factions in other historical films by Orduña. Manuel Luna (Don Juan Manuel) is the wicked Jew, Isaac, in *Alba de América,* the epitome of the anti-Semitism that characterized the Franco dictatorship. In *La Leona de Castilla* he plays Manrique, a traitor who infiltrates the comuneros (individuals who banded together to defend their rights against the arbitrary encroachment of the Spanish monarchy in the 1520s) and sexually assaults the virtuous Doña María de Pacheco, who personifies the motherland in the film. Eduardo Fajardo (Marquis de Villena) plays Gastón in *Alba de América,* the archetypical lust-filled, scheming Frenchman who conspires to hand Columbus's enterprise in the West Indies over to the French kings. In *La Leona de Castilla* he plays another traitor, the cynical Tovar, who infiltrates the Comuneros and promises to undermine the unity of the Castilian nobles. Not only do the same allegorical archetypes and situations repeat themselves from film to film, but even in the manner in which the scenes are staged become repetitive. All of this strengthens the allegoric sub-text, allowing the audience to immediately recognize the same actors in their recurring roles within an identical plot: Spain's eternal fight against anti-Spanish forces. As a result, the dual redundancy that Llinás emphasizes becomes even more evident. The audience, already familiar with the events portrayed in the film, is presented with a story line in which the ending is revealed at the beginning of the film through various prolepses, thereby creating a visual loop between the first and last frames, accompanied by an off-camera narrator that acts as an omniscient guide throughout the story. The flashbacks that narrate the background events of the story are used to emphasize one aspect or another of the plot, whose subtext is virtually identical in all the historical films produced by CIFESA. By utilizing the same actors in similar roles (Aurora Bautista and Amparo Rivelles as personifications of the motherland and Manuel Luna and Eduardo Fajardo embodying the anti-Spanish faction) favors the audience's identification with or rejection of the characters and the forces they represent. This formula could not last forever, and certainly due to its own redundancy, it was quickly exhausted. After the economic fiascos of *La Leona de Castilla* and *Alba de América* in 1951, CIFESA abandoned the historical genre and so began the decline of the production company from Valencia.

CONCLUSION: THE MADNESS OF A REGIME

Locura de amor was produced at a time when CIFESA was the official promoter of the Franco dictatorship and in a year (1948) when Franco's regime saw the restoration of a figurehead monarchy (the

Law of Succession had passed the year before) as a solution to the problems of domestic stability and international recognition. In Juan de Orduña's film the kings, Felipe and Carlos, are invariably depicted as weak dignitaries who require the protection and tutelage of soldiers with political experience. Queen Juana stands opposed to these puppetlike characters as a figure who rises above political matters, while demonstrating the archetypal characteristics of the heroic Spanish women depicted in CIFESA's historical cinema. Juana is the personification of the motherland in danger, driven mad by the conspiracies of foreign powers; her personal sacrifice will make Spain's salvation possible.

As with all historical fiction, especially that created for propaganda use, Juan de Orduña's film reveals more about the time of the film's production than the historical period to which it alludes. Historical cinema during Francoism fulfilled the need for iconographic legitimation and political propaganda of a regime imposed by force. CIFESA's culminating period (1945–51) coincided with a time of political crisis. Franco had to reorient his governing philosophy in a way that would progressively distance itself from the fascist ideology that he adopted immediately following the civil war (1939–45), as a means of acquiring the international recognition he so desired and that had been systematically denied to him by the world community up until that point.

As in all of the historical films produced by CIFESA, *Locura de amor* presents the coded allegorical worldview of Francoism, according to which Spain finds itself besieged by foreign powers and is compelled to recover its true identity from its sixteenth-century imperial past. Juan de Orduña's film portrays more than a madness of love; it reveals the madness of a regime that saw cinema as an ideal instrument for the legitimation of its imagined "New Spain" and the perfect vehicle for the exaltation of nationalist sentiment by means of allegorical celebrations of its own apotheosis.

NOTES

1. The allegorical dimension of Spanish cinema during these years can be explained by its role as the ideal transmitter of the government's ideology. As Domènic Font points out, during the autarchy, cinema, "along with education," represented "a very systematic, ideological, Francoist design" (1981, 293). Although many critics have mentioned this aspect of Spanish cinema in passing (Gubern 1990, 58; Heredero 1993, 171; Fanés 1982, 181; Sánchez Biosca 1989, 77), until now no one has produced a monographic study on the topic, which from our point of view is an essential element in understanding cinema during the autarchy.

2. The nature of CIFESA as an organ for state propaganda is beyond doubt. In its mission statement, the promoters of the company expressed their will "to continue the economic policy guidelines that inspired the Franco dictatorship" (Font 1976, 107). In 1942, the president of the company, Vincente Casanova, received the Cross of Military Valor from the minister of war himself "in recognition of his unselfish devotion to collaboration between the State and the cinematographic industry in promoting propaganda" (Font 1976, 107). Four years later (and two years before the production of *Locura de amor*), Casanova was elected to the Union's Executive Council and as a representative of the film production industry in Spain's Parliament.

3. Franco rose up through the military ranks during the African wars and his personal guards were referred to as his Moorish guard until the time of his death. Never in Spain's modern history had relations with the Arab world been so good. The closeness of this relationship was due in large part to the radical anti-Zionism of Francoism, as well as to the many political and cultural similarities between the two. Shannon Fleming points out that, "among the Arab states Franco recognized like minds: conservative, traditional monarchical regimes that opposed the 'godless' teachings of communism and the rootless secularism of Western liberalism" (1980, 133).

4. Javier Tusell points out that "the influence of the Undersecretary to the President was much greater than befitted his administrative post. . . . He played a decisive role in the formation of Franco's attitudes regarding certain political questions, and those attitudes turned out to be very important for the survival of the regime during its early years" (1993, 177). To a large extent Carrero was responsible for the marginalization of the Falange after 1941, and for the establishment of the regime within the structure of an authoritarian monarchy.

WORKS CITED

Algora Weber, María Dolores. 1995. *Las relaciones hispano-árabes durante el régimen de Franco: La ruptura del aislamiento internacional (1946–1950)*. Madrid: Ministerio de Asuntos Exteriores.

Blinkhorn, Martin. 1979. *Carlismo y contrarrevolución en España, 1931–1939*. Barcelona: Crítica.

Cano Ballesta, Juan. 1994. *Las estrategias de la imaginación: utopías literarias y retórica política bajo el franquismo*. Madrid: Siglo XXI.

Fanés, Félix. 1982. *CIFESA, la antorcha de los éxitos*. Valencia: Institución Alfonso el Magnánimo.

Fernández, Carlos. 1984. *El almirante Carrero*. Barcelona: Plaza & Janés.

Ferrer Benimeli, José A. 2000. "Franco y la masonería." In *España bajo el franquismo*, edited by Josep Fontana, 246–68. Barcelona: Crítica.

Fleming, Shannon. 1980. "Spain in the World: North Africa and the Middle East." In *Spain in the Twentieth-Century World: Essays on Spanish Diplomacy, 1898–1978*, edited by James W. Cortada, 121–54. Westport: Greenwood Press.

Font, Domènec. 1976. *Del azul al verde: el cine español durante el franquismo*. Barcelona: Avance.

———. 1981. "El cine español durante la autarquía." In *Arte del franquismo*, edited by Antonio Bonet Correa, 291–313. Madrid: Cátedra.

Gubern, Roman. 1990. "La decadencia de CIFESA." *Archivos de la Filmoteca* 4:58–65.

Heredero, Carlos. 1993. *Las huellas secretas del tiempo: Cine español 1951–1961*. Madrid: Filmoteca Española.

Llinás, Francisco. 1998. "Redundancy and Passion: Juan de Orduña and CIFESA." In *Modes of Representation in Spanish Cinema*, edited by Jenaro Talens and Santos Zunzunegui, 104–12. Minneapolis: University of Minnesota Press.

Ortega y Gasset, José. 1972. *La España invertebrada*. Madrid: Espasa-Calpe.

Monterde, José Enrique. 1995. "El cine de la autarquía (1935–1950)." In *Historia del cine español*, edited by Roman Gubern et al., 181–238. Madrid: Cátedra.

Palacios, Jesús. 1996. *Los papeles secretos de Franco: de las relaciones con Juan Carlos y Don Juan al protagonismo del Opus*. Madrid: Temas de Hoy.

Preston, Paul. *Franco*. 1994. New York: Harper Collins.

Primo de Rivera, José Antonio. 1930. "España: la lanzadera duerme en el telar." *Unión Monárquica* 102 (December 15).

———. "Justificación de la violencia." 1936. *No importa* 2 (June 6).

Richards, Michael. 1996. "Constructing the Nationalist State: Self-Sufficiency and Regeneration in the Early Franco Years." In *Nationalism, and the Nation in the Iberian Peninsula: Competing and Conflicting Identities*, edited by Clare Mar-Molinero and Angel Smith, 149–67. Oxford: Berg.

Rivière Gómez, Aurora. 2000. *Orientalismo y nacionalismo español*. Madrid: Instituto Antonio de Lebrija.

Sánchez Biosca, Vicente. 1989. "Fotografía y puesta en escena en el film español de los años 1940–50." In *Directores de fotografía del cine español*, edited by Francisco Llinás, 56–91. Madrid: Filmoteca Española.

Seguin, Jean-Claude. 1997. *"Locura de amor."* In *Antología crítica del cine español*, edited by Julio Pérez Perucha, 230–32. Madrid: Cátedra.

Tusell, Javier. 1993. *Carrero: La eminencia gris del régimen de Franco*. Madrid: Ediciones Temas de Hoy.

Villacañas Berlanga, José Luis. 2004. "Ortodoxia católica y derecho histórico en el origen del pensamiento reaccionario español." *Journal of Spanish Cultural Studies* 5.2:187–99.

Zumalde Arregi, Imanol. 1997. *"La llamada de África."* In *Antología crítica del cine español*, edited by Julio Pérez Perucha, 309–11. Madrid: Cátedra.

Woman, Nation, and Desire in Juan de Orduña's *Locura de amor* and Vicente Aranda's *Juana la Loca*

María Asunción Gómez

MANUEL TAMAYO Y BAUS (1829–98) IS CONSIDERED BY SOME CRITICS THE best Spanish playwright of the nineteenth century. His historical drama *La locura de amor* [The Madness of Love] premiered in Madrid in 1855 and soon became his best known work and a box office success whose far-reaching repercussion in time and space is due, in great part, to its filmic adaptations: Ricard de Baños and Albert Marro's *La locura de amor* (1909), Juan de Orduña's *Locura de amor* (1948), and Vicente Aranda's *Juana la Loca* [Juana the Mad] (2002). From these three adaptations, only Orduña's and Aranda's have reached wide audiences. Both film-makers appropriate Tamayo y Baus's appealing plot of politics, passion, and jealousy to their own ends. While Orduña transforms Tamayo y Baus's work into a piece of conservative political propaganda, Aranda focuses overtly on the politics of desire and female sexuality. This chapter explores these two filmic representations of Juana of Castile and other female characters (Aldara and Aixa) both during Francoism and at the dawn of the twenty-first century.

HISTORICAL-HISTRIONIC MELODRAMA

Exacerbated feelings and excessive, irresistible passion that turns the loved one into something irreplaceable were commonplace in nineteenth-century Romanticism, and at first sight Tamayo y Baus endeavors to faithfully reproduce these elements with accuracy. In Orduña's film adaptation, the representation of the mad queen's crazy love remains intact. However, the director adds an allegoric framework with unmistakable political reverberations. Juana is presented as the embodiment of the motherland, harassed and driven mad by foreigners who, in their boundless ambition, employ intrigue and deception and put the unity of Spain in danger (Seguin 1997; Juan-Navarro 2005). Several critics have pointed out the allegorical character of a good portion of the Francoist historical cinema produced during the 1940s and 50s (Gubern 1990, 58; Heredero 1993, 171; Fanés 1982, 181; Sánchez Biosca 1989, 77). The subtext in *Locura de amor* is the autarchical discourse of Francoist dictatorship: "Here, the sacrificial task of unifying the empire, represented by the daughter of Isabela the Catholic, is compared to the Machiavellian and foreign-favoring (both terms used synonymously in many instances) character of the Flemish Court" (Company 1997, 12). Francoism always defended a kind of antiliberal, extreme Catholic nationalism founded on the base of a strongly centralized government. In order to legitimize its fabricated country, Francoist rhetoric frequently returned to the time of the Catholic Monarchs, a crucial moment for Spain in her formation as a nation state. Juana of Castile lived during a time characterized by events that would play a decisive role in the construction of a centralized government and the emergence of a nationalist spirit. The end of the reconquest, the expulsion of the Jews and the Counter-Reformation that separated Spain from the rest of Europe were seen as just the prehistory to the New State, whose ideology began to be defined at the end of the 1940s.

One of the typical devices of nationalistic discourse was to refer back to remote time periods and to transform them with the manipulative lens of ideology. Thus, national identity was formulated in terms of a cultural and political continuity (Spencer and Wollmann 2002, 84). The reformulation of the past as justification of the present calls to mind the dynamics of the origins of myths, just as Roland Barthes describes them: "To go from history to nature, myth undertakes its own economy: it manages to abolish the complexity of human acts, it awards them the simplicity of essentialism, omits dialectics, suppresses anything that is not obvious and creates a world without contradictions since it lacks profundity" (1957, 239). The defense of "destiny's unity in the universal" (Primo de Rivera 1974, 564) was something more than an entelechy that the catechism of the Falange, Spain's paramilitary Fascist party, used in order to define Spain. Furthermore it represented the perfect explanation for the naturalizing power of the myth. Myth purifies things, "it brings them back to innocence, bases them on nature and eternity and grants them clarity not from explanation but rather from verification" (Barthes 1957, 239).

Through its culturally propagandistic political machine, Francoism came to encapsulate an ideology that more than just simple, it could be labeled "simplistic." However, the regime conferred on that ideology an eternal and essential value. Historical cinema played a very important role in constructing this essentialism of the nationalist discourse whose culturally constructed nature was to be concealed at all costs.[1] Among the historical films produced by CIFESA, the ones directed by Juan de Orduña particularly stand out: *Locura de amor* (1948), *Agustina de Aragón* [Agustina from Aragon] (1950), *La leona de Castilla* [The Lioness from Castile] (1951), and *Alba de América* [The Dawning of America] (1951). These films comply with other CIFESA productions not only in their propagandistic bias, but also in the use of strong female characters. The first of these was the only one that achieved resounding success and led to what was known as CIFESA's historical cycle.[2] Orduña achieved such a success by intertwining political propaganda with a story of passionate love, jealousy, and madness. In Orduña's *Locura de amor* the nationalistic discourse is immersed in an economy of desire in which nation, race, and gender play a crucial role.

The complicated plot of Orduña's movie reflects the strong melodramatic component that brings together, and sometimes displaces, the political message. Captain Álvar de Estúñiga recounts Queen Juana's story at the request of Emperor Carlos V, who arrives at Tordesillas to visit his mother, by then victim of absolute dementia. This meeting between mother and son emphasizes the allegoric interpretation: the young emperor shows a mix of fear and distrust upon entering Juana's chambers and Juana does not appear to recognize her son. Carlos I of Spain and V of Germany is a "stranger" to his mother and a "foreigner" to his people. Neither his mother nor Spain recognizes a king that, like his father, was born abroad and was raised by Flemish advisors. This initial repudiation is also extended to his companions. When Juana sees the Golden Fleece on De Chievres's chest, she remembers the betrayal she was a victim of in her youth and she feels threatened. What follows is a flashback that takes us back to Juana's early years in Flanders and Felipe's unfaithfulness in the Flemish court, an unfaithfulness that continues in Castile with a Moorish princess, Aldara. Aldara is in love with Captain Álvar, who at the same time secretly loves Juana. In this complicated network of stories of unrequited love one can observe a clear contrast between the Castilians (Juana, Álvar, and the admiral) and the Flemish (Felipe and his advisor Filberto de Vere). The Castilians personify the defense of Spain as well as the affirmation of a series of traditional values in which one finds the true essence of Spanishness. The latter characters embody the danger that all foreigners represented to Spain. Between these two irreconcilable factions is the character of Aldara, who plays a role as ambiguous as the one the Arab World played during the Franco dictatorship. Aldara goes so far as to threaten to kill the queen, yet, in the end, she saves Captain Álvar's life.

In turn Captain Álvar evokes the image of a loyal, disciplined soldier. As in the rest of CIFESA's historical films, this is a new depiction of Franco as the "hero-leader that represents the driving force of History and the subject of paternalistic relationships with the people" (Monterde 1995, 235). Captain Álvar's loyalty to Spain, personified by Juana, is reaffirmed by his platonic, pure, and impossible love. Unlike the lasciviousness that Felipe exhibits, only worried about satisfying his carnal desires despite the betrayal that those desires entail at a personal and political level, the ascetic Álvar (half monk and half soldier) sacrifices his love for his patriotic duty and suffers in silence.

Juana, the motherland, is virginal yet desirable and desired. This paradoxical combination of purity and restrained eroticism can be seen in the scenes in which she appears with Captain Álvar. In Juana's relationship with her husband Felipe, on the other hand, histrionics overshadow eroticism. The representation of the motherland should remain magnified and Orduña found the best way to accomplish this was by means of the grandiloquent and overboard performance of Aurora Bautista, which corresponded to an aesthetic that could be classified as neoexpressionist. Excessiveness affected everything in *Locura de amor,* and as Company very skillfully points out, what was supposed to be an inspirational embodiment of Spain, dangerously borders on the ridiculous:

> In *Locura de amor,* starring Aurora Bautista in 1948, Orduña's staging not only submitted to the dramatic game of the actress but also openly emphasized all the excessive gestural dimensions of her movements and the dramatic projection of her voice. So before the eyes of bewildered viewers, moments of turmoil and rage unfold when Juana's character fluctuates between the sublime and the ridiculous; for example, when Juana prefers madness to indifference. Or when she enters the cathedral in Burgos, followed by traveling royalty, and a courtier announces her titles and honors. As well as in the end when Juana demands silence so that no one disturbs the deep sleep of death that the King just gave in to. (1997, 5)

Furthermore Company adds that in this film both the editing and the composition served to extol Juana's character in such a way that they became "vehicles for the construction of a mythical space where this character is presented as an illustration or icon subjected to devotion" (5).

In contrast to Aurora Bautista's overacting, the solemnity of Sara Montiel, in the role of Aldara, the sensual Moorish queen, serves to create an illustration or icon but with a very different meaning. Vicente Sánchez Biosca compares the way in which José Fernández Aguayo, the director of photography for *Locura de amor,* organizes the close-ups of Aurora Bautista and Sara Montiel:

> The first character is pensive and is illuminated by means of an abstract tone that enhances and separates her from the rest of the frame. She listens to Flamenco music that causes her pain since it reminds her of her husband's unfaithfulness. She is seized by delirium. . . . The second close-up is of Sara Montiel's face, of the Moorish queen whose whole body exudes hate and who shouts for revenge. The photography impregnates this face with a connotative gesture, yet, in spite of everything, it does not appear distorted by shadows. A face untarnished by history, one that has not suffered. On the contrary, it is a pristine, pure face. It is not the face of the character but rather the face of the actress. (1989, 65–66)

Through framing and careful lighting, Juana's face is the representation of a suffering nation betrayed by foreigners. By means of an almost expressionist aesthetics, both in the performance and the photography, Aurora Bautista becomes the epitome of mythical Castile. On the other hand, Sara Montiel does not transcend the representation of herself. Curiously enough, this movie is the first superproduction that Sara Montiel took part in. Her career reached its climax with another film by Orduña, *El ultimo cuplé* [The Last *Cuplé*] (1957) and with that role she became a national sex symbol. If the persona embodied by Aurora Bautista is characterized by delirium, then Sara Montiel's role is characterized by desire. Aldara's gestures are full of restrained eroticism (as restrained as society's repressed sexuality under Francoism) that quickly became the most characteristic and exploited feature of Sara Montiel's performances.

Aldara's character is typified by lust and sensuality. Insincere, lewd, and restless with jealousy, she manages to enter the palace posing as a Castilian lady-in-waiting in order to take revenge on Juana. In the end she redeems herself by killing De Vere, thus saving the life of her beloved captain and, therefore, the life of the defender of the country that she clearly wants to belong to. In the Moorish woman's love-hate relationship two types of desire are intertwined. Her unrequited love for Captain Álvar fits into the private spectrum, but her collective desire to take revenge of the colonizer has national significance and conflicts with subjective desire. As a result, her jealousy has a dual dimension: amorous and patriotic. Aldara envies Juana because the captain loves her, but she is also envious of what Juana represents: the grandeur of the Spanish Empire. Sumathi Ramaswamy explains that nationalism "is a structure of sentiment that turns around longing

and belonging" (1997, 10), so that the patterns of desire that eroticize the imagined community are essential to the formation of
nationalist ideologies. Aldara "longs," yet "does not belong" to that
invented and mythologized country that Franco's dictatorship tried
to keep alive.

Aldara's final destiny departs from the original model. In the play
by Tamayo y Baus, Aldara ends up entering a convent while in
Orduña's film she decides to return to her homeland in Africa where
a suitable fate awaits her as a completely subordinate, colonial entity:
to exist as a fiction imagined by the mother country. The movie's deviation in relation to its literary source is symptomatic of the urgent
interest demonstrated by Francoism in reaffirming the illusive concept of "empire," precisely at the moment in which the last remnants
of Spanish colonialism in Africa started to collapse. Likewise the
aforementioned deviation allowed the discourse on Western national
identity to be strengthened by opposing a fabricated Orient: "European culture gained in strength and identity by setting itself up
against the Orient as a sort of surrogate and even underground self"
(Said 1979, 3).

The two main characters of Orduña's film are national allegories.
Juana represents the motherland, betrayed by the greed or jealousy
of foreigners. Aldara is the allegory of the imagined colonized Other.
Her revengeful desires are transformed, thanks to the erotization of
her relationship with the colonizer, into irresistible attraction. The
gracefulness, and bravery of the Spanish knight obliterates her old
rancor. By renouncing to revenge, she also renounces to her position
of superiority and complies to forgiveness and submission as the bul-
warks of the motherland

THE EROTIZATION OF HISTORY

Vicente Aranda's interpretation of Juana's "madness of love" deviates
from Tamayo y Baus's romantic perspective. Even though at first
glance it could seem like a remake of Orduña's work, Aranda's film
displays a completely personal and modern point of view on Juana's
character. Aranda portrays Juana's madness not as pathology but
rather as a cultural construct. Juana was not crazy but was treated as
though she was because she did not accept the unfaithfulness of her
husband nor did she adhere to the tacit norms of women's sexual passivity of her time. Aranda deconstructs the romantic myth of Juana's
madness of love in order to relay his own modernized version of it.
Aranda's Juana is far from being the epitome of spiritual love in its

most exalted form. The viewers have before them a flesh and blood woman whose passion is manifested not by means of grandiloquent speech but rather through physical pleasure. Overflowing romantic passion now becomes a sort of sexual addiction in which the woman becomes an active agent, but within an unfortunate relationship of dependence on the man that jeopardizes her emotional stability.

While sexuality and the body have an insignificant role in the works of Tamayo y Baus and Orduña, Aranda gives them a prominence that is in keeping with all his films, whose main constants are: representations of unfaithfulness and jealousy, love-hate relationships, tragic triads of jealousy-madness-death, and sexuality as a source of pleasure as well as a dependence or addiction.[3] Enrique Colmena summarizes the repertory of themes related to sexuality present in Aranda's films:

> lesbianism, fellatio, cunnilingus, losing ones virginity, working as a pornography actress, impotence, shaving the pubis, male homosexuality, transsexualism, incest, sodomy, sexual dependence or addiction, necrophilia, voyeurism, transvestitism, urination on others, masturbation, intercourse while standing, fetishism . . . and in a changing world in which sex, cruelty, violence, male and female emasculization, genital self-mutilation, rape, sadism, masochism and the real offspring of both: sadomasochism, sexual harassment, sexual blackmail, erotic whipping, kisses stained with blood, psychological self-flagellation and torture converge. (1996, 25)

Next to this comprehensive list of what socially and institutionally could be labeled as perverted and marginal sexuality, *Juana la Loca* is presented as a candid movie in which, surprisingly, there is an almost total absence of sexually explicit scenes. What is the reason for Aranda's sudden restraint? In an interview, the director explains that he has grown tired of explicit eroticism and now he searches for "the eroticization of the soul" (Ibáñez 2005).[4]

In spite of, or maybe thanks to, Aranda's self-censorship, the movie exudes eroticism and explores women's sexual pleasure. After almost forty years of Francoist sexual repression (1939–75), any fleeting trace of anarchist free love of the 1930s had been erased. Liberalization of sexual practices and the vindication of sexual pleasure for women are perceived as historical achievements that started during the transition period to democracy (late seventies and eighties), but that have not been completely assimilated even today.[5] Nevertheless this alleged vindication of women's active role in seeking sexual pleasure remains distorted by the reaffirmation of the myth that a woman's sexual pleasure is associated with phallic penetration. The prominence of the phallus as having paramount importance is stretched to the extreme and in some scenes it borders on the ridiculous. After Juana's first sexual encounter with Felipe, she seems to be mysteriously hypnotized by the supposed power of the phallus. The manipulation of the camera's point of view and a careful editing of the scene contribute to phallic mystification. Aranda's protagonist moves away from the sexual passiveness that patriarchal societies attribute to women, yet Juana still tumbles into the stereotypical identification of sexuality and genital stimulation that is still current in such societies.

Curiously enough, even though the excitement and eagerness of the love between Juana and Felipe seems to respond solely to the obsessions of the director, Ludwig Pfandl, perhaps the most well-known biographer of Queen Juana, also presents a fictionalized version of the story that surely serves as the basis for the recreation of some of the key moments in Aranda's film. This seems to be the case in the scene where Juana and Felipe meet for the first time. Pfandl narrates the scene in terms that hardly seem appropriate for what is supposed to be an objective, historical account: "At first sight the natural sexual appetites of the two young people (she was seventeen years old and he was eighteen) were inflamed with such eagerness that they did not wait for the wedding that was planned for two days later. Instead, they sent for the closest priest that could be found to pronounce the blessing so that they could consummate their marriage that same afternoon" (1943, 51–52). Neither Tamayo y Baus nor Orduña take advantage of this historical fact of indisputable dramatic potential. In Orduña's *Locura de amor,* this deviance in protocol could have been too risqué for the prudish, moral Francoists. However, Aranda fully utilizes the implications of that historic event and in a very effective way depicts the awakening of their "natural sexual appetites." After exchanging looks and a hasty blessing, Felipe takes Juana in his arms and prepares to consummate their marriage, but not before saying goodbye to the members of the court gathered there: "We will see you in a week." Juana's becomes fatally attracted to Felipe's sexuality and her innocence is thus transformed into harmful passion.

The destructive character of Juana's passion is commented by several historians. Manuel Fernández Álvarez's biography uses Pedro Mártir de Anglería's words to describe Juana as "a very passionate woman" who later becomes "a terrible woman," due to jealousy: "Felipe, her young husband, began to be alarmed and he went so far as to try to put limits on a true battle of the sexes. In his Flemish tongue, Juana was becoming a *schrecklich,* a terrible woman" (2000, 62). Aranda is undoubtedly attracted to the myth of the castrating, terrible woman (taken to an extreme in one of his first films, *La novia ensangrentada* [The Bloody Bride] (1972) and he illustrates it in an explicit way in several scenes of *Juana la Loca*. One of those episodes is especially meaningful because of the new view Aranda presents of the theme of the castrating woman. In this case Felipe is not portrayed as a victim of Juana's jealousy, but rather he feels a special attraction to the actions that his wife carries out due to her jealousy. With the purpose of finding out the identity of the woman with whom Felipe has just committed adultery, Juana sniffs the bed sheets as if she were a hunting dog. In the subsequent scene she is able to recognize the same scent on one of her ladies-in-waiting and Juana immediately cuts off the woman's hair, displacing her castrating fury on the woman's body. When Felipe asks her to explain her actions, Juana replies, "I hate everything that comes between your body and mine, even if it is the air. . . . I am the sovereign of Borgoña and I made you king of Castile, but I also want to be your wife, your woman and your whore." Juana sets aside her role as queen and offers her body as a wife, as a simple woman or if neither of those suffice, as a prostitute. Juana succumbs to the loss of her dignity because of her overwhelming desire, while Felipe feels a kind of sadomasochistic attraction toward her. When Juana, knife in hand, begins to outline the reasons for her supposed madness, Felipe experiences a morbid pleasure from observing the suffering and the harm that desire is causing to her body and mind: "Mad, because I love you to madness. Mad, because I want you to be mine. Mad, because I do not want you to seek in another woman what I will give you with more to spare. Mad, because I seek to engender and give birth to your children. Mad, mad for love. Yes, mad." The phallic symbolism of the knife that Juana puts against Felipe's neck while stating these words points out the power dynamics of attraction-repulsion that exist between them.

Besides the clear connection between Juana's vindication of sexual pleasure and her alleged madness, another issue comes into play: Juana's body and her reproductive function. Like the representation of Juana's sexuality, the theme of motherhood is portrayed as a cultural construct. Aranda presents a mother whose behavior could appear transgressive in the sixteenth century, but not for present times. Juana sees procreation not as the result of her matrimonial duty, but rather as the palpable fruit of her passion. Aranda does not allude to the political consequences of Juana's remarkable fertility or her physical endurance. It is well known that in the period, after the death of Philip, Juana's body was treasured precisely for having achieved something that in the sixteenth century was unsual: the survival of all six children that she bore.[6]

As seen earlier, Juana exhibits the connection between motherhood and madness: "Mad, because I seek to engender and give birth to your children." Oddly enough Juana vindicates not her right but rather her political duty since as queen she had to bear children to succeed her to the throne. Furthermore since the Catholic church maintains that the main function of a marriage is procreation, Juana's vindication has moral approval, which was of great importance in Renaissance Spain. Behind Juana's affirmation, lurks the request for a right: if she cannot have Felipe's body as a lover, she seeks it as her husband.

Aranda presents how Juana's vindication fell to the wayside because her rebelliousness confronted some tacit rules that controlled social customs and that consequently delimited the borders of common sense and insanity. Her status as queen entailed certain cultural restrictions that limited the uses of her body as a lover or as a mother. This also appears in another aspect intimately related to Juana's "maternal body." Maternal breast-feeding was a taboo practice within certain social classes since it was a function associated with animals, and by the sixteenth century, high-class European women had given up the practice and left the job in the hands of wet nurses. Juana violates the norms once again and in Aranda's film expresses the absurdity of this custom that aims to keep high-class women from an allegedly humiliating practice that links them to female mammals.[7] Continuance of these taboos throughout the centuries demonstrates to what point social norms had relevance and control over women's bodies. In the case of a woman's breasts, the patriarchal culture had assigned, almost exclusively, its worth as a sexual organ whose function is to give pleasure to men. Any other practical function that could put in danger this allegedly essential function had to be limited and controlled as much as possible.

This dual importance of women's breasts, as an organ at the same time associated with sexuality and motherhood, has functioned in art as a complex signifier of femininity. Traditional artistic representations have attempted to separate these two functions of the breasts. Since the Renaissance, poetic works tended to represent the breasts in a metonymic form. Women's breasts are ivory, lilies, or snow. These metonymic invocations that eroticize the breasts as objects of masculine desire are carried over to the present day, but Aranda deconstructs them in order to highlight the fusion between motherhood and eroticism. The result is a provocative scene that, even nowadays puzzles the viewer. While Juana breast-feeds her daughter, she experiences a sexual arousal that she does not hide in Felipe's presence.

He reproaches her saying: "With good reason they whisper that you are crazy."

In this scene two very different stances in regards to female sexuality are presented. Felipe's attitude reflects the dichotomous definitions of sexuality that mark an incompatibility between the maternal and erotic functions of a woman's breasts. On the contrary, to Juana, reproductive practices are a source of eroticism. By portraying breasts in their erotic function—yet not to provide pleasure for the male viewer, but rather for the mother—Aranda deviates from the patriarchal point of view that opposes the two functions of the female organ, while at the same time undermining the myth of Juana's madness.

Aranda's Juana is a modern woman, vehement and passionate, for whom jealousy is a consequence and almost a condition for love: "Those that are not jealous, do not love," she affirms. In the fifteenth and sixteenth centuries, Juana's jealousy is considered pathological because society expected a more tolerant attitude from the queen in regards to her husband's unfaithfulness. During that time period, it was a common practice among monarchs to have sexual relations outside of their marriage. The legitimate wife did not necessarily applaud these adulterous relationships, even less so if she was a queen, but she was expected to resign herself to the facts without making a fool of her husband. Juana's jealousy and her supposedly pathological behavior have to be considered not only as something personal, but rather as interpersonal or social issues, since the ways in which one experiences and expresses jealousy reflect the norms and the institutional structure of society.

CONCLUSION

The majority of the differences between *Locura de amor* and *Juana la Loca* come from the historical and cultural context of the production of these movies. Orduña's film has the trademark of CIFESA, a production company that specialized in formulaic historical films with a distinct nationalistic air. By means of a skillful manipulation of the popular genres of the time, especially melodrama, and through the use of allegoric plots, these films broadcast the propagandistic message that legitimizes the consolidation process of the new Francoist government. In contrast, Aranda's movie emerged during a time in Spain in which the process of democratic normalization was already an irreversible reality. This explains why Spanish cinematographic production and directors like Aranda have experienced an ever-increasing process of depolitization during the last twenty years. In spite of the film-makers's combative attitudes during the final years of power of the Partido Popular (People's Party, a conservative political party in Spain) and the emergence of a new outpouring of social realism, the fact is that, unlike what happened during the first stage of Francoism, Spanish directors were no longer the spokespeople for the authoritarian regime nor were they radical antagonists like those who formed the group of the so-called New Spanish Cinema. So, during the last few years, within national cinematographic production, many new possibilities have been generated that tend to distance themselves from large-scale, general viewpoints on history as well as schematic allegories in order to go more deeply into the individual psychology of the characters and to explore social reality from a critical rather than militant point of view.

If the context of the two films by these directors could not be more different, then equally dissimilar are their aesthetics. Orduña and Aranda share an interest in violent passion and have a special fascination for female characters with strong personalities as central figures in the majority of their films. However, while Orduña embraces melodramatic romanticism to conclude his stories, Aranda's aesthetic viewpoint is clearly antiromantic. Therefore Orduña comes closer to Tamayo y Baus's world view and sensitivity, while Aranda accepts Tamayo y Baus's play and Orduña's filmic adaptation as pretexts that allow him to impart a radically different world view. Aranda eliminates the romantic elements of the play and the allegoric interpretation of the film adaptation in order to focus on erotic desire and its excesses. Thus once again the popular themes of his filmography are reiterated: pleasure and pain, sex and cruelty, possessive love and alienation. Aranda simplifies the historical context and complex interweaving of personal and political interests in order to provide viewers with his personal viewpoint on this historical character whose complexity is still being debated.

Aranda is very aware that the body is a powerful image. Juana's (Pilar Pérez de Ayala) body takes on an unparalleled starring role in order to emphasize her ability to feel and arouse erotic pleasure, her maternal function, and in short her essential role in what could be called the "fabrication of madness." *Juana la Loca* is a good example of how social and cultural determinants that control a woman's body can also be influential in the construction of pathological mental behaviors. In other words, Juana's alleged madness is linked to how she makes use of her body and her sexuality. Since the regulation and control of a woman's body changes with every time period and society, each one has defined in very different ways the limits between sanity and madness. For Tamayo y Baus's protagonist, her passion and madness of love are not found in the body but rather in her heart: "What sickness is this that everyone speaks of to me and whose name I know not? What purpose does it serve to search the body for something that is in the heart?" (1978, 45). A century and a half later, Aranda looks to the body, rather than the heart, to offer viewers another point of view on a woman that lived in the sixteenth century and yet in the dawn of the twenty-first century continues to captivate our imagination.

Translated by Christine Jenack

NOTES

1. The usefulness of historical cinema as a transmitter of political propaganda is brilliantly exhibited in these two editorials from the magazine *Primer plano:* "In order to expand the outline of our triumphs and to execute, with more vivacity and force, than books do . . . it would be worthwhile to illustrate cinematographically the greatest events and most important historical figures from the grandeur of the Spanish Empire. In order to make them understand and so that we may be better understood than the way we are currently known" (Fanés 1982, 165). "The stature and responsibility of historical cinema is such that it is not comparable to any other genre. . . . The importance of the historical genre on the screen contributes to the development of a national spirit. . . . No other moment like this, in which the praise of the national essence is a fundamental and inevitable duty of all Spaniards. Directors and producers should feel an unavoidable, imperative obligation to teach, domestically and abroad, about the magnificent, glorious course of Spain throughout the centuries" (Editorial, *Necesidad de un cine histórico español* [qtd. Monterde 1995, 234]).

2. Félix Fanés observes that in the majority of the movies by CIFESA "the protagonists were strong female characters: Marie Anne de Tremoilles in *La princesa de los Ursinos* [The Princess of the Ursinos]; Countess Albornoz in *Pequeñeces* [Trifles]; Agustina Saragossa y Doménech in *Agustina de Aragón;* María de Toledo in *La leona de Castilla* [The Lioness of Castile] (1951), and Lola in *Lola la Piconera* [Lola, the Parlormaid]. The masculine characters were not only superfluous counterparts to the true 'protagonists,' but they also tended to die before the end of the film" (1982, 180). Curiously, as Fanés himself explains, this pattern was not a reflection of Spanish society in the 1940s, in which "the protagonist in real life was the man and the woman was assigned the role of submission and acceptance" (180).

3. The relationship between unfaithfulness, jealousy, masochism, and death are central themes in *Amantes* [Lovers] (1990), the film that earned Aranda international fame. *La pasión turca* [Turkish Passion] (1994) equally revolves around the strong sexual dependence Desideria has on Yamán. Other problematic relationships can be found between: Esther and the editor in *Las crueles* [Cruel Women] (1969); Fanny and the man from Galicia in *Fanny Pelopaja* [Fanny Straw-Top] (1984), the captain and his daughter in *El crimen del capitán Sánchez* [Captain Sanchez's Murder] (1984), Joan and Norma in *El amante bilingüe* [The Bilingual Lover] (1993), and Luisa, Ángel and Ramiro in *Intruso* [Intruder] (1993). In one of his first films, *La novia ensangrentada* [The Blood Spattered Bride] (1972), he also presents a rela-

tionship of sexual dependency, in this case vampiric and lesbian, that ends with the lovers's murder.

4. Aranda was also influenced by the qualms and discomfiture of the actress that played Juana, Pilar Pérez de Ayala, who confessed feeling uncomfortable filming certain scenes, since she is still discovering her body. In addition to these factors, there is another significant reason that would explain the omission of scenes with pornographic tendencies. At all costs Aranda wanted to avoid problems with the prudish Academy of Motion Picture Arts and Sciences since he hoped that his movie would be nominated for an Oscar.

5. Aranda had addressed this theme on several occasions, for example in *Amantes* and *El amante bilingüe,* and he uses it now as starting point to explain his interpretation of Juana's character.

6. After Philip's death, due to her fertility and her physical strength, Juana's body was prized. There were negotiations for her to marry Henry VII, but she always refused to remarry.

7. *Lo Libre de les Dones* [The Book for Women] was found in Juana's library. It was written in the fourteenth century by the Franciscan Francesc Eiximenis and was translated to Spanish in the sixteenth century with the title *Carro de las donas* [Women's Duties]. It was an instruction manual for women originally published in the fourteenth century that achieved a sizeable readership. In this manual, it is explained that morals and good customs are transmitted through breast milk and therefore it is advisable for noblewomen to breast-feed their own children (Aram 2005, 46).

WORKS CITED

Aram, Bethany. 2005. *Juana the Mad: Sovereignty and Dynasty in Renaissance Europe.* Baltimore: Johns Hopkins University Press.

Barthes, Roland. 1957. *Mithologies.* Paris: Seuil.

Colmena, Enrique. 1996. *Vicente Aranda.* Madrid: Cátedra.

Company, Juan Miguel. 1997. *Formas y perversiones del compromiso: El cine español de los años 40.* Valencia: Ediciones Episteme.

Eoff, Sherman. 1940. "The Spanish Novel of Ideas. Critical Opinion (1836–1880)." *PMLA* 55:532–58.

Fanés, Félix. 1982. *CIFESA, la antorcha de los éxitos.* Valencia: Institución Alfonso el Magnánimo.

Fernández Álvarez, Manuel. 2000. *Juana la Loca: La cautiva de Tordesillas.* Madrid: Espasa Calpe.

Font, Domènec. 1976. *Del azul al verde: el cine español durante el franquismo.* Barcelona: Avance.

Gubern, Roman. 1990. "La decadencia de CIFESA." *Archivos de la Filmoteca* 4:58–65.

Heredero, Carlos. 1993. *Las huellas secretas del tiempo: Cine español 1951–1961.* Madrid: Filmoteca Española.

Ibáñez, Norberto. January 20, 2005. "Vicente Aranda." Available at: http://contrastes.uv.es/seis/aranda.html.

Juan Navarro, Santiago. 2005. "La Madre Patria enajenada: Locura de amor, de Juan de Orduña, como alegoría nacional." *Hispania* 88, 1:204–15.

Monterde, José Enrique. 1995. "El cine de la autarquía (1935–1950)." In *Historia del cine español,* edited by Roman Gubern et al. Madrid: Cátedra.

Pfandl, Ludwig. 1943. *Juana la Loca: su vida, su tiempo, su culpa.* Buenos Aires: Espasa Argentina.

Primo de Rivera, José Antonio. 1974. *Obras de José Antonio Primo de Rivera.* Madrid: Delegación Nacional de la Sección Femenina del Movimiento.

Ramaswamy, Sumathi. 1997. "Virgin Mother, Beloved Other." *Thamyris: Mythmaking from Past to Present* 4, 1:9–39.

Said, Edward W. 1979. *Orientalism.* New York: Vintage Books.

Sánchez Biosca, Vicente. 1989. "Fotografía y puesta en escena en el film español de los años 1940–50." In *Directores de fotografía del cine español,* edited by Francisco Llinás. Madrid: Filmoteca Española.

Seguin, Jean-Claude. 1997. *"Locura de amor."* In *Antología crítica del cine español,* edited by Julio Pérez Perucha. Madrid: Cátedra.

Spencer, Philip, and Howard Wollman. 2002. *Nationalism: A Critical Introduction.* London: Sage Publications.

Tamayo y Baus, Manuel. 1978. *La locura de amor.* Madrid: Espasa Calpe.

Appendix I: Portraits and Paintings

Pedro López Gómez

Although they are not wearing the rich, pompous clothing that appears in Jacob van Laethem's triptych, in this representation they do not lack luxurious jewelry. Philip has the chain of the Order of the Golden Fleece around his neck, and a jewel is fastened to his hat. Juana is wearing a beautifully embroidered circlet on her head and a pendant around her neck that seems to be the same one from another portrait.

The Order of the Golden Fleece was founded by Philip, archduke of Austria, in 1430. An example of its emblem or chain can be found in the Museum of Art History in Vienna. The founding was at the time of Philip's third wedding, when he married Isabella of Portugal. The Order had a political and religious goal: defense against the Turks. Its leader was the Archduke. However, with the legacy of Burgundy, it passed to the Habsburgs with what remained of his very rich treasure. The Fleece refers to the Greek legend of Jason and the Golden Fleece, with the image of lamb's wool hanging from the necklace, but it also refers to Gideon, the biblical warrior chosen by God.

Juana's circlet, dress, pendant, and posture, including her interlocked hands, can be compared to the portrait of Jane Seymour, queen of England, painted in 1536 by Hans Holbein the Younger. This lady was at the service of Catherine of Aragon and of Anne Boleyn as a lady-in-waiting. She married Henry VIII of England in 1536 and gave birth to Edward VI, the future heir to the throne. Excepting the superior quality of the latter painting and the psychological introspection it presents into the firm character of this woman, the supreme ostentatiousness of her finery and jewelry in essence correspond to the same style and disposition. This young beauty with an oval face, sensual lips and azure eyes, hair parted down the middle and pulled back, perhaps in braids or a low bun, bedecked with jewels, supposedly is Juana of Castile. A pendant that hangs from a thin chain is buried in her generous bosom. Her delicate hand extends its index finger upward, suggesting communication with the viewer.

According to Fernández Álvarez, Juana, the princess of Spain at that time, is presented in all her arrogant beauty: her hair pulled back with two bands, her beautiful eyes, her fleshy mouth, attention called to her bosom by a low-cut neckline. "A body made for love, with the fire that would change history."

The painting is attributed to Juan of Flanders, one of Isabella the Catholic's favorite painters, whose origin is revealed by his name. The young

Figures 3 and 4. *Juana of Castile and Philip "The Handsome"* as they appear in the famous triptych in the Museum of Ancient Art in Brussels. Images courtesy of the Museum voor Oude Junst, Brussels.

Figure 5. *Johanna die Wahnsinnige* by Juan of Flanders, c. 1497. Image courtesy of the Kunsthhistorisches Museum, Vienna.

Figure 6. *Philipp der Schöne* by Juan of Flanders, c. 1497. Image courtesy of the Kunsthhistorisches Museum, Vienna.

Figures 7 and 8. *Portraits de Philippe Le Beau et de Jeanne La Folle.* Image courtesy of the Musées Royaux des Beaux-Arts de Belgique, Brussels.

man with elongated face and nose, thick lips and light eyes, short hair falling in a bob partly covered by a dark hat, is Philip, archduke of Austria. Around his neck, he wears the chain of the Order of the Golden Fleece, and his hand seems to rest delicately on an object that we do not see.

The painting is attributed to Juan of Flanders, and it is kept at the Museum of Art History in Vienna. It can be compared to the very valuable portrait of Philip's relative, Anthony of Burgundy, painted by Rogier van der Weyden circa 1460, which hangs in the Museum of Ancient Art in Brussels. There is a striking resemblance between the two, although the nickname "handsome" suits the ancestor better than the descendant, at least in this painting.

According to literature from the Museum of Ancient Art in Brussels, these two panels form the doors of a triptych, whose central part, "The Final Judgment," is of lesser value. It comes from the city of Zierikzee, where it would probably have been found in the courtroom of the town hall. Indeed, it portrays a "tableau of justice" such as those found in other courts of the Low Countries, and the idea of "final judgment" was intended to inspire judges to hand out fair sentences. Both husband and wife are adorned with all the symbols of royal power. Philip, called "The Handsome," is wearing full armor. Coats of arms of Burgundy, Austria, and the kingdoms of Spain decorate his cuirass. He is covered by a luxurious cape with an ermine collar, and over his helmet he wears a crown. Around his neck, he wears the chain of the Order of the Golden Fleece. In his right hand he holds a sword, a symbol of his supreme worldly authority.

Juana, called "The Mad," wears a rich, brocaded dress with a white doublet, and she is draped with a royal cloak, decorated with the same coats of arms. On her head she wears a black circlet, richly adorned along the border. Around her neck is a pendant hanging from a chain, most likely gold. If, as Fernández Álvarez notes, the artist captured Juana during her first pregnancy, as the position of her delicate hands suggests, the painting would have to date back to about 1498, but this is in contradiction with her clothing and accessories. Furthermore, although Juana's countenance is full of melancholy, it would be a stretch to think that it is the countenance "of a woman wondering about her uncertain fate."

Philip, son of Marie of Burgundy and Maximilian of Austria, was born in 1478, and in 1496 he married Juana, daughter of Ferdinand of Aragon and Isabella of Castile (the Catholic Monarchs). When Isabella died, in 1504, Philip claimed the throne by right of succession. Because he died shortly thereafter, in 1506, and in the painting he is covered with symbols of royal power, the triptych can be dated fairly precisely.

In the background, a typical, conventional, Flemish landscape makes it possible to identify the gardens of Coudenberg, the Palace of the Austrian Dukes in Brussels, where tournaments were held. Also in the background, the walls of the city and the two towers west of St. Michael's Cathedral, today St. Gudula's Cathedral, can be seen.

The painting is attributed to the Master of the Joseph Legend. However, that it could be the work of Jacob van Laethem has not been ruled out; van

Laethem was accepted into the Antwerp Guild in 1493, and he accompanied Philip on his trips to Spain.

Juana la Loca frente al cadáver de su esposo Felipe el Hermoso (see Fig. 1 on page 176) is an utterly romantic interpretation by Francisco Pradilla of Juana's trip through Castile, toward Tordesillas, carrying her husband's body. It was done on a very big canvas, consistent with the historical painting genre of the time. According to P. Mártir de Anglería's analysis, the procession included ecclesiastics, nobles, and knights. On one of the days, from Torquemada to Hornillos, "the queen demanded that the coffin be put in a monastery where she believed monks resided, but later she discovered that it was a convent of nuns. She was horrified and instantly demanded that the coffin be taken out of there and brought to the field. There she made the whole procession stay, out in the elements, suffering the immense cold of the season." Juana, wearing a habit and widow's circlets, looks at her husband's coffin with possessed eyes, while the members of her entourage make themselves comfortable around a bonfire, or watch the spectacle from a distance. In the background, a stormy sky and a typical plateau landscape give more impact to the composition. Of course, it is an idealization, not intended to be a portrait of the queen, who at that time was pregnant.

Philip's body is buried together with Juana's in the Royal Chapel in Granada, to where it was moved from Tordesillas by order of Philip II in 1574. In the chapel, in the middle of the nave, are the tombs of the Catholic Monarchs, a beautiful Renaissance work of the Italian Fancelli. Next to them are the tombs of Juana and Philip, even more splendid, the work of Bartolomé Ordoñez.

Appendix II: Juana as a Palimpsest

WORKS ABOUT JUANA OF CASTILE

Plays

Felipe el Hermoso (1845), Eusebio Asquerino and Gregorio Romero
Locura de amor (1855), Manuel Tamayo y Baus
Doña Juana la Loca (1864), Ramón Franquelo
La reine Juana (1893), Alexandre Parodi
Jeanne la Folle (1895), Louis-Lucien Vermeil
Santa Juana de Castilla (1918), Benito Pérez Galdós
¡Castilla por doña Juana! (1920), Juan de Arzadun
Love Possessed Juana (1939), Angna Enters
Jeanne la Folle (1949), François Aman-Jean
El corazón extraviado (1957), Aberto de Zavalía
Jeanne la Folle (1958), Frédéric Feusier
Donna Juana, Infantin von Spanien; oder, À la recherche de l'absolu. Eine unhistorische Historie in fünf Akten (1959), Max Gertsch
Johanna die Wahnsinnige: historisches Schauspiel in 3 Akten (1959), Franz Dubsky
Le Cardinal d'Espagne (1960), Henry de Montherlant
Juana creó la noche (1960), José Martín Elizondo
Los comuneros (1974), Ana Diosdado
El engañao (1976), José Martín Recuerda
Juana del amor hermoso (1984), Manuel Martínez Mediero
Un château en novembre (1984), Emmanuel Roblès
Falsa crónica de Juana la Loca (1985), Miguel Sabido
La reina loca (1988), Wenceslao Godoy
Retablo de là pasión y muerte de Juana la Loca (1996), Manuel Rueda
Razón de Estado o Juego de reinas (1997), Concha Romero
Jeanne de Castille, ou La reine qui n'aimait pas Dieu (2003), Christine Wystup
The Lunatic Queen (2005), Torben Betts

Novels

Jeanne la Folle, reine d'Espagne (1825), Antoine-Jean-Baptiste Simonnin
Jeanne de Castille: nouvelle historique (1843), Antoinette Henriette Clémence Robert
La reina loca de amor (1863), Francisco José Orellana

252

Juana la Loca: Seis novelas superhistóricas (1944), Ramón Gómez de la Serna
Seek the Darkness: The Story of Juana la Loca (1955), Amarie Dennis.
The Prisoner of Tordesillas (1959), Lawrence L. Schoonover
La reine folle d'amour (1961), Janina Villars
Ma fille Marie-Hélène Charles Quint (1974), Jeanne Champion
Un amour fou (1991), Catherine Hermary-Vieille
Joana (1991), Guillem Viladot
Satrapia: El libro de memorias de Juana la Loca (1991), Julio Rodríguez
Juana la Loca (1992), Carmen Barberá
La leggenda di Juana I (1992), Adriana Assini
Los silencios de Juana la Loca (2003), Aroní Yanko.
El pergamino de la seducción (2004), Gioconda Belli.

Poems

Juana of Castile (1910), May Earle
"Elegía a doña Juana la Loca" (1918), Federico García Lorca

Opera

Doña Juana la Loca (1848), Manuel Tamayo y Baus.
Giovanna la Pazza (1890), Emilio Serrano
Rage d'amours (2003), Rob Zuidam

Coreographies

Juana la Loca: Vivir por amor (2002), Sara Baras.

Paintings

Juana la Loca ante el féretro de su esposo Felipe (1858), Gabriel Maureta
Juana la Loca ante el féretro de su esposo [sketch] (1860), Eduardo Rosales
Doña Juana la Loca mandando abrir el féretro de don Felipe el Hermoso (1862), Carlos Giner
Llegada a Tordesillas de doña Juana la Loca (1866), Ibo de la Cortina
Demencia de doña Juana (1866), Lorenzo Vallés
Juana de Castilla ante el cadáver de su esposo (1868), Juan Martínez
Doña Juana la Loca en el castillo de Illescas (1873), Eduardo Rosales
Juana la Loca frente al cadáver de Felipe el Hermoso (1877), Francisco Pradilla
Juana la Loca recluida en Tordesillas (1906), Francisco Pradilla

Films

Locura de amor (1909), Ricardo de Baños
Locura de amor (1948), Juan de Orduña

Juana la loca . . . de vez en cuando (1983), José Ramón Larraz
Juana la Loca (2001), Vicente Aranda

Biographies and Historical Studies

Altayó, Isabel, and Paloma Nogués. *Juana I: La reina cautiva*. Madrid: Silex, 1985.

Aram, Bethany. *Juana the Mad: Soverignty and Dynasty in Renaissance Europe*. Baltimore: Johns Hopkins University Press, 2005.

Barberá Puig, Carmen. *Juana la Loca*. Barcelona: Planeta, 1992.

Brouwer, Johannes. *Johanna de Waanzinnige: Een tragisch leven in een bewogen tijd*. Amsterdam: Meulenhoff, 1940.

Buyreu Juan, Jordi. *La Corona de Aragón de Carlos V a Felipe II: Las instrucciones a los virreyes bajo la regencia de la princesa Juana (1554–1559)*. Madrid : Sociedad Estatal para la Conmemoración de los Centenarios de Felipe II y Carlos V, 2000.

Carrilero Martínez, Ramón. *Colección documental albacetense de la reina doña Juana (1505–1519)*. Albacete: Diputación de Albacete, 2002.

Fernández Álvarez, Manuel. *Juana la Loca 1479–1555*. Palencia: Diputación Provincial, 1994.

———. *Juana la Loca: La cautiva de Tordesillas*. Madrid: Espasa Calpe, 2000.

Ferri, Edgarda. *Giovanna la Pazza: Una regina ribelle nella Spagna dell'Inquisizione*. Milano: Mondadori, 1996.

Fuente, Vicente de la. *Doña Juana la Loca vindicada de la nota de herejía*. Madrid: A. Perez Dubrull, 1870.

Godoy, Wenceslao. *La reina loca*. Salamanca: Editora Regional de Extremadura, 1988.

Hillebrand, Kart. *Un enigma della storia: La prigionia di Giovanna la Pazza*. Palermo: Sellerio, 1986.

Höffer, Constantin von. *Donna Juana, Königin von Leon, Castilien und Granada*. Viena: Karl Gerold's Sohn, 1885.

Horst, Eberhard. *Die Spanische Trilogie: Isabella, Johanna, Teresa*. Düsseldorf: Claassen, 1989.

Hulst, Henri d'. *Le Mariage de Philippe le Beau avec Jeanne de Castille á Lierre le 20 Octobre 1496*. Anvers: Imprimeries Generales Lloyd Anversois, 1958.

Ladero Quesada, Miguel Angel. *La armada de Flandes: Un episodio en la política naval de los Reyes Católicos, 1496–1497*. Madrid: Real Academia de la Historia, 2003.

Lanz, Johann. *Die Nachkommen der Johanna der Wahnsinnigen*. Wien: Heraldisch-genealogische Gesellschaft "Adler," 1993.

Mares, Roberto. *Juana la Loca*. Mexico, D.F.: Grupo Ed. Tomo, 2003.

Maurenbrecher, Wilhelm. *Bergenroth's Johanna von Kastilien*. Berlin: G. Reimer, 1860.

Miller, Townsend. *The Castles and the Crown: Spain, 1451–1555*. New York and London: Coward-McCann, 1963.

Montero, Rosa. *Pasiones: amores y desamores que han cambiado la historia*. Madrid: Aguilar, 1999.

Neumann, Harald. *Johanna die Wahnsinnige—geisteskrank und nekrophil?* Sternenfels: Wissenschaft and Praxis, 2000.

Nishikawa, Kazuko. *Kyojou fuana: Supein oke no densetsu o tazunete.* Tokyo: Sairyusha, 2003.

Obregón, Antonio de. *Juana la Loca, más mujer que reina.* Madrid: Ediciones B. Bureba, 1955.

Olaizola, José Luis. *La vida y la época de Juana la Loca.* Barcelona: Planeta, 1996.

Pardo Bazán, Emilia. *"Un drama psicológico en la historia de España: Doña Juana la loca según los últimos documentos." Teatro Crítico* 2.14 (Feb. 1892):67–105.

Penella, Manuel. *Juana la Loca.* Madrid: Amigos de la Historia, 1975.

———. "La reina Juana no estaba loca." *Grandes enigmas históricos españoles.* Madrid: Amigos de la Historia. Editions Ferni Genéve, 1979.

Pfandl, Ludwig. *Johanna die Wahnsinnige: Ihr Leben, ihre Zeit, ihre Schuld.* Freiburg: Herder, 1930.

———. *Juana la Loca: su vida, su tiempo, su culpa.* Buenos Aires: Espasa Argentina, 1943.

Prawdin, Michael. *The Mad Queen of Spain.* Boston: Houghton Mifflin Co., 1939.

Rodríguez Villa, Antonio. *Bosquejo biográfico de la Reina Doña Juana.* Madrid: Sucesores de Rivadeneyra, 1874.

———. *La Reina Doña Juana la loca, estudio histórico.* Madrid: M. Murillo, 1892.

Roesler, E. Robert. *Johanna die Wahnsinnige, Königin von Castilien: Beleuchtung der Enthüllungen G.A. Bergenroths aus dem Archive zu Simancas.* Wien: In Commission bei Faesy and Frick, 1870.

Sanz y Ruiz de la Peña, Nicomedes, and Antonio Vallejo Nágera. *Doña Juana I de Castilla, la reina que enloqueció de amor.* Zaragoza: Ediciones Luz, 1939.

Silva, Alberto. *Doña Juana la Loca, 1479–1555.* Madrid: Ediciones Cultura Hispánica, 1957.

Tighe, Harry. *A Queen of Unrest: The Story of Juana of Castile.* London: S. Sonnenschein, 1907.

Vostell, Wolf. *Omaggio a Giovanna la Pazza.* Napoli: Il Centro, 1980.

Zalama, Miguel Angel. *Vida cotidiana y arte en el palacio de la reina Juana I en Tordesillas.* Valladolid: Universidad de Valladolid, 2000.

Contributors

BETHANY ARAM teaches Spanish History at the International College of Seville in Spain. She is the author of *Juana the Mad: Sovereignty and Dynasty in Renaissance Europe* (2005) and has recently completed a monograph on gold and black legends in the conquest of America.

BECKY BOLING is Professor of Spanish at Carleton College. Her research focuses on contemporary Spanish-American narrative and theater with a strong interest in women's writings. She is also on the editorial board of *Latin American Theater Review*. Since the completion of her thesis on Carlos Fuentes's *Terra nostra*, she has remained intrigued by counter-hegemonic rewritings of history in Spanish-American literature.

TARA FOSTER is Resident Instruction Assistant Professor at the University of Missouri in Columbia. She recently earned her doctorate in French with a specialization in medieval literature from Rutgers, The State University of New Jersey. Her dissertation focused on the portrayal of feminine discourse in a corpus of female martyr saints' Lives composed in Old French and Occitan between the eleventh and thirteenth centuries.

ELENA GASCÓN VERA is Marion Butler Maclean Professor of History of Ideas at Wellesley College. She is the author of *Don Pedro, Condestable de Portugal* (1979) and *Un mito nuevo: La mujer como objeto/sujeto literario* (1992) and coauthor of several books including *María Luisa Bombal: Apreciaciones críticas* (1987), *Homenaje a Justina Ruiz de Conde en su ochenta cumpleaños* (1992), and *Signos y fábulas: Ensayos sobre Pedro Salinas* (1993). She has written numerous articles on topics that range from Spanish medieval literature and feminist studies to Spanish postmodernism and hispanic cinema.

DAVID R. GEORGE, Jr. is Lecturer in Spanish at Bates College. He has read and published papers on various aspects of nineteenth-century peninsular literature, as well as on film and popular culture in the early twentieth century. His most recent work appears in the edited volume *Visualizing Spanish Modernity* (2005). Currently he is working on an annotated edition of Leopoldo Alas's *Doña Berta.*

MARÍA A. GÓMEZ is Associate Professor of Spanish and Director of the Spanish Graduate Program at Florida International Univesity. She is the author of *Del escenario a la pantalla: La adaptación cine-matográfica del teatro español* (2000) and is currently working on a manuscript on the representation of motherhood in Spanish literature and film.

SANTIAGO JUAN-NAVARRO is Associate Professor of Spanish at Florida International University. He is the author of *Archival Reflections: Postmodern Fiction of the Americas* (BUP, 2000) and coeditor of *A Twice-Told Tale: Reinventing the Encounter in Iberian/Iberian American Literature and Film* (2001). He has also published over forty articles on various topics of Hispanic literature and film.

PEDRO LÓPEZ GÓMEZ is University Full Professor of Library and Documentation Sciences in the University of A Coruña. He holds a PhD in History from the Universidad Complutense of Madrid. He is the author of *La Real Audiencia de Galicia y el Archivo del Reino* (1996), *José Cornide, el coruñés ilustrado* (1997), and *La expedición Iglesias al Amazonas* (2001). From 1988 to 1990, he was Head of the School of Archives of the Archivo del Reino de Galicia and has been director of state archives in Pontevedra (1974–1985), A Coruña (1986–1995), and Barcelona (1996–97).

JOSÉ LUIS MORA GARCÍA is Professor of Philosophy and Humanities in the Universidad Autónoma of Madrid (Spain) and president of the Asociación de Hispanismo Filosófico. He is the author of *Hombre, sociedad y religión en la novelística galdosiana* (1888–1905) and *Benito Pérez Galdós (1843–1920),* He is editor of *Artículos, relatos y otros escritos de Blas Zambrano,* and coeditor of *Obras Completas de Manuel de la Revilla.* Vol I y II (2006). His essays on nineteenth- and twentieth-century Spanish iLterature nad Philosophy have appeared in numerous anthologies and journals.

VILMA NAVARRO-DANIELS is Assistant Professor of Spanish at Washington State University. She earned her PhD (2003) in Spanish at the University of Connecticut. Her research interests include nineteenth-century peninsular Spanish literature and contemporary peninsular Spanish literature, film, and culture. Her approach bridges the fields of literature, social sciences, and film studies. She has published on peninsular Spanish film, theater, and novel.

SALVATORE POETA is Associate Professor of Spanish at Villanova University in Pennsylvania. He earned his PhD from the University of Pennsylvania with specialties in early modern and modern to present-day Spanish literature. In addition to publishing numerous articles in his areas of expertise, he has authored *La elegía funeral en memoria de Federico García Lorca (Introducción al género y antología)* (1990). He has also published his own poetry in Spanish and in English in numerous academic journals.

MARÍA ELENA SOLIÑO is Associate Professor of Spanish at the University of Houston. She has published *Women and Children First: Spanish Women Writers and the Fairy Tale Tradition* (2002), a study of the literary fairy tale tradition in Spain and its impact on women writers brought up during the Franco regime, especially Martín Gaite, Matute, Tusquets, and Moix, and is currently working on a book about historical film, a project that began with a study of the two popular films on Queen Juana, the 1942 *Locura de amor* and Aranda's 2001 *Mad Love*.

MERCEDES TASENDE is Professor of Spanish at Western Michigan University. She is the author of *Palimpsesto y subversión: Un estudio intertextual de* El ruedo ibérico (1994), as well as several articles on authors such as Emilia Pardo Bazán, Miguel de Unamuno, Ramón Gómez de la Serna, Ramón del Valle-Inclán, and Manuel Rivas. She is currently working on Unamuno's writings dealing with the Spanish civil war.

JAN REINHART is the manager of the film and music libraries at Rutgers, The State University of New Jersey and a graduate student of literary translation. Prior to coming to Rutgers in 1998, he worked for a decade as a journalist for daily newspapers in the Midwest and East Coast. He studied opera singing and classical guitar at the University of Toledo in his Ohio hometown.

PHYLLIS ZATLIN is Professor of Spanish and coordinator of translator/interpreter training at Rutgers, The State University of New Jersey. She has published widely in the areas of theater and theatrical translation, film adaptation, and the narrative of contemporary Spanish women writers. Among her books are *Cross-Cultural Approaches to Theatre* (1994), *The Novels and Plays of Eduardo Manet* (2000), and *Theatrical Translation and Film Adaptation* (2005). Her previous studies related to Juana I of Castile focus on plays by Martínez Mediero, Emmanuel Roblès and Martín Elizondo.

Index

Admiral of Castile, Don Fadrique
  Enríquez de Cabrera, 15, 216, 219,
  220, 222, 230
Agustina de Aragón, 212
Alba de América, 212
Alexander VI, pope, 38, 43n. 16
Alfonso XII, king of Spain, 26, 184
Algora Weber, María Dolores, 226
allegory, 26, 28, 72, 84, 210–27, 233
Altayó, Isabel, 41, 44, 254
Álvarez Junco, José, 75
Aman-Jean, François, 144, 148, 156–57,
  252
Amour fou, Un, 144, 157, 161, 252
Anchieta, Juan de, 198
Antwerp, 251
Aragon, Catherine of, 47–57, 243
Aram, Bethany, 28, 44, 56, 75, 105, 116,
  157
Aranda, Vicente, 10, 21, 26–27, 106,
  110n. 1, 194n. 9, 228, 233–42, 254
Arteaga, Almudena de, 56

Baños, Ricardo de, 212, 228, 253
Baras, Sara, 253
Barberá Puig, Carmen, 117, 254
Barcelona, 153, 207–8
Barthes, Roland, 134, 143, 229, 241
Bataillon, Marcel, 129
Beatriz, daughter of King Pedro I of
  Castile, 83
Begoña, José, 105
Belli, Gioconda, 10, 21, 194n. 7, 196,
  253
Benavente: fortress of, 37
Bergenroth, Gustav, 22, 39–41, 43nn.
  30, 31, and 32, 44–45, 82, 90, 254
Bethlehem of Brussels: convent of, 38,
  43n. 16
Betts, Torben, 252
Blanquat, Josette, 90
Blinkhorn, Martin, 214, 226

Blockmans, Wim, 44
Boling, Becky, 117
Borja, Francisco de, duke of Gandía,
  marquis of Lombay, third general of
  the Jesuit Order, 45, 83, 85–86, 88–
  89
Brant, Sebastian, 155
Brouwer, Johannes, 254
Bruges, 38, 43n. 17
Brussels, 12, 38, 201, 207, 244–45,
  248–50, 250
Burgos, 13, 15–16, 34, 38, 62–63, 74,
  104n. 7, 112–13, 160, 166, 213, 220,
  231
Burgundy, Mary Duchess of, 11, 49,
  198, 250
Busette, Cedric, 117
Butler, Judith, 57
Buyreu Juan, Jordi, 254

Calderón, José Manuel, 56
Calvino, Italo, 90
Calvo, Armando, 212
Camón Aznar, 105
Campbell, Roy, 117
Campos Marín, Ricardo, 69, 75
Camus, Alfredo Adolfo, 90
Cano Ballesta, Juan, 226
Cardinal d'Espagne, Le, 144, 157, 252,
  163, 170n. 6
Cardona, Rodolfo, 90, 105
Carlos, Don, prince of Asturias, son of
  Philip II, 107
Carrero Blanco, Luis, 215–16, 219–21,
  226n. 4
Carrilero Martínez, Ramón, 254
Carrillo, Mary, 212
Carthusians, 42n. 10, 43nn. and 17, 44
Casanova, Vicente, 221, 226n. 2
¡Castilla por doña Juana!, 252
Castro, Eduardo, 117
Catalina, queen of Portugal, 166

261

Catalina (Catherine) of Aragon, queen of England, 11, 23, 47–60
Champion, Jeanne, 25, 144, 151–57, 253
Charles V, king of Spain, Holy Roman Emperor, 9, 13–14, 16–17, 25, 34–37, 40, 44, 66–68, 82, 88–89, 101, 105 n. 10, 109–10, 116 n. 2, 128, 135, 150–55, 157–58, 165, 168, 177, 192, 193 n. 2, 194 n. 3, 198, 202–3, 207, 253
Charles "the Bold," duke of Burgundy, 38
Charlot, Jean, 143
Château en novembre, Un, 158–72
Cilly, Claude de, 42 n. 7
Cixous, Hélène, 143
Claires, of Rejas, 38–39
Clémence Robert, Antoinette Henriette, 64, 144, 157, 252
Clement, Catherine, 143
clothing, 169, 181, 187, 243, 250
Cohen, Margaret, 157
Coloma, Padre, 90
communism, 211, 214, 219, 226 n. 3
Comunero rebellion, 14, 17–19, 28, 37, 82, 85, 88–89, 116, 119, 128, 156, 164–65, 193 n. 2, 207, 224, 252
Comuneros, Los, 17, 28, 252
Conchillos, Lope de, 87
Connor, Joan, 117
constitutional monarchy, 177, 183–84, 207
corazón extraviado, El, 252
Córdoba, Martín de, 56
Corneille, Pierre, 158
Cortes, 13, 154, 195 n. 13
Cortina, Ibo de la, 253

degeneration, 23, 61–76
Demencia de doña Juana, 15, 253
Denia, marquis of, Sandoval, Don Bernardo de, 14, 16, 36–37, 82, 88, 109, 119–21, 123, 128
Dennis, Amarie, 44, 151, 157, 252
Dennis, Nigel, 95, 105
De Nora, Eugenio, 105
Díaz-Diocaretz Myriam, 56
desire, 15, 19, 27, 40, 49, 52–53, 55, 61, 66, 72–73, 97, 108–9, 123, 126, 128, 139–40, 142 nn. 6 and 7, 146, 153–54, 179, 184, 186, 194 n. 10, 222, 228–42

Diosdado, Ana, 17–18, 28, 252
DiPuccio, Denise, 129
Donna Juana, Infantin von Spanien, 252
Doña Juana la Loca, 253
Doña Juana la Loca en el castillo de Illescas, 253
Doña Juana la Loca mandando abrir el féretro de Don Felipe el Hermoso, 253
Dousinague. José M., 56
Downing, Lisa, 76
dowry: Juana's, 34
Dubsky, Franz, 252
Durán, Rafael, 213

Earle, May, 20, 253
Echegaray, Alfredo, 213
Eiximenis, Francesc, 49, 56, 241
Elam, Keir, 143
"Elegía a doña Juana la Loca," 18, 20, 24, 107–18, 164, 253
engañao, El, 17, 18, 28
Enrique IV, king (of Castile and Leon), 57, 179
Enters, Ana, 110, 116 n. 2, 117, 252
Erasmus, Desiderius, 11, 16, 19, 24, 54–55, 57, 79, 85–89, 119–32, 155
Escorial, El, 42 n. 12
Esquer Torres, Ramón, 76
Evrad, Franck, 157

Falange, 210, 226 n. 4, 229
Falsa crónica de Juana la Loca, 25, 116, 133–43, 252
Fanés, Félix, 226
Fantazzi, Charles, 56
fascism, 153, 210–11
fasting, 39, 129
Febvre, Lucien, 129
Felipe el Hermoso, 252
Fernández, Carlos, 220, 226
Fernández, Justino, 143
Fernández Alvarez, Manuel, 28, 44, 85, 90, 99, 105, 254
Fernando, king of Castile and Aragon, 9, 11, 13, 15, 19, 23, 33–35, 37, 40, 42 n. 1, 43 nn. 21 and 26, 47, 53, 63–66, 82, 88–89, 101, 106, 108, 110, 126–28, 133, 135–38, 150, 152–56, 158, 163, 166–68, 179, 181, 187–88, 192, 194 nn. 3 and 8, 195 n. 13, 198, 200, 202–4, 250

Ferrer, Mosen Luis, 13, 43
Ferrer Benimeli, José A., 226
Ferreras, Juan Ignacio, 76
Ferri, Edgarda, 254
Feusier, Frédéric, 144, 157, 252
Finkenthal, Stanley, 91
Fleming, Shannon, 22
Fonseca, Juan Rodríguez, bishop of
    Córdoba, 34, 42 n. 2
Font, Domènec, 226
Franciscans, 38, 43 n. 20, 45, 121, 241 n. 7
Franco, Francisco, 21, 26–27, 68, 91,
    116, 163, 170 n. 8, 194 n. 3, 210–27,
    228–35, 239
Franquelo, Ramón, 82, 252
Freemasonry, 214, 219, 220, 226
Fuente, Vicente de la, 254
Fuentes, Carlos, 143

Gabriele, John P., 129
Gachard, Louis Prosper, 22, 40, 42 n. 2,
    44–45
Galíndez de Carvajal, Lorenzo, 43 n. 21,
    45
Galindo, Beatriz ["the Latinist"], 83
Gallop, Jane, 143
Ganivet, Ángel, 214
García de Catrojeriz, Juan, 56
García Lorca, Federico, 18, 20, 24,
    107–18, 164, 253
Gardiol, Rita Mazzetti, 117
Garrido, Carlos, 105
Gibson, Ian, 117
Gies, David T., 76
Gil, Rafael, 213
Giovanna la Pazza, 201, 253
Gómez de Fuensalida, Gutierre,
    ambassador, 34–35, 42 n. 5, 45, 47, 56
Gómez de la Serna, Ramón, 20, 22, 24,
    117, 92–106, 253
Granada, 13, 16–17, 48, 53, 92, 104 n. 7,
    108, 110–13, 117, 123, 127, 146, 166,
    181–82, 188, 192–93, 199–200, 251
Gubern, Roman, 225 n. 1, 226

Henry VIII, king (of England), 11, 47,
    54, 56, 243
heresy, 16, 22–24, 33, 40, 41, 82–89,
    119, 121, 147, 149, 163, 192
Hermary-Vieille, Catherine, 144, 157,
    161, 252

Hillebrand, Kart, 254
Hispanidad (Spanishness): 211, 230
Höffer, Constantin von, 254
Horst, Eberhard, 254
Hulst, Henri d', 254

impiety, 33, 179
Impresiones y paisajes, 108, 112
Inquisition, 11, 48, 146, 147–49,
    152–53, 156, 166–67, 194 n. 2
Isabel I, queen of Castile, 9, 11–13, 15,
    19, 23–24, 33–34, 36, 40, 42 n. 1, 47,
    49, 50, 53, 55, 64, 66, 84, 89, 92, 94,
    104 n. 7, 110–11, 119–26, 159,
    162–63, 170, 178–80, 182, 186–88,
    192, 194, 243, 250
Isabel II, queen of Spain, 26, 177–79,
    182–84, 186–87, 190, 193, 195 n. 14

Jeanne de Castille: nouvelle historique, 64,
    144, 157, 252
Jeanne de Castille, ou La reine qui n'aimait
    pas Dieu, 252
Jeanne la Folle (1895), 144, 157, 252
Jeanne la Folle (1949), 144, 157, 252
Jeanne la Folle (1958), 144, 157, 252
Jeanne la Folle, reine d'Espagne, 144, 157,
    252
Jews, 11, 24, 48, 119, 123, 152–53, 163,
    166–67, 169, 224, 229
Jiménez de Cisneros, Francisco,
    archbishop of Toledo, 121
Joana, 253
Johanna die Wahnsinnige, 252
Jover, José María, 91
Joyce, Rosemary A., 57
Juan Carlos I, king of Spain, 219
Juan-Navarro, Santiago, 229, 241
Juana creó la noche, 18, 25, 28, 158–60,
    163–66, 168–72, 252
Juana de Castilla ante el cadáver de su
    esposo, 253
Juana del amor hermoso, 18–19, 22,
    24–25, 28, 86, 116–17, 119–32, 159,
    161, 163, 166, 171, 252
Juana la Loca (Mad Love), 10, 21, 26–27,
    110 n. 1, 194 n. 9, 228, 233–42, 254
Juana la Loca . . . de vez en cuando, 254
Juana la Loca frente al cadáver de Felipe el
    Hermoso, 16, 176–77, 185, 190–93,
    215, 253

Juana la Loca ante el féretro de su esposo [sketch], 253
Juana la Loca ante el féretro de su esposo Felipe, 253
Juana la Loca recluida en Tordesillas, 253
Juana la Loca: Seis novelas superhistóricas, 24, 117, 92–106, 253
Juana la Loca: Vivir por amor, 253
Juana of Castile, 20, 253

Ladero Quesada, Miguel Angel, 48, 56, 254
Landa, Ochoa de, 43
Lanz, Johann, 254
Laredo, 34
Larraz, José Ramón, 254
Leggenda di Juana I, La, 253
León Tolosana, Carmelo, 56
leona de Castilla, La, 212
Llegada a Tordesillas de doña Juana la Loca, 253
Llinás, Francisco, 227
Locura de amor (1885), 10, 15–16, 20–23, 26–28, 61–76, 82, 116n. 1, 117–18, 181–82, 194nn. 6 and 9, 201, 212–13, 217, 222–23, 228, 233–35, 239–40, 252–53
Locura de amor (1909), 212, 253
Locura de amor (1948), 10, 21, 26–27, 67–68, 210–42, 194, 253
Lola la Piconera, 212
Love Possessed Juana, 110, 117, 252
Lunatic Queen, The, 252

Ma fille Marie-Hélène Charles Quint, 25, 144, 151, 157, 253
Machado, Antonio, 117
Machiavelli, Niccolò, 137, 144, 158, 222, 229
Magnarelli, 117
Mallo, Tomás, 91
Manuel, Don Juan, 34, 217, 223
Mares, Roberto, 254
Marías, Julián, 106
Maureta, Gabriel, 253
Martín Acosta, Emelina, 56
Martín Elizondo, José, 18, 25, 28, 158–60, 163–66, 168–72, 252
Martín Recuerda, José Martín, 17, 18, 28
Martínez, Juan, 253

Martínez Mediero, Manuel, 18–19, 22, 24–25, 28, 86, 91, 116, 117, 119–29, 159, 161, 163, 166, 171, 252
Martínez Nadal, Rafael, 117
Martínez Pérez, José, 75
Mártir de Anglería, Pedro, 45, 155
Mary Tudor, queen of England, 50
Matienzo, Fray Tomás de, 12, 34
Maurenbrecher, Wilhelm, 254
Maximilian of Austria, Holy Roman Emperor, 11, 34, 37, 49, 51, 198, 250
Mayo, Alfredo, 213
Mazzeti Gardiol, Rita, 106
Medina del Campo, 12, 57
Mendoza, Francisco de, 182
Mendoza, Juana de, 36, 46
Miller, Townsend, 9, 97–99, 104–8, 110, 117, 156, 157, 158, 171, 254
Mink, Louis O., 106
Miraflores, Cargthusian Monastery of, 13
Miranda, Fray Andrés de, 38, 39, 45
Moi, Toril, 56
Monterde, José Enrique, 227
Montero, Rosa, 11, 28, 116, 118, 254
Montherlant, Henry de, 144, 148, 157–58, 160, 163, 170n. 6, 171, 252
Moors, 15, 48, 62, 66, 104n. 6, 110, 119, 123, 127, 146–47, 149, 166–67, 182, 187, 190, 198, 199–200, 214, 216, 218, 222–23, 226n. 3, 230–33. *See also* Muslims
Mota, La: fortress, 12, 57, 162, 188
Moxica, Martín de, 104n. 6
Muñoz Fernández, Ángela, 45
Muñoz Molina, Antonio, 91
music, 11, 22, 26, 27, 49, 133, 168, 198–209. *See also* opera
Muslims, 147, 156. *See also* Moors

Naccarato, Frank, 56
Naples, 10, 13, 55
nation, 15–17, 20, 25–27, 41, 65–68, 70–75, 175–97, 210–27, 228–42
National Catholicism, 211
necrophilia, 23, 42n. 10, 44, 53, 61–76, 137–38, 166, 210, 234
Neumann, Harald, 255
Nicolás, César, 106
Nieto Soria, José Manuel, 56
Nieto Soria, José Manuel, 48, 56

Nishikawa, Kazuko, 255
Nogués, Paloma, 44, 254
Núñez D., 91

Obregón, Antonio de, 255
Olaizola, José Luis, 50, 56, 91, 104, 106, 255
opera, 10, 21–22, 26–27, 64, 104n. 2, 159, 190, 198–99, 253. *See also* music
Orduña, Juan de, 10, 21, 26–27, 67–68, 210–42, 194, 253
Orellana, Francisco José, 253
orientalism, 190, 218, 223, 227, 233, 242
Ortega y Gasset, José, 214, 227
Ortiz, Alonso, 56

Padilla, Juan de, 14, 19, 119, 194n. 2
paintings, 10, 15–16, 175–97, 243–51
Pardo Bazán, Emilia, 81, 91, 255
Palacios, Jesús, 227
Paris, 40, 64, 70, 168, 170n. 7, 176, 190, 199–201
Parodi, Alexandre, 144, 157, 252
Paul, John E., 56
Paz, Octavio, 143
Penella, Emma, 170n. 4
Penella, Manuel, 255
Pérez Bustamante, Rogelio, 56
Pérez Galdós, Benito, 16–17, 23–24, 28, 77–91, 118, 252
pergamino de la seducción, El, 10, 21, 194n. 7, 196, 253
Perry, Elizabeth M., 57
Pfandl, Ludwig, 17–18, 22, 28, 41, 45, 86, 91, 96–98, 102, 104n. 2, 105n. 9, 106–7, 118, 235, 242, 255
Philip II, king of Spain, 85, 251
Philip III, king of Spain, 36, 42n. 13, 45
Philippe, duke of Burgundy, king of Castile (Philip I), 9, 11–13, 15–17, 26, 34–40, 42nn. 4 and 6, 49–54, 56, 61–66, 68–69, 72–75, 82, 93, 97–105, 108, 110, 112–13, 122, 124–26, 145–47, 149–53, 156, 158, 162, 166–67, 175, 177, 181–82, 188, 191, 194n. 8, 195n. 13, 198–99, 202–4, 206–7, 213–25, 236, 241n. 6, 243–45, 247–48, 250–51
Pick, Daniel, 76
plague, 14, 37, 150

Poeta, Salvatore, 118
Pollin, Alice, 118
portraits, 27, 122, 153–54, 181, 194n. 7, 243–51
possessions, 119, 123, 146, 166, 251
Pradilla, Francisco, 16, 176–97, 215, 251, 253
Prast, Antonio, 57
Prawdin, Michael, 22, 97–99, 104nn. 5, 6, and 7, 106–7, 109, 118, 255
Prescott, William H., 106
Preston, Paul, 227
Primo de Rivera, José Antonio, 214, 227
Princesa de los Ursinos, La, 212
Prisoner of Tordesillas, The, 118, 253
Protestant Reformation, 120–22

Quilligan, Maureen, 57
Quirini, Vicenzo, 34

Rage d'amours, 205–7, 253
Razón de Estado o Juego de reinas, 20, 252
regenerationism, 214
Reina loca, La, 254
Reina loca de amor, La, 253
Reine folle d'amour, La, 253
Reine Juana, 144, 157, 252
Rejas: monastery of, 38
Retablo de la pasión y muerte de Juana la Loca, 118, 252
Rey Briones, Antonio del, 106
Reyero, Carlos, 76
Ribera, Diego de, 43n. 24
Richards, Michael, 227
Rivelles, Amparo, 212
Rivière Gómez, Auror, 227
Roach, Joseph, 76
Robert, Clémence, 144, 157
Roblès, Emmanuel, 10, 18–20, 25, 28, 144, 157–72, 252
Rodríguez, Julio, 116n. 1, 118, 253
Rodríguez-Fischer, Ana, 118
Rodríguez Villa, Antonio, 22, 40–41, 45, 118, 181, 255
Roesler, E. Robert, 255
romanticism, 9–10, 15–16, 20, 22, 24–26, 33, 39–41, 61–75, 146, 177, 181, 189–93, 198–202, 208, 210, 215, 218, 228, 233–34, 239, 251
Romero, Concha, 20, 22, 252

Romero, Gregorio, 252
Rosales, Eduardo, 187, 253
Rubin, Nancy, 57, 118
Rueda, Manuel, 116, 118, 252
Ruiz Ramón, Francisco, 76
Rummel, Erika, 57, 129

Sabido, Miguel, 25, 116, 133–43, 252
Sabugo Abril, Amancio, 106, 144
Saint Claire of Tordesillas: royal
    monastery of, 39
Samuel, Charles, 157
Sánchez, José, 213
Sánchez, Magdalena S., 45
Sánchez Biosca, Vicente, 227
Santa Juana de Castilla, 16–17, 23–24,
    77–91, 252
Santiago (Saint James), 39
Sanz y Ruiz de la Peña, Nicomedes, 41,
    45, 94, 96, 102, 104 nn. 2 and 6, 106,
    255
Satrapía: El libro de memorias de Juana la
    Loca, 118, 253
Schoonover, Lawrence L., 118, 253
Seek the Darkness: The Story of Juana la
    Loca, 44, 157, 253
Séché, Alphonse, 157
Seguin, Jean-Claude, 227
Segovia, 12
Serrano, Emilio, 201, 253
Serrano Ajenjo, José Enrique, 96, 106
Seville, 123
Shoemaker, William H., 91
silencios de Juana la Loca, Los, 118, 194 n.
    7, 197, 253
Silva, Alberto, 255
Simancas, Archive of, 40, 42 n. 1, 44, 90,
    255
Simón Tarrés, Antonio, 57
Simonnin, Antoine-Jean-Baptiste, 144,
    157, 252
slaves, Moorish, 104 n. 6, 146–47, 163
Smyth, Edmund J., 157
Soldevila-Durante, Ignacio, 106
Somerville, Margaret R., 57
Sommé, Monique, 42 n. 14, 45
Soto, Domingo de, 85
Spanish Civil War, 26, 92, 96, 116, 163,
    221, 225
Suárez Fernández, Luis, 45, 57
Succession, female, 11–12, 50, 213

Surtz, Ronald E., 46
Szásdi, István, 46

Tamayo y Baus, Manuel, 10, 15–16,
    20–23, 26–28, 61–76, 82, 116 n. 1,
    117–18, 181–82, 194 nn. 6 and 9, 201,
    212–13, 217, 222–23, 228, 233–35,
    239–40, 252–53
Taylor Woods, Jeremy, 118
testament: of Diego Gómez Manrique,
    36; of Isabel I, 13, 187
Thibaudat, Jean-Pierre, 157
Tighe, Harry, 255
Tordesillas: castle of, 9, 13–14, 16–17, 19,
    23, 25, 28, 37–38, 46, 55, 82, 85, 86,
    88–89, 93, 101–2, 105–6, 118–19, 121,
    128, 144–45, 154, 157, 164, 166–68,
    171 n. 9, 180, 191–92, 194 n. 8, 196,
    198, 205–7, 215, 230, 241, 251, 253–55
Toledo, 38, 119, 122, 127, 221
Toledo, María de, 240 n. 2
Toro, 195 n. 13
Toro, José López de, 42 n. 8, 45
Torquemada, Tomás de, 181, 251
Torre, Antonio de la, 57
Tudela de Duero, 15, 62
Tusell, Javier, 227

Urraca, queen of Castile, 92, 95
Ursula, Saint, 38, 43 n. 20

Valencia, 213, 224, 226, 241
Valladolid, 13, 42 n. 1, 45, 46, 56, 57,
    196, 255
Vallejo Nágera, Antonio, 255
Vallés, Lorenzo, 15, 182, 253
Vermeil, Louis-Lucien, 144, 157, 252
Veyre, Philibert de, 35, 40, 181, 213,
    217, 220, 222–23, 230, 232
Viladot, Guillem, 253
Villacañas Berlanga, José Luis, 220, 227
Villapalos, Gustavo, 57
Villar Toldán, Miguel, 212
Villars, Janina, 144, 157, 253
Villena, marquis of and duke of
    Escalona, Don Diego López Pacheco,
    217, 223–24
virgin martyrs, the eleven thousand, 38,
    43 n. 20
Voragine, Jacobus de, 46
Vostell, Wolf, 255

Walters, Gareth D., 118
White, Hayden, 106
Winston, Jane, 157
Wystup, Christine, 10, 25–26, 158–61, 165–69, 170 n. 6, 171 n. 9, 172, 252

Yanko, Aroní, 116, 118, 194, 253
Ynduráin, Francisco, 106

Zalama, Miguel Angel, 41, 46, 96, 106, 255
Zatlin, Phyllis, 144, 157
Zavala, Iris M., 57
Zaragoza, 38
Zavalía, Alberto de, 252
Zuidam, Rob, 205–9, 253
Zumalde Arregi, Imanol, 218, 227
Zweig, Stefan, 129

Wedded to Crime

Wedded to Crime

MY LIFE IN THE JEWISH MAFIA

Sandy Sadowsky

with H. B. Gilmour

G. P. PUTNAM'S SONS   NEW YORK

The following is a true story. In some instances names have been changed to guard the innocent or for reasons of legal and personal protection. Hattie Prince, Reefer May, Peter Knossos, Muttel Diamond, Bea Spizer, Lila Navarro, Peter Von Shlemme, Milty Heinz, Tom Sullivan, Tony and Charlie North, Ziggy Schwartz, Chalky Lefkowitz, Giorgio the Jaw, Iris, Enid and Lido are pseudonyms.

G. P. Putnam's Sons
Publishers Since 1838
200 Madison Avenue
New York, NY 10016

Library of Congress Cataloging-in-Publication Data

Sadowsky, Sandy.
Wedded to crime: my life in the Jewish Mafia / Sandy Sadowsky,
with H.B. Gilmour.
p. cm.
ISBN 0-399-13614-2
1. Jewish criminals—United States—Case studies.
2. Mafia—United States—Case studies. 3. Sadowsky, Sandy.
4. Wives—United States—Biography. I. Gilmour,
H. B. (Harriet B.), 1939–. II. Title.
HV6194.J4S23 1992   91-42058 CIP
364.1′06′092—dc20
[B]

Printed in the United States of America
1 2 3 4 5 6 7 8 9 10

ACKNOWLEDGMENTS

It would never have occurred to me to write a book, except for a fabulous happening on a rainy day at the hairdresser's. I was telling a story about one of the funnier episodes in my life as a gangster's wife, and two other women came out from under their hair dryers to listen. One was Lee Klein, a neighbor, who said, "If you were a book, I would read you"; and the other was Bernice Chardiet, a well-known book producer, who said, "You *should* write a book and I'll *help* you work on it. You have a terrific story to tell." From the moment we met, Bernice had faith in me and in my story, not only for its "insider" view but for what it might say to other women. I'm very grateful to Bernice and her partner, Daniel Weiss, for their diligent efforts to make this book a reality on my behalf. I would also like to thank Lisa Wager, my editor at Putnam, for her enthusiasm and her wonderful editing skills, and H.B., my collaborator, for her wit and humor, and her dedication to this project.

And to all my dearest family and friends, who have been there for me and shared my life, a very special thank you, and all my love!

*To Jeffrey, the greatest! My joy,
my friend, my beloved son, and to
Tillie, my mother. Wish you were here!*

Contents

	Prologue	9
1	A Nice Jewish Girl	15
2	The Velvet Room	29
3	Bernie's Princess	39
4	Playing House	55
5	Easy Come, Easy Go	64
6	Mrs. Wise Guy	74
7	Changes	93
8	Roman Holiday	108
9	The Gold Coast	114
10	The House of Yenom	134
11	A Stand-Up Broad	144
12	A Birthday Present for Bernie	157
13	Life and Death	175
14	My *Gutta Better*	192
15	Alone	205
16	The Merry Widow	222
17	Living Dangerously	236
18	Courting Trouble	250
19	Sadie, Sadie	259
20	The Long Goodbye	269
	Epilogue	287

Prologue

"I've got a little business to take care of before we hit the Copa, kid," Bernie Barton said, ushering me into the back of the limo that had been waiting to pick us up at his Greenwich Village supper club.

It was an unusually warm June night in New York. We were on our way uptown to catch Billy Daniels's opening at the Copacabana—the popular singer was a personal friend of Bernie's—and I was dressed for the occasion in five-inch heels, a tight little black cocktail dress, and a single strand of pearls. My thick auburn hair was pulled back in a high ponytail. Between the heels and piled-up hair I was just about Bernie's height. And I was wearing my makeup the way I'd learned to during my brief stint as a Vegas showgirl—bright red lipstick, thickly drawn doe eyes, and spiky false black lashes.

It was about a week before my twentieth birthday and a week after Bernie's forty-first.

"Stop at Chesty's, the cocktail lounge over on Thirty-eighth Street," he told the driver.

I'd only been dating Bernie Barton for about a month, but already I knew better than to ask what business he was going to take care of.

"This is Sandy Sadowsky," he introduced me to the four men waiting for us at a table at the back of the bar. Despite the oppressive weather, they were all in suits. Diamonds flashed when they shot their cuffs. Diamond-studded gold watches glinted at their wrists. Diamond rings—one in the shape of a horseshoe—circled their pinkies.

Two of the men were bookmakers, one tall, nervous, skinny; the other short, fat, and bald. The third person at the table looked like a fireplug in a sports jacket. He was the bodyguard. And the body he was guarding belonged to the fourth man at the table, Tommy Dio, a stocky, immaculately groomed man with thick worker's hands and manicured fingernails.

Tommy was known as the nice Dio—compared to his brother, the celebrated Teamster boss, Johnny Dio. The Dioguardi boys were "labor relations experts," soldiers in the Lucchese crime family. They were also the cherished nephews of James Plumeri, better known on the pages of The Daily News *as the mobster Jimmy Doyle.*

"Uncle Jimmy," who was several years older than Bernie, was a friend of his from way back, from when Bernie was a spunky, blue-eyed kid driving bootleg trucks for Meyer Lansky on the Lower East Side. It was probably Uncle Jimmy who had suggested the sit-down meeting with Tommy Dio. Tommy was considered a gentleman. If anything needed straightening out in New York's Garment Center, he was the man to talk to.

What needed straightening out that night was a debt some woman owed to the Mutt and Jeff book-making shylocks across the table. They had fronted a girl named Bunny several thousand dollars in betting capital—at the going mob rate of interest. Bunny lost the bets. The vigorish, the interest, was mounting like mad. By this point it was about five times the original loan.

"I don't want no more fuckin' jewelry," the tall, nervous bookie said, then shot me an apologetic glance. *"Excuse my language."* Then he turned back to Bernie. *"I got jewelry coming out my ass already. I ain't a fence. I don't work on Forty-seventh Street. I want the cash, or her old man's going to be shitting out of a second asshole. Excuse me,"* he said again to me.

Bernie reached for my hand under the table and gave it a little squeeze. I smiled at him, then ducked my head and went back to stirring my screwdriver.

"BB, what's your interest here?" Tommy Dio asked Bernie.

"Bunny's an old friend. Her husband's a nice guy, Tommy. Small potatoes. Straight. A dress manufacturer—"

Tommy Dio glanced at the short bookmaker. *"You went up to see him last week, am I right? What did you do, you threatened the man?"*

"Tommy, Tommy," the bald guy said, mopping his brow with his paisley silk handkerchief. *"The broad owes us up the wahzoo. It's going on months already. What do you want me to do?"*

Tommy Dio brushed imaginary crumbs off the white linen tablecloth and shrugged at Bernie, waiting for his response.

"I'm godfather to their kid," Bernie said. *"Just stop the clock on the vig, that's all. Give her some time to clean up the loan . . . to handle the vig she's already run up."*

"The woman is still betting," the short, fat guy said.

"She can't bet no more," Tommy Dio decreed. *"That's the first thing."*

"Okay," Bernie agreed.

"This girl, this Bunny—you used to fuck her, right?" the tall bookmaker asked Bernie. *"Excuse me,"* he said again to me.

Bernie's hand tightened on mine. *"So?"* he said softly, in his genial, gravelly voice. But I knew he'd come close to swinging at the man.

"So, you still shtupping her? That's why you're so concerned?"

"Watch the mouth," Bernie warned, still smiling. *"Here's what I'm*

asking," he said. *"The woman's a friend of mine and she's in trouble. Stop the clock on the vig. Now. Today. Give her a year to pay up. Leave her old man alone. And take the goddamn jewelry she's offering as collateral. Give the woman a break."*

"Done," Tommy Dio said. *"BB, you're personally responsible that she holds up her end. It's a done deal."*

"He's still fucking her. Got to be," the short, fat guy laughed.

"Don't talk that way in front of the kid, okay?" Bernie said. This time, he wasn't smiling.

"Okay. Okay," the bookmaker said. *"No offense, kid, right?"*

I was the kid.

George Raft, the movie star, who was also a friend of Bernie's, always called me the kid. And when I was pregnant with Bernie's son, Raft said, *"Look at that, the kid's going to have a kid."*

Many Junes later, almost to the day, the kid's kid was graduating from college.

The 1989 graduating class of the John Jay College of Criminal Justice was so big that the ceremony was held in Carnegie Hall that year. And the day was so swelteringly hot that Carnegie Hall looked and sounded like the F train. Despite the air-conditioning, wilted parents were fanning themselves with graduation programs. Little kids were squirming, shouting, tugging at the ties they'd been forced to wear or their new, too tight shoes.

I was glad I'd arrived early to get a decent seat. I'd hurried up the steps and through the lobby, not knowing whether it was my high heels or my heart making the racket. Before I'd even gotten to my seat, I'd felt tears brimming. But I made it, mascara dry, head held high, as if Bernie were gripping my arm, leading me through the chaos.

I lost it when the graduates marched in. The families and friends who'd waited so impatiently fell silent for a moment, awed. Then we all stood and started applauding wildly. I spotted my son among the capped and gowned graduates filing into the hall. That did it. The flood gates gave way. The tears came, the makeup streaked. I didn't care. Jeffrey looked so handsome, so much like his father—ramrod straight, with Bernie's muscular build and dark, good looks.

And how proud of him Bernie would have been, I thought, as the graduates took their seats. Jeffrey's father hadn't gone to college. He hadn't even graduated from grade school. Everything Bernie Barton had needed to survive as a kid, he'd learned on the streets of New York's Lower East Side. Back then, the neighborhood—from Allen Street to Avenue A— teemed with Jewish immigrants, and the streets stunk of herring, pickles, and poverty. When Bernie was a boy, Meyer Lansky ruled the Lower East Side and guys like Farvel the Stick and Red Levine could help a smart kid bring home a buck to his family instead of wasting his time in school. College? Where Bernie grew up, having a son in the sixth grade was a luxury most families couldn't afford.

Now, here was Bernie's son receiving a college degree in Criminology. Bernie's son, Jeffrey, sitting on the stage of Carnegie Hall as the president of John Jay talked about the graduates' future in law enforcement. Some would join the New York Police Department, he said. Others would go into drug enforcement work, join the FBI, or go on to law school and perhaps become district attorneys, lawyers, judges. Today, there were more opportunities than ever in law enforcement, the president pointed out ironically, because there was more crime. And the young people graduating, he said, would be among those responsible for changing that daunting statistic, for fighting the war on drugs, for combating crime, for making our society safe and our country a better place to live.

Proud? You could practically hear the buttons popping off the parents' vests. I was *kvelling,* bursting with pride and joy. Bernie, I asked silently, did you hear that? That's your kid he's talking about, the one you never really got a chance to know.

What a party he'd have thrown today, I thought as I watched Jeffrey on the stage, waiting for his diploma. Bernie would have pulled out all the stops, jammed our Upper East Side apartment with friends and family. Cokey would have come down from Harlem. Uncle Vinny would have come up from Florida. Josh would have been there, the Park Avenue lawyer who—as Bernie had always warned him he would—had finally gotten disbarred for consorting with criminals. There would have been huge platters of food, champagne flowing, people singing and dancing and toasting, "Mazel-tov!"

The *gantse* wise-guy *mishpocheh* would have showed up for Bernie's boy. From Vegas, Detroit, Miami, Cincinnati, Chicago. Guys with $50 haircuts and $1,000 suits, diamond pinky rings, gold Rolexes, and shoes as soft and shiny as their silk ties. Mobsters with names like haberdashers—Manny, Moe, and Dave. Tough guys who talked business in the steam room of the Luxor Baths and then cried at Molly's on Rivington Street when the violinist played "My Yiddishe Momme." And it would never have occurred to Bernie Barton that there was anything strange about a room full of gangsters celebrating his son's graduation from a school for law enforcement.

Watching our son accept his diploma now, watching Jeffrey wave the rolled parchment over his head in triumph, I suddenly felt the terrible loss again. Right there in Carnegie Hall, at what should have been—and was, really—one of the happiest, proudest moments of my life, I needed Bernie beside me. Twenty-four years after his death, I still missed him.

Oddly, though, I noticed that I was not crying now. I shook my head, and smiled. Sandy, I said to myself, look at that—all you have to do is *think* of the guy and you go from wimp to stand-up broad again. I could almost hear him saying it: *Tough guys don't cry, baby. Stand-up broads don't, either.* His words, his thoughts, his way of life. When had they become mine?

I was a kid when I met Bernie Barton. And though I didn't know it at twenty, I'd been desperate for everything this man had to offer. His strength, certainty, and protection. His desire to mold me, teach me, turn me into his kind of woman, perfectly matched my need to be shaped, led, and loved.

I guess it was right there, in Carnegie Hall, the day of Jeffrey's graduation, that I began to understand. I seemed to have the beginnings of an answer to the question I'd asked myself countless times in a life where excitement, danger, and violence were as commonplace as Corning Ware: What's a nice Jewish girl like you doing in a place like this?

CHAPTER ONE

A Nice Jewish Girl

There's a joke about a little boy who comes home from school and tells his mother he was in the class play. "I played a Jewish husband," he says. "That's okay," his mother tells him. "Next time, you'll have a speaking part."

Contrary to belief, all Jewish husbands are not mild-mannered accountants.

My father was a gambler. He embezzled from his brother. Borrowed money from the mob. Had an affair with my mother's best friend. And, when I was fifteen years old, he ran off and left us penniless—my mother, Tillie, my eight-year-old sister, Marlene, and me. We were so flat busted that when the loansharks, the "shylocks," came to our house to collect the money he owed them, they felt so sorry for my mother that they gave *her* money. He got in touch with me months later and conned me out of a small inheritance that was in trust for me. His name was Sol and I worshipped him.

It was his father's old apartment in Flatbush that we moved to in 1949, when I was ten. It was near Ebbets Field when the Dodgers still played there, a big, airy apartment with high ceilings and lots of light in a tree-lined, middle-class Jewish neighborhood in Brooklyn. My sister and I shared a pink room. We slept in twin four-poster Colonial beds. At night, with the door open at the right angle, I could look into our dresser mirror and watch the living room TV.

We lived on the fifth floor of a six-story apartment building. Our neighbors down the hall were Enid and Mervin. Enid was a knockout. She had false eyelashes, hairpieces, hats, and gloves for every occasion. She was a great cook. She drove her own car. Her husband Mervin didn't drive. He was kind of a *shlep*.

Enid taught my mother how to dress, how to put on makeup. My mother would sit at Enid's dressing table and Enid would powder, paint, and perfume her, show her how to use eyeliner, how to glue on the lashes, pluck a sophisticated arched brow, pencil in fuller lips. They'd try on clothes together. And whisper and laugh. I was wild for Enid. I idolized her.

After school, if my mother wasn't home, I'd go down the hall to Enid's for milk and cookies. Sometimes, I'd try on her shoes. She had more shoes than A.S. Beck's and Kitty Kelly's combined: suede ankle straps, open-toed wedgies, creamy, soft leather, and glass-smooth patent leather in "smart" colors, gay colors, with grosgrain bows and satin trim, and flat, medium, and break-your-ass high heels. Enid was our own Joan Crawford. I hung on her every word, and a couple I wasn't supposed to hear.

Sitting at her kitchen table, my chin in my hands, I'd listen to the confidences she shared with my mother . . . and, one day, discovered the secret of the shoes. Enid, glamorous wife of the *nebbish,* Merv, was a kept woman. Everything she had, from her home to her hairpieces, she owed to her lover, "a big man in the shoe union."

Enid and Mervin were my parents' best friends. The couples went out a lot together. Dressed to kill, they hit the New York night spots. They drank, danced, and dined together, had their pictures taken against zebra-skin covered banquettes, toasted one another, argued over which couple would pick up the check and who should tip the hatcheck and cigarette girls.

My father loved the high life. He loved to see my mother done to the nines. Her beautiful, pale face brightened with red lipstick and amber rouge. Her hair swept up, held in place with fancy combs and crocheted snoods. Sol was one of the original slaves of fashion. He loved clothes, loved shopping, loved to spend lavishly on us, his girls. He'd take my mother and me into the city to carpeted dress shops on Madison Avenue, where he'd supervise our selections. A handsome, tall, and burly man with striking, prematurely white hair, he'd sit on little gilt chairs surveying us, squinting through the smoke of his ever-present cigar, as we modeled for him.

Clothes. Broads. Cigars. Gambling. Sol was passionate about them. He borrowed the cash to support his passions wherever he could—whether it was from shylocks on the street or the till of the bindery he owned with his brother, Meyer. My father loved excitement, tumult, the wildness of the streets. From the time he was a kid, he always had to be where the action was. As a boy, he'd idolized gangsters. As an adolescent, he'd driven a bootlegging truck for Al Capone. He knew how to melt down gold. He hung out at the track. He loved the horses and could not keep a buck in the pockets of his elegant, double-breasted suits if there was one around to bet on. Clothes. Broads. Cigars. Gambling. He loved them. But most of all, he assured me, he loved me. Most of all, I was the love of his life. His favorite. His girl.

And the day he left was the day I stopped being a girl. February 1954. I was fifteen years old. On Friday night, my father packed a suitcase. It was no big deal. He kissed us goodbye. He was going out of town on business. It was bitter cold out. From the kitchen window, I watched him walking toward the Oldsmobile on Lincoln Road. Under the street light, I could see his coat blowing, the breath coming from his mouth as he opened the car door. He didn't look up at me or wave. It was no big deal.

On Monday afternoon, I walked home from Erasmus Hall High School. It was still cold out, but the books clutched against me were more an unconscious shield for my breasts than a way of staying warm. My legs were bare except for the bobby socks and white bucks I wore with my pleated navy skirt. My long, wavy hair was tucked into the hood of the white and plaid reversible parka my father had bought me in the fall. And if my lips were quivering with cold, they were quivering under the requisite Milkmaid pink lipstick we all wore that year.

I opened the door to our apartment. The warmth in the hallway felt good. I shook my head out of the parka hood. Something was wrong. From the vestibule, I saw men in the living room. They were waiting for me.

I recognized Dr. Horowitz first. "Is Mommy sick?"

My uncle Jakey was there. He answered before Dr. Horowitz could. "No, she's asleep." He was angry.

"The doctor gave her a shot," my mother's other brother Leo explained, nodding at Horowitz.

"She got a letter from your father today." Jakey said *your father* like it was the polite form of *that bastard*. "He must have mailed it before he left. He's not coming back."

"The money," Leo prompted.

"He took it. All of it. Every cent your mother had in the bank for his *fahcocktah* gambling. He owes 'the shylocks.' From his family's mouth he'll steal to pay the shylocks! Look," Jakey said, snatching up the letter that had been sitting on one of the end tables. He held it out to me. He smacked it with the back of his hand. "Look. This is what he says. I owe the shylocks. I'm not coming back. So Leo goes to the bank as soon as your mother calls and, sure enough. Nothing. *Gornisht.* He emptied the account. He left you to starve!"

Enid came out of the bedroom and put her arm around me. "Sit down, Sandy, honey," she said. She took the letter from Jakey and handed it to me. I skimmed it. I couldn't really focus on it. All I knew for certain was that it was addressed to my mother. It didn't mention my sister or me. I handed it back to Enid.

"It'll be all right, Sandy," she said. "You've got to be strong for Marlene and your mother. She came to my door sobbing. I called Dr. Horowitz and he gave her a tranquilizer. She's sleeping now, but she's going to need you when she wakes up." Enid took my hand and squeezed it. "It's okay, honey. Everything will work out. You'll see."

I didn't respond aloud. I became aware of a suddenly deafening pulse in my ears. It took a little while to realize that the sound was coming from the thudding of my heart. I don't know if anyone said anything else. I wouldn't have heard it. My mind was dead; my body, my emotions had taken over. All I felt was rage. As if I'd caught Jakey's anger like a cold.

I walked into the darkened bedroom where my mother was sleeping. I stood beside the bed, staring at her. I hated her. It was her fault that he'd left, that he'd left *me*. It had to be. I hadn't done anything, had I? I was the one he loved. He'd never have left me. I hated her. I hated her in the wedding picture on the dressing table, the one standing on the doily next to her glass perfume tray. I wanted to smash the picture of her holding calla lilies, standing next to him, in her long white satin gown.

She was seventeen years old in that wedding portrait; and he was twenty-six. They had been secretly married for more than two years.

My mother, Tillie, was only thirteen years old when Sol Sadowsky swept her off her feet. He was tall and handsome, armed with a quick smile, a facile phrase, and the raw energy and ambition of an American. A big man, relentless in pursuit of what he wanted. And, at thirteen, Tillie was it—a beautiful child, a refugee from Eastern Europe who spoke English gamely but haltingly, a pale, fragile-looking girl with blonde hair and coal-black eyes. To him she must have seemed a treasured and protected child, but at thirteen she'd already had enough sorrow and adventures to fill a normal lifetime.

Her mother and father had been murdered in a pogrom. At three years old, she'd gone to live with her mother's sister, Tohba, and her husband, Sholem. Orthodox Jews, they'd been forced to flee Russia, and Tillie's childhood was spent wandering through a Europe crushed by poverty and hostile to Jews. When finally her aunt and uncle managed passage to America, they adopted Tillie. Despite the fact that she was always called "the orphan child," she was adored by her adoptive parents and, reared in their Orthodox household, was considered pious, loving, and sensible. The brothers born after her, Jake, Marty, and Leo, had always been protective and respectful of her.

And she of them. So much so that although she was a married woman at fifteen, she went home to her aunt and uncle's house every night and told no one of the marriage until she turned seventeen. Then she announced that she was engaged to Sol Sadowsky. Everyone knew she'd been seeing him for years, knew how unaccountably constant he'd been, probably marveled that a man of his reputation had acted with such faithful restraint. Pleased and undoubtedly relieved for her, the family threw Sol and Tillie a mighty wedding. It was years before anyone discovered that on her wedding day, the orphan child was already married.

She was not a child anymore. She was, to me, that day and for years to follow, my enemy—the woman whose ignorance of fashion, coquetry, compromise had driven my father away. I turned from the wedding portrait remembering the nights they'd fought. It was her voice I remembered, her shrill, unforgiving anger. Her tears and outrage at his broken promises, the gambling debts, the increasing, unexplained absences. It was the terrible feeling of helplessness I remembered, of lying in bed and listening and knowing, somehow, that my future was being decided by my mother's unhappiness.

I left her—in the room that Monday afternoon and in the wreckage of my adolescent heart. I turned to Enid for consolation. And so did my mother. And Enid was always there for us, helping with a few bucks, a little food, words of comfort and encouragement. My uncle Meyer, from whom my father had stolen, also sent money and food. It was true what my mother's brothers had said: Sol had cleaned us out. He'd taken every cent he could get his hands on. There was no money for rent, for clothes, for food. He'd left us to starve.

It was the end of normalcy. I'd never loved school, but I'd had friends there. If I wasn't a great student, I had other attributes. I was admired for my personality and spirit and sense of humor. I dressed well. I was tall and maybe a bit self-conscious about my height and developing body, but I was reasonably attractive and, under Enid's tutelage, getting good at making the most of my dark eyes and pale skin and dark, auburn hair.

Now, shame bowed me. My eyes were bloodshot and swollen from crying night after night, and dark from lack of sleep. My skin grew sallow. My shoulders were rounded with despair. I felt and looked like hell.

Shame kept me from my friends, too. Just being around kids who had normal, two-parent families caused me pain. I felt separate, different, cast out. My father had abandoned me. My flamboyant, high-living father had run off leaving us destitute. Potatoes mashed with *shmaltz,* eggs and onions became our nightly protein-balanced meal. My mother, half mad with grief, got a job in a dry-cleaning store, handling other people's dirty clothes. I worked part-time at a shoe store. Every cent we earned went toward helping us survive. And I thought everyone knew and everyone believed—as I must have in my deepest, secret heart—that I'd done something to deserve it.

My best friend, my only friend now, was Leona, who had, by my reckoning, as screwed up a family life as I now did. She was a Polish-Greek Catholic with three bizarre brothers—the nine-year-old walked around the house in high-heeled shoes—and a bus-driver father who made Ralph Kramden look like a Rhodes scholar.

I began to cut school regularly. I couldn't study or concentrate on anything. Almost every day, I'd break down crying in class. Run out, mortified. Find Leona. Go with her to Garfield's Cafeteria and smoke and drink coffee among the old men until it was time to go home. I had avoided my friends. Now they began to gossip about me, to shun me. Rumor was I stayed away from school because I was pregnant. There was no other way for them to explain my sudden tears or why I hid from them. And there was no way for me to explain the separateness and shame I felt.

Finally, the truancy and misery overwhelmed me and I dropped out of Erasmus Hall High. I had turned sixteen. There'd been no celebration, no sugar corsage or birthday cake. My father had left and taken my childhood with him.

From the lofty height of my high-heeled shoes, I looked down on my school girlfriends. I was still sixteen but I was a working woman now, wearing nylon stockings and earning $45 a week at the shoe store. I'd enrolled in adult evening classes to get my diploma. I contributed my salary to the household. Still, there was never enough money at home, and that was not the only scarcity. Energy, laughter, optimism, and joy were also in short supply. So that fall, at the invitation of my mother's cousins who had a big house in Beverly Hills and two kids approximately the same ages as Marlene and I, we moved to California.

If I'd felt like an outsider among my Brooklyn classmates, I felt like a Martian among the blue-eyed blondes of Beverly Hills, who drove their own convertibles to school, dressed like they'd stepped out of *Seventeen* magazine, and lived the kind of lives I'd only seen in movies. It was as if I were watching some blinding Technicolor extravaganza from the last row of a dark theater.

Nearly every morning I'd leave our cousin Helen's sprawling Tudor mansion and find a bench along the way to school. There I'd sit, in all my angry, adolescent New York-ness, cutting school, staring out at brilliant sunlight, turquoise cars, tanned people, palm trees. And I'd long to return to Flatbush, to drink coffee with Leona in the smoky comfort of Garfield's Cafeteria, to be back in Brooklyn where I knew who was who, what was what, and how to pronounce it.

One day, when we'd been in California about a month, I saw someone sitting on one of *my* benches. A kid hunched over like a little old lady, with a couple of school books and a loose-leaf binder beside her. As I got closer, I recognized the dejected little girl. It was my sister, Marlene, who was nine years old then. I was shocked to discover that she was as miserable and lonely in Beverly Hills as I was.

That night at dinner I announced to my mother that I was leaving. "With you or without you," I said, "I'm going back. I can't stand it here. I ask for a cup of coffee 'regular.' It's bad enough that I say, 'caw-fee' and they say, 'calf-ee.' But they think 'regular' means *black*—with milk on the side!"

"Big deal," she said. "You'll get used to it."

"I don't want to get used to it. I want to go home! If I have to beg, borrow, or steal the airfare I will. But I'm going back to Brooklyn."

"Stop it, Sandy." My mother shook her head and sighed. "You're just a kid. Who's going to take care of you? Where are you going to live?"

We'd given up the apartment on Lincoln Road. Home was no longer a place.

"I'll get my job back in the shoe store," I said. "I don't need you or anyone to support me. I can do it myself and I will."

Two weeks later, after a lot of screaming and fighting, my cousin gave me the airfare. I packed a suitcase and returned to New York alone. I got a job—in a training program at AT&T. I even re-enrolled in night school. And I lived with any friend or relative who'd put me up for a night or two. It was lonely and exhausting. I lived out of the single suitcase I'd brought with me. It was a fierce winter, and I was still in aching shock over the sudden destruction of our family. Between the weather, work and school, and the gypsy life I was living, I was constantly tired. And very relieved when, a couple of months before my seventeenth birthday, my mother and Marlene returned from California.

We moved into a single room with a kitchenette and bathroom a couple of blocks from our former, two-bedroom apartment. It was cramped and ugly, but I was grateful to have a home base, a place where I could finally hang up my clothes.

The relief and gratitude I felt were secrets I kept from my mother. I no longer trusted her. The shabby apartment where we all slept in one room I added to my list of grievances against her. I still held her responsible for my father's leaving, for the devastation of our family. Not only had he gone, but he might as well have taken her with him for all the good she was doing us now. She'd become useless, a depressed drudge incapable of anything but anger or tears. She clung to her family. She had no friends left. And, in my terrible, callow cruelty, I let her know it every chance I got.

I knew what would make her wince. "You drove him away," I'd shout at her. "He's probably found another woman."

Enid was no longer our neighbor. My mother stopped seeing her. And with work and school occupying all my time, I hardly ever visited our old building where Enid and Merv still lived. One day, I saw Enid's green Buick parked across the street from our new place.

"Sandy!" She rolled down the window and called to me. "Come over here, honey. I want to talk to you."

I climbed into the front seat beside her.

"Your father wants to see you," she said.

I was stunned. I turned and looked over my shoulder, half-expecting to see my father in the backseat. "Where is he? You know where he is? You've talked to him?"

She was lighting up a Pall Mall. Her manicured fingernails were blood-red against the white cigarette. She shrugged and stuck the lighter back into the dashboard. "He wants to see you, Sandy. I'll take you to him. But don't tell your mother. Okay?"

Dumbfounded, I nodded my head. "Where are we going?" I asked, as she pulled away from the curb. "How did he get hold of you? Did he call? Have you been in touch with him all along?"

"He's talked to Merv a couple of times," she said uncomfortably.

We parked on a Brooklyn street near a luncheonette my father had liked. As we walked toward the shop, I saw him. He was standing just outside the luncheonette, handsome as ever in a dark overcoat, his thick white hair ruffled by the wind. He was smoking a cigar and he gave me a crooked smile. "Hi, sweetheart," he said.

I ran to hug him, my heart bursting with joy and relief. He was back. His troubles were over. He was coming home!

But he turned to Enid who was standing a few steps off to the side and put his arm around her. "There's something you should know, Sandy," my father said. "Enid and I are in love—we have been for many years. We're going to get married as soon as our divorces come through."

I stared at him, incredulous. For years? "You were having an affair before you left us?"

My father nodded, the cigar bobbing merrily up and down.

"We didn't want to hurt you or your mother, Sandy," Enid said. "These things happen. I hope when you're older you'll understand."

I found myself nodding as if, sure, I understood. I couldn't speak. My main concern was that my father was going away again.

He pulled away from Enid and bent toward me, taking the cigar out of his mouth. "You'll always be my angel, Sandy," he said. "What happened between your mother and me has nothing to do with you. But now, I need your help. Can you help your old man, Sandy?"

I nodded again, waiting.

"Your grandfather left you a little money, sweetheart. Twenty-five hundred, right? I need you to lend me some. Not a lot. Just half of it. I'll pay you back, Sandy. Just as soon as I'm on my feet again. I promise."

"But I can't touch that money till I'm twenty-one—"

"You can with my consent. I'm your legal guardian," my father explained. He took my hand and we all walked to the bank together. Inside, he helped me fill out the necessary forms, told me what to say, and where to sign. And I withdrew half of my inheritance and gave it to him.

"Daddy," I asked him outside the bank, "do you think I could come live with you? I'm working now. I could help out."

"Sure," he said. "I'd really like that, sweetheart." He kissed me on the forehead. "I'll call you, Sandy. Soon."

I didn't see him again for twenty-six years.

* * *

My father had his gambling debts. My mother had her broken heart. And suddenly, I'd had enough of both of them.

For more than a year and a half, my life had been decided by *their* problems, their secrets and misery: where and how I lived, what I wore, who I saw, and who I hid from. I'd been shlepped from coast to coast, from security to destitution, from childhood to adulthood with no time out for adolescence. Sadness and anger had become my constant companions: They woke me in the morning and put me to sleep at night. Then, shortly after my father let the I-Love-Enid cat out of the bag, everything changed.

Fun was what I wanted. And I didn't care how fast or far I had to run to find it. Where there was a good time to be had, that was where I was going to be.

Garfield's Cafeteria on Church Avenue was just the starting gate. It was open twenty-four hours a day. You could sit around with a cup of coffee for at least twenty-three of them before someone would wipe yesterday's food off the table and give you the boot. After nine at night, the *alter kockers* and the squares cleared out and the cool crowd took over. Leona and I met there nearly every night.

After dinner—which I'd have at home to save a couple of bucks—I'd put my hair up into a long ponytail, pencil in thick black doe eyes, and slip into a cardigan sweater buttoned down the back and tight black Toreador pants. In black flats (which took me from my workday high-heeled five-ten—too tall for the neighborhood boys—to a nearly normal five-eight), I'd run to meet Leona at Garfield's.

Sitting at a table at the back of the blue-tiled cafeteria, we'd nurse our coffee and chain-smoke and alternate laughing too loudly with trying to look blasé—blasé was a cool thing to be. And blowing smoke rings was a blasé thing to do. Seductively, we'd pout circles of smoke into the air and stab at them with the lit end of our cigarettes. "Don't let it die a virgin," we'd laugh. Sometimes, we'd ask one of the guys for a light. Wreathed in blue smoke, we schemed and dreamed and watched the guys with Marlboro packs rolled up in their T-shirt sleeves, combing back their DAs— Duck's Ass hairdos—and hiking up the collars of their black leather motorcycle jackets.

It was 1956. I was almost eighteen. Brando had already won his first Oscar for *On the Waterfront*. Elvis had just made his movie debut in *Love Me Tender*. But for Brooklyn girls, the boy of the moment was our home-grown native son, Tony Curtis. And Arnold, who leaned over from the next table and lit my cigarette in Garfield's one night, was a perfect Curtis clone. Brilliantined black hair, swept back at the sides and cresting over his forehead. Blue eyes surrounded by thick black lashes. A smoldering smile. A Brooklyn accent. And he was in acting school in the city. *The* city—Manhattan. Arnold was irresistible. And of all the leggy, big-breasted girls in Garfield's, it was me he reached for through the smoke.

Arnold introduced me to Manhattan nightlife. His favorite hangout was Jilly's on Fifty-second Street. He knew everyone in the small, dimly lit piano bar where Nicky DeFrancis played "Fly Me to the Moon" and guys in sharkskin suits and pinky rings bought Manhattans and Seven-and-Sevens for Garment Center models. Arnold told me my body was as good as the suit-and-coat models' who hung out at Jilly's. Hell, I was tall enough, and I had a great bust, a tiny waist. I was a perfect size eight. And, come on, did I want to be a telephone operator for the rest of my life? Arnold was all for self-improvement. Hey, why did I think he was taking acting lessons?

The girls I met at Jilly's seconded the motion. Marilyn, who was twenty-one and modeling for Miller and Shulman Coats and Suits, thought I'd do great in the Garment Center. Judy, a hairdresser from Glascow, Kentucky, who worked in a famous New York salon, absolutely agreed with her. "With yo' looks, honey," she'd drawl, "why you bustin' that pretty little butt for peanuts?" I was earning about $65 a week at AT&T. Marilyn made twice that for walking around a showroom looking pretty.

So I signed up for a night course at the Barbizon School of Modeling. And now when I walked into Jilly's to meet Arnold, I was toting the round black patent leather Barbizon Model's hat box the school had given me—along with lessons on how to walk, wear a hat and gloves, diet, makeup, and exercise. In those days, exercise meant getting strapped, with a sling around your butt, onto a machine that shimmied you till your breasts banged against your arms and your teeth felt loose. And, boy, was I proud. I was studying to be a model. I had a boyfriend who was going to be an actor, who looked just like Tony Curtis, and knew everyone from the drop-dead gorgeous greasers at Garfield's to the celebs at Jilly's. Arnold even knew Cole Porter's body guard and masseur, Steve.

One night, the three of us went up to Porter's apartment in the Waldorf Towers. A valet let us into a spacious entry hall that led to a huge living-room with floor-to-ceiling windows overlooking the Manhattan skyline. A grand piano sat near the windows on thick gold carpeting. The furnishings, like the scale of the rooms, were oversized. Deep velvet club chairs and an enormous plush sofa. Cole Porter looked almost lost in the upholstery. He hoisted himself out of the sofa to greet us. I was surprised to notice that he limped. He was very gracious, very warm, and almost shy.

At Steve's or Arnold's suggestion, he showed me through the suite. It was the first time I'd seen a private library—an entire room filled with shelves of books, a leather-paneled desk, a wooden pedestal on which stood a rotating globe of the world. The bathrooms—any one of which was larger than our entire apartment—were carpeted. There were gold-flecked mirrors on the bedroom ceiling. Porter had his own massage room.

He offered us drinks, which his valet fixed. And, as I sunk sleepily into one of the big club chairs in the livingroom, Cole Porter sat at the piano and played "Begin the Beguine" and "Night and Day." Later, I woke in that chair and listened to Steve, Cole, and Arnold talking. I couldn't hear every word, but there was an intimacy in their tone and manner. I remember thinking that they must all be very good friends. I remember wondering whether Steve was gay—queer, we called it then—and then, a fleeting, silly thought, whether Arnold might be AC/DC.

When Cole Porter was out of town, Steve threw parties in that magnificent eight-room apartment in the Waldorf. The crowd was wild, mixed, young, and trashy. Broadway dancers, starlets, whores. The women all seemed to be named Nikki, and came in carrying little dogs in their hands. The guys were gorgeous, mostly gay. I'd stand in a corner hanging on to a drink, my brown eyes as wide as they could get through the stinging smoke, staring at the scene and hoping Arnold would find me soon and take me home.

A few months before my nineteenth birthday, after I'd become a genuine Seventh Avenue showroom model, Arnold and I broke up. His mother stormed our Brooklyn apartment demanding back the friendship ring he'd given me.

Arnold got to keep the ring; I got to keep the terrific friends I'd made at Jilly's. A couple of nights a week I'd stay in the city at Marilyn's apartment—she was Jewish and still lived with her parents. Or at Judy's when her boyfriend, the guy who owned the renowned salon she worked in, went home to Scarsdale to spend a night with his wife and kids. He was paying rent on the apartment, which was just above his shop in the East Fifties. It was a simple arrangement. He paid the rent, he got first dibs on the bed. One of the things that made his salon famous was that it was open very, very late to accommodate celebrities, showgirls, call girls, and other clients who lived a reversed night and day existence. It was one of them, a stunning redheaded friend of Judy's, who decided at Jilly's one night that I had just what it took to be a fabulous Las Vegas showgirl.

Sure, it made sense to her, I thought. And if she drinks two more screwdrivers, she'll decide I ought to run for Miss Rheingold. "I don't sing, dance, or act, and I've got a Brooklyn accent," I reminded her. "And anyway, I'm making nice money modeling now."

So, okay, my legs were getting palsied from walking around in five-inch heels a hundred hours a day. My arms were starting to look like Charles Atlas's from lifting seven-pound coats—putting them on, taking them off, twirling, shlepping them back to the dressing room and reappearing a minute later in a five-pound, two-piece suit under yet another seven-pound coat. Ah, the glamour of the showroom model's life. But what the hell, I was taking home close to $125 a week, which in 1957, 1958, was a month's rent on a nice little three-room apartment in Manhattan.

"Showgirls don't sing and dance, silly. They just walk around in fabulous costumes and earn three hundred a week."

"Three hundred . . . A week?!" I was floored.

"Three hundred, three fifty . . . And that's just salary," Judy's friend explained. "They fly you there and you get room and board free."

"Over my dead body," my mother said when I told her.

I'd answered an ad. The Desert Inn wanted me. "Ma, I'll be able to send home about two hundred fifty a week. And it's like camp, for God's sake. We stay in *dormitories*."

"You know what a *courva* is?" she asked.

"A hooker. But Ma, I'm going to be a showgirl, not a hooker. I'll live in a dorm with other girls. We'll be supervised. I'll be as safe as if I were in a girls' boarding school."

"A showgirl. You'll walk around naked on high-heeled shoes with fruit on your head. This is a job? For *shiksas,* for *courvas* this is a job, not for nice Jewish girls," my mother said.

We were at the kitchen table. On the daybed behind us, my open suitcase was packed. All I needed to add before snapping it shut was the cosmetic case that pear-shaped Noah, one of my Garment Center admirers, who ran the drugstore in the lobby of the building where I worked, had given me as a going-away gift. I was stuffing cotton balls into the pretty pink case as fast as I could. My mother was pushing crumbs from our breakfast rolls around a plate, and shaking her head, and sighing with exasperation. "Las Vegas, *feh!*" she said. "Who knows what you'll meet there, the kind of men waiting to take advantage of a girl like you. A girl? No, a baby!"

She was right. In Las Vegas, I was a baby. I was not just chronologically younger than most of the girls I lived and worked with. Emotionally, I was an infant. From the moment I stepped off the plane into the white desert sunlight, I became a homesick, nervous wreck hiding behind a perpetual, dazed smile.

The showgirls and dancers lived behind The Desert Inn in a two-story annex that looked like a motel. I shared a room with a pair of tough little blonde Barbie dolls from the midwest who'd been in Vegas for a while, knew the ropes and how to wind them around the wallets of heavy hitters in the casino after hours. I thought three hundred a week plus room and board was sumptuous. Donna and Lureene thought it was chump change.

They, and some of the other more experienced girls, were very patient and protective with me. They teased me about my accent, my innocence, the bounty of my breasts. They taught me how to make up like a showgirl. Enid's false eyelashes and over-the-lip-line penciling was conservative, subtle compared to the bigger-than-life-showgirl look we were after. Max Factor Pan-Cake makeup slathered from the dark roots of your hair to the deep cleft of your cleavage—applied with damp sponges in which the makeup oils had long ago turned rancid. Soft, coal-black eye pencil drawn heavily across the top lids of your eyes, sweeping up halfway across your temples. Bright red lipstick emphasizing the brightest, whitest, seductive smiles money could buy.

We wore the makeup on stage a couple of hours a night. We wore it with our amazing sequined-and-spangled costumes, in Merry Widow corselettes that could cinch a twenty-two-inch waistline down to a mere nineteen inches—because looking great was more important than breathing. In flesh-colored tights and stiletto heels we moved into the blinding spotlight. We walked gracefully, desperately, under elaborate headdresses that soared up out of tiny sequined skull caps anchored with bobby pins that made you feel like a human pin cushion balancing a chandelier on your head.

I loved being on stage. After the initial terror had passed, of tripping or having the great plumed headdress tilt or tumble, moving into that spotlight, walking out of the wings to center stage, was a fantasy come true. A transformation. I was no longer Sandy Sadowsky of Flatbush, Brooklyn. I was a performer, a glamorous Vegas showgirl.

We wore the makeup on stage a couple of hours a night, but, more importantly, we wore it after the shows to let the big spenders in the casino know that we were showgirls.

The stage shows I'd been so apprehensive about turned out to be the easiest part of life in Vegas. I'd work until close to three in the morning, grab a quick, free meal at the casino coffee shop, sleep for a few hours, and then get up to rehearse for most of the day. It was a grueling schedule, even for an energetic nineteen-year-old. But the money was great—or so I thought until Donna set me straight.

"Three hundred bucks?" She looked at me and shook her head as though I were a drooling embarrassment.

We were putting on our makeup, sitting alongside half a dozen other girls at the long, mirrored table we shared in the dressing room. It was noisy, chaotic, and warm. And I'd said something about how nice it was to be making *real* money.

"Compared to what you could be raking in—with that body and those big brown eyes, Sandy—three hundred bucks is nothing," Donna concluded.

"Well, sorry. But I'm not a hooker," I said.

"Well, sorry!" She laughed. "I wasn't talking about hooking. Listen, after the show, we'll change and walk through the casino and I'll show you what I mean."

That night, between the first and second shows, we walked out to the vast carpeted casino, past rows of clanging slot machines and green felt-covered blackjack tables crowded with players who were drinking, smoking, and betting with equal intensity. As Donna led me toward the craps tables, she gave me the drill: "Okay, now, you'll stand on one side of the guys and I'll be on the other. All you have to do is ask me if I'm going to play. Got it? We just mosey over and you give it a half a minute and then you say, 'So, Donna, are you playing tonight?' "

The craps table we stopped at was jammed with high rollers. There were guys standing behind piles of chips, pushing one, two, three chips, blues, reds, yellows, onto the numbers and watching the dice hit the felt and not even blinking as the croupier raked in the chips they'd lost. Donna moved toward a guy whose eyes were pinned to the table action. He had rolls of chips in his hands and he was toying with them, as if he couldn't wait to put them down on the next number. He polished off a glass of booze and ordered another from a passing waitress as Donna sidled up next to him.

I worked my way up to the table, a couple of players away from her. "Donna," I called, "are you going to play?"

She ran her fingers through her long blonde hair and gave a little shrug. "I can't tonight," she answered. "I don't have any money."

The guy standing next to her looked up. He gave her the once-over, then, boom, he pushed a stack of chips in front of her. "You're in, babe," he said, and turned back to the game.

My mouth fell open.

Donna slid a couple of the chips onto the felt. And, cautiously, quickly, scooped the rest into the little handbag she was carrying. She played the chips on the table, then moved on.

"See, the thing is these guys stop thinking of chips as real money. And it's part of the game to give chips to pretty girls, especially showgirls," she said, as we hurried back to the dressing room for the next show. "They're smoking, they're drinking, they're bombed, they get generous. On a good night, you can pick up an extra couple of hundred dollars . . . and, baby cakes," she added with a wink, "you don't have to unzip a thing."

Needless to say I did not mention this newfound skill to Tillie during my weekly phone calls home. And, to tell the truth, while it made me feel grown up and glamorous for a while to walk through the casino at three A.M. in full showgirl makeup, gold hoops dangling from my ears, in tight black Toreador pants, black ballet slippers, and a blouse unbuttoned to flash just enough Max-Factored cleavage to rake in a roll or two of chips, the game never countered my homesickness. Las Vegas was very exciting, very full of wise guys and easy money in the late fifties but, to tell the truth, the generous guys weren't always so befuddled with booze and gambling that they didn't want a pound of flesh for a handful of chips. And, to tell the truth, which I never did to my mother, Donna, Lureene, and some of the other girls who'd befriended me did "date" for money from time to time, and if they weren't certified hookers, they lived with a similar contempt and desperation for men and money. For the most part, the Vegas showgirls I met were there for one of two reasons: to land a husband or to move up in a performing career; and in both areas they were ruthlessly competitive.

Nights were days and days were nights. There were no rules. I was a nervous wreck most of the time. And twenty minutes a night in the spotlight didn't balance out the fear and loneliness I experienced daily.

So six weeks after I left New York, I telephoned Tillie and made her the happiest Jewish mother in Flatbush. "Ma," I said, "You were right. It's a *shiksas'* life out here. I'm coming home."

CHAPTER TWO

The Velvet Room

In Vegas, the girls sometimes called me a bookworm because I'd stay in the Annex reading instead of cruising the casino at night. Some of them thought I was crazy. Most of them figured it was because I was Jewish and that along with having horns, killing Christ, and barbecuing gentile babies for Passover, Jews were just naturally brainy.

But I left my reputation as a bookish recluse in the desert. Back in New York, I jumped into nightlife with a new vengeance.

Judy or Marilyn, Patty or Nikki would say: "Okay, where are we going tonight?"

We'd be gathered around the piano bar at Jilly's, or filling little plates with steaming free hors d'oeuvres at the El Borracho on East Fifty-fourth, or fixing our makeup in the ladies' room at Billy Reed's Little Club.

And someone would call out the name of a nightspot in town. And within five minutes, we'd bat our eyelashes at whoever was picking up our tab and move on to the next, better, newer, hotter club. Then as now, many of them were owned, run, or frequented by the mob.

It was the spring of '59. Eisenhower was golfing away his last term as president. Nobody cared about Nixon, least of all Ike who, asked to name one of his vice president's outstanding accomplishments, said: "Give me a week and I might think of one." Hardly anyone outside of Massachusetts had heard of John F. Kennedy. But if you walked into a Manhattan supper club or after-hours joint, you'd hear people whispering:

"Wow, there's Anthony Strollo, the one they call 'Tony Bender.' Runs the Jersey waterfront."

Or: "That's 'Tony Ducks' from the Teamsters, the blue-eyed guy in the horn-rimmed glasses."

Or: "Oh my God, is that Johnny Dio?"

And you'd stare in awe at the faces you'd seen on the front page of yesterday's *Daily News*. Celebrities.

One of the hottest new spots in town that boasted such "celebrities" was an elegant supper club in the Brittany Hotel on East Tenth Street in Greenwich Village.

"It's called The Velvet Room," Judy's redheaded friend Nina told us. "Right, baby?" She was toying with the suit lapels of a guy named Zippy, who had something to do with the International Ladies' Garment Union.

About eight of us had assembled at Jilly's, and now we were hungry and eager to move on. Noah the pear-shaped druggist, my old admirer from Seventh Avenue, was picking up the bill for Marilyn, Judy, and me. With one of the three little black cocktail dresses I owned, I was wearing the artificial pearls he'd given me a couple of weeks before—to celebrate my promotion from off-the-rack modeling to couture suits and coats.

"The Veyl-vet Room," drawled Judy. "Sounds sexy."

It was. A big, tufted black leather door opened onto a red carpeted entryway, behind which sprawled a long, polished mahogany bar. Walls flocked in a red and cream fleur-de-lis pattern were reflected in the huge, gold-specked mirror behind the bar. Chandeliers and crystal wall sconces bathed the room in a soft pink glow.

Beyond the lounge area, the dining room curled around a little piano bar and dance floor. An elaborate mahogany and glass divider separated the two rooms. The tables were set with white linen, candles, and flowers.

Nina's boyfriend, Zippy, had phoned ahead. The maitre d' led our party of eight to a long table at the edge of the dance floor.

We'd just gotten our drinks and were checking out the menus when, "Sandela! Yoo-hoo, Sandy!" a husky voice bellowed.

"Oh, shit," I said.

It was Helen, one of my mother's few still-loyal friends.

Although she was classically beautiful with fine chiseled features, deep-set eyes, and pale hair swept back in an elegant chignon, when Helen drank she became a wild woman capable of anything. I froze at the table and raised my eyes to heaven—or the nearest thing to it—the cream-colored ceiling of the dining room. God, please, I prayed, don't let her embarrass me.

It was too late.

"Who is that?" Judy asked as Helen careened from the banquette against the back wall toward our table, thudding against chairs, wine buckets, and waiters along the way.

"A friend of my mother's from Brooklyn."

"She's gorgeous," Marilyn said.

"She's bombed out of her gourd," said Nina.

"She's your mother's friend?" Noah, whose attention was riveted to the creamy front of Helen's low-cut dress, couldn't believe it.

"She used to live downstairs from us. She's ten years younger than my mother. About thirty, I think."

"Sandela! What are you doing here? You look gorgeous. Come, sweetheart. Come, *shayna*—" She grabbed my wrist and started pulling me to my feet. "I want you to meet my fiancé," she said, pointing to the man she was with. To avoid a scene, I got up and walked her back to the banquette. "Sandy, this is my fiancé, Bernie Barton," Helen said. "He owns the place."

The man in the booth smiled and rose slightly. The most amazing pair of baby blue eyes I'd ever seen fastened onto mine.

"Bernie," Helen said. "This is my friend Tillie's daughter, Sandy. Is she gorgeous, or what?"

Never taking his eyes off mine, he nodded, amused. "Hey, kid," he said. His voice was gravel. His hand in mine was soft and cool.

I sat with them for a few minutes. I don't remember what I said. Nice to meet you. Your restaurant is beautiful. I don't remember what he said, except that he made me laugh, made me feel comfortable and nervous at the same time: comfortable because I felt that he liked me; nervous because he was Helen's boyfriend, old enough to be my father, and I found him very attractive. People stopped by the table. People treated him with deference and respect. You could tell they were pleased when he kidded with them, or stood to shake a hand.

I excused myself and returned to my friends. "He owns the place," I told Judy. "He's a doll. He's funny and bright. I can't figure out what he's doing with Helen, though. She's been married and divorced twice already and she's got a new boyfriend every other day."

Sometime later, I went to the powder room. The banquette where Bernie and Helen had been sitting was empty. Scanning the room quickly, I didn't see either of them. I was disappointed.

To get to the bathrooms, you had to walk out of The Velvet Room and into the Brittany's lobby through a corridor of telephone booths. The booths were the old-fashioned kind that had wooden doors with glass panels in the top half. There was a bald guy with a phone to his ear in one of the booths. He wasn't speaking, just grinning. When I came out of the powder room, ten minutes later, he was still leaning back against the wall of the booth, holding the receiver. He was still grinning, but his expression had changed to one of glassy-eyed ecstasy.

Curiosity got the best of me and, as I passed, I peered cautiously into the booth. And saw that he had company, a woman on her knees who was giving him . . . reason to smile.

I kept walking and started to laugh.

"Hey, kid." The gravel voice stopped me in my tracks. Bernie Barton was standing in front of me. "Give me your number," he said. "I'd like to take you out."

There was no doubt in my mind that I wanted to see him again. But it wasn't as easy as all that. "I can't," I said. "You're engaged to my mother's friend."

Bernie laughed. He had big, perfect white teeth. His amazing blue eyes crinkled at the corners. "Helen? Come on," he said. "She's everyone's fiancée."

I tried not to smile but I knew what he'd meant.

I was wearing my highest heels that night and he was just a bit taller than I, built strong and solid as a prize fighter, with thick dark hair that was not exactly gray but lighter at the temples.

Bernie Barton took my hand. The shirt under his Glen Plaid suit jacket was powder blue, almost the same shade as his eyes. The collar and cuffs were white and, as I looked down at his hand holding mine, I noticed the monogram on his cuff, "BB." That's what they had called him—"BB" or "Mr. B"—the guys, the cigarette girl, who'd come by the table while I was sitting with him and Helen.

"You've got to," he said, teasing. "I own the joint. You're on my turf, you do what I say."

Under the grin was a will of iron.

He handed me a matchbook from the club and I wrote down my number for him. "Okay," I said, "but I don't know if I can go out with you."

"Sure, kid," he said, pocketing the matchbook. "I understand."

He called me the next day.

"I'm sorry, Mr. Barton," I said, "I told you yesterday. I'm not the kind of girl who goes out with another woman's man."

I wasn't trying to be coy or cute—I wouldn't have known how with this man. I'd seen him in action, on his own turf as he'd called it. The people who'd stopped by his table at The Velvet Room last night had done everything but bow or curtsy to him. He excited and intimidated me. He seemed so sure of himself, so determined about what he wanted. And that he wanted to see me seemed an enormous compliment.

But Helen had called him her fiancé and, no matter how we'd joked about it last night, I couldn't go out with a man who belonged to someone else. Not after what Enid had done to my mother.

"Listen, kid," Bernie said, with just a trace of impatience, "I told *you* yesterday that I'm not going with the lady. Now, why don't you give her a ring and ask her. I've got to get back to work. I'll talk to you later."

It took me an hour to get up the nerve to call Helen. I kept playing through the scene, imagining Helen as my naive and loyal mother and me in the evil Enid role. Finally, I stubbed out my cigarette and dialed the number.

"Bernie wants to go out with me," I blurted out, close to tears. "Is he really your fiancé?"

Helen burst out laughing. "Oh, baby, poor baby," she said. "No. Go out with him if you want to. I called him my fiancé? Oh, my God, he'll never speak to me again. You want to see him, be my guest. But, Sandy baby, listen—Bernie Barton is not someone to take seriously. You know how old he is, baby? Forty. And he's been around. He's a gangster. He was in the rackets. He's been in jail. For a good time, a little fun, he's fine. Just don't get serious with him."

So Bernie Barton was a gangster. What did that mean? Helen might just as well have said he's exciting, dangerous, he's a man with a past. That's what I knew about gangsters. They weren't real. They were celebrities. Stars. Bigger than life. The eight-inch black and white screen of the Philco television console in our old Brooklyn living room on which I'd seen the Kefauver hearings had seemed too small to contain them.

While other kids were mesmerized by Howdy Doody and Winky Dink, I'd watched Frank Costello's hands fooling with the water pitcher at the senate hearings table. And listened to guys "take the Fifth"—the Fifth Amendment—and respectfully refuse to answer questions on the grounds that the answers might tend to incriminate them.

What I remembered most of all about the hearings, which I'd catch when I came home from school, was Virginia Hill. She was a beautiful hillbilly who'd gone out with some top mobsters. They said she'd been Joe Adonis's girl and then Bugsy Siegel's. And there she was in her low-cut black dress and wide-brimmed black picture hat, in sunglasses with a silver fox jacket draped across her shoulders. Notorious, glamorous, mysterious were the words most used to describe her. And when they questioned her about the nightclub she owned and all her other assets, Virginia didn't take the Fifth. She said, "Men lahks to give me money."

I was only twelve or thirteen when the racketeering hearings were televised and that was what I remembered: Virginia Hill saying, "Men lahks to give me money." I thought she was sensational.

When Bernie called me later, just as he'd said he would, I agreed to go out with him the next night. He said, "Good. Okay, kid. I'll send a car for you." And when, at exactly eight o'clock, the doorbell rang and a well-dressed older man announced that he was Mr. Barton's driver and that the car was waiting at the curb, I kissed my frowning mother's face, gave my wide-eyed little sister, Marlene, a hug, and swept grandly out the door thinking, wow, this is the life.

Mr. Barton's driver held open the car door and for the first time in my life, I climbed into the plush backseat of a beautiful black limousine. Bernie was going to meet me at the club, but he'd sent flowers and arranged to have a bottle of champagne chilling in an ice bucket in the limo and Frank Sinatra crooning through the speakers. Feeling alternately sophisticated and like a kid playing movie star, I poured myself a glass of champagne and settled back against the velour seats for the trip from Brooklyn to Manhattan. A trip, I gleefully reminded myself, that I'd made countless times—in my unfortunate former life—by subway.

I had finished two glasses of champagne and was feeling pretty good by the time the limo pulled up in front of The Velvet Room. I smoothed back my hair and readjusted the black ribbon around my high ponytail. I smoothed down the snug black sheath I was wearing and adjusted my string of pearls so that the clasp was at the nape of my neck where it belonged. I slicked on a fresh coat of bright red lipstick, made sure the doe eyes weren't smeared or the false lashes hanging askew. But somewhere between the curb and the big tufted leather door I became suddenly stone-cold sober and very unsure of myself.

I was totally unprepared for the way Bernie Barton's eyes lit up when I walked into the lounge. He was at a table up front, in the bar. He was in conversation with another guy and he looked up, straight at me, as if radar had told him I was in the room.

He stood and came toward me. "You look great, kid," he said in his husky voice. He looked me up and down. "Beautiful, baby," he said, walking me over to the table. "Isn't she beautiful?" he said to the heavyset older guy he'd been talking with. It thrilled me to hear the pride in his voice. "This is Ziggy Schwartz," Bernie said. "We grew up together."

"We did a lot of things together," Ziggy said good-naturedly. He laughed and shook his head. *"Oy-oy-oy,* Bernie. You're gonna do time for this one."

"She's worth it," Bernie kibitzed back. "What're you drinking, kid?"

I asked for something fruity—I think grapefruit juice and vodka—and Bernie raised his eyebrows a little, then smiled. He snapped his fingers and someone was there in a second to take the order.

We sat down with Ziggy who, it turned out, was the head of a Teamsters local. He was a little drunk and said a lot of things that Bernie shook his head over, and told me a lot more about Bernie than he wanted me to know in the first fifteen minutes of our first date: They'd been to jail together. Bernie had a daughter my age. Bernie had been a big shot, a *macher,* in the union, but he'd screwed up, gotten popped for something stupid, something, Ziggy said, "only *shvartzas* get popped for."

Bernie was annoyed, but only once did he reprimand Ziggy Schwartz. That was when I said, "You know, my mother's maiden name was Schwartz." And Ziggy, with a cockeyed, drunken smile, shrugged and said, "Yeah? Maybe I fucked her."

"You don't talk to this one like that," Bernie said angrily.

Ziggy paled. Then he nodded, and grinned again. "I'm sorry, Sandy. I'm just a dirty old man. I don't remember how to talk to nice girls anymore."

We left Ziggy in the lounge and walked through the dining room toward the banquette, where he'd had dinner with Helen. People called out to Bernie as we passed: "BB, how's it going?" "BB, let me buy you a drink." "You robbing the cradle, BB?" And Bernie had a smile, a handshake, a wink, or a wisecrack for each of them.

At the table, too, we were interrupted by a constant stream of men—men dressed as elegantly as Bernie, with manicured hands, perfect hair, monogrammed cuffs, gold watches, platinum ID bracelets, diamond cuff links, star sapphire pinky rings. And, at least three times between the shrimp cocktail and the filet mignon, Bernie was called away to handle something in the bar, in the kitchen, in the backroom.

Once, he came back to the table and told our waiter, "See the guy at the bar with the shiner? Get him a raw potato from the kitchen."

'Yes, Mr. B," the waiter said, and took off.

"Are raw potatoes good for black eyes?" I asked.

Bernie laughed. "No. That guy, Joey, up there. He likes to do bar tricks. He's got one—where he pushes a straw through a raw potato. He gets them to bet him he can't do it. And he takes their money, too. The guy's a maniac. Holds up taxis on the way over here for drink money."

The guy at the bar was Joey Gallo. "I'm a tough guy," he used to say. He'd come into The Velvet Room with his brother Albert, who they called "Kid Blast," and a couple of other wise guys—they were like a little wolf pack, ferocious and unpredictable. Black eyes, skinned knuckles, scraped cheeks. But they wore suits at the club and if their fingernails weren't always spotless their long-collared white shirts and pocket handkerchiefs and silk ties were. "Crazy" Joe Gallo was their leader. "I'm tough. I'm a really tough guy." I remember him saying it all the time. And this was before he read Camus and Gide in jail and became the darling of swinging sixties café society.

"So what's a kid like you doing hanging around with Helen? She's got a few years on you," Bernie said when he'd returned to the table for the fourth time in fifteen minutes.

"She's a friend of my mother's," I told him. "Actually, she's ten years younger than my mother and ten years older than me. When she was falling apart over her second divorce, she'd come to my mother for advice. They became very good friends. She used to live in the same building as we did in Brooklyn."

"What'd she tell you about me?" he asked.

"Nothing," I said.

"Nothing?" He laughed.

"I mean, that you weren't her fiancé, of course. And that she didn't have any objections to my seeing you."

"I owe her one."

"And not to take you seriously," I added, staring down at the ravages of my steak and baked potato.

"Good advice. So what are you, Jewish?"

"Yes. Are you?"

"Sure," he said, then smiled. "You want to see proof?"

I laughed. "No, thanks. I'll take your word for it."

"Good girl."

"But 'Barton,' " I said, "that's not a Jewish name."

"Used to be Blaustein. You know who Barton MacLain is? He played the heavy in a lot of old gangster movies and cowboy movies. Him and Bruce Cabot—I used to love them. That's where I got Barton. From Barton MacLain."

"That's interesting—that you liked the bad guys, not the heroes," I said.

"They had more character. They were tough guys. Heavies always have more character, don't you know that? So, are you Orthodox?"

"My mother keeps kosher. I don't."

"That's nice. Coming from a good Jewish family is nice. So, listen, kid. I've got to do a little work in the back now. Order yourself a nice dessert, some coffee, cognac, whatever you like. The car'll be ready whenever you want to go back to Brooklyn."

He stood up. I couldn't believe it. He was leaving me. My heart sunk. I felt tears welling. And all I could think of was, moron, why did you tell him your mother keeps kosher? As if that had somehow been the deciding factor in his dismissal.

He tilted my chin up and, bending, kissed me lightly on the lips. "Same time tomorrow night?" he said. "I'll send the car."

My mother saw more of me now than she had in months. I came home every night after work to shower and change and get ready for my date with Bernie.

"Who is this man?" she wanted to know. "Where does he get the money to send a car all the way to Brooklyn twice a night?"

"He's a very nice man, Ma. He owns a supper club in New York."

These conversations would take place while I rushed around the cramped apartment, getting dressed, doing my hair, and putting on makeup.

My sister, Marlene, would be sitting at the kitchen table trying to study, but most of the time she'd get caught up in the Cinerama soap opera playing around her. She'd give me a wink or a grin or an A-OK circle if I got in a good line.

"A very nice man who is twenty years older than you. What kind of *very nice man* goes out with a girl young enough to be his daughter? And what do you have in common with this fine gentleman? He buys you malt-eds, maybe? He wants to hold your hand? And you, you ride him around his fancy supper club in a wheelchair?''

My mother would be at the sink or stove, preparing Marlene's dinner. She'd toss her remarks over her shoulder, casually, like someone flinging a scarf dripping acid.

"We have dinner, we talk— He's smart, Ma. He's lived a very interesting life."

"Oh, you talk. I see. And he's smart, your good friend with the car and the money and the fancy New York supper club. Of course, why didn't I figure that out. Of course, that's what he wants from you—conversation! Especially because he's smart, right? And he must be a very educated man to have such deep conversations and discussions with a high-school drop-out."

"A high-school dropout who pays your rent, Ma!"

I was still contributing most of my salary to the family. As a showroom model in the Garment Center, I earned about four times what my mother did at the cleaning store. And Bernie was impressed with this—not that I was a model, but that I supported my family.

He'd done the same when he was a kid. His mother and her sister had worked twelve hours a day in the candy store on the ground floor of their tenement building on First Street and Avenue A. To help support them, Bernie had taken a job as a hat boy at Moe Penn's, an elegant men's shop on Grand Street. He was twelve years old at the time.

The haberdashery catered strictly to a moneyed clientele. And among those with cash to flash on the Lower East Side in the early thirties were some of the most notorious gangsters and gunmen of their day. At Moe Penn's Bernie got to know them. Two who took a special liking to him were Meyer Lansky's lieutenants, Sam "Red" Levine and Philly "Farvel the Stick" Kovolick.

Years later, I met them. They were in their late fifties, early sixties by then, which was ancient to me. But in their twenties—about the time Bernie was talking his way into that job at Moe Penn's—Red and Farvel were making big names for themselves in what used to be called "The Outfit."

Rumor had it that it was Red, using a squad of imported Jewish hitmen dressed as Federal tax agents, who engineered the 1931 murder of Salvatore Maranzano, the self-proclaimed Boss of all Bosses of the Italian mob.

Farvel, who was busted in '33 at a "crime conference" at the Hotel Franconia, along with Bugsy Siegel, Lepke Buchalter and Gurrah Shapiro, was known even among those strong-arm men as a shakedown artist of exceptional greed. He was called "Farvel the Stick" because he drove for Lansky—stick shift getaway cars and bootlegging trucks—and did anything else with a stick that Meyer needed done.

Another dapper dresser from the old neighborhood, another one of the well-connected "older" guys who shopped at Moe Penn's, was James Plumeri, better known as Jimmy Doyle, whom Bernie introduced to me two decades later at The Velvet Club as Uncle Jimmy. In the late fifties when I met him, Jimmy owned and lived above a nightclub on First Avenue called the Ali Baba—which Bernie always called The Bucket of Blood. In the sixties, Jimmy disappeared. Years later, pieces of him were still turning up in garbage cans all over New York.

Farvel, Red Levine, Jimmy Doyle. They were the guys Bernie met when he was twelve and working at Moe Penn's, the ones who taught him the ropes and had him running numbers and driving bootleg trucks when he was thirteen, the men who became his friends and called him "kid" for the rest of his life.

Bernie told me about them long before I met them. Not how they had made their reputations, but that they'd helped him out when he was young and needed to make money to help support his family. And, forgetting that I was supposed to be a sophisticated model in my little black dress and string of pearls, elbows on the table, chin in my hands, I hung on his every word.

I wanted to tell my mother how wrong she was about Bernie. How he respected me because I gave her money and was Jewish and came from a good Orthodox home. I wanted to tell her how wrong she was about why he liked me. She was afraid that Bernie would take advantage of me. I couldn't tell her that I was getting worried that he wouldn't.

Every night Bernie sent his car for me promptly at eight and every night for two weeks, after a chaste kiss, he sent me back home alone to Brooklyn.

And every night at his club I became more impressed with him, with the amazing range of people who were drawn to him, who'd known him for years and told me benevolent little secrets about how BB had bailed them out of a jam or done some thoughtful little thing for their sick mother or kid brother or cousin Shlomo from Delancey Street. And every night of those first two weeks I became more infatuated with Bernie Barton, every night a little more in love.

Then one Monday we'd finished dinner and were sitting at Bernie's table in the lounge, when two men came by to say hello. Bernie asked them to join us. One of them was a stocky guy he'd grown up with, who we'll call Milty Heinz. Milty, Bernie said, was one of Johnny Dio's right-hand men in the Teamsters. I'd heard of Johnny Dio. Anyone who picked up *The Mirror, The News,* or *The Herald Trib* had read about him at one time or other. He was one of the mob's "labor relations experts," who'd been accused of plotting the acid-throwing attack that blinded a newspaperman named Victor Riesel in 1956—supposedly to keep him from testifying before a special federal rackets grand jury.

The other guy, Steve Crane, a tall, attractive man who owned restaurants in California and New York, turned out to be the ex-husband of Lana Turner, the movie star. His daughter had recently gotten into trouble for knifing a small-time hood named Johnny Stompanato. The headlines had talked about an argument in the movie star's bedroom that escalated to violence, and the daughter had been acquitted on the grounds of justifiable homicide because she'd only killed the hood to save her mother's life.

So there I was, nineteen years old, resting my ponytail against the tufted leather banquette at Bernie's table in the bar, listening to Johnny Dio's right-hand man telling Lana Turner's ex-husband what a "ballsy bastard, a real stand-up guy BB is," when a good-looking, grinning man with a great tan swept into the place, a blonde on each arm, and hollered, "Mr. B—my main man!" And there I was looking right up into Billy Daniels's incredible smoky blue eyes. Eyes I'd only ever seen before in black and white, on television, where Billy was always introduced as "That Old Black Magic man," because that was the song that had become his trademark.

Billy set the blondes up at the bar and came back to our table. He teased Bernie with affection and familiarity and talked with Milty Heinz and Steve Crane for a while. Then he kissed my hand and returned to his girls.

"You know Billy Daniels, too?" I whispered, awestruck.

Bernie nodded, no big deal.

"How do you know him?"

"From uptown, from Fifty-second Street, jazz joints, around," he said. "Let's go up to the apartment."

"What?"

"The apartment. My place, dummy."

"Candy man, you've got to come see me at the Copa," Billy Daniels called after us as we left the club. "And bring the princess with you, baby."

CHAPTER THREE

Bernie's Princess

The apartment occupied the entire second floor of a beautiful brownstone on Seventy-ninth Street between Fifth and Madison.

"Oh, my God, I don't believe it," I said as Bernie led me through a gorgeous set of tall, solid wood double doors into a carpeted hallway.

"What's the matter?"

"My father used to take me shopping right around the corner from here."

"Yeah? That's nice."

"No, but I mean, you don't understand. This is the street I always wanted to live on. In this neighborhood. On this street. In a building just like this."

He was walking ahead of me, up a flight of red-carpeted stairs and down the hall. He stopped in front of the door to his apartment and glanced skeptically at me over his shoulder.

"Honest," I said, as he began working on the locks. There were at least six, including a thick deadbolt and a police lock. "Isn't that amazing? This is where I've always wanted to live."

"Maybe you should look around first," Bernie said, without cracking a smile. He threw open the door and I followed him into the apartment.

Then suddenly I thought about how I must have sounded, like I had my bags packed in the back of the limo and if he just gave me a minute, I'd move right in. I got very flustered.

"You want a drink?"

I followed Bernie into a huge room with a dining table and chairs in one corner and, in another, a lavish mirrored cabinet housing a TV, radio, stereo, and record collection. The room was tiled in black and white squares and, in front of the Murphy kitchen—a little hideaway closet that contained a tiny sink and half-refrigerator and stove—was a giant white tufted-leather standup bar.

"Listen, I didn't mean it like it sounded. I mean, it's true. We used to drive in from Brooklyn. My father used to take us shopping on Madison Avenue. I always loved this neighborhood—"

"You nervous?" he said, walking over to the bar. "Don't be nervous." He poured himself a drink, then handed one to me. "Come on," he beckoned with a hitch of his head.

A set of large black and white doors with etched-brass knobs led into the living room, a spacious room carpeted blood red. The ceiling was black, the walls were white and, at the far end of the room, two huge floor-to-ceiling windows looked out onto the wide street. The furniture was also red, white, and black, and there was a big fireplace with a white marble mantel.

Across from the fireplace, partially screened by a tall black lacquered cabinet, was a large mirrored alcove that held, like a diamond in a platinum setting, Bernie's king-sized bed. In which, I thought, the apartment I shared with Marlene and my mother could have laid down to rest. I took a big swallow of the scotch he'd poured me. "Wow," I said.

Bernie laughed and turned me around so that I was facing him. With a hand on each of my shoulders, he held me at arm's length and looked at me quietly for a minute. "So?" he said.

"So," I echoed, my voice breaking, my head bobbing philosophically like an old rabbi thinking it over: "Yeah, so . . ."

"You going to sleep with me, kid?"

"Yeah." My head was still bobbing, my brown eyes staring into his baby blues.

"It's late."

"You sleepy?" I asked.

Bernie turned me around and pointed me toward the bathroom. "Go." He laughed.

Forty-five minutes later I was wide awake staring up at my reflection in the mirrored ceiling above the bed. Bernie was sound asleep beside me. He hadn't laid a glove on me. Well, a glove maybe. A sweet, gentle, sexy hugging hand or two, yes. A pair of very nice loving lips, yes. And then, he'd said, very softly in that raspy, sexy voice, "Okay, baby. Sleep, honey." And rolled over. And that was that. He was out. I was up.

I spent the few remaining hours before dawn wondering whether I'd done something wrong, whether Bernie really cared for me, whether he found me attractive. I took breaks in the worrying by imagining what it would be like to live with him, to live in this apartment, to sleep every night with him in this bed.

It was the first time I'd ever spent the night with a man. I got up early in the morning for work and, when I had showered and dressed, Bernie was still asleep. I had no idea about the etiquette of the situation. I decided not to wake him. I spent a while composing a little love note to him, then left it on the pillow and tiptoed out of the apartment.

Later, he called me at work. "How you doing?"

"Fine," I said, grinning at just the sound of his gruff voice.

"Good. Listen, I'll see you later at the club. Only don't say anything, you hear me?"

"Sure," I said, not sure at all what he meant.

"You tell anyone about last night, I'll kill you."

"Oh," I said. "Oh, Bernie, of course I won't. But it was nice. You were sweet."

"Sweet?" he growled. "What's wrong with you?"

That night at The Velvet Room, we were very careful with one another, trying to behave as though nothing had changed between us. But every once in a while, we'd catch each other's eye across the table and I'd start to smile. And Bernie would shake his head like, cut the crap, kid. But you could see him trying not to grin. He'd turn away fast, or get into a sudden, intense conversation, or order someone around.

Another old union friend of his showed up close to closing time, a guy named Moishe Pickles. If Bernie had wanted to prove to me that night what a tough guy he really was, Moishe was the best PR man he could've asked for.

"What a temper this man has," Moishe told me, clapping his hands together and laughing. "You remember the shirt buttons?" he asked Bernie. "One night we're in a bar uptown. A shmuck, a square, a guy named Alby, right, Bernie? He comes over to the booth. BB's talking to a couple of people. He tells this customer, wait. But this Alby needs to see him. Right away. He don't get the message. Guy wanted money, a loan, something. Bernie says, 'Alby, I'm talking business here,' right, Bernie? The shmuck still don't get it. 'I gotta talk to you,' he said. Three times. Four times. Finally, BB gets up. He's got that little nail-cleaning knife of his. He says, 'When I tell a guy to wait, he's supposed to wait.' And with one stroke, he moves down this Alby's shirtfront and one, two, three, he shaves every single button off this square's shirt. The guy went nuts. He took a swing at BB."

"What happened?" I asked.

"He went nuts," Moishe repeated. Then he shrugged. "Bernie broke his jaw."

"You broke his jaw?"

"And my thumb. You forgot that part, Moishela."

"Oh, yeah. It was disgusting. His thumb was hanging off like it didn't even belong to his hand. Watch out for this man, Sandy. What a temper!"

"Hang out. Have another drink. We're going home now," Bernie told Moishe.

When we got into bed, and I was curled up against Bernie, lying in the crook of his arm, examining his thumb, he said: "You think I'm a tough guy?"

"No."

"You're wrong," he said.

We made love that night. And every night after. I started hanging out at the apartment. I moved a few things into Bernie's closet. A couple of evenings a week, I bathed and changed there after work, then went down to meet him at the club. Flatbush Avenue was where my mother and sister lived. East Seventy-ninth Street was where I felt at home.

I loved walking around barefoot on the deep pile carpeting. I loved sitting at the tufted white-leather bar. I loved taking long, leisurely bubble baths with the stereo on in the living room and a glass of champagne on the rim of the tub. And, most of all, I loved being in love with Bernie Barton. I'd known him a little more than a month, but it was a new adventure every day.

One afternoon I was sitting in his apartment, waiting for him to get dressed. I was on the bar stool with my legs crossed, swinging my foot.

Bernie crossed the room knotting his tie. "You've got a hole in your shoe," he said.

Embarrassed, I looked at the sole of my black pumps. "I'll have to get it fixed," I said.

"Forget about it. Tomorrow afternoon you meet me after work."

He called me at the showroom at three the next day. "I'll be at Fifth Avenue and Forty-ninth Street in twenty minutes," he said. "Meet me."

"I don't know if I can leave so early."

"You want me to talk to your boss for you?"

Less than an hour later, we left The Ansonia shoe store. It was a beautiful, bright spring day and I was wearing a brand new pair of open-toed, brown-and-white, high-heeled spectator pumps. With my purse tucked under my arm, I stepped out of the store into the sunlight of Fifth Avenue swinging a stack of tied-together shoe boxes with each hand. A clerk, whose hands were similarly filled, followed me out to the curb. Bernie had bought me *twenty-seven* new pairs of shoes!

"Who's Enid?" he asked. He had hailed a cab and was peeling off a couple of bills to hand the clerk.

I hadn't even realized I'd said her name aloud. I settled into the backseat of the taxi surrounded by stacks of shoe boxes. "Oh, a woman I knew a long time ago who loved shoes," I said.

A few days later, I walked into Bernie's apartment after work. A man I'd never seen before was sitting on the black sofa in the living room with a big brown paper shopping bag at his feet. He glanced up, grinned, and toasted me with the tall glass in his hand.

He was a light-skinned black man with a little mustache and slicked-back red hair. He was wearing a bright Hawaiian sport shirt, orange linen slacks, and pointy light brown alligator shoes. I had never seen anyone like him in real life. He looked like a cross between Cab Calloway and Nathan Detroit.

"You've got to be Sandy," he said.

Bernie was nowhere in sight and I must have looked as nervous as I felt.

"He's in the bathroom. He'll be right out. Relax. I'm an old friend," the man said pleasantly.

I'd never known a black man before, never seen one sitting back with a drink in his hand in a white man's living room calling himself an old friend. This was in the fifties. The Civil Rights movement was still a couple of years and several states down the road. Blacks couldn't vote in the South, couldn't go to the same movie theaters or drink from the same water fountains as whites. They were expected to step off the curb to allow a white person to pass. Up North, and certainly in the Brooklyn Jewish world I came from, there was another kind of segregation that kept us just as separated, just as ignorant and prejudiced about the people we politely called Negroes and more familiarly called *shvartzas*.

Billy Daniels, with his blue eyes and $600 silk suits, didn't count. He wasn't a man, anyway. He was a star.

Bernie walked into the room before I found my voice. "Baby, this is Red. Red, Sandy." He was in a terrific mood.

"Hello," I finally said.

"Hot Dog here is my main man. Wait till you get to know him, Sandy. You're going to love this guy."

Red nodded modestly.

"Hot Dog?"

They laughed. "That's what they call me," he said. "My real name's Harrison Allen."

"You know at baseball games, how they'll pass a hot dog hand to hand and by the time it gets to you it's ice cold and you missed five great plays? That's Red. That's how he blows a joint." Bernie could see I was confused. "Smokes tea . . . marijuana," he explained. "The time it takes for him to pass it to you, man, the crowd's gone home and they're rolling up the infield."

They both thought that was pretty funny. "Excuse us a minute, baby," Bernie said, signaling Red to follow him into the alcove.

"You didn't lie, man," Red said, chuckling, hauling his skinny self up from the couch. "She sure is a fine-looking girl." And off they went behind the black lacquered cabinet, laughing up a storm.

I didn't know whether they were laughing at me or had been smoking funny cigarettes before I'd gotten there or what was going on, but there was a bond between them that made me feel naive and left out. I walked out of the living room, over to the bar.

"Listen, baby," Bernie called to me. "I need you to work for me tonight. At the club."

I couldn't believe it. I'd just spent a full day on my feet in a Seventh Avenue showroom and now he wanted me to work another shift. He had never ever even suggested such a thing before. What was going on here?

"The cigarette girl can't make it. I need you to fill in for her."

He and Red were still in the alcove and I was close to tears. But I said, "Okay. Whatever you want."

"Your uniform's in that shopping bag Red brought over. That's all you're going to wear. Go on, get it. Try it on."

I walked over to the couch and looked into the shopping bag. At first all I saw was a swatch of silky fabric. I reached into the bag to get the uniform. Bernie and Red poked their grinning heads out of the alcove in time to see me pull a gorgeous Breath-of-Spring mink stole out of the brown paper bag. The fur was soft and thick, light as a feather, and lined in exquisite pale satin.

I thought I'd gotten the wrong bag. "Bernie?"

"What's the matter? You don't like it?"

"Like what? This is a mink stole, Bernie."

"It's your new uniform, baby," he said. "And there's something for you on the fireplace."

In a little white jewelry box on the marble mantel was a pearl and sapphire ring.

"So? You like it?"

"Oh, Bernie, it's gorgeous." A ring, I was thinking. Oh, God, he's given me a ring. And a *mink stole*! I ran to him and kissed him. "Thank you," I whispered.

"Thank Red," he said. "He went shopping for me. Of course, if you don't like it," he teased, "we can always send it back, right?"

"We aim to please," Red said, delighted.

And they meant it, too. Through the years a lot of shopping bags and boxes showed up. Bernie loved to surprise me. And, for the most part, I loved his gifts. Nothing ever came close to that first Breath-of-Spring mink, though. Once he got me a long white mink stole. He thought it was sexy and fabulous. I thought it looked like something a stripper would wear. I mean, it was *white* and long. Tall as I am, I could've wrapped it around me twice.

We were in the car. The white stole was lying on the front seat between us. Bernie said, "You hate it."

I said, "No. I just don't love it. It's fabulous, but not for me."

We were waiting for a traffic light on Park Avenue. An elderly, heavy-set black woman was at the curb, waiting to cross the street. "Okay," Bernie said. "It's not for you. Maybe it's for her. Here," he called to the woman. He tossed her the mink. The light changed. We drove away.

Bernie's birthday was May twenty-eighth, just a couple of weeks before mine. And only a couple of days after he gave me that first mink stole. I was nineteen years old and, believe me, I wore that little mink every chance I got. That first night, I wore it to the club and never took it off for a minute, not through dinner or drinks after. I hugged it close to me all night. It was the most glamorous thing I had ever owned, the most extravagant gift I'd ever received. It was practically a pet. And when Bernie told me we were going to the Copacabana for his birthday, the mink and I were in seventh heaven.

The Copacabana was famous as a celebrity hangout. Almost every gossip column you read in the morning covered who was seen with whom at the Copa the night before. Plenty of FBI files were filled with the same information. Not all the Copa celebs were movie stars.

The club was owned by Julie Podell, a little Jewish man with a voice like landfill. There was enough gravel and ground glass in it to bury New Jersey. Downstairs at the Copa, in the main room, Julie used to stand at the back of the club watching his people work. He didn't mix much unless he knew you and then it was mostly, "How's it going? You got everything you need?"

Bernie introduced me that first night as his lady. Julie gave me a little nod, said, "Nice to meet you, Sandy." Then, "Everything okay, Bernie? You got a table? Carmine, take care of Mr. Barton."

I don't remember who was playing in the main room that night. It might have been Joe E. Lewis or Jack E. Leonard or Steve Lawrence and Edie Gorme. They were the headliners of that time. Or it could have been Billy, whom we saw there several times and who never failed to get an embarrassed smile from Bernie by teasing him, shouting out affectionately from the stage: "There he is, one of the good bad guys . . ." Or, "One of my dearest friends . . . a nice white Jewish man." But I remember we just peeked in on the main room, that night, then went upstairs to the lounge.

Ruby Stein waved us over to his table. I had never met him before. I had never even heard of him, but by the 1960s, Ruby and his partner, Jiggs, were notorious as big loanshark bankers. They lent money to some of the most dangerous shylocks on the street. Guys who paid them one and one-half percent interest and, in turn, lent the money at five times that rate to doctors, lawyers, stockbrokers, and corporate types desperate to cover gambling debts or other emergencies. Ruby's clients included guys who used leg breakers as enforcers, guys who'd threaten whole families to get their "vig" or take over a man's business if he couldn't pay up, and suck it dry of cash and into bankruptcy in a couple of months.

As I said, I didn't know anything about Ruby the night of Bernie's birthday. He was just a nice Jewish man to me, about ten years older than Bernie, wearing glasses. His well-groomed hair was brown with pronounced reddish highlights. He was a perfectly ordinary-looking guy— except for one thing. Ruby had a twitch, an eye tic that looked like he was winking at you. The more he drank, the worse the tic got.

He was with Jiggs Forlano that night at the Copa when he called us over to his table. Jiggs was a black-haired Italian, as tall, dignified, and silent as Ruby was drunk and wild. The night was young for Bernie and me, not quite midnight, but Ruby had obviously been drinking for a good couple of hours. He always drank brandy. And when Bernie introduced me to him, he started winking at me. This made me extremely nervous. Not only did Bernie have a temper, but there was a big bosomy blonde rubbing up against the sleeve of Ruby's sharkskin jacket, and who knew what kind of temper she had.

Bernie said, "This is my lady, Sandy."

Ruby said, "Hiya, kid," and winked. He was too far gone to remember his friend, so she introduced herself. "I'm Beryl," she said pleasantly. "Glad to meet you." And Ruby winked at me.

"Beryl. That's my Hebrew name," Bernie said.

"Look at that, he's my namesake," Beryl told Ruby. He winked at her.

Jiggs, who was known as "the shylocks' shylock," talked softly to Bernie for a while. Then Ruby and Bernie started talking ballgames and horse-races, Vegas and Puerto Rico. A little warning bell went off in my head. I listened as they talked and kidded with each other. Their words seemed familiar and so did the subtle change in their tone and energy. Gamblers. I had a flash of déjà vu. An uh-oh, here-we-go-again feeling. And I wondered if Bernie loved gambling the way my father had.

Of course, the minute the topic changed, Ruby was winking up a storm at me again.

"Honey, let's go," I whispered to Bernie at the first opportunity.

We went to our table and ordered a bottle of champagne to celebrate Bernie's forty-first birthday. When the waiter brought the tall ice bucket to the table, he said, "That gentleman would like to buy you a drink."

Bernie craned his neck. His face lit up with recognition and he waved to a well-dressed man in tinted glasses, who was toasting him from a booth against the wall. Then he said, "Excuse me, baby. I've got to go say hello to someone. I haven't seen these guys in years. They're from Chicago."

Bernie went over to the booth and I watched him pumping the man's hand. Then he was introduced to the others at the table. He was wearing his best grin, every one of those perfect white teeth on parade as he chatted with the aging boys from Chicago. I was fine. I wasn't bored at all. It was my first night at the Copa and there was plenty for me to gape and gawk at. Then I heard, "Sandy, come here. I want you to meet someone," and he signaled for me to join him.

"This is Rocco Fischetti, and his brother, Charlie. And you might know this guy over here."

Frank Sinatra stood up. He took my hand and kissed it.

"Oh, my God," I said.

"She'll never wash it again," Bernie teased.

We sat with Sinatra and the Fischetti brothers for a couple of minutes. It turned out that in some circles Rocco and Charles were as famous as Frankie. They'd made names for themselves in Chicago serving the legendary "Scarface" Al Capone. Now they ran the town. Of course, that night, when I asked Bernie who they were and what they did, he said, "They're in the fish business."

Someone had told Rocco that it was Bernie's birthday and they bought us a round of drinks. I took just a sip or two. I couldn't drink. I could barely breathe. I excused myself and ran to the phone to call my mother. "Guess who I'm with?" I said.

"Why, you left the old one, the *alter kocker*?" she asked dryly.

"Frank Sinatra!"

There was a silence on the line.

"Ma?"

"Which Frank Sinatra?" she said. Then she laughed.

In the back of the limo, riding up Madison Avenue at dawn, Bernie kissed me. "Did you have a good time, *mamela*?" he asked.

"The greatest."

"You think this was good, wait till your birthday," he promised. "I don't know what we'll do yet but, guaranteed, it'll be something special."

It was. I never cried so much in my life.

On June 13, the night before my birthday, I woke up to the sound of Bernie wheezing and gasping. He could barely lift his head off the pillow. "What is it?" I asked, frightened.

His hair was soaked, his face was beaded with sweat. The bed was drenched. He couldn't catch his breath. I was petrified, paralyzed. I didn't know what to do—whether to pound his back, dry him with a towel, put ice on his burning forehead.

"Bernie, should I call Red? What should I do?" I asked frantically. "Oh, Bernie, I love you. Help me. Tell me."

He couldn't speak. He signaled for me to give him a pencil and paper and, still coughing and wheezing, he wrote down his doctor's name and phone number.

By the time Dr. Sealy arrived, Bernie's fever had reached 103. I was rubbing his shivering body with washcloths soaked in cold water and alcohol. And I was very relieved when the doctor asked me to wait in the living room while he examined Bernie. The tears I'd held back flowed down my cheeks as I chain-smoked and paced. Every ashtray in the place was filled by the time Dr. Sealy came out to talk to me. You could hardly see the red carpet for the Kleenex.

"Are you his daughter?" Sealy asked.

I was embarrassed. "No, I'm his . . . friend?" I suggested.

The doctor sighed. "Well, I hope you're aware of his condition. Bernie is a very sick man. He had rheumatic fever as a child and developed a heart condition. He's got to be very careful about colds. He's prone to pneumonia and that's very, very dangerous for him."

"Is he going to die?" I was twisting a tissue in my hands trying to make them stop shaking.

Dr. Sealy noticed and frowned. He took my hands in his. "He'll be fine tonight. I gave him a shot. I'm going to write a prescription for penicillin. I want you to get it filled in the morning. I'll call later and we'll see how he's doing. I may want to hospitalize him tomorrow."

I smoked and cried till the sun came up, and then I turned twenty.

It was too early to call in sick at work. Too early to get the prescription filled. Bernie was sleeping. He still sounded terrible to me. He was still wheezing, but it was much better than the coughing fit, and he wasn't gasping for breath anymore. I got dressed and looked in my wallet. I had about eight dollars. I went to the dresser where Bernie kept his spare change. There was a couple of hundred dollars in the drawer. I took a twenty and Bernie's keys and went to the little gourmet deli that was open all night on Madison Avenue.

I bought Campbell's chicken noodle soup and Jell-O and Wonderbread for toast. I bought ginger ale and Lipton's tea and a little jar of honey that, on Madison Avenue, cost half a day's salary. I bought whatever I could find that my mother gave me when I was sick. The only thing I left out were coloring books and Crayolas.

Bernie was still asleep. He still felt very hot. I sponged him down with alcohol and changed the pillow cases. He was very pale and his breathing was so noisy it was frightening. I busied myself around the apartment for a while, cleaning up. I opened a can of soup and put it in a pan on the stove and waited, thinking he'd get up. I read the Jell-O instructions and, finally, pessimistically, tried my hand at making a bowl. And every time I walked back into the alcove and saw him struggling to breathe, I'd break down and start crying all over again. I had known him less than two months. I was afraid I was going to lose him forever.

I called work and then I called my friend Judy at her boyfriend's beauty salon.

"He's so sick," I said. "He really looks bad, Judy. He looks like an old man. Like that movie where Ronald Coleman takes the girl out of Shangri-la and suddenly she turns two million years old."

"Don't cry, honey. He'll be all right. That doctor said so, didn't he? So what are you crying for? What's the worst that could happen?"

"Oh, Judy," I said, "what if he dies before I get a chance to marry him?"

Dr. Sealy stopped by that afternoon. Bernie was just barely awake. He hadn't eaten all day. He'd had a couple of sips of tea and honey to wash down the penicillin tablets, that was all. And, in spite of my sponging him down with alcohol every twenty minutes or so, his fever was still pretty high.

"I'm going to put him in," Sealy decided. He called Cabrini Hospital on Nineteenth Street and made the arrangements, then gave me the address and left.

I'd called Hot Dog Red for Bernie earlier in the day. Red was going to take care of some business for him uptown and then, he said, he'd come by the apartment to help me out. He arrived shortly after Dr. Sealy left. I'd been holding it together for Bernie. I'd managed not to cry for about fifteen whole minutes. But as soon as Red rang the doorbell, I fell apart again.

"Take it easy, kid. The Dog is here," Red announced, laughing, trying to cheer me up. "You just go in there and get BB dressed and I'll drive you down to the hospital."

In the front seat of Red's caddy, Bernie rested his head on my shoulder. "You sorry you got involved with an old man?" he teased.

"She told *me* she was," Red said.

I wanted to kill him. Bernie started to laugh and had another coughing fit.

I checked him into the hospital. They put him in a wheelchair. It really scared me. He looked so weak. And it reminded me of what my mother had said about riding him around his club in a wheelchair. And now, there he was slumped down in a wheelchair and he did look old and helpless and I felt young and useless. And then, the nurse said, "Are you his daughter, dear?" And, *again,* I started crying.

I stayed at the hospital all day. Finally Dr. Sealy sent me home. "Go on," he said, "Bernie's asleep. There's nothing you can do for him now except get some rest yourself." Before I left, I tiptoed into Bernie's room. He had tubes running into his arms and an oxygen mask over his face. But he looked better than he had when we'd checked in. At least his brow wasn't creased with worry and pain.

Red drove me back uptown. "Bernie said take whatever money you need from the drawer. And if you need more, if you need anything, you just call me."

I thanked him and went inside. I started cleaning things up—I changed the bed linen and hung up Bernie's clothes and threw out the uneaten soup and emptied the ashtrays and picked up the Kleenex. And then I caught a look at myself in the mirror behind the bar. I wasn't wearing any makeup. My hair wasn't even combed. I was wearing a shirt of Bernie's that I'd thrown on when I went shopping at six in the morning.

"Happy birthday, kid," I said to the girl in the mirror. My voice was so hoarse from smoking and crying all day that I sounded just like Bernie. He'd promised me a special birthday, I remembered. Well, I thought, he'd delivered.

The next day, I slept later than usual. I phoned in sick again at work and rushed down to Cabrini Hospital. When I got off the elevator at Bernie's floor, I saw a pretty nurse come giggling out of his room. Then two guys with cigars in their mouths came out. Then a big woman, a candy striper, carrying a stack of magazines. It was like one of those little circus cars out of which comes an endless parade of clowns. He'd been in the hospital less than twenty-four hours, but the room was already filling with flowers, candy, and coffee cups. And Bernie was propped up in bed with the oxygen mask over his nose and a telephone nestled against his ear.

"You're feeling better?" I asked.

He nodded and held up his hand for me to wait. He listened at the receiver for a while, then hung up and pulled off the oxygen mask.

"Bernie, don't!" I protested.

He gave me a great big smile. "Come here, baby, and give me a kiss," he said. He didn't sound as good as he looked, but it was a big improvement over yesterday.

"Who were you talking to?" I asked.

"I wasn't talking. I was listening," he said. "I made a couple of bets."

That was the day after he almost died. By the next day, the traffic in and out of Bernie's private room was unbelievable. If there'd been a turnstile at the door, he could have raked in a fortune. Wise guys in shiny suits took turns squeezing into the space between the bed and the window. Nurses had to nudge past the visitors. The television was on, the ballgame was blaring. There were open Chinese food containers on Bernie's bed tray. The little chest of drawers under the TV set was as well stocked as The Velvet Club's bar. Red was on the phone placing bets for Bernie. And Bernie, in his hospital gown, was sitting up in bed in the middle of all this chaos scribbling in a little notebook.

"My God, what are you doing?" I asked him.

"Keeping track," he said cryptically, and stuck the book under his pillow.

Later that night, when there was a dinner-time lull in the crowd, Bernie took out the notebook again. He was jotting down names. Again, I asked about the book.

"I'm writing down who was here, who came to visit me," he explained, "Who came to give me *koved.*"

"*Koved?*" I'd never heard the word.

"It means respect. Honor. You've got to keep track of these things, of who shows up to pay respect."

The fourth day when I came to visit after work, Bernie threw everyone out of the room. "I feel better," he said, grinning.

"Oh, honey, I'm so glad."

"Lock the door and I'll show you," he said.

I thought he was kidding. I laughed. He wasn't kidding.

We made love in his hospital bed. I was afraid someone would barge in and catch us and throw me out. I was afraid the embarrassment would kill me and the excitement would kill him. I had my eyes squeezed shut the whole time, praying that he wouldn't die, and thinking, this can't be good for a heart condition.

* * *

The week following Bernie's hospitalization, I stayed home from work to take care of him. We were together day and night. I think it was the most time I'd ever spent alone with another human being and it was never boring.

I discovered how much Bernie loved to read. He sent me to the library with lists of books. It was the first time I'd ever really used a library, and I was almost as proud of myself as I was of him. He read Shakespeare's plays aloud to me. We'd act out some of the scenes together. Elizabeth Barrett Browning was his favorite poet. Bernie recited her work from memory. We played cards and board games like kids. And we talked and talked and talked.

I learned more about him that week than I had in the nearly two months we'd been seeing each other.

I lit a cigarette one night while we were playing Monopoly. "Did you know I used to smoke? You want to know how I quit?" he asked, laughing. "When I was in prison. The doctor told me I had to stop smoking, but I didn't. They made me an auxiliary fireman. I had my own room in the firehouse, my own bathroom. And one day this muscle-bound giant, this *bulvon,* knocks on the door. And he says he's been watching me and he likes me and he wants to be my girlfriend. I say, thank you very much, a girlfriend with testicles I don't need; however, I could use a maid. And we cut this deal for cigarettes. He did my laundry, kept the place nice, and I paid him off in cigarettes. That's how I quit smoking."

Another afternoon, Bernie was in bed reading to me. He started coughing and put down the book. "I always liked to read," he said, after he'd caught his breath again. "But in prison, that's where I first had the time. That's also where I found out about this heart condition. In Atlanta. I'd catch a cold and be laid up for weeks. Finally, the prison doctor discovered that one of the valves in my heart was shriveled from the rheumatic fever I had when I was seven. I still remember being sick when I was a kid. My mother laid me out on blocks of ice on the kitchen table to get the fever down. Ice from the ice box. That was before refrigerators. An old man used to come a couple of times a week with the ice and shlep it up the three flights of stairs on his back. He'd have a gunny sack over his shoulder with a three-foot square block of ice lying on top of it. Each block weighed about a ton. I still remember how it felt, laying there on top of the ice."

"What happened," I asked tentatively. "I mean, with prison. Why were you there?"

"I'll show you. Behind the bar, there's a scrapbook. Bring it here."

I did. It was an old-fashioned scrapbook. The black pages were filled with scotch-taped newspaper clippings and snapshots fastened at the corners with little white triangular picture holders. The newsprint on most of the articles was yellowed. The stories were headlined: *Teamster Official Indicted. Mobster Convicted. Union Boss Charged with Racketeering.* We sat on the bed and looked through the pages together. But to this day, I don't remember the specifics of Bernie's case, only that it had to do with crooked union activities, and once he'd been convicted and sent away, he couldn't be reinstated. And that was that, as he put it, for his short career as a rising labor leader.

The scrapbook included lots of pictures of friends, from his days on the Lower East Side to his bid in Atlanta. "I used to sit with the old man," he said, meaning New York City's Boss of all Bosses, Vito Genovese, who was serving time on a narcotics rap in the same prison. "Ziggy Schwartz was there, too. And a Jewish guy, a swindler called Tiny who must've been twelve feet tall," Bernie reminisced.

That started us kidding around about the difference between the Cosa Nostra and the Kosher Nostra. "Sure, everyone thinks, the Jews are the brains and the ginzos are the brawn," Bernie said, "Well, *mamela,* it ain't necessarily so." And he rattled off the names of Jewish mobsters as famous for their muscle as their minds—Legs Diamond, Dutch Shultz, Monk Eastman, Big Jack Zelig, Lefty Louis Rosenzweig, Waxy Gordon, Bugsy Siegel, and even Meyer Lansky, the most famous business head in the mob. He had stories about them all.

I'd listen, with my mouth hanging open, seeing the crowded, shadowy streets of the Lower East Side as he talked, and the bootlegging trucks and the *shtarkes,* the strong-arm men, making their weekly collections from the shopkeepers or fighting with baseball bats and blackjacks, one day on the side of labor, the next with management.

One of my favorites from that time, from the week Bernie was recuperating, was his story of how "racketeering" got its name. "Did you ever hear of Dopey Benny Fein?" Bernie asked me. "He had droopy eyelids, that's why they called him 'Dopey.' Started out as a pickpocket, a little street hustler selling 'protection' to the neighborhood greenhorns . . . This guy practically started labor racketeering single-handed. In fact, the whole thing with 'rackets'—the word 'racketeer' started when Dopey Benny Fein used to hustle money from little Jewish shopkeepers on Grand Street by muscling them to buy tickets to a dance. In those days, dances were called 'rackets.' And, believe me, Benny made a fistful of money on the 'rackets.' "

That was how Benny got started, Bernie told me. Then, as the Jewish labor movement began to grow, "the Dope," he said, hired himself out as a head-basher to any union local that needed help during a strike. From the butchers and bakers to the rag pickers and umbrella makers, nobody crossed the picket lines while Dopey Benny Fein's gangs patrolled them. And no workers voted against the leadership if the leaders had hired Dopey. He even put together a gang of women who used umbrellas weighted with lead to convince nonunion women workers to join the movement.

I remember I asked Bernie if he still saw Dopey. He gave me such a look, and then he laughed. "I'm not that old, baby," he said. Dopey Benny Fein's time was around the turn of the century. Bernie hadn't known him; he'd heard stories and he'd read about the original racketeer. But the way Bernie Barton told a story, not only would you have sworn he was there, you felt like you were right there with him.

Our time together during that week after he got out of the hospital brought us closer than ever. When he told me he was going away for about six weeks to a spa in Connecticut, it was all I could do not to cry. He left for Bill Hahn's and I went back to work. But I still spent a couple of nights a week at his apartment. I'd take the long, luxurious bubble baths I loved and listen to the stereo. And I'd sleep in Bernie's T-shirts, sniffing the cool white cotton, trying to catch a trace of his aftershave around the collar, hoping for a scent of him.

We talked on the phone almost every night. He sounded better and better. Finally, near the end of July, he said he was feeling great and he thought he'd be back in a week.

The next day, he called me at the showroom. "I'm home," he announced. It was maybe two o'clock in the afternoon. I threw my dress on over the little light satin modeling slip we wore and tore out of Midwest Couture.

Bernie was sitting at the white tufted-leather bar having a drink. He looked up at me as I came through the door. He had a spectacular tan, and his eyes seemed twice as blue as I remembered them. His face was relaxed and his body back to its youthful strength. "What are you waiting for?" he asked, as I stood, suddenly speechless and awkward, in the entry hall staring at him. "Did you miss your daddy, baby? Are you my girl?"

At the end of that summer, he asked the question again. "Are you my girl?"

We'd spent most of August together. Almost every night, I'd meet Bernie at the club and we'd have a late supper and go uptown to his place. Once in a while, he'd be busy or have to go somewhere on business, and he'd send me home to Brooklyn in the limo.

One night in August, Carmine Lombardozzi, who was very connected with the Gambino family and very married, came in with a tall, gorgeous platinum blonde.

Carmine, a warm, darkly handsome man in his mid-forties, had fallen in love with a wise guy's twenty-three-year-old kid. She was about five-eight in her stiletto heels, with a body that could stop a B59, and was wrapped skin tight in a teeny-weeny, thigh-high dress. Her name was Rosemary. She was as sweet as could be and crazy about Carmine. And Carmine couldn't keep his hands off her. Bernie kept asking him to quit it. "What're you feeling her up in my place for?" he said. "Come on, Carmine, does this look like the backseat of your car?"

Bernie introduced Carmine Lombardozzi to me as "The Doctor," but some people called Carmine "the King of Wall Street" because of the stranglehold he was supposed to have—through loansharking, gambling, and stolen securities—on some of the stock exchange's biggest traders.

"Why do you call him the doctor?" I asked Bernie.

"Because he's an operator," Bernie said.

But Ziggy or Moishe Pickles or maybe it was Red had another explanation. "Because he puts people in the hospital," one of them said.

We went to the Copa a couple of times with Carmine and Rosemary. We spent a weekend at a dude ranch in New Jersey, The Sakasooner Ranch, with friends of mine, and a weekend at the Concord Hotel in the Catskills with friends of Bernie's. All summer long I'd met more of the club—the racket club, as some of the wives used to call it.

And on Labor Day, Bernie said to me: "So, are you my girl?"

I said, "Of course I am."

"Okay," he said. "Then go home and pack. You're going to live with me."

CHAPTER FOUR

Playing House

It was like a Jewish joke—a bad Jewish joke. It was like being caught up in a melodrama from the Yiddish Theatre on Second Avenue or suddenly turning the television on to a bizarre sitcom in which the Goldbergs enter the Twilight Zone.

It was the best of times. It was the worst of times. It was the day I packed my bags and left Brooklyn.

"Er zol ligen in drerd! He should rot in hell!" my mother shouted. Rage lifted her onto her tiptoes, wrath hauled her arm up, forefinger pointed to heaven, God as her witness. "In *drerd!"* she screamed as I dumped the contents of my two dresser drawers into shopping bags.

"I love him, Ma," I shouted back. "And he loves me!"

"Pah!" she spat. "This is love?! What do you know about it? This is a gangster, a hoodlum, a man capable of God knows what kind of *mishegaas,* what kind of insanity and lies! This man loves you? *Vi a lokh in kop*—like a hole in the head! What did I raise? What kind of moron? If a man loves you, he marries you!'' She paced and spun and shouted behind me in the crowded kitchen while my little sister cowered on her daybed, holding her ears and crying.

"Don't worry, Ma. I'll still pay the bills,'' I hollered.

She gasped. "This is what you think I'm talking about? Money?!'' and she gave such a bloodcurdling scream that I whirled around. She was tearing her hair.

"Ma, don't! Stop it, please!'' I begged her. I put my arms around Marlene. "Don't look at her. She's crazy,'' I said.

"Sandy, don't go. Please,'' my little sister sobbed.

"I love him, Marlene. You don't understand. Mom will be all right after a while. She's just crazy now. She'll be okay and I'll still pay the rent and there'll be enough money for you, for your clothes, for whatever you want, baby. But I've got to get out of here. I'm leaving this mad house. There hasn't been a minute's peace between Mom and me since Daddy left. You get along with her. It won't be bad once I'm gone, Marlene.''

"You'll see! You'll see,'' my mother raged. "You think he loves you? You think he's going to marry you, Mrs. Wise Guy? No man buys a cow when milk is cheap!''

I slammed shut my little suitcase. I stuffed the last sweater into the shopping bag. "What do you know,'' I said. "What do you know?'' But I saw the pain cross her face, as if she'd read my mind, and I bit my lip and didn't finish the thought: You're so smart you're alone!

I grabbed whatever I could carry and ran for the door. But she let out a wail that stopped me in my tracks. "Nooo!'' she screamed. And I watched, in stunned silence, as my mother threw herself onto the floor! She threw herself onto the green floral kitchen linoleum and started to flail like a dying fish. She banged her head against the floor. She screamed and prayed and flopped around. *"Got in himmel, Gotenyu, Vey isz mir, Gevalt!''*

I was beyond feeling now. I flew out the door and ran down the hall to the elevator. All the way down to the ground floor, I could hear her.

The driver Bernie had sent was leaning against the front fender of the car, reading a newspaper. He saw me shoot out of the apartment building. God knows what I must have looked like, but he threw down the paper, grabbed my suitcase, and yanked open the car door for me. Then he jumped into the front seat and we sped off into the night—just like in a gangster movie.

The first couple of months we lived together, I was Barbie, Bernie was Ken, and the brownstone on Seventy-ninth Street was our doll house. Or so it seemed to me. Ponytail swinging, high heels clacking, I went to work every day in the Garment Center, no longer a subway shlepper from Brooklyn but a real New Yorker now. The spacious apartment in one of Manhattan's best neighborhoods, the silk-stocking district as it was known, was where I really lived, where I slept and woke every single day. And I adored coming home to it. The man I loved was strong, handsome, rich, and if not famous at least well-known and liked among a select circle of celebrities.

Most evenings, we'd have dinner at the club. But if Bernie said, "Baby, don't come down tonight. Relax at home and I'll call you later," it was no problem—because I loved being in that apartment alone. Bernie had shown me the secret hiding places: the dresser drawer where a couple of hundreds were always stashed; the white Moroccan leather hassock in the living room with the false lid on it in which Bernie kept thick envelopes of money, private papers, a gun, jewelry, and God knows what else. I even had a set of keys to Bernie's big green Cadillac with the swept-back tail fins that sat parked right outside our building day and night. Bernie rarely used it. He preferred taxi cabs or hired cars. And, of course, I never drove it. I didn't know how to drive. I didn't know how to cook. I didn't know how to iron. And these were some of the things that almost brought the doll house tumbling down.

At first, Bernie thought it was cute that I didn't know how to boil an egg. I didn't even know how to boil water. Literally. He bought me a glass pot and actually had to show me that when the water bubbled, that meant it was "boiling hot."

Rock Hudson's butcher, at Schaffer's on Madison Avenue, where customers waited in chairs for their meat to be trimmed, was not as thorough a teacher as Bernie. Don't get me wrong: He sold me a fabulous filet mignon, thick and beautifully marbled. A steak for a king, he kidded me, after I told him I wanted to fix a perfect dinner for my boyfriend. I asked him the best way to cook it, and he said, just put it under the broiler.

Bernie came home from the club early that Thursday. I showed him the steak and he was very proud of me. "That's a gorgeous cut of beef," he said. "How much did it cost?"

I told him and he gave me one of his are-you-out-of-your-mind looks.

"Why, is that a lot?" I asked innocently.

"Naw," he said sarcastically. "Not if you got the rest of the steer cooling in the fridge."

My feelings were hurt and I huffed away. He shook his head and walked off to the bar and made himself a drink while I turned on the broiler.

The butcher never told me to turn the steak over. And every time I looked into the stove and lifted the piece of meat up, it looked terribly raw on the bottom. So I let it broil and broil and, finally, when it was nice and brown and there was no blood oozing from underneath it, I put it on a plate and carried it in to Bernie.

He went crazy. He looked at this little curled black knob of steak I'd brought him and you could practically hear the whistle tooting and see smoke shoot from his ears. That was my personal introduction to the highly touted Barton temper. Moishe Pickles hadn't lied.

He threw the plate across the room with all his might. The steak flew like a hockey puck. The plate shattered. The baked potato, half raw, cold, and hard as a rock inside its tepid skin, landed with a thud, then skittered across the bar, bowling over a couple of glasses and an ashtray. And before all that registered, Bernie's mouth went off.

I had never in my entire twenty years ever heard such language used, let alone directed at me. I was not just frightened, I was embarrassed by the words. "Stupid bitch. Cunt," he screamed. And "dumb douche bag."

I couldn't believe it. This was my Prince Charming, my Ken doll? I stared at him, incredulous, as he leapt up from the chair and went from pounding the table to pounding the walls. I watched dumbfounded. I trembled in fear and stood still and said nothing as Bernie, biting his fist, ran past me out the front door.

It was obvious that I had a lot to learn. And despite that frightening explosive temper, Bernie was a terrific teacher. Like my father, he enjoyed taking me shopping. We'd go to Lily Rubin or Wilma's on Fifty-seventh Street and he'd sit on the little gilt chairs or Victorian settees as I modeled tailored suits and flowing fitted evening gowns for him. With a nod or a shake of his head, he'd make the final decision on every item. Bernie had an opinion on everything I wore, the way my hair was done, the kind of makeup that was right for me. Sometimes he liked me looking sophisticated; sometimes innocent and young.

He liked me in elbow-length gloves and elegant hats—the same big-brimmed picture hats that I'd admired as a kid on the ultimate gangster's moll, Virginia Hill. I had a dozen of them in a rainbow of colors in velvet, felt, and straw.

Poor Jimmy Doyle, Johnny Dio's uncle, went to his grave with a scar on his skull from one of my picture hats. Bernie and I had lunch with him in a restaurant one Mother's Day and, as we were leaving, I bent to kiss him goodbye. I was wearing a stiff-brimmed straw picture hat, red, I remember. And as I straightened up, the brim ripped a hole in his forehead. Blood started gushing out. Everyone at the table stared in shock. A couple of guys tried to mop Jimmy up with linen napkins dipped in ice water. I just stood there, white as a sheet, stunned and horrified, as they rushed him out of the restaurant to an emergency room where it took three butterfly stitches to stop the bleeding.

Of course, at Bernie's, clothes in plain brown bags would appear from out of nowhere. Coats and sweaters. Suits and gowns. Shopping bags would show up in the living room. Hat boxes and shoeboxes and garment bags that were left like orphaned babies.

There were a couple of brothers from Little Italy, Tony and Charlie North, who'd come by from time to time, always together, with suitcases full of designer gowns. Ceil Chapman was a big label in those days and, unbeknownst to her I'm sure, Tony and Charlie were her best customers. They were short and stocky. They looked and dressed alike in dark shirts and shiny suits. A couple of wise guys Walt Disney could have created, they were so ugly they were cute. Fences and loansharks for most of their lives, they'd been in and out of jail countless times. Bernie knew one of them from prison.

In addition to handling some of the most beautiful and elegant evening gowns I'd ever seen, the North brothers helped me understand one of Bernie's strangest habits. He talked in his sleep. He didn't just talk. He fought, cursed, and yelled. "You bastard, I'll kill you!" "Back off, fucker!" "You're a dead man! I'm going to get you!" I'd awaken with a start, my heart pounding violently, only to find Bernie sound asleep, fighting some invisible dream demon.

It wasn't until I heard Tony North teasing Charlie about the same kind of nightmares, the same loud, violent conversations in his sleep, that I began to realize that Bernie's bizarre and frightening outbursts were common among men who'd spent time in prison. Later, other women, girl-friends and wives of guys who'd been inside, told me they had the same experience.

As furs and clothing seemed to appear at the apartment out of thin air, so, one day, did Raven with her magic pink cosmetic box. Raven was one of the stars of Club 82, a mob-controlled nightspot in Greenwich Village with a floor show that featured men dressed and made-up as women. They were so good at it that customers always gasped at the end of the show when the wigs came off and the sexy girls they'd been drooling over all night turned out to be boys in drag. Of course, the tuxedoed, crew-cut waiters at Club 82 were women—women every bit as tough and stocky as the North brothers.

Raven was a make-up artist, a thin boy with reddish black hair, a pointy face, and a beak that left no doubt where he'd gotten his stage name. He was a sad-looking unattractive guy. In drag, he became a sad-looking un-attractive girl. But he was a wizard with cosmetics and, at Bernie's request, he taught me all his favorite make-up tricks. Talking a mile a minute, Raven would drape a towel around my neck and, hands fluttering, open his prized pink leather cosmetic case.

"So you're gawn to the Concord? So what'ya wearin'? Black? Wha'four? Y'need a little color, Sandy. Oooooh!" he'd scream when I'd show him the dress or gown or suit du jour. "Oooooh, my Gawd, gorgeous! Like Rita Hayworth, Sandy! With that hair of yours and those long kid gloves. I can't stand it! Just like Rita in *Gilda*. You could drive Glen Ford wild. So—" He'd swoop down on a lipstick brush, a compact of Pan-Cake, a lightening sponge. "We'll give you that Gilda look! The luscious lips. The flashing eyes!" Raven could build bones and sink cheeks and create what he liked to call gypsy-goddess-eyes-to-die-for.

There was so much Bernie wanted to show me, so much about life he got a kick out of and wanted to share with me. He was at home everywhere. And wherever he was, he picked up the pulse, the accents, the style of his surroundings. At The Velvet Club, he was genial, the best host in the world, nodding and waving and shaking hands, taking care of business with that big Chiclet smile of his. At the Copa he was stylish, generous, bright. With the North brothers, he was strictly street. With guys from the old neighborhood, his conversation was suddenly spiced with Yiddish words and humor. And up in Harlem, where he took me one crisp and sunny fall afternoon, he was as loose and alive as I'd ever seen him anywhere.

I'd never been uptown before. I don't remember why we went, but sitting beside Bernie in the green Caddy, I was dressed to the nines in a stylish new blue suit with a navy blue picture hat. The car radio was on. The windows were open. The big Caddy made a U-turn on 125th Street and pulled right into a perfect parking spot just waiting in front of a storefront with a Take Out Chicken sign hanging over its door. Bernie said, "Just sit there, baby. I'll come around and open your door." He got out on the street side of the car and by the time he walked around the front grill, guys were drifting toward us, coming from across the street and out of the chicken shack.

Men were calling out, "Hey, mah man." "BB" "Mr. B, where you been?"

And Bernie started grinning from ear to ear like he was home. "Hey, man," he'd say. "How you? How you been?" He acted just the same as everyone else. There was no mockery or mimicry about the change that came over him. He was in Harlem, behaving like he'd been born there, looking proud and pleased and welcome. He opened my side of the door and gave me his hand. I stepped out, high heels and nylons first.

"How'do?" men mumbled. Some tipped their hats. "Look what Mr. B's got." They smiled and nodded approvingly. Bernie helped me up onto the front fender of the Caddy. I sat there, fishing in my purse for a cigarette. The minute I found my cigarette case and drew one out, a match appeared under it. "Light?" one of Bernie's friends offered. "It's BB's princess," I heard.

"Who's that?"

"It's BB's princess."

Big eyed, I watched as Bernie talked to people outside the Chicken Take Out. I felt so proud of him. Everywhere we went, he had friends, people liked him, trusted him, slapped him on the back or hand, grinned and joked with him. And every other guy would sneak a peek at me, and touch his cap and say, "How'do?"

Bernie had friends in Harlem. He also had business in Harlem. As we made the rounds that first day, conversations that began with laughs would turn suddenly serious and hushed. Even as I sat on the fender of the Caddy, I noticed a tall black man touch Bernie's elbow and the two of them kind of faded back over toward the Chicken Take Out storefront. Bernie's smile changed just a little. He was listening to the man, nodding his head. The smile was still on his lips, but you could tell it was his ears and eyes that were doing the real work now—alert, at attention, all business. And then, of course, the thick white envelope in which by now I could nearly smell the cash was passed. Bernie tucked it into his breast pocket, clapped the guy on the shoulder, and we were off again.

We drove around and Bernie pointed out the sights to me. That was where the old Cotton Club used to be. A bootlegger named Owney Madden controlled the place. Lucky Luciano was supposed to have had a piece of it. So had a white political boss named Arnold Rothstein. And a black numbers banker named Bumpy Johnson. Did I know that *shvartzas,* colored people, were not even allowed inside the Cotton Club back in its heyday? Only the stars among them—the rich, famous, and dangerous.

I met Bumpy Johnson at an afterhours club uptown a few months later. He was dark and clean, immaculately well dressed with processed straight hair. An elegant-looking man who spoke in a quiet, refined way and never used the popular language of jazz or the streets. Bernie introduced him to me as though he was an elder statesman, with great respect and pride. He had balls. He was honorable. He'd organized unions in Harlem. He'd bank-rolled everything from numbers operations to neighborhood bars. And back when black folks couldn't get in the front door of the Cotton Club, Bumpy Johnson could and did. And back when black folks were supposed to take a backseat to the wise guys from downtown, Bumpy Johnson sat where he pleased.

We continued our tour of Harlem and pulled up outside Sugar Ray's, the bar owned by boxing champ Sugar Ray Robinson. Purple was Robinson's favorite color. His big purple Cadillac was often parked right outside the bar, which was, of course, decorated in purple from its lilac and lavender walls to its deep purple leather bar stools and tufted banquettes. That day, my first in Harlem, the champ's car wasn't outside the bar, but Cokey's Cadillac was.

Cokey was one of Bernie's favorite uptown running mates. Bernie had known Cokey almost as long as he'd known Hot Dog Red, but the two men were very different. Where Red was mellow and easy-going, Cokey was quick and electric. He was a wiry, light-skinned black man who owned some chicken and ribs places in Harlem and had a string of prize fighters.

What else Cokey was into only God, Bernie, and the D.A.'s office knew for sure. But I had my suspicions about his nickname. We picked Cokey up at Sugar Ray's and the three of us went over to the gym where some of Cokey's fighters were training.

Bernie was wild about boxing. He also owned a fighter or two. But he was a lot more successful betting on fights than owning fighters. The gym on the second floor of a rickety corner building was steamy, loud, and exciting. Both Cokey and Bernie quickly got caught up in watching the training bouts. Again, I was surprised at how many people knew Bernie and came by to say hi. Some ribbed him about one of his fighters who'd taken a terrific licking at Sunnyside Gardens a couple of weeks earlier.

The kid's name was Carlos. Bernie had been excited about taking me to the fights, especially when one of his boys was on the bill. It was yet another world he was eager to introduce me to. But Carlos, the fighter whose food, rent, and training bills Bernie paid, had put in a short and miserable performance before getting knocked down in the second round and Bernie went nuts! He actually pushed up to the ring and started pounding the mat with his fist, screaming, "Get up, you bum. I feed you, I dress you. How can you do this to me?! Get up or I'll kill you!"

The kid tried, I'll give him that. He looked at Bernie pleadingly through his one good eye. The other was swollen shut. "Please, Mr. B," he managed.

"Get up!" Bernie roared.

Carlos tried, made it to one knee, then collapsed.

Bernie bellowed like a wounded bull: "Noooo! You bum, you dog, you dirt bag bastard! Where's your balls? Where's your pride?! How can you do this to me?! Get up!" He started scrambling into the ring. It took a couple of security guards to stop him from crawling under the ropes. I don't know if he was going to fulfill his threat and go after Carlos or if he intended to show the kid how to fight by taking on the winner. I was just glad somebody stopped him.

Despite his threat to kill the kid, Bernie eventually got Carlos, who clearly didn't have what it took to stay alive in the ring, a job in the Garment Center.

None of Bernie's fighters amounted to anything. His judgment in this arena was a joke. One time, Cokey tried to interest him in a new young guy up at the gym. Bernie looked the kid over. "Nah," he said, instantly. "He's too big, too awkward. No way. He'll never make it."

Cokey said, "You're wrong. The kid's got the goods. He can go the whole way."

"Too gawky, too big," Bernie insisted. "What's his name?"

"Cassius Clay," said Cokey.

"Forget him," Bernie said.

A few years later, the kid took a new name: Muhammad Ali.

Bernie loved Harlem. He knew its ins and outs, from neighborhood bars and little chicken and rib joints where thousands of dollars in numbers money changed hands to the celebrity spots, jazz clubs, and luxurious afterhours places where gambling, smoke, and coke were openly indulged from midnight through the wee small hours. After a night's work at The Velvet Club, he'd go uptown to unwind at places like Reefer May's, a town house in Harlem's classiest section, Sugar Hill.

Reefer May's was like a decadent Disney Land, a sprawling adult theme park for urban vampires. One never arrived before midnight. After the witching hour, the place began to fill with wise guys, slumming socialites, jazz musicians, and the occasional rich, adventuresome college kid. People came in every color and many of them came with guns. Weapons were like accessories, as important as cufflinks or tie pins, no more. Women floated through the rooms in every stunning style of dress. Models in sequined gowns dragging floor-length furs behind them. Square girls in blonde page-boys and ankle-length taffeta skirts. Actresses, dancers, entertainers still in their stage makeup, their heads covered in Audrey Hepburn-type scarves. Older women in good jewels and dark glasses.

And, of course, there was Reefer May herself. She was an enormous and beautiful middle-aged black woman, who wore floor-length caftans and her thick, still-dark hair pulled back tightly in a large, neat bun. She was extremely sweet-faced with flawless, shiny cocoa skin. According to Red, she'd been a breathtakingly handsome girl, the mistress of a white numbers banker. An Irish or Italian guy, a nice man, Red said, who'd been wildly in love with her. Reefer had put away the money she'd gotten from him and with it, after he died, she'd bought her place.

There were at least eight huge rooms at Reefer May's and each was decorated differently. You would wander from the purple, red, and gold-cushioned Arabian Nights room into the brass, mahogany, and red velvet decor of a turn-of-the-century bordello; from a jungle setting of tropical plants and tigerskins to the elegant, pleated fabric walls of the gambling casino. In one room musicians would be jamming, passing joints, getting up to chat or take a break, and their seats would immediately be filled by new musicians, whose girls would sway against the wall or carry fresh glasses of scotch, bourbon, vodka, or cognac over to them. If the jam didn't smell of marijuana smoke it smelled of Gitanes or Gauloise, the musky French cigarettes so many of the jazzmen had gotten used to in Paris. At the bar, people would knock powdered lines of cocaine onto the backs of their hands and snort them up or offer them around in the ritual way one might suck on a lemon after a shot of tequila.

I continued working in the Garment Center, but it was hard showing up early in the morning after spending time either with or waiting for Bernie.

His schedule, his way of life, was never going to be conventional, I realized, but I did the best I could to keep up with it. Sometimes, he'd come home at six in the evening, with a little bag of food for me from the club. He'd have a drink and unwind while I ate dinner. We'd talk, cuddle, catch up, and he'd leave again at ten to go back to work. And he might not come back until three or four in the morning. Some days, he was walking in the door as I was walking out. Some nights, he wanted me to be with him when he visited an afterhours club in Harlem or a gambling joint downtown. All in all we spent more time together than most couples I knew back then. It was great for our relationship, but deadly for my career. In late October, I got fired.

CHAPTER FIVE

Easy Come, Easy Go

My nose was running and my eyes were red from crying when Bernie came home that night. "Baby, what's the matter, are you sick?" he asked.

I was in bed, surrounded by tissues. "No. I got fired."

"Thank God," he said.

"What do you mean, thank God? How am I going to support my family. They need my help. My mother makes *bubkes* at that dumb cleaning store. Marlene's too young to go to work, even part-time. She's only twelve. She's got to study to get decent grades. How can you say, 'thank God'?"

"Thank God it's your job, not your health," he said, and sat down next to me on the bed. "Look," he said, taking my hand. "You got fired. You'll collect unemployment. You'll send Tillie your unemployment check and I'll make up the difference. It's nothing. It's just money, baby."

He was as good as his word. My mother despised him and he knew it. But he never took it personally. "Why should I," he'd ask. "She's never even met me. When she meets me and hates me, *then* I'll start worrying."

He gave me cash every two weeks to send home to Brooklyn. And, for a long time, I didn't tell my mother where the money was coming from. I didn't want to worry her about my losing my job. I knew how awful she'd feel about it. How afraid she'd be of my total reliance on Bernie, a man in whose love for me she had no faith at all.

It took me a little while to get used to depending on Bernie for money. I felt very uncomfortable asking for cash, although he never made a big deal about it. "Go to the drawer," he'd say. That was it. He never said, take five dollars or take five hundred. Just "Go to the drawer. Get what you need."

There were always a couple of hundreds in that magical drawer. Even during sports seasons, when Bernie's betting fever really took off. That's when both TVs and the radio would be blasting off and there'd be hot and cold running bookmakers in the apartment all day long. A guy would walk in with an envelope of money and hand it to Bernie. Fifteen minutes later, another guy would walk out with two envelopes. And Bernie wouldn't blink one way or another. He'd just grab the phone and lay the next bet, shushing me, shushing Red, running from one room to the other checking the game scores, from the NFL on ABC to the NHL on CBS.

A few weeks after I lost my job, and the maple trees lining Seventy-ninth Street shed the last of their leaves, I looked out the window one morning and saw that the green Caddy was gone. "Bernie," I called, rushing back to the bedroom where he was still asleep. "The car's missing."

"It's okay," he mumbled.

"What do you mean, 'it's okay'? You lent it to someone?"

"No. I *gave* it to someone."

"I don't understand."

"I owed the guy. I gave him the car. Now you understand?"

It was Hot Dog Red, that afternoon, who explained that the guy Bernie had given the car to was a bookmaker and the Cadillac was payment for a gambling debt.

A week later, the Caddy was back.

A couple of weeks before Christmas, a white-haired old man showed up in our livingroom. His name was Sonny, not Santa. And he didn't have a beard. Outside of that, the resemblance was uncanny. Bernie had been caught up in football action for a while and there seemed to be more fat envelopes leaving the house with bookmakers or their runners than coming in. So I was surprised when he suggested that I do some holiday shopping. "Go with Sonny. Get whatever you want for yourself, for Marlene and your mother. Buy stuff for everybody. Go. Sonny'll take you."

"Okay, fine," I said, and got ready to go out. "How much money should I take?"

"No, babe. You don't need money," Bernie said. "Sonny'll handle it."

We went to Saks Fifth Avenue. Sonny was a sweetheart. He was very patient. He'd lean against a pillar or when there was a chair available, he'd sit and wait with the growing pile of boxes and shopping bags while I examined each new item. "Is this worth it?" I'd ask him. Or, "I don't know, do you think it's too expensive?"

And Sonny would always encourage me. "It's beautiful. Buy it. Don't worry. Bernie'll pay for it." So I bought gifts for my mother, my sister, my cousins, my friends and, of course, for Bernie. I bought cashmere sweaters, suede belts, leather pocketbooks, silk scarves, magnificent shawls, shirts, jewelry, perfume. "Beautiful," Sonny would say. "Buy it. It's a bargain. Don't worry about it." And Sonny charged everything.

We took a cab back to the brownstone. It took Sonny two trips up the stairs to get all that I'd bought into the apartment. It added up to several thousand dollars' worth of gifts. Sonny had a drink with us. "Okay," Bernie said to him. "So what's the damage?"

Sweet as ever, smiling kindly, Sonny held up the fingers of his right hand.

"Five," Bernie said, peeling off the bills.

Five thousand dollars. Oh, my God, I thought. I didn't know I'd spent that much! But Bernie didn't blink.

"Five hundred," he said, slapping the last bill into Sonny's outstretched hand. "Thanks, man."

"Take care," Sonny said, draining the drink. "Sandy, you've got wonderful taste, honey. It's a pleasure going shopping with you."

I waited until Sonny was gone. Then I said, "Bernie, I added up the sales receipts. I know it comes to much more than five hundred dollars."

"Forget it. It's nothing. It's a credit card thing, a fugazy." Then he stopped and reconsidered. "Don't worry about it," he said evenly. "You're better off not knowing. Anytime you want to go shopping, just let me know and I'll call Sonny, okay?"

"Okay," I said. But later, on the phone with Toni, a friend of mine who was also seeing a wise guy, I said, "Did you ever hear the word 'fugazy'?"

"Sure," she said. "It means phoney. Phoney. Fugazy. It's just another word for it."

In January, Bernie and I were having steak at the Hickory House and one of the bookmakers I'd met a couple of times came in. Bernie asked him to join us. What does he want to drink? How's the family? They're just sitting there shooting the breeze and, casually, Bernie pulled a pink piece of paper out of his wallet, signed it, and handed it over to the guy. Then he took a couple of keys off his key ring, handed those over, too. The bookmaker smiled, nodded, put the pink slip and the keys in his jacket pocket. Then he finished the drink Bernie had bought him, and got up with an "Okay, Bernie. So long, Sandy. You're looking great. Prettier every day." And off he went.

Before I could say, "What was that?" Bernie said, "I just signed over the car." He was cutting his steak. He didn't even look up. "You've got cash for a cab, right, baby?"

The money came. The money went. Two weeks after he gave up the car, Bernie was flush again. He decided to take me out to a new French restaurant he'd been hearing about, a small, romantic, elegant place on the Upper East Side. It held no more than sixty people and, at nine, when we got there, it was already packed. We had a drink at the bar, which sported gleaming brass and etched-glass fixtures and huge bouquets of fresh flowers.

I wore a beautiful pantsuit, a sort of silk pajama outfit with a tunic top and gorgeously tailored loose-fitting trousers. The silky fabric moved wonderfully and Bernie thought it was not just chic but sexy as hell. He couldn't have been happier when the maitre d' led us to a secluded table at the back of the restaurant.

Bernie ordered a bottle of wine. We were on our second glass, teasing each other, fooling around under the table like kids. It must have been ten or ten-thirty when two men at a table near the front stood up suddenly, pulled out guns, and announced, "This is a stick up."

Immediately, Bernie started to get up. I put my hand on his thigh and he stayed put, but his fist closed dangerously around the table knife. "They've got guns, baby. Don't," I whispered.

Some of the diners had their hands up in the air, others were shaking visibly. At the table next to ours, a good-looking, gray-haired woman was crying. Her husband was trying to comfort her in a frightened whisper. "Shhh, Belle, it's all right, darling."

The well-dressed gunmen quickly locked the front door. One of them, a guy with a blond crewcut, started barking out orders: "Empty your wallets. Cash on the table. Take off your jewelry."

The second man, dark-haired and tall, emptied the register, then stayed at the front of the restaurant as the blond went from table to table throwing the cash and jewelry into what looked like a pillowcase.

"A square joint," Bernie was muttering. "This is what happens when you go to a square joint. You don't get robbed in a wise guy's place. Okay," he said to me. "Take off all your jewelry like he said. But under the table. Very carefully. Put your hands under the table. Here," he said. He slipped me a stack of money. "It's about a grand. That top you're wearing is nice and loose. Put the money in your pants, okay? And the jewelry, too. The blouse'll cover it. Just leave the earrings on the table. I've got about five hundred in my other pocket. Let that bastard have it."

I did exactly as Bernie told me. Very, very carefully, with my hands under the table, I pulled off the rings, my watch, and gold bracelets. And put them into my panties, along with the thousand dollars he'd handed me. Then I began to take off my earrings, with big, exaggerated gestures, trying to show the blond guy with the sack that I was doing what he'd said to do.

"Shit," Bernie grumbled as the crew cut headed directly for us. "I think the guy at the door must've seen you and signaled the other one."

No sooner were the words out of Bernie's mouth than the blond banged a fist on the table. "You think you're smart, right? You think you're being a very clever fellow. Get up!" he ordered me. "I'm taking the broad into the ladies' room, smart guy. And I'm making her strip, and if I have to I'm going to shake her and everything can fall out of her cunt. I don't care."

"You son of a bitch," Bernie said.

The guy had a gun pointed at us. "Bernie, please, don't," I said. "It's okay. I'll go. Don't say anything, please."

But Bernie was half out of his mind. He talked very softly, more like a growl than language, and I knew he was hanging on to that temper of his by a cuticle. "You don't know who I am, buddy, and you're better off not knowing right now. But you're dead, fucker. You hear me?" A scary, soft growl.

The guy got nervous. He started waving the gun under Bernie's nose. "This is what I know, asshole. This. You see this. Now shut up. You," he said to me, "stand up. Move."

And thank God Bernie controlled himself. His fingers were white from how hard he was pressing them against the tablecloth. His face had drained of color. But he let us go.

In the ladies' room, the guy was all business. He pointed the gun at my face and said, "Take your pants off." The waistband of the slacks was elastic, so I just pulled them down with my underwear, and everything I'd hidden inside the pants went clattering to the floor: rings and watches and money and bracelets. It was incredibly noisy. Things were bouncing on the tiles and Bernie's money fanned out all over the place. The gunman swept the stuff up and put it into the pillowcase and walked me back to the table.

The police showed up about ten minutes after the thieves left. Everyone was questioned about what had been taken. Bernie played it very, very square with the cops. He told them exactly what had happened, including how he had told me to hide the jewelry and some cash in my pants. He had to tell the truth because other people had already told the police about the man taking me into the bathroom, which had scared most of them to death because they hadn't heard the exchange between Bernie and the gun-man and had no idea why he'd singled me out. In fact, the gray-haired lady from the next table put her arm around me and said, "You were very brave." I was touched. I told her that she had been, too. And we hugged.

All the way home, Bernie couldn't stop ranting about how this would never have happened if he hadn't decided to try a square restaurant. Nobody would've walked into a mob-run joint and pulled a couple of guns, he said, unless they were prepared to use them—and quick!

In the apartment, he was on the phone before he had his coat off. "You hear anybody pulled off a heist like that, you get back to me right away," he said. He described the guys. Then, "WASPs," I heard him say. "They looked like WASPs, but I feel it in my gut they were guineas. Yeah, the blond prick, too. Italian."

He hung up. "I'm sorry, kid," he said to me. I was sitting in a heap on the sofa. I'd thrown water on my face to try to calm down. My mascara had run and I didn't care, so I was collapsed on the couch with big black smudges running down my cheeks. Bernie sat on the arm of the sofa. He pulled out his handkerchief and wet a corner of it in his mouth and, almost absentmindedly, started to wipe the mascara off my face. "It's not so much what they took," he said. "It's what they did to you. You don't know how it felt sitting there. I had all kinds of fantasies. I should have killed the bastard."

So word went out on the street. Two weeks later Bernie got a phone call from someone who said, okay, all the jewelry and the thousand in cash was going to be returned. But Bernie wanted a piece of the guys. The middleman on the telephone said, "Look, we don't want to give these guys up. They know who you are now, but they didn't know in the restaurant. They're sorry, Bernie. They know you now."

"Okay," Bernie said. "Fine. You don't want to give them up. That's up to you. But if I ever see them walking the streets, I'm going to put a couple of shots into them." He sounded as cold and deadly serious as I'd ever heard him.

But when he got off the phone, he shrugged his shoulders and said, "Hey, at least we played it square for the night, didn't we?" It was as if the whole thing were a Halloween prank and we'd been costumed as normal people for an evening. Looking down the barrel of a gun was just part of the everyday trick-or-treat setup squares had to live with.

Tough guys lived by different rules. And at an engagement party one Sunday afternoon at Ben Masich's Town and Country Club on Ocean Parkway, Bernie decided it was time for me to learn a couple of the basics. The Town and Country was to Brooklyn what The Copa was to Manhattan—a supper club setting for the borough's rich and famous, which included politicians and crooks. I can't remember whose daughter had gotten engaged at the black-tie party, a councilman's or a consigliere's, or if the band, after a run of mambos, lindys, and fox-trots, finished up with a hora or tarantella. I don't remember whether the solid-gold *chais* and diamond-chip-trimmed Stars of David outnumbered the Florentined holy medals and jewel-encrusted crucifixes.

I just remember that the band was good and that I wanted to dance. I sat, searching the room for Bernie, at a big, round table with people I didn't know. All of them were much older than I. Most of them were heavyset women in pastel chiffon and bright hair, whose husbands were making the rounds, drinks in hand, cigars lit, breast pockets bulging with gift envelopes of cash for the father of the betrothed. I had on a new black beaded cocktail dress that had arrived in the traditional shopping bag and was wearing my Breath-of-Spring mink stole, of course. Bernie was bent out of shape about being in a tux on a Sunday afternoon.

When finally he returned to our table, I said, "Honey, dance with me. The music is terrific." It was a slow dance. Bernie sighed and gave me a look. "What?" I said. "I just asked you to dance with me, that's all."

"Okay. One," he said.

He wasn't a terrific dancer, but it felt good being in his arms. I liked the thought of how nice we looked together. I imagined other people watching us, thinking, what a handsome couple—Bernie with his rugged good looks and pale blue eyes, me in my glamorous black beaded dress, auburn hair piled high on my head twisted in a fashionable French knot. The music was slow and sexy.

Then the song ended and Bernie started walking me back to the table. "Wait," I said. "Maybe they'll play another slow one."

He shook his head and kept on going. I stopped and held on to his hand. "Come on, honey. Just one more."

"Sandra," he said. He'd used that name, that warning tone, only a couple of times before. I rolled my eyes waiting for the lecture. "I don't dance," he said. "You get it? I danced with you once because you asked me to. And I told you just once, I'd do it. And I did. And that's it."

I'd had a couple of screwdrivers. I felt a little playful. I hurried after him as he walked away. "And that's it," I repeated, mimicking him. "What's it? What's 'that's it'?"

We were off the dance floor now. Bernie pulled me along to a quiet corner just outside the banquet room. "I'm going to set you straight now," he said with strained patience, like a teacher talking to a dull child. "Tough guys don't dance, you understand?"

I was embarrassed by the way he was speaking to me. "Oh, yeah," I said with bravado. "Tough guys don't cry. They don't go down on broads— they don't eat anything unless it's on a platter. And they definitely don't dance."

"You got it," Bernie said and walked away.

The band played a drum roll. The lights dimmed. And a dozen waiters sailed out of the kitchen carrying trays of flaming cherries jubilee.

I'd left Brooklyn at the end of August. In early February, Bernie went to Florida on business. My mother and I hadn't exactly resumed "normal relations"—we'd been fighting since I was thirteen—but we did speak regularly now on the telephone. And Bernie, with his Jewish sense of family, never missed an opportunity to promote peace between us.

When George Raft came into The Velvet Room one night with a couple of wise guys, it was Bernie who suggested my mother might get a kick out of hearing about it. "Oh, Mr. Raft," I'd gushed, "I've loved you since I was a little girl." Everyone at the table laughed. It took me a while to realize I'd implied he was old. "Thanks a lot, kid," he'd said. From then on he always called me kid. And it was Bernie who said, "Go call your mother, tell her you just met George Raft. Let her *kvell* a little."

If he bought me something new that I loved, he'd say, "Why don't you give Tillie a call? Tell her what I got you. Make her happy." He'd always remind me to buy Marlene a birthday gift or send my mother a couple of extra dollars for whatever special occasion was coming up.

In February, before he left for Florida, Bernie left me extra money and suggested that I invite my mother to come into the city and stay with me for the couple of days he'd be gone. "Make sure she takes a taxi," he said, tossing the extra cash into the drawer. He wanted her to see where and how I was living. He wanted her to know that I was safe and being well cared for.

Much to my surprise, my mother accepted. "He's not going to be there?" she asked three times.

"No, Ma. He's going to Florida."

"But not with you."

"It's business, Ma."

"Business? What kind of business does a man like that have? Monkey business, maybe. But you, you're sure it's business."

"What are you saying, he's lying to me? He's going for pleasure?"

"Excuse me. Did I say pleasure? For his *health,* maybe. A man his age—I thought maybe he's got rheumatism, maybe arthritis like the other *alter kockers* and he's going to take the waters in Miami Beach."

"Take a cab, Ma. I'll pay for it when you get here."

The apartment was spotless. But I spent the morning compulsively straightening things anyway, fluffing the pillows on the black sofa, picking lint from the red velvet side chairs and red carpeting, blowing ashes off the gold-flecked glass coffee table top and imaginary dust off the ornate mirrors and brass and crystal lamps with their towering pleated shades. Between chores, I paced and smoked and peered out the tall livingroom windows, watching for my mother's taxi.

My mother was a short woman, blonde, stylish, and neat. It hadn't been that long since I'd seen her, but she looked smaller than I remembered as she stepped out of the cab in her good wool coat and leather gloves. Standing there with her pocketbook tucked under one arm and her little overnight bag in her hands, she looked tiny, vulnerable, and lost. And I found myself thrilled and close to tears at the sight of her.

I knocked on the window for her to tell the driver to wait. I waved the money Bernie had left for the cab and signaled that I'd be right down. I saw her joy at the sight of me—for just an instant she let it show. Then she made an annoyed face and waved me away. By the time I ran downstairs to the front door, she was snapping shut her change purse and the taxi was pulling away from the curb.

She allowed me to kiss her cheeks. "Why'd you pay him, Ma? I have the money. I told you I was going to take care of it."

"Seven dollars and fifty cents with the tip. You'll send it with the unemployment money, all right?"

I wrestled her suitcase out of her hand and took her arm and we walked inside together. "You look great, Ma."

"You're too skinny," she said.

"Isn't this a gorgeous building? Look, Ma," I said, leading her upstairs, toward our apartment door. "Isn't this pretty, wallpaper in the hallway, carpeted stairs, and everything. Wait until you see the apartment."

"Very nice, very nice," she acquiesced. The hallway was neutral turf.

I threw open the apartment door. "And this is our place."

She sighed and walked inside. "Oh, my God," was the first thing she said, and that only when she was standing in the middle of the black, white, and red livingroom. She turned slowly. There was a little grin on her face and she was fighting it all the way. *"Oy, oy, oy.* Look at this. Like Ali Baba and the Forty Thieves!"

I cracked up. I don't know why, but instead of being hurt or angry I thought it was the funniest thing I'd ever heard. It was clever, sarcastic, and awestruck—just like my mother. And I'd really missed her. Not just for the couple of months since I'd moved to Manhattan, but for all the years we'd fought and grieved. I just started laughing. She did, too. From that moment on the weekend was just us, a couple of girls laughing and being sarcastic and clever and, once in a while, annoyed with each other, and awestruck, too.

I took her on a tour of the house. She was not impressed by the tiny kitchen. She stared at the half-fridge and shook her head in disbelief. "Such a rich man can't afford a real refrigerator?" She clicked her tongue over the mirrored bedroom walls and ceiling. "Whoever saw mirrors like this? What for? He likes to look at himself in bed?" The telephone in the bathroom floored her. "Why? Very nice. It's very nice. But for what?" I couldn't tell her Bernie didn't like to be too far from his bookmaker.

I took her to Stark's on Madison Avenue for lunch. And then we went shopping, stopping in at all the beautiful shops on Madison and Fifth Avenue. We walked over to Rockefeller Center. As we watched the ice skaters in the rink below, I said, "I'm going to take you to Bernie's club for dinner. I can't wait for you to see The Velvet Room." My mother shook her head.

"But why, Ma?" I was so eager for her to see it, to see me in it and how well I was treated and how many famous people came there. But she flat refused.

"Don't ask me why, Sandy. I don't know. When he marries you, then I'll go there. Until then, it's like asking me to eat *trayf*."

So we went to dinner in Little Italy at a place a friend of Bernie's owned. We had a bottle of wine and ordered lavishly, and I saw her flush when the check came and I laid a hundred dollar bill on top of it. But the owner came over quickly and stopped the waiter from taking the money. "Sandy, what's the matter with you," he said sadly. "You know your money's no good here, kid. Here, let me buy you and your beautiful sister here a Zambuca. Did you have enough of everything? You liked the fish? Tommy," he called to the waiter, "pack up a couple of cannolis for the girls to take home."

We slept together in the king-sized bed. We were both a little high and very, very happy and it was like a kids' pajama party. Then, in the middle of the night my mother's screams woke me up.

"What?! Ma, what's the matter? What happened?"

She was cowering under the covers. "Ma," I started whispering, afraid there was someone in the house. "Ma, what happened? What scared you? Is someone here?" I was afraid to put on the light.

"I saw someone looking at me," she said.

"Who? Where?"

There was a moment's silence. Then, sheepishly, she stuck her head out from under the covers. Pointing at the ceiling, embarrassed and still shaken, "There," she yelled. "In that *meshuggene* mirror, where else?!"

My mother had to go back to work on Monday. Sunday evening, we kissed and hugged and she said, "Thank you for a wonderful weekend."

"You know, Ma. You could call Bernie sometime and tell him thanks, too," I said. "It was really his idea. It's his money, his apartment."

"When he marries you," she said. Then she stroked my cheek and got into the cab. I waited outside until the car was out of sight.

That night, when Bernie called me from Florida, he asked how the weekend had gone.

"Great," I said and sighed.

"So why do you sound like you're dying?"

"It's nothing. We had a great time."

"Sandra . . . What's going on?"

"Baby," I said, "when are we going to get married?"

CHAPTER SIX

Mrs. Wise Guy

We were in bed the night Bernie came home from Florida.

"Did you miss me?" I asked, snuggling up against him.

He had just showered. His dark hair was slicked back and damp. He looked tan, clean, healthy, and very sexy. He moved up against me and, laughing, said, "You have to ask?"

Against my better judgment, I wriggled closer. I could feel my resolve melting. I tried again. "Do you love me?"

He put his arms around me. "Yes, baby. Of course I love you. Can't you feel how I love you? How I missed you? What do you think is going on here?"

"Then why can't we get married?"

"Sandra!" he hollered. "What the hell's the matter with you? I just got home. It's my first night back. What are you trying to ruin it for?"

"I want to get married, Bernie."

"Good," he said. He threw back the covers. "Great!" He got out of bed. "Go, get married. Good luck to you."

"I want to marry *you*!" I screamed after him as he stormed into the bathroom and slammed the door.

I was crying when he finally came back out. "Now, listen, kid," he said. He sat down at the edge of the bed and hugged me. "You know I love you. You're my baby. You're my girl, aren't you? But this isn't a good time for me. I'll tell you the truth, *mamela*, business is lousy. I may have to give up the club. I've been losing on the games. I need some peace around here. I need, well, you know, baby. I'm a man. You know what I need. Come on, Sandy, don't go nuts on me here. You love your daddy, don't you, baby?"

I fell apart. I loved him so much. I felt so sorry for him. I wanted to be his good little girl, his stand-up broad, the one he could count on. "Yes," I said.

We made love.

"Bernie," I said the next day. "I want to get married."

He was coming out of the bathroom rubbing his hair with a towel. He stopped. He tilted his head and looked at me as though he was unsure he'd heard right.

"Seriously," I said.

He walked back into the bathroom and shut the door.

A couple of nights later when we were in bed and I began *hocking* him, nagging him about marriage again, he rolled away from me and reached over to his night table. He pulled open the night table drawer. For a split second, I wondered if he was going to pull out a gun and shoot me. Instead, he pulled out two wads of cotton and made a big show of putting them in his ears. Then he rolled back over to me and picked up where he'd left off.

But I was a woman with a mission now. And Bernie had been a better teacher than he thought. Along with the lessons he constantly gave me on everything from elocution, manners, and morality to makeup, hairdos, and homemaking, Bernie had taught me more than he knew about persistence, stubbornness, fighting for what you want, standing up to an adversary, hanging in against the odds. Everything I'd heard him say and watched him do I tried now. And I was getting good at it, too.

I even enlisted my mother in the cause. My sister Marlene had told me how impressed she'd been with her weekend in the city. "The minute she got back to Brooklyn," Marlene said, "she got right on the horn and called up all her friends. 'Such a gorgeous apartment.' 'Such a fine neighborhood.' 'A phone in the bathroom yet!' " So when Bernie suggested that I invite my mother to join us on New Year's Eve, I did it with more urgency than usual.

"Ma, you've got to come," I insisted. "I need you. You want him to marry me, you've got to get to know him and he's got to meet you. Let's start the new year right. Let's be together. I need your help, Ma."

It was an amazing evening. Bernie handed me his tuxedo and told me to get it pressed. I had no idea he meant professionally. I assumed he wanted me to iron it. So I did. And handed it back to him about twenty minutes before my mother was due at the apartment. He took one look at the shiny, crooked creases I'd ironed into the trousers and hit the roof.

"What the hell is wrong with you? Where do you come from, Mars?" He picked up a bedside book and hurled it at the bathroom door. He flipped a big glass ashtray off the dresser, and when it stopped bouncing and rolling he jumped on it with two feet. "You never heard of a dry cleaner? Your mother works at a cleaning store! What do you do, sit on your fucking brains all day?" He slammed his fist into the wall and God was with him— or with me—because the spot turned out to be plasterboard, not concrete, and his fist went right through it. "God damn New Year's Eve and I'm going to wear pleated fucking trousers to the fucking club tonight?! What the hell is the matter with you?!"

I was still getting dressed when my mother arrived. Bernie, with an ice pack on his knuckles, answered the door. They had spoken a couple of times on the phone. They had bantered back and forth, Bernie perhaps a little more good-naturedly than Tillie. Now, five minutes into their first face-to-face meeting, he said to her: "Tillie, didn't you teach that kid of yours anything? She can't cook. She can't iron—"

My mother cut him off. "I didn't raise her to be a cook or a laundress," she said icily. "She only has to be good in one room."

Bernie couldn't believe his ears. He broke up laughing. "Well, there you did a gem of a job," he said.

Boy, was he wrong. I was pretty naive about sex when I met Bernie. But even more naive about birth control. It wasn't long before I became pregnant. I was frightened and frantic and I didn't dare tell Bernie. I knew the last thing he wanted right then was a baby. And I didn't want one. I was too young and I wasn't married.

And as far as abortions went, not only were they not legal but, well, I had seen how Kirk Douglas responded to the news that Eleanor Parker had had an abortion in *Detective Story*. He'd said he wished he could rip his brain out of his head and hold it under cold water to wash it clean of the thought of her.

I called Judy at the beauty salon and sobbed the bad news to her over the phone.

"Now, darlin'," she soothed, "you just come right on down here and we'll think of something."

You'd think two heads were better than one. Not when they belonged to Judy and me. I was filled with fear and she was filled with folklore.

"Okay, I borrowed a car," she said when I burst into her apartment over the shop on East Fifty-fourth Street.

"Good. Where are we going?"

"You want to get rid of it, don't you?"

"Yes," I said. "But where are we going?"

"For a ride," Judy said with an air of cunning.

I had no idea what she was talking about. "Okay. Good. But what about, you know, Judy, my being pregnant?"

She was gathering up her purse and keys and getting into her coat. "Sandy, that's why I borrowed the car, for christsake. We're going to ride over every bump and pothole in New York City until we get rid of it."

"You're kidding."

"Let's go."

True to her daffy Southern-accented word, Judy started up the little black two-seater sports car she'd borrowed from her boyfriend and, with me tearfully riding shotgun, she pulled away from the curb. She was a bad driver at best. Now here she was grinding gears and practically whooping out rebel yells as we sped, bumping and bouncing, over the worst ruts in the city. I was white-knuckled with fear. Only the fact that the car was a convertible kept my skull from being shattered as we hurtled along.

"What if this doesn't work?" I managed to holler through clenched teeth.

"It'll work. Don't worry. Trust me, honey."

We went to Jilly's for a drink after the ride. I was sick to my stomach. It was clear that all we had gotten rid of was my lunch.

"Do you remember Hattie Prince from the beauty shop?" Judy asked.

With prompting, I recalled a very tough lady with short, curly, bleached blue-white hair and big black eyes whom I'd seen at Judy's salon a couple of times. I remembered a throaty liquor voice, a blinding jewelry collection, a commanding, almost masculine manner, and a lot of makeup. Hattie Prince was a *zaftik* little bulldog of a woman. And Judy or someone else at the shop had described her as an ex-madam and a bookmaker.

"I hear she's doing abortions now," Judy said.

"I don't have money for an abortion. Isn't there anything else we can do?"

"Lysol," Judy said, draining her Southern Comfort. "Douching with Lysol."

We wobbled back to her apartment as the sun was setting. "Are you sure?" I asked in the old brass-trimmed elevator heading up to her fifth-floor apartment.

"Well, not one hundred percent. But it can't hurt to try, can it?"

So I douched with Lysol. Which was a little like charbroiling my womb. My insides felt like hamburger meat on fire. I could barely walk to the curb to call a cab. "Well, that should certainly do the trick. Call me when you get home and let me know what happens," Judy urged as she helped me into the taxi.

Nothing happened. I was in great flaming pain for about a week. I developed a vaginal infection. I was still pregnant.

Judy and I called Marilyn and she mentioned my old pharmacist friend Noah from the Garment Center. He suggested Urgatrate, a drug that was supposed to bring on menstrual bleeding. Marilyn and I went down to see him. The pills he gave us were black and big as bullets. I thought if one Urgatrate was good, three would be better. And I got desperately, but bloodlessly, sick.

Bernie was out when I got home. I crawled into bed and curled up, holding my aching stomach. I had the chills and was burning up at the same time. Sweating and shaking, I fell asleep and woke as Bernie got into bed at about four in the morning. He tried to hug me and I groaned and pulled away. "What's the matter?" he asked.

"Nothing. I'm sick."

"From what? Do you have the flu?"

I was too exhausted to get into it. "Yes," I said. "Just let me sleep."

The next day, still queasy, I was leaning against the little Formica kitchen counter waiting for water to boil for a cup of tea, when the doorbell rang. I shuffled to the window and looked down. A slender young guy in a gray overcoat, hatless, his thick dark hair ruffled by the wind, was calling his name through the intercom. Peter something. I'd never seen him before. "Who's that?" I asked Bernie.

"Shit," he said. "It's my P.O. Give me a hand, Sandy. I've got to clear the house quick."

Quick was not in my body's vocabulary that day. I watched as Bernie began to tear around the apartment tossing gold, silver, and crystal ornaments, ashtrays, candlesticks and other valuables into drawers and closets.

"What are you doing? What's a P.O.?"

"P.O.—parole officer. It's the Greek," Bernie said, stuffing a shopping bag full of recently delivered cashmere sweaters under the bed. "He's doing one of his little surprise check-ups and if he sees any of this, I'm screwed. He knows how much I'm supposed to be making to the penny. I can't have expensive stuff like this around."

I was wearing what I'd slept in, one of Bernie's T-shirts. "I'd better change," I said.

"You'd better hide," he said. "Just hang out in the bathroom for a couple of minutes. It won't be long."

"Bernie, I'm sick," I protested.

"Five minutes. I promise."

By the time Peter Knossos, the P.O., entered the apartment, it was stripped to essentials. Never mind that even in its bare state it looked like Liberace's guest room, at least the real high-ticket items were out of sight.

"Hiya, come in, how're you doing, Peter?" Bernie greeted the probation officer like an old friend. "Can I get you a drink? Cigar? What brings you to the neighborhood?"

Either Knossos was soft-spoken or Bernie was effusively loud, but I only heard mumbled replies. Sick as a dog, clutching my belly, I still couldn't resist sneaking a peek at the guy. After a couple of minutes, I opened the bathroom door a crack and peered out. Just in time to see Bernie taking this dark-haired kid's arm, leading him toward the door. "Here," he said, stuffing a wad of bills into the guy's gloved hand. "Buy your kids something nice, Peter. I'll see you next Wednesday."

I waited until the front door closed, then I came out of the bathroom. Bernie came flying into the bedroom. He was wearing just the white undershirt and shorts he'd had on under his scarlet silk Sulka robe when the P.O. had first rung the bell.

"What the hell was wrong with you? I asked you to help me clear the place out and you were just standing there staring at me." Bernie reached under the bed and pulled out the robe which he'd balled up and tossed there a minute before he'd let Peter Knossos into the apartment. "Do you understand this guy could put me away again?" He put on the robe and tied the tasseled silk sash. "Sandy, when I need you, you've got to be there, baby. You're either a stand-up broad or you're not. Now what's going on?"

"I'm sick," I shouted back at him.

"You're not that sick."

"I'm sicker than sick, Bernie. I'm fucking pregnant." That stopped us both; I was as shocked by what I'd said as he was.

"You're what? You're pregnant? How?!"

"What're you, crazy? What do you mean, 'How'?! How does someone get pregnant?"

"I'll tell you how," he yelled, pacing the bedroom like a caged tiger. "By not taking care of themselves, Sandra. That's how. I trusted you. I thought you took care of that."

"I did!" I hollered. "I was using rhythm!"

Bernie screeched to a halt. "Rhythm? What the hell is rhythm?! I'm talking prevention here, precautions. I'm not talking about the goddamn rhumba!"

"It's what the Catholics do!"

"Did you ever notice that Catholics have twenty kids apiece?"

"Stop yelling!" I screamed at the top of my lungs.

"It's fucking hot in here," Bernie said, opening his robe. "It's hot here, right? I'm burning up."

I sat down on the bed, my head in my hands.

He sat down beside me. "Don't cry, baby. I'm sorry I'm yelling. I'm just hot."

"I'm not crying," I said, looking him right in the eye. "I have a headache from all your screaming. We'll have to get married."

He leapt up from the bed. "Impossible. Are you out of your mind? I'm not ready. Not like this." He took off his robe and hurled it into a corner. "It's hot in here. Listen, Sandy, sweetheart, listen to me. Now is not the time to do this—not like this. We're not getting married because you're pregnant. It's not right."

"Oh, and it's more right for me to be pregnant and not married?"

"First we'll take care of one thing, then we'll talk about the other," he said, going suddenly and conveniently philosophical. "I've got a friend, an excellent, competent woman who also happens to be a close personal friend who does abortions. She's got a dozen places all over the city. Clean places with good doctors."

"Bernie, I'm afraid," I said honestly. In my mind abortions meant dirty old men in bloody smocks squinting at you through cigarette smoke. Butchers who used coat hangers and knitting needles. I had heard showgirls in Las Vegas talking about the pain and horrors they'd gone through and how friends of theirs had actually died as the result of botched abortions. I thought about girls who'd wound up infected, who'd been deathly ill for months after or, worse, could now never have a baby. I was very scared.

"It's nothing. Don't worry about it. I'll give Hattie a call—"

"Hattie Prince with the blue poodle cut?"

Bernie's eyes narrowed suspiciously. "How do you know Hattie?"

"She used to get her hair done at Judy's." I narrowed *my* eyes suspiciously. "And what kind of 'close personal friend' is Hattie Prince to you?"

"We went out a couple of times. No big deal. Anyway, I hear she's got a great operation now. I'll call her."

"Is that supposed to make me feel better—an ex-girlfriend of yours is going to kill our baby?"

Bernie was actually sweating now. He tugged at his undershirt collar. "Sandy, baby. I really love you. You've got to believe me. We can live together forever if you want. But now is not the time to get married and you can't have a baby unmarried. It would be a disgrace, a *shande*. So that's it. That's all we can do now. Goddamn it," he cried suddenly, and ripped off his undershirt. "Why does this always happen to me?"

"What?!" I said.

"I can't look at a woman without her getting pregnant! If you knew how many times I've been through this!"

"You bastard!" I said.

"Yeah, yeah, you're right."

"You son of a bitch!"

"I'm sorry, baby."

"You prick!"

"You having fun?" he asked.

Bernie put in the call. Within half an hour, the ubiquitous Hattie Prince phoned us back. It turned out that one of her "clinics" was conveniently located just two blocks away, in a townhouse on Madison Avenue and Eighty-first Street. She was so pleased to hear from Bernie, he made the mistake of telling me later, that she said she'd do the abortion free of charge. Normally her fee was $1,000.

I got back into bed when he told me that and I stayed there, crying and shaking with fear, anger, shame, and despair. A couple of days later, Bernie took me over to Hattie's. It was a freezing cold day in March. The sky was sunless, overcast with threatening gray clouds that echoed my own cheerlessness. Even Bernie had run out of jokes and wisecracks. The two of us bundled together against the wind and walked the two blocks to the townhouse in silent, sad resolve.

Bernie kissed me, mumbled, "I'll make this up to you, kid. I swear," and left me at the door.

I took the small elevator up to the designated apartment. A girl in a white nurse's uniform let me in. The place was much bigger than I'd imagined it from the outside, and far more luxurious than the cold, green-walled institution I'd expected. I was led into a spacious livingroom with big, plush sofas covered in bright chintz on which some girls were resting. Two of them were asleep. One was curled up, holding her belly. It looked like a terribly homey hospital recovery room. There were bowls of fruit and pitchers of orange juice on a mahogany sideboard that looked every bit as attractive as the rich still-life oil paintings ornately framed on the walls.

A second nurse came in and introduced herself as Mary. She took me to a small examining room off a carpeted corridor. She told me to undress and lie down and she draped a white sheet over me. The room was clean and very professional-looking, but as I waited alone for the doctor my fear returned. My heart began thumping again so loudly, I was sure others could hear it and, when the door opened and the doctor came in, I thought he was going to ask me to please be quiet, that my heartbeat was disturbing the other patients.

The doctor was a woman. A short, stocky woman in a white uniform complete with sterile cap and mask. She was perfectly silent as she made her preparations. Pulse pounding, I watched her closely, but her large black eyes never made contact with mine. Then I noticed that distinctive bluish-white hair peeking out from under her cap.

"Hattie, is that you?" I said, my voice quavering with fear.

"Relax, kid," Hattie Prince said. "I can give an abortion better than any of these Park Avenue quacks. And I'm doing you personally."

I was not reassured. That she could drink and swear like a man I never doubted. That she was a financial whiz who owned at least one full-length chinchilla coat was impressive. That she had run a big bookmaking operation and had been a successful madam when she was just a few years older than I was now—none of these things, which Judy had told me about Hattie Prince, qualified her as a competent physician.

"Here." Hattie handed me two pills. "Take these, they'll relax you."

I didn't argue. I gulped them down. After a while, two women entered the room. One of them was Mary, who took my hand and said kindly, "You just squeeze if you need to. I'll be right here." The second nurse laid a cold compress over my eyes and then it was Hattie, I guess, who moved my feet into the stirrups. I remember feeling a searing, stabbing pain, a sudden churning of my insides. Then Hattie said, "It's over, kid. Mary'll help you get dressed and into the other room. You just lie down there and relax with the other girls for a while. We'll get you some hot soup."

I was too groggy to focus on anything, to feel anything. "It's over?" I remember asking Mary as she helped me off the operating table. "Is that it? Is that all? Did I have a baby?"

She was brusque but not unkind. "You're fine," was all she said. "You need to rest.'' There was a lot of blood. I felt terribly weak. Finally, I stopped asking questions and just let her clean me up and dress me and walk me into the room with the big, soft, floral couches. There were still a few women lying there; a couple of them were moaning. I wanted to lie down. I was exhausted and now my feelings were coming back, waking up slowly in my bruised, churning belly.

"Just lie down now,'' Mary said, and left me.

A girl moaned. Another one was crying and clutching her stomach.

Suddenly I was afraid to lie down, afraid to close my eyes in this room full of sick, deathly pale strangers. A wave of nausea swept over me. I needed to rest, but not there. Bernie was supposed to pick me up in an hour or so, but I couldn't wait for him. I had to get out of there. I found my coat and it was hard to just lift my arms and slip them into the sleeves. The motion, every movement, felt connected to my womb, tugged nauseatingly at my insides. But I had to get home. I figured I could make it the few blocks on my own.

On Madison Avenue, the icy wind bit through my coat. I hunched against it, walking nearly doubled over. Despite the freezing cold, my insides were boiling. I stopped at a little delicatessen and bought an ice-cream pop, but it didn't cool the burning sensation, it didn't stop the sweat from pouring off me. By the time I reached our building on Seventy-ninth, I was pretty sure I was going to die. I rang our apartment bell and Bernie buzzed me in.

The single flight of stairs to the second floor seemed higher than Mount Everest. Bernie was standing at the top. He looked down at me and I knew how bad I looked by the stunned, scared expression on his face. "What the hell are you doing here?'' he shouted. "Are you crazy?''

I held on to the bannister with all my strength and looked up at him. Then I passed out.

Hours later, I woke up in bed. Bernie was sitting beside me holding a bowl of chicken soup. I remember thinking how sweet it was of him, how Jewish and sweet and typically Bernie. And the fact that it was Campbell's Chicken Noodle Soup instead of homemade somehow made it even sweeter. If it had been homemade, it would have meant he'd bought it somewhere. With Campbell's I knew he'd had to open the can and add the water and cook it himself.

"Hiya, kid,'' he said very gently. "You hungry, baby?''

I shook my head.

"Sandy, I'm sorry,'' he said. "About the baby. About what you went through.'' Suddenly, there were tears in his eyes. The tough guy was crying. I wanted to reach up and wipe away the tears, but I could barely move my arm. I managed to take his hand. He brought it to his lips and kissed it. "It's just that the time wasn't right, baby. But I promise you, I'll give

you what you want, Sandy—everything, love, marriage, a home. We'll
have kids, baby. Just be patient.''

It turned out that Hattie's high opinion of her skills was not misplaced.
She knew her business. She gave Bernie antibiotics for me. I took them
and, about a week later, saw an excellent gynecologist and told him the
entire story. After examining me, he said I was a lucky girl, that whoever
had performed the abortion had done an excellent job, and that I was
perfectly healthy for a young lady who had gotten off the operating table
and walked home in subfreezing weather.

Easter Sunday the air was crisp, the sun was shining, the city was thaw-
ing out of winter. The ice had melted in Central Park and from every little
patch of urban earth in which a tree or tulip had been planted, from window
boxes to brownstone gardens to squares cut in the concrete streets, the
smell of wet earth signaled spring. It was a perfect day, Bernie assured me
as we drove north through the park, to see the Easter Parade in Harlem.

In the big new Oldsmobile he'd showed up with a couple of weeks after
he bet the Caddy and lost, we pulled up in front of the bar and grill Cokey
owned on the corner of Seventh Avenue and 125th Street. Folding chairs
and barstools had been set up outside in the sunshine. It was early, not yet
noon, but Hot Dog Red was already there smoking his Luckys and looking
like spring in a powder-blue suit and vest, with a tan straw hat on his head,
spotless new white 'gators on his feet, and a frosty mimosa, a tall glass of
orange juice and champagne, in his hand.

"What's shakin', sis?'' he said, standing to buzz me on the cheek. He
shook hands with Bernie. "Lookin' fine, Mr. B,'' he teased. Red was
family. When he called Bernie Mr. B, it was almost a parody of the def-
erential way others used the term.

"Mr. Dog,'' Bernie kidded him back.

Cokey came out of the bar to greet us. With him were two locals I'd met
before. Red Dillon, tall, skinny, light-skinned, who'd been a mob power
around Harlem almost as long as Bumpy Johnson had and was almost as
well known. But where Bumpy was a figure of awe and respect, famous
and venerated, Red Dillon was notorious and feared. "He'll shoot you first
and ask questions later,'' I'd heard Bernie say of him. The second man
with Cokey was a numbers runner named "Parks,'' a very amiable, very
black man who was always bowing and who, Hot Dog had hinted, did a
little dealing on the side.

"Miss Sandy,'' Parks said, touching his cap to me. "You are a vision
in red today. You do your man proud.''

I was wearing a red linen dress with a white collar and navy-blue piping.
And, of course, I had on one of my floppy straw hats, navy blue with a
navy and white polka-dot ribbon round the crown. I used to get these

terrific headaches from the hat pins. Also, the brims were so wide that I often had to tilt my head back to see. Now I peered out at Parks and thanked him for the compliment.

Cokey, Bernie, and Red Dillon had a little business to discuss inside. "Let them nappy-haired niggers go," Hot Dog said as the men went into the bar. I was used to Red's outrageous mouth by now, but it still jolted me to hear him say "nigger." And he knew it. Grinning, he winked at me and patted the folding chair next to his for me to sit down. A waitress brought me a mimosa. And for the next hour or so, I watched the parade, which was an informal procession of men, women, and children dressed in their spring finery on their way to or from church to celebrate the resurrection of Christ.

Pastels were the order of the day. The women, in magnificent hats garlanded with artificial flowers, fruit, ribbons, and feathers, strolled by in high-heeled shoes dyed lavender, lime, pink, or yellow to match their Easter suits and dresses. Many of them wore square-shouldered fur jackets or stoles from another era, pearly gray Persian lamb and red and silver fox or, draped over their shoulders, a rope of needle-nosed, beady-eyed furry creatures biting each other's tails.

Gloved hands clutched a rainbow of bibles, red, black, royal blue and white; or held the gloved hands or squeaky-clean collars of beautifully dressed, immaculate children. Some of the women, sometimes three generations of them, walked along with their arms linked. Men walked in family groups or lagged behind in twos and threes, in snap-brimmed summer hats and pale patent leather shoes.

So many different faces, so many colors—black, brown, beige and creamy white—walking in the sunlight of Seventh Avenue. Here and there music could be heard, a little school band would appear. Children in rich purple or white satin uniforms with gold braid trim played hymns and marched under the solemn watchfulness of adult chaperones. A group of women in black choral robes, their brightly colored high-heeled shoes visible beneath the hemlines, walked and clapped and sang spirituals.

In time, Bumpy Johnson showed up, as conservatively dressed and elegant as ever. "Here comes the Exterminator," Hot Dog said. I thought he was referring to Bumpy's dark past and tried to shush him, but it turned out that Bumpy Johnson had actually gone into the bug extermination business up in Harlem and was doing quite well at it. Of course those, like Hot Dog, who'd known him as a powerful mobster were especially struck by the irony of his new title.

Shortly after Bumpy arrived, Iris showed up. She was Cokey's girlfriend, and one of the few other women I could count on seeing when the boys got together. Iris was a tall, thin, gorgeous black woman in her early forties. Her face was all dark and silky skin pulled tight as a drum over these amazing African bones. Iris was a sharp, educated woman, an ex-madam, ex-numbers runner, and current restauranteur, whose fabulous soul food place was right around the corner from Cokey's bar.

The way Bernie loved Harlem, Iris loved the Lower East Side. We went shopping for furniture down there one afternoon and, at Benson's, Iris bought a bedroom set that made Bernie's mirrored alcove look like a nuns' retreat. It was white and gold and I think the headboard lit up. It had inset mirrors and shells and velvet panels and cupids and God knows what. I watched Iris count out and hand over seven grand in cash for that big *ungepotchket* bedroom set, and then she dragged me to the pickle barrels and halvah and herring merchants and finally, to Yonah Shimmel's Knishes, where she bought up half the store to take back to Harlem and freeze.

Cokey walked over while Iris and I were in the middle of a conversation. And then something strange happened. I was talking about my friend Toni's "colored girl." It was what I'd always called the cleaning woman who worked for Toni. Colored. Cokey, who'd been drinking for several hours and doing whatever else he did, shot me a terrible silencing look. I'd never seen him angry before, certainly never at me.

"Don't say colored," he said. He held out his hand. "Is this colored? Is it blue? Green? Purple? I'm not colored," he said. "I'm Negro. You got it? Negro, Sandy. Not colored."

"I'm sorry," I said, flushing with embarrassment.

Cokey walked away. Iris winked at me. "He's loaded, honey," she said. "Don't worry about it."

Hot Dog tried to comfort me. "He don't mean a thing by it," he said. "He just blows hot and cold that way. Probably won't even remember it tomorrow. Nothing you can do about it, Sandy. Times are changing," he said with a philosophical shrug.

Hot Dog had it right. Times were changing—up in Harlem and down South where Martin Luther King, Jr., was sentenced to four months at hard labor for sitting at a Whites-Only lunch counter. Richard Nixon was running for president. He said he had no opinion on King's sentencing. John Kennedy, on the other hand, behaved like a *mensch*. He personally phoned King's wife, Coretta, and offered to help any way he could.

Hot Dog Red, the last person in the world I'd expected to pay attention to politics, suddenly knew all about Kennedy and Nixon and how Martin Luther King's father, a Protestant minister, had announced he was voting for Kennedy, even though he never thought he'd vote for a Catholic president. And John F. Kennedy said, "Imagine that, Martin Luther King, Jr.'s father is prejudiced."

That was what Hot Dog meant when he said times were changing. As for me, this is the way I remember events:

A couple of Bernie's friends were dating girls my age. Milty Heinz, the Teamster official and pal of Johnny Dio's, whom I'd met with Lana Turner's ex-husband, had a twenty-five-year-old girlfriend named Diana. And a guy named Whitey Diamond, whom everyone called by his Jewish name, "Muttel," was going out with a cute kid named Trudy. Both Milty's girl and Muttel's in that election year were campaigning hard for marriage.

King got out of jail. Kennedy won the election. Diana and Trudy won *their* campaigns. It was like the new president said, "The torch has been passed to a new generation." And, as if they were afraid of being left in the dark, Milty and Muttel married into that new generation.

And Bernie came home one afternoon. I was sitting at the bar, smoking, flipping through a magazine. I looked up. "You want to get married?" he said before he'd even taken off his coat.

For months I had been nagging, hollering, praying, and *hocking* him. "Oh, my God. Yes!" I said.

"Okay. That's it. No questions. We're getting married."

I jumped off the barstool and flew into his arms. "You really mean it? Oh, God, I'm so happy. You're not kidding, right? We're really going to get married?"

"Sure," Bernie said, grinning now. "You want to get married, we'll get married." He kissed me. Then, "Go," he said, peeling my arms from around his neck, "call your mother. Tell her."

I did. "Ma, you want to go to a wedding?" I said.

Bernie was at the bar, pouring himself a scotch. He looked over at me on the telephone and shook his head indulgently at my childishness. I started to laugh.

"What?" he said. "What'd she say?"

"She says, 'Thank God,' " I told him. "She wants to know when."

"Of course." Bernie laughed. "Okay, Saturday," he said. "Tell her we're getting married next Saturday night, all right?"

Tears stung my eyes. "He says Saturday, Ma," I told her. It went on that way for a little while. She'd ask me a question. I'd ask Bernie. He'd tell me. I'd tell her.

"She wants to know what happened," I said. "What made you decide?"

"I ran into Muttel on Park Avenue," Bernie said distractedly. He'd picked his coat up from the couch and was searching through the pockets for something.

"He says he ran into Muttel. Whitey Diamond, whose Jewish name is Muttel. He's a friend of Bernie's—"

"He was in a limousine," Bernie continued. "With Trudy. He said, 'We just got married.' I said, 'Okay, that's it. I'm doing it.' "

"What?!" I said, putting my hand over the receiver. "Bernie, are you telling me you decided to get married because Muttel got married?!"

"What?" my mother wanted to know.

"What?" Bernie called to me.

"What are you talking about?!" I asked him.

He hardly heard me. He was at the closet, hanging up his coat. "Tell her it's not going to be anything fancy," he hollered. "I have no money for a big wedding right now. I owe everyone. I'm even thinking about getting out of the club. So it'll just be family. A couple of friends. Who knows, maybe this'll change my luck. We'll go downtown tomorrow and get the blood tests. Then we've got to go see my P.O. I'm still on parole. So we need the Greek's permission—"

I took my hand off the phone for a second. "Hang on a minute, Ma," I said, then slammed my palm back over the receiver and, suddenly breathing hard, tried to make sense of the barrage of information Bernie was casually tossing over his shoulder.

He was broke? That meant *we* were broke; that meant Bernie's betting had taken a bad turn again. So why didn't he say what he always said when the money temporarily dried up—I may be broke but I'm not poor? I almost bolted for the window to see if the Oldsmobile was still outside. And the club, The Velvet Club? I knew he'd been aggravated about the place for a while, but this was the first I'd heard about him getting out of the business. And now that he'd finally asked me to marry him—never mind that I wanted to kill him because it was a chance encounter with Whitey Diamond that had somehow convinced him to marry me; never mind that I felt like a mother who wanted to say, "And if Muttel jumped off the roof, Bernie, would you jump, too?"—now that I'd gotten what I'd wanted for so long . . . *now* he told me we'd need to get permission from a parole officer! We couldn't even get married unless Peter Knossos said it was all right.

Not for a minute, not for a million bucks, was I going to pass along one word of this information to my mother.

"Got to go. 'Bye, Ma. I love you," I said, "I'll call you later."

Bernie walked back into the living room as I hung up the phone. "So, we're going to get married. How's that make you feel?" he said, grinning at me. "You happy, baby?"

"Yes," I said, and burst into tears.

There was no doubt in my mind that I loved Bernie with all my heart. I had never known anyone as exciting or generous as he was. I had never felt as desired, protected, or cherished as I did with him. I was happy. But I was also suddenly terrified—that he'd change his mind, that he'd get sick again, that the rollercoaster he called life would come unhinged one day and we'd wind up destitute or dead.

I spent the afternoon phoning friends. I called Judy and Marilyn and even Leona, who still lived in Brooklyn. I called Toni, an ex-showgirl like myself, who was being kept by a big mob guy. I called Iris uptown and Bernie's mom downtown, and I did my best to hide my fears from myself as well as from them.

* * *

We were broke but we weren't poor. We still had the big, shiny new Oldsmobile, I reminded myself as we drove downtown the next day to see Peter Knossos, the parole officer.

"Okay, let's go over it again," Bernie said. "Where did we meet?"

"Oh, Bernie, he's never going to believe me."

Bernie shook his head, frustrated at my lack of confidence. "Sandra, don't start with me today, okay? Just let's do it like I told you. We met at a dance at the synagogue."

I burst out laughing. I couldn't *hear* it with a straight face much less say it. Bernie shot me a look.

"Okay, okay, sweetheart," I capitulated. "I'll tell him we met dancing the hora." I took out my compact and checked my face for the tenth time.

"Don't," Bernie warned.

"I'm not putting on makeup. I'm just looking, okay? God, I look ridiculous. Bernie, I look about twelve years old. The ponytail's okay, but do I have to wear a ribbon?!"

Bernie had supervised my dressing that morning. My long hair was slicked back into a high ponytail with a ribbon wrapped around the rubberband: a *pink* ribbon. And I was wearing a little plaid dress with a Peter Pan collar and very plain little black pumps. I'd left all my jewelry at home, except for a simple Star of David on a thin gold chain, which Bernie insisted I wear. All that was missing were the bobby socks and loose-leaf notebook, I thought.

"You look terrific," Bernie said. "What's with you today? All of a sudden you're teaching the teacher?"

It was one of his favorite expressions—teaching the teacher. And it seemed particularly apt today. I felt as if I was on my way to school and it was pop quiz time.

"No, baby. I'm sorry," I said. "I'm just a nervous wreck. It's like going to take a test or something. I was never good at test taking, Bernie."

He patted my thigh affectionately. "I always thought you were, *mamela*. You passed my tests, didn't you? Sandra—" His tone of voice changed abruptly. He became the teacher again. "Where are the gloves? Put on the fucking gloves, will you?"

"Very nice, Bernie. Fucking gloves. Is that the way you're going to talk in front of Peter?" I said, fueled by raw nerves rather than courage. I put on the white gloves he'd insisted I wear. My palms were perspiring and my hands were shaking with nervousness.

We found a lucky parking spot less than a block from the courthouse. "Remember. We met at *shul*," Bernie said. "At a dance, you got it?"

Bernie waited in the outer office while I went in to see Peter. The parole officer, the same man to whom I'd seen Bernie slip cash, was sitting behind his desk looking very cocky. For a start, he had his foot on the handle of his bottom drawer. He didn't stand up to greet me, but simply motioned for me to have a seat in the wooden chair at the side of his desk.

"You're Sandy?" he said.

My gloved hands were toying with the clasp of the purse in my lap. I couldn't find my voice; I just nodded respectfully.

"I'm Peter Knossos," he said. "I'm Bernie's P.O. Do you know what P.O. means?"

I nodded again.

"Parole officer," Knossos said, just to be sure I understood. On his desk was a wooden picture frame in which there was a photograph of an attractive, dark-haired young woman holding a little boy. Beside the picture was a milk glass vase with a single red rose in it. The rest of the green metal desk was covered with papers and folders.

With the toe of his shoe, Knossos pulled open the bottom desk drawer. Staring at me the entire time, he reached down into the drawer and pulled out a thick manila folder and threw it down on the desk where it landed with an impressive thump. The whole thing was pretty dramatic. "You know what that is?" he asked.

I shook my head no.

"It's your future husband's rap sheet. His file," he explained.

"Wow," I blurted out. "It's pretty thick."

The P.O. laughed. "It sure is," he said. "It dates back to when he was thirteen years old. Do you have any idea what's in it?"

"Of course," I said, trying to make up for the petty disloyalty of being shocked by the thickness of Bernie's arrest record. "He's told me everything."

"Oh, really? I'm just curious," he said. "Did he ever say whether he'd killed anyone?"

I gripped the clasp on my purse so hard it snapped open. "I asked him that," I answered honestly, almost shouting at the parole officer.

"And?" Knossos said, waiting.

"I said, 'Bernie, you never killed anyone, did you?' and he said, 'Naw, babe.' "

"That's it?"

"Yes."

"Good. That's good," Knossos said, unimpressed. He nodded at the Star of David on its chain around my neck. "You're Jewish?"

"Yes."

"Have you ever been married before?"

So much for looking twelve, I thought. "No."

He asked a few more questions about my background, where I came from, my schooling. I answered honestly and, I hoped, demurely. Then Knossos said, "So how did you meet Bernie?"

"At a Jewish dance," I said. "I met him at a dance at the synagogue."

The parole office cracked up, busted out laughing. Before I knew it, I was laughing with him. Something snapped in me. All the tension that had held me rigid broke and the two of us cackled and shook with uncontrollable laughter. "That's good. That's really good," Knossos gasped, trying to catch his breath.

Finally, he leaned back in his chair and wiped his eyes. "You know, sweetheart," he said. "You really love this guy, that's obvious. So I guess I'm going to give you permission to marry him. Who knows, maybe you can straighten him out. After all, he's still young," Knossos teased. "Just be sure I get a copy of the marriage license. I want to make sure you aren't lying to me."

We both stood up. To my surprise, Bernie's parole officer pulled the rose out of the vase on his desk and handed it to me. Then he gave me a kiss on the cheek. "Good luck," he said. "You're going to need it."

I thanked him and rushed out to the waiting room and into Bernie's arms. "He said yes," I said, elated. "Come on, we can go now. I passed!"

"See, I told you," Bernie said. "Good girl. I'm proud of you."

We left the building holding hands and walked to the car. As we were about to get in, Bernie snapped his fingers. He turned and looked back up to the building. "I knew it!" he growled. "The son of a bitch is watching us!"

I turned to look and, sure enough, there was Peter Knossos leaning out his window. Without thinking, I waved to him.

"Get in," Bernie said, holding the driver's door open for me.

"You want me to slide over?"

"No. I want you to drive. That's why he's watching. The bastard is trying to set me up. I'm not supposed to own a car, much less drive one."

"What are you, crazy?" I whispered, as if Knossos, three stories up and half a block away, could hear me. "I can't drive, Bernie. I don't know how!"

"Get in," he insisted in a strangled voice. I took one look at him and knew he was on the verge of a temper tantrum. That was all we'd need. For his P.O. to watch him jump up and down screaming and biting his fist. I got into the car and sat staring helplessly at the wheel while Bernie walked around to the passenger side.

"Okay, okay." He was trying to calm down. "There's nothing to it, baby. You'll do fine. Okay, breathe," he said. "You're turning blue."

I breathed. The steering wheel felt huge. The car seemed as big as a bus.

"Turn the key," Bernie said. I did. The motor started. "Good girl. See, you're doing great. Now slowly, Sandra, slowly—put your right foot slowly on the gas pedal."

We lurched forward.

"Stop! Hit the brake. No, the other foot. Slowly!!!"

Step by step, Bernie instructed me on how to move the car out of the parking spot and into street traffic. I was sweating like crazy. Now that I'd found the brake, I pumped it for reassurance every two seconds. As soon as the car moved forward, I'd hit the brake—slowly, slowly, I thought. But no matter how slowly, how gently I tried to step on the brake pedal, we sort of bounced down the street. "Okay, good," Bernie tried through clenched teeth to be encouraging. "Okay, keep going. Just go slow, baby. Good. Okay. You're going two miles an hour, Sandra—leave the brake alone! Okay, good. Stop. Sandra, stop! Stop now!"

I hit the brake. Bernie hit the windshield. "You said to leave the brake alone!" I complained.

"The light was red!"

"Oh."

Finally, Bernie said, "Turn here, then pull over to that pump and stop. Slowly stop."

I tried. We jerked around the corner and kind of bounced over to the curb. I eased my foot onto the brake pedal. Bernie was hanging on to the dashboard this time. "Slowly," he cautioned.

I did it with no more damage than the crunch and squeak of tires scrapping the curb. I took my sweating palms off the steering wheel. And I waited—for one complaint, one nasty remark. I was so keyed up that I think I would have slugged him had he said anything but what he did say, which was: "Okay, sweetheart, move over."

With immeasurable relief, I traded places with him and lit a cigarette. Smoking it was like learning to breathe again. I felt like a guppy gasping for air. My head was light; my heart was thudding. After we'd put a few blocks behind us, Bernie reached over and affectionately mussed my hair. "You did good today," he said. "But you've got to learn to drive, kid."

"Marry in beige you'll be in a rage," Judy recited, standing back to admire my hair which she'd just teased and patted into place. "That's how it goes, right, Marilyn?"

The three of us were in the bathroom of the rabbi's apartment on the Upper West Side where, in less than ten minutes, Bernie and I were going to be married. Outside, in the living room, the rest of the wedding party, about eight relatives and friends, waited on folding chairs for the ceremony to begin while the rabbi's children chased each other from room to room.

"Rage? Judy, what are you talking about?" I asked.

"You know, honey. 'Marry in white your life will be bright. Marry in red you'll always be in bed. In blue your love will be true. In beige, you'll be in a rage.' That's how it goes."

"Gee," Marilyn said, impressed, "I never heard that. But it's a pretty suit, Sandy. You really look gorgeous . . . even if it is beige."

Bernie had given me $100 two days before the wedding and I'd rushed over to Ohrbach's and picked up a beige shantung knockoff of a Jackie Kennedy suit and some lacy new underwear. At Bakers I got beige shoes and a purse to match. Now I saw myself in the mirror, a vision in beige.

"It's a good thing I'm not superstitious," I said, managing a laugh. But I was. And the only thing I had on that wasn't beige was the *royta bendle,* the red ribbon I had tied to my bra for good luck. So Judy's little poem did nothing to quiet my wedding-day jitters.

Bernie had made all the arrangements. Because of how broke we were, he hadn't told many people that we were getting married. Still, the few friends who knew had wanted to make us a big reception. Bernie wouldn't hear of it. His tremendous pride dictated that we wouldn't accept cash presents or a party he himself couldn't afford to throw. It was ironic given all the fat envelopes, the hundreds of dollars, I'd seen him press into the hands of brides or stuff into "bridal pillowcases" at the weddings we'd been to. I didn't care, though. I was getting my wish. It wasn't the big fancy wedding I'd dreamed of, it was being married to Bernie. My only regret at that moment, big deal, was the color of my suit.

The rabbi's wife knocked at the door. "All right, missus. It's time."

Judy squeezed my hand. "You look jes beautiful, honey," she said, suddenly close to tears. Marilyn kissed me on the cheek, then quickly wiped away a trace of her bright red lipstick. "Oh, Sandy. I love you," she called, grabbing Judy and rushing out. Judy blew me a kiss for luck.

The rabbi's wife was not much older than I, but was short and stout with dimpled arms that looked like they'd already spent a lifetime bathing children and kneading dough. She was wearing an apron over her print housecoat. "Come," she beckoned. She untied the apron and hung it on the back of the bathroom door. "Your man is waiting."

And he was. In a handsome three-piece blue suit with a carnation in his lapel and a white satin yarmulka on his head, my man was standing in front of the rabbi, practically tapping his foot with impatience. The rabbi's wife managed to grab a couple of the running children on our way into the living room. Those heavy hands of hers were faster than they looked. The rabbi himself silenced the rest of the kids with an ominous, dark look. He began the ceremony with the same angry intensity. When it was over, Bernie and I kissed and then he looked around for the glass.

Traditionally, the groom is supposed to step on a glass and that signals the end of the ceremony. Some people said the number of pieces the glass broke into would show you the number of years you'd live in health and happiness together. Some people said stepping on the glass was a way to commemorate the destruction of the temple—to remember at the height of your joy the sadness of your people. Whatever its true meaning, it was tradition at a Jewish wedding for the groom to break the glass and have everyone yell, "Mazel-tov!"

So Bernie said to the rabbi, "Where's the glass?"

The rabbi's wife held up her dimpled arms. "No, no. We can't do it," she said, and started explaining how it would ruin her carpeting. And the rabbi said, "Don't worry, it's only tradition."

"It's supposed to keep away evil," Bernie said. "You know, you shatter the evil spirits."

"No, no. Don't worry, you won't have evil spirits," the rabbi insisted. "Here, we'll have wine and sponge cake and that's it."

Between the beige/rage couplet and not stepping on the glass, the two of us were off to a great start, I thought. I could see that Bernie was annoyed about it, too. "Leave it to Muttel to recommend a rabbi who cares more about his goddamn carpeting than about Jewish tradition," he grumbled, as my mother, Marlene, and I piled into the car after the wedding.

But if the ceremony didn't end traditionally, at least the night did. After a lovely wedding supper with friends and family, Bernie and I picked up the Sunday papers, the *News* and the *Mirror,* and walked home with our arms around each other. It was what we did almost every Saturday night, only this Saturday night, April 15, 1960, we were married.

CHAPTER SEVEN

Changes

The boys were coming over. In the middle of the afternoon, Bernie would come home with a bag full of deli—pastrami, corned beef, chopped liver, pickled red peppers, potato salad, the works. "Listen, babe, just put this out on serving platters. Fill the ice bucket. Make sure there are plenty of ashtrays around. And then, why don't you call Judy or Toni or your mother. Go for a walk. Read a book. You know."

I knew. Bernie had always liked to use the apartment as his club house. He loved having friends over. The "boys"—Hot Dog Red, a rich young Jewish lawyer named Josh, and Uncle Vinny, a dapper Italian about Bernie's age—would put their feet up on the furniture, light cigars that smelled like burnt rope, aim the ashes at the nearest glass or plate, dribble chopped liver onto the carpeting, and put all the big events of the world to bed.

Before we were married, when the boys stopped by, I'd set out the drinks and deli and then, at a high sign from Bernie, discreetly disappear. Now I resented being sent off to bed like a child. It wasn't Bernie's apartment anymore, it was my home. And I found myself wanting to hang out with the grown-ups. Especially when they'd start talking about someone called Lido.

They'd have a couple of drinks, a hit or two of grass. They'd settle the space race, offer their two cents on Kennedy, Khrushchev, and Castro, and on who was in and out of prison and politics—Joey Gallo was in, Carmine DeSapio was out. And then they'd start:

"How can you believe Lido's crap, B?" Hot Dog would say.

Bernie'd laugh. "You think Lido's full of shit? How come you won't look him in the eye, Dog?"

"Just 'cause he's full of shit don't mean the nigger can't give you the evil eye."

Vinny, who was called "uncle" because of his mania for straightening magazines and organizing activities—more like a maiden aunt than an uncle—heart-of-gold Vinny, who owned a couple of little bars and was mostly supported by women, would shake his head and say, "Calls himself a priest? It's a fuckin' sacrilege!"

"Afro-Cuban priest, Vinny. Lido's a Santoro. It's not a Catholic thing."

"Santoro, shmantoro." Josh the lawyer, who idolized Bernie, would shrug skeptically. He was from a very rich family, good people from the Garment Center who'd struck it rich and gotten into the movie business. His cousin was a big Hollywood producer. With his relatives and his law degree Josh could have lived easy in the straight life, but he was nuts about gangsters, especially Bernie, whom he looked up to like a father or an older brother.

"Nigger's a coke machine, that's all," Hot Dog Red declared. "You give him enough toot, he'll tell you whatever you want to hear."

"Who's Lido?" I'd ask Bernie, exchanging a clean ashtray for one filled with Red's ground-down Lucky Strike butts.

"Nothing. None of your business." He'd signal with his eyes, dart his baby blues toward the bedroom. "Go, Sandy. Go read."

"What does Santoro mean?" I'd ask, sweeping a crushed red pepper off the coffee table into my palm.

"Sandra!" Bernie'd give me his best dismissive glare.

But now that I was Sadie-Sadie-Married-Lady, my knees didn't buckle instantly at his every angry glance. I didn't scurry to the bedroom on command. I'd find excuses to hang around and listen.

I knew that Bernie was superstitious. If he won at the track, he'd wear the same shirt the next five times he placed a bet. He made a big deal of kissing the *mezuzah* when he walked out the door. He lit green "money candles'' in the house. And I suspected that he was a lot more upset than he'd let on about not breaking the glass at our wedding.

I was superstitious, too. The red ribbon I'd worn on our wedding day was just one of the *royta bendles* in my life—I had red bits of fabric hidden in every closet and cupboard of the apartment. On my birthday, June 13, Saint Anthony's Day, I'd go to church with Uncle Vinny and make a novena to the patron saint of the poor and the foolish. I believed in the power of those novenas and prayers. I believed in the evil eye, fortune-tellers, gifted people, astrology, good vibrations, men with mustaches. I was always waiting for a miracle, waiting for someone to wave a hand, mumble ''shmaydray,'' make all the bad disappear.

I'd never discussed any of this with Bernie. But I was determined to find out more about Lido. And the more Bernie put me off, the more determined I became.

In bed, after I'd vacuumed the chopped liver out of the carpeting and wiped the last trace of pickle juice from the coffee table, I'd curl up against him and begin:

''Honey, who's Lido?''

''Come on, Sandy. I'm tired, baby. Aren't you tired?''

''No. Bernie, why did Red say that about the evil eye? Is he really afraid to look at this Lido?''

''You know Red, he's superstitious.''

''Are you?''

''Sandra, are you going to knock it off already?''

''Yes, baby. But are you? I mean, do you believe in séances? You know, my mother used to go to seances. She believes in all that stuff—fortune-tellers, curses, the works.''

''Tillie?'' He laughed. ''No kidding.''

''And my cousin Francine, the one I lived with in Beverly Hills when I was a kid, she used to do automatic writing, you know, like when a spirit speaks through you, guides your hand.''

''And what about you?'' Bernie asked cautiously. ''Do you believe in that stuff?''

''Some of it, sure.'' I shrugged. ''Do you?'' It felt very strange talking about this aloud. It was almost embarrassing, more intimate than sex.

''Yeah. Some,'' he confessed, sounding as sheepish as I felt.

''What's Santoro?''

''A priest in an Afro-Cuban religion—a kind of voodoo called Santeria, very powerful. And very interesting,'' he said, backing away from it, getting objective.

''And Lido is a priest in this religion?''

''Yeah, I guess, something like that.''

''Bernie, can I go with you sometime?''

"What, are you crazy?"

"Why, is it just for men?"

"No. But it's . . . Take my word for it, baby. It's not for you."

It took about two months. It was in June, on the anniversary of Bernie's father's death. Two months after we were married, Bernie put on a yarmulka, lit a memorial candle for his father, recited the *Kaddish,* the ritual Jewish prayer for the dead, then turned to me and said, "Okay, I'm going uptown tonight to Lido's. You want to, you can come with me."

I had to work very hard at acting cool as we drove up to Spanish Harlem. There were a million questions I wanted to ask Bernie, but I was afraid that he'd get annoyed with me and change his mind about taking me along. So I sat silently beside him in my black turtleneck and slacks, smoking, and trying to distract myself by looking out the car window at the men sitting on milk boxes, playing dominoes, women leaning on pillows, watching the street from their kitchen windows, guys washing cars with water from opened fire hydrants. Along with the sounds of people and traffic, Latin music blared from parked car radios and stereo speakers set up in doorways.

Maybe it was the prospect of meeting Lido, at last, that took me back. Maybe it was the swarming neighborhood we'd passed through or the grandmotherly woman I'd noticed moving through the crowd, a black babushka on her head, an urgent mission in her rolling, hurried gait. But, as Bernie pulled into a parking space on 108th Street, I found myself remembering something that had happened when I was just a little kid.

My mother had taken me with her to see a rabbi's wife who was supposed to have psychic powers. The *rebetsn* was going to read the cards for my mother. I was about eight years old. I remember having to reach up to hold my mother's hand. Normally, it made me feel more grown up to walk at a distance from her and pretend I was on my own, a big girl walking along alone. But that day I held her hand with no argument because the neighborhood was strange, a bustling unfamiliar place.

My mother and the rabbi's wife sat at the dining-room table, which was covered by a lace cloth. There were silver candlesticks on the table. And there was a bowl of fruit and a dish of hard candies on the sideboard next to the straight-backed chair that I was sitting on, separate from them, watching from a distance. The *rebetsn* laid out the cards for my mother and was studying them. I waited expectantly, straining to hear before she'd even said a word.

Suddenly the rabbi's wife jumped back from the cards. *"Oy, oy, oy,"* she screamed. "I have to run to the *shul*. Someone is dead."

We all three rushed from the apartment and separated on the street. The rabbi's wife, moving like the elderly woman in Spanish Harlem, hurried toward the synagogue. My mother and I tore away in the other direction, to the subway that would take us home. When I asked my mother about it days later, she shook her head sadly. *"Oy, nebech,"* she said. "She was right. The rabbi had a heart attack and died in the *shul."*

So I was probably thinking of the rabbi's wife as Bernie led me across the street and down three steps into the ground floor of Lido's East Harlem brownstone. I had no clear image of him in my mind before he opened the door to greet us. I just felt spooked and spiritual and eager to meet the man I'd heard so much about, the gifted Afro-Cuban priest whom Bernie regarded with the same awe and reverence my mother had felt for the rabbi's wife.

"Lido," Bernie said, "this is my lady, Sandy."

He looked like Little Richard. He had pale brown skin, pomaded hair, a pencil mustache, and more show-stopping jewelry than the entire orchestra section of a Hadassah matinee.

"Sandy," he said, clasping my hand. I could barely tear my eyes from the diamond in his pinky ring, which had to be about seven carats in a gold gypsy setting that made it look even bigger. Not that this stone needed any help. It was the size of a grape.

"Come in, B." He was all in black, from his velvet slippers and flowing trousers to his wide-sleeved satin shirt. Jangling gold necklaces and bracelets, Lido led the way into a pretty normal-looking living room. Against his black shirt, on top of about ten other necklaces, lay a huge, diamond-studded cross on a thick gold link chain. Fingering that cross after a few minutes of gossipy small talk, Lido said, "What have you brought me, B?" His neatly manicured nails were long; his pinky nail longest of all, and he soon put it to use.

Bernie pulled a small cellophane packet out of his back pocket and clapped it into Lido's hand. And Lido's long pinky nail dipped into the packet and came out carrying a heap of white powder, which he promptly tossed into his nose and snorted with gusto.

Cocaine. I remembered what Hot Dog had said about Lido. Lido was a coke head. It helped him reach his "outer vibrations," he claimed. What vibrations Bernie was reaching for I have no idea, but the two of them were making short work of that packet. Finally, Lido said, "What's bothering you, B? What's the problem?"

And Bernie, who'd forgotten I was even in the room by then, said, "I'm thinking of selling the club. I need cash. My partners'll buy me out. I don't know—it's just not working anymore, Lido."

Lido hadn't forgotten me. He gave me his hand and pulled me to my feet. "We'll look into the bowl," he said to Bernie, leading me to a door at the far end of the living room. "We'll look into the bowl, then we'll see."

The door led to a linoleum-covered basement. There were coins scattered all over the floor—pennies, dimes, nickels, quarters, half-dollars. There were four or five big pillows on the floor, pushed up against the walls. Lido signaled for us to sit down on them. Between the pillows, and in wall alcoves as well, stood brightly painted plaster statues of Saints and Indians. And before the statues were little dishes of food, cigars, money, and leaves, herbs I guess.

"Give me eight cents for the Blessed Mother," Lido said to me. "It's got to be a nickel and three pennies," he insisted, as I rummaged in my purse for the money. When I found the right change, Lido put it into a tin cup, then put the cup at the base of one of the statues.

I remember that he and Bernie talked for a while. I was still enthralled with Lido's jewelry. A couple of the chains around his neck had diamonds running through them, and every time he moved they sparkled. At some point my attention wandered to the change on the floor of the basement. I began counting it, and the process became hypnotic. There were coins everywhere, heaped in corners and thicker around the feet of some of the painted saints. The next thing I knew, Bernie was getting up. Lido, again, helped me to my feet. He led us both to the middle of the room and had us kneel down together. I noticed that there was African music playing. I guess it was African—voices chanting over a quiet, repetitive drum beat.

Lido set down a bowl and wooden spoon in front of us. Talking the entire time, he tossed a handful of what looked like leaves and dirt into the bowl. I can't remember what he was saying, nothing terribly spiritual or hard to understand, but it was like a shower of sounds.

At some point, he left us, Bernie and me, kneeling in that basement room and returned carrying a live chicken. It happened so fast, I didn't have time to know that I knew what was going to happen next. Chanting, Lido laid the chicken on the linoleum in front of us and chopped off its head with a machete knife. I gasped. Lido held the flailing headless carcass upside down and let it bleed into the bowl, then he tossed it away.

He was busy throwing more leaves and dirt into the bowl and seemed not to notice the headless chicken flapping around the room. But I noticed it! I screamed and tried, because we were still on our knees, to roll out of its way. I half rolled, half crawled, and finally scrambled to my feet and started dodging the poor doomed bird as best I could. Bernie and Lido paid no attention to this at all. Not to me. Not to the bird. They were concentrating on the voodoo stew Lido was brewing. He dipped his fingers into the mess and smeared some on Bernie's forehead.

Bernie looked over his shoulder at me cowering in the corner next to the painted Indian. "Sandy, come here, baby," he said very calmly.

Lido lowered his head and looked at me as if he were peering over the rims of a pair of eyeglasses. Was this the famous evil eye Red had talked about? Shaken to the bone by the chicken, I shuddered violently. Lido smiled, then signaled for me to kneel down again next to Bernie. And, of course, I did. And, of course, he smeared my forehead with the same bloody mud.

I don't know what was in the bowl, besides fresh chicken blood, of course. I don't know what blessings or curses the boys were trying to conjure. I know that the blood should have been hot, but it felt incredibly cool on my forehead and that, as repulsive as the mixture was, it worked like a Valium. My fluttering heart quieted down. I took Bernie's hand. And I felt safe.

Despite my upset about the chicken, Bernie was very proud of me. I think he'd half-expected me to tell him he was crazy to put any faith in Lido's mumbo jumbo but, while I had my doubts about the man, I was too superstitious to put him down.

As we were leaving the brownstone that first night, we ran into a couple of heavy hitters from Little Italy going in to see Lido. It was a funny scene. The first jolt of recognition. The guys and Bernie smiling, shaking hands, saying, "Hey, how you been? What're you doing up here?" Then the sudden embarrassment. They were very flustered, all three of them, like kids caught with their fingers in the cookie jar. These were tough guys. Mobsters. The Italians were killers—literally. A couple of connected, respected, street-wise hit men. And here they were bringing drugs or diamonds or bundles of money to a chicken killer who looked like Little Richard and needed cocaine to jump-start his psychic powers.

We went to see Lido a number of times and eventually, at least in part because of the flamboyant Santoro's advice, Bernie did sell his piece of The Velvet Room to his partners. With the exception of that first night, there were always other people around, limousines double-parked outside or cars with bodyguards waiting in them. Bernie saw nothing strange about saying Jewish prayers in the morning and kneeling in front of Lido at night. And, apparently, neither did half of New York's most notorious mobsters and madams. These might be people who thought anyone who read Jeanne Dixon's astrology column in the newspapers was soft in the head or square. But Lido who, for a couple of hundred dollars and a spoon or two of coke, would call down curses on an ex-lover or an enemy, they considered a smart investment. I think for Bernie and his friends to feel comfortable, even their psychics had to be crooked.

Bernie had been bugging me to learn how to drive since the day I almost killed us both getting away from Peter Knossos's office.

"You're not working now. You've got nothing to do. If you wanted to, you could take a drive to Brooklyn, see your mother or Leona. You get your license, it'll give you a little freedom. Plus," he added as if it were an afterthought, "you never know when I'll need you to run an errand for me or drive me somewhere."

What else was he going to say? The truth was that Bernie hated to drive, wasn't legally supposed to, and having a licensed chauffeur handy at home couldn't hurt. So I went to driving school and did very well.

The day before I was scheduled to take my driving test, he decided the master should see if the school was giving him his money's worth. And, of course, if I fell short, he was prepared as always to teach me what I needed to know.

Whenever Bernie had taught me anything in the past, I'd always been a willing pupil, as eager as a puppy to earn his praise. I had also always been terrified by his temper. So the instruction process was definitely a carrot-and-stick affair. The carrot was earning a pat on the head from Bernie. The stick was that temper, and I'd do almost anything to avoid its being loosed on me. But now that we were married, even that began to change.

Over my weak objection that it was almost dark out and that my learner's permit was for day-time driving only, Bernie drove the Olds over to Sutton Place. The neighborhood was less than a mile from where we lived, but it was so rich, quiet, and exclusive that it had its own police force. It was a low traffic area with streets wide enough for me to practice U-turns. Which was what Bernie wanted me to do.

We traded seats. I got behind the wheel. "Okay, let's see you do it," he said. And I did, exactly the way my instructor had shown me—looking both ways even though it was a one-way street, double-checking in the mirror as I pulled out, looking over my shoulder, being extremely cautious . . .

"Come on already," Bernie grumbled. "There's nothing coming. It's a one-way street. Hit the gas and go!"

I did but with a bit of my confidence chipped away.

"Watch out for the station wagon. You almost clipped it."

"I saw it, Bernie. I had plenty of room."

"You think so, huh? Okay. Again. Try it in one motion instead of turning, then backing up."

"The instructor told me to back up first."

"Sandra, don't start. I'm telling you to try it this way, okay? In real life you've got to be able to maneuver fast. Come on, try it again."

I tried to do it the way Bernie wanted, but I turned too wide and had to back up again. I wanted to look over my shoulder to be sure I could see everything behind me, but I thought that would annoy him, so I just used the mirror and started backing up.

"Stop, stop, stop!" he shouted. "What are you, a moron? You've got to look over your shoulder or they'll nail you."

"Bernie, you're making me nervous," I said softly between clenched teeth.

"Park," he barked.

"Where?!"

"What the hell's the matter with you? Where? In a parking space, that's where. Go. Over there."

"There's a hydrant there. It's illegal."

He sighed. Actually, it was more a snort of disgust than a sigh. "We're not leaving the car there overnight, Sandra. You're just practicing parking."

"Okay, okay. Stop yelling already. Please!" I pulled parallel to the car in front of the space, checked the mirror, turned the wheel sharply, and began backing up. I was afraid I was moving too slowly—not for me, but for him—so I accelerated.

Bernie had a vein on the side of his neck that used to start jumping when he was really losing it. Out of habit, I glanced over at him to see how far gone he was. The vein was doing the Cha-Cha-Cha even before the Olds jumped the curb and rammed into the fire plug. The car was like a tank. The pump broke. Water shot out of the hydrant. Bernie whirled around, saw what had happened and started cursing at me.

"Shut up!" I heard myself scream. "*You* made me do that, you shmuck! If you hadn't been yelling at me the whole time, it never would have happened. It's your fault. *You're* the moron! *You're* the dumb cunt! *You're* the stupid bitch! Not *me*, Bernie! So just shut up!"

"Are you out of your fucking mind?!" was the gentlest part of his response—and just the beginning.

I put my hands over my ears. "Yeah, yeah, yeah!" I screamed. "I must be out of my fucking mind. I married you, didn't I?"

I was wild. I was gone. I had never opened a mouth like this to anyone ever in my entire life. But something had snapped inside me and suddenly I was a force to be reckoned with. I was a mad woman! I jumped out of the car and slammed the door with all my might. He screamed at me first from his side of the car, then he slid over to the driver's seat to curse me closer up. I think the only thing that prevented his getting out of the car and coming after me was the water shooting out of the busted pump, soaking everything. Dripping wet, I started jumping up and down, hammering on the hood of the Olds.

"Stop it, you bitch, or I'll get out of this car and brain you," he threatened.

I tried to tear the antennae off the Olds to defend myself.

"You didn't do enough damage?! Leave it alone! You touch that again, I'll rip out the steering wheel and wrap it around your fucking neck!"

Sutton Place had never heard anything like this. Suddenly there were sirens and flashing lights added to the melee. Someone had called the cops, the private police patrol. They arrested us. They threw us into the cruiser, put me in the front seat and Bernie in the back like a drowned cat and a rabid dog collected by the ASPCA.

At the Sixty-ninth Precinct we were charged with disturbing the peace and held for about half an hour until we quieted down and the desk sergeant heard our story and discharged us. A domestic quarrel, they called it.

The next day my driving instructor picked me up and I took the test in the driving school's car. When it was over, the inspector told me that I had passed. I returned home in vengeful triumph. "You see," I announced, sweeping past Bernie into the livingroom. "I do know how to drive! I passed the test on my first try!"

I was prepared for all hell to break loose again. Chin out, hands on my hips, I whirled around to face him.

He was smiling. "I knew you'd do it, baby," he said with pride and affection. "I even got you a present." He gave me a hug, a kiss, and a beautiful little diamond bracelet. And, the next day, he gave me a hundred dollars and told me to drive out to Brooklyn and take my mother and sister to lunch.

The Olds was a mess. A couple of weeks after I got my license, a sleek, brown Caddy replaced it. It was a beautiful car that looked like a big chocolate candy bar with caramel leather seats and a burled wood dash. It was Bernie's baby, his new toy, and it sat gleaming and gorgeous in the parking space in front of our building.

Bernie was both proud of me and dismayed by my new policy of talking back. Sometimes it drove him crazy. And now I had another ace in the hole. One he'd delivered on a silver platter—a driver's license and the freedom he'd promised it would bring me. One night that first summer we were married, after a quarrel that escalated to name-calling again, I picked up the car keys, waved them in his face, and literally ran out the door. Only the fact that Bernie was in his shorts stopped him from scrambling down the steps into the street after me.

"Get back in here!" he yelled from our window as I started up the car. "Sandy, I'm not kidding! Get up here! This minute!"

I gave him the finger and drove away.

I had no place to go. It was a hot night. I rolled down the windows, turned on the radio, and cruised into Central Park. The breeze was wonderful, the smell of jasmine filled the air. I had just about forgotten Bernie when police sirens went off behind me. I pulled over to get out of the way of the cop car. But it was me they were after. Two officers came over to the car. One of them had his hand on his holster, which really freaked me out. "Let's see some identification, lady," the other one said.

I showed them my driver's license.

"I'd like to see the registration," he said.

"What's going on?" I asked.

"You're driving a stolen vehicle, lady," the itchy trigger finger announced.

My heart started pounding. My hands shook as I searched the glove compartment for the car registration. Of course, I thought. Where else would Bernie get a car like this? I couldn't begin to figure out the consequences of my being arrested or even questioned about how I happened to be driving a stolen car. Between Bernie and the cops, suicide seemed like the best bet. I handed the registration papers over to the police.

The cop looked from my driver's license to the registration. "And you're Sandra Barton, right?"

"Yes, Officer," I said, close to tears.

"Well," the first cop said to his partner, "it's registered in her name. Who called in the complaint?"

"Excuse me," I said. "What complaint?"

"This car was just reported stolen."

I knew who called in the complaint! "But it's registered in my name and here's the insurance card," I said, on the offensive now. They apologized and drove off. Shaken, I headed home, knowing that Bernie had called the cops on me. He'd reported the car stolen but forgotten that he'd had it registered in my name and, of course, he'd never bothered mentioning anything to me about where he'd gotten the Caddy or in whose name it was registered.

He was standing at the window, waiting for me, when I returned. He was standing there, grinning, with his arms folded across his chest.

I walked into the house. "You happy now?" he said, smirking, satisfied that he'd given me enough trouble to call it even.

"Shmuck," I said, brushing past him. And we never mentioned the incident again.

Lido's chicken didn't die for nothing. By August, Bernie was out of The Velvet Room and we'd moved from Bernie's bachelor pad to a spacious, one-bedroom apartment, with a terrace overlooking the river, in a new luxury building on East Seventy-fourth Street.

We had a real home, at last. And I was having a ball fixing it up. With my mother, Marilyn, or Iris I shopped the Lower East Side for furniture, carpeting, curtains, beautiful new sheets and pillowcases and, the pride and joy of my new powder-blue bedroom, a white, custom-made, trapunto-stitched bedspread.

I had gone downtown with Iris one hot August afternoon to buy some pillow shams. I'd taken a swatch of white quilted fabric with me to Benson's so that the ruffled shams I was searching for would perfectly match the bedspread. Hot and tired, I came home loaded down with pillows, sheets, white, blue, and mauve shams, and a new dust ruffle for the bed. It was about five o'clock. All the way up in the elevator all I could think about was the cool shower I was going to take and the big glass of iced tea I was going to fix for myself before Bernie got home.

The minute I turned the key in the door, I knew there was something strange going on inside. And that was *before* I saw the shotgun in the foyer. I heard noises in the bedroom. My arms were filled with packages. I remember seeing the gun resting against the coat closet door. I remember wondering if Bernie had taken up hunting. I'd seen guns around the apartment before, but never a rifle. And then there were these weird grunts and moaning noises.

Bernie called out, "Sandy, is that you?"

"Of course," I said, annoyed, wondering who was groaning in the bedroom with Bernie. "Who were you expecting?"

"Come in here, quick. I'm glad you're here. I need help," he called.

I threw the bags onto the sofa, hurried into the bedroom, and gasped.

A stranger in an undershirt and dark pants was bleeding to death on my new bedspread. A bright red stain was spreading out from his shoulder. His thin gray hair was matted with blood. One side of his face was smeared with it and he was sweating like crazy. There was blood seeping down the side of the bedspread, pooling onto the powder blue carpeting.

"Oh my God, oh my God, oh my God," I chanted, taking a step back, wanting to run from the room but paralyzed with fright.

The man's eyes had been closed. At the sound of my voice, he opened them and tried to look at me. He was so far gone he couldn't focus. His eyes were out of control, rolling wildly. The part of his face that wasn't covered with blood was ashen, slick with sweat, practically paler than the bedspread.

Bernie was standing next to the bed holding a bloody rag that turned out to be the guy's shirt. "Listen to me," he said. "I need your help. I've got to get the bullet out."

"What bullet? What happened? Who is he?"

"Never mind who is he. Get me some water. Towels. The sharpest steak knife you can find—"

"No. No. No." I was shaking my head. I was afraid to look at Bernie. I was afraid to look at the stranger in the bed. I just watched the stain on the carpeting grow. "No, Bernie. We've got to get him to a hospital, call an ambulance, get help. He's bleeding, Bernie. He's dying."

"Sandy. Not now. Don't go nuts on me now. Just do what I ask, okay?" He was eerily calm and serious. "He's been shot. We can't take him to a hospital. It's out of the question. I'm going to take care of him. Now, get me the knife."

"Who is he? Who shot him? Is that his gun out there?"

"Why, is it bothering you, the gun? Don't touch it. Leave it exactly where it is. Don't touch the gun. Don't question me. Just do what I told you and do it right now, Sandy."

I raced to the kitchen, crying and shaken. Fumbling in the kitchen drawer looking for the sharpest knife I could find, I began ranting aloud. "He's going to die," I said bitterly, "on my side of the bed! Bernie killed him and laid him out on my side? Why didn't he put him on his own side of the bed!''

"Sandy, hurry up!''

I was a crazy person, a lunatic. But Bernie's voice cut through the insanity. I grabbed a knife, filled a big pot with hot water from the sink. Put another pot of water up to boil. Grabbed a couple of clean dishtowels and ran back to the bedroom.

"Okay. Hold the water. Just stand there,'' Bernie said. He took the knife and bent over the guy on the bed and started to cut into him like a surgeon. The bleeding man screamed bloody murder. I closed my eyes and started trembling so hard that water washed over the top of the big pot, splashing my blouse and skirt and shoes. When the screaming stopped, I opened my eyes and saw that the guy had passed out.

Bernie was still hunched over him, digging into his shoulder. I remember thinking how calm, almost professional, Bernie seemed. The nerve in his neck was absolutely still. Then a wave of nausea nearly knocked me to my knees.

Bernie said, "Got it.'' And started mopping the guy up. He took the bullet into the bathroom and flushed it, I think. I was still standing there, paralyzed, holding the pot of water with the bloody towels in it.

"You look a little green,'' Bernie said when he came back into the room. "You did great, babe. Go ahead, get out of here. I'll finish up. Make me a cream cheese and onion on a bagel.''

I had two cigarettes going and a scotch in my hand when Bernie came into the kitchen. I'd left a cigarette in the living room next to the couch where I'd sat with my head between my knees for five minutes after leaving the bedroom. Bernie brought the lit cigarette into the kitchen with him. When he saw that I had another one going in my mouth, he frowned at me, shook his head, and doused the first one under the tap.

I handed him the plate with his favorite supper on it—toasted bagel, cream cheese, tomato, and red onion. If he had a lecture prepared on leaving lit cigarettes around the house, he never got a chance to deliver it.

"Who is that man?'' I asked. "Bernie, I have a right to know. What if he dies here? What if the police come? What am I supposed to say? I live here. I'm your wife. You want me to make believe a guy I never saw before in my life isn't lying in there bleeding to death on my side of the bed? Who shot him? How did he get here?''

"Don't ask me about my business, Sandy,'' he said.

Terrific, I thought. Standard wise guy answer. I was all set to start in on him again. My nerves were as raw as the red onion on his plate when, suddenly, Bernie did what Bernie did best—a 180-degree turn. "Listen, baby,'' he said, in a suddenly exhausted voice. "I'm really glad you showed up. I needed your help. You did a good job. You're a stand-up broad, Sandy. I'm proud of you.''

He walked out of the kitchen with the sandwich.

I knew Bernie's don't-ask-me-about-my-business spiel by heart. I knew, also, that for the most part it was to protect me, to keep me ignorant of anything that could get *me* in trouble as well as him. And, for the most part, I did try to stay out of his business. I wanted to be a good "racket club" wife. And that meant, no questions.

But I was also a Jewish wife. And that meant, no secrets.

Bernie had the same problem. He was a wise guy, he lived a tough life by a tight code. He was supposed to be careful who he trusted, careful who he talked to. There were certain things he wasn't supposed to tell me—for my own good, for his safety, for the sake of preserving the rules and rituals of a certain way of life.

But he was Jewish, too. And he wanted a real wife, not just an armpiece; not just a kid who looked up to him, but a partner he could respect and trust. I wanted so much to be that person. I knew he was training me to be that person. But it was a slow, cautious process and in an emergency, like the one we faced that night, neither of us was sure I was ready.

Although I hadn't stopped asking questions or demanding answers since I'd laid eyes on the bleeding man, when all was said and done, I wasn't sure I really wanted to hear the truth, the whole truth and nothing but . . . I was very scared. All I wanted was for Bernie to reassure me that we were safe.

It could have been him in that bed, I thought. It could even have been me.

Later that evening while Pinky, which was what the wounded man's name turned out to be, slept in our bed, Bernie and I camped out in the living room—and talked.

"Is he going to live?"

"Yeah. He'll be fine. I'll get him out of here in the morning."

"Good," I said. "Could you move the gun at least? Get it out of the foyer, get it out of my sight?"

"Leave it. It's not bothering you."

We'd had a couple of drinks by then. Bernie had smoked a little grass. We had a long L-shaped couch in the new apartment and I was lying down on the loveseat part of it and Bernie had the four-cushion side. "What happened to him?" I asked again.

"He's a jerk. He tried to hit Red Dillon."

"Red Dillon from uptown?" I remembered the tall, thin, light-skinned gangster I'd met at Cokey's bar. I remembered being told he was quick and dangerous. "The one you always say would shoot you first and ask questions later?"

"Red owed Pinky money. Pinky decided to collect. He knew Red would be at this garage uptown. Pinky is all balls, no brains. He pulled a rifle on

Red Dillon in bright daylight in the middle of Harlem. Dumb bastard threatens Red. Red's bodyguard put a hole in him.''

The telephone rang. Bernie said, "Only if it's Hot Dog or Vinny. Otherwise, I'm not in." The phone always rang a lot—it was Bernie's lifeline to the world; to business, betting, breathing. That night, it rang more than usual. And each time, I'd answer it and say the caller's name aloud. "Oh, hiya, Carmine," I'd say. And Bernie would shake his head no. "Sorry, he's not here," I'd say. "I'll tell him to call you."

"Are the cops going to come, Bernie?" I asked him.

"I hope not."

"Is anybody else going to come here?"

He shrugged. "I don't think so. If they do, you don't know Pinky. You don't know Red Dillon. You never heard these names."

"How did he get here?"

"He was in trouble. He called me."

"Everyone calls you when they're in trouble," I said. "Everyone comes to you. You're too good. You'll get in trouble."

"Nah," Bernie said. "It doesn't matter, anyway. As long as I do the right thing."

We must have talked until five in the morning. Every fifteen minutes, Bernie would get up and check on his patient. He did a hell of a job. Pinky walked out on his own steam about noon the next day. I never saw him again.

Bernie made a phone call in the morning, then he got Pinky a clean shirt and a raincoat. I think they wrapped the shotgun in the raincoat. I think they must have gone down to the basement garage and that a car—sent by whoever Bernie had spoken to that morning—was waiting there to whisk Pinky away, because Bernie returned to the apartment alone less than fifteen minutes later.

In the short time he'd been away, I'd peeked into the bedroom, seen the blood again and broken down sobbing uncontrollably. I was making a pot of coffee when he returned. He saw that I'd been crying. He put his arms around me.

"I can't live this way, Bernie. It's too scary. This isn't the life I want," I blurted out, almost ashamed to admit it, as though I were letting him down.

"I know, baby. It's okay," he said, as my tears spilled onto his shoulder. "You're right. It's no way to live. Sandy," he said, "it'll never happen again. I swear to you. I'm going to give you the life you want and deserve. Just be patient, baby."

"Really?" I said, stepping back and studying his face. "Really, Bernie, you'll go straight? We'll live like normal people?"

"I swear it to you, Sandy. I promise," he said.

CHAPTER EIGHT

Roman Holiday

I reminded Bernie of that promise every chance I got. But to be honest about it, I didn't always hate the crazy life we were living. It took me places and taught me things "normal" people never experienced. And while danger was the downside—coming home to find guys bleeding in your bed, hearing that a friend you hadn't seen for a while was turning up in pieces around the city, keeping secrets, telling lies, being constantly careful of what you said to whom—it was almost always mixed with a sense of excitement and adventure that was elating and addictive.

For the most part, Bernie kept me out of his business. I was the one who'd ask too many questions and catch him half-asleep or trick him during a fight into telling me more than he wanted me to know. As much as I wanted a decent normal life for us, I also wanted the fun, excitement, and privileges of life in the fast lane.

Of course, I didn't admit that to myself as a twenty-two-year-old new-lywed. And if I didn't have absolute faith in Bernie's commitment to re-form, at least I had hope. After all, he had said we'd be married one day, and we were. How much more nagging could it take for him to make good on this new promise? My fantasies of living a normal life blossomed.

So, of course, when Bernie came home all excited one afternoon in early September and announced that we were going to Rome, Italy, I jumped on him with gratitude and joy.

"Oh, honey, we're going to have a belated honeymoon!" I cried, like any upstanding citizen of Picket Fence, Suburbia. "I'm so excited. When are we going?"

"Tomorrow," he said.

"Oh, my God, so soon? I can't. I don't have clothes. I've got to shop, pack. And what about passports? Don't we have to get passports?"

"Not necessarily," Bernie said. He was carrying a leather briefcase. He put it down on a barstool, opened it, and pulled out two passports. "Hot Dog's bringing over your wig in a half-hour—"

"Wig?" I asked cautiously. I could feel those fantasies withering on the vine.

"I want you to put on some makeup," Bernie continued, tossing one of the passports to me. "A lot of makeup, baby. And the wig. Then the Dog'll take you to get the photo made and we'll put it on your passport."

I opened the passport book. "Who's Sally Mason?" I asked.

"That's you."

"Bernie, why do we need this? Why can't we just go like normal people?"

" 'Cause we're not doing something normal, baby. This is a very special trip. Listen, I've got to run out for an hour. Don't let that bag out of your sight, okay? And don't let anyone in here but Red. And, Sandy, you can't tell anyone we're going, you understand? Not even your mother. Now, move, sweetheart. *Shmear* on that makeup. I'll be back soon."

I stared at the door as it slammed shut after him. Then I looked at the briefcase sitting on the barstool.

Okay, don't ask questions. Just do what he told you to do. Go into the bedroom, sit down at your dressing table, and turn yourself into Sally Mason, said my mob-wife mind. But my Jewish feet made a beeline for that briefcase. What I saw inside confused me. Paper. Not money but certificates of some kind, in denominations ranging from $5,000 to $50,000. I was a kid. I'd never even heard of bearer bonds, but that's what they were. Payment notes entitling the bearer to hard cash—to the tune of hundreds of thousands of dollars.

I closed the briefcase and carried it with me into the bedroom.

Forget it, I told myself as I attacked my makeup with trembling hands. Who knows what they really are or why he's got them. Maybe he's holding them for a friend, maybe they have nothing to do with this trip. My mind and heart raced as I pencilled on thick black doe eyes, and pasted false eyelashes big as spiders onto my aquamarine shadowed lids.

Hot Dog Red rang the bell about five minutes before Bernie returned. He handed me a hat box in which was a long, trashy, platinum-blond wig.

"So you're going off to meet the Pope," he said, chuckling, as I pinned up my hair to try on the wig.

"We're going to Rome. I've never been to Europe, Red. This is my first trip ever. I'm so excited," I said honestly. "There's so much I want to see! I want to go to all the museums. And see the fountain where you throw in coins and make wishes like in the movies. And shopping!"

To tell the truth, I was even excited about stealing towels and bringing home soap from the best hotels. I thought about being pinched on the street by men who looked like Marcello Mastroianni and about kneeling before the Pope wearing a black lace handkerchief on my head like Jacqueline Kennedy.

"Who knows, maybe we *will* have an audience with the Pope," I kidded Red back. But in my extravagant daydreams, even that was possible.

When Bernie walked in, I said, "Do they let Jewish people meet the Pope? Do you think we could do that?"

He winked at Red. "Well, baby," he said. "I don't know about the Pope, but you might get to meet a couple of friends of his."

I could barely sleep that night.

"I can't wait to see Rome," I said, snuggling against him in bed. "It'll be so romantic."

On the plane the next day, my head was itching like mad from the blonde wig. I had to go into the bathroom every fifteen minutes to scratch my scalp. Grabbing every headrest en route for balance, I tottered up the aisle of the plane in the dark glasses, five-inch heels, and tight skirt Bernie had me wearing. He thought it made me look like a typical American tourist. I thought I looked like Bimbo the Wonder Whore.

"Do I have to wear this wig and stuff the whole time we're in Rome?" I asked.

"You can take it off when we get to the hotel," he promised.

We were staying at the Hassler, which was next to a beautiful church at the top of the Spanish Steps. Our room was comfortable and clean, not the presidential suite, but with a breathtaking view of Rome.

As soon as we were alone, I took off the wig and threw it onto the bed. "Oh, God, I want to take a shower and then I want to go for a walk. Did you see the city? It's gorgeous. So many fountains and statues and bridges and scooters!"

"We're not going out today," Bernie said.

"But it's still early. Why not?"

"We're here for business, not pleasure," he said. "Tomorrow morning, you'll put on that little black dress I got you. And the wig and the sunglasses. And then we're going to the Vatican—"

"The Vatican? That's the first place you want to see? What's wrong with you?"

"We're not going there sightseeing, Sandra. I told you, it's strictly business."

"In the Vatican? We're Jewish. What kind of business?"

"I've got to pick up some money," Bernie said.

I waited. I thought he was going to say: I've got to pick up some money *and then* we're going over to the Vatican and . . . But no, apparently it was a complete sentence. I didn't get it. "What's that got to do with the Vatican?" I asked.

We'd both had a couple of drinks on the plane. Now Bernie pulled out a joint he'd had stashed and lit up. "You looked in the briefcase," he said, with a little grin. It wasn't a question. He knew me. "You saw the bonds."

"That's what they are? Bonds?"

"Go shut the curtains, Sandy."

"I want to see the city. It's bad enough I can't go outside. Can't I at least *look* at Rome?"

"Not this trip, baby."

"I know, I know." I sighed and drew the curtains shut. "Strictly business, right?"

"Right. Go ahead, now. Count the bonds."

"I don't feel like it." I threw myself onto the bed and started pulling out the bobbypins that had held my real hair up inside the wig. "Anyway, I know there are a lot of them. So what does the Vatican have to do with it?"

"The Vatican has its own bank. You didn't know that, did you?"

He was teaching me again. And I was in no mood now. Still, what he was saying was news to me. "They have a bank?"

Bernie nodded. "They've got one of the richest portfolios in the world."

"So what are we going to do there, cash in the bonds?" I was being sarcastic.

That little grin widened. "You got it," he said.

"I don't believe it. You're kidding," I insisted. And even when Bernie shook his head at my naiveté I was still dumbfounded, I still thought he had to be joking. "We're taking the bonds to the *Vatican*, Bernie? We're going to cash them there?"

He took another toke of pot, then knocked off the ash on the bottom of his shoe. "First thing tomorrow morning," he said. "We go get the money. We're back in the room. One-two-zipola, then we're out of here. We never were here. Strictly business." Bernie dove onto the bed next to me. He was in a terrific mood. "It's a lot of money, baby. More than you've ever seen."

"Is it yours?"

"Not all of it."

"So who does it belong to, the racket club?"

"The racket club?"

"You know, the organization, the outfit—"

Bernie started to laugh. "That's what you call the boys, 'the racket club'?" He couldn't stop laughing.

"You're stoned," I said.

"You think so?" he said, brushing the bobby pins off the bed. "Come here. You know, you don't look half bad as a blonde. Maybe you ought to put that wig back on."

I did, the next morning. I wore the wig, the black dress, the sunglasses and, at Bernie's suggestion, I stuck two sticks of chewing gum into my mouth, the consummate tourist.

A car was waiting for us outside the hotel. The driver was a young Italian who looked more like a peasant than a jet-set Roman. His face was brown and lined from the sun. He was wearing a cap, baggy pants, and a black vest over shirtsleeves. He drove us to Saint Peter's Square, right through the wrought-iron gates into Vatican City. The car stopped in front of a beautiful church.

Bernie had a gold charm he always wore around his neck on a long gold rope. It had a Jewish star on one side and a Saint Christopher's medal on the other. The minute the car stopped in front of the church, he took off the necklace and turned it around.

"What are you doing?" I asked.

"Putting the Saint Christopher's medal face out. It's wrong for a Jewish God to walk into another God's house," he said.

I hadn't thought about it, but now I agreed with him. And, suddenly, I felt like it was wrong for a Jewish human to walk into another God's house, too—chewing gum, no less. Worrying and half-waiting for one God or another to show up and strike me dead, I held Bernie's hand and entered a magnificent chapel filled with gold ornaments, marble statues, and beautiful paintings.

There were worshippers in the church, kneeling at dark polished wooden pews. And there were a number of priests dressed in plain black cassocks. While I stared open-mouthed at the stained-glass windows and beautiful arched ceiling, Bernie stopped one of the priests and spoke to him in English. The priest signaled for Bernie to wait. And then he brought a younger priest over to us. The second man spoke English with a lovely Italian accent. Bernie mentioned a name to him and the young priest nodded and said, "Come with me, please."

He led us through the side door of the chapel down a long corridor, then showed us into a study. It was a big, high-ceilinged room with a large wooden desk that had a huge, velvet-covered armchair behind it and two highbacked wooden chairs in front of it. I sat in one of them. Bernie stood. The priest asked if we'd like some coffee and I said yes. And he left us.

All this time, Bernie was clutching the briefcase under one arm. The priest returned with a tray of coffee for me. A second priest entered. Bernie said, "Baby, I'll be right back," and he left with both of them.

I was terribly nervous. I sat there sipping the espresso, I guess it was, and looking at the brocade hangings and the beautiful red patterned rug and the oil paintings of saints and churchmen, cardinals, maybe—what did I know about Vatican rank?—and thinking the most ridiculous thoughts. I wondered, did Jews do the same thing? Did they have their own bank or was it just the *goyim*? I wasn't sure about the bonds, either. Was Bernie doing someone a legitimate favor or were the boys involved? There'd been a Wall Street heist in the papers a couple of months back, a really big one, and there'd been a lot of talk about mob involvement in it. Were these the stolen bonds, was this a mission for the mob? Then I started wondering if cops would bust in suddenly. And I was very nervous and staring at the door and then I thought, well, maybe the Pope will walk in instead. By mistake, even. That would be interesting.

When the door finally did open, it was Bernie with the young priest. He was holding the case in front of him. He patted it and winked at me and I knew he had gotten the money.

The same driver was waiting for us just outside the church. In the car, Bernie signaled me not to say anything and we rode back to the hotel in silence. The briefcase on his lap seemed almost spotlit to me, so hot it was practically smoking. He hugged it to his chest as we entered the hotel, rode up the elevator, and finally returned to our room.

In the car on the way back it began to hit me about this business trip. Bernie had taken a briefcase full of bearer bonds into the Vatican and come back out again with cash. Though I hadn't seen the money yet, I was sure of it. I wondered again whether the bonds belonged to "the boys." And if they had, did that mean the Vatican was fencing for the mob?

Yes, and they'd been doing it for years, was what Bernie said back at the hotel.

"Where did the bonds come from?" I asked him, tearing the wig off again and throwing it onto the bed.

"You don't need to know," he said.

"Is it from the heist that was in the papers?"

"You don't need to know. You don't want to know. Case closed, baby."

"Okay. So *now* can we go out?" I said, I think just to irritate him.

"No."

"Isn't there a safe in the hotel where you can leave it?"

"No." Bernie set the briefcase down on the bed. "It stays here and we stay here." He drew the shades again.

I'd been edgy all morning. I'd become almost desperate to do something normal, walk around without the goddamn wig, see the city, be a real tourist. Anything to get rid of the nervousness, the fear, I guess, the sense of danger that had walked into the Vatican with me. Now I knew absolutely that I wasn't going anywhere but home tomorrow, that I was really stuck in the hotel room. I was annoyed, angry, frustrated. "Great," I griped. "Join the mob and see the world!"

"Don't say I never took you anywhere," Bernie teased me the next morning on the plane.

"When can we come back and do it for real?" I asked. We were sitting side by side, holding hands.

"It's not over yet," he said. "Now, listen. When we get home, don't talk on the phone. If anyone asks where you were, where we were, we were in and out. Anyone tried to reach us, we were just around. You don't tell anyone about Rome. Tillie you can tell. Your mother's okay. But not on the phone, Sandy. The phone is your worst enemy. The phone is a weapon."

"Again with the teaching?" I said.

"You think I'm going to be around forever? What're you going to do when I'm gone?" Bernie said. "You've got to be smart. You've got to learn. I don't want anyone taking advantage of you."

I didn't want to hear it. I didn't want to know it. Sure, Bernie was more than twenty years older than I. Sure, he was a sick man with a dangerous heart condition and a life-style to match. But death wasn't what I wanted to think about right then, right there.

I pulled away from him and stared gloomily out the window at the field of clouds we were plowing through—a field that suddenly took on the sinister look of heaven.

"I thought you said we were going to live like normal people," I grumbled. "You promised me. So what good will all this information do me, knowing stuff like 'the phone is a weapon'?"

He gave me a look. Then he shook his head and sighed. "Normal?" he said. "Sandy, for me, this *is* normal, baby."

CHAPTER NINE

The Gold Coast

A couple of weeks after our Roman holiday, Bernie was restless and ready for action again. It was late September. The weather was lousy. He'd been hanging around the house a lot. He'd caught a cold, which made him irritable and demanding. And also meant that Dr. Sealy practically moved in with us.

Autumn in New York was no picnic for Bernie. And Bernie, hanging around the house, restless, irritable and demanding, was no picnic for me. Bored, he was like a tiger in a cage. Bored *and sick* he was like a tiger with a toothache—snarling, growling, pacing, unpredictable, dangerous. When I wasn't shopping for him, cooking for him, running errands for him, answering the phone for him, delivering messages for him, giving him his medication and making coffee, drinks, and putting out ashtrays, pastrami, and pickles for the condolence callers, and cleaning up afterwards, I gave him plenty of distance.

About a minute before that first sneeze laid him low, Bernie had been talking about going to Miami for the winter. And boy was I thrilled when

Dr. Sealy gave him the go-ahead. I'd never been to Florida. And if Bernie's descriptions of broad white beaches, palm tree-lined avenues, palatial hotels, kidney-shaped swimming pools, and endless sunshine had enticed me before he got sick, after three weeks locked up in the house with him, I was ready to take off on my own.

Late October, we packed up the car, let the street dirt and dying leaves whirl away behind us, and drove South leisurely, in great spirits. Bernie was very relaxed and feeling good. The trip took five days. And as he drove, Bernie pointed out the sights, and talked about Florida, what we'd do and who we'd see.

"You'll get to meet Farvel," he promised. "And who knows, maybe even Meyer." Bernie loved Farvel, whose real name was Philly Kovolick, his mentor from the Lower East Side ghetto decades ago. Farvel was Meyer Lansky's wall, Bernie said. Thick, dependable, hard as stone. You had to go through him to get to Meyer.

Bernie loved Farvel, but he revered Meyer. He called him "the old man." The old man, he said, had been a postwar pioneer, practically single-handedly transforming Florida into "the Gold Coast." Everyone who was anyone had followed Meyer Lansky south in the late forties and early fifties—from Cleveland, Philadelphia, Boston, New York, the *gantse mishpocheh,* the whole family, had bought homes and real estate there and wintered in splendor near where their money was invested.

Meyer had left them for Cuba. If the old man had made Florida "the Gold Coast," he'd turned Havana into a diamond mine, Bernie said. But Fidel Castro's revolution had defeated Lansky's partner, the Cuban president, and closed the lavish clubs and casinos. The "syndicate" had been forced to leave everything.

Now Meyer was back in Florida, living with his second wife, Teddy, whom he'd met while she was a manicurist in a mob-run hotel. Bernie had never met Teddy. He'd never really socialized with Meyer Lansky. He knew of her only through Farvel. But you never could tell, he said, maybe we'd get a chance to meet her this trip.

I can still remember my first palm tree. Bernie pointed it out to me somewhere above Palm Beach. And then, farther south, we began to see the hotels along the ocean. We drove down Collins Avenue past the Thunderbird and the Castaways, down toward the soaring, sprawling hotels of Miami Beach. In the waterway across the road from the Fontainbleau was a huge, gaudy, Chinese-style houseboat.

"Guess who owns that?" Bernie asked. It turned out to be the loveboat our friendly neighborhood abortionist Hattie Prince had built for a well-known New York saloon keeper she was keeping. And next to Hattie's junk was a yacht called *Ocean's Eleven,* named for the recent movie that had starred Frank Sinatra and his "rat pack" pals.

From Collins Avenue, we drove into a beautiful street aptly named Pine

Tree Drive and there, at the end of a circular driveway, was the house Bernie had rented for us.

"Oh, my God, is it really ours? It's gorgeous, Bernie!" I cried. And when I say "I cried," I mean it literally. As he led me from room to room through the spacious, airy house, my eyes misted. I was utterly overwhelmed. Not only were the rooms twice the size of those in our New York apartment, but there was a full dining room, a pantry, a laundry room and a "Florida Room" with a pink and gray terrazzo-tiled floor and three walls of jalousied windows that opened onto a big backyard with palm trees and exquisite hibiscus plants and a blue, kidney-shaped swimming pool.

Our first weeks in Florida were spent seeing the town. We had steaks at the Epicure, overstuffed sandwiches at Wolfies, blintzes at Pumperniks. We ate ribs and chicken at the piano bar in the Barnfire, bet bundles at the dog track, the race track, the trotters, and Jai Lai, caught the shows at the Fontainbleau and Eden Roc, had drinks at the Racket Club and watched, through a plate glass window at the bar, people swimming underwater at the Castaways.

But as we began to settle in, Bernie would disappear for hours during the day. Sometimes he'd have to go back to New York for business. I was left by myself for long stretches of time in a strange place where I knew no one. Or else Bernie and I were constantly together for days on end and that could drive me crazy, too. I had no friends of my own in Florida. I didn't know how to get around. It wasn't like New York, a place where you could walk practically anywhere and take a bus or subway everywhere else. So when Bernie took the car I was stranded, and when Bernie was home I had to depend on him to take me places. Weeks became months and I became as bored, restless, and irritable as he'd been before we left New York.

"Do something with yourself. Get a hobby. Learn something," advised Mr. Self-Improvement.

"Like what?"

"Like what would you like to do? What do you wish you could do?"

"Play the guitar," I decided.

"Okay," Bernie said.

"Well, I don't have a guitar. And I don't know how to play, so I guess I'd need lessons."

"Fine," he said.

Bernie being Bernie, two days later the equipment came rolling in: a metallic-red electric guitar, speakers, an amplifier, what looked to me like enough electrical equipment to short-circuit the East Coast. And the day after that, a guitar instructor showed up. A very nice, very serious young man who meant well and had tremendous patience.

I was very attentive. I worked hard at it. The instructor said I had to cut my fingernails if I wanted to play. With tears and trepidation, I cut my fingernails. I practiced chords. I strained to hear if the guitar was out of tune. I tried to learn how to tune it. I had no aptitude whatsoever. Two weeks and thousands of dollars later, the only thing I could play was "My Dog Has Fleas."

"What counts is you tried," Bernie consoled me. "Take off that halter top, it's too low-cut." He had an appointment with Farvel up at the Castaways. I was going to do a little shopping in Surfside, then pick him up after the meeting.

"I'm going to be in the car the whole time, right? I'm just dropping you off."

"Like that, you are. Get dressed. Put on a nice blouse. Maybe I'll introduce you."

I hadn't met Farvel yet. I hadn't met any of the real players, just a couple of nightclub owners, numbers guys, bar flies, and track touts. I changed into a pretty white pique blouse with candy-striped pink and white Toreadors and high-heeled sandals. I put on a pair of hoop earrings, tied a pink bandana around my head, and teased the hair behind it until I looked like a real Miami Beach lioness.

"That's better," Bernie approved. "Now I'm proud to show you off."

"I feel bad about the money we wasted on the guitar lessons," I said as we drove up Collins Avenue. "But I've been thinking about what you said. About learning things, improving myself."

Bernie laughed. "I can feel the pain in my wallet now. How much is it going to cost me this time?"

"I want to sing."

"I'll shut off the radio."

"Stop it. You know what I mean. I want to take singing lessons. I think I could really do it, Bernie. I'm young, I'm pretty. How hard can it be to sing?"

"We'll talk about it later," he said, as we pulled up to the Castaways. "Right now, I've got to meet Farvel for lunch and a *shvitz*. Pick me up in an hour."

It was just like in New York. Bernie used to go down to the Luxor Baths to talk business in the steam room with guys who'd come in from out of town. Jewish guys from the midwest, New England, Las Vegas, and Florida steaming together like *kreplach* in soup. The *shvitz,* they called it. The sweat box. They'd sit with cigars clamped in their teeth, towels wrapped around their bellies, sweat pouring off them, attendants dousing them with cold water, while they caught up with world and local events. And then, pink and shiny, they'd waddle into the restaurant at the Baths and load up on pickled herring, borscht, and chopped egg salad.

The Castaways in North Miami Beach looked nothing like the Luxor

Baths, however. It was a big, luxurious, sprawling hotel that had its own yacht basin and was designed to resemble a shipwrecked pirate's palace. The Teamsters owned it. And when I drove up to get Bernie, he was standing outside talking to someone I figured was a union official from up north. His skin was so white that I assumed he was just down for business. No one who lived in Florida could be that pale, I thought.

Bernie waved me over and I got out of the car and walked toward them. The union guy barely looked at me. He was about B's height and thickly built—like a wall—which should have given me a clue. The man was several years older than Bernie, but his hair was still thick and dark. He had thick Edward G. Robinson lips, which were wrapped around a forgotten cigar that waggled as he talked with Bernie.

"Farvel," Bernie said, "this is my little girl, my baby."

Farvel the Stick shook his head from side to side. "This is some baby," he said, grinning approvingly. I nodded at him. I *was* a baby, a twenty-two-year-old kid who, if you said hello to me, would be stuck for an answer. Especially in front of a man I'd been hearing about for years.

Bernie was beaming at me.

"Nice to meet you," I managed.

"Come on." Farvel took my arm and said to Bernie, "He's right inside. He should meet her." He led me into the hotel lobby.

Two men, deep in conversation, were walking toward us. One was tall, slender, and elegant-looking. The other was very short and tan, wearing moccasins with a cabana suit of beige shorts and a matching jacket. He had a lined face and long nose and looked like a mild-mannered accountant who'd spent a hard-earned vacation day sunbathing beside a pool.

"Meyer," Farvel said to him, "this is the kid's wife. Ain't she a cutie?"

Meyer Lansky nodded his head at me. "A pleasure to meet you," he said. "Bernie says you're going to be a singer."

Bernie and Farvel laughed. The tall, lean man extended his hand to me. "Good luck," he said.

"Sandy, this is Jimmy." Bernie introduced me to Jimmy Blue Eyes, one of Meyer's Italian associates.

I'm sure I blushed. "How do you do?" I said.

"Okay, kid," Farvel said to Bernie, deftly steering us toward the lobby doors again. "Good to see you. Sandy, don't be a stranger." Without taking the cigar out of his mouth, he leaned forward and buzzed my cheek. "You need something, call my Minnie. What the hell's she got to do all day anyhow?"

Bernie was very proud of me. He was also proud that I'd seen him with Meyer Lansky and Farvel and Jimmy Blue Eyes, men he idolized but rarely saw. He was in a terrific mood, full of gossip and inside information, as we drove back home. I could see how thrilled he was to have spent the afternoon with the old man. "Oh, does he hate Castro," I remember Bernie saying. I remember it because it was hard for me to believe that a little, slight man like that could hate anyone. He seemed too peaceful to be that passionate.

"I can't believe you told Meyer Lansky that I was going to be a singer," I said.

"Why not? You are, aren't you?"

Of course, within a week, I was taking singing lessons. Some mornings my voice coach would come to our house; some mornings I'd meet him for my hour's lesson at the club where he sang nights and played the piano. I thought I was coming along fine. But I was probably so busy belting my heart out that I never saw him wincing.

One morning, as I was getting ready to go out for a voice lesson, I heard men's voices in the kitchen and the sound of things being scraped along the floor. I walked into the kitchen just as the men were leaving and saw three crates that looked like coffins piled one on top of another in the corner of the kitchen.

"What's going on?" I asked Bernie, who was hurrying past me on his way to the bedroom.

"I'm going out of town for a couple of days and I want you to stay in the house and not leave."

"What do you mean, 'not leave'?" I said, following him. "I've got a singing lesson in fifteen minutes."

He was tossing clothes into a small suitcase. "I mean not leave today, tomorrow, the next day. I need you to watch those boxes for me. I mean do not set foot outside this house until I get back."

"What's in them?"

"None of your business," he replied predictably.

I thought about it for a minute. "Okay, then, I'll ask Barry to come here for my lessons."

"Over my dead body. You don't talk to Barry or anyone but me. You don't let in anyone but me. You don't go out for anything until I get back. You need food, order it over the telephone. And I'm going to be calling to make sure you're here, Sandy, so don't fool around, okay? If anyone else calls looking for me, I'm out fishing. I'm sleeping. I'm at the track—just don't make conversation."

"Yeah, I know. The phone is my worst enemy. The phone is a weapon," I recited sarcastically.

He raised an eyebrow at me. I checked his neck for vein movement. I thought I could see a little twitch getting started. I left the bedroom.

The first day and night went by. I watched TV, I practiced singing in the mirror. I started to get claustrophobic. The next day, I left the kitchen and sat outside on the patio, I went swimming, I tossed coconuts around the backyard and cut flowers. The third day, I thought about just taking a walk around the block. But by then I knew I couldn't. Bernie was phoning me about ten times a day to make sure I was home.

The miracle was that it took three whole days before I broke into the crates. I found some tools in the garage and, standing on a kitchen chair, I pried open the top box. My worst fear was that there might be a body inside. No, maybe my worst fear was that there'd be *parts* of a body inside. I never even considered what was actually in the crates—guns. There were enough guns inside those coffin-sized boxes to start a new revolution in Cuba.

"Shit," I said aloud to myself. "I'm baby-sitting guns!" Then, "Shit," I said, staring at the splintered top of the crate, "he'll see that I looked in and he'll get all excited." I ran back out to the garage, and got a hammer and nails and repaired the top as best I could. Bernie kept phoning. I kept my vigil. I walked in circles around the pool like a guy exercising in a prison yard. And as I walked, my imagination went wild. I thought of how Meyer hated Castro and how Bernie loved Meyer and I wondered if, indeed, the guns were destined for Havana.

I know that Bernie did occasionally do favors for Meyer, personal favors. I remember in New York a few years later, he got a telephone call in the middle of the night and ran out of the house with a raincoat on over his pajamas to get Meyer's daughter, whose name was also Sandy, out of a jam she'd gotten into at the Copa.

I never found out about the guns, though. Within an hour of Bernie's return, the crates disappeared from the kitchen. He was in a great mood and I was relieved that he was back and that he hadn't noticed the boxes had been tampered with.

"I've got a surprise for you, baby," he said. I'd been *hocking* him about singing in public, about launching my career. "I spoke to Moey," he said, mentioning a friend of his who owned a disco in Hallendale. "And you're going to open at his place. It's all arranged."

My singing teacher wasn't sure I was ready. Finally, he capitulated, saying that I'd probably make up in enthusiasm for what I lacked in skill. He worked out arrangements for me and instrumentals for the little backup group we'd hired. Bernie helped me pick out a stunning full-length gown. He bought out the disco for the night and packed it with every local character he could find. He didn't invite Meyer or Farvel, thank God. But there were enough people sitting out front when I peeked before the show to drive me to drink.

The champagne Bernie had bought me was already open in the dressing room. I sipped and paced and sipped and touched up my makeup and refilled the glass and sipped and stared at the blurring words to the songs I'd taped onto the mirror. I was so scared that my hands started shaking as I poured and sipped another glass of champagne.

By the time the M.C. announced, "And here, making her singing debut, is the lovely Miss Sandy Barton!" I was totally bombed. In my showstopping evening gown, I stumbled on stage and stood clutching the microphone, swaying, petrified. The band played the opening bars. I opened my mouth. Nothing came out. The group started over. Still nothing. My heart started thudding. My eyes blurred. The last thing I saw was Bernie sitting ringside, all dressed up in his tuxedo.

"God, let the earth open up and swallow me," I prayed. Then I passed out cold.

I came to in the dressing room and started crying. But Bernie took me in his arms and soothed me. "Don't worry, sweetheart. It's okay," he whispered, smoothing back my hair, patting my cheek. "Everything's okay, *mamela*. Don't cry."

Bernie knew how lonely and bored I'd been. He'd gone along with my wild schemes, he'd given me guitar lessons, tried to help me launch a singing career, and even flew Marlene and my mother down to Miami and entertained them royally, all so that I might be happy in Florida. But what I needed were friends and a social life of my own. Even this, Bernie tried to arrange for me.

He came home one day all excited. "We've been invited to lunch on Davey Yaras's yacht," he said, about a month after my singing career was nipped in the bud at Moey's disco. "Farvel and Minnie are going to be there. And Davey's wife, Blanche, who's like this," Bernie crossed his fingers, "with Teddy Lansky."

He was really pleased—for both us. Yaras was a heavy hitter from Chicago, a colleague of Meyer's, and a good friend of Farvel's. Socializing with Davey Yaras was a big step up from the run-of-the-mill Miami characters we'd been seeing.

Again, Bernie supervised my dressing. No shorts, no halter top. You didn't go to show off your legs on Davey Yaras's yacht. For slumming around at the dogtrack with the girlfriends and mistresses of low-level wise guys, shorts were occasionally permissible. But we were in the big time now. I was going to meet The Wives.

Yaras's yacht was docked at a boat basin somewhere between Fort Lauderdale and Hollywood. The first sight of it took my breath away. It was gleaming white and big as a ship, and carried its own full-sized speedboat aboard. A uniformed captain greeted us.

At the top of the steps was Farvel, white as the yacht and wearing a straw porkpie hat against the sun. An unlit cigar was clamped in his teeth. The only time I ever saw Farvel without a cigar was at his daughter's wedding, and only for the short time it took him to walk her down the aisle.

"It's the kid and his Mrs.," Farvel hollered, extending his hand and practically yanking Bernie onto the boat. "Minnie, come here. What the hell's the matter with you? Come say hello."

So the first of the Florida wives I met was the motherly Minnie Kovolicks, Farvel's heavyset, comfortable, long-suffering partner. *Hamisch* was the word for Minnie. Her expressions, the raised eyebrows, the shoulder shrug, the thin smile, ran a narrow gamut from accepting to tolerant. Decades of Farvel's good-humored Jewish abrasiveness had rounded off any edges Minnie might have had. "Look, a baby," she said of me. "Very pretty, Bernie. You got yourself a sweet little girl. And you," she confided, "you got some prize here."

As plain and soft-spoken as Minnie Kovolicks was, that's how extraordinary, outspoken, and fabulous Blanche Yaras seemed to me. She was a beautiful blonde, twenty years older than I and twice as glamorous. She was dressed in an exquisitely tailored, spotless linen pantsuit. Her brilliant blonde hair was rolled in a perfect soft page-boy. When she spoke, everyone listened. When she moved, a constellation of diamonds caught the sun. When Minnie walked me over to her, it was like being introduced to a spotlight.

"Blanche," Minnie began.

"What Blanche?" Farvel hollered. "Call her by her real name, her Jewish name. Bleema, Bleema we call this beauty. Am I right, Bleemela?"

Blanche Yaras smiled fully and graciously. "Of course, Farvel, darling," she said, laughing. "And you're Sandy? Oh, my God, Bernie, you robbed a cradle." Blanche patted my teased auburn hair and chucked me gently under the chin. "A beautiful little cradle. Davey!" Blanche commanded her husband before whom grown men and investigating senators quavered. "Get this gorgeous little girl of Barton's a drink."

I felt like a child, an awkward, starstruck kid. The minute I met Blanche Yaras I wanted to be her. She intimidated me and I remember watching her that day and thinking I want to grow up to intimidate a kid like me someday.

There was another couple on the yacht as well. The eight of us sat down to a beautiful luncheon around a handsomely set table on the forward deck. There were fresh flowers on the table, linen napkins in tortoise shell rings, crystal goblets for Farvel and Davey's seltzer, silver salt and pepper shakers, and a silver bread tray. And plenty of wine and laughter. Davey Yaras was a very good-looking man, tall and implacable. Every now and then he'd shake his head at Blanche's irrepressible comments and pronouncements, but it was clear that she was her own woman, brash, beautiful, and commanding.

When I admired a pin she was wearing, she said, "I'll give you my jeweler's name. Make him get you one." She tossed her head at Bernie.

She didn't lower her voice, either. "Get him to spend that money on you, honey. Get it before it's gone. And wear it."

Teddy Lansky gave me the same advice.

I don't know if it was Blanche Yaras's doing or Farvel's, but about a week after we spent the day on the Yarases' yacht, we were invited to dinner at the old man's house.

"What old man?" I asked Bernie, who'd come crashing through the hibiscus bushes and palmetto leaves with the happy news. I was sitting at the edge of the pool, swinging my legs in the water. He came around from the garage, beaming his big toothy smile at me.

"What old man?" He laughed. "Meyer," he said. "Meyer!"

I scrambled to my feet as if Meyer Lansky, himself, had entered the backyard with Bernie. "What do I wear? How am I supposed to look?"

I wasn't surprised when Bernie had the answer already. "Nothing low-cut. Nothing showy." But his teaching tone ended right there. "What am I going to bring him?" he wondered aloud, sounding almost as awestruck and uncertain as I felt. "Flowers, dessert, booze? What can you bring to a man like that?" And I was surprised to discover that this was Bernie's first invitation to Meyer's home, too.

For years, he'd been one of the boys, "the kid," a well-liked character but a floater, a loner, a rebel. Now that he was married, he was respectable. Like Farvel, like Meyer, he was a family man again. I'd become an asset he hadn't counted on. I was a sweet kid, a good girl—not a hooker, not a sharp broad—a wife.

I decided on a turquoise linen sheath and heels. I wrapped a turquoise bandana around my hair and pulled back the front and teased the back into an auburn explosion. Very chic, very "swinging," very sixties. Bernie decided to send flowers to Meyer's home, which I thought was a very sophisticated thing to do.

Meyer and Teddy were living then in a handsome, surprisingly unpretentious house up in Lauderdale, I think it was. The neighborhood was quiet and suburban, not one of the elegant gate-guard communities. And the house was spacious but very simple. A nice Florida home. Not a mansion.

Because of what I'd seen of the Yarases' life-style, I think I expected a servant to answer the Lanskys' door. I certainly didn't expect Farvel. But there he was, all spruced up in a loose-fitting dark suit and tie. Even his cigar seemed better dressed than usual. It wasn't the cold chewed stub he traditionally held in his teeth, but a full, freshly lit Havana.

"It's the kid," Farvel announced, leading Bernie and me into the Lanskys' ornately furnished, plushly carpeted livingroom where several couples were having cocktails and hors d'oeuvres. At Meyer Lansky's house this didn't mean champagne and caviar. Cocktails meant scotch and hors d'oeuvres meant chopped liver, which Minnie Kovolicks had prepared according to the old neighborhood recipe and shlepped over to the dinner party in a Tupperware bowl inside a brown paper bag. Minnie's *gehakte leber* was served in a cut crystal, silver-trimmed chalice with a silver bread basket full of cocktail rye.

Farvel walked us over to where Blanche Yaras was in the middle of telling a joke to Georgie Gordon. Georgie, who ran casinos for Meyer in Las Vegas, was called Geo and that was how, after she got to the punch line, Blanche introduced him to me. Bernie already knew Geo. While they did their "Hey, how you been? You look great," Blanche took my arm and walked me around, introducing me to some of the other women.

"Meyer's with Davey in the Florida room, they'll be back in a minute," she said. "Have you met Meyer yet?"

"Just once. Just to say hello," I admitted.

Blanche took my breath away all over again. She was larger than life—with jewelry to match. She patted my hand and said, "You look adorable. Smile, *mamela*. Don't be nervous. You're among friends here. Wait'll you meet Teddy." And, on cue, this incredible little doll came toward us from the dining room.

Blanche had beauty, a stunning figure, and great flair, but you could still think of her as a basic Jewish broad. Minnie looked like a Jewish Mother. But Teddy Lansky was a porcelain doll, a perfect blonde-on-blonde miniature. She was bone-thin and perfectly proportioned with fine features, a tiny nose, pale eyes, and a ready smile. Even in the high heels she wore under her floor-length brocade caftan and with her platinum hair piled on her head in a high French knot, she was tiny. Maybe four feet ten inches tall to my hulking five foot eight.

"So you're Sandy, Bernie Barton's wife," Teddy said. "Well, isn't he a lucky guy? Such a pretty girl. Isn't she, Blanche? I'm glad you could make it tonight," she said. "And thanks for the flowers. It was very thoughtful of you to send them."

"Oh, that was Bernie's idea," I said, then started blushing.

Teddy Lansky laughed. Then someone caught her eye and she patted my hand and excused herself. "Would you like a drink? Blanche knows where the bar is."

"Blindfolded," said Blanche.

I followed Blanche around that evening. I was excited but lost, definitely out of my element. A shy, smiling silence was the best I could do to hide the way I felt about myself, which was uncomfortable, tongue-tied, dull, dumb, and unattractive. The women around me were all older, all married to men of power. They'd raided their safety deposit boxes for dinner at Meyer's.

"This is Neddie from Boston. Yetta from Cincinnati. Ruchel from Detroit. Malka from New Jersey," Blanche would introduce them. I'd totter from one incredibly bejeweled wife to the next and, grand and glowing, they'd coo over me like pigeons in peacock's clothing.

"So young . . . So pretty . . . I'd kill for that skin!" they cooed.

It didn't matter what they said to me. They treated me kindly, protectively, like a little girl. But it was all I could do to walk with them, sit down to dinner with them. I wanted to learn how to be like them. And they tried to teach me.

"How cute," said one of the midwest wives, viewing the pearl and gold ring that had been Bernie's first gift to me. The hand that lifted mine to examine the ring was weighted down with about $50,000 worth of blindingly "cute" equipment. "You've got to meet Alan Pincus, my jeweler down here, Sandy. He's got a pair of diamond and pearl earrings that would be perfect with that ring. And don't tell me about 'can't afford it,' " she said, waving away my unspoken objection. "If that *mamzer* of yours won't give you the money, you'll stick your hand in his change pocket while he's sleeping and take what you need."

I was shocked. "Oh, I couldn't do that." I practically gulped.

Blanche winked at me. "You're young yet, sweetheart. You'll learn."

Meyer appeared just before dinner. He came in from the Florida room with Davey Yaras. He was wearing a very handsome double-breasted blue blazer with a silk tie and well-tailored navy linen trousers. He was only in his fifties then, but he looked like a really old man to me, small and frail. He appeared to be almost shuffling as he entered the room with Davey. Then I noticed that with his elegant outfit, he was wearing bedroom slippers and white socks!

Teddy, who was in her forties, was like the fountain of youth to Meyer. His whole appearance changed when he was around her. He was only five-four and, soaking wet, weighed maybe one thirty-five but standing next to Teddy he looked toweringly robust. You could tell he really adored her. His face changed when he looked at her, his tone of voice changed. He called her "darling" and "dear." It sounded so loving to me, so tender and sophisticated.

I couldn't help comparing Meyer and Teddy with Blanche and Davey or Bernie and me, who were the more commonplace "baby" and "sweetheart" kind of couples. And we were a touch of class compared to Farvel, whose terms of endearment to Minnie ran more to "What are you, crazy? What're you, deaf? What're you, stupid?"

We sat down to dinner at a long, handsomely set table in the dining room. Meyer was at one end and Teddy at the other. Beside Meyer's plate was a dinner bell, which he rang as soon as we were all seated. Two servants, a man and a woman, came in from the kitchen with a tureen of matzo ball soup. Everyone talked and tore pieces of bread and challah from the silver baskets while the soup was ladled out. Then there was a lot of laughter and slurping of soup and Farvel calling everyone by their Jewish names. I was down near Teddy's end of the table and she was extremely hospitable to me, asking me questions and smiling and generally trying to put me at ease.

All of a sudden I heard this bell ringing. Then clanging. No one stopped eating or speaking. No one seemed to have heard anything but me. I looked down at Meyer's end of the table and there he was ringing that dinner bell with all his might. "Where the hell are they?" he shouted. "What the hell's wrong with them. Clear away the goddamn soup already! *Zolst ligen in drerd, genavisha mamzers!*" he cursed the servants in Yiddish. And no one stopped eating for a minute but me. People were reaching across one another for the bowls of sauerkraut and pickled tomatoes, or passing bottles of seltzer with silver siphons or refilling their wine glasses.

Between every course, between the brisket and noodle pudding, the chicken and potatonick, there was Meyer in his handsome jacket with the jaunty handkerchief in his pocket, turning red and ringing the bell and letting loose a stream of Yiddish curses that would make a borscht belt comic blush.

Meyer was not really a typical loudmouth gangster. For the most part, he was conservative, quiet, and commanding. His Yiddish cursing was much funnier than it was frightening. And just as Meyer could lapse into a peculiar crudeness, so Farvel had a streak of gentility in him. He extended his love for Bernie to include me. And when he came up to New York, he often invited me to go shopping with him. Of course, I never said no.

We'd stroll the streets of the Lower East Side where Farvel had grown up with Meyer. Many of the merchants they'd known from their boyhood were still in business there. And Farvel, who always wore a hat in New York, a battered fedora that was as recognizable as his trademark cigar, would walk briskly through the narrow streets receiving greetings and nodding hello like royalty visiting a far-flung empire. I had to hurry to keep up with him. We'd stop into one shop after another along Rivington or Allen Street and Farvel would shmooze and bargain.

"What're you getting for seltzer now?" he'd ask a shopkeeper.

"For you, Mr. Kovolicks," most of them responded, "don't worry."

Farvel would smile his thick-lipped smile and order cases of seltzer, tuna fish, herring, jars of pickles and sauerkraut, cartons of toilet paper.

"Okay. Put it away. I'll have someone pick it up later," he'd say, and off we'd go to the next store. "How much do you pay for ketchup?" he'd ask me.

"Gee, Farvel, I don't know."

"Tuna fish—what're they getting up here for a can of tuna fish these days?"

"I don't know, Farvel. I just go to the supermarket and get what I need."

He couldn't believe it. "What kind of housewife are you?" he'd demand.
I'd hang on to his arm, scurrying alongside him as fast as I could while he
grumbled affectionately about me, about Bernie. "What's wrong with him?
You're married to a kid who doesn't know how to save two cents. He
spends crazy. Five-hundred-dollar suits?! Feh. The kid doesn't know the
meaning of money!''

Both his hands would be stuck in the pockets of his blue double-breasted
coat. The battered hat was pulled down low over his eyes, the cold cigar
waggled as he spoke. "You know, I put these guys in business years ago,"
he'd say, tossing his head at a two-by-four jewelry shop or clothing store
with Hebrew lettering in the windows. Or "I got his brother-in-law out of
a jam." Or "This one owes me a favor from World War II yet!"

On one of these outings Farvel dragged me into Robbins Handbags and
asked me to help him choose a pocketbook for Minnie and two for his
daughters. I did. Each bag cost over a hundred dollars. And Farvel said,
"All right. Now you. Pick out what you like for yourself."

"Oh, no," I protested. "I can't. Really, Farvel, I don't need a new
bag."

"Come on, come on. What's the matter with you. You don't refuse a
gift. It's an insult. So which one you like?" After I chose one for myself
he insisted that I pick out one for my mother.

When I got home, I showed Bernie the bags and praised Farvel's generosity.

"He doesn't pay for them," Bernie said. "The food and toilet paper and
clothes. He gets them for free. He shakes down the shopkeepers. They
don't charge him for that stuff. He picks it out and then, when he's ready
to go back to Florida, he'll send two guys with a U-haul downtown with a
list. They drive from store to store picking up the crap he ordered. It sits
in his garage in Florida. Wait. Next time we go down, I'll show you. We'll
go over to Farvel's house and you'll see."

Sure enough, a month later when Bernie and I went to Florida for our
second season, we drove over to Farvel's up in Hollywood. Like Meyer's
house, Farvel's was big and attractive but not what you'd imagine from a
man with the kind of power and money he commanded. Very low key. The
most ostentatious thing about the house was the sweeping circular driveway
and the four cars parked in it that belonged to Farvel, Minnie, and their
daughters. There was no room in their huge garage for cars. It was stacked
floor to ceiling with cartons of tunafish, pickle jars and cases of seltzer and
Dr. Brown's Cream Soda and Celery Tonic.

These men were full of contradictions. Meyer Lansky's estimated personal wealth was around three hundred million dollars. But everything
about his home and life-style, at least everything I saw firsthand, was simple, unassuming, and very Jewish. One of the richest men in the world

wore bedroom slippers at an elegant dinner party, spoke softly and lovingly to his wife, and then, during dinner, rang a bell for servants and, when they didn't show up instantly, cursed them like a punk from Pinsk.

And Farvel, whose cheapness was legendary, threw a wedding for his daughter of mind-boggling extravagance. To begin with, he paid the airfare and hotel bills for all the guests who flew in for the affair. And, oh, that flight from New York to Florida. "If this plane went down," Bernie said, "there'd be no one to run the underworld." Everyone was aboard. Ruby Stein and Uncle Jimmy Doyle, Milty Heinz from the Teamsters, Jimmy Blue Eyes, and there were Gambinos, Giordanos, Gallinas.

Farvel had put together an incredible guest list and it looked like no one had rsvp'd regrets. Even Cab Calloway and his wife were there. The tables were assigned with the wisdom of Solomon. Great care and thought had been given to who sat where and with whom. At every table were the brands of cigarettes the guests at that table smoked and the right bottles of booze. Farvel circulated collecting *koved* and envelopes of cash. The guys teased him, called out to him, "Hey, Farvel, you going to give the kids the right shake?" Envelopes poured in from around the country. Men who couldn't be there or hadn't been invited sent their tribute with others. Geo must have brought ten stuffed envelopes with him from Las Vegas. At one point, Farvel was carrying around a cigar box filled with envelopes. Every ten minutes he'd rush off to the safe and return with the empty box again.

Bernie had bought me a dress in New York which I just hated. To this day, I have no idea what B-movie he was making in his mind when he envisioned me in this sleeveless Empire aqua chiffon extravaganza with elbow-length satin gloves. I felt as though I'd shown up at the wedding of the decade in my nightgown. I spent half the evening trying not to run into Blanche, who was wearing a sexy, skin-tight beaded gown with about an acre of well-tanned cleavage showing, or Teddy Lansky, who took the prize for dazzling class in a bronze sequined gown under a matching Chanel jacket with sable cuffs.

For me, the most beautiful part of the evening came when the band played "Hava Nagila" and, unexpectedly, men wandered over from the tables and the bar to the dance floor. The dinner and partying had gone on for hours. Most of them had their ties loosened by then, a collar button undone. Some had removed their jackets and rolled back their cuffs. Faces were flushed. Here and there a strand of slicked-back hair fell over a warm forehead. And when the *hora* music began, intense conversations ended, raucous laughter faded, the tight little groups loosened and drifted almost automatically onto the dance floor. As if by some magical unspoken agreement, the women and children who'd begun the traditional Jewish dance moved into the background. And only the men, the wise guys, the tough guys who didn't dance, held each other's shoulders in a big circle and began this amazing, hypnotic, slow step-kick that gradually became a glorious half-serious, half-wild *hora*. Some faces were stern with concentration; others were totally open, grinning, glowing. From the sidelines, squashed between the wives and children clapping time at the edge of the circle, I searched for Bernie. My heart leapt with pride when I saw him in the ring of dancers. Laughing aloud, his face and shirt soaked with perspiration, he was moving with a joy, grace, and pride I'd never seen before.

The party lasted for a whole weekend. Farvel put everyone up at The Hollywood Beach Hotel. The place was like Gangster Heaven. From the snack bar to the spa, everywhere you went you ran into heavy hitters. Bernie got telephone calls from men he hadn't seen in years. They met for a swim, a *shvitz,* a card game, an afternoon at the track. He was like a kid with every invitation. These were the major players he was running with, not the pimps, pushers, numbers runners, and everyday *pishers* he dealt with in the city. And Bernie's being there, being invited, meant that Meyer had given the okay. Again, it was confirmation that he was no longer regarded as a renegade kid.

While he *shvitzed,* I shopped.

"You going to buy it or not?" I was in the hotel boutique admiring a very expensive pearl-trimmed cashmere sweater when I heard the booming voice behind me. I turned and there was Blanche Yaras grinning at me. Laughing beside her, pert and beautiful, was a radiant Teddy Lansky.

"I don't know," I said, thrilled to see them but instantly intimidated by the dynamic duo. "It's a lot of money."

"What do you care?" Teddy asked. "Buy it! Spend it. If he doesn't spend it on you, he'll gamble it away."

"Are you alone here?" Blanche asked, taking my arm. "Come on, Sandy. We'll shop later. Join us for lunch."

The three of us sat out at a table under an umbrella near the pool. It was a terrific lunch. We laughed and gossiped, just me and my idols, a trio of girls with nothing to do but shop and spend their husbands' money. It was Cinderella Time poolside.

"With most of them," Teddy told me, "the money comes and goes. You've got to get it while they've got it."

"Steal from his pockets or from what he leaves you," Blanche advised. "And always tell him everything costs more. He won't even notice."

"Honey, you're young now, but this life eats you up and sucks you dry. Who's going to take care of you? Him? Get it now, while you can. Because you'll need it later—guaranteed."

I laughed and loved being with them, but I could never do what they said. Steal from Bernie? It was inconceivable to me. "But he's my husband," I said. "It's wrong."

I really wanted to be an honest kid. And I was. I never stole from him.

Looking back on the money that, exactly as Teddy said, came and went and was gambled away, I'm sorry now that I didn't take their advice. Our little hassock, over the years, probably held huge amounts of cash, jewelry, and other valuables. If there wasn't enough in our "petty cash drawer," the drawer in the night table on my side of the bed, I'd take what I needed from the hassock. But I always wrote down the exact amount on a slip of paper and threw it into the hassock when I took the money out.

Temptation was all around me—in the night table, in the hassock, and there was also Bernie's "pocket money." He would empty his pockets onto the dresser each night and there'd be $2,000 or $3,000 lying around. If I'd taken $100, would he have missed it? If I'd put a couple of grand into a safety deposit box, I would have had it instead of the track touts and bookies from New York to Puerto Rico—and, oh yes, the croupiers at the Desert Inn.

I'd already seen Bernie hand over the keys to our car to pay off a debt. Not too long after Teddy and Blanche tried talking sense to me, Bernie made a bundle of money and bought me a magnificent diamond ring. It was close to fourteen carats. "You see," I told myself. "Good things come to good people. I didn't have to steal from him. Look at this gorgeous ring." To tell the truth, I couldn't wait to go down to Florida that year and show it off to Blanche and Teddy.

I never got the chance. We flew out to Vegas about a week after I got the ring. Bernie hit the crap tables. "Stay with me, baby," he said. "I need you for luck." I stayed. I watched him betting big. I heard people all around us start yelling, "High roller! High roller!" Bernie started losing. My heart started thudding against my rib cage. He broke out in a cold sweat. The little vein at the side of his neck was jumping. Beads of perspiration poured down his face. In eighteen minutes flat, he blew $18,000. His voice was raw. He said, "Eighteen grand. That's it. I quit," and I fainted.

I woke up in Geo's private office at the Desert Inn. The first thing I noticed was that my beautiful, brand-new, fourteen-carat, emerald-cut diamond ring was gone. "I've been robbed, I've been robbed," I screamed.

Geo's bodyguards were just outside the door. They quieted me down. One of them went to get Bernie. "Oh, God, thank God you're here," I cried, and fell into his arms. "Bernie, my ring's been stolen. Oh, God, what are we going to do?"

"No, no," he said, trying to comfort me. "It isn't stolen, baby. Don't worry. I took it off your finger while you were out and gave it to Geo for the money I lost."

Needless to say, I never mentioned the ring to Teddy Lansky, Blanche Yaras, Minnie Kovolicks, or the other Jewish racket club wives who had tried to wise me up. And if, in my twenties, I'd thought they were cynical or callous about their husbands, if I'd felt shocked and scandalized by their advice, they were Pollyannas compared to the Italian mob wives I ran into later.

Mostly, I met them at weddings. It was strange, but I actually felt more at ease with the Italian wives than I did with the Jewish. I think it was because I so idolized women like Teddy and Blanche, that it was nearly impossible for me to feel equal to them. But I was a good mimic. I learned how to look like them, and that, I thought, gave me an edge among the older, and to me less glamorous, Italian veterans.

It wasn't that the Italian mob wives didn't have the diamonds. They'd hit the vaults before the weddings, too, and truck out their best—knuckle rocks, they had. Enormous rings and diamond, ruby and emerald necklaces and bracelets and gem-encrusted gold charms marking every occasion in their lives from their mother's first communion to the high school graduation of their fifth grandchild. And tiaras! These women owned diamond tiaras.

At the wedding supper, the bride would shlep around a bag the size of a pillowcase, which was made of the same satin or silk fabric as her gown. This enormous sack they called the *busta,* or "the wedding purse." And couples would walk up to the dais and drop in the envelopes.

What was amazing to me was that you'd be sitting at the tables and all of a sudden the men would start asking one another, "Hey, what are you giving?" "You think six bills is good?" "His mother is my sister's aunt's god-daughter, so that'll cost me another fiver."

Sometimes, as the discussion went on—and the open bar booze flowed— men would decide they'd been stingy. They'd take out the sealed envelopes right at the table and tear them open. Then they'd dig into their pockets, pull out a bankroll, and peel off another couple of hundred for the bride's wedding purse. "That's enough," I heard a guy say, "we don't give a penny more than a grand. Who's kid is this anyway?"

I once asked Bernie, "How much money could kids like this get?"

"Oh, maybe fifty, sixty thousand dollars," he answered.

"My God, what a place for a robbery."

Bernie laughed. "Look around. You see those guys in tuxedoes stationed along the walls? They've got guns, Sandy. There aren't a lot of stick-ups at mob weddings."

At one wedding, the father of the bride had an adding machine sitting next to his dessert plate on the dais.

And just as I'd seen happen at Farvel's daughter's wedding, I noticed that a lot of envelopes would come in from out of town. Men would pull out six or seven envelopes from their pockets and drop them into the wedding purse. The money was a token of respect. It was never really spoken of as giving cash; it was "giving respect." Of course all the money in the envelopes was cash. Although you could tally up the price of the suits and boots and pinky rings, the gowns and furs and tiaras into tens of thousands of dollars, most of the wedding guests didn't know what a checking account looked like. Checks could be traced. Questions of income could be raised. Checks were an invitation for the FBI and IRS to climb into bed with the newlyweds.

There were no more Gene Kellys or Fred Astaires among the Italian mobsters than among their Jewish counterparts. Oh, maybe you'd see a grandfather twirling a little girl or once in a while a father dancing with his daughter or daughter-in-law, but for the most part "tough guys don't dance" was a nonsectarian slogan.

What was different about the Italian mob weddings was that the women danced together. The first time I saw this, I was really surprised. The first time an Italian mob wife asked me to dance, I was speechless. I finally shook my head and said, "No, thanks." And then I got crazy with guilt thinking I'd hurt her feelings.

After the last food course, just as the coffee was being served, the men would leave the tables and head over to the bar or gather in little groups to discuss business. And then the wives would get going.

"Thank God, they're gone so we can have coffee in peace," someone would always say.

"I'll have another drink now. He's not watching me," I heard more than once.

The women were nervous wrecks. Each one had her own tic, eccentric mannerism, or nervous habit. Angie, whose father had been a lieutenant in the Bonanno family and whose husband ran a couple of afterhours spots downtown, wore her jet-black hair pulled back tightly into a high chignon. She had long fingernails, polished translucent white, with which she constantly dug into her scalp, prying loose and twirling one thick strand of hair after another. Another woman, Tina, the wife of a Brooklyn mob boss, had a solid gold Dunhill lighter which she tapped compulsively on the table. Still another endlessly drummed her long, thick fingernails. They scratched. They twitched. They cursed their husbands.

"Let them stay away," they said. "Let them talk forever!"

Their husbands were lousy lovers, they said. They cackled and called them "The Minute Men."

Angie said, "If he stinks at home, you think he's going to do better for that pig he's got over on East Eighty-fifth Street?" That was another thing that surprised the hell out of me. These women all knew the addresses and telephone numbers of their husbands' mistresses. If they were pushed too far, they called. It was because Italian men, they said, were stupid, careless, or just plain didn't give a damn. They left the addresses and telephone numbers in the pockets of shirts they gave their wives to launder; on the dressers where they left their money at night; on matchbook covers and pieces of torn menus from nightclubs.

"When the FBI comes looking for him, they come to *my* house," said a tall, dark, attractive woman I'd never met before. "My children get involved. They have to hear this. They never bother his girlfriend. It's my house they go through."

A woman sitting across the table at a wedding took a seat next to me after our husbands had gone off to the bar together. "How old do you think I am?" she asked out of the blue. "I'm forty-two." She looked ninety-two. "You see me," she said. "I've got a bleeding ulcer from him. You can't take what they say to heart. It'll kill you."

"I was happier when he was in prison." Boy, oh, boy, did I hear that a lot. And that particular line was not exclusive to the Italian wives.

If Farvel's was the most extravagant wedding I'd ever been to, Freddy the Greek's was indisputably the strangest. Freddy was a very well-respected guy among his peers. He'd pulled off some of the most ingenious and well-known heists of his day. Among them was one of the biggest jewel thefts in New York. On a Sunday, exactly as planned, Freddy snatched several million dollars' worth of uncut diamonds from a midtown exchange. He had a car waiting on Forty-seventh Street and a truck with a ramp ready around the corner. He drove to the truck, backed the car up into it, stowed the ramp, closed the backdoors of the truck, and went tear-assing up Eighth Avenue, a street of potholes to rival the Grand Canyon. As he bumped and banged along Eighth Avenue, the backdoors of the truck were jarred opened and the car, carrying the diamonds, rolled out.

Needless to say, police showed up and Freddy was arrested.

While he was doing time in jail, a nun from his old neighborhood would visit him with messages from his friends. She came once or twice a week and after she delivered the messages, she stayed to talk and they got to know one another. In time, they fell in love.

Freddy was probably in his fifties. The nun, whose name I think was Agnes, was close to forty and had spent her entire life in the service of God. Convent-educated from girlhood, she was from a devout Irish Catholic family teeming with nuns, priests, and cops. But she and Freddy were in love and there was nothing to do about it but make it legit. So here she was, married to God and engaged to a gangster.

The wedding was planned for the day after Freddy the Greek got home from jail. And it went off better than Freddy's last heist had. The ex-con and his virgin bride were married in a huge midtown church just off Ninth Avenue. I remember walking into the chapel at high noon on a Saturday and being absolutely staggered by the crowd. There must have been more than three hundred people packed into the pews and lining the aisles. And of the three hundred at least a third of them were in uniform. There were priests, bishops, a cardinal, nuns, novices, and police brass. At the reception after the ceremony, the guests sat at segregated tables. At some tables were members of the clergy, at others members of the police force, members of the bride's family, members of the groom's family, and then there were tables of members of the five families—the top echelon gangsters who ran New York City at that time.

The strangest thing about this very strange wedding was that everyone had a terrific time. The nuns were thrilled for their "Little Sister." They teased her and laughed and were full of fun and happiness. The priests and the cops got on fine with the mobsters. Many of them had nodding acquaintances before the wedding. Everywhere I went I heard guys saying things like, "I went to school with that red-headed cop," or, "There's Father Joseph, from St. Mary's where my kid goes," or "Isn't that Fat Tony Salerno's bodyguard who did a bid at Dannemora?" And Freddy and Agnes practically needed his truck again, just to haul away the wedding purse.

Not all the marriages I witnessed ended as grandly as they'd begun. Farvel's daughter's marriage to her "plain guy" didn't last. That's what everyone called him because he wasn't mob blood. You'd ask, "Whose son is he?" and someone would say, "No one's. He's a plain guy." Anyway, they wound up divorced. The daughter of a major Jewish mob boss married the extraordinarily handsome son of the owner of one of New York's renowned Jewish dairy restaurants. Her father stopped by their house one afternoon and found his son-in-law in bed with another man and, with remarkable restraint, had the marriage, not the groom, dissolved. And only a couple of years after his wedding, poor Freddy was gunned down in the streets.

CHAPTER TEN

The House of Yenom

Our second season in Florida, Bernie got sick and had to be hospitalized. As soon as he was well enough, we returned to New York. We weren't back in town a day before our apartment became the convalescent clubhouse again. Both telephones were in constant use. Gifts arrived. Guys arrived. Ashtrays filled. Scotch bottles emptied. And I couldn't wait for him to get on his feet again and out into the world.

Bernie always had something going. Even while The Velvet Club was hot, he and Red were partners in a string of Harlem numbers joints. He had a piece of half a dozen different bars. With Cokey he owned a couple of fighters. He was always looking for action. Sometimes he'd fall into wild schemes and quick money. And sometimes the ship he was waiting for sank before it sighted land. Some of his ventures were inspired and some were plain pipe dreams. One of them was both. It began a week after we got back to town. Bernie was sitting around with Cokey one night, passing a joint and watching TV.

The famous evangelist Billy Graham was big then. He'd recently held a rally in Yankee Stadium and was all over the news. "How much you think he rakes in at one of those tent shows?" Cokey asked.

"Plenty. And he doesn't pay taxes, either. Some gig, right?"

"Unreal," Cokey marveled.

"You know, that's what we ought to do. We ought to go into the preacher business," Bernie said. "Get that non-profit license and run it semi-legit."

They talked about it for a while, had a few laughs, kicked around ideas about how it could be done. A couple of days later, Cokey called all excited and said, "Tell B I found our boy. I'm bringing him by tonight."

His name was Tito and he was gorgeous. Dazzling might be more like it because there was something about him, a glow, a warmth, that lit up the room the minute he walked in. With a smile that was shy and seductive at the same time, he looked like a cross between Billie Dee Williams and Jesse Jackson. "Pleasure to meet you, ma'am," he said with this incredible soft Southern accent.

Bernie started grinning the minute he saw him. "Where did you find this kid?" he asked Cokey in the kitchen. Tito was making himself at home on the L-shaped sofa, cleaning some pot and expertly rolling up a couple of joints.

"I know his family. He's up from Alabama. He's got some kind of preaching certificate. Says he got ordained somewhere down South. He's our boy, B."

"Kid's a hustler," Bernie said, "*and* a pothead."

"Yeah, but he's a preacher, too. We could do this, B. We could make this happen."

And they did. Josh, the lawyer who yearned to be a hood, researched the non-profit status for them. A couple of days after Tito showed up, Josh came by and dumped a thick pile of papers on the coffee table for Bernie to read. And Bernie did. He studied the requirements. He made phone calls. He put out the word that he was looking for space uptown. By the time he was well enough to leave the house again, mutual friends had tipped him and Cokey to a beautiful deal on Lenox Avenue.

There was a "superette" that had gone out of business on Lenox and 123rd Street. It was a space smaller than a supermarket but bigger than a large grocery store. Bernie called the landlord and they picked up the lease on it for practically nothing. If the rent was maybe three, three-fifty a month it was a lot. It was a big, raw storefront and the challenge was to turn it into a church.

They had the preacher. They had the place. They needed the name. Bernie and Cokey went back and forth on it for days. We were surveying the boarded-up superette, stepping carefully over broken glass and busted shelves and warped linoleum, when Bernie hit on a winner.

"The House of Yenom," he decided.

"Solid," Cokey said. "Where'd you pull that one from?"

"The House of Yenom," I repeated. It sounded nice, exotic yet solemn. Then I got it and I cracked up.

"What?!" Cokey asked.

And Bernie explained that in Yiddish *yenom* means "Joe Shmoe's, the other guy's, not ours." And in English yenom is money spelled backwards. Perfect. So that was the name of the church, The House of Yenom.

When it was time to renovate the building, Bernie's union connections got them the best skilled labor working off-hours at bargain rates. Guys sent by friends from the Plumbing Union, the Carpenters Union, painters, plasterers, kids who wanted to get into the Teamsters. In the blink of an eye, the place started humming. Some afternoons I'd go uptown to see how the job was coming. It was like walking onto the set of an old MGM movie, the kind where Mickey Rooney says to Judy Garland, "Hey, I've got a great idea—let's build a house of worship in Harlem!"

Everybody got involved, excited, carried away. We'd sit around at night, after the workmen left, Bernie, Tilly, me and Cokey, and sometimes Iris or Josh or Hot Dog Red, and we'd have coffee and talk and laugh and come up with wild new ideas.

Personally supervising every detail of the renovation, Bernie was like a great big kid, a cross between Mickey Rooney, Michelangelo, and, when it came to decor, Father Divine. He ordered black floors and blond wood panelling, ornate prayer benches with royal purple pew cushions, gold wall sconces in the shape of cupids dripping crystal beads, and on the starry sky-blue ceiling he installed colored spotlights focused on a big, step-up pulpit. An arched chapel-style entrance with stained-glass panels replaced the store windows, and then they shlepped in a huge white pipe organ that looked like someone had ripped it off from Ringling Brothers.

In the back, behind the altar area, Bernie had two offices built and an oversized kitchen. He felt that it would be a good gesture for the church to feed some of the neighborhood people once or twice a week at a small soup kitchen. So, in addition to all the glitter up front, big stoves and refrigerators and other appliances were installed.

Bernie wasn't satisfied with just turning the storefront into a religious wet dream; next he went to work on Father Tito, which is what the kid started calling himself—Father Tito or Preacher Tito. They got him these gorgeous white robes with gold and purple trim. And Bernie laid down the law to him.

"A preacher is always on call," he told the kid who had an apartment a couple of blocks from the storefront. "During the day you look like a business man. Shirt and tie, all the way." He took Father Tito up to Lester's, one of the legendary uptown tailors favored by the Harlem mob boys, and ordered him half a dozen suits and bought him a closet full of shirts and ties and a few fancy pairs of alligator shoes. "And you don't get high during the day," he told him. "If you want to get high, just get high a little bit. But you've got to be straight most of the time."

Father Tito got caught up in the thing fast. He felt he had a true calling. He thought he should have a choir. So a couple of neighborhood kids were recruited, street kids, and they decked them out in beautiful robes, too. Then Cokey got hold of some of the local talent—hookers. High-class, gorgeous call girl hookers, but hookers. And they were going to work Sunday nights, wearing white gowns and these big imitation gold crosses. They were stunning girls and they were going to be called "The Virgins of Father Tito" or "Father Tito's Princesses."

Bernie and Cokey were careful to set everything up legally, to get the proper permits and registrations so The House of Yenom would have tax-exempt status. And though the permits and renovation and choir robes and, finally, even the meat, milk, fruit, and vegetables that he bought through his wholesale connections, all came to a pretty penny, Bernie believed it was worth it. "You have to invest money," he kept saying. "You've got to speculate to accumulate."

The week The House of Yenom was set to open, Bernie had fliers printed and neighborhood kids were hired to stick them into mail boxes, on lampposts, on the sides of buildings, under the doors of apartments, and handfuls were left with local merchants to be given out to customers. They were everywhere, and they announced the Sunday opening, "a mass at high noon," followed by a breakfast.

It was late spring, a beautiful morning. We arrived at the "chapel" at about ten o'clock. A huge banner hung above the entrance and a red carpet had been rolled out over the sidewalk. Spotlights were set up, even though it was a sunny morning. They lit the carpeted sidewalk in front of the arched entrance where a choir of beautifully robed children swayed and clapped and sang hymns. With the spotlights and red carpet, with the choir rocking and singing, when people started showing up, started actually *thronging* into the place, done up in their Sunday best—the furs and flowered hats, the starched shirts and suits pressed to a blinding shine—it looked like a Hollywood premiere.

The house was packed. The organ was playing. And, finally, Father Tito appeared and he was a sight to behold. Robed in white and gold, he walked along a path of rainbow lights followed by his "princesses," eight breathtaking hookers, a rainbow of colors themselves, from ivory to ebony, decked out in flowing white satin gowns. People gasped. "Praise the Lord," you could hear one or two call out. It was astounding.

I looked at Bernie and I started to laugh—out of sheer excitement, out of awe, I think. If I hadn't laughed I would have cried. Father Tito looked so impressive and the whole church was so beautiful. Seeing it filled, seeing people's faces all lit up with pleasure, with joy, it really was like a religious experience. It was almost as if we had succeeded in creating a real church.

Tito was a powerful preacher. Cokey was right about the kid's ability to rock out a crowd. It seemed clear that he really did have a calling. And Bernie was right, too, because it was equally clear that Father Tito was a terrific pothead and he had certainly turned on before he hit the pulpit. People stood and swayed and shouted out to him. They cried "Amen!" whenever he said something they really agreed with, or they shouted, "Preach!" or "Yes, tell it!"

Tilly was having a ball. "It's not so different," she said to me. "Look." She jutted her chin toward a standing man who was rocking back and forth as Tito spoke. "Like *davening*," she said, meaning the swaying prayer stance of Jewish men.

The sermon was a great success. The little black collection boxes were brimming with donations. And after the service, a beautiful brunch was served—ham and scrambled eggs, lox, cream cheese and bagels, and there were even collard greens and black-eyed peas and fabulous soul food because Iris had gotten a couple of terrific bar chefs to come down and do the cooking.

At the end of the day, we went into the office and tallied up the collections. We had a couple of thousand dollars' worth of coins and bills— ranging from pennies and singles to the hundred-dollar bills some of the Harlem wise guys who'd showed up for the opening had tossed in. I counted the money as Bernie had taught me, all the bills facing the same way, presidents up, ranging from low to high denominations.

"Okay," I said, writing down the amount of coins I had to cash in for bills at the bank the next day, "now that we have this money and we're officially open, I'll have to keep records of how much we take in and how much we're spending. I'll need receipts for what everything costs, even if you're paying cash for the food or booze or the coffee. Whatever you do here, you've got to know what you're laying out so you can be reimbursed. Whatever you spend I need to know—the food, toilet paper, washing the robes, everything."

Bernie was crouched in front of the old-fashioned four-legged safe he'd bought. Only he, Cokey, and I knew the combination. His mouth fell open. "What're you out of your mind?" He shot me a look. "Since when did you become a fucking bookkeeper and such a business woman?"

"Well, somebody's got to do it," I said. "Even if it's tax exempt, you have to keep books. You need a record of what comes in and what goes out. It's just common sense."

Little did I know then that what came in and what went out was sometimes a load of television sets or stereos or other fast-moving merchandise that eventually turned the backroom of that little store of God into a Grand Central Station of hot items. After getting Bernie's usual response to questions about what was going on, I learned how to close my eyes to the traffic. And, apparently, so did the neighborhood cops who had to be blind not to notice trucks pulling up to the side entrance and racks of clothing, and huge, sealed cartons being wheeled in and out every half hour.

But that first day I argued forcefully enough to be made the official bookkeeper. And, oh, did I take that job seriously. I was so proud of myself. I felt like a real take-charge kind of business woman, like the controller of a big corporation. I loved it. Controller of The House of Yenom. I could make myself believe that it was a real business; that we were legit, at last. Well, ninety-nine percent legit.

I was up at the church three days a week working on the books. It was impossible, of course, since Bernie and Cokey were used to accounting systems that were a little looser than what I was trying to do. Bernie would hand me a fistful of money and tell me to stash it in the safe. I'd say, "Okay, what does it go under? I've got to record it before I put it in."

"Never mind, just stash it," he'd say. Or "Charge it to sausages, for God's sake!"

I definitely got carried away with myself. But nothing like the way Father Tito started getting carried away.

Tito was good, no two ways about it. But he was only self-ordained. And after that first day, when we were all sitting around after the chapel was swept and the dishes cleaned and the food and money put away, Tito started talking about television. How we could probably do a deal to have the services televised. And maybe open up other Houses of Yenom in different parts of New York. Make a whole chain of them. Like Mc-Donald's. The kid had lit up the minute the doors were locked and he was ripped. But high as he was on grass, he was higher on himself. Success was like a drug to him—he'd gotten a taste and right away he wanted more.

The House of Yenom was a going concern, a quiet little gold mine that gave the neighborhood people much of what they wanted from it—a place to meet and pray and sit down together for community breakfasts with their families, friends, and neighbors. Things ran pretty smoothly for months. After a while I gave up trying to keep the books straight. But it wasn't the merchandise in the backroom or financial crisis that brought down the House. Ultimately, it was Father Tito's success.

The kid got a lot of attention. Not just through word of mouth, but an uptown newspaper had covered the opening and gave him, a great review. The more good things that happened to him, the more he began to believe his own press. He started thinking that he was a real preacher. He began performing wedding ceremonies.

Bernie didn't know anything about this until, one day, two kids whom Tito had married started having trouble. They wanted to get divorced. They'd come to the church to see Tito about it and, when Bernie walked in, Tito tried to shush the kids, get them to make up fast, get them into the other office. Bernie followed them and asked what was wrong. And that was it!

"That son of a bitch is marrying people!" he roared at me. "There are children that are going to be walking around as bastards. And what happens when a couple wants to get a divorce? Do you know the heat that could bring down on me? I'm doing *business* out of that place. I don't know how many marriages he's performed. Sandy, there are people living together who are not married in the eyes of God, and that is one thing I won't go for!"

Bernie tried talking to the kid, tried to set him straight. But Tito had really gone 'round the bend on this thing. He started screaming at Bernie, that he had a divine right to perform weddings, that God had given him the go-ahead. He was screaming and preaching. Bernie got crazy and decked him. Father Tito flew over the desk, out for the count. Within a week, Bernie shut the place down. And that was it, a sweet deal gone sour. Or, as Josh the lawyer used to call it, "the fall of The House of Yenom."

I was sorry to see it go. It was a scam, a hustle, a front for fencing stolen goods maybe. But it was also as close to going straight as we'd gotten, which made it close to heaven for me. After Yenom, when I'd ask, "When are you going to give up the rackets, baby? Aren't we ever going to try to go legit?" more and more, Bernie would just shake his head.

"What do you want me to do, babe? Open up a candy store on the Lower East Side and sell two cents plain, and you can help me stuff the newspapers on Saturday night? No, baby," he'd say with this sad little smile, "I only know one way. Putting my back against the wall. Whatever I make, I can call it my blood money. If I have to pay or do time, that's okay. 'Do the crime, pay the time,' that's the saying. And I accept that."

An exciting idea, a scheme that worked, a pipe dream that came true, The House of Yenom had been hatched while Bernie was home recuperating. It was one of the few good things that ever came out of his sickness. And he was sick now at least twice a year. Because of his heart condition, he'd catch a cold, it would turn into pneumonia and, the next thing you knew, he'd be fighting for his life.

It wasn't something you could get used to. He got weaker after each bout. It took longer for him to get well again. And, when he struggled for breath, so did I. Watching him rigged up to an oxygen tank, seeing the color and life drained from his face, it got so that I could hardly breathe, I was that scared of losing him.

I was angry a lot, too. Because when he was sick, Bernie could become incredibly impatient and demanding. Here was a man who prided himself on never asking for help. But, when he was hospitalized, he had to depend on doctors, medicine, and machines to keep him breathing. And, when he came home, he had to depend on me for everything else. He hated it. It made him crazy. And I was the one he took his frustration out on. He wanted me to learn and do everything in five minutes and get back in time to empty the ashtrays and put up fresh coffee for his friends.

Sometimes I hated him. Sometimes I felt sorry for myself. Sometimes I'd watch him struggling for breath in his sleep or just breathing quietly and peacefully, and I'd be overwhelmed with love for him. I'd want to wake him up with kisses, wake him up just to tell him how much I loved him.

He did what business he could from home during these times. He spoke to Hot Dog Red on the phone five times a day and saw him at least two. "All right, listen. I need you to go to the bank and rent a safety deposit box," he said to me after Red stopped by early one morning and dropped off a brown paper grocery bag.

"I don't know how," I said, which of course was not his favorite response.

"It's simple. I'll tell you how." He was sitting up in bed with his legs crossed like a snake charmer's. "You just walk in and you say you want to rent a safety deposit box, and when they ask what your name is you make up a name. They'll give you a card to sign," he said, dumping the contents of Red's paper bag out onto the bed. Dollar bills rained down onto his crossed legs. "You tell them the box is for you and your husband and you bring home the card for my signature, too."

"It's all legal, right?"

"What the hell do you care what it is? Just do it. Just make up a name—"

"Like what?"

"Like Henny Penny. Like Desdemona Finkelstein. A name, Sandra. Any name but Barton, okay?"

When I'd showered and dressed, Bernie handed me three envelopes. One was full of money—the cash Red had dropped off. The other two were fat and taped shut. I stuck them into my handbag and all the way to the bank, I was racking my brain for just the right name. Opening the box was as simple as Bernie had said. No one asked for identification. No one mentioned a social security number. When they asked my name, I blurted out, "Sadie Green."

I brought the signature card home for Bernie to sign. He shook his head and looked at me as though I were crazy. "Sadie Green? Where did you come up with that?"

"I don't know. It's a name, isn't it? You said make one up. That's it."

He laughed and signed "Hymie Green."

Over the years, I opened five different safety deposit boxes at Bernie's instruction, four under different names—all of them Jewish. We were Anne and Ben Fine. Sara and Abe Weissman. Miriam and Meyer Katz. Only one box belonged to Sandra and Bernie Barton. The safety deposit boxes were our hassocks-away-from-home and worked the same way. Envelopes in; envelopes out. Take a thou, leave a note. But it was my job to keep tabs on what went into which box. I wrote it all on a slip of paper, including the names and numbers of the boxes, and stuck it away in a safe hiding place.

My cousin Francine had moved to New York from L.A. and lived not too far from us now. "Give the keys to Francine," Bernie said. "I don't want them around the house if I'm ever arrested or the place is searched. I don't want the FBI or anyone else finding safety deposit box keys here." So when I needed to make a deposit or withdrawal from the boxes, I just stopped by Francine's first.

I'd been uptown with Bernie to the numbers joint Red ran for him. It was not an impressive setup. The apartment was a fifth-floor walkup on Pleasant Avenue and 116th Street. It was a threadbare railroad flat with a bathtub in the kitchen and a toilet in a closet so small your knees hit the door if you tried to sit down. In the middle room was a long piece of plywood laid across a couple of sawhorses. On top of that makeshift desk were three or four telephones which never stopped ringing, a bunch of adding machines and notebooks in which the bets were recorded. Hot Dog's contribution was the clock on the wall. It was his idea to write down the time a bet came in and he'd go crazy if anyone forgot to do it.

The first time I was there, I just helped myself to a cup of coffee from the percolator on top of the stove and sat quietly on a chair until Bernie and Red had finished talking business. Now Bernie sent me back to the place to pick up a bag from Red, who he said was short-handed and couldn't deliver it himself. I went. I drove up to Harlem alone and shlepped up the five rickety flights of stairs and knocked on the door. Red let me in. The place was jumping. The phones were ringing off the hook. The guys at the plywood table were writing down numbers as fast as they could, and checking the clock. But every one of them took the time to tilt his head or tip his hat in my direction and say, "Afternoon, princess." "Mrs. B. How you doing?" "Miss Sandy, how's BB today? You tell him Sonny says hello."

"You want a soda or a cup of coffee?" Red offered.

"No thanks. Gee, it's busy here."

"Here, sit down, baby," Red said, sliding back a chair in front of one of the phones at the desk. "Let me show you how this works." He slid over an opened notebook and handed me a pencil. "When it rings, you just say, 'Yeah?' and the guy'll give you a number and an amount. You say them back aloud to be sure you got it right, then just write them down right here, look at the clock and jot down the time, and that's it."

The phone in front of me rang. "Go on," Red nodded.

"Yeah?" I said.

The voice at the other end said, "Gimme a dollar on 592." There was a racket behind him. It sounded like he was calling from the subway or a pipe factory. I repeated the number, repeated the amount, his name, wrote them down. Red was grinning, nodding encouragingly at me.

I took a couple more calls. One was from a numbers runner. He reeled off about twenty different combos. "A dollar on 295, two bucks on 826, a fiver on 007, a dollar on 721 . . ." and on and on.

"You did great," Red said when I'd hung up. Then he explained how the winning number was chosen. In the back of the newspapers, in the sports sections, there was a daily tally of "the mutuel handle," or how much money a given racetrack had taken in for the day. In the winter, when the northern tracks were closed, they used the totals at Gulfstream or Hialeah. If a track took in $2,150,657 for the day's races, the last three numbers, 657, in any of six possible combinations, were the winning numbers for that day. That was how they figured "the Brooklyn number." There was a more complicated recipe for what was called "the New York number," which involved the amount of money laid down on the one, two, and three horses in the first race at a particular track. To work that one out you practically had to be a CPA.

"But these people are betting *bubkes*," I said. "A dollar here, a big two bucks there. How can you make a living on that?"

"It adds up," Red assured me and, just to prove it, handed me a sack full of money to take back to Bernie.

I decided that I wouldn't say anything to Bernie about working the phones or learning about how the winning numbers were picked. I knew how he hated to have me nosing around his business, and I didn't want to get Red in trouble. But the minute I walked in the door, Bernie was already grinning, already waiting. "So, how do you like taking bets? Think you got a career in the numbers?"

He'd wanted me to learn. He'd told Red to sit me down and stick a phone in my hand and see how I did. He wanted the boys uptown to get to know me, to get to know that I was him when I showed up, I represented him. Later that night, after I'd thought about it a little, I felt awful. I realized, or thought anyway, that Bernie was getting me ready to be without him. To know who to go see and what to do. To collect what was due him when he couldn't go anymore. It scared me. I couldn't fall asleep. I locked myself in the bathroom and cried.

CHAPTER ELEVEN

A Stand-Up Broad

All this activity, my learning how his businesses worked, and how to stand in for him, opening the safety deposit boxes, handling the money, all this was rewarded with the ultimate compliment: "Baby, you're a stand-up broad." Being a stand-up broad had almost as many rules as being a tough guy. Stand-up broads didn't ask questions, didn't look at other men. And if her guy looked at other girls, a stand-up broad looked the other way. Stand-up broads made no scenes, no demands, no waves. A stand-up broad stood by her man.

I'd do almost anything to earn that praise, to get that little pat on the head. I almost gave my life for it.

Among his other businesses, Bernie had a piece of an afterhours club in Harlem. It was as classy as the Copa and as wild as Reefer May's. The place was done up like a nightclub from a thirties movie, and on opening night a lot of the patrons dressed that way, in dinner jackets and full-length gowns. The club would start filling up after midnight. The crowd was mixed: politicians, high-priced lawyers, the show biz crowd, sightseers and sights to be seen, underworld characters in assorted colors and affiliations.

For me it was the best thing since The Velvet Room. Bernie and I had our favorite spot—a cozy corner at the crook of the sweeping L-shaped bar. From it we could watch the players and the games. In keeping with the 1930s look of the place, the bar top was deep blue glass and it was as often laced with lines of cocaine as it was ringed with drink coasters. Beyond the bar was a huge gambling room with baize-covered tables for blackjack, craps, and high-stakes poker. The dealers and croupiers all wore dark suits and ties. At four in the morning, the limos would be parked three deep outside.

In the early winter of '63, the place had been open and doing a booming business for a couple of months. It was close to four in the morning. Bernie and I were kibitzing, shooting the breeze, with Uncle Vinny and Hot Dog Red at the bar. We were wedged into our favorite corner. I don't remember what I had for breakfast this morning, but I remember exactly what I was wearing that memorable night. It was a gray peplum suit, nipped in at the waist and, as my old friend Raven would have said, very, very Rita Hayworth.

I was feeling pretty Rita Hayworth, too—sitting there, looking sultry with my long legs crossed, a cognac in my hand, surrounded by the guys I loved best in the world—when the unthinkable happened. Six men walked into the place, a place owned, operated, and usually jammed with some very connected characters. The guys were very well dressed. They looked like any other patrons and they would have blended perfectly into the crowd except for the ski masks they were wearing and the guns they held.

"Oh, God, here we go again," I said, grabbing Bernie's arm.

He froze. His eyes, blue ice, followed them as they went around shoving people, ordering them to the floor, yelling, "Give it up. Empty that wallet. Take off the jewelry. Throw it here, throw it here!" The guys were everywhere at once. The guns were like extensions of their hands, pointing, gesturing, jabbing. A couple of the guys were holding tommy guns, automatic weapons, crooked in their arms like television gangsters'. Some of them hit the gambling room. The rest fanned out near the bar.

We'd been sitting perfectly still, but I could see Bernie's rage building. That telltale little vein in his neck was throbbing. The tops of his ears were red. And then I got the one unmistakable clue. He started muttering. "What're you out of your motherfucking minds you pricks coming in here the fuck you think you are shit for brains bastards you're dead assholes cold meat motherfuckers out of the game . . ."

Mumbling, grumbling, muttering. I couldn't believe it. Neither could the guy with the gun working his way down the bar toward us.

"Shut the fuck up," he said to Bernie. "Shut your fucking mouth right now, dickhead or I'll—"

Let me be honest. I had knocked back a few Remys. And I was scared for Bernie. How else can I explain why I jumped off the barstool, arm raised, finger pointing at the ceiling, and yelled, "Don't you talk to my husband that way!" The gunman was almost as startled as I was. He shot me.

"Oooo, Bernie," I said. I reached inside my peblum jacket and found the wetness that turned out to be blood.

It was a small gun. I don't even remember hearing the noise, but it must have shook everybody up because the guy who shot me took off fast. "Let's go, let's go, it's done, let's split, it's over!" he hollered to his pals, and they pounded out of the place.

Suddenly, I was surrounded by people. Everyone was shouting. Bernie had one arm around my waist, the other was pulling my jacket off my injured shoulder. "Hang on, sweetheart. Hang on. Uncle Vinny's getting the car. You'll be okay, baby. Here, drink this. Go on, baby."

He was pouring scotch down my throat. The bartender was popping open bottles right and left, spilling the alcohol onto handkerchiefs that people were handing over. Red and Bernie took turns putting these compresses on the wound, mopping up the blood. Everything hurt. Everything stung. Everything felt and tasted and smelled like alcohol.

Uncle Vinny drove us to a doctor in the neighborhood, a nice Italian guy he knew named Dr. Milardi or Moretti. Anyway, he said it was a flesh wound. In and out. No muscle or nerve damage. He just scooped the little sucker out, and cleaned up the wound.

It was daylight by the time we got home. When I woke the next afternoon, Bernie was on the phone in the living room. I could hear him laughing. "I'm not kidding, that's what she said, 'You can't talk to my man that way,' " he was telling someone. "Oh, yeah," he added, after a pause. "Sandy's a stand-up broad. Always was."

Please. A moron was what I was.

It took me months to stop shaking. Every time a door slammed or I'd be around a crowd of noisy people, my heart would start slamming against my chest and my shoulder would throb an aching little reminder of how close I'd come to death. I don't even know what made me do it, what I was thinking of, or whether I was thinking at all. But my reputation was made in the stand-up ranks. I was a heroine. It became known in high places that BB had some wife. Look how much she loved him, that she took a chance on getting herself shot just to defend him. What a gutsy girl. What an idiot! I was a complete fool to do that. But stand-up broad sounds better than sucker.

"Tell Chalky what happened," Bernie said. "When you send him the *pesach* basket, in the note, write about how you got shot." Chalky Lefkowitz was a childhood friend of Bernie's who was doing ten-to-twenty in Trenton for armed robbery. We'd send him holiday gift baskets and cards, and Bernie always insisted that I write the notes to Chalky. "Wait till you meet him, Sandy. When this guy gets out, we're going to take over the town. There's nothing Chalky and I couldn't do together. This man is closer to me than my own brother. I've known him since we were two years old. White hair, he had, like chalk, he was so blond. Our mothers used to wheel us in carriages together. Write to Chalky, baby. Let him know what a stand-up broad I got."

I did, of course, I wrote to Chalky Lefkowitz and, at Bernie's bidding, I told the shooting story to Johnny Dio's uncle Jimmy Doyle, to Hot Dog's wife, Thelma, to Iris over drinks at Cokey's bar, to Farvel on the phone and Milty Heinz at a birthday party and Billy Daniels in Atlantic City. Bernie even made me tell the story to Della Reese, whose boyfriend, a bald black man who wore a wall-to-wall rug, he knew from uptown.

Even Lido, the Santeria high priest, got into the act. He sent word that
we should light the same candles for me as he'd advised for Bernie's re-
cuperations: a white candle for light and good spirits; a green candle for
money; and a red candle for well-being. Bernie lit the candles. He put
pieces of fruit near them, and a lump of sugar and a white handkerchief
and he chanted the prayers that Lido recommended.

Bernie always believed deeply in Lido's power and prescriptions. In fact,
when we were about to get involved in a deal that could make us legitimate
millionaires overnight, a deal that would actually take us to Africa, Bernie
insisted that we go up to Spanish Harlem first for Lido's blessing.

Through Hot Dog Red, Bernie met two black diplomats from Abidjan,
the capital of the Ivory Coast, which turned out to be wedged between
Ghana and Liberia. The men, who spoke with beautiful clipped English
accents and dressed as elegantly as British lords, were very connected in
their country, all the way up to the prime minister and the minister of
commerce. The way they told it the Ivory Coast was very rich in certain
commodities, but lacking in some pretty basic others like baby food, soda
pop, laundry detergent, paper products, and even underwear.

Bernie started romancing these guys in order to go into business with
them. He wanted to be the purchasing agent for dry goods, appliances,
clothing, and other items for their country. Of course, Bernie had great
connections for getting hot merchandise, the kind that fell off trucks and
into mob hands every day. But the more he researched the project, the
more convinced he became that he could do the job on a semi-legit basis
and make it pay big. So he and Red were all over the guys, as they used
to say, like white on rice.

They wined them, dined them, got them the best smoke in town and the
sexiest hookers. And while the boys from Abidjan were getting laid and
loaded, Bernie was running to fruit companies, paper products manufac-
turers, freight outfits, Garment Center connections, guys who ran the docks,
and he was busy comparing prices and compiling lists and checking out
every aspect of the deal. He'd met the diplomats in June of '64. In August,
he came home and said, "Baby, get the passports in order, we're going to
the Ivory Coast."

But first, Lido.

It was a steamy night at the end of August. As directed, we arrived at
Lido's East Harlem townhouse at midnight. After his traditional greeting,
the warm handshake followed by the outstretched open palm waiting for
cash and cocaine, Lido snorted up a couple of lines of inspiration and led
us down into the basement. He asked about my shoulder. It had been about
half a year since the shooting. He asked B whether he'd lit the candles and
laid out the fruit and sugar according to directions. Then he checked my
wound and nodded, pleased with the healing process.

Bernie and I knelt in the center of the floor as Lido went around the room lighting candles and mumbling prayers. When several candles were lit, dozens of white candles, in every corner of the basement, he shut the overhead light and returned to us carrying a wide white candle. He set it down before us and laid his hands on our heads.

The drumming, thudding, conga music began. Lido's face was dark and shadowy, his white silk sleeves billowing. His huge rings, the gold and diamond chains, the big diamond-encrusted cross, sparkled and shimmered in front of our eyes. Lido chanted a prayer, then cut off a piece of my hair and a piece of Bernie's and put the locks into a bowl. He threw in some dried herbs, added various colored waters, and while he mixed up the potion, he had us close our eyes and recite some special words. Everything was very, very dark except for the candles which were all white; white candles everywhere.

He stirred and we recited. He mixed new ingredients and gave us new words to say. This went on for several minutes, fifteen, twenty. Then, out came the chicken. Lido wrung its neck. Then he held the poor limp bird by its legs and spun it around our heads. He had the chicken in one hand and these sort of makeshift maracas in the other, rattles and feathers and beads and whatnot hanging off them. And he was shaking them and throwing himself around and screaming and carrying on and singing and talking loudly in a language I couldn't understand. Twenty minutes he carried on like a maniac and then it was all over.

He stuffed the dead chicken into a bag and told us to throw it into water. And that was it.

"How much did you give him?" I asked as we left the townhouse with this chicken in a brown paper bag. It smelled awful in the car, sitting on the seat between us.

"Don't ask," Bernie said.

"What, a lot? A hundred? Two?"

"Sandra!"

We left the car with our doorman and walked over to the East River. "What's the big secret? Why can't you tell me?"

It was two, three o'clock in the morning. Dark and hot out. Not a breath of air, not a soul in sight. According to Lido's instructions, we each had to have one hand on the bag. We'd been staying even with one another, but Bernie didn't want to talk to me about the money, so he started to speed up and I was huffing and puffing alongside him, trying to hang on to my end of the chicken.

"A lot, okay?" he grumbled.

"More than five hundred?"

"Yeah."

"You're kidding. Was it a thousand—or more?"

"More. Now stop."

"Holy shit," I said, as we reached the guard rail that ran alongside the river. "This better be good."

"Enough, Sandra," Bernie warned. "Just shut up and read the words, okay?" Lido had written down some prayers for us. He'd written them phonetically and we recited them several times as he'd instructed. And then we heave-hoed the chicken right into the river. According to Lido, we were now spiritually prepared to make a killing on the Ivory Coast.

Hot Dog Red was going with us. He was Bernie's partner in the deal. The three of us had been invited to stay at the prime minister's palace in Abidjan. While the boys shopped for gifts to shmear the officials and their wives with, I went to Abercrombie and Fitch and bought myself an authentic-looking safari outfit. I mean, what did I know about Africa? Nothing that I hadn't seen in the movies, and that meant snakes and lions in the daytime and mosquito netting and drums at night. In Bermuda shorts and a pith helmet, I was ready for the jungle. It never occured to me that Abidjan might be a bustling city. I thought Bernie was crazy when he told me to pack a couple of good dresses and high-heeled shoes. But, of course, I did it. And, of course, Bernie booked us all first class.

The tickets cost a fortune. It was the most expensive and longest plane ride I ever took in my life. But, what the hell, we weren't going to Miami, we were going halfway around the world to become millionaires. We started off happy, excited, raring to go, three amigos shlepping a ton of luggage, most of it filled with gifts for the Ivory Coast bigwigs, pens and pencils from Tiffany's, jewelry which B had gotten from friends in the business, silk scarves, gorgeous sweaters, perfume, booze, all beautifully gift-wrapped. But the flight seemed to take nine hundred hours. I think it was actually twenty—twenty hours in the air. And hour by hour, we lost our enthusiasm, got bored and quiet, and drank more and more.

When I say *we* got quiet, I mean Bernie and I. Red became a maniac on fire. When he got drunk, he got very hyper. For a little while, Bernie tried going through some papers with Red, going over prices and contracts and agreements that Josh had drawn up. Then he saw that Hot Dog was getting wilder by the minute, that he was too loaded to focus on business. I remember Bernie, finally, giving up and saying, "Okay, now listen. When we get there, you're going to give very little to the conversation, Red, you got me? All you've got to do is stand there and look black and listen and nod, okay?"

By this time Red had at least two cocktails and half a bottle of wine in him and who knew what else he'd thrown into the mix. A drink at a time, he had turned into a crazed cartoon of himself—louder, faster, blacker, more frantic and friendly than I'd ever seen him before. He was all over the place, laughing, chatting, jiving up a storm with anyone who'd look at him.

Bernie went to sleep. After a while, I conked out, too. But from the way he looked when we finally landed, I'm sure Red kept up his insanity for the rest of the flight. His wavy, processed red hair was sticking up all over the place. His pale brown skin was ashy, almost green. His eyes were bloodshot, the bags under them looked like they weighed as much as our luggage. He reeked of alcohol, smelled like it was oozing out of every pore; fumes curling up out of the tangerine and green racetrack-patterned shirt he was wearing and his shiny forest-green pants and even his pride-and-joy, pointy-toed beige 'gators.

We landed late at night, about ten o'clock, I guess. The diplomats Bernie and Red had befriended in New York had gotten in touch with their superiors, who had insisted on meeting the men who were going to be their purchasing agents in the U.S. A big limousine had been sent to the airport for us accompanied by another car, which was full of uniformed soldiers. They whisked us off the plane, piled our bags into the limo, and off we sped to the prime minister's palace. An assistant was waiting for us inside. He apologized for the prime minister's not being there to greet us personally, but he'd been called away to another part of the country on business and would be back the next day. The assistant showed us to our rooms, which were spacious and beautiful. Bernie and I had our own bedroom and sitting room. Red had the same set up next door. "Man, this is living," he kept saying. "Down here, the rich are rich and the poor are poor. These niggers know how to live."

There was food waiting, fruit and native dishes in beautiful covered platters, vegetable pies and tea. We ate and showered and slept until noon the next day and woke to find the sun streaming in through our windows. We were served an American breakfast in our rooms—bacon, eggs, coffee, and toast—and told that the prime minister was back and waiting for us.

The gifts Bernie had brought were very well received. The prime minister, the minister of commerce, secretaries, assistants, military men, everyone and their wives and children were lined up to meet us. And they oohed and aahed over the gifts Bernie handed out. Then we were escorted to a big terrace out back, a huge patio area where we sat and sipped tea and chatted like old friends. Only a few of the women and none of the children sat with us. Most waited at the edge of the lawn, staring and smiling shyly at us. The women were wearing beautiful bright turbans and long gowns. And, as I returned their quiet smiles, I couldn't help noticing that the entire backyard was ringed with military men, soldiers with guns. Lots of guns.

The minister of commerce, a dignified, gracious man, told Bernie that he didn't want to discuss business on the first day. "Tomorrow is soon enough," he said. "Perhaps you'd care to see a bit of our country today. And tonight we'll welcome you officially with a feast." So off we went to explore the countryside, again escorted by a car full of uniformed, gun-toting soldiers. As for the feast, I was very glad that Bernie had made me pack some dressy clothes. Everyone was done up to the nines for this extraordinary little dinner party the prime minister threw for us. Some of the men wore suits and ties, but most were in fabulous long robes with turbans and lots of gold bracelets and rings. The women looked exquisite in their tribal gowns. The food, native vegetable and fish dishes, was absolutely delicious and, of course, the booze flowed. They served Dom Pérignon and brandy and French wines with dinner. Hot Dog was in seventh heaven. "Man," he kept saying, "these niggers do live right."

"Shush, Red," I said more than once that night. "You can't talk that way. You're going to get us in trouble."

But he was buzzing. His eyes, glistening with pleasure, darted everywhere at once. "Um-hum," he said, smacking his lips. "We have fallen into the old honey pot this time, girl."

If I didn't know better, I thought to myself, I'd say Red was ripped on cocaine. He was speeding, drinking like booze was going out of style, and he could not stop talking.

Bernie had packed boxes of the best American cigars. The men enjoyed an after-dinner smoke. Conversation was pleasant, light, and friendly. The women were quiet, shy, almost subservient. They covered their mouths when they giggled. We had a terrific evening and went back to our rooms tired, happy, and full of optimism.

The next day, we were scheduled to meet with the prime minister after breakfast. We were shown into his office, which was big, sunny, and serious-looking. Aside from the ceiling fans and tall louvered doors, it could have belonged to the chairman of AT&T. Flanked by his minister of commerce and two aides, the prime minister waited in a tall mahogany leather chair behind a big polished desk. Bernie, Red, and I sat down opposite him.

Everything started out fine. Everyone was smiling. Bernie began to explain his business plan, telling them how he had access through his contacts to many kinds of goods. Hot Dog was beautiful, grinning, hadn't said a word, just backing Bernie up with nods and grins. And then Bernie pulled out some of the papers that Josh had drawn up. He passed them over to the prime minister, who gave them to the minister of commerce, as Bernie started to explain the financial arrangements. He sounded so legit, so calm and business-like, I was very proud of him. Then he said, "For obvious reasons, of course, we've got to handle the whole deal in cash."

The minister of commerce looked up from the papers. He kind of cocked his head like the RCA dog but didn't say anything, just waited and listened. And Bernie went on about how it had to be cash.

I don't know what happened. From the question of cash it started to move very quickly into other problem areas and, finally, the minister of commerce said, "I believe there's a misunderstanding about the question of your fee.'' He tapped the contract Bernie had given him and showed it to the prime minister and things heated up a little.

Then all of a sudden the prime minister said something to Bernie that Red didn't like. He sort of called him a crook. Bernie didn't like it, either, of course, but he kept cool. The next thing I knew, Red jumped up and started waggling his finger in the prime minister's face, yelling, ''You nappy-haired nigger, what are you trying to do, lay some jive on us?''

I could feel the blood drain from my face. I could see it leave Bernie's. We're sitting there, whiter than white, shaking, and all of a sudden, I notice that the prime minister's got a jumping jugular vein that makes Bernie's look laid back. Bim, bam, boom, the minister of commerce calls Bernie a thief or something to that effect. The prime minister rears up, points to the door, and says, ''You are to leave my country immediately. Get out!''

Red is already standing, already leaning across the PM's desk, and talking to the head of the Ivory Coast like he's some two-bit uptown numbers runner who's holding out on him. Red really gets into it, waving his hands and shaking his shoulders and really carrying on, when suddenly the door to the office bangs open and soldiers come running into the room with their guns pointed right at us.

Oh, my God, I'm a young girl. I haven't even lived yet. Now I'm going to die in Africa, I thought. My poor mother! No kidding, this is what I thought. I was crazy with fear. Half a dozen uniformed soldiers were standing there, nervous, angry, pointing rifles at us and you could see their hands shaking on the triggers.

From there, it got wilder. We were marched out of the office and made to sit in a small waiting room. Someone said our bags were being packed for us. The soldiers watching us never lowered their rifles. While they stood staring at us, holding guns on us, Bernie and Red started to argue. Bernie said out of the side of his mouth, ''Listen, I know what he was accusing me of and I could have handled it. You and your stupid mouth. I told you to keep quiet.''

Red was still revved up. ''You were going to let some jive-assed nigger fuck up the sweetest scam I ever saw. You think I'm going to sit there like a dummy watching this nappy-headed sucker steal my deal?''

''Please stop,'' I begged them. ''They're watching us. They're going to shoot us soon. Please stop yelling.''

''Look what you did,'' Bernie growled at Red. ''You see how you set us up? You couldn't listen to me. You couldn't keep your mouth shut. I told you, give nothing to the conversation. But you had to carry on! Now we'll either be shot or arrested. You don't listen! You don't learn!''

Within a matter of minutes, our luggage was brought down. The prime minister came in, followed by more soldiers. ''You are going to be driven to the airport and you are to get on the plane, which will be here in two hours," he announced in that cool, clipped voice. "The plane will return you to your country. If you aren't on that plane, you will be shot."

I thought I would die. But Bernie wanted to try to talk to him, charm him, change his mind. He started his spiel and the prime minister cut him off. "I don't do business with white trash," he said. I don't know where he learned that expression, but he said it with an ice-cold British accent.

Bernie's eyes narrowed and *his* vein started popping. "*You're* calling *me* white trash?!" He took a step toward the prime minister. And all you could hear in the room were guns clicking into place.

We were driven to the airport in the same limousine that had picked us up, followed again by a car full of soldiers. All during the ride, Red and Bernie were going at it. Then Red said, "Aw, the hell with this. I'm going to light up a joint." He pulled out some pot.

Bernie's eyes almost fell out of his head. "You traveled through Customs with pot?! What are you, crazy?"

"Why, you think I'd come to a hole like this without a stash? I got smoke, I got coke, I got what it takes. Yeah, that's right, you heard me, B. I got some toot here, too!" Red shouted back.

I thought Bernie would kill him. Instead, he got quiet and just shook his head. "You're really out of your fucking mind, you know? I was a fool to get involved with you, to bring you here. I should have known better." He was really stunned. It didn't stop him from taking a toke when Red passed the joint, though.

Red just shrugged at Bernie and rolled his eyes. He passed the joint around and the three of us got high in the back of the limo. It didn't take long before the driver got into the act. "What's that smell?" he asked. Red offered him the joint, told him it was a special tobacco grown in New York. So, the driver got loaded, too. By the time we got to the airport, the four of us were totally tilted.

The soldiers marched us through the place into a private room and we waited for the plane under guard. Instead of two hours, it took almost three for the plane to arrive. The entire time, except for brief smoke breaks when Red lit up another joint, Bernie and Red were at each other's throats. In the end, even I got into it.

"Look, it was a mistake, it wasn't meant to be, okay? What's the big deal?"

"Who asked you?" Bernie yelled at me. "Who the fuck asked for your brilliant opinion on this?"

"Brilliant? Sure, like throwing a chicken into the fucking East River is going to make us millionaires, right? Now, *that's* brilliant."

"Shut up, Sandra."

"Yeah, when you get back to New York and get your money back from Lido, I'll shut up."

"Stop, Sandra. Now!"

It was World War III. The soldiers were staring at us with their mouths open. They'd had three hours of Bernie pacing and grumbling at Red and at me, and me changing chairs trying to get comfortable and yelling at him, and Red just ranting non-stop, calling everybody names. They were nervous wrecks from being locked up with us and ready to put us out of our misery—or shut us up permanently to end theirs. Red's parting shot to the soldiers when the plane finally did arrive was: "When you get back, you tell your main man that I'm going home to Harlem and I'm getting my main man and we're going to come down here with mortars and machine guns and do you right!"

On the plane ride home we were so exhausted that we slept for almost the entire twenty hours. And, of course, once we got back to the United States, Bernie made me shut off the phones. He wouldn't take calls from anybody. He gave Red strict instructions to stay off the streets and not answer his phone and not show his face anywhere. Bernie was terrifically embarrassed at having been thrown out of the country. But after a day or two went by, he started to see the humor in the situation. And, the next thing you knew, he was telling everyone about it, cracking people up with his account of the *gantze megillah,* the whole deal. He was a great story-teller and, really, people used to fall off their chairs when he told this one.

By fall, when Farvel came up to New York, the Ivory Coast adventure had become such a classic that he insisted Bernie tell the story over dinner at Molly's on Rivington Street. It was a command performance—and what an audience! Once or twice a year, the heavy hitters would come into New York. Usually, Bernie would get a call from Farvel, from Florida, heralding the gathering. Within a week, they'd arrive from all over the States—from Boston, Minneapolis, California. There'd be Davey from Chicago, Geo from Las Vegas, Moe from Cleveland, old-timers like Red Levine and Farvel, who'd come up together on the Lower East Side, and younger guys who were learning the business.

Bernie would run down to the Luxor Baths to meet them. Sometimes he'd be away for a day or two. He'd stay over at the baths, spend the days steaming and talking business and eating in the restaurant down there. And then I'd get a call saying, "Okay, babe, get dolled up tonight. I want you to look gorgeous for me. We're going to Molly's," and I'd know that business had been concluded and the unwinding was about to begin.

The guys would put on their expensive suits and diamond tie pins and huge gold pinky rings. They'd be perfectly polished, barbered, manicured, and each of them would have a woman on his arm, an accessory as glittering and valuable as a cuff link. Oddly enough, most of the women these men brought to Molly's were wives. They just weren't married to the men they were with. Their husbands were straight guys; their boyfriends were gangsters.

My age—I was in my twenties, about ten years younger than the rest of the girls—and the fact that Bernie always called me his "lady," never his wife, made me a sort of honorary mistress. But the women I met at Molly's were fun-loving, sweet, *haimisha* girls and they always treated me very nicely, like a little sister or a favorite doll. And did they get *fahpitzed* to spend a night with their fellas? For a little middle-of-the-week dinner at Molly's, out would come the furs, the sequined sweaters, and low-cut, tight black dresses, the pointy-toed shoes with rhinestones stuck in the stiletto heels, the teased hair adding two to twelve inches to their height.

If the customers looked like a million, Molly's didn't. It was just a Jewish restaurant on Rivington Street on the Lower East Side. But when the boys from out of town wanted a place to unwind, to eat the food their mothers had fed them, to hear the songs and voices of their childhood, to take strength from their Jewish roots again, it beat the Copa by a mile.

Molly's was nothing to look at. Two steps down from the street, it was a narrow space with high ceilings and white walls. Behind the cash register was a Jewish calender and a framed photograph of Chaim Weizmann, the first president of the State of Israel. The tables were covered with plain white cloths. The blond wood chairs were scarred, darkened by time and grime, with inset leather seats and backrests. Very plain. And on the table would be bottles of seltzer, the old-fashioned kind that could double as a fire extinguisher, and bowls full of briny pickles and red peppers. There were no bread baskets, just white plates piled high with sliced rye. Hot tea was served in glasses. The sugar containers were tall cannisters with built-in metal funnels. And the white-aproned, singing waiters, who could pour chicken soup from thick metal cups into shallow bowls without losing a *lokshin* or spilling a drop, were wise-cracking, sour-faced veterans. There was a square stand-up bar near the entrance that dispensed everything from Mogen David to Moët.

Molly, herself, was a big-mouthed, bleached blonde made of the same stern stuff and loose flesh as Sophie Tucker. Her breasts bulged over the plunging necklines she wore. Her makeup was as abundant. She was crude, loud, and loving, knew every customer's preferences and peculiarities and those of his father before him. Molly was the original stand-up Jewish broad. And to add a touch of class to her place, she insisted that the musicians who played the whiny, joyous Jewish numbers her customers loved, the cigarette smoker hunched over the upright piano, the sad accordion player and the pasty-white violinist, all wore tuxedos.

"Sandela, *shayna,* how are you? You look so pretty tonight," Farvel would shout out, as we approached the big round table against the wall where the gang was gathered. "The kid's treating you good?"

"Very good, sweetheart," I'd say, kissing the cheek he extended to me.
Sometimes he'd remember and take the cigar out of his mouth first; sometimes not.

"You know everyone, right?"

By this Farvel meant the men. The women would introduce themselves.
"Hi, honey. Bea Spizer, we met last year when Harry was in town."

That night, that September after the Ivory Coast fiasco, Red Levine—
whose last name was pronounced to rhyme with divine—was sitting across
from Farvel. What they had in common, aside from their ever-present
cigars, was Meyer. They were his, they'd grown up in the shadows of the
same tenements; they'd served him. They were, as the newspapers and
television programs called them, his "lieutenants," his "trusted aides."

Red still had the full, if thinning, head of wavy reddish-blond hair that
had won him his nickname. He was about my height, no more, and very
thin. And sitting beside him was Sylvia, the good-looking woman who'd
gotten drunk at another of Molly's dinners and whom I'd had to escort
home to a very impressive apartment on Second Avenue. Red was in his
late fifties, early sixties then and looked like a kindly Jewish uncle, a nice
guy, a sweetheart—which he always was to me. It was hard for me to
believe that this was the same man who supposedly carried out one of the
most notorious hits in gangland history, the man Meyer assigned to direct
the squad of Jewish gunmen who murdered Salvatore Maranzano. After
Maranzano's death—four bullets and six knife wounds after—Meyer and
his boyhood friend, Lucky Luciano, were supposed to have organized the
new mafia, The Syndicate or The Outfit as it was called. The syndicate
was run by five "families" rather than one "boss of all bosses"—which
was the title Maranzano had reserved for himself.

When Bernie first introduced me to Red Levine, you could always find
him hanging out at the bocci courts over at First Street and Avenue A.
He'd just be standing there, talking to old friends, patting neighborhood
kids on the head. A sweet man. A *ziskite*. And, years later, when Bernie
was gone and Red was really an old man, I drove down to the Lower East
Side with Jeffrey in the car. Jeffrey was a baby then. We were in the car
together and something went wrong. The car started rolling. I couldn't stop
it. I screamed for help. And Red Levine, who had to have been in his
seventies, ran down the street, threw open the driver's door, and forced the
brake down until the car finally stopped. If it hadn't, I'm convinced Red
would have done something else, even if it meant hanging on to the bumper
until his shoes left skidmarks on the street.

Red knew Bernie from the old days, from when Bernie was an eleven-
year-old kid working at—and, as Red never failed to remind him, stealing
hats from—the best haberdashery on the Lower East Side. He had a real
fondness for Bernie. So when Farvel gave Bernie the high sign and said,
"Go on, kid. Tell 'em how the *shvartzas* threw you out. Out of Africa,

Red! Wait, this you're not going to believe!'' Red started grinning right away.

"Still a *mamzer*," he said, affectionately. Still a little bastard.

The guys never talked business at Molly's. They laughed. They drank. And when the little *klezmer* band played the old favorites, "Bei Mir Bist du Schön" or "Orchu Chonya" and, especially, "My Yiddishe Momme," the men's eyes would mist over. "Oy," they'd sigh. "You remember that song, Farvela? *Gedenkt?*" Do you remember? Sometimes they'd cry. And late at night, fueled by memories and J&B, they'd leap to their feet when the band played a *hora* or a handkerchief dance.

And they ate. Boy, did they eat. The waiters would cruise out with course after course of plates piled high with herring and boiled beef, chopped liver, potato latkes, roast chicken, unborn eggs, brains, stuffed derma, *lokshin kugels*—noodle puddings—and a chopped tenderloin cutlet they used to call "mush steak."

"You don't get food like this in Vegas, do you, Geo?" someone would say. Or, "Go try to find a decent stuffed derma in Cleveland."

Everything was washed down with seltzer, bottle after bottle of bubbly, stinging, belch-inducing seltzer. And when the gatherings got a little wild and the guys a little frisky, it was not unknown for them to have seltzer fights, *shpritzing* each other like schoolboys until Molly trundled over, flesh heaving, hammy fists on her hips, to demand: "What the hell is going on here?!''

I loved it. I loved the old songs. I loved the Jewishness. I loved the food. When I knew we were going to Molly's for dinner, I'd starve myself all day and really go to town.

"Look how skinny she is," Red's girl Sylvia would marvel, watching me put away the food. "So, Bernie, when are you going to fatten her up so I don't have to eat my heart out with jealousy? Tell me, *mamela*, when are you going to get pregnant? When are we going to see a belly on you?''

CHAPTER TWELVE

A Birthday Present for Bernie

Sylvia wasn't the only one who asked. Some of the wives would tease me about it. My friend Judy, who'd finally traded in her famous hairdresser for the piano player from Jilly's (not poor Nicky "Fly Me to the Moon" DeFrancis, who'd thrown himself out a window, but a stunning young Latino named Nino) and now had a beautiful little girl, mentioned it every time I visited her. "Sandy, you're so good with the baby," she'd say in her unconquerable Kentucky drawl. "When are you going to have one of your own?" And, of course, my mother never stopped hoping and hinting. "Maybe you should get a nice two bedroom place, sweetheart. Maybe, if there was room for a baby—"

But nobody asked the question more than I did. It was 1964. I was already twenty-five years old. If not now, when? I began to wonder. "Soon, babe," Bernie would always answer. "I promise you, Sandy. Soon."

He didn't seem to be against the idea, I reasoned during my solitary walks along the river, where I'd see women wheeling baby carriages, or when I sat alone on a bench in the sunshine of the little park behind our building watching nannies and mothers chasing toddlers, or in the supermarket when I'd push my cart full of grown-up food past the grinning baby faces on the Gerber and Beechnut jars.

Bernie was doing well at the time. His health seemed to be holding up. He hadn't been hospitalized in nearly a year. He was running around like crazy, busy day and night. The hassock was stuffed with cash. It was one of those rare times when there was more coming in than going out. I'd carry envelopes to the safety deposit boxes a couple of times a month.

And sometimes when I asked myself, "If not now, when?" it wasn't just the baby I meant. It was "If not now, when will we be *normal*?" Having a baby began to seem like the first installment on that dream.

It was summertime. We were all dressed up, on our way to an engagement party or a wedding. It was an afternoon affair, which meant there'd be kids around. "Bernie, I really want to have a baby," I said. "I'm twenty-five already."

"Yeah, I know," he said, eyes on the road, not even looking at me. "I'm thinking of trading you in for a couple of seventeen-year-olds."

I burst into tears.

"What?" he said. "What the hell's going on with you?"

"You're not kidding," I sobbed.

I believed it. I believed that soon I would be too old to be glamorous to him, that he'd take a mistress like the other mob guys—if he didn't already have one! He was away so much. How did I know he wasn't running around on me? It was part of the life. There were always glamor girls who hung out around mob guys. They had more groupies than rock-and-roll stars—gorgeous young girls turned on by the action, money, and power, as attracted to the scene as I'd been. And hadn't I spent evenings with the guys and their girlfriends—at the Copa, at Molly's, at after-hours joints and racetracks, lowlife bars, and pricey restaurants? I even knew and loved some of the girlfriends. My friend Toni was being kept by a big-deal Italian mobster and had been for years. Even Red Levine, who always seemed so *haimish* to me, had his Sylvia. I'd be with the guys and their girlfriends one night, and two nights later, in the same restaurant, I'd be sitting there with them and their wives.

Once I even asked a friend of Bernie's, "Why do you run around? Why do you cheat?"

"For the glamour," he said. "You've got to have a broad by your side and she's got to be the best." He pointed to some of the girls in the nightclub we were in. Most were sitting beside men who were talking to one another or focused entirely on sawing through their sirloin steaks and wolfing down their baked potatoes. The men barely looked at the women sitting next to them, as beautifully made-up and decked out as they were— with jewels sparkling from their earlobes, around their necks, on the fingers that held the cigarettes, or gold lighters or drink stirrers that they toyed with. "You see how they sit, they listen? Not one of them is smart. You tell them where to stand, where to sit, and you tell them how high to jump."

"Very nice," I remember saying sarcastically.

But now the idea that Bernie might view things the same way, might want, or even have, a decorative little girl to tell how high to jump, drove me crazy.

Sometimes tears infuriated Bernie; sometimes he was moved by them. That afternoon in the car, he pulled his handsome Sulka handkerchief out of his breast pocket and handed it to me. "What the hell's wrong with you today? I was teasing you, that's all," he said. "You want a baby? We'll have a baby. I told you we would. Soon. I promised you, didn't I, that I'd give you the life you wanted?"

"You mean it?" I wrapped my arms around his neck and hugged him. "Oh, sweetheart, you really mean it, right?"

"Yeah, yeah. Take it easy." He grinned and pulled himself free of my grip. "I'm driving, baby."

"But you mean it."

"Sure," Bernie said. "Soon."

That was the last day I took the Pill. I didn't say anything to Bernie about it. I just went off birth control and onto sex. I took him at his word. Soon meant soon. Within three months, I knew I was pregnant. But the urine test I took came back negative—three times. "I don't care what that test shows," I told Tillie in the luncheonette where we were having coffee. "I know when I'm pregnant, Ma. And I'm pregnant."

"From your mouth to God's ear," she said, clasping her hands together dramatically. "But, *mamela,* this time, if the doctor says no, I mean, this time you took a blood test, right? So, if he says no today, don't worry. You'll just forget about it and you'll keep trying."

"Is it time yet? What time is it, Ma?" I was supposed to call Dr. Truppin at five o'clock to find out the results of the blood test.

"You've got time. It's four-thirty."

"I'm going to call him right now. I'm pregnant, Ma. I just know it."

Truppin was in. "Good news," he said.

"I'm pregnant?!"

"You're pregnant, Sandy. You were right." When he gave me the due date, I whooped with joy.

"What?!" my mother said when I came back to the booth.

"Bingo! I'm having a baby, Ma."

"No!"

"Yes! And you'll never guess the due date. May twenty-eighth, Ma! I'm going to give birth on Bernie's birthday!"

"Mazel-tov! Oh, my God, I'm going to be a grandma!" We both laughed.

"It's a boy," I said. "I know it like I knew I was pregnant even when the tests said no." This was before amnio or sonograms, before it was possible to know the sex of the baby in advance.

"Whatever it is, as long as it's healthy, you'll be happy," my mother assured me. "And, Sandy, wait. Now you'll see. Things'll change."

"What's it like," I asked, as we left the coffee shop together, "having a baby, Ma?"

She squeezed my arm and shook her head. "*Oy,* don't ask," she said. "Better you shouldn't know." But not even that could daunt me. I put Tillie in a cab to Brooklyn and rushed home to Bernie.

It was a beautiful October day. The terrace door was open and he was sitting near it, at the bar, having a drink before he went out for the evening. His hair was slicked back, still wet from the shower he'd taken. The top button on his monogrammed powder-blue shirt was open; his silk tie was unknotted. He looked relaxed, comfortable.

"Do you have to go out tonight?" I asked.

"Why? You want to come along? Come with me, I'm going uptown for a couple of hours, then we'll stop in and see Cokey—"

"No, honey. That's not what I meant. I mean, can't you stay home with me? Bernie, there's something I want to tell you."

He looked at me and sighed and shook his head. "Here we go," he said. "I hate surprises, Sandra. And I can tell you've got a beauty cooking."

"Well, you're right," I blurted out, laughing. "I'm pregnant, Bernie. I'm giving you a son on your birthday!"

He gave me a long, stunned look, then set his drink down on the bar. "You're pregnant?"

The laugh began to stick in my throat. Suddenly, I was ready to cry, ready for him to blow his top. "Yeah, I am," I said, and nodded.

"We're going to have a baby?" he said, and slowly his face broke into a huge smile. "No shit?"

"A boy, Bernie. On your birthday. The doctor said the due date is May twenty-eighth."

He jumped up off the barstool. "How do you know it's a boy?"

I shrugged. "I just know."

"A baby. A son. You think I'm going to have a son?" He was definitely warming to the idea, getting excited. I nodded and he gave me a great big hug, then he leapt away from me. "Oh, my God, did I hurt you? Are you okay?"

"I'm fine."

"This is great. Great, baby! We've got to do something. We've got to celebrate!" Within fifteen minutes, he'd hit the phone and told the world that we were expecting, that *he* was expecting an heir. "This is it," I heard him tell Vinny. "No more fooling around. I'm going to get my act together." He'd said the same or similar to at least four other friends he'd called. "I'm going to put aside a little bread, then go legit," he'd told them. "This kid is going to have a decent life, the best of everything. Come on over, we're going to celebrate."

Oh, my God, I thought. Tillie was right when she said things would change. Here was Bernie making promises, not just to me, but to Vinnie and Josh and Red. He even put in a call to Trenton, to tell Chalky in prison that night.

The gang assembled and it was party time. After the last guest had left, and it was probably Hot Dog at three or four in the morning, when we were finally alone in the apartment, Bernie put his arms around me. "I'm so happy, baby. And I don't want you to worry about a thing," he said, earnestly. "Everything is going to work out for us now. I know things have been rough for you. But it'll be different now, Sandy. This baby is going to change our luck. And I'm going to take good care of you, both of you. You wait and see. I'm going to take care of everything."

He meant it. In the next couple of months, Bernie went into high gear. He became obsessed with getting ready for the baby, but in his own way, in his own style. A two-bedroom apartment became available in our own building, a beautiful, sunny place with a terrace overlooking the river. The rent was outrageous, but Bernie snapped it up immediately. "He's got to have the best, our kid," he'd say. "I've got to put the money together now because you never can tell what'll happen down the road."

We went shopping for baby furniture. And again, of course, nothing but the best would do. At a very exclusive showroom on lower Fifth Avenue, which featured British baby furniture and carriages, we chose everything we needed for the nursery and a Royal Coach baby carriage. It was a huge, extravagant carriage—"The kind you see British nannies wheeling in Hyde

Park,'' the salesman in the three-piece suit and uptown accent assured us.
"It'll take a month to arrive from London, but it's well worth the wait."

"Bernie," I whispered. "It's so expensive."

"I keep telling you, Sandy, this kid's going first class. He's got to start
out right, baby."

The bigger I got, the more tenderly Bernie treated me, and the harder
he worked. I asked him to slow down, stay home. "First, I want to put
together a couple of big scores," he'd say. "You never know. I'm not going
to leave you young with a baby to take care of and no money."

He started talking about the future that way more and more. How he
had to run and set up this little deal downtown, put out a couple of loans
uptown, take a trip here, make a call there . . .

"Because what are you going to do if something happens to me,
baby?'' . . . "Because I'm not going to be around forever and you're going
to need a nest egg to bring my son up right." . . . "Because there's no
telling what's in the cards, Sandy, and then where would you live? What
would you do?"

"Stop it!" I'd wind up shouting at him. "I don't want to hear it, Bernie!" I was pregnant. I was superstitious. I was in love with him. I couldn't
think about living without him. I sure as hell wasn't going to talk about it.
The sickness and danger were behind us, I told myself. This was a time of
joy. We were having a baby, taking a step toward the good life, the straight
life. And that meant Mommy and Daddy and baby makes three, not two.

Like a harbinger of doom, like a bird of prey, slimy Hymie the Sleazeball
showed up. Hymie was a cousin of Bernie's from the Lower East Side. He
was a nervous, chubby, pear-shaped little *shlemiel,* whom Bernie had helped
out of a jam years ago. Hymie, who talked a mile a minute and whose
eyes shifted just as fast, had been caught embezzling from the men's clothing store he'd managed. Bernie had paid back the money—$20,000 or
$30,000 it was—out of his strong sense of family loyalty and he'd gotten
the owner to drop the charges.

Except for their blue eyes, there was no family resemblance at all between Bernie and Hymie. Hymie was older, shorter, paler—he had the
pasty white skin of a *yeshiva bucher.* What hair he had left was a washed-
out reddish-blond and his balding head was always beaded with sweat. Hot
Dog Red couldn't believe they were related by blood. He hated Hymie on
sight—which wasn't that hard to do. The guy oozed flattery and deceit.

But he was family. In Bernie's book that made him trustworthy. And the
way Bernie was setting up new deals and businesses now, he needed more
help than Hot Dog could give him. He'd even started putting out a little
shylock money and he assigned Hymie to keep track of the loans and pick
up the payments.

"I don't understand it," I'd tell Red. "Bernie knows how sticky this sleazeball's fingers are. How can he trust him? How can he bring him into the business, into our home?''

Hymie's marriage was on the rocks. I'd met his girlfriend, who looked more like a whale than a homewrecker. She towered over him. With a little heave, her breasts, which were enormous, could've rested comfortably on his hunched shoulders. Breasts aside, she looked like a guy in drag.

Because he hated to go home, Sleazeball used to hang around our place. He'd poke around, look in the medicine chest, in the kitchen cabinets, the refrigerator. He'd walk behind the bar and fix himself a nice stiff scotch. He started answering the phone when it rang.

"Hymie, this is my house," I'd say. "You can't answer the phone."

"What's the difference, Bernie's expecting an important telephone call," he'd say in that voice like a chipmunk on speed, "so I picked it up, what's the harm, relax, Sandy." This round-shouldered, pear-shaped, pasty-faced, sweat-soaked loser was suddenly swaggering around my apartment doing gangster imitations. "Relax, Sandy. I'm just trying to help out. Remember, if anything happens to the big guy, you can count on me."

I wanted to kill him. I'd complain to Red or my mother, but I never said anything to Bernie about Sleazeball, which was what I'd taken to calling him. Bernie had enough on his mind. He was running himself ragged. I could see it coming. "You're going to get sick if you keep up this pace, Bernie. You've got to get some rest."

"You're the one who needs the rest, sweetheart. I'm doing fine. Never felt better in my life. Hey, I'm going to be a father, right? A father works hard, gets things set up for his kid, right? So you go lay down, baby. I've got to make a couple more calls. Then Hymie's stopping by and we're going downtown for an hour or so."

Bernie was doing a lot of things I hadn't seen him do before. Although, in the old days, on East Seventy-ninth Street, he'd sometimes ask me to wait in the bedroom alcove or even in the bathroom while he talked a deal with a couple of visitors, he'd never asked me to leave the house. Now, it was getting to be a habit. A squat, dark-haired Spanish-speaking man would show up from time to time. He'd come in with suitcases and Bernie would ask me to take a walk. I saw this dark-haired guy maybe four or five times in the apartment or I'd pass him in the hallway or the lobby as I was leaving. He spoke no English. He was always shlepping those suitcases. I didn't ask Bernie what was in them. I had a feeling it was drugs, pot maybe, maybe even cocaine. I never asked. And Bernie never offered an explanation.

Of course, *I* also did a couple of things I hadn't done before. We were going out to dinner with Cokey and Iris one Friday. I had a beauty parlor appointment that day. It was supposed to be just for a manicure, but I decided to get my hair cut—short. My hairdresser tried to talk me out of

it, but I'd made up my mind. With great reluctance, he gave me what I'd
asked for. The shop was in the lobby of our building. I thought I looked
great until I got upstairs.

Cokey and Iris were already there. Bernie was at the bar fixing them
a drink. I walked in, or waddled—I was close to six months pregnant
then—expecting oohs and aahs. Cokey and Iris were kind enough just to
go slack-jawed. Bernie was more expressive. "What the hell did you do?"
he demanded.

"Why? I like it. I think it's cute," I protested.

"You look like a fat boy!" Bernie said.

"Bastard," I mumbled, biting back the tears.

"I swear, a fat *boy*! Look at her. Tell her. Come on, Cokey. Iris, tell
her the truth. Cute, she says!"

"It is cute. I think it's cute," Iris soothed.

I steamed off into the bedroom to change for dinner. "You're late,"
Bernie called after me. When we were ready to leave, he grabbed my coat
and held it up for me to slip into. Instead of sliding an arm into the sleeve,
I made a fist and pushed through hard and punched Bernie in the nuts.
"Jesus!" he gasped and went down on one knee behind me.

"Oh, honey, I'm so sorry," I said sweetly.

Iris took my arm and hurried me out the door while Cokey waited, trying
to keep a straight face, for Bernie to catch his breath again.

I was having a very healthy pregnancy. I felt good most of the time. But
I was gaining weight like crazy. I don't know if I looked like a fat boy
but, boy, was I fat! My belly, at five months, stuck out so far I used to
rest my arms on it. Which Bernie hated. It made him nervous. "Stop that,"
he'd beg me. "Look how you're pressing down on your belly. You'll crush
the baby's head."

I was in my sixth month when Bernie had another attack. He caught a
cold that quickly turned into pneumonia and he went into congestive heart
failure. Red and I rushed him to the hospital once again. I was distraught.
I was hugely pregnant, super-sensitive, and very scared. I knew how much
these bouts with illness took out of Bernie. I knew how much his conva-
lescences took out of me even when I was normal, how much running
around I'd have to do. I knew the house would fill up with his friends
again, and I was in no condition to trundle around emptying ashtrays and
cleaning up after the boys.

I was at the hospital, sitting outside Bernie's room, feeling sorry for
myself when Dr. Sealy finished his examination and came out into the
hallway.

"How are you, Sandy?" he asked gravely.

"Fat," I said, and laughed. "Other than that, I'm okay. A little tired.

A little nervous about Bernie. He's really been running around like mad these past few months, Doctor Sealy. He got himself really run down.''

"If you're feeling up to it, come take a walk with me. I want to talk to you." Sealy helped me up out of the chair. He kept a hand on my elbow as we walked along the corridor on the way to his office. "You know, you were right. Bernie has exhausted himself. He's always been a very sick man, Sandy, and he's gotten worse."

He opened the door to his office and we went inside. "I'm sorry, Sandy. I hate to have to tell you this, especially now, at a time like this. This should be a happy time for you. Your first baby. But Bernie is very sick," Dr. Sealy said, once we were seated. "The hole in his heart has gotten too big."

"What does that mean?" I asked, afraid that I already knew. I sat there with my hands crossed on my belly. I'm crushing the baby's head, I thought, as if Bernie were inside my brain, as if I could hold on to him by becoming him, thinking his thoughts instead of mine.

"Sandy, I'm sorry," Dr. Sealy said. "I don't think he'll live out the year."

For a minute, I just sat there. Then I shook my head no.

I kept on shaking my head as if that could change things, as if I could shake out Sealy's words. My head whirled with noise—I was thinking a thousand things at once, feeling a thousand feelings. Fear. Terrible, raw fear gripped me.

No, I kept thinking, this isn't true. How can he do this to me, I thought, as if Bernie's being sick was just some mean thing he was doing to hurt me, to frighten me. I shouldn't have cut my hair, I thought, as if that had something to do with his sickness, as if the hair I'd cut off had held whatever magic it took to keep Bernie healthy. I won't live through this, I thought. I don't know how to live. I couldn't take care of Bernie; how can I take care of a baby? I don't even know how to take care of myself. Who'll tell me what to do? Who'll teach me? And I could hear Bernie saying, "Don't forget, kid. I taught you everything you know. But I didn't teach you everything *I* know."

And underneath the jumble of thoughts and feelings, I heard myself sort of chanting. "He can't die, it's not true, he can't die, it's not true, he can't die."

Finally, I said, "Does Bernie know, Doctor Sealy? Did you tell him what you just told me?"

"No."

"Does anyone else know?"

"No, Sandy. No one knows but you."

"I want to tell my mother," I said, "nobody else."

A nurse was carrying a basket of fruit into Bernie's room when I got back. There were already two or three more bouquets of flowers than when I'd left, and almost an entirely new shift of friends. Hot Dog was gone, but Uncle Vinny had showed up. Bernie was propped up on the pillows. He winked at me. His face creased with pain.

"He looks like shit," Vinny said to me, not bothering to lower his voice.

I walked past him to the side of Bernie's bed. There was a needle in his hand attached to an intravenous tube. I just put his palm onto mine and held his hand for a little while. "Baby, I'm going to call my mother, then I'm going home. I'm very tired. But I'll be back later."

"No. You take it easy. You're carrying precious cargo. Stay home tonight. Give Tillie my love. I'll see you tomorrow."

I kissed his head and went home.

"He's dying, Mama," I said when Tillie came over to our apartment that evening. I'd asked her to spend the night with me. I didn't want to be alone.

"Sandy, if it's God's will, he'll get to see his baby born. Then, we'll see. We'll just take it one step at a time."

Bernie was in the hospital for about three weeks, which was the length of his usual stay. Hot Dog drove us home. This time, Bernie didn't even walk to the car. He was taken by wheelchair to the lobby and then he had to use Red and me as crutches to get from the hospital doors to the curb. He was in a great mood though, tipping the nurses and attendants as usual, basking in their smiles, handshakes, and words of farewell: "Good luck, Mr. Barton." "Pleasure to meet you, Mr. B." "What a nice man, isn't he, Mary?" But he'd really begun to deteriorate.

He looked old and tired. His skin was sallow and seemed to hang loosely on him. His eyes were ringed with purple circles and so creased with worry or pain that he seemed to be squinting. Even with his sunglasses on, you could see the wrinkles fanning out from the corners of his eyes, carving into his empty cheeks. His lips were dry, chalky-white; the corners were red, raw, and ulcerated when he smiled. Ah, but that smile, those beautiful, big white teeth—it lit up his face the same as ever.

In the car, he grinned. "Home, Mr. Dog," he commanded in a softer but still gravelly voice.

"You feeling fine, B?" Hot Dog asked.

"I'm going home, aren't I? Can't feel better than that."

He was retaining water. He wouldn't stay on the diet the doctor had recommended. So Dr. Sealy taught me how to inject him with silverate of mercury, which was supposed to handle the bloating. I had to practice by injecting an orange.

Every other day, crouching on my swollen legs, leaning over the bed with my big belly, I injected the solution into Bernie's thigh. Then I'd fix his breakfast and get out the pills he had to take, and clean up the dishes Sleazeball Hymie and his girlfriend had left in the sink the night before, and answer the second phone because Bernie was already talking on the first one, and answer the door because Dominick S. was stopping by on his way home from an after-hours joint with a couple of girls he'd just met and a big stinking cigar stuck in his mouth, and Carlos from uptown had a couple of bags of merchandise he wanted B to take a look at, and Billy Daniels who'd just finished his gig in Atlantic City at three A.M. was downstairs in a limo wanting to know if B was awake yet. I didn't get to take a shower or put on makeup or just sit down with a cup of coffee until Hot Dog showed up around eleven or twelve each day.

Bernie and Red had built their friendship and trust through the years, but my love affair with Hot Dog, because that's what it was, this amazing friendship infused with laughter, respect, and love, had blossomed in adversity. It was a relationship I couldn't have imagined that very first day when I found him sitting on the sofa in Bernie's livingroom all duded up in his orange slacks and beige 'gators. Back then, with my prejudice and ignorance, it was fear at first sight. But Red had been there for me through thick and thin ever since. From Bernie's first illness before we were married when I was scared to death that he would die in my arms and Hot Dog had appeared like a genie from a bottle to drive us to the hospital, to the insanity of our three amigos Ivory Coast adventure, to the way he showed up day after day now, during Bernie's illness, never entering the house empty-handed, always bringing fresh bread or milk or juice or phoning first to ask what I needed—I'd never have survived without him.

My mother, too, was there for me. She had a good job then. A customer from the dry-cleaning shop where she'd worked in Brooklyn had gotten her a clerical position at a brokerage house on Wall Street. From there, on her own, Tillie had worked her way up to office manager. I called her a hundred times a day. And, if I needed her, she'd drop everything and come uptown to sit with me, talk with me, help out in any way she could. Sometimes she'd stop by after work and stay with me for the evening; sometimes she'd sleep over. We'd have ourselves little pajama parties and talk about everyone and everything but how sick Bernie was.

The one topic on which Tillie was less than helpful turned out to be childbirth. Whenever I asked her what it would be like or how it had been for her, she went into a melodrama, she gave a monologue, that would've been held over forever at the Yiddish Theatre on Second Avenue.

First would come the baleful look, the eyes beseeching heaven as her witness, the tight mouth pulled down at the corners. Then she'd start with the clucking tongue, "tch, tch, tch." And finally, it went something like this: "A labor I had from you, don't ask. Twenty hours, maybe more, tearing out my *kishkas*. And it was miserable out. Raining. And the wind was blowing. And they came in to me—I was screaming. And did they bring me even a glass of tea?!'' And so on.

Red and my mother were the two people I depended on during that frightening time when I was pregnant, big as a house, and emotionally wrung out from trying to nurse Bernie back to health while carrying the most terrible secret of my life. And as comforting as Hot Dog and Tillie were, that was how irritating Hymie was. More and more he came to resemble a vulture, a miserable fat bird circling, sniffing around, waiting to make his move.

He sidled up to me in the kitchen one day with half a pastrami sandwich in his hand. Josh and Uncle Vinny and some of the other guys always made sure there was plenty of food around. As soon as one platter started to look depleted, they'd phone out and order more from the deli. So the Sleaze came in carrying this huge, overstuffed half of a sandwich and, again, he started with his big plans for the future. ''Sandy, I just want you to know that if anything happens to Bernie, we'll keep the businesses going, you and me, just like Bernie would want. We'll keep everything in the family and we'll take care of that baby in your belly, because I know you really know a lot about Bernie's businesses.''

Although I had a miraculously healthy pregnancy, I was very depressed that day. I hadn't had my home to myself, except for a few hours while we slept, in weeks and weeks. There were always strangers coming and going and friends dropping around. Even when Red or Josh would drive Bernie uptown or to someplace out of the house when he had an appointment, there'd usually be a couple of people hanging around waiting for them to come back. So I'd gone into the kitchen to get away from the tumult for a minute, and here came Hymie, his pasty face oiled with sweat as usual, bringing with him the future that I tried so hard not to think about. I despised him at that moment. But, oddly enough, I didn't let loose on him.

''Thanks, Hymie,'' I said. ''I know I can count on you. But, you never know, life changes from minute to minute. Let's just wait and see what it brings us.''

Sleazeball left the kitchen and I was amazed at the way I'd handled myself. Later that day, I told Red what had happened. ''You're turning into 'my man,' '' he said, and laughed. ''You handled that roach exactly the way B would have done it.''

As the weather got nicer, Bernie would sometimes sit out on the terrace. He'd take the phone out there with him and make his calls and shmooze for hours. He was physically weak but his mind—and his mouth—were working a mile a minute. My mouth was going, too. Mostly to the kitchen, where I'd nosh on the leftover appetizing and deli and Chinese food. I was eating out of nerves and I was very nervous and very big. I was also always tired.

Sometimes Bernie would wake me in the middle of the night and ask me to make him a cup of tea. I wanted to sleep. I needed my sleep. Sometimes, I'd just turn my back on him and say, "No, you go do it yourself. I'm exhausted." Sometimes we'd have screaming fights in the dark over such garbage. And sometimes, I'd just climb out of bed and shuffle into the kitchen half-asleep and put up the water and lean against the refrigerator door with my arms crossed and resting on my huge belly, and wait for the water to boil for his tea.

One afternoon, I remember, I'd gone into the baby's room, probably to find a moment's peace and quiet. The furniture we'd ordered from England hadn't arrived yet but the blue carpeting was in and the pretty wallpaper Tillie and I had picked out. I ran my hand over the teddy bear pattern on the wall and I walked over to the closet and opened the door. The closet was empty, of course. I stepped inside and closed the door behind me. The next thing I knew, I was sitting on the floor of the empty closet in the baby's room, sobbing. I felt like a little girl in a secret hide-away trying to find a place where no one could find me and nothing could hurt me. But all I could think about was how alone I felt and how lonely I was going to be without Bernie.

Halfway through my seventh month, the baby's room was still bare. The fine furniture and fancy carriage we'd ordered had arrived from England, but a dock strike had shut down the New York piers. No one dared cross the stevedores' picket lines. No cargo was being unloaded.

Finally, Bernie made a phone call. "Okay," he said to me, one icy morning in March, "here's the story. You go down to the docks on the West Side, go to Pier #21, and ask for Tommy P."

My belly had outgrown my widest winter coat, but I wore the coat anyway, open, of course, over a couple of layers of sweaters and, in slacks and flats and gloves and a woolen hat pulled over my still short and choppy hair, I caught a cab down to the docks. I waddled onto Pier #21 clutching the piece of paper on which I'd written Bernie's instructions.

Crates were stacked high in front of every ship. The ships were as tall as buildings and the pier seemed endlessly long. With my belly sticking out of the coat, I shlepped the length of three city blocks before I found Tommy P. He was a rough-looking guy in his fifties, with a nose full of broken veins and a full head of salt-and-pepper hair that whipped around in the wind. He was standing outside a little wooden shack. He helped me inside and asked where the baby furniture had come from and the name of the store where we'd bought it. With large, scarred, and callused hands he rifled through endless papers. Then he took my arm and together we shuffled along another mile or so of oil-stained rotting boards until we got to the ship.

There was a man in a pea coat and Navy watch cap standing next to the boxes piled in front of an enormous ship. Tommy P. talked to him. The guy went scurrying up onto the ship and Tommy said to me, "Stay here and don't move. They're going to bring a chair for you, and then we'll get your stuff."

Well, they sat me down, belly and all, right there on the dock amongst the cartons and crates and ropes and dollies and picketing stevedores and sailors gaping down from the ships. They even brought me hot tea. And, for about forty minutes, I sat there, alone, in a chair on the dock, sipping tea in the wind. It was the most luxurious, relaxing time I'd had in weeks.

Tommy came back with six *bulvons*—six of the biggest, strongest, most strapping men I'd ever seen—and while they carried carton after carton of baby furniture off the ship, a truck pulled up and a couple of other *shtarkers* started loading our stuff onto it. "Okay," Tommy said when everything was accounted for and waiting in the truck. "Just give me the address and we'll deliver it."

I gave him our address and then took out the envelope full of cash Bernie had given me. "How much do I owe you?" I asked.

He put up his palm like a traffic cop. "Don't worry about it. It's all been taken care of." Then he put me in a car and I was driven home. The truck arrived moments after I did. Six guys carried in the crates and cartons. They put together every piece of furniture and assembled the magnificent baby carriage for us and, refusing anything but a couple of beers, they left.

We were ready.

About a month before I gave birth, Bernie started to feel better. The color returned to his face. He could breathe normally again. Even his voice seemed stronger. I thought a miracle had happened. But Dr. Sally warned me against optimism. However wonderful Bernie felt or looked at that moment, nothing had changed inside. The hole in his heart was as dangerous, and inevitably fatal, as ever.

The baby was due on May twenty-eighth, just before the Memorial Day weekend. Dr. Truppin, my obstetrician, had plans to go on vacation. He had me come in for an examination on May twenty-seventh, and he said, "You're ready. We'll deliver you tomorrow."

I was shocked. "What do you mean? How can you tell?" I asked.

"If the water hasn't broken by tomorrow morning, you come into the office and I'll do it for you. Then we'll put you in the hospital."

I went home and, of course, I told Bernie. We had plans to go to the Copa that night, to celebrate his birthday at midnight. It was a Thursday, the night the Copa opened its new acts, and the whole world was there. We ran into Hattie Prince at the bar. "Mazel-tov." She grinned at my belly. "See. I told you you'd be fine, kid, didn't I?" she whispered to me after extending her cheek to Bernie for a kiss. "So when are you due? You look like you're going to have it tonight."

"Tomorrow," Bernie said. "It's my birthday gift."

Uncle Vinny waved us over to a table near the dance floor. He was wearing a three-piece suit and his usual immaculate pin-striped shirt. Vinnie believed pin-stripes made him look taller. He was considered a stylish dresser, a bit of a trend setter, because he wore vests before anyone else we knew did. And because, on a gold chain hanging from his vest pocket, he wore his father's watch. And hanging from the chain was a tiny fourteen-carat-gold box with a teeny, tiny gold spoon attached to it. In 1965, this opulent little coke stash was considered terribly cool. The medical establishment had not even begun to talk about cocaine as "the only non-addictive drug." That joke went off half a decade later.

Vinnie pulled out a chair for me and, after Bernie introduced me to the other men at the table, I gratefully lowered myself into it. I knew Ruby Stein of the twitching eye, of course. "BB, you look like a million bucks," he said to Bernie. "Jesus, I heard you were dying, and look at you."

I must have flinched, but I laughed along with everyone else. It was one of those times when it was almost impossible to believe Dr. Sealy's dire prediction. Bernie had really had a miraculously good month. He was eating, sleeping, and breathing normally again and, tonight, flushed with excitement about the baby's birth, grinning, shaking hands and kibitzing with the guys, he did look like a million.

Next to Ruby was Gribbs Tremonte, a neat but not dapper gray-haired man who was, Uncle Vinny later confided, "very connected," a lieutenant in Fat Tony Salerno's family.

When the second or third round of drinks came, Vinny toasted Bernie's birthday. Everyone at the table joined in. "Tonight's your birthday?" someone asked.

"No," Bernie said. "Tomorrow. And guess what my lady's giving me for my birthday—a baby. She's having a baby on my birthday."

Everybody laughed. Someone said. "How do you know it's going to be tomorrow?"

"Hey, she's got an appointment," Bernie answered.

"You're kidding," Ruby said. "What kind of appointment?"

"I never heard of such a thing," someone else commented. "Who ever heard of having an appointment to have a baby?"

"No such thing," another skeptic chimed in.

"Leave it to my girl," Bernie said. "She knows how to do things right. She's having the baby tomorrow morning. On my forty-sixth birthday, she's going to give me a son."

Well, that was too much for them. "A son?! How do you know it's going to be a boy?" Gribbs Tremonte asked.

"Sandy said so, that's how."

"Well, I tell you what," Gribbs said. "You're a sporting man, Bernie.

I'll make you a bet. I'll bet you twenty thousand dollars that you have a girl.''

A couple of people had been laughing, teasing, shmoozing. They stopped. A hush fell over the table.

"Take it or leave it."

"You got it," Bernie said. "Twenty grand that I have a son."

Gribbs said, "Twenty thousand says it's a girl."

And that was it. The bet was made. I almost fell off my chair.

"You better have a boy," Bernie whispered to me when the chit-chat began again.

"But what if it's a girl? Bernie, this is the craziest! I've seen you take some pretty cockeyed bets, but twenty thousand dollars on the sex of your child?!''

"Baby," he said to me, all blue eyes and big white grinning Chiclets, "tomorrow, on my forty-sixth birthday, I'm going to have a son *and* an extra twenty thousand dollars."

It was a good bet.

The next morning, we went to the hospital. Five hours later, I was the very tired but happy mother of a nine-pound baby boy.

After Tillie's great tales of childbirth, I'd opted for total unconsciousness. And the first thing I saw when I opened my eyes after the delivery was a crowd of men standing in the doorway of my hospital room. They looked like a jury. And the verdict was in. The moment I stirred, they started grinning and laughing and calling out congratulations. "He's beautiful," Josh the lawyer said. "You did great."

"We saw him," Uncle Vinny hollered.

"A bruiser," someone else called out. "Big, he's big."

And Red said, "Wait till Bernie sees him. He'll be here soon, Sandy. He sends his love."

There were twelve or thirteen men crowded around the door but Bernie wasn't among them. "He was sick, Sandy," Red explained after he'd shooed the others out of the place. "He hung in for a couple of hours. We were downstairs waiting for the news, but the doc said it could be hours yet and he told B to go home. Just between us, baby, he's not well. He's looking really bad, Sandy. You think he wouldn't be here right this minute if he was feeling okay?''

It was not what I wanted to hear. Whatever happiness I'd felt when I woke up disappeared at Red's words and a chilling ache set in. Tears welled as he spoke and, from that moment on, they came with baffling ease and suddenness. The private room overlooking Central Park that Bernie had ordered for me was filled with flowers. There were nineteen bouquets and floral arrangements already there when I opened my eyes and more arrived hourly. People sent baskets of fruit and jams, different kinds of salamis and assorted cheeses. There was even a box of grapefruits and oranges from some of the Florida *mishpocheh*. But there was no Bernie.

"Your mother's throwing a little birthday party for him this afternoon," Red said. "Then he'll be by. He'll see you tonight, Sandy. He's so proud of you. And he's so happy, kid. You did great. Have you seen your son yet?"

I shook my head. Bernie was sick again. Too sick to visit me. Too sick to see the son he'd been so excited about.

"So what are you going to name the kid?" Hot Dog asked, trying to cheer me up. "You got something picked out yet?"

"Jeffrey," I said. "We're naming him for Bernie's aunt Jenny, the one who owned the candy store his mother worked in. He loved her so much. She helped raise him. So we're naming him with a 'J' for Jenny. Jeffrey or Jason. I think it'll be Jeffrey. I like that best."

"Yeah. Jeffrey." Red rolled the name around. "Jeffrey Barton. Very slick. Very distinguished. What a kid."

"Jeffrey *Allen* Barton," I said.

"Allen. Nice," Red said. "Like my last name." Though hardly anyone we knew ever used it, Hot Dog's real name was Harrison Allen.

"Not 'like,' " I said. "We're naming him for you, Red. Allen is for you."

"Sandy. Come on," he said, shaking his head as if I were putting him on.

"Ask Bernie. We already decided on that a long time ago. Jeffrey for Bernie's aunt Jenny. Allen for you."

"For me?" Red's grin nearly split his cheeks. "No shit," he said, and laughed. "You named him for me."

I was dozing when the nurse brought Jeffrey to me for the first time. "Mrs. Barton," she called. "It's feeding time. I brought you a bottle and your baby."

I opened my eyes. Each time I'd opened my eyes since Red had gone I'd felt that breath-sucking blueness, that empty-hearted ache. "I can't," I said, barely looking at her, turning away from the little blanket-wrapped creature in her arms.

"Of course you can, Mommy," she said. She looked like a kid, a little Puerto Rican nurse, with big dark eyes and long pretty hair trailing down the back of her uniform. "Here you go." With the authority of someone twice her age and size, she adjusted my arm and laid Jeffrey down onto it.

And once she did, once I looked at him, it was over. I was in love. I'd never seen or felt anything like it in my life. Here was this absolutely perfect, unblemished child with so much silky black hair that someone had made him bangs and tied back the rest in a bow to keep it out of his eyes.

He was big, gorgeous, and clean with not a mark on him. And he went at the bottle like a chip off the old block. My side of the block, not Bernie's. At that point, even after the delivery, I was up to well over 170 pounds.

Jeffrey was an angel from the beginning. Tillie used to say it was like he knew he had to be good, that he knew he'd been born into a time of chaos and crisis and that his job was to give no trouble. He was the most peaceful, placid, loving baby, the blessing in a cursed family. His father met him later that day, at the evening feeding, and was as quickly smitten.

Bernie looked *shvakh*—pale and sickly, washed out, like a limp, wrung-out rag. He walked into the hospital room slowly because his legs were terribly swollen and aching. And he apologized for coming empty-handed, although he'd already sent a magnificent, huge floral arrangement that had arrived earlier in the day. I could see that it was all he could do to get himself to the hospital. But he apologized for not bringing a gift or flowers—just as during his recuperation before I gave birth he'd begun to apologize for not making love to me. He'd been too weak to walk, then. Too weak to get himself a drink of water. But he felt he should have made love to me. Like it was the tenth commandment of the Tough Guys Torah. I was seven, eight, and nine months pregnant at the time. The doctor had told me my husband was dying. Sex hadn't been a priority issue for me.

"So how are you, kid?" he asked. "You did good. I just saw him. What a beauty. He's the biggest one in the nursery. And that hair."

"More than me." I tried to laugh. "What about you? You feeling lousy?"

Don't, my mother shook her head, signaling me from the door.

"I'm okay. Tillie made me a nice little birthday party. She and Marlene brought over a cake. It said, 'Happy Birthday, Dad.' It was terrific."

"I'm glad," I said, swallowing back the tears. I couldn't think of anything that didn't make me more depressed. Even Bernie's mentioning the birthday party made me think, of, my God, what if this is his last birthday? I wasn't there for the party. I'll never celebrate another birthday with him.

CHAPTER THIRTEEN

Life and Death

The Friday we brought Jeffrey home, Bernie was ecstatic and uncharacteristically shy.

We'd hired a baby nurse—you guessed it, nothing but the best. She was good enough for Steve Lawrence and Edie Gorme's children; she was good enough for Bernie Barton's son. And she really was good—a good, competent woman who almost wound up taking care of three patients instead of one. Her name was Ruth. Bernie asked her, would she mind very much if he put Jeffrey into the crib instead of her doing it. He was so happy and eager and heartbreakingly humble with Ruth.

"I don't mean to bother you, but you understand," he kept saying to her. "This is my first child in how many years—twenty-five? I have a twenty-five-year-old daughter. And this is the first boy born in my family in forty-six years. I don't mean to bother you, Ruth, but I want to spend time with him. I don't want to get in your way, Ruth, but I'd like to rock him for a while."

And he did. He took Jeffrey from my arms and put him into the magnificent blue and white canopied cradle. Then he sat because he was very weak. He sat in the white rocking chair and talked to his son through the crib bars. He called him Tiger. He'd say, "Tiger, I'm going to walk you in your carriage in the park and I'm going to sit with you in the playground."

Twice that day, with Ruth's approval, of course, he took Jeffrey out of the crib and fed him. He gave his son his first bottle at home. And he couldn't stop talking to him. It was like, in one afternoon, Bernie was trying to describe to that little week-old baby the lifetime he wanted them to have together. Every time I popped my head into the room, he was talking to Jeffrey: "And wait until you're old enough to play ball . . . And I'm going to read to you. You're going to love Shakespeare, Tiger."

My girlfriend Judy was at the house. By that time, she knew how sick Bernie was. She'd walked into my hospital room when I was crying uncontrollably. I'd been hysterical for hours. It was Judy who'd made the nurses phone Dr. Truppin. He gave me a sedative and stayed with me, holding my hand for forty-five minutes while I spilled out my tears and sorrow. And, of course, Judy heard everything. She became one of my rocks. She came to see me every day and called in between times and she was there when I brought Jeffrey home that first day.

Sleazeball Hymie was waiting for us, too, and my mother, and my sister, Marlene, I think. And, thank God, Red was there. He'd driven us home from the hospital.

But for most of the afternoon, Bernie sat in the baby's room talking to Jeffrey, hanging out with him, like he was one of the boys. Around sunset, we sat down to eat and Bernie said, "I don't feel well."

I asked, "Should I call the doctor?"

"No." He stood up. "I just don't feel well," he said again, and then he collapsed.

My mother stayed with Ruth and the baby while Hot Dog, Hymie, and I got Bernie to the hospital. It was Mount Sinai, the hospital from which we'd brought home his son that morning. Dr. Sealy had been called. He was waiting for us. We checked Bernie in and, four or five hours later, we left. He was alive. He was hooked up to the oxygen tank again with tubes running in and out of him and a mask over his face. He was very weak. It had been a close call. But he was alive.

The next three weeks were so hectic that I was almost too busy to be depressed. I was a new mother, brand new. I had an infant at home. Every morning I'd go marketing, clean the house, then rush over to the hospital to be with Bernie.

"Did you know he was taking amphetamines?" Dr. Sealy asked me one day. "All last month. That remission we saw—he was taking pills."

Red knew about it. He'd tried to stop B. "I said, 'Man, that speed's going to kill you with your bad heart.' I didn't find out about it till the day Jeffrey was born and he was coming by the hospital to see you, Sandy. I said, 'B, you're crazy popping those pills.' But he said he needed that get up and go. He wanted to see his boy, he said. He'd never make it to the hospital without them."

So he hadn't gotten better. He'd only tried to convince me that he was feeling fine, tried to keep me from worrying about him during the last month of my pregnancy, tried to make life easier for me and for his son. But at a terrible price.

And he didn't seem to have learned a thing.

The day after his collapse, the party was in full swing again. Bernie's hospital room was crowded with friends, flowers, forbidden booze, and food. He was doing business from his sick bed. Now and then, I'd arrive to find his door locked. On those days, he might give me five or ten thousand dollars to take home; some days he'd ask me to bring him that amount. We had no health insurance. Guys like Bernie didn't apply for Blue Cross or Blue Shield. So, often the cash he gave me to take home one day— thousands of dollars stuffed into envelopes—I'd bring back the next to pay the hospital and doctor bills.

The hospital staff was crazy about Bernie. He'd send me out to buy perfume for his favorite nurses; there was always food in his room—not just the fruit and candy baskets friends had sent, but the coffee and fresh rolls, lox and bagels, deli sandwiches, Chinese food, chicken and ribs, and even charbroiled sirloin steaks that his visitors phoned out for or brought to him—and no nurse, orderly, technician, porter, or intern (or their families and pets, for that matter) ever went hungry when Bernie Barton was around. They'd drop into his room for a snack day or night.

Some came to nibble, some came to gawk. The hospital staff was never sure exactly who Bernie was or what he did, but they were awed by both the quantity and quality of his visitors. As usual, an endless parade of characters showed up, dressed in everything from jeans and lumber jackets to tuxedos. And the floor staff had their favorites.

The nurses were wild for Billy Daniels. They'd find excuses to come into the room while he was there and ask for his autograph. One evening, one of them asked Billy to sing "That Old Black Magic," the song he'd made famous. Then all the nurses started begging him to do it. And the wise guys were kidding Billy, and egging the nurses on. Finally, Bernie said, "Go ahead, Billy. Make them happy." Well, if someone had been dying down the hall there'd have been nobody to help him, because everyone on the floor was either squeezed into or lined up outside Bernie's room listening to Billy's little concert.

And that wasn't the only command performance held there. Bing Crosby's brother was in the room next to Bernie's. And one evening, while I was sitting in the lounge, Bing came in and we started talking. He told me how sick his brother was and I told him a little about Bernie and about just having had the baby. The next thing I knew, Bing was dropping into Bernie's room every now and then. And one night, he said something like, "If there's anything I can do for you, just let me know." And Bernie said, "Well, I'd love to hear you sing 'White Christmas.' "

Bing Crosby turned to me. "This is some guy you got here." He laughed. And then, "How can I refuse?" he said. So Bing Crosby sang "White Christmas" in Bernie's room. And, again, the hospital staff gathered 'round to sway and swoon.

Please. By the time George Raft showed up, they were ready to nominate Bernie for President.

One evening, I got off the elevator and everyone at the nursing station was eating Chinese food. I went down the hall to Bernie's room and there were nurses and orderlies and wise guys squeezed into the place among the flowers, fruit baskets, scotch bottles, racing forms, bags of ice, and what seemed like hundreds of white take out food containers.

Bernie had ordered up from Bill Hong's, one of the best and most expensive Chinese restaurants in the city and, naturally, he'd bought enough to feed the entire eighth floor. Just as naturally, no ban on eating the forbidden, heavily salted food was going to stop him from enjoying it. So there he was, sitting up in bed, holding court, laughing and eating Chinese food.

I was in the doorway, about to say, "What are you doing?!" but Dr. Sealy beat me to it. He pushed past me into the room. "What the hell are you doing?" he shouted at Bernie and, without a moment's hesitation, he cut through the crowd, wiped his hand across the hospital tray on Bernie's bed, and sent the containers flying. The walls were covered with Chinese food. Wise guys scattered like scared schoolboys. The nurses practically crawled out the door.

"What the hell is wrong with you, Bernie?" Dr. Sealy demanded. "Are you trying to kill yourself?"

Bernie looked at him. "Come on, Doc," he said, with this lopsided grin, this resigned smile. "Let's stop the bullshit. I'm not going to live much longer. Leave me alone and let me enjoy the time I've got."

The second week of Bernie's hospitalization, Uncle Vinny, who was a devout Catholic, stopped by to give me a lift to the hospital. "I've got an idea," he said. "Let's go to your synagogue first and have a prayer said for Bernie."

So we did. We drove to the *shul* where Bernie used to go for High Holy Day services and to say Kaddish for his father. I spoke to the rabbi and gave him some money and he said they'd make a prayer for Bernie at the temple that night.

"Thanks," I said to Vinny. "I'm glad we did that. Now let's go to the hospital. I want to see Bernie."

"In five minutes," Vinny promised. "Now, I want to go to my church and light a candle for B. What's the difference? Let's have all the gods going for it."

Vinny was so good to me. He was there like my right arm. All of Bernie's friends were. Usually I'd drive to the hospital by myself, but if I didn't feel up to it one of them would always show up to give me a lift. They'd take turns staying with Bernie. Hot Dog and Josh and Uncle Vinny were keeping a sort of tag-team vigil at the hospital. If one of them left the room to run an errand or to bring me to the hospital, another would stay with Bernie until I got there. They never left him alone.

Hymie was hanging around, too. He'd either be at the hospital or at our apartment. In fact, he was at the house a lot while I was out. When I'd come home from visiting Bernie, Ruth would tell me that Hymie had been there using the phone and cleaning out the refrigerator. I didn't like it. I remembered how he'd sniffed and snooped around when the house was crowded with people. I didn't even want to think about the liberties he'd take there on his own.

About this time, Bernie's childhood friend, Chalky, got out of prison. Now, at Bernie's request, I had written letters to Chalky for years and sent him Jewish New Year's cards and birthday gifts. I felt as though I knew the guy. But as fate would have it, I never ran into him at the hospital. I'd leave for twenty minutes to run an errand or I'd show up after dinner and Bernie would say, "Chalky was here. You just missed him, baby. Wait till you meet him, Sandy, you're going to love him."

"If I ever get out of here, Chalky and I are going to tear up this town," he'd say. "You can trust him, Sandy. If you ever need something, he's one of the people you'll be able to count on."

But one day I walked in and, again, Chalky had been there and gone. Only this time, Bernie shook his head. "There's something wrong with him. He's changed," he said. "But what the hell can you expect? A man does twelve consecutive years from the age of thirty-two to forty-four—he's got to come out bent."

Every now and then, Bernie would send everyone home and we'd just sit together in his room and watch TV. It was one of those nights. We were alone together. Out of the blue, Bernie turned to me and said, "You know, babe, I'm going to die. I'm going to be leaving you sooner than I thought—"

I started to protest, but he said, "No, don't say anything. Just listen to me, okay?" So I nodded, but I didn't want to hear anything he said. I couldn't stand the fact that he could mention his death, talk about it calmly, when I couldn't even think about it without being overwhelmed by fear and despair.

"I hope you've learned the things I taught you, Sandy," he said, and rattled off a couple of lessons: Don't get mad at anyone, get even. And be careful of people. You can trust but don't trust that much. And then he said, "When I die, baby, you and Red'll carry on the numbers business as much as you can. Red will look after you. Him you know you can depend on. Hymie's been taking care of a couple of loans I put out. He'll tell you who owes what and where the book is." He said there were a couple of other businesses I could expect money from and there were some that might dry up without him because they might not want to deal with a woman. And then he said, "And, of course, it goes without saying, if you need anything, you can trust Chalky. I hope you get to meet him before I die."

"Stop," I finally said. "You're not dying." But he brushed off my words.

"All of a sudden the pupil is smarter than the teacher? Stop kidding me," he said. "We both know what's what. I just thought we'd have more time, kiddo. I'm sorry."

I was fighting back tears, but I was also relieved that Bernie knew how sick he was and that he didn't seem scared or angry. He was doing what he always did—trying to take care of me. Trying to teach me. Trying to prepare me to take care of myself. And his son.

He was heavily medicated. Sometimes he'd be a little woozy. His thoughts would wander, his conversations would start and stop abruptly.

"I know sometimes you've been unhappy," he'd say, "and I'm sorry, Sandy. I wish I could've done better by us. But this is the way our life is. This life-style. It's almost like being in a maze. You can't find which way is out.

"Maybe I didn't do it right all the time but I did it my way, on my own," he'd say. "Yeah, I'm a member of the mob, a gangster, whatever. I only know one kind of life. But I've never been beholden to anyone; I never took orders. And you know what, baby, it's how I am. I can't help it. What's wrong with me, they can't fix.

"Take good care of my son, Sandy. Maybe from him you'll get what I promised you. A decent life. You'll raise him to be a man, a good man, an honest man."

And he said that when he met me he fell madly in love and that he'd meant it when he promised me all those things—a house, marriage, and a baby carriage. And he said he was sorry now that he'd probably never see his son grow up. He'd never be able to walk in the park with him or talk with him or teach him things. He was sorry that life did this to him and to me.

While I was grateful that he could tell me these things, needless to say, these conversations often left me shaken and depressed. I'd leave the room and hurry down the hall to the lounge to have a cigarette, and I'd wind up either staring at the wall or crying uncontrollably. I was crying one afternoon and there was an elderly lady in the lounge. "What's wrong?" she asked me.

"I have a very sick husband who might die," I said.

And she said, "My husband is definitely dying. It's any day now." She said to me, "Don't cry now. Don't let him see you cry. Don't let anybody see you crying now. When he does die, you'll have all the time in the world to cry."

I never forgot what she said. She was right.

Three weeks. Three weeks was the time Bernie usually stayed in the hospital during a bout of illness. And now that he'd been at Mount Sinai exactly three weeks, he wanted to go home. It was a Friday night. Everyone else had left. Bernie said to me, "I feel all right. I want to get out of here. If I'm going to die, I want to die at home."

"You can't be serious," I said.

"Don't tell me I can't be serious. Who the hell do you think you're talking to. You know better than me all of a sudden? Is that what you're saying? I feel fine. And I'm going home.''

We argued a little and then, to placate him, I said, ''Well, at least wait until you see Doctor Sealy later on tonight or tomorrow morning and just ask him what he thinks.''

''Sure. Okay,'' Bernie said. The little skirmish had tired him out. Or else, he was pacifying me. But he agreed to check with Dr. Sealy before doing anything.

Saturday morning I was in the kitchen warming the baby's bottle. It was a hot day at the end of June. The terrace door was open. Ruth was in the nursery getting Jeffrey dressed for a stroll in the park behind the house. In the three weeks since I'd brought him home from the hospital I'd had so little time to spend with this beautiful little boy. I was lamenting that fact, looking forward to feeding him his bottle and just sitting with him for a few minutes before rushing back to Bernie, when the doorbell rang. Barefoot, in a housecoat, I shlepped my 170 pounds over to the door, opened it, and almost went into cardiac arrest.

Standing there, in a trenchcoat and bedroom slippers, with nothing else on underneath, was Bernie. He shoved past me into the apartment. ''Don't say a word!'' he fumed. ''I don't want to hear a fucking word out of your mouth about the goddam hospital or what am I doing here. I told you I was coming home. This is my house and if you don't like it, you can get your ass out of here. Not a word, Sandra. I'm warning you.''

Typical. He was yelling at me so that I wouldn't yell at him. ''All right,'' I said. ''Calm down. Are you naked under that?''

''Don't do it, Sandra.'' He waved a finger under my nose, cautioning me against laughing at how he looked. ''I spoke to Sealy and he said 'no way.' And I told him I've got things to do here. Important things—''

''And you left against his advice? You just walked out?''

''Of course I did. I have a son I don't even know yet—''

''Okay, okay. Stop yelling. You want to scare your son to death?''

''No. I want to see him. Where is he?''

''Put some clothes on first, Bernie. You look like a pervert.''

''Don't start!'' he hollered, but he went into the bedroom and changed his clothes and then he went right into the baby's room and started buttering up Ruth to let him feed Jeffrey. So twenty minutes after the great escape, there he was sitting in the rocking chair cooing to Jeffrey and giving him his bottle.

I stood in the doorway for a second, watching them, and Bernie saw me. ''Can you deny me this?'' he asked. ''If I'm going to die, first I'm going to spend some time with my child.''

After a while, Ruth took the baby out to the park and Bernie, who was clearly exhausted, got into bed and fell asleep.

I didn't know what to do. I was scared stiff. The minute he dozed off, I

called Hot Dog and Vinny and Josh and told them what had happened.
Then I got on the phone with Dr. Sealy, who by this time, of course, knew
that Bernie had bolted. He said, "I don't like it. I told him not to do it,
but we've got to deal with it the way it is for now. We'll keep him in the
house and see how it goes."

I was shaking. I whispered into the phone. "Doctor Sealy, what if something happens? What if he—"

"I'll be by this afternoon with his medication and I'll have a talk with
him. Try not to worry. You've been through a lot in the past month, Sandy.
With Bernie. With being a new mother. You've got to take care of yourself,
too. You need some rest."

"Doctor Sealy, I don't think I can do it," I said softly. I didn't want
Bernie to hear me. I was ashamed. I didn't want anyone to hear me. "I
don't think I can take care of him now. I don't have the strength left or the
energy or the mentality for it. I'm afraid of what will happen here. I don't
want him to die in this house. I know I sound selfish, but I really don't
want that. I have a baby here. A newborn son I haven't spent two minutes
with. Doctor Sealy, please, I don't want to be selfish, but this apartment
is all I have. It's the only place I've had where I could find a little peace
and quiet in the past three weeks. And I'm afraid to look at him, Doctor
Sealy. I can't live with that feeling of gloom and doom every time I look
at Bernie."

"I know," Sealy kept saying. "Just hang on, Sandy. I'll be there as
soon as I can. Take it easy. Try to get some rest yourself."

Dr. Sealy arrived about four in the afternoon. He examined Bernie, then
read him the riot act. That he was to take it easy. He had to only eat what
I gave him and I was to watch his diet. No salt in his food. No excitement.
He was supposed to stay in bed and rest, quiet and calmly.

I knew it would never work. Bernie was incapable of being still, of
sticking to a diet, of not getting excited. But I didn't say anything. When
Dr. Sealy was leaving, he took me aside and said, "The first sign of any
difficulty, no matter what it is—if he sneezes too often or goes to the
bathroom more than normal, anything—you're to call me right away."

Later that day, Uncle Vinny came by and then Hot Dog and Josh showed
up. My mother came over. Only the close friends were there and they kept
up my morale and they made Bernie laugh and they fussed over the baby
and kept saying how much he looked like his father. Which was true. The
resemblance was uncanny then and now.

So Saturday ended quietly.

On Sunday the telephone started to ring. Everyone who'd gone to the
hospital to visit Bernie and been surprised to find someone else in his
room, or who'd phoned him there and been told the patient was gone, had
by Sunday discovered that he was home. Flowers started arriving, baskets
of fruit, boxes of candy. The buzzer from the lobby went off every ten

minutes to announce another delivery. The doorbell never stopped chiming. The telephones rang so constantly that by ten A.M., I had to take them both off the hook.

Then people started dropping by. Hymie showed up with the enormous woman he'd left his wife and children for, and the wise guys came, the union *machers,* the bookies and numbers runners, the uptown crowd in their snappy clothes and pointy alligator shoes, the boys from Little Italy all dressed for church, the madams and ex-madams, some mistresses, some wives. And out came the cigars, the cigarettes, the grass, the booze. People would come in, look around and head straight for the phones to tell their friends to come by.

Bernie was home. The party was on.

Only the nursery was off-limits. Thank God for Ruth, who stood guard and forbade anyone to enter baby's room. Other than that, there was no privacy anywhere. It was as if I was on public display. It was only a month since I'd given birth. I was heavy and depressed. I walked around constantly in a housecoat. I hadn't bothered about a manicure or had my hair done since the delivery. And I didn't care. I didn't care how I looked or dressed or behaved. There were some men I had to be polite to and I was. There were medicines I had to give to Bernie at the right times and I did. I had to inject him. I had to prepare his food the way the doctor had ordered it prepared. I did all this mechanically, like a zombie. And I served coffee and cleaned up the drinks and cups and the cake plates.

The party lasted from Sunday through Tuesday. Tillie came as often as possible to help out. And Red and Vinny and Josh were almost always there and there was another friend of Bernie's, Marty, and a couple of other guys I could depend on. They were the only ones I spoke to at all. The others, the ones who came to pay respect or talk business, I hardly acknowledged. At one point, in the kitchen with my mother, I cried. I didn't care who might walk in and find us. I couldn't hold it together anymore. I couldn't even get into my own bathroom to cry in privacy because the door was locked and who knew who might be in there or what might be going on.

I was feeling very sorry for myself. I said, "Ma, I'm coming apart. Why is this happening to me, Mama? I just had a baby. I waited my whole life to have a home and a husband and a baby. Why is this happening now, why to me?"

"It's an old Jewish expression, *mamela,*" Tillie said, wiping my tears with a corner of the dishcloth. " 'This is the way God voted the day you were born.' *Vos is geshribed, is geshribed.* What is written, is written."

Wednesday was a bright and sunny day. That morning, the nurse was getting Jeffrey ready to go out. She'd sit with him in the sunshine in the little park behind the house for a couple of hours each day. About eleven o'clock, Bernie said to me, "I want you to be out of here between twelve and two if you can. Red will be here with me, so I'll be okay. I'm expecting some people."

Because of the way I looked and felt, I hadn't left the house in days. But I put on a pair of sunglasses and told Ruth I'd be going downstairs with her and the baby. We were walking toward the elevator. Ruth was wheeling the carriage and I was holding on to the bar like a second child, like a frightened but obedient sister, when I saw the short Spanish-speaking guy with the suitcase coming toward us. He had company this time. A second man with a second suitcase. I just kept walking and the men passed us and, of course, headed right for our apartment.

When we returned a couple of hours later, Bernie called me into the bedroom. He was wearing a white T-shirt and shorts, but there was a pair of trousers lying at the foot of the bed. I could tell he'd gotten up and dressed for his visitors. Now he was stretched out again, propped up on two pillows, looking pretty worn out. There were two wrapped packages next to him. "How's the kid?" he asked.

"An angel. He slept in the sun. Ruth is going to feed him now."

"Good. That's good," Bernie said, but I could see he was distracted. "Sandy, I want you to take these packages to the vault tomorrow. And there's a message in there from me to you, in with the packages. If I die, the message tells you what to do with the contents of these packages, all right?"

"All right," I echoed flatly. I didn't ask questions. Intuition told me what Bernie didn't need to anymore—that I was better off not knowing. I didn't want to ask or argue anything. I did what I'd been doing since Bernie had come home from the hospital—what I knew I had to do, automatically, mechanically, without thought or question. It was the way I'd made it through the past four days and, so far, against my expectations, I was still moving. I hadn't collapsed or broken down in front of anyone but my mother or started screaming—all of which I'd felt like doing almost every waking minute of the four days.

It was a quiet afternoon. For some reason, the house was empty. Maybe Bernie had asked everyone but Red to stay away. Whatever the reason, there were no strangers around that afternoon and, thank God, because shortly after the Spanish guys left Lido paid us a call. And he was dressed up not to be believed—all in white with his biggest and best jewelry sparkling and clanging with every velvet-slippered step he took. The four thousand gold and silver bracelets, neck chains studded with diamonds and emeralds, rings on every finger, diamonds and star sapphires set in platinum and rubies in pink gold. The jewelry, oh, the jewelry!—it crossed my mind to take Bernie's gun down from the closet and hold Lido up. Oh, yes, and he had brought a gift for Jeffrey. He was standing there in all his splendor carrying a floor-to-ceiling teddy bear he'd just bought at F.A.O. Schwarz for the baby.

Anyway, Ruth, whose eyes almost fell out of her head at the sight of this man, took the bear and I ushered Lido into Bernie's bedroom. After a few pleasantries, Lido asked me to make the room dark. He'd brought a tape over with him which he asked me to put on the stereo. If was African music, soft, very, very soothing. While the music was going, Lido chanted and prayed and shook rattles over Bernie's sick bed. The Santeria's eyes rolled and his body was waving back and forth like cattails in the Jersey swamps. After a while, he tied a red ribbon entwined with herbs around my waist and told me to wear it for twenty-four hours. He put *santos,* plaster saints, and pots of incense, and herbs and God only knows what else under Bernie's bed. And he said this would make Bernie well and protect the house from evil. "You will not die," Lido promised. "You will recover at once to full health and take up your lives as before."

Bernie thanked him. Then Lido sat around and chatted and had black coffee laced with brandy and smoked some pot.

After he left, I said, "What did he charge you this time?"

Bernie said, "Absolutely nothing. His showing up here today was a complete surprise. I never called him. I never said a word to him about being sick. And he wouldn't take a cent from me today."

It had been almost one week since Bernie came home. During that week, Dr. Sealy had come by once a day, sometimes twice to check him. Technicians came to take blood. A young doctor showed up with a portable cardiograph machine. And all in all it seemed that Bernie was holding his own.

"Let's call this a state of remission or a quiet period," Sealy said. "But, Sandy, the slightest show of anything wrong, day or night, you call me."

"Is it possible that he'll be all right?" I asked. "I mean, he's home. He walked out of the hospital. You say he's doing okay. Maybe he'll make it."

Dr. Sealy shook his head. "The tests we did in the hospital show that his heart muscle is deteriorating." He could see that I didn't understand. "His heart isn't pumping right. It's getting weaker. Eventually his kidneys will go and there's no way he can be put on a machine. It just wouldn't work. What will probably get him is encephalitis, or what's commonly called sleeping sickness. When the heart and kidneys are damaged this way, waste matter backs up and causes brain damage. Eventually, he'll go into coma. He's not strong enough to fight this, Sandy. Though God knows he's trying. He's putting up a hell of a fight. But he's not going to make it, Sandy. I'm sorry."

* * *

The very next day, Bernie started to cough. By mid-day he was running a high fever. By Saturday night, Sealy rushed over and wanted to put him back in the hospital. Bernie refused, fought him tooth and nail. "No way. You're out of your mind if you think I'm going back there."

"This is serious, Bernie," Sealy said. "You're sicker than you know."

"Come on, come on. You're not getting rid of me that fast," he said, trying to laugh, trying to joke, through the coughing spasm.

I walked Dr. Sealy to the elevator. He said, "I don't care how you do it or what you have to do, Sandy, you get that man back into Mount Sinai. Leave a message on the service and I'll meet you there. He's had a relapse. He's got to be hospitalized."

I went back into the apartment. "Bernie," I said. "Sweetheart, you've got to go back. I can't take care of you here. I'm scared, Bernie. Really, I am. I have the baby to take care of. And I'm so tired, sweetheart. I can't give me what you need now, Bernie. You've got to go back where they have nurses twenty-four hours a day and the right medicine and machines right there. I can't do it."

He went crazy. He began cursing me, accusing me of not caring about him. "No, it's not that you can't take care of me. You don't fucking want to. You're too goddamn lazy. Don't give me that shit about the baby. The baby, you've got nothing to do with him. You've got a nurse. A housekeeper. You've got your mother and Marlene to help out. You've got everything you need. You're trying to get rid of me, that's all. What, am I ruining your fun? You can't stand looking at me? No, when I'm flush, when I got money coming out of my ass, then you'll be happy to hang around, right? You're no damn good. You and that fucking quack, Sealy. You're trying to dump me. Both of you! Well, fuck you. Fuck you both. I'm home. This is my home! You don't want to nurse a sick man, get the fuck out!"

It went on like that for two hours. Screaming. Coughing. His face was bright red. He was having trouble breathing, but he wouldn't stop shouting. Finally, he took a couple of sleeping pills and fell out.

I got on the phone and spoke with Uncle Vinny and Josh the lawyer and I talked to Hot Dog. I called all his close friends and told them what was going on. And they all said, Sandy, you'll just have to do it. "Throw him out," Vinny said.

"How can I throw him out? The man's in bed. He's dying."

"No matter what. No matter how sick he is. Throw him out," Vinny advised.

The next day, he was sicker. The fever was higher. He was coughing more. Dr. Sealy said he'd send an ambulance.

"But he won't go," I tried explaining again. "Doctor Sealy, what do you want me to do? I can't physically lift him and put him in an ambulance. You'll have to take him out with a derrick."

"You'd better do something," Sealy said. "Carry on, scream, rant and rave. Do whatever you have to do to get Bernie out of the house and back into the hospital where he belongs. Or else, Sandy, he's going to die right there in your bed.''

Bernie and I fought all that morning. I was out of my mind, crying, begging, screaming and, finally, cursing, too.

''That's it,'' Bernie shouted suddenly. He threw back the covers and hauled himself out of bed. ''Get out of here this minute, or I'll kill you.''

I cowered in a corner but I wouldn't leave. I thought he was going to keel over right then and there. He was that weak. Oh, but what a set of lungs on him and oh, the power of his anger. It was like a drug, like speed—it turned him sharp, raw, and fast. He got on the phone to Hot Dog and, staring daggers at me, demanded that Red come over and get him out of the house immediately. He slammed down the phone and started getting dressed and then he ran over to the hassock and took whatever cash was in there.

All the while, he screamed at me. ''You want me out, you bitch? I'm out of here. I don't have to listen to you anymore. I'm checking into a hotel.'' He was opening and closing drawers, throwing things out of them, looking for money. ''I'm taking everything. I'm going to clean out the vault. You'll have nothing. You're no damn good, you whore. You cunt.'' Slamming closet doors. Stuffing cash into his pants pocket though the zipper wasn't even zipped yet. ''I'll get even with you for this. You want me out? You want to throw me out in the street when I'm dying? I'll get you! Even if I die, I'll get you for this!''

In the middle of this insanity, Hot Dog showed up. He was sitting on the sofa watching Bernie fly around the place cursing me, grabbing money and shaking his fist. Red winked at me as if to say, Let him talk. Don't worry, I'll get him to the hospital.

''Let's go!'' Bernie hollered. And he was out the door, with Red loping along behind him.

A couple of frantic phone calls to Dr. Sealy and a couple of hours later, Hot Dog called.

''Where are you? Is Bernie with you? Is he all right?''

''Oh, Mr. B is fine and dandy. We are in the Presidential Suite of the Plaza Hotel is where we are. Your man says if he's dying, he's going to die in the Presidential Suite no matter what it costs him. You've got to admit Sandy, our boy has style.''

''Should I come over?''

''Not if you value your life. Woman,'' Red said, in that very emphatic tone of voice, ''he says he hates your guts right now and he's going to kill you. And he is just wild enough, Sandy. Do not come, do not call. Give me time alone with him. He brought his medication with him, so he'll be okay. By Monday, I'll have him back in the hospital.''

I didn't sleep much Sunday night. My mother came over and she and

Ruth and I were up for most of the night talking. We were in the living room having coffee. It was past midnight when something hit me.

"Mom," I said. "I bet he took the vault key and he's going to clean out our box."

"Don't be crazy," Tillie said. "How would he even think of that? The man was angry, crazy, but he's sick, Sandy. You think he's going to stroll into a bank and take all your money?"

"I'm right, Ma. I've got a feeling, an instinct about this." I went into the bedroom to the drawer in which I kept most of our keys. The only vault key we had in the house was the one to the Mr. and Mrs. Barton box. A duplicate of it, along with all the other vault keys, was at my cousin's house. Sure enough, the vault key was missing.

"He's going to clean out the vault. He said he was going to take all the money and, I guess, he meant it."

"Well, he's sick. He's just being a little *meshugge*."

"I know. But when he's back in the hospital and there are bills to pay, what then? He's checked himself into the Plaza. He's living it up. I know this man. He could blow every cent we have in a fit of spite and there'd be nothing left for the hospital and doctors."

"What can you do?"

"What can I do? I can beat him at his own game. I'm going to Francine's to get the key tonight and first thing tomorrow I'm going to the vault."

Tillie laughed. "Look at you, Mrs. Tough Guy."

The next morning, Monday at a quarter to nine, in sunglasses with a kerchief over my unwashed hair, I was waiting outside the bank. The minute the doors opened, I hurried down to the vault and cleared out our safety deposit box. I didn't close the account. I just cleared out all the money and then, as an afterthought, I threw in a single that I had with me. I left one dollar in the box. I didn't want to take the money home, so I told the man I wanted another box under the name of Sandra Barton, alone. I paid for it, signed the signature card, locked the money inside, and left the vault.

I walked up the steps, breathing a sigh of relief and wondering where I'd gotten the nerve to do what I'd just done, where I'd gotten the brains to open a new box and leave the money where it would be safe. I heard voices, footsteps. I looked up. And there was Bernie, all pumped up, with Red on one side of him and a black man I'd never seen before on the other, coming down the stairs. A brass rail separated us.

I kept walking up and they kept coming down. "You!" Bernie screamed. I thought he'd have his final heart attack right there. But I was as angry as he was and as arrogantly pumped up. "You thieving, no-good bitch," he screamed. "Conniving cunt! Did you take the money? It's not enough you want me dead, you want me broke, too?!" Red grabbed his arm.

"Tough shit, tough guy," I hollered back at him. "The early worm wins!'' It wasn't till later, in the taxi headed home, that I realized I'd gotten it wrong, that I'd meant the early *bird*. ''I was here first!'' I shouted, and then I ran out of the bank as fast as my legs could carry me.

Tillie couldn't stop laughing when I told her what had happened. She was holding her belly. Tears were running out of her eyes. And she kept gasping and saying, ''God forgive me, I know it's not funny. It's not nice. God forgive me.''

I wasn't home ten minutes when Bernie called. I heard the street noises in the background and I knew he was at a payphone. ''I'm going to kill you, Sandra,'' he growled. ''I'm not kidding this time. You think you're going to get away with this stunt? You're crazier than I thought. And you're dead, lady. You and your mother and you better get the kid out of the house because I'm going to blow up the whole fucking place!''

With that, Red got on the phone. He was hysterical laughing. ''You should have seen your face. What a look when you saw us. Woman, you were wild. I'll never forget that scene as long as I live!''

''He's going to kill me?'' I asked.

''Just keep cool. I'm going to try to get him back into the hospital,'' Red said.

That afternoon, Bernie collapsed at the Plaza. Red reached Dr. Sealy and they returned Bernie by ambulance to Mount Sinai. I rushed over to the hospital to find out that Bernie had asked Security to bar me from the room.

Red walked me to the lounge and filled me in on what had happened. After his phone call to me, Bernie had gone back to the hotel. ''He was steaming,'' Red said. ''You know how he gets, he couldn't shut up. The more he thought about it, talked about it, the wilder he got. He hit the phones and called Vinny and Josh, Cokey, Frank, Muttel, Farvel. He was calling the whole world, telling them how you robbed him and how he's going to get even with you. Sandy, he even tried to put a contract out on you. He called a guy to put a hit on you and then he went crazy because the guy he called wouldn't do it. He'd already heard what went down and refused to get mixed up in the shit. I think that was the last straw,'' Red said. ''He started coughing and spitting up and then he collapsed.''

Uncle Vinny came into the lounge. I was crying. ''He hates me, Vinny. He tried to put a hit out on me.''

''He doesn't hate you,'' Vinny said, putting an arm around me. ''He's just running scared now. He knows it's over, but he doesn't know how to lay down. So he's blaming you. But I'll tell you something, Sandy. He's also proud of you. He said to me, 'Look how her mind works, Vinnie. I taught her too well.' ''

''It must be terrible for him to believe I would rob him. I wasn't robbing him, Vinny. I'm going to need the money for the bills, his bills. Do you think I'd hurt him?''

"Of course not. And you did the right thing. I've known this man for years. He had that money, he might've gotten on a plane and gone off to Europe. He could've hit Vegas and lost it all on a throw of the dice. No one thinks you robbed him, Sandy. You did the right thing."

Josh the lawyer drove me home. "He can't believe it. He can't get over how you beat him." Josh laughed. "He says you should have worked for the CIA. So Red says, 'What about the FBI?' And Bernie said, 'Naw, they're too dumb.' "

It only took two days for him to relent. Red walked me into the hospital room. "So how's my son?" Bernie asked.

"Gorgeous and good as gold—what else?" I said.

We never mentioned what happened at the bank.

Bernie was in the hospital for seven weeks. Specialists came from Boston to try to put him on a kidney machine, but just as Dr. Sealy had predicted, it didn't work. I went to Mount Sinai every day. It was like going to a job. I'd get up early, shower, dress, make sure the house was stocked with whatever the nurse and baby needed. Ruth had only been able to stay with us for six weeks before moving on to her next baby, her next commitment.

Jeffrey's new nurse was a wonderful Jamaican woman named Nora who was in her mid-forties and had a son in the Navy. So clean she smelled like fresh laundry. Nora was as gentle and caring to me as she was to the baby. Her good-natured disposition and lilting accent enchanted everyone who met her. So I'd leave Jeffrey in Nora's capable hands and then I'd drive over to the hospital, almost always with cash in my bag to pay the bills, which mounted as he got sicker.

Between the heavy medication and the progression of the illness, Bernie was in and out of consciousness most of the time. People still came up to see him. They'd come and go. Sometimes, he'd be able to talk and kid around. Sometimes, now, he'd want to be alone. Chalky called while I was there one day. I answered the phone. "No," Bernie said. "I don't want him here. I'm not in the mood. He's gone stir-crazy, Sandy. I love that man. I'd do anything for him. But I don't want him hanging around now."

There were many nights when I slept at the hospital. And there were many nights when Red or Vinny stayed over, too. They'd sleep in the lounge. I'd sleep in the room with Bernie, but it was a different sleep he had now. He was in a semi-coma and I'd talk to him. "You've got to hang on," I'd beg him. "You can't die. You can't leave me this way. You promised we'd have a regular life—a house and baby. You promised me, sweetheart. You've got to hang on."

It was weird. I felt so attached to him. I felt that I was dying with him. And I wanted to live, to continue, to have a life. And I believed that it would be over, my life with his, when he died. So I wished he would stay in a coma forever. Because it would give me something to do. I'd have to come to the hospital. I'd talk to him. I'd comb his hair. I'd do anything so that I could still be married to him. I'd realized that once Bernie died, I wouldn't be married anymore. I know how simple, how stupid, that must seem, but it left me breathless with terror. I wouldn't be Bernie's wife. I wouldn't be married. Then what would I do, who would I be? I'd be nothing. Nobody. Alone.

I got into this funny habit. Every night after I left the hospital, before I went to bed—and it could have been one or two in the morning, it didn't matter—I'd have to find out if Bernie was all right. It was too late to call his room. But there was a wonderful old woman who was the floor nurse on duty after midnight. I'd call her. Her name was Mrs. Zimmerman. I'd say, "Mrs. Zimmerman, this is Mrs. Barton. Is my husband still alive?" And she'd say, "Stop that, relax yourself. He's fine." It was unbelievable. I couldn't sleep unless I heard this kind woman's comforting voice.

Bernie slipped into a coma. All his close friends still came to the hospital every day. We'd take turns clapping hands, making noises, to see if he'd respond. I'd play music and talk to him, but it was no good most of the time. Once in a while, though, he'd stir and come awake. Once he said, "Sandy, we had such little time together. I thought we'd have more." Another time, he opened his eyes and I said, "Do you know who I am?" "Yes," he said. "You're the mother of my beautiful son. Take care of him."

It was a Friday night, August 6, 1965. Bernie had been in a coma ninety percent of the time for the past three weeks. But that evening, everybody was there. Hot Dog, Vinny and Josh, of course. But there were many other visitors, as well. In fact, my uncle Meyer, my father's brother who'd kept in touch with us for all those years, showed up at the hospital that night. My mother came with him. It was like one big party again. People were walking in and out of the room. Some of the staff brought us coffee and hung around to chat. Of course, the place was still bright with flowers and gift baskets. And in the middle of everything, Bernie woke up. His blue eyes were clear, alert. He said hello to everybody as if nothing had happened. He looked beautiful. He looked rested, as if he'd just woken from a long sleep.

We were all talking to him. "I heard you were sick," Uncle Meyer said. "But look at you. You look better than me."

"That's not so hard to do," my mother teased. And Bernie actually laughed.

He was chatting with Red and Vinny when I pulled my mother out into the hallway. "Mom, you see, it's a miracle!" I said. "He's going to make it. He'll live to see his son Bar Mitzvahed, yet. I know he will. It's a miracle!"

She shook her head. "No, sweetheart, this won't be. There's an old

Jewish superstition, Sandy. When someone is ready to die, God gives them a chance to say goodbye. That's what's happening, *mamela.* He's ready."

I thought she was crazy. I didn't believe her. I couldn't. When we left the hospital that night, my uncle, my mother, Vinny, and I went out for coffee together. I was so happy. "A miracle is taking place," I said. "Something wonderful is happening."

At seven-thirty Saturday morning the hospital called. "You'd better come over," one of our favorite nurses said. "He's bad. I'm sorry. I think you'd better hurry."

By the time I got there, Bernie was dead.

CHAPTER FOURTEEN

My *Gutta Better*

I walked out of the hospital and stared numbly into the sunlight at Central Park across the street. The pills Dr. Sealy had given me were making me light-headed. My eyes felt raw from crying. My throat hurt from scream-ing, aloud and silently. Hot Dog was at my elbow. Vinny and Josh followed us through the door. I was very tired. I didn't feel like I had the strength to stand. So Red and I sat down on the hospital steps, and Vinny and Josh leaned up against the railing.

"What do I do now?" I asked.

Josh said, "Let's go home."

Vinny nodded. "We'll go home and get some coffee, then you'll make plans."

I didn't want to move. Every step took me farther from Bernie and closer to a terrifying uncertainty. I didn't want to lose sight of the hospital. Sitting on the steps kept me attached to it. To a life that was receding faster than I could think. I'd had my baby and left my husband here. From this build-ing, I'd brought home a new life and lost my old one. I doubled over suddenly, clutching my stomach. The ache was there. The loss. The feeling I'd first known as a girl when my father left. It had grown with me, that yawning emptiness. It was too big now ever to be repaired.

"Come on, Sandy," Red said, standing, offering me his hand. "Let's go home. There's nothing left for us to do here."

The boys took me home and stayed with my mother and me. She was terribly sad, Tillie. She had grown to love Bernie so much and now she grieved for him. But she was also my tower of strength. Nora put up coffee and we all sat down together and stirred the cups listlessly. Red was pacing. Everyone was stunned and sad. But at least we were together.

In less than an hour, the phones started ringing. Josh answered one of the first calls. I heard him say, "Yes, he's dead," so I assumed it was a friend. But Josh's voice was off, he sounded annoyed, snappish. "Yes, I'm sure," he said. Then, "This is Josh Loew. I'm an attorney and a friend of the family. And if you've got a problem, why don't you go over to Riverside Chapel and pry open the coffin!" He slammed down the phone.

Vinny looked up when Josh came back into the room. "FBI?" he said.

Josh said, "How did you know?"

Vinny said, "I thought something was going on. Sandy, when I'd pick you up to drive you over to Mount Sinai, I knew it. I saw the bastards. I didn't want to worry you. They were parked right outside your door for weeks."

"Scum," Josh said. " 'Are you sure he's dead?' the guy kept asking. Scum bastards."

"Did he say why?" Red asked.

Josh looked over at my mother. "Naw," he said. "He didn't say."

I knew he was lying to protect Tillie's feelings and probably mine. Later, Vinny told me that the FBI was setting Bernie up for a drug bust; a conspiracy charge of some kind. They'd had a tap on the house phones and on Bernie's hospital room telephones, too. He said Josh had told him the FBI agent who'd called an hour after Bernie died had sounded almost pissed off that he'd been cheated out of a bust.

After that, the telephone just started ringing. People had heard that Bernie had died. The FBI weren't the only ones who cared or found it hard to believe. After a while, I gathered my strength and changed my clothes, and the boys took me crosstown to Riverside Chapel on Amsterdam Avenue to make the funeral arrangements.

"When do you think you want to have it?" Hot Dog asked on the way over.

"Right away. Sunday," I said. "He's Jewish. I want him buried according to tradition, right away."

"Tomorrow?" Vinny was surprised. "That soon?"

I looked at Josh, who came from a good Jewish family. "That's how it's done," Josh told them. "But Sandy, there'll be a lot of people from out of town who might want to come."

"He was very well-liked," Vinny added. "He had friends everywhere. I think he would've wanted them to have a chance to say goodbye."

"I don't care," I said. But by the time we got to the chapel, I'd come up with a compromise.

I picked out a beautiful casket and reserved the largest chapel, which held about two hundred people and, just in case the boys were right, I asked the funeral director for the latest possible time on Sunday, which turned out to be two-thirty in the afternoon, so that anyone who wanted to come in from out of town to pay respects to Bernie would have at least twenty-four hours to do it. It was also a Jewish tradition that time be made for people to gather the night before the funeral, and so the last thing I arranged at Riverside that morning was for the viewing, as it was called, from seven to ten that night.

The boys brought me back to the apartment and left. My mother, the baby, and my sister were there, but I felt very alone. I wandered from room to room. I tried not to look at anything. Bernie had been right when he'd shouted, "This is my house!" He was dead, but everything in the apartment belonged to him. And everything that caught my eye reminded me that he wasn't coming home—from the portrait of him in the living room to the cuff link tray on the bedroom dresser to the shaving gear in the bathroom to the highball glasses on the kitchen sink drain that Marlene had used for milk but Bernie'd always used for scotch. Everything looked as lonely and abandoned as I felt. So I tried not to look or feel or think.

When finally I did break down, it came out cockeyed—not about the loss of Bernie but about my not having a dress to wear to the viewing. I'd caught a glimpse of myself in the bedroom mirror during my aimless pacing. And suddenly I was crying uncontrollably. Tillie rushed into the bedroom and put her arms around me.

"I have nothing to wear," I sobbed. "Look how fat I am. Look how terrible, how disgusting I am. I have nothing to wear. I've been wearing maternity clothes." What I'd thought but didn't dare say aloud was that Bernie's casket would be open at the viewing and I kept thinking: He'll see me like this. He always cared so much about the way I looked, he tried so hard to teach me how to take care of myself, how to put on makeup, how to dress. Now, with his casket open, he'll see me and be repulsed. "I want to be beautiful for him, Ma," I tried to explain, in a ragged voice.

I borrowed a black chemise from a girlfriend and someone gave me a black lace kerchief for my head. And I did the best I could. By six o'clock, I couldn't wait any more. "Let's go now. I want to be with him," I told my mother. "I don't want him to be alone."

I wanted to get to the funeral parlor and see his face. I felt as long as I could look at him, he wouldn't really be dead. I'd have a husband.

So we went to the viewing early. And, God, the sight that greeted me. There were so many people already there. It was a stifling hot August night and people came in three-piece suits and ties and many of the women wore long-sleeved dresses. The casket was open and draped over it was a *blanket* of red roses. I had never seen anything like it, hundreds of red roses! And the walls of the room, the biggest viewing room they had, were lined with flowers. We'd arrived early and there were at least twenty or thirty extravagant floral arrangements, from towering bouquets to a horseshoe of white roses with a gold sash across the middle that said, "Love ya, Ricky."

"What is that?" I said to Josh. "It looks like something they'd send to Sea Biscuit for winning the Kentucky Derby. What are all these flowers doing here? This is a Jewish funeral home. Jewish people don't send flowers to the chapel. Get them out."

"Don't," Josh whispered to me. "They're obviously from friends who aren't Jewish and this is how they show their love. So let it be, Sandy. Bernie would have liked it."

And you know what? The minute Josh said that, I thought, I bet he does like it. I could just picture Bernie watching the whole affair, checking out the inscribed ribbons and the cards and *kvelling* at the crowd he'd drawn. He looked beautiful, handsome, and comfortable, as if he were just sleeping, but so much more peacefully than he'd slept in the past several weeks. And I thought how nice it must be for him to finally lie back on a satin pillow and be covered in sweet-smelling roses.

Vinny and Hot Dog took me back to the house and stayed awhile. The baby had a bad night. He was crying a lot, which was very, very unusual for him. And, of course, it was the day his father died. Ten weeks old he was, and fatherless now. Why shouldn't he cry? "There goes the Jab," Red said that night.

"Jab?"

"Mr. Jeffrey Allen Barton," said Red. "That's J.A.B. The Jab."

Well, Hot Dog went home to Thelma. Vinny stayed over on the couch in the living room. The poor guy didn't get much rest because the Jab and I cried through most of that night. The sleeping pills the doctor had given me kept me from getting up and walking around, but they didn't stop the tears. And Nora who, walking and rocking the baby, was Jeffrey's sedative, didn't have much luck, either. The Jab and I cried, each of us in our separate rooms, each of us mourning our separate loss. And then the sun came up—it was a hot and horrible Sunday—and I got ready to bury my husband.

I sat in the little private room in the funeral parlor staring at Bernie, knowing it was going to be the last time I saw him. Again, I had the strange feeling that as long as I could see him, nothing had changed, but that when the coffin lid closed it would be on my life as well as his. "You know this is it, Ma," I'd said that morning. "Today it ends. What do I do after today is over?"

"You'll worry about it tomorrow," she'd said.

"Like Scarlett in 'Gone With the Wind'? What will I do? I'll worry about it tomorrow?"

"Yes," Tillie said firmly. "That's exactly what you'll do."

The rabbi came into the family room. He said a prayer for us and then he cut *schnear*—he made a tear in a little piece of black ribbon—and handed it to me to pin on my dress. It was my mourning badge. I had to wear it for seven days.

I didn't want to be in the room when they closed the casket lid. I took Josh's hand and my mother's and I said, "Come on, I want to see who's here. We'll just take a peek."

I was amazed! The entire chapel was full. The room held two hundred, maybe two hundred and fifty people. And it was standing room only. Every seat was filled and people were lining the aisles. Josh had been right about giving people time to get there. I saw the boys from Vegas, who'd clearly spent the night on the Red Eye and rushed over from the airport still in their white slacks and rumpled jackets, and the Florida crowd in seersucker and patent leather white loafers. I recognized friends of B's from Boston and from Cleveland. Half of Harlem was there. There were some old black women sitting at the back of the chapel, rocking back and forth. I nearly burst into tears! Bernie, I wanted to say, look! Can you see this? Do you know how loved and respected you are?!

Lido was there draped in purple and bright gold with some friends we'd met at his townhouse. There were people done up like they were going to a wedding and people who'd rushed over in jeans. My childhood friend Leona from Brooklyn was sitting next to Judy, who'd been with me the night Bernie and I met. High-ranking members of the five families had all showed up. They were shaking hands, turning slightly this way and that in their seats, to acknowledge one another and their constituents. Their body guards in shiny suits and dark glasses kibitzed among themselves.

Toward the back, a balding, blond-haired man was standing against the wall. He seemed very solitary, very self-contained yet self-conscious, as if he expected attention but was above caring about whether he got it or not. He was about Bernie's age and coldly attractive, dressed to the nines on that sweltering summer day in an immaculate suit with a pale blue shirt and silk tie. "Who's the blond guy in the back?" I asked Josh.

"Oh him? That's Chalky Lefkowitz. Bernie's friend who just got out of Trenton State. I thought you knew him."

"No," I said. "I've only spoken to him on the phone. But Bernie adored the man."

"Yeah, I know." Josh shrugged. "Not my kind of guy," he said cryptically.

Vinny, who'd gone outside for a cigarette, had spotted us peeking through the door. He shouldered his way up the aisle toward us.

"Look at this," I said to him. "Every seat in the house is taken. It's standing room only. Like an opening," I said. "Or a closing."

"Yeah," Vinny said angrily. "They're even crawling around outside, taking license plate numbers."

"The FBI?" Josh asked.

"Unbelievable. Cars are triple-parked outside and these jerks are stepping over bumpers and crouching down to get the numbers. They've got no respect."

I went numb again once the service began. I sat through the eulogy conscious of people crying around me, of murmured agreement with some of the things the rabbi said and even a little relieved laughter every now and then. And then Vinny took my elbow and helped me up and we went outside to the waiting limousines.

There were two limos for the family and close personal friends. The heat outside was awful. The streets looked yellow and were practically steaming in the glaring daylight. I followed my mother into the first car and sat back in a daze. It wasn't until we were on the Long Island Expressway that I turned around and looked back.

"What is that?" I asked Vinny, who was in our car. "I hear music."

"It's Red," he said.

I looked out the back window and there was a procession of seventeen cars following us. And first among them, filled to capacity with mourners, was Hot Dog's white Cadillac convertible. Red had the top down and the tape deck on full blast. He was playing "When the Saints Come Marching In" for Bernie. And he played it, full blast, all the way to the cemetery.

I stood unsteadily in the oppressive heat and watched my husband's casket lowered into the grave. When the rabbi signaled, my mother had to remind me what to do. At her whispered instruction, I tossed a shovel of dirt onto the casket. What a wrenching sound, that sad little hail of earth and pebbles on mahogany wood. Most of the flowers from the funeral home were at the gravesite. When I stepped back into my mother's arms, people began to walk past the grave. They'd throw in bouquets or just take a flower and toss it onto the casket. A couple of men blew kisses as they went by. Then a guy reached into his pocket and pulled out a handful of pot and sprinkled it over the grave. Someone threw in a little cocaine. A woman came up and tossed in perfume. Guys cried. It was an unbelievable procession of people, Bernie's people, which meant rich and poor, young and old, black and white, Jews and gentiles, street and straight.

"He would've loved it," everyone kept saying back at the house. The seven days of sitting shivah, of mourning, began right after the service. People came from the cemetery and crowded into the apartment. Some who hadn't made it out to Farmingdale were already waiting at the house. Platters of food had been delivered. Liquor and champagne was sent up. Some friends had even sent over their housekeeper to help with the serving and cleaning. The wooden boxes on which the family was supposed to sit were set up; the mirrors were covered so that the soul on its journey to heaven wouldn't catch a glimpse of itself and despair. For seven days, the lost loved one was supposed to be remembered, spoken of, wept over, even laughed about; and his bereaved survivors were not supposed to mourn alone.

So the party was on again.

People were coming and going all day and long into the nights. The doormen of the building were in seventh heaven. Every time someone tossed his keys to a doorman or left a limo double-parked he'd tip the building guys extravagantly. The doormen would phone up in voices so happy they were almost laughing and they'd say, "Mr. Gruzetti is on the way up. And I'm watching his car!" They made out like bandits.

And everyone who showed up brought a gift for the baby. Stuffed animals of every size and species were piled up in his room, silver rattles, cups and spoons, clothing—the wardrobe was not to be believed. It was during this hectic time that I began to learn how to take care of my child.

There were only two places I could find peace during that week when the apartment was constantly filled with people. I'd sit out on the terrace in the evenings, the way Bernie had, and smoke a cigarette and stare out at the city lights or I'd hide in Jeffrey's room and, sometimes, just rock and watch him breathe. I began feeding him his bottles, learning how to change his diapers, how to bathe him, hold him, cool him. From the time I'd brought him home from the hospital, I hadn't had much of a chance to get to know my son. It was strange, but that terrible mourning period brought at least that blessing.

The apartment was crowded most of the time. People came up to me. They kissed me. They patted my hands. They reminded me of things Bernie had said or done. They talked about how honorable he was, how loyal, how funny. "A lovable lunatic," more than one guy called him.

"He was an original," his friend Morty said. "We'd meet the Italian guys downtown. Bernie'd be sitting at the table. A guy would say, 'Who you wit? I'm wit Bonanno. Who you wit?' And Bernie'd say, in the same way as them, 'I'm wit everybody. I don't stand alone. I stand wit everybody.' And you know," Morty said, shaking his head, sighing, "he was, Sandy. He was there for whoever needed him."

"He was always there for me," Josh the lawyer told me. He came and found me out on the terrace. He looked rumpled. His sport shirt was wrinkled, the collar lying kind of cockeyed, one side up, one side down. "He'd say, that shingle of yours is worth everything. He wanted me to do better, to be better. He always said that, Sandy. You can do better than this, barrister, he'd say to me. Make a living off us, but don't become one of us," Josh remembered. He looked so sad.

After a while, he sat down next to me and put his feet up on the railing. And the two of us stared out into space.

God bless Red. That first week after Bernie's death, that week of sitting shivah, a lot of people treated me as though I were very fragile—which I was. To tell the truth, they treated me as though I were crazy—which I also was. I never knew when I'd laugh, when I'd cry, when I'd scream. But Hot Dog treated me as though he had total confidence in me. As if he needed me. Oh, do I remember his slicked-back red hair and pale-coffee skin, his pencil mustache, those little laughing eyes, and that big Cab Calloway grin.

In the middle of mourning, with the house constantly crowded, with people smoking, drinking, eating, laughing, and grieving, Hot Dog would call me into the bedroom or the kitchen, wherever it was momentarily quiet, and we'd go into a huddle. He'd hand me the brown paper bag full of numbers money. He's start talking to me about the business, about what he'd done and what he thought we ought to do. He'd ask my opinion. And for a couple of minutes each day, I'd have to pull myself together. I'd have to think like a rational human being. And what would I think? I'd think, what would Bernie say in this situation? What would Bernie do?

Hymie was at the apartment every day. He'd even offered to stay over. He was a close relative, he reminded me. It was his duty to be near, to watch out for me. And with him, too, I thought, what would Bernie do? And I tried to be nice to him. "No, sweetheart," I told him. "You must be exhausted, too. Go home. Come back tomorrow, in the day time. Come every day. But I don't want anyone sleeping in the house."

Hot Dog and Vinny, our real family, Bernie's and mine, the ones he truly loved and left to watch out for me, did stay over. They'd fall out on the floor or the living room couch. And, of course, my mother was with me, and Nora and the baby. But not Sleazeball. During the shivah week, the fat little man who'd walked hunched over for most of his life began to strut around the apartment as if he owned the place, trying to hold court, trying to chat up the *machers* and wise guys, playing the big shot.

I would not allow him to spend the night. I would not allow him to answer the phones anymore. For Bernie's sake, I'd start out nicely with, "Hymie, thank you very much, sweetheart, but don't answer the phones for me," but I'd wind up with, "This is my house now. Mine alone, Hymie. Keep away from my phones!"

Hymie wasn't the only one I shouted at. One of Bernie's ex-partners from The Velvet Club, we'll call him Georgie Mahoney, Mahoney the Phoney, had moved down to Florida. He'd come back to New York for the funeral and decided to hang around for a little while.

Georgie was an attractive guy. He had a great tan. He took excellent care of himself—every and any way he could. He paid a shivah call at the apartment one afternoon. After he'd made the rounds, shook hands, shot the breeze with the boys, he came out to the terrace and, carefully hiking up his linen trousers at the knees, sat down next to me to chat.

"What are you going to do after all this is over?" he said to me.

"Georgie, I don't know," I said. "It's one day at a time at this point in my life. I have to get through the mourning period. I have an infant to take care of. Why?''

"Well, you're a young girl yet. You're beautiful. I always said you were beautiful, Sandy. You'll take off all the weight you've put on. And then, you'll meet a man. You'll get married again. A girl like you—you'll have another life. You could have any life you want.''

He went on that way for a while. He made me nervous, uncomfortable. I blurted out, "What are you saying, Georgie? Are you propositioning me or proposing?''

"A little of both,'' he said.

"I'm sitting shivah for one of your friends, Georgie, and you're sitting her making a pitch for me? Georgie,'' I said, "do you think I was left a lot of money?''

He gave a little wink. "Well,'' he said, "we know B had tons of money.''

I said, "Is that what you think? Who says so? I'm not saying he did or didn't. That's no one's business, Georgie. It's definitely not your fucking business!''

He gave me a look, like how dare I speak to him that way. But before he could come up with the words, I hauled off and smacked him across the face so hard his head shook. Then I started to scream.

I had Georgie put out of the apartment. Vinny came running. A couple of the other *shtarkers* sitting around stuffing their faces dropped everything and ran to help me. I pushed past them into the apartment and ran through the living room shouting, "Get that bastard out of my house!'' Then I spun around and looked at everyone who was staring at me. "And if anyone else here thinks Bernie left me money . . . If he did leave me money . . . If he left me a dollar or a million dollars, he put his back up against the wall for it! It's blood money! And it's nobody's business but mine!''

And all these big men, these tough guys, they looked down at their feet. They looked up at the ceiling. They were embarrassed because they knew what I meant. I'd heard them guessing and gossiping. They'd be sitting around the dining room table and their favorite topic of conversation was how much money Bernie might have left me. One would say, "Oh, he was loaded. The guy had millions stashed away.'' Somebody else would shake his head and say, "Get outta here, the guy didn't have two nickels to rub together. He was a gambler. He lost his shirt.'' And then I'd hear, "BB knew how to live. He lived big. He left a bundle.'' They sounded like a bunch of *yentas*.

Bernie's old friend from the Teamsters, Milty Heinz, came by one day. The house was crowded. I was in terrible shape; just moving was an effort. I looked up and there was Milty at the bar. "Sandy,'' he said. "I need to talk to you, baby. You know B borrowed a nice little piece of change from me a couple of months ago. And I know you're good for it.''

"What are you saying, Milty? That I owe you money?''

The big *shlub,* the hot shot who blew money at the Copa like it was dust. "Well, yeah," he says. "Twelve grand to be exact."

"I don't believe you," I said. "Bernie made you one of Jeffrey's godfathers. Doesn't that mean you're supposed to help look after his kid, not try to steal the milk from his mouth. Excuse me, I've got to talk to someone," I said.

I found Josh and dragged him into the bedroom and told him what Milty had said.

"That bastard! He's trying to make a move on you. He's trying to shake you down. Did he show you a piece of paper? Is he holding a note? He's lying, Sandy. Tell him to go fuck himself."

I marched out of the bedroom. "Milty," I asked, "do you have anything with B's signature on it that says he owes you?"

"Hey, we didn't need paper—" He started giving me what good friends they were, trust, favors, all the nice words.

"Milty, you're lying," I yelled. "On the advice of my attorney, go fuck yourself!"

The whole place sucked air for a second. There was this collective gasp. Then tongues clucked and tongues wagged and people came to put their arms around me and some guys tried to make Milty feel better as he headed for the door. Personally, I don't even think he took it hard. He was one of the guys who believed Bernie had left me a fortune. So what would a measly twelve grand mean to me? Hey, no hard feelings was his attitude as he walked out the door.

He was just another *gonif* looking for an easy score.

One of the reasons all the talk about money got to me was that I didn't know myself what Bernie had left us. Certainly there was no will. Other than the cash I'd taken from our joint safety deposit box—most of which had gone to pay medical bills—I had no idea whether I'd have a dollar or a dime to live on. I had the apartment rent to pay and, for those days, it was an expensive place. I had the baby to support. It scared me. Red always said not to worry. But I knew we weren't going to live on a paper bag full of singles and fivers. I tried to push the fear out of my mind, but it would creep back in.

I began sitting shivah on Sunday, as soon as we got back from the cemetery. All day, every day, people came up to pay their respects and they all brought cakes, liquor, casseroles of food, platters of deli, and gifts for the baby. They'd kiss me, they'd say something to the other members of the family, and quite a few of them would make a point of spending some time with my mother, too. It was about Tuesday when Tillie called me into the bedroom.

"Sit down," she said, locking the door behind us. "I've got something to tell you." She opened the closet and pulled out a plastic bag full of envelopes. "From the day of his funeral people have been giving me these envelopes. There's money in them."

"For what?" I asked.

"For you and the baby."

We began to open the envelopes.

"I didn't know what to do," Tillie said, as if she'd done something wrong.

"No, Ma," I said. "It's good. Take it. Because Bernie would have done the same thing for anyone else's widow. You always give widows money."

"Well," said Tillie, not entirely convinced. "I heard about them doing this at Italian funerals, but not at Jewish."

"Maybe it was the Italian guys that gave them to you."

"To tell you truth, I don't knew who they were. Men kept coming over to me that Sunday in the funeral parlor, people that were here yesterday. I lost track. I'm sorry. I don't even know who they were. And I'm sorry because they didn't even write their whole names on the envelopes. Look," she said. "Here's initials. Here's first names only. In two days, you got from four different Sals and even more Jimmys. This is it."

There was close to $8,000 dollars in that first batch of envelopes. "Ma," I said, smiling for the first time that day. "If anyone else hands you an envelope, just take it and tell them 'God bless you.' "

She laughed at me. "Sandy, you'll never get to heaven this way," she said.

"Is there really a heaven, Ma?" I asked her later that day. She'd found me out on the terrace and sat down beside me. She looked exhausted. "Do any of us really get to heaven? Do you think Bernie is up there looking at us?"

"Absolutely," she said. "He's up there in heaven and he'll be a *gutta better* for you." She saw that I didn't know what she meant. "A *gutta better* is an angel," she explained. "Someone who has died and gone ahead to look out for your interests. He'll argue and pray for you—and for his son and even for me. He'll talk to God for all his loved ones, that God should take care of them. He'll help to see that it'll be okay."

"A guardian angel," I said.

"Exactly. It's like having the best lawyer money can buy; a defense attorney who pleads your case before God. And with that mind of his, and that mouth, how can we lose?"

About a second later, Josh poked his head outside and said, "Excuse me, Tillie. Sandy, can I see you for a second?"

"Speaking of lawyers," I said. "Stay, Ma. I'll be right back." Josh put his arm around me and we walked through the partying crowd. "I've got good news for you. I was just in touch with one of the FBI agents who was on Bernie's case. They called me. They wanted to let me know that I was on record as Bernie's attorney and that the tap's been taken off your phone, so your phone is clean now.''

"Josh, what the hell are you talking about?''

"The FBI had Bernie under surveillance, Sandy. They had a tap on your phones for two months before Bernie went into the hospital. I told you about it the day he died, remember? They thought he was involved with drugs. Well, the tap is off now. Your phone is clean.''

"You mean, all the months he was in the hospital, everything I said to anyone on these phones—they were listening?''

"Yeah. They have tapes of everything.''

It had not registered before. Now I felt nauseated with humiliation and shame. I remembered the anger and exhaustion, the disgust and hopelessness I'd felt about Bernie during that terrible time. I remembered every rotten thing I'd said about my dying husband to intimate friends, who I knew would understand the stress I was under and not take me too seriously or judge me too harshly. Now I was mortified. To think that strangers had been listening, men who had wanted to bring harm to Bernie had heard his wife bitching about him as he lay dying.

"They were taping conversations?'' I asked Josh, sick with shame. I tried to remember whether Hot Dog and I had talked business on the phone. Or the men who'd been here night and day—had they known our phones were tapped?

Josh was saying that he hadn't trusted the agent who'd called him, so he had phoned a friend of his who was with the FBI and that the friend said, yes, the tap had been released, the lines really were clean now.

I realized again, how different our life had been from other people's. It was a very strange way to live. I wondered if I'd ever find a better one.

Smack in the middle of the shivah week, I was sitting with Judy and Nino and I glanced up and saw that Hot Dog had arrived. He was nervous, dancing around in the restless way he had. As soon as I looked up, he signaled for me to come talk. "A couple of the kids got pinched this afternoon,'' he said. "We've got to bail them out.''

"Runners?''

"Yeah. Good kids.''

"Okay, let's get Josh,'' I said.

"No,'' Red said. "They don't need a lawyer. We just gotta bail them out.''

It was about ten at night. There weren't too many people still hanging around. Even Hymie had gone home. I looked for my mother and saw that the door to Jeffrey's room was ajar. "God, Red,'' I said. "I don't know. I'm sitting shivah. I don't think I can do it.''

"Sandy, they might get panicky. Someone's got to go down and bail them out. I can't go on record like that. You've got to do it.''

"Okay," I decided. "How much is it going to be?"

"About seven bills. Here," Red said, handing me the nightly brown paper bag.

"All right," I said, as Tillie tiptoed out of the baby's room and carefully pulled the door shut behind her. "Let me just tell my mother. I'll be right back."

I took her into the big bedroom and told her as I changed my clothes. She hit the ceiling. "What are you crazy?!" she hollered at me. "It's a *shande,* a shameful thing! You can't leave a shivah house. You're in mourning!"

"I know. But I've got to do it, Ma," I said, struggling to get my size 18 body into my size 16 jeans, hopping around on one foot, then the other. "Bernie left me this business. And Red needs me. I'm going to bail out a couple of kids who run for us."

"God will punish you," she shouted.

That did it. I zipped up and broke into tears. "God will punish me?" I said. "Why, Ma, you don't think He's punished me enough already, that at twenty-six years old I have to sit shivah for the man I love, the father of your new grandchild?!"

The night air was stale but sweet to me. I hadn't been out of the house in days. I looked up at the sky as Red's convertible carried us downtown to night court and I wondered what my *gutta better* would say to God to square this one for me. She's just doing what I would have done, Your Honor, I thought Bernie might say. She's my stand-up girl and she's doing what I taught her.

Whatever excuses he might have to make for me, I realized that for the first time in weeks, I felt okay. I had a purpose, a mission. People were counting on me—Red, the runners. I even felt that Bernie was counting on me in some weird way and that he'd be proud of me. A man's got to do what a man's got to do, I remember thinking. And then realizing that, for the moment, I was the "man" I was talking about.

Down at night court, I sat on a back bench and spilled hundreds of dollar bills out of the brown paper bag Red had given me. I counted the money the way Bernie had taught me to, presidents up, all facing the same way. I counted out $700 in singles. When I signed the bail form, I was asked about my relationship to the guys. "I'm a friend of theirs," I said. "I know them." I surprised myself with how cool and efficent I was. I did what I had to do and I felt very good about it. I felt, to tell you the truth, guided from above. And I knew I had done what Bernie would have in the same circumstances. If he'd been sitting shivah, he'd have done exactly the same thing.

It was a very temporary respite from the sorrow. Red dropped me off in front of our building and, by the time the elevator got to our floor, I was frightened, lonely, and depressed again.

Shivah ended officially that Sunday, one week after Bernie had been buried. Following another custom, my mother and I and Hymie and other relatives went downstairs and walked around the building from left to right. We made a full circle to ward off the evil spirits. Then everyone went home.

CHAPTER FIFTEEN

Alone

I remember lying in my mother's arms and sobbing.

"Ma, there's a hole in my heart. Will it ever go away? I feel as if I can't breathe."

She said, "I promise you it will. But when I don't know. It will go away, *mamela*. One day at a time. And that's how you'll live your life. Go dry your eyes, wash your face, sweetheart. You'll feel better."

"I can't," I said.

Hot Dog, Vinny, Josh, and big, burly Morty, the guy who'd told me how Bernie use to say "I'm wit everybody," came over in shifts to keep me company. Morty would say, "Get out of that *shmatte,* that rag you're wearing. You'll feel better."

"I can't," I said.

"Sandy, just put a comb through your hair. Put on a little makeup. You'll feel better," Judy urged.

"Come walk with us, your beautiful child and me," Nora would say, "Come down to the park for a little air."

"Eat real food. Stop stuffing yourself with junk."

"Don't lay around in bed so much."

"Of course you can go to the supermarket. You've got yourself and the baby to feed."

"What do you mean, you're afraid to stand in the stall shower alone? It's ninety-five degrees out, Sandy. Take a shower, you'll feel better."

Bernie had been dead for two weeks and my vocabulary seemed to be reduced to two words: "I can't."

For some reason I'd had tremendous physical strength while he was ill. Only days after giving birth I was running to the hospital, shopping, cleaning, cooking, entertaining friends. I'd done whatever needed to be done—

not graciously, not without anger, self-pity, and tears, but somehow I'd found the energy. Now, two weeks after his death, I moved like a zombie. I couldn't stop crying. I'd fall to my knees doubled over with a sense of loss and fear so deep it literally stole my breath away. My mother had to teach me how to breathe into a paper bag so that I wouldn't pass out.

Alone was how I felt. Terrified, inadequate, alone.

But I wasn't alone. Each day Vinny would stop by. Hot Dog would deliver the brown paper bag. Morty would clown for me and try to teach me card tricks. Josh would phone daily and visit whenever he could. My little sister Marlene hung around, tried to help. And most of the time, Nora took care of Jeffrey and me as though we were brother and sister. And, of course, Tillie slept over every night and spent as much time during the day with me as she could.

"Just give me a month," I told Red one day, "then I'll come out swinging."

Hymie wanted to talk business. "Not now. Not yet," I said. "Give me a month to mourn."

One day, we gathered up all of Bernie's belongings. There's an old Jewish superstition that says no one should walk in the shoes of a dead man. So we threw all the shoes into the incinerator. The clothing we gave to the doormen and to charity. The jewelry I kept, except for a couple of special pieces that went to those Bernie had loved best, family and friends. It must have been the beginning of the third week. I looked around the apartment and, except for the portrait of him that hung next to mine in the living room, the portraits we'd had painted in Florida, there was nothing left of the man. Even the smell of him was gone from the bedsheets. I used to lie down in bed and I couldn't smell him anymore. The only thing left of Bernie in the house was that little boy lying in the crib.

I wanted to die. I wanted to die so badly that I made a half-assed attempt at slitting my wrists. It was one morning after Tillie had gone to work. Mornings were the hardest, waking up with that thump of fear, that first terrible consciousness, the dread. I heard Nora in the kitchen talking to Jeffrey. I knew she was getting his bottle ready, then they would go out. I knew Jeffrey would be better off without me. I was useless, crazy, incapable of taking care of anyone. I couldn't even brush my teeth anymore. I was standing at the sink holding a razor blade. It was as much of an effort to drag it across my wrist as it had been to drag my 170 pounds out of bed. I cut my wrist very carefully. I stared down at what looked like a little scratch dotted with red droplets and watched the blood begin to ooze out of it. I was crying. And suddenly, I thought: "Hey, what am I doing? This hurts. I'm not strong enough to kill myself. I'm a fucking coward."

It was so weird. I went from this dull, aching, definitely wanting to die feeling to sudden clarity. I wouldn't be able to do it and, what was more, I didn't really want to.

I hadn't done much damage. I cleaned myself up and then I started swabbing the blood in the sink. And I looked in the mirror. I remember taking off my housecoat, the loose-fitting sleeveless cover up, the *shmatte* I'd been wearing. I looked at myself in the mirror, at this fat body, the hanging breasts and flab, and I thought: But the face is young, the girl's face is young. It's still a pretty face.

I thought: You know what, you'd better shape up, baby.

Then I looked up at the ceiling, as if I could see right through it to heaven. And I screamed, "BERNIE!" Oh, how I wanted him. How I wanted to hear his deep, gravelly voice again. I screamed his name at the top of my lungs. And Nora came running into the bathroom. There was still some blood on the sink and she saw it.

"It's all right," I said. "Don't worry about it. Please believe me, I'm all right. Everything is fine." I walked her out of the bathroom. "Nora, it's over," I said. "From here on in, it's got to be up because I've reached the bottom. My mother told me, you can only go so low in life, you can only be so crazy and miserable, and that when you reach the bottom there is only one way to go after that because you have no choice."

I made a promise to myself that day in the bathroom. I reminded myself of what I'd told Red and Hymie and everyone else who was either worried about me or wanted to talk business. I'd said, "Let a month go by and I'll come out swinging." Bernie had died August seventh. It was now September first. That morning with the razor blade, I reminded myself that it was almost time.

"Ma, I'm taking the car and driving out to see Bernie," I said that weekend.

"What are you talking about?"

It had begun to dawn on me that he was really gone, that he hadn't just left for a little while. He was never ever coming back. The realization was absolutely intolerable. I wanted him. I needed to be near him. "I'm going to the cemetery," I said.

"You can't do that. It's not even a month yet. You don't do that in the Jewish religion until the headstone is put up."

"The hell with the Jewish religion, Ma. I want to see him. I want to be close to him." I put some coffee in a Thermos, I took a sandwich along, and I drove all the way out to the Island. I parked in front of his grave and sat there and ate and spoke to him.

"Why did you leave me?" I asked. I was a little scared and tentative, at first, as if Bernie were really listening to me and, because he'd been sick, because he'd been dead, I didn't want to yell at him about it. I wanted to be nice. But as I spoke, I gathered force. The sadness and loneliness gave way to anger. And, boy, was I mad. I had no idea how pissed off I was until the words came pouring out.

"Shmuck, you couldn't take care of yourself? How many times did Doctor Sealy tell you to lay off the fucking salt, Bernie? How many times? Was it worth it, the goddamn Chinese food and the deli? The cigars and speed? Speed, you took! Jerk! What the hell was the matter with you? Was it worth it to never see your son again? I'm so mad at you," I said. "You could have had it all, if you'd just been straight—with yourself, with Doctor Sealy, with me. You could have enjoyed the good life. Watched Jeffrey grow up. You could have been with me. I miss you so much, you moron! Oh, Bernie, what am I going to do? How am I going to raise our son? I don't know how to do it, baby. I'm scared. What do I do now, Bernie? Tell me!"

All this between bites of a bologna sandwich and sips of coffee from the Thermos cup. I laughed at myself. I cried for Bernie. I expected him to answer my questions, to consider my side of things. I ran my hand over the warm earth and knew he was beneath it. Strange as it seems, it was comforting to know that he was there. He was somewhere real in the world, near enough for me to drive out and talk to. I needed to know he existed, that he had lived and been real and was real still. And, finally, I forgave him. "I'll live," I promised. "And you know what, Bernie, I'm going to make you proud of me." When I drove home in the early evening, I felt much better. I felt that I had been with him.

Later that week, I took off the piece of black ribbon that I'd pinned to my bra every morning, and I put it away in a drawer. And I took out Bernie's necklace, the gold medal with Saint Christopher on one side and the Star of David on the other, and put it on. And that day, Vinny and Red and Morty took me marketing. It was the first time I'd gone shopping since Bernie died. Nora dressed Jeffrey and I put him in his carriage— not the Royal Coach baby carriage, which had turned out to be totally useless; it was so big we could only fit it in the building's freight elevator—but a nice, normal little stroller. And the five of us went to the supermarket.

The five of us went everywhere together that fall, the guys and Jeffrey and me. The boys stayed close. God forbid Jeffrey shouldn't have a male image around. Here came the volunteer squad, the proud godfathers: Red, a reed-thin rainbow in his straw fedora, Hawaiian shirts, and green, orange, or electric blue pants; Vinny, immaculately coiffed, shooting his cuffs, always clean and crisp; and hulking Morty, all six-foot-three of him, wreathed in cigar smoke, dark, wavy hair slicked back, long rambling nose in the air. They came with me to the pediatrician for Jeffrey's checkups. They wheeled him in his stroller in the little park behind our house. They'd sit in the playground for hours and watch over him while he slept in the sunshine. They'd prop him up in the supermarket cart and wheel him along the aisles while I shopped. They had loved Bernie. Now they were taking care of his wife and kid.

I was still breaking into uncontrollable tears a couple of times a day. Knowing that his closets were empty, his side of the medicine chest, his side of the bed, his foods were not in the kitchen cupboards anymore caused a sick ache in my gut. And if, for a minute, I was able to forget him, the next minute I was beating myself up for being so selfish and uncaring. I was very lonely and lost. But I had promised Bernie I'd live. I had promised myself I'd come out swinging. Bills had been piling up. Ready or not, it was time to take care of business.

"We've got to talk, Red," I said when Hot Dog came by to drop off the numbers money.

He grinned. "I've been waiting for you, partner. Let's do it."

We sat down and, for the first time since Bernie's death, we really discussed finances. The business was healthy. Red ran it right. The runners were good neighborhood kids, loyal, honest, competent. So were the guys who manned the phones in the walkup. There'd never been a doubt in Red's mind that he and I were now partners, that I was in for fifty-fifty just as Bernie had been. "But what do I have to do?" I asked.

"Just come down to the place for a while," Red said. "Let people see you around. Let them get to know you're in for Bernie. Let them get to know you're not the boss's old lady, you're the boss."

Did I hear Red's brain ticking? You'll have to get out of that housecoat, woman, he might just as well have said. You won't be able to sit around and mope all day, or break down crying, or feel sorry for yourself.

"So what would I do? Take numbers, make coffee, what?" I asked, warming to the idea.

"Yeah. That. And whatever you want. Just stop up. Kibitz with the boys. Hang out."

The next people I contacted were Shorty and P.D., two of the dozen partners in another of Bernie's businesses, a seedy but profitable neighborhood bar on East Ninety-sixth Street and Second Avenue. We'd driven past the place countless times on our way up to Harlem and stopped in for drinks occasionally. The neighborhood then was Italian and Irish. There'd be grandmothers sitting on the stoops shelling peas, or leaning out the windows on fat feather pillows. Lots of kids around. The old men would sit around the bar watching the ball games and eating the free hardboiled eggs.

Shorty and P.D. had paid a shivah call and been very sweet about telling me that, as far as they were concerned, Bernie's share of the profits now belonged to me. What that meant, I didn't know. So I phoned the bar one afternoon and Shorty was there. He said, "You want to talk? Great. Come over in half an hour, P.D.'ll be here. It'll be a pleasure to see you, honey."

Shorty was, what else? short, and chubby with salt-and-pepper hair that he wore in what they used to call a Caesar cut—which meant that what was left of his hair he combed forward in a little Frank Sinatra-style fringe. P.D. was tall and skinny. What made him unique was his passion for climbing greased poles. He'd talk for hours about the flag-pole shimmying contests he'd been in and the techniques he used to win them. People would run when he got started. P.D. would open with, "First you gotta grease your palms—"

And never mind that this was a connected guy, a gangster talking, half the bar would knock back their drinks in one gulp and disappear.

I got dressed and drove over to the bar. P.D. and Shorty were waiting. "You're in," Shorty said. "You'll get your piece same as like when Bernie was alive."

"Good," I said, even though I still had no idea whether he was talking about $5.00 a week or $500.

"It'll vary," P.D. read my mind. "Depending on the action in the place. Some weeks a hundred. Some weeks three bills—"

"And the action is?"

"Aw, you know, kid. A little numbers biz. A little a this, a little a that. It varies."

"Tell you what," said Shorty. "You come in a couple days a week. Bring the kid. How's that big boy? Bring him with you anytime. Come in, help out around the place a little. Get to know the action. That's the best way."

"It may not look like much," P.D. said, "but this here's a little gold mine, Sandy. And it ain't a half-bad place to hang out."

How can I explain how good it felt, sitting there in a dark booth in a musty old bar that stank of booze and sawdust, talking to a couple of wise guys who were treating me as an equal? Here I was, yesterday a weepy young widow, today a full partner in two of Bernie's businesses.

There was only one other person I had to see—Sleazeball Hymie, who was supposed to be collecting interest and keeping the books on the loans Bernie had put out.

At the end of shivah, when I was giving away some of Bernie's jewelry, I remembered that I'd left my diamond wedding band and a couple of other good pieces of jewelry in the secret hiding place in the hassock. I'd put them there during my pregnancy, when my fingers had gotten too swollen to wear the ring anymore. So the day I was cleaning out Bernie's things, I'd gone to the hassock to get my jewelry. And it was gone. I searched the whole house. I thought I'd gone crazy. I knew I'd put the ring, a diamond-studded gold watch and my good diamond earrings into the hassock. What the hell had happened to them? Who knew about the secret compartment in the hassock besides me and Bernie? No one. Not Hot Dog. Not my mother.

Hymie!, I thought. During that period when Bernie was sick at home and Sleazeball first started running errands for him, Bernie had probably told him about the hassock. He's blood, he used to say. Bernie trusted blood.

I remembered how Hymie had been hanging around the house while I was at the hospital with Bernie. I remembered Ruth, the baby nurse, always telling me that he'd been at the apartment, making phone calls, cleaning out the fridge, and poking into everything.

Well, no sooner did I think Hymie! than I got this full-blown picture of Hymie's full-blown girlfriend showing up at the house the week after the funeral wearing a gorgeous new cocktail ring on her pudgy finger, a ring that cost far more than a haberdashery clerk could afford. Hymie was still working days in a men's clothing store, not the one he'd embezzled from, of course. I'd commented on his girlfriend's new ring, which she immediately said Hymie had given her along with a beautiful diamond pin and a pair of earrings to match. "Very nice," I'd said to the Sleaze that night. "Must have cost you a fortune."

"Oh, um, ah," he went. "I got lucky gambling."

I almost laughed in his face. The man was the worst gambler, the biggest loser, the *shlemiel* of the century. But I was on good behavior with him during that shivah week. I was trying to treat him the way I felt Bernie would have wanted me to.

Now I thought, yeah, Hymie, you got lucky. You're lucky Bernie is dead. I could not shake the notion that Sleazeball had stolen my jewelry. I knew it in my head and I knew it in my gut. But I'd never confronted him. I'd never suggested that I didn't trust him. Now it was time to find out what was going on with the business he was supposed to be taking care of. And now was the time, also, to remember Bernie's advice: Don't get mad. Get even.

I phoned him at the clothing store. "Hymie, it's time," I said. "I'm ready now for us to have our little talk." He was so excited. This was what he'd been waiting for. He felt that he was the rightful heir to Bernie's kingdom. Who was I, what was I? A kid. A girl. Bernie would never turn his business over to a woman. Like everyone else, Hymie had speculated on how much money Bernie had stashed away, how much his schemes and dreams brought in. And like everyone else, Hymie thought the figure was astronomical. He was practically giggling when he said, "Sure, sure, Sandy. Right away. The sooner the better. Tonight's no good? How about tomorrow?"

The next evening, after dinner, Hymie came to the house. I poured the coffee and asked my mother to excuse us, and he and I sat down at the dining room table to talk business.

"Hymie, I don't know exactly what you were doing for Bernie while he was so sick and then after, these past few weeks, well, I really didn't want to know. But now I'm ready, sweetheart. You tell me.''

"I'm glad you're feeling better, Sandy. And I'm glad you're asking. You know I wanted to have this talk before, but I respected your feelings. He was my blood. It's been a terrible loss. But life goes on. And all I want is what Bernie would have wanted. For me to help out you and the baby. And you can count on me one hundred percent,'' Hymie announced, struggling to keep his gaze steady and sincere, his watery blue eyes focused on me.

"Thanks.''

"You know Bernie had a little loan money out on the streets. Nothing. A couple of bills. It's no big business, believe me. And whatever little money he lent he asked me to collect the juice, the vig—you understand vigorish? The interest, Sandy—he wanted me to collect it and so I did and I'm still doing it.''

I knew that near the end, Bernie had gone into loansharking. He'd lent money at mob rates. I also knew that he'd kept a black book somewhere because at one point he'd showed it to me and said, "You see this. This is money, baby. This is a record of who I've lent money to and how much they owe.'' I hadn't seen the book when I'd cleaned out his things, but I knew one existed. "Hymie, you keep a record, don't you?''

"Of course,'' he said, a little indignant that I'd question his competence.

"I'm only asking, Hymie. It's a black notebook, right?''

"No. It's not black. But, don't worry, I have every cent written down. And I even have some money for you tonight—''

"What else did you do for Bernie?'' I asked.

"Well, whatever else I did, it's over with. I can't do more about it unless you get involved.''

I had a hunch Hymie had delivered some of those packages from the Spanish suitcases and that he'd be happy if I knew where we could get some more. "Good. Then that's over,'' I said. "Because whatever else you did for Bernie I'm not getting involved in. Just the loans, that's all. So what percentage was Bernie giving you, Hymie?''

"Oh, you know Bernie. He was a generous guy. He'd throw me some here, throw me there. He took good care of me.''

I said, "Hymie, I'll take good care of you. Don't worry about it, sweetheart. The people Bernie lent the money to, I have no interest in meeting them. You take care of it. You just continue on with it. But, Hymie, the rest of Bernie's business, what Bernie had going with Hot Dog and his other investments—Hymie, that you cannot touch.''

He didn't like it. "Come on, Sandy. This is family talking. I just want to take care of business the way Bernie would have wanted. I'm just trying to look out for you. Somebody's got to keep an eye on Bernie's interests for you and the kid.''

I said, "You know what, Hymie, we'll be okay. Don't worry about it. So you said you have some money for me?"

"Yeah." He wasn't happy, but he dug out his wallet and pulled a banded bankroll out of it. "It's what mounted up the past couple of weeks while you were out of commission. I was holding it for you. Friday nights I usually go collecting. I'll bring you the juice."

"Hymie, you'll let me see your records," I said.

His blue eyes blazed for a second. "I don't have them on me now. You worried? I'll bring them to you."

Without Bernie's little black book I was at Hymie's mercy. He'd bring me what he brought me. Whether it was the right amount or not I'd never know. Plus, I was still steaming about the stolen jewelry. For the moment, there was nothing I could do about it. So I smiled and stood up. "Okay, Hymie. Don't worry about it now. I'm very glad we had this talk. I feel much better," I said. I picked up his coffee cup and mine and took them into the kitchen and left him with his mouth hanging open.

So what could I count on? A little money from Red here, a little from the bar there and, from Hymie, as little as he could get away with. It was time to answer the question on everyone's mind: How much did I really have? It was time to hit the vaults.

In the next couple of days, I got the keys from my cousin Francine and the paper telling me what my name was at which bank, and off I went to discover what my future held.

Believe me, the *yentas* would have been disappointed.

Most of the cash had gone to pay doctors and hospital bills. Most, but not all. There was enough left to live on for a while, although it wasn't going to be in the lap of luxury. Still, as my mother said, "It'll buy a lot of milk and diapers for Jeffrey. Plenty of young girls with babies have been left off worse." And there was a surprise. The jewelry that had disappeared from the hassock was not in any of the vaults, but in an envelope I'd thought contained cash, was Bernie's black book—complete with the names and interest rates on every loan on which Hymie was supposed to be collecting juice.

All in all, it wasn't bad.

And then it got better.

At the end of September, I got a phone call from a man named Nathan. "I'm a friend of Meyer's," he said. "I'd like to buy you lunch and—" I was instantly nervous. "Meyer who?" I asked, although of course I knew who he meant.

"Meyer Lansky," said the man. "My name is Nathan and I'd like to discuss something with you. It's good. Don't get upset, it's only good."

"How did you get this number?" I asked. It was an unlisted line.

"Meyer got it from Farvel."

"Oh," I said. "Do you know Farvel?"

"Of course," said Nathan. "I had dinner with him and Minnie last week at—"

"Have you ever been to his house?" I asked.

"Many times."

"You've seen his garage?"

Nathan laughed. "You mean the warehouse?"

That did it. "Okay," I said. "I'm sorry I asked you so many . . . questions."

"Please," he brushed off my apology. "I understand. So you'll meet me for lunch? It's a good surprise. I don't want to talk over the phone."

"Of course," I said. I was still huge, but I worked hard at making myself look decent. I squeezed into a dark dress and high heels. I put on some makeup, did the best I could with my hair, and I drove down to Little Italy to meet Meyer's emissary at the Villa Penza, an Italian restaurant on Grand Street.

Nathan turned out to be a couple of years younger than Meyer and older than Bernie. He was a tall, tanned, heavyset man with a full head of hair that was graying at the temples. Conservatively dressed in a blue blazer and charcoal gray trousers, he stood as the head waiter led me to his table in the backroom.

"Nice to meet you," he said, patting my hand solicitously, "even under these sad circumstances. Sit, please. How's the baby? Such a terrible thing," he said in a *haimisha* way that was nevertheless politely formal. "I knew Bernie from years ago. A lovely man. I always liked him."

We made small talk for a while, ordered lunch. Finally, Nathan said, "I have a present for you, from Meyer himself. It has nothing to do with anybody else. It's a personal thing he's doing on his own. A baby gift."

"But he already gave us—" I began.

"No, no, take it." He laid a plain white envelope onto my palm and closed my fingers over it with his two hands. "So you'll keep it for the Bar Mitzvah. Meyer wants you to have it. Also, he asked me to call up your building management, which I did. Sandy, Meyer liked Bernie very much. Bernie was dear to him. And we know he didn't leave you millions. You're a young woman on your own with a newborn baby to raise. So Meyer sent them a check. So you shouldn't have to worry about that."

"About what?" I asked.

"About your rent, Sandy. Meyer paid your rent for the remainder of this lease and the next. That's three years, I think. So, your rent is paid in advance. Don't worry about it. Meyer owes this to Bernie. We don't want you to think it's charity."

I was overwhelmed. I wasn't sure what I ought to say, how I was supposed to behave. Three years' rent! I thought of the little man I'd seen sitting at the head of his table, ringing the dinner bell and cursing in Yiddish. I thought of him grinning, his thin lips stretched almost ear to ear, his head dipping in a self-deprecating, modest gesture. The long, bony nose. The bright, twinkling eyes. Meyer's class and generosity overwhelmed me. I tried to refuse the gift. "No, no. It's too much," I protested. But Nathan insisted it was money due Bernie, that Meyer would be hurt if I turned it down, that it was already a done deed, the building management had been contacted, the check had probably already cleared.

I remembered how Bernie had always lit up in Meyer's presence, how he respected, *revered,* the man. I wondered if he'd ever realized how much Meyer cared for him. Enough to make this extraordinary gesture, to free his widow and son from worrying about how they'd pay the rent—for the next three years!

"Okay," I said finally. "Please tell Meyer, 'Thank you,' " and Nathan, clearly relieved, winked at me and nodded his head as if to say: good girl, that's better.

The money in the plain white envelope, Meyer Lansky's gift to Bernie's son, turned out to be five thousand dollars.

"Five thousand dollars and three years rent!" I told my mother as soon as I got home. "Can you believe it, Ma?"

"Very nice." She tsked and clucked and shook her head in admiration of Meyer's gift. "Very nice." Then she clasped her hands together. "Oh, my God, I almost forgot. Wait. Wait, Sandy, sweetheart. Come, quick."

She dragged me into the bedroom. "What?" I kept saying, starting to laugh because Tillie was grinning all of a sudden, almost giggling now.

"Oy-yoi-yoi, can you believe it, to forget this?" She opened the closet door and, standing on her tip-toes, pulled down two shoe boxes from the shelf.

"The cards from the *t'alainas,"* she said. "The Italians. They kept bringing me envelopes and you told me to keep taking—so here they are!"

She took the lids off the boxes. Each of them was stuffed to the brim with envelopes bearing sympathy cards and cash! I spilled the contents onto the bed and kicked off my high heels. Then my mother and I sat down and started ripping open the envelopes. There was money in every single one. As Tillie had told me before, most of the cards were signed with just a first name or initials. The ones I knew how to contact, I did, and they were very, very sweet, almost embarrassed by my thanking them. Forget it, this is what we do, they said. And if you need anything else, we're here for you.

September, October, November—the months rolled by. I started taking care of myself. I went to a doctor, who put me on a diet, and I stayed with it. I was very determined, very gung-ho to get skinny and look gorgeous. And it was working. It was a miracle. It was like watching a real human being begin to take shape out of a great lump of flesh. It wasn't just the weight loss, of course. I was coming back to life. It was visible in my face, my hair, the way I walked and sat and even talked on the telephone.

I started taking care of the baby, spending real time with him. I'd dress Jeffrey up in one of the beautiful little outfits friends had given us—little shorts and T-shirts that made him look like a miniature boxer in training. I'd tuck his silky dark hair under the tiny baseball cap Red had bought him. The Jab was big, bright, good; and goofy-looking when he smiled. And he smiled as soon as he saw me now, he knew me.

I'd take him down to the park and sit there with the other mothers. Not with them exactly, but near them. I didn't really have many single friends or girlfriends to hang out with. Leona worked. Judy had Nino and the baby to take care of. So I remember sitting on the wooden benches in the concrete playground, watching the other mothers and trying to pretend that I was just like them. That I had to go up at four o'clock or five to feed the baby and get dinner started for my husband. I don't know who I was trying to fool, myself or the harried but efficient-looking young women who seemed so normal, whose lives I imagined with envy. I wondered what they talked about to one another. I tried to hear what they said to their children. Sometimes, I'd say the same things to Jeffrey, just to see how it sounded, how it felt. "Okay, time to go upstairs, *tateleh*. Daddy'll be home soon and you've got to have your supper and your bath and you'll be all clean and smell so beautiful when he comes in."

Sometimes, I'd take Jeffrey with me to the bar on East Ninety-sixth. P.D. or Shorty or the other guys would fuss over him and call him "Champ," or "Little B," but no one called him "Tiger." Eventually, I cut Nora down from full- to part-time and, when she was there, I'd sometimes drive up to Harlem and hang out with Red at our numbers place. A couple of evenings a week, I'd work at the bar. I'd serve drinks and sit around and kibitz and laugh with the old Italian and Irish guys and their women. It was good to have somewhere to go and something to do.

My mother would stay over for one week now, then spend the next week at home in Brooklyn. She was a working woman and she'd been doing two big jobs for over a month—her real one on Wall Street and the even more exhausting one of being there with me, for me, while I cried and screamed and mourned. She needed a rest and, boy, had she earned it.

When my mother wasn't around, Hot Dog was. He and his wife, Thelma, stayed close, and took care of me. Thelma was in her forties, a smart, good-natured, light-skinned, top-heavy woman who owned a beauty parlor in Queens. She adored Red, loved him dearly, and kept a great home up on the Riverdale/Bronx border. And, working as hard as she did six days a week, she'd invite me and the baby to dinner early every night and lay out a home-cooked feast that came as close to tempting me off my diet as anything ever did. Red and Thelma had no kids of their own. Jeffrey was their delight. My man, my namesake, Mr. Jab, the prince, Hot Dog called him.

So time passed. I tried to keep busy. I took care of business. I lived . . . and I learned.

Every week on Friday night, Hymie used to come over and give me the interest, the vigorish, on Bernie's loans. One week it would be one figure, the next another. He said he'd taken out his piece, the amount he and Bernie had agreed upon. I didn't even try to figure out what his deal had been with Bernie. Fine. I had the book. Most of the names in it belonged to men I didn't know. But the way it worked, many of them would be legitimate businessmen who'd needed money fast and couldn't get it from a bank. Some were people who didn't have any kind of collateral to put up. I wasn't going to call them and ask what they'd given Hymie on Friday. And, although I'd considered it once or twice, I had enough sense not to ask anyone to intervene for me.

First of all, I remembered what Bernie used to say about keeping up a good front. "Never let anyone know you're hurting. Let people think you have more than you have. That way they'll never think you want something from them. And when you do go to them, they feel that your credit is good." So, I figured if the time came that I really needed help, I'd ask. For now, I'd save the muscle.

Well, one afternoon I got a phone call from a guy whose name was in the black book. He was very straightforward. He said that he owed Bernie money. He knew I was B's wife and that I was well-connected. So he wanted to let me know that he was going to pay off the entire loan the following Friday. He'd be giving Hymie $17,000 and that would complete his loan.

Okay. Fine. I called Hymie and told him what to expect. "When you meet this man on Friday, Hymie, he's going to give you the full amount," I said. "Seventeen thousand dollars."

"Terrific. Super. That's great," says the Sleaze.

"And Hymie," I said, "keep two grand for yourself. And fifteen you bring back to me. Okay?"

"Okay. Very generous of you. Super. Don't worry."

Right. So, Friday night I'm watching the clock. Normally he'd show about eight. It's nine, ten, eleven. No Hymie. Finally, eleven-fifteen, they buzz from downstairs to say he's on his way up and I can hear in the doorman's voice that something's wrong. And in comes Hymie. His hair is a mess, washed-out, reddish-blond tufts standing up all over his head. His face is not just pasty and sweating, it's shmeared with dirt that looks like axle grease. There's a little blood on his cheek—something red, any-way. Maybe it's his girlfriend's nail polish. He's huffing and puffing. His coat is open so you can see his shirt, which is ripped with a couple of buttons missing. White, heaving blubber showing through. Not a pretty sight.

I could have mouthed the words right alongside him: "I've been robbed!" Right.

"Eighteen grand!" he hollers. "They took everything. The week's vig. The payoff. Every cent!"

Poor thing.

"Hymie, calm down, sweetheart," I said aloud. To myself I'm chanting, You dirty motherfucking lying bastard, this is how you're going to rob me?!

Well, he was entitled. He hated my guts. He was jealous of Bernie. He was a low life. Fine. Of course, he'd try to rob me. And, of course, I thought about calling in a couple of specialists who'd give Hymie's knee caps a remedial course in debt collecting. Instead, I brought the fat man a drink. I gave him a washcloth soaked in cold water to put on his bruises. And then I went into my bedroom and brought out Bernie's little black book.

"Hymie," I said, making sure he saw the book. "Don't worry about it. You know what, Hymie, you don't have to do this anymore. It's over with."

His fat mouth went slack. I thought he'd throw a blood clot to the brain from all the effort he was making trying to figure out what that would mean to him.

"Hymie, I'm going to call up everyone in this book and tell them, the hell with it, their debts are canceled. They owe me nothing!"

His wormy lips started working; there were sounds, but no words came out.

"Or better yet, I'll have one of the big guys from downtown, one of Bernie's friends, intervene. Hymie," I said tenderly, "I never want this to happen to you again."

"I can't think. I'm too upset," he said, and left.

The next day, like a good in-law, I called him at home to see how he was feeling. He said, "You know, Sandy, we really shouldn't stop this. Why should people get away with taking Bernie's hard-earned money?"

"It's over with," I said. "I'm going downtown this afternoon and putting out the word. I'm giving them the book and telling them to call up everyone who can't pay and tell them that all debts are canceled. I really don't want to be a part of this anyway," I said. "It's dirty and I really don't want it."

I could hear this bastard gulping, but there really was nothing he could say. In any case, I figured he was sitting on eighteen grand and whatever else he'd managed to embezzle from Bernie's business. So he'd be all right for a while. And I wouldn't have to put up with seeing him on Friday nights and having him try to wheedle and whine his way into any little piece of action he caught wind of. He could keep the bread and good riddance.

Well, a month later, I got a call from a guy who handled junkets to the

Desert Inn in Las Vegas. He said that Hymie had called him up and said that he was a close relative of Bernie Barton's and he'd like to go on a junket. This man said, "I'm calling to find out if he's legit. And what do you want me to do?"

"I'll call you back," I said.

I thought about it for a while. All I kept remembering, aside from how angry I was at the fat weasel, was what an unlucky *shlep* Hymie was.

I phoned the man back. "Look," I said. "Yes, he's a relative. But he's also a bastard. I think he ripped me off for close to twenty grand. Put him on the junket, why not? But don't give him credit. Just let him travel free, let him eat, drink, let him stay in a gorgeous room and see the shows, but don't comp him any credit at all, because the guy's a stumble bum. He stole from me."

"In that case, we won't put him on at all."

"No," I said. "Whatever he stole from me, let him go for it. Maybe his luck will turn and he'll win money. Maybe. But if I know Hymie, he's going to lose and lose big. Maybe twenty's worth. Maybe more. No matter what, though, no credit."

"You got it," the guy said.

So Hymie drank Dom Pérignon for breakfast and ate sturgeon for brunch. And he dropped a bundle bigger than his belly. He let it slip like sand through his fingers. He came back from Vegas dry-cleaned.

Revenge was definitely tempered by regret. *Eighteen grand*—I'd let it get away from me. So, six months later, when my friend Lila phoned with a sudden cash-flow problem, I was determined to help her claim what was rightfully hers.

Let me tell you about Lila.

Lila Navarro was stacked. She was a leggy blonde with a pair of doe eyes that made Bambi look like he was squinting. And she was as bubbly and upbeat as she was beautiful. In addition to her physical and temper-mental assets—or maybe because of them—Lila had enviable assets in jew-elry and hard cash. These she'd collected from a very big wise guy who'd kept her for years, and kept her very well. Duke was a major mob *macher*. So when you said, "Lila, those diamonds are to die for," you weren't that far off the mark.

About half a year after Hymie lost his shirt and my money in Vegas, Lila called me, sounding uncharacteristically blue. "Well, I don't have anymore jewelry," she said. "Duke's under investigation, and the lawyers told him to put it all in the vault."

"All of it?" I groaned, thinking of the blinding rocks, the exquisite rings, pins, necklaces, and earrings that kept Lila lit up like Christmas twelve months a year. "But you've got access to the vault, right?"

"No," she said. "But, what the heck. It's just for a couple of weeks.

Just in case the FBI busts into my place one night while he's here. Just so they don't find the jewelry or take it. You know how the FBI can be. It's no big deal, Sandy. What's a couple of weeks?''

A lifetime, as it turned out.

While Lila's jewelry was buried in an iron box in the basement of the First National Savings Bank, Duke had a massive heart attack.

I dragged Lila out of her apartment and shlepped her over to the hospital. Duke was trussed up like a turkey ready for the oven, and looked about the same color. He was gray. He had tubes running in and out of him. Lila didn't want to do it, but I made her ask him about the vault. Which one had he put her jewelry in? I didn't feel that great about about doing it, either—but she was my friend, lost in grief and fear, a couple of things I knew a little about.

Duke understood. He told us which vault and the name it was under. Lila had the keys to all his safety deposit boxes at her apartment. Then he tried to give her a hard look. "What's the matter," he said. "You worried? You think I'm going to die?''

I was holding Lila's hand. "Yeah," we both blurted out. And he cracked up.

Five weeks later he was dead.

After the funeral, Lila was wild with panic. Duke had supported her for years and years. The gifts he'd given her, her retirement fund—hundreds of thousands of dollars' worth of jewelry, and the fifty or sixty thousand dollars that had been in the house—were now locked away, lost to her forever.

The two of us sat around Lila's place drinking J&B and pondering the mess. Lila was an ex-showgirl. The walk-in closet in her bedroom held a couple of wigs. She was dynamite with makeup. We drank, we wandered around her house. On the chaise in her bedroom lay a suit of Duke's she couldn't bring herself to throw out. I must have passed the suit ten times going to and from the bathroom. Passed the wigs on their wooden stands. Passed the makeup on her dressing table. And I still don't know how it all came together. How we hatched the scheme.

What I do remember is waking up to the alarm one Friday morning and thinking: It's dark out, it's too early—what the hell am I doing up at this hour? And then I thought about what Lila and I were supposed to do that day. I sort of smiled, thinking in that foggy, not-quite-awake way that it was a dream, a joke, right? Then my heart kicked in like a jackhammer. I knew it was real. Lila and I were going to get the diamonds today.

In front of the mirror, at Lila's dressing table, the transformation began. The men's wigs she'd gotten from the theatrical supply house were good. Hers was auburn, mine a darker brown, like mink almost—dark with a couple of lighter strands running through it. It looked prematurely gray and very real.

As she pinned my hair up close to my head, Lila's hands were shaking. And why not? She was lucky her fingers worked at all. She'd spent the better part of two days practicing Duke's signature. The cream-colored carpet was littered with crumpled sheets of paper on which was written— in Duke's childish scrawl—the bank alias he'd confided at the hospital.

The thick hairpins Lila used did a good job of flattening my thick hair. She put a stocking over the top of my head and we both burst into nervous laughter. I looked like Dopey of the Seven Dwarfs until she slipped my wig on. I shut my eyes. Lila slopped a coat of gummy glue all over my cheeks, pressed my upper lip, chin, temples. I opened my eyes a minute later—presto!, I had sideburns and a nicely trimmed beard and mustache. Then she thickened my eyebrows. The whole thing looked pretty good, but putting on a pair of shades, these masculine-looking sunglasses she'd picked up, really finished the face trick.

The morning was almost gone by the time she had herself done up. We wrapped bandages around our breasts, flattening them as best we could— two *zaftik* ex-showgirls, better endowed than the Rockefeller Foundation, trying to pass for men. Barrel-chested men. Lila'd bought extra padding from the theatrical place, too, to make us look bigger, fleshing out our shoulders, chests, arms, even our necks. Lila was going to wear a scarf. I had on one of Duke's cashmere turtlenecks.

We put on our suits, hats, dark glasses and studied ourselves in her mirrored closet doors. It was a great look. "A couple of inches taller," I told her, "and I could fall for me." We left Lila's place giddy with self-confidence.

The bank was on West Forty-seventh Street, in the crowded heart of the jewelry district. We got out of the cab and shouldered our way through the lunch-time noise and chaos. The narrow street was filled with rushing people—solid-looking women in fur coats and jackets and pale-skinned orthodox Jews, many of them dressed in long, shiny black coats, with beaver hats and sidecurls tucked behind their ears; but, surprisingly, there were plenty of guys who looked a lot like us. Pale, bearded men of medium height in business suits and hats, walking with their heads down, in a hurry.

Just outside the bank, Lila grabbed me. "I can't do it," she whispered, dragging on my arm. "Let's not do this, Sandy. Forget it."

I wavered for a moment, but then I thought of my own vault adventure and how I'd never have made it without that money. That got my blood pumping. But I spoke very calmly. I didn't want to make a scene in the street. "No way," I said. "We're going for it."

In we went, straight through the bank without another word, and down the stairs to the vault room. Lila gave a nod and a grunt to the officer in charge of the vault. I slapped down the safety deposit box key authoritatively as Lila, gloved hand trembling only slightly, quickly signed, in that cramped, practiced scrawl, the name Duke had given us.

The guy picked up the signature tag, went to check it, and said nothing to us. Next thing we knew, he'd swung open the door to the vault room and we were in like Flynn.

There was about $72,000 in cash in the box—along with all of Lila's jewelry. What a treasure chest. What a sight. It reminded me of the pirate movies I'd seen as a child. I didn't dare look at Lila's face. I was trying with all my might not to burst into gleeful laughter. It was way too soon to relax. I furrowed my brow and played my role straight and did just what we'd planned to do.

We'd brought along handkerchiefs to wrap the jewelry. We put them in the inside breast pockets of our jackets and in our slacks pockets. We divvied up the money and stashed it as evenly as possible so we wouldn't leave the bank bulging lopsidedly, and we sauntered out of the vault.

Back at her apartment, Lila and I poured the treasure trove onto her coffee table and screamed and hugged each other and literally danced with delight. Then we poured ourselves some stiff drinks—in part to celebrate our triumph; in part to numb us against the agony of removing the false beards.

Sitting there, half-plotzed on scotch, I had a sudden sense that Bernie was near, that he'd been with us all along, laughing, approving. Maybe it came from the sweater, the turtleneck I was wearing. The smell of cigars, a pale whiff of aftershave that clung to the fear-dampened cashmere. It was Duke's sweater but it could have been Bernie's. Putting together some wacky plan, risking his neck for a friend, it was something Bernie would have done. I looked at Lila, all flushed with excitement. I thought, Bernie would have been proud of me today.

CHAPTER SIXTEEN

The Merry Widow

Wise guys were my friends. Wise guys were my partners. Wise guys were practically the only men I knew. But I was determined not to be swept off my feet by one ever again. Mahoney the Phoney might have been the first of Bernie's old pals to hit on me, but he certainly wasn't the last. Almost a year after Bernie's death, I was slim and trim again. Now that I could wear high heels, form-fitting dresses, short skirts, and hip-hugger jeans, now that my auburn hair was long and lustrous again, now that laughter didn't feel like a foreign language, the wise guys came out of the woodwork.

If I showed up in a restaurant with Morty or Hot Dog, they'd float over to the table with stars in their eyes. If Vinny took me to a wedding or even a funeral, guys who'd treated me like the invisible woman were suddenly my lost friends and last hope. It wasn't that *I* was so irresistibly attractive. But a slim, pretty, possible naive, young widow with maybe millions stashed away sure was. And it wasn't just that most of these sudden suitors were *cafones,* jerks, shmucks—though they were. I still wanted what Bernie had promised me but hadn't lived to deliver—a normal, picket-fence life.

I wasn't the only wise guy widow on the block. A girl named Doris, whose husband, Lenny the Dentist, had died half a year before Bernie, called me while I was sitting shivah to extend her condolences. It turned out that she worked for a company that booked gambling junkets. We talked once in a while and, almost a year after Bernie's death, she invited me to join her on a junket to Monte Carlo. Five days, four nights, in the South of France, with everything free except the casino gambling. And, would you believe it, my mother and Red and even Morty had to help convince me to go. As the anniversary of Bernie's death drew near I'd begun to slump again into sadness. "Go," Tillie commanded. "Don't look a gift horse from God in the mouth."

Our very first evening on the glamorous Côte d'Azur, Doris and I, who were sharing a beautiful two-bedroom suite overlooking the yacht-filled harbor of Monte Carlo, shimmied into floor-length basic black and headed over to the legendary casino.

I was bent over a hot craps table, when a European-accented male voice said, "Do it, cupcake."

I had hit a seven and then another seven on the first roll-out, and my third throw had just been an eleven. The casinos in France are much quieter than those in Vegas. The deep, accented voice sounded very loud and forceful. It threw me off. My hand and luck wavered. I threw a point—a five, I think. And then, annoyed, I turned and looked up. And up. And up. And there was the Marlboro Man in a tuxedo, a towering blond god, a six-foot-six Dutchman named Peter Von Shlemme.

I quickly forgave him for blowing my winning streak. We chatted and laughed. He staked me to black jack, craps, champagne, and, within hours of our meeting, a diamond bracelet. Not a big-deal diamond bracelet, just a cute, delicate little one, padded with rubies and lesser stones. He was tall, gorgeous, a gentleman to his well-clipped fingertips *and* he had a yacht parked outside that made Davey Yaras's boat look like a toy. It was three stories tall.

We wound up watching the sun come up from the deck of this ship.

Then, Peter escorted me back to the hotel where Doris was frantic, ready to get the police to drag the Mediterranean for the poor, depressed widow she'd talked into coming to France. I thought we'd need her dead husband, Lenny the Dentist, to wire shut her jaw when I introduced her to Peter, who was, as my mother would've said, a gift horse from God.

Peter and I were inseparable for the next few days. We danced, gambled, dined at the best restaurants, drank Dom Pérignon, and saw a lot of dawns from the deck of the yacht. During the day, we'd swim, sunbathe, and listen to music on deck or sleep in one of the countless luxurious cabins below.

On our third day together Peter had to go into town on business. He left me aboard the yacht alone. After a while, I started exploring the rest of the place.

The yacht was amazing. Bedrooms, dining areas, sitting rooms—all exquisitely put together, very glamorous, with gold fixtures, paintings, antiques, ankle-deep carpeting, and fresh flowers in huge crystal vases. And as I explored, I kept saying to myself, "This is how the other half lives—the really rich, one hundred percent legit."

Two flights below deck, I opened a door and there were the crates. Coffin-shaped. Big. Instantly familiar. I stepped into the room and flipped up the top on one of the boxes. I didn't have to pry it open this time, just lifted the lid and there they were. Guns. A cabin full of them.

I ran upstairs as fast as my feet could carry me, determined to head straight back to the hotel. Peter was just stepping back aboard.

"Listen," I said, tossing my suntan oil and cigarettes into my beachbag. "I didn't mean to pry, but I saw the crates downstairs. The guns. Peter," I said, "are you a gun runner? A dope smuggler?"

He laughed. "I'm in munitions, guns, various enterprises. Let's just say I am an entrepreneur."

But I knew better. I just knew it. "You don't do anything really legal, do you?" I asked.

Again with the laugh. "What do you know about these things?"

Well, in a couple of choice words, I told him.

He was thrilled, delighted. It was the best news he'd had all week. At last, someone who could understand. Share his life. Travel the world with him.

"What is it?" I said, angrily. "Do I have a sign on my back that says, Wise Guys Apply Here?!"

I scrambled off the yacht and headed back to the hotel full steam ahead. Two days later, I flew back to the States with Doris. I was glad I'd met Peter, glad we'd had our fling. I felt more like a woman than I had in a long time and I was grateful for the fun. But I didn't need anyone new in my life who wasn't one hundred percent kosher.

I'd had it with wise guys.

* * *

During the shivah period, I'd made friends with a couple who lived down the hall, Margo and Warren Steiner. Margo was as short as I was tall. She was a bright, personable, stylish girl, no more than five-foot-two, and every inch a *mensch*. The first time she spoke to me, we were both carrying bags of garbage to the incinerator at the end of the hall. "I'm sorry about your loss," this lovely girl said in a voice filled with such sincerity that I almost burst into tears. "I don't know how you'll manage, with a brand-new baby and everything. If there's anything we can do to help, please come by. Just knock on the door."

She and her husband, Warren, a short, wiry, attractive young stockbroker, had no children. She oohed and aahed over Jeffrey, who gave her a great big drooly grin. And from then on, through the months of mourning, their apartment became my haven. They were bright, successful, and straight. They became my friends.

Two weeks after I got back from France, I threw a great big party for Jeffrey's first birthday. It was Memorial Day weekend. I ordered dozens of bottles of champagne and platters of smoked fish and deli from Zabar's. There were breads and bagels, strudels and cookies, and a great big birthday cake with a huge blue candle in the shape of the number one. Tilly, Marlene, and I, with a little help from Margo down the hall, blew up balloons and strung crepe paper around the place. And we crowned Jeffrey with a little blue party hat.

The birthday boy's proud godfathers were there—Red, Vinny, big Morty. Margo and Warren came over with some of their friends. Shorty, P.D., and a few of the guys from the bar stopped by. Judy and Nino brought their little girl. Thirty or forty people showed up, all of them bearing gifts. The baby's room was piled high with huge stuffed animals, alphabet blocks, Legos, trucks, planes and pull toys, little footballs and baseballs and whiffle ball bats. And, again, some of the guys came up to me or my mother and pressed envelopes filled with birthday cards and cash into our hands.

It was a joyous occasion but it was Bernie's birthday, too, and his friends remembered it. All afternoon, guys would walk up to me and say:

"He would've been forty-seven today, right?"

"Great party. B would've loved it."

"You know, Sandy, I miss him, too."

Toward sunset, I stepped out onto the terrace. The apartment was noisy with talk and laughter. With Thelma at his side, bearing a cotton cloth to wipe Jeffrey's drooling mouth, Red was toting the baby around. Jeffrey had begun speaking early and one of his first words was "hat." He loved Hot Dog's hats and now he was peeking out from under Red's straw fedora as one adoring friend after another took turns tickling him, tossing pretend punches at him, kissing his sweet cheeks and wet chin. And the Jab was giggling and grinning. My mother was talking with Margo and Warren.

Morty was showing Marlene card tricks. I saw all this from the terrace and I remember feeling very blessed and content and proud of the party I'd put together. Then I turned away and looked up at the pink-streaked twilight sky. "Thanks, babe," I said. "Happy birthday."

I'd had my batteries charged in Monte Carlo and I was speeding through everyday life now. A couple of times a week I'd go uptown to help Red out. And at the end of the day, when the two of us ambled along 125th Street on our way to Cokey's bar or one of our other favorite places, I'd feel special again—the way I used to with Bernie. The older guys who'd known him and the new guys who'd gotten to know me would call out, "Hey, princess. How you doin'? How's it going? Lookin' good, woman." And I loved it. I loved being known, feeling safe, walking tall.

I had that same good feeling in the bar on Second Avenue when the wise guys and the squares treated me with respect and deference. No one minded that I couldn't mix a decent drink. It was easy enough to pour straight shots and sit around making small talk. I liked the dank, shady atmosphere, the characters, the gamblers and tough guys, the players and pretenders. It was a world that was totally separate from my life at home, from sitting in the park with Jeffrey or wheeling a shopping cart through the supermarket. And I loved it, too, because it was a world that kept me connected to Bernie. It was a way of keeping him alive for me. At the bar or up in Harlem, ten times a day, I'd catch myself thinking, "What would Bernie say in a case like this? What would Bernie do?" And when I drove, I'd realize that I was checking the rearview mirror because Bernie always said to make sure no one was following me.

Nights I'd spend quietly at home with Jeffrey. My mom or Nora kept me company. Some evenings, I'd take Jeffrey with me to Margo and Warren's apartment and we'd hang out there and he'd fall asleep on their big, soft sofa. Warren was teaching me how to play the stock market. He was very bright and very busy in those boom days. He'd take companies that were shells and build up the value of their stock and get out with bundles of money. I started off with $2,000 and Warren gave me a tip on an over-the-counter stock that all of sudden started going up and up. I got out, a couple of weeks later, with a terrific profit and an addiction to playing the market. I started reading *The Wall Street Journal*. I'd listen very carefully to Warren's stock conversations and advice.

In that era of Day Trading, when you could buy a stock in the morning and sell it in the afternoon, Margo and I decided to form an informal little corporation, to pool our money and play. A couple of days a week, Warren would send a limo to take us down to the trading floor and we'd buy and sell and go to lunch with friends we'd made at the exchange.

Margo and I might have looked as different from one another as day from night, but we were kindred spirits and became fast friends. She was an Argentinian Jew who'd been raised in Buenos Aires. She'd come to America as a young girl and one of the things we discovered we had in common, even though I was born here, was a feeling of being different and of working hard to fit in. Another thing we discovered about each other, to our mutual delight, was that we both believed in psychic phenomena. In fact, Margo had a Santeria priest she'd go to occasionally who was fresh off the boat from Cuba.

I was in seventh heaven, meeting bright new people, making money hand over fist one week, then throwing it away the next. And I was working hard at improving myself, my vocabulary and diction. I was trying to absorb everything about this new and exciting world. And, best of all, to these people, I was just a rich widow—a *normal* rich widow.

One of the people I met through Warren and Margo was Sybil Burton, who'd recently been divorced from Richard Burton, who'd left her for Elizabeth Taylor. Now she was trying to put together financing for an elegant new kind of club in New York—a discotheque. She'd borrowed $1,000 each from hundreds of people and Warren, Margo, and I became three of them, three of the countless investors in Arthur's, Manhattan's first glamor and glitter, celeb-haunted disco.

And who did I invite to be my escort for opening night? None other than Hot Dog Red, himself. Margo and I in our floor-length gowns, Red and Warren in tuxedos, drove up to the spotlit entrance, where it looked like thousands of wild celebrity stalkers were bunched behind ropes, gawking and screaming at the entering stars. There was a red carpet leading up to the doors and plenty of dark-suited muscle holding back the barricaded fans.

We stepped out of our big, black limo and walked toward the doors and suddenly people were shouting, "Cab Calloway! Cab Calloway!" Red waved graciously to the crowd, then started signing autographs until I dragged him away. Roddy McDowall, Sybil Burton's main partner in the club, was greeting people at the door. As we walked in, he said, "Hello, Cab." And Red said, "How do!"

I'd begun to feel like I was in control of my life—and that it was a pretty good life. I did what I wanted to do when I wanted to do it. I ran my house that way. I ran the businesses that way. I ran my social life that way. I slept when I wanted to sleep, ate when I wanted to eat, I had no one to answer to except myself, right or wrong. For the first time in my entire life, I was footloose and fancy free.

Morty was not. The poor guy had been busted on a narcotics thing and he knew he couldn't beat the rap. He was destined to do time.

"You know, Sandy," he said during one of our evening card games, "you're doing okay now. But you never know what could happen. When you might need someone to help you out of a jam. A guy with connections. Look at me. Out of the blue, I'm going away for a year. But you know who always asks for you—and he really never met you; only saw you from a distance at the funeral—is Chalky.''

"That's strange, Morty," I said, "the man never called me or anything, never showed up at the house when I was sitting shivah. He was supposed to be such a close friend of Bernie's. I know how much Bernie loved him, but I don't know him."

"Well, being that I'm going away and being that Chalky is interested in meeting you, how about one night the three of us get together for dinner? Would you like that?''

I wasn't sure and I said so.

About a week later, Warren was out of town and Morty decided to take Margo and me to dinner at Gatsby's on First Avenue. At that moment in time, Gatsby's was the place to go—a big, beautiful restaurant where you'd always find a couple of wise guys thrown in with the Upper East Side thrill seekers, the big-money garmentos, lawyers, brokers, wealthy college kids, and slumming socialites who mobbed the place on weekends. So I wasn't totally surprised to see Chalky Lefkowitz already there, sitting silently at a table with a glum-looking blonde at his side.

"Hey, there's Chalky," Morty said, trying to make it seem like a stunning coincidence. "Why don't we ask him to join us?''

He was such a bad liar, no wonder he was going to do time. "Join us? Morty, they're sitting alone at a table set for five. Maybe we should join them.''

Chalky perked up as we approached his table. It didn't take two minutes for him to invite us to sit down and order drinks. He was a couple of years younger than Bernie and there wasn't much left of the white-blond hair that had given him his nickname. But he was tall, tanned, slim, and fit-looking and, in a crisp pin-striped shirt and an elegant dove gray suit, he was dressed in that squeaky clean, tightly buttoned-up way he'd been at Bernie's funeral. The girl with him was a standard issue mob playmate—attractive, young, nervous, and quiet.

It was a pleasant evening. Chalky was charming. He didn't laugh as much as Morty did. He didn't tell jokes. He wasn't clever. But he was nice and, at Morty's prompting, he started to tell stories about the old days on the Lower East Side with Bernie. I'd heard how their mothers had pushed them side by side in carriages before they could walk, how they'd known each other practically from birth. But Chalky brought me glimpses of Bernie's childhood. They stole together, he said. They were never athletes, Chalky and Bernie. While other kids were playing stickball and stoop ball, they'd be shooting pennies, playing cards, and stealing apples off neighborhood pushcarts.

"And Bernie," Chalky said, "was the best-looking kid in the world. A lot better looking than me," he said. "Even as a kid, he had the *shtik* to get girls. The talk, the style, the balls. I'd tag along with him when I was ten, eleven and he was, what, a bit shot of thirteen? We'd get dressed up and go uptown to pick up girls. Our neighborhood was First Street and First Avenue. Uptown to us was Fourteenth Street. Then Bernie found out there was a Forty-second Street and that was that!"

What Chalky didn't say that night was that his own childhood had ended at seventeen when he'd done his first bid at Dannemora. Morty told me that on the way home. He also told me that Chalky was connected, feared, and respected. He was closer to Meyer than Bernie had ever been. And he was tight with the Italians, the old Luciano mob that had been taken over by Vito Genovese. Also, the fact that he'd done time bought him an edge. Hard time, too. He'd fucked up good, but he'd paid his dues.

Chalky had been to prison a couple of times. The last bid he'd done, he and a friend had set out to rob the New Jersey home of a bookmaker reputed to hold millions in his safe. The friend had clocked the comings and goings of the mark, knew when the guy was home, when he was away, knew the family went out to dinner every Thursday night at the same time, and knew exactly how long they'd be gone. Easy pickings.

So one Thursday night, after the family left for dinner, Chalky and his pal broke into the house and were meandering around the ground floor feeling safe and comfy, utterly oblivious to the fact that one of the bookmaker's kids was sick and had stayed home with a maid that night. The little girl surprised them coming down the stairs. The maid called the cops. And the easy pickings turned into a grotesque shootout under the Hudson.

With cop cars in close pursuit, Chalky's friend drove into the Lincoln Tunnel, headed like a bat out of hell for New York. The cops were shooting. Chalky returned some of the heat. Meanwhile, the NYPD had been alerted and the tunnel was sealed on the Manhattan side. So they were ducks in a barrel, and Chalky's partner's face was blown off in the crossfire. Chalky wound up with the guy's blood and brains all over his jacket. And a cop was killed.

They couldn't pin the cop's death on him. With all the bullets flying, nobody knew who'd killed who. But New Jersey definitely had him for armed robbery and a couple of other things. He was sentenced to twenty years in Trenton and had done twelve when he was paroled.

I didn't know any of this at the restaurant, of course. I said, "What puzzles me, I mean, you loved Bernie so much and he was always talking about you— Why didn't you come by the house during shivah? Why didn't you ever get in touch after the funeral?"

He fumbled and bumbled for an answer and then he finally said, "That's in the past. Now, with Morty going away . . . and I know how close he's been to you, a good friend . . . I'd like you to have my phone number and know at all times where you can get in touch with me. Just in case you ever need a favor."

So I filed it—under friend in need. I had no interest in the man romantically. He was respected, he was connected. Maybe he could even do card tricks like Morty. Great. My motto was: No More Mobsters.

Then my girlfriend, Lila, introduced me to Eddie.

One night Lila and I decided to go out dancing. We were at Arthur's, hadn't been in the place ten minutes, when she started tugging me toward a small table off the dance floor where a guy was sitting alone with a bottle of champagne cooling in an ice bucket. "It's Eddie," Lila bubbled. "I've been dying for you to meet him, Sandy. He's gorgeous. He's loaded. He's in the trucking business. And he owns a couple of horses."

She was right about gorgeous. Sitting there was a young Greek god who, as it turned out, was Italian. He was thirty, maybe thirty-one years old, with olive skin, thick dark hair, and the kind of green eyes that look up at you out of a black forest of lashes. He was beautifully dressed and, when Lila introduced us, he extended this cool, brown, manicured hand and tugged me gently toward the seat beside him.

We had a lovely time, talking, laughing, drinking champagne. I asked whether it was true that he owned a couple of racehorses. He said absolutely, and he invited Lila and me to go out to the track with him the next day. Lila said she'd love to. Eddie took my hand and said, "And you— you're mine. You're definitely coming with me."

I was flattered. I loved his looks, I'd enjoyed the conversation and laughter. It was time to leave. I stood up. Then he stood. He came up to my shoulder. In flats, he was maybe only an inch or two shorter than me. In heels, I towered over him.

It didn't seem to bother him, not that night nor the next day at the track. The three of us had a fabulous brunch, lost most of the races we bet on, and then went down to the stables where Eddie, with an iron grip on my hand, kibitzed with and introduced us to everyone from the owners to the stable boys. It was a terrific day and, before it was over, Eddie was in love. And that was okay with me.

We started seeing each other. He had a beautiful light-filled apartment on the Upper East Side and he was as fastidious about it as he was about his clothes, which he changed a couple of times a day. He was a good cook. He enjoyed fixing dinners for us. Jeffrey was small and portable then and it was nice for me, having the three of us together. In fact, one of the quirky things about dating Eddie was that I'd never met any of his friends except for Lila. We'd have dinner with her at a nice restaurant once in a while, but mostly it was just the two of us, or Eddie would cook at home for Jeffrey and me.

Inevitably, I moved away from my friends and associates. I didn't want Eddie connecting me with the racket club. Red understood. "You just go and have a good time," he said. "You deserve it, woman. I'll take care of business and when you can help me out you will." He even arranged to cover for me at the bar.

Six months into the relationship, Eddie took me to dinner at Monsignor, an elegant Italian restaurant off Park Avenue in the Fifties. When the waiter came over, Eddie said, "We'll order drinks now, but we'll wait with dinner." Then he turned to me. "My uncle's going to join us," he explained.

Before I could ask him more about it, in walked a consiglieri of the Gambino family, a tall, graying man of sixty, who in his youth had been a noted mob enforcer. He'd recently finished a bid in Atlanta. Of course, the table he was heading for was ours.

"Sandy, this is my uncle Aneillo." Eddie beamed.

"I know him," I said. "Hello, nice to see you."

"I was sorry to hear about Bernie. He was a good man. I always liked him," the big man said.

"It's been over two years."

"I was away." He shrugged philosophically.

I could hardly look at Eddie through dinner. My head was spinning. I'd prided myself on keeping the past out of this new relationship, and here it was, sitting across the table in gray hair and a neat suit. And Eddie didn't seem the least bit flustered.

"What's going on?" I demanded after we'd said goodnight to the consiglieri. "You didn't act surprised at all that I knew your uncle—or that he knew me! You knew all about me, everything, who my husband was? Talk to me, Eddie. Tell me how, what, where?!"

"Of course I knew," he said. "Sandy, when I met you, after I realized I liked you, I went downtown and asked permission to start seeing you—"

"You got permission to date me?! From who?!" I wanted to know. Later I found out that it was the North brothers he'd gone to, the short, stocky guys who used to show up at Bernie's apartment on East Seventy-ninth Street with suitcases full of Ceil Chapman gowns.

"What's the difference who?" Eddie said. "I told them my intentions were honorable and they are. I'll probably marry you."

"No!" I hollered, scaring the hell out of him, I think. "I mean, I don't know what's going on here. I'm in shock. I can't talk about it now."

Marriage? I had told my friends, "I like this man. He's good to me. He's good to my son. It's nice to have a boyfriend—but I miss Bernie. When I'm in bed with him, I miss Bernie. When I think something's funny and he doesn't get it, I miss Bernie. When I have a problem and I ask his advice, I miss Bernie. He loves me. He takes care of me. But he's not sweet, he's not passionate like Bernie was."

And friends would tell me. "Get that out of your head. Nobody and nothing'll ever be like Bernie was."

Oh no, oh shit, I was thinking all the way uptown in the cab, how did I wind up again with a connected guy, an *Italian* connected guy? Not my life, but all the Italian wives' lives I'd seen, flashed before my eyes: the nervous wrecks watching their macho men strut; the women who drank on the sly and phoned their husbands' mistresses in the middle of the night; the ones who made fun of what selfish bastards their husbands were in bed.

Eddie was selfish in bed. Eddie was a gambler, a big loser, who owed money to everyone. His family was always bailing him out with the shylocks. And he had that macho way about him that sometimes fascinated but more often frustrated me. He had very rigid, old-fashioned Italian ideas of how everyone should behave—especially me. And he had this thing about my being Jewish. He'd say things like, "You know, you're very beautiful, for a Jewish girl," or "You're great, for a Jewish girl."

I could almost hear Bernie asking, "Is this the man you picked to replace me? Is this the kind of 'substantial' man you think is good enough to be a father to my son?"

I knew I'd never marry Eddie. I knew I should stop seeing him, end it. But I didn't know how quickly and terribly fate would do for me what I couldn't do for myself.

A few weeks after the restaurant encounter with his uncle, Eddie and I had plans to go to dinner and the race track. That day I came down with a virus. I ran a high fever, I was practically delirious. I called Eddie and told him I couldn't make it, then I slept for the rest of the day and through the night. At eight the next morning, I got a phone call from Eddie's brother, whom I'd met at the trucking office once or twice. He told me Eddie was dead.

I learned from the newspapers as well as from friends that he'd been shot "gangland style," a bullet hole in the back of the head. His car had been found somewhere out on the Island. It was front-page news. GANG-LAND NEPHEW SHOT the headlines read. And there were pictures of Eddie's bloody body on the cover of *The Daily News*.

As the first shock subsided, the realization that I was supposed to be with him that night set in. It could have been me in that car on the front page of *The Daily News*—or, God forbid, Jeffrey—lying dead beside Eddie right on the bloodsoaked seat of the Lincoln we'd ridden in so many times before.

God had to have been watching over me that night, God or my *gutta better.* Because hit men, contract killers, don't spend a lot of time worrying about who's sitting next to their target. If the hit's set, it goes. And if I hadn't come down with a twenty-four-hour flu, I'd have been sitting right next to Eddie, and Bernie's son would've been an orphan. I was grief-stricken, petrified, and grateful all at the same time. And I kept saying, over and over again, "What is with me? What's wrong with me? Why do I get involved with these men? How do they find me? How do they know?"

Four or five months later, on a beautiful mild day in early fall, I decided, on a whim, to treat myself to lunch at Tavern on the Green. I asked for and was ushered to a quiet table where I could lunch alone, looking out at the garden and the still lush lawns of Central Park. Midway through the meal I noticed a table of three men. I looked at them and said to myself, mafiosi, wise guys having a meeting at a safe place in the afternoon where mostly elderly people or tourists go. Smart, I said to myself, and I went back to minding my own business.

When I'd finished lunch and looked up to signal the waiter, I saw they were gone. "I'm ready," I said to the waiter.

"Your check was picked up by the men at that table," he said, nodding at, what else, the one where the wise guys had been sitting, the table with the cigar butts still smoldering in the ashtray. I laughed to myself. Maybe I even looked up to heaven to ask Bernie to witness my innocence. See, I was just sitting here minding my own business. They find me.

I walked back out into the sunshine, ready to hail a cab. One of the men from the wise guy table was waiting. He took my arm and said, "Did you enjoy your lunch?"

Was he good-looking? Would God with his sense of humor tempt me with anything less than a stunning, tall, dark, and handsome wise guy? He was gorgeous. A cross between Robert De Niro and Vic Damone.

"Do I have to thank you for it?" I asked.

"You do," he said, and started making small talk.

"Excuse me. Here's a cab. Thanks again for lunch," I said.

He held on to my arm. "No, don't. I'll drive you."

I pulled my arm out of his grip, smiling pleasantly. "Very nice of you. No thanks."

"Why not? I don't get it? I've got some time to kill—"

"I said no thanks and I mean it," I interrupted him. "I don't get into cars with strange men."

He laughed. "Okay. Fair enough." He opened the cab door for me. "You take the cab and I'll follow you home."

"Don't be ridiculous," I said, and got into the taxi. He closed the door and gave me a smile and, fifteen minutes later, as I was getting out of the cab at my building, he pulled into the driveway behind us.

His name was Nicky.

"Let me guess," I said. "You're Italian."

"You got it. You like Italian men?"

"I've really got to go. Thanks for lunch."

Ten minutes later, with my phone number scrawled on the back of a matchbook in the pocket of his overcoat, he waved goodbye with a great big smile. And, with my emotions turned on and my brain shut off, I went upstairs to wait for his call.

I liked him. I liked the way he'd come on to me, the way he looked, the sound of his voice. I liked him so much that when he phoned later that night as he'd said he would, I told myself, *really* did I know he was a wise guy? How could I be so sure? Was it just because he was Italian? Had I been jumping to conclusions, making a federal case out of nothing? I told myself a lot of things. Him I told, "Yes, I'd love to have dinner with you."

Friday night, when he picked me up, we fell right into easy conversation, teasing and bantering like old friends. Then five minutes into the ride, he said, "Do you like Italian food?"

"I love it."

"Okay. We'll go downtown for dinner."

"Downtown?" I knew he meant Little Italy. But there were lots of restaurants downtown. I thought, maybe we won't bump into anybody who knows me. I said, "Great," and kept the conversation light and breezy—which was no piece of cake after Nicky parked, took my hand, and started walking me toward a restaurant owned by a guy named Sammy who'd been one of Bernie's best friends.

Okay, here goes, I thought, as we walked through the door. He'll find out who I am and I'll find out who he is. And I clung to the diminishing possibility that Nicky would turn out to be a tourist who just liked the Italian atmosphere downtown.

He'd made reservations and they'd picked out a nice corner table for us at the back of the restaurant, where Nicky immediately took the seat facing the door. "You feel safer with your back up against the wall?" I teased.

He raised an eyebrow at me.

"I read a lot of books and see a lot of old gangster movies," I explained.

"Then we have something in common. I love old gangster movies," he said.

About twenty minutes into the meal, a familiar voice called out, "Well, hello Nicola, how are you?" and I realized that Bernie's friend Sammy, the owner of the restaurant, was on his way over to our table. I got very involved with my veal chop and, while Nicky and Sammy conversed in Italian, I kept my head down and pushed food around on my plate. Finally, I had to look up. Sammy did a double-take.

"Sandy, princess, baby, how are you?" He bent down and kissed me hello.

Nicky's mouth fell open. "How do you know him?" he asked, and I could see the macho storm clouds gathering on his brow. He thought Sammy was an old lover of mine.

"Friend of the family," I said.

Sammy sat down with us and started shmoozing with me—how was I, how'd I been, how was my beautiful son? "If BB was around, he'd be so happy with that kid," Sammy said. "But of course, he is looking down at us from heaven, God bless him." The next thing I knew, Sammy had Nicky joining us in a toast to Bernie who, Sammy let him know, was somebody special, a man of respect.

A few minutes after Sammy left us, Nicky excused himself. By the time he came back to the table he knew everything about Bernie and me that he needed to know. He returned with a smile on his face. He looked at me and said, "You know, kid, you're my kind of broad. You and I are going to get along very, very well," he said. "This could be the beginning of a beautiful friendship."

Yeah, he loved gangster movies. He talked gangster movies. He tried to live gangster movies. But he was a bookie. He was in his early thirties and ran a successful bookmaking operation. That's all he did. It was almost legal, I told myself. And though that pleased me, it sure didn't thrill him. Nicky wanted to be a hot shot, a heavy hitter, a made man. He definitely wanted to be bigger and better connected than I—but he wasn't. Poor man, he wasn't a wise guy, he was only a disappointed hood. And when we had arguments, I'd let him know it.

We argued a lot—for me it was almost recreational. Bernie had enjoyed arguing, disagreeing, battling and, as he loved to say, he'd taught me everything I knew. So shooting off my mouth and standing up for myself had become like a sport for me. And I was good at it. I'd learned from one of the best. For Nicky, it was shocking for a woman to talk back, let alone yell back, stand her ground, or even threaten. He was very macho, very used to women, if you'll pardon the expression, jumping when he said jump and humping when he said hump. And, wildly jealous and possessive as he was, he definitely didn't play by the same rules he laid down.

Which is why it ended badly.

He was always checking up on me. Always giving me grief about where I'd been and what I'd done. If he called and I was out, he was sure I was with another guy. If I met one of Bernie's friends at a club or restaurant, he'd sulk while we spoke and give me the fifth degree the minute the guy left. I was totally loyal to him. It never occurred to me to date more than one man at a time.

So, when Nicky got a little loaded one night in a restaurant and started paying a lot of attention to a girl at the bar, I got annoyed. And when I saw him writing down his number on a matchbook and handing it to her on the sly, I got loud. One thing led to another. A shouting match ensued. I spilled a drink on him. He overturned the table. And as he made a move for me, I growled: "Try it, buddy. You think you're connected? You don't know connections. Try it and you'll get to know a couple of mine!"

I looked into his face and he was really frightened. I turned on my heels and walked away.

No more wise guys. No more wanna-be wise guys. I'd had it. From the gunboat buccaneer, to poor Eddie to Nicky the Weasel, my record for picking the wrong men—or having them find me—was three for three. I was through with romance for a while.

CHAPTER SEVENTEEN

Living Dangerously

Bernie had called me his baby. When I was married to him, that's what I was. After he died, I felt like a frightened, rebellious teenager. It was obvious that I didn't know what I was doing when it came to men. In friendships, too, I tended to go overboard. Like every new kid on the block I had to learn through my mistakes. Most of them were merely embarrassing, but some of them were murder. Almost.

Friends showed up after Bernie's death whom I hadn't seen in years. One of them who paid a shivah call was a guy called Tutti, from my old Brooklyn neighborhood. Tutti was a big bruiser, into the martial arts before they became fashionable in America. He'd been a wrestler. He'd studied kung fu. He looked like a samurai warrior. And he came from a very religious Orthodox Jewish family. He and his two brothers owned small neighborhood bars all over Brooklyn. They were strictly legitimate guys, Wall Street players. When disco fever hit New York in the late '60s and clubs were opening all over town, Tutti and his brothers expanded into the security business. They'd collect the night's money from the clubs and drop them at the appropriate vaults.

Tutti had become a pal. He'd stop by, like Morty had, to play with Jeffrey and sit around and gossip over endless cups of coffee. It was an easy-going, brother-sister kind of thing. We'd talk about who we were seeing. When Tutti found a new girlfriend, he'd always bring her to me for approval. If I shook my head, no, he didn't see her anymore. Nights when I was restless, I'd ride shotgun with him as he drove from club to club picking up the day's receipts.

One afternoon he showed up at my house ripping mad. Someone owed him close to $100,000, he said, pacing back and forth in my living room. He'd lent the guy the money to go into business and, sure enough, the business had really started taking off. Now, four or five times, the guy had promised to give Tutti back the hundred grand and every time he went to meet him, the guy either didn't show or showed up with some lame excuse and no bread.

"Tonight," Tutti said, pounding his hammy fist into his palm as he spoke—a fist that could chop through a pile of bricks. "I'm supposed to meet him again. Only this time, if he screws around with me, I'm going to fucking kill him."

"What kind of guy is he?"

Tutti knew what I meant. "He's straight. He says he's legitimate. But he's got a cousin who's supposed to be connected downtown."

"If you want me to, Tutti, I'll find out. You can have a roundtable meeting downtown, see what's been going on with your money. In fact," I offered, "I'll say it's my money, if you want, and let's see who his cousin is."

Tutti said, "No. Thanks, anyway. He's supposed to give me fifty grand tonight and he just better be there with it."

I wanted to calm him down so that he wouldn't get into trouble. The best I could come up with was: "Listen, you're in a bad mood, Tutti. Let me go with you. Let me ride shotgun with you. You know I get a kick out of hanging out with you and I've got nothing else to do tonight."

He was supposed to meet the guy around eleven o'clock all the way out in the Red Hook section of Brooklyn. Neither of us knew the area. Anyway, I conned him into taking me along, then I changed my clothes. I remember it was early fall. I put on a pair of jeans, boots, my short leather jacket, a turtleneck, and I wore my dark glasses pushed up on my head, holding back my hair.

I'm a big girl and Tutti had a little car. It was one of the first foreign cars I'd ever seen—a Porsche or an Alfa Romeo, I don't remember. But it was a little bitty low-slung thing and when I sat in it, my knees would come up to my throat. We took a nice long ride to Red Hook with me folded up this way, and all I remember is endless blocks of row upon row of dark warehouses. About five minutes away from the meeting place, Tutti says, "Here's my gun. I don't trust this guy. If anything happens, Sandy, just start shooting. Cover me, baby."

I said, "Are you out of your mind?!"

"No. I don't trust the guy. I've just got a hunch," he said.

We pulled up in front of the address—a warehouse. When Tutti cut the car lights, it was jet black outside. I couldn't see my hand in front of me. I began to get a very bad feeling. Then another car wheeled into the street and a man carrying a suitcase stepped out. Tutti got out of our car. And, with my eyes adjusting to the blackness, squinting through the dark, I could see him going to meet the guy. Then they came over to the car where I was sitting with Tutti's gun in my lap. I grabbed it and quickly lowered my hand so that the gun was hidden between the seat and the door, and I just held it there with my knees knocking up against my chin.

Tutti opened up the suitcase and started counting. The money was all there. He tossed it into the car's trunk, then handed the empty satchel back to the man. The second he closed the trunk, another car pulled up. Three guys jumped out. And Tutti hollered to me through the window, "I'm getting into the car! Start shooting!"

I rolled down the window, picked up the gun, and, as Tutti backed out with tires squealing, I started shooting up into the night sky. Like a bat out of hell, we flew. And I just kept shooting and shooting until Tutti finally yelled, "Okay. We made it. Okay, stop!"

"Oh, my God, what if I hit something?" I screamed. "It was so dark. I don't know what the hell I was shooting at."

"The goddamn *moon*," Tutti said. "If they'd parachuted in, you'd *maybe* have nicked one!"

I was shaking when we got upstairs. "That's it!" I ranted. "You're going to find out who this cousin is and I'm going to set up a roundtable meeting downtown. That bastard still owes you fifty grand. Say it was my money that you gave to him. Say whatever you have to!"

I went into the bathroom and threw up.

The next day, the very next evening, Tutti and I sat down with six elderly men at a bar on Mulberry Street. I had called Shorty at Second Avenue as soon as Tutti found out who the cousin was. Shorty recognized the name and contacted the guy's boss, who in turn called his boss, who among a lot of less public assets owned a couple of restaurants in Little Italy. Everybody agreed to sit down to a roundtable meeting, which was what these problem-solving sessions were called.

We went with the story that it was my money on the line. Apologies were tossed like bouquets. Roses to Tutti, orchids to me. And, of course, the cousin said, "The guy took this on his own to do. If I would have known about it—" He shrugged, he shook his head. "Never."

I said, "I think you knew. I think you helped him set it up."

The old men looked back at him. He said, "I apologize." Another bouquet landed in my lap. "I'd like to help you. I knew nothing about this until I got the telephone call last night. But I'd like to help because he is my cousin and I feel responsible even though I'm not."

The old men looked at me. I had dressed very carefully and well for this occasion. I was wearing my full-length mink coat and as much jewelry as I could flash without looking flashy. I was decked out as a lady. But the mouth was strictly Bernie Barton's. I might as well have been channeling him at a séance. It even surprised me. I knew just what to say, how far to take it. I was sure the cousin had been in on it from the beginning, and I could tell the others believed that, too, though they couldn't take sides against him in front of me.

Anyway, Tutti walked away from that meeting with the other $50,000 due him—which they thought was mine—and an extra $25,000 for the grief. Real flowers were sent to my home; toys were sent to Jeffrey. Tutti was so grateful that he bought me a color TV and then decided to buy one for my mother, too. Of course, word went out on the street again that Bernie's princess was some ballsy chick; some stand-up broad. And, as much as I enjoyed the accolades, I felt as if it had been Bernie, not me, sitting around that table with the old men. Or that, at the very least, it had been his reckless, rebellious spirit guiding me.

My neighbor Margo's Cuban guru as much as said so.

After Margo and I discovered our shared belief in psychic phenomena, we visited Ormando, the Santeria priest she'd told me about. He was a refugee and spoke only Spanish. Margo had to interpret for me. But the first thing he said when I walked through the door of his little apartment uptown was: "Who is the dead man with the blue eyes who sits on her shoulder?"

Ormando was tall and thin with big black eyes, yellow skin, a bony nose, and stringy, pomaded shoulder-length hair. His small apartment was decorated with the same statues, candles, feathers, and offerings I'd seen at Lido's place, but he was much, much less expensive. He charged only three dollars, I remember. And he didn't need to suck an extra hundred up his nose to get the session going.

Ormando impressed the hell out of me with his question about the blue-eyed man. He also knew that I had a baby son, and he said quite a few other startlingly accurate things about my past. Then he predicted that I was going to get married within two years and described the man I would marry: tall, blondish, good-looking, debonair, macho, rich. Just as I was beginning to feel optimistic, Margo said, "But it's not going to be a good marriage, he says. In fact, he thinks you know him now. Oh, you know him," Margo continued to translate, "but you are . . . *unaware* of him. He's not actually in your life now."

"Sandy," I remember she said later, "maybe it's that fellow Morty wanted you to go out with—what's his name who we had dinner with at Gatsby's?"

"Chalky Lefkowitz?" I said. "No. Ormando said good-looking. Do you think Chalky's good-looking? I'm not attracted to him at all."

With Morty gone, Chalky had begun checking in with me. He was a bit of a *yenta,* a typical mob mouth. He'd always tell me what he heard on the street about me and I'd tell him it was an understatement. If he said, "I hear you're always running around up in Harlem," I'd say, "Twenty-four hours a day." If he said, "Bernie must have left you a bundle. A couple of million," I'd say, "A billion." If he said, "I hear you're seeing three different guys," I'd say, "No, seven. A different one for every day of the week.'' Whenever he tried to find out anything about me, I deflected it by saying, ''You're absolutely right. Only more so.''

We developed this rough repartee on the telephone and, gradually, we became buddies. Like Tutti, like Josh and Uncle Vinny, Chalky would stop by once in a while just to shoot the breeze. He'd talk to me about the women he was dating. He was going with two different girls at once.

''You'll get caught and wind up all alone,'' I warned him.

''Well, one of them is Eurasian. Very quiet, sweet, pretty girl. But she's half-Chinese, so I can't marry her. And the other one's a Jewish girl, sharp as a tack, but she's got a little bit of mileage on her, been around the track once or twice.''

''How do you do it? I mean, do you see them on a schedule?''

''Yeah,'' he said. ''Every other day. And one day a week I rest.''

Actually, he didn't. I'd run into him once in a while on his days of rest and there'd always be a young cocktail waitress or some other Barbie Doll-type on his arm.

And he'd tease me. ''When are you going to get married and make someone happy?'' he'd ask.

''I tell you what. You get married first and I'll give you a great wedding gift. And then you give me one twice as nice.''

''Nah, I'm too cheap,'' he'd say. Or, ''Okay, whatever you need, I'll get you for your wedding—a blender, an iron, a toaster.''

''Yeah, the sky's the limit with you, right, Chalky?''

Sometimes he'd call me up in the middle of the day. ''I'm bored. Do you want to go to lunch?''

''Well, I was going to take Jeffrey out for the afternoon.''

''Bring him along,'' Chalky would say. So the three of us would lunch, and go for walks and drives together. And, after a time, Jeffrey started calling him Uncle Chalky which—considering his relationship with Bernie, their mothers having been as close as sisters—Chalky sort of was.

After a while, my girlfriends started asking me about him. Lila would say, ''Why don't you try to hook Chalky?''

''Because he's my friend, my brother. I don't think of him in those terms.''

Judy thought he was attractive.

''Maybe he is,'' I'd say, ''but he's not my type. He doesn't turn me on at all.''

Margo said, ''He's never been married. He seems to be crazy about you. And Jeffrey. He'd make a good father for Jeffrey. Don't you ever think of marrying him?''

''Never,'' I said.

And when my girlfriend Leona encouraged romance, pointing out how much like Bernie Chalky was, I'd tell her, ''That's just the point. I don't want to marry a man that much older again and have him get sick and die.

And also, he's a wise guy. He's connected. Even more than Bernie was. He's been to jail three times already. He'll either get sick and die or go to jail. And anyway,'' I'd say to Leona or Judy or Margo or Lila or even my mother, "I want a normal life and a normal man who works normal hours. I want to be Sadie-Sadie, Married Lady. I don't want to be Mrs. Wise Guy anymore.''

As a pal, Chalky Lefkowitz was fine. He'd call, he'd visit, he'd pledge his friendship and promise that if I ever needed anything, if I ever got into a jam, he'd be there for me, no questions asked. But he was just one of the guys I hung out with. My main man was still Hot Dog Red.

While I'd been having my flings and things, Hot Dog had been taking care of business. On a beautiful evening in early spring, he came down to meet me and the Jab at the bar on Second Avenue.

"Sandy, you know we had a very good week. We're better than even. We've covered expenses and we're way ahead,'' Red said. "We've got eleven thousand dollars to play with. What do you want to do with it?''

We were sitting in a back booth. Jeffrey was propped up on the bar and Shorty was playing clap-hands with him. "What do you mean?'' I said, distractedly. "Put it away in case next week's a bad week.''

"Well,'' Red said sheepishly. "I've got to tell you something. Someone gave me a tip on a horse and I think we should—''

That got my attention. "Hold it right there,'' I said. "I used to hang around with a guy who had horses. He got tips all the time—from jockeys, stableboys, bookies, even God. He never won.''

"Yeah, but this is a boat race,'' Hot Dog said. "And I've got a very good feeling about it, Sandy.'' A boat race is a fixed race. Like a submarine, the competition is going down, taking a dive. Red said, "Saturday afternoon at Belmont Park. I got the name of the horse and she's going off at good odds.''

"It's not kosher,'' I said. "What'll happen if someone hits it big next week and we have to pay off—''

"Don't worry about it,'' Red insisted. "I'll hock my jewelry if I have to. I'll hock my Cadillac. We'll make it. I've just got a feeling about this.''

So that Saturday, a lovely spring day in April, we drove out to the track and sat tight until the boat race. Then, while I waited in the stands chain-smoking, Red put the entire $11,000 on a filly named Pride of Rahemia.

The tip had been good. You could practically see the jockeys on the other horses yawning as Pride of Rahemia sailed past them. Red and I jumped up and down, hugging each other and screaming at the top of our lungs. "We won! We won!''

"It's a sign!'' he shouted.

"Of what?'' We were jostling through the crowd on our way to collect our money.

"That we ought to buy a boat."

"What are you talking about?" We breezed up to the payoff window.

"I've been reading about boats. There's one I saw. It's over in New Jersey. A thirty-two-footer."

"Stop. Hold it right there!" I tugged the short sleeve of his lime-green shirt. "What do you mean, 'we ought to buy a boat'?"

"It's a sign," Red said again. "We won on a boat race. We've got to buy a boat."

"You're insane."

"Just wait till you see the one I've got in mind. You're going to fall in love with it, too." He stepped up to the teller and turned in our tickets and collected the money—which he counted carefully and then tucked away in his pants pocket. "Come on. We'll drive out to Jersey," he said.

Easy come, easy go. All the way out to the boat yard in New Jersey Red is *hocking* me about this incredible yacht that he's been checking out for months and now we've got to have it. And I'm hollering that he's crazy and what the hell are we going to do with a boat? I can't even swim, let alone drive a boat. And Hot Dog is smiling, smoking, driving, nodding, giving me prices and statistics, reasons and excuses, facts and figures and, less than an hour later, we owned a yacht.

This was early April. The boat, a thirty-two-foot Owens that slept six, and would have a state room, galley, shower, depth finders, sonar, radar, even dishes with a nautical pattern, was made to order and delivered to us two days before my mother's birthday, the weekend of July Fourth.

Red and I had gone to school and gotten our captain's licenses by then. And, through a friend of Bernie's, we'd rented prime space, a gorgeous end-of-the-pier slip at the Seventy-ninth Street Boat Basin, which was a five-minute crosstown drive from my door. We christened the yacht *Pride of Rahemia,* in honor of the boat race that had bought her, and on her maiden voyage up the Hudson, we threw a fabulous, catered birthday party for Tillie.

Now, when I wanted solitude, I'd strap on a life vest, make sure the coast guard radio was on, and take to the river. I never really took the boat more than ten miles up the Hudson in either direction. But once out there on the water, I'd drop anchor and loll in the sunshine. Sometimes I'd pour myself a glass of wine and, holding one of the weighted crystal goblets Red and I had ordered for the boat, just stare out at the Manhattan skyline or the Jersey Palisades.

I loved to be alone on the boat. It made me feel very strong, very powerful. I'd think, look at this, look at me, I've got a captain's license. I own a yacht. Years ago, my mother made us mashed potatoes and chicken fat for dinner. And today, look at me.

*   *   *

It was heaven, that hot summer, having a big, beautiful boat with a telephone and TV aboard, docked right in Manhattan. I took Jeffrey down there every chance I got. The slips on either side of us were empty and we'd hang out with a friend or two in voluptuous, breezy privacy. Then one day, Jeffrey, my girlfriend Judy, and I arrived at the boat basin to find a cabin cruiser bobbing in the slip alongside ours. *Pride of Rahemia* was practically eclipsed by her luxurious new neighbor, the *Chicita*.

There was Latin music blaring from the huge cruiser though it was barely noon. Clearly, there were people partying aboard, but we made ourselves comfortable and were minding our own business, sunbathing on the deck of the *Rahemia,* when a man's voice called out, "Hey Sandy! Is that *chew,* baby? Where you get *Yewish* food around here?"

Judy and I sat bolt upright. "Oh, my God," she said. "It's Spanish Ray!"

"Spanish Ray. The King of Harlem. Oh, no," I groaned. "That's all we need!"

Spanish Ray's father was one of the richest men in Harlem. And Spanish Harlem. He owned grocery stores, apartment buildings, street blocks. And Ray was one of the biggest numbers bankers in town. God only knew what else he dealt and did. But if you owed Ray, you had to pay. He was known to walk into bars and actually shoot off men's fingers over broken promises. A very good-looking Puerto Rican, a mustachioed man of Bernie's age but tall and reedy with thick, slicked-back black hair and a dazzling, dangerous smile, Spanish Ray was notorious and nuts.

He and Bernie had been friendly. Whether they'd ever done business together, I didn't know; nothing that ever came into my home, so I assumed they'd just known one another and hadn't really been close. But here was Spanish Ray looking at Judy and me like he'd found his long lost sisters.

"I didn't know you knew Ray," I said to Judy as we made our way over to the *Chicita*. We shot the breeze boat to boat for a few minutes and then accepted Ray's invitation to come by for a drink and a tour of his yacht.

"He goes with my friend Suki, the ice skater."

"That pretty little Japanese girl?"

"Yeah," Judy said. "He drives her crazy. When they go to bed, he wears socks and a gun strapped to his ankle."

Spanish Ray was constantly bringing food over to *Pride of Rahemia,* and booze, and cartons of cigarettes. If we were both on line to get gasoline, he would have paid for mine before I even pulled my boat in next to the pump. And he threw the most extravagant parties. He'd send out for food—"Yewish" food from Zabar's, Chinese food from the Gold Coin, soul food, Spanish food, steaks, and lobsters.

He had the best wine, the best food, and the wildest assortment of people on his boat. Models, centerfolds, and wanna-be's in Band Aid-sized bathing suits would rub shoulders, and whatever else was handy, with stars of show business, mob business, and, yes, even *Fortune 500* business, who'd drop in to slum in opulence. I met Malcolm Forbes on Spanish Ray's yacht. By five P.M., come rain or shine, hell or high water, there was a party going aboard the *Chicita*.

One morning, when my mother and I were sunbathing on my boat, Ray appeared on the deck of the *Chicita* holding a full-length chinchilla coat. It was brand new. The labels were still on it. "Hey, preencess. You like this? Here," he called, tossing me the coat. "Try it on."

It fit me like a dream. "Keep it," Ray said. "It's a present."

I argued with him a little bit but, despite the fact that it was easily eighty-five degrees out, I didn't take off the coat. "Thank you, thank you, thank you. I love it," I finally said. "It's incredible. It's gorgeous, Ray."

He laughed and waved off my excitement. "Okay," he said. "It looks good on you," and he disappeared back into his boat. Twenty minutes later, he came out again, this time with a mink coat. Same drill. Full-length, exquisite, labels dangling off it. "Hey, mami—" he called to my mother. "You like it?"

What else was she going to say? "Beautiful," she cooed.

"Okay. Here. It's yours," Ray said and threw the mink onto our boat.

"Ma, don't take it off," I whispered. "Wear it." Eighty-five degrees, not a breeze in the boat basin, and my mother's little shoulders were sagging under the weight of the full-length mink coat.

"I love you, mami," Ray called. "Enjoy. Keep it. It's yours. I love you, Sandy. I love the baby. I love your mama. I love the whole wide world!"

About two weeks later, I arrived at the boat basin in time to see Spanish Ray being led off the *Chicita* in handcuffs by four gun-toting men in dark suits—cheap dark suits. FBI agents. Ray winked at me as they marched him away.

One afternoon in late summer, I ran into Chalky. I hadn't seen him for a while or even spoken with him. We stood on a street corner and played catch up. He was engaged, he said.

"So which one turned out to be the lucky lady?" I asked.

"Both of them. I bought them both identical rings. Three carats each."

"Both of them?!"

"Sure. This way, they both stopped *hocking* me about marriage. I figure I've bought at least a year's time."

I shook my head and laughed. "Listen, why don't you come down and see the boat?" I said.

"What boat?"

"Come down and find out. At the Seventy-ninth Street Boat Basin. Here's the number. Call or just come by."

One September afternoon he showed up unexpectedly, as if he were just in the neighborhood looking for a cup of coffee. I was pleased to see him.

A couple of friends were on board. Jeffrey was there, of course. And my mother, I think. The weather was still beautiful. We were in our bathing suits, and Chalky was wearing a starched shirt and long pants. And you could see that he was very surprised, very impressed with the boat, especially when he found out it was mine.

"Where'd you get the money for a boat?" he asked.

"None of your business," I said.

"I'm just asking. What's the harm?"

"Hey, if I tell you everything, you'll be smarter than me. You'll know everything I know and everything you know."

It was one of Bernie's lines. Chalky smiled, recognizing it. "Yeah, right," he said, giving me an appraising look. It wasn't just my mind and mouth he was appraising either. I was at fighting weight, wrapped in a bikini, and tan as a berry. And for one moment, I saw him eating me up with his eyes. Sparks passed between us, but I let it go. I didn't want to start anything. As a pal, Chalky was perfect; as a boyfriend—well, for starters, he was already engaged . . . twice.

He was my brother, my father, my friend. Aside from that brief moment on the boat, I didn't look at Chalky through the eyes of a woman. So it surprised me when, in November, he telephoned and started hemming and hawing.

He had a big affair to go to—a legitimate deal—a union fund-raiser at the Plaza. He didn't want to take his Jewish fiancée. She was to loud, too brassy for this bunch. And he didn't feel like showing up with the Eurasian. So, he was thinking and he was wondering and it had occurred to him and . . . Five minutes it took him to *krechtz* out the big question: Would I go with him to the fund-raiser? I'd have a good time, he assured me. Maybe I'd even meet someone.

"Sure," I said, puzzled over why he'd made such a big deal about it.

My girlfriends had never stopped trying to romanticize my friendship with Chalky. To them, he seemed like the perfect guy for me. They knew how in love with Bernie I'd been. They'd seen me come apart after his death. I was doing okay now but—a woman alone, a woman with a baby to support—for how long, they asked, did I think I could I make it on my own in a man's world? And here was Chalky Lefkowitz, an attractive bachelor who seemed to enjoy my company and who just happened to be Bernie's best friend.

"It's like it was written this way," Lila would say. "Like a story. Bernie dies and here, Chalky shows up ten minutes later."

"It's a very odd coincidence," Margo, with her belief in fate and the spirit world, agreed. "That he should appear the way he did, just as Bernie was dying."

But the one whose opinion I valued most was Gloria's.

Right after Bernie died, Josh showed up at my house with her. She was in her thirties, beautiful, bright, and Jewish. And she ran the best high-class call girl operation in town. I trusted Gloria. She was tough. She'd made it on her own. She knew how to navigate in this so-called "man's world." And when I told her how awkward Chalky had sounded on the phone, she decided that it was time I made a move on him.

We were shopping for a dress for me to wear to the gala. I'd picked out a couple of hot numbers, but when I tried on a long beaded gown with a side slit the contest was over. It was outrageously expensive, but I'd never worn anything that felt as luxurious or looked as glamorous. And Gloria was unrelenting, insisting that if I couldn't afford it, she'd buy it for me.

"Think of it as an investment," she urged. "I've got a funny feeling about this, my vibes tell me it's going to be the start of something good. You're either going to meet someone at the affair or Chalky will fall madly in love with you."

I bought the dress and I ticked off the reasons Chalky was out of the question for me. When I got to my biggest and best—I don't want a mob guy again; I don't want a mob life—Gloria said, "Sandy, face facts, baby. Have you ever thought what would happen if you did meet a totally straight guy and he found out all about you? You know," she said, "that could turn a legitimate guy off." Then she countered every other objection I had to Chalky, ending with what was to become her anthem: "I think you ought to go for it."

I have never felt as beautiful as I did that Saturday night. I'd had my hair done. I'd taken great care with my makeup. Gloria had lent me a pair of long diamond earrings and a single diamond bracelet to wear with the long-sleeved, body-hugging, floor-length beaded gown. In my high heels, my legs looked a couple of yards long through the side slit. I threw my mink coat over my shoulder and went down to the lobby to meet Chalky.

He had rented a limo. When he stepped out in his tuxedo, he looked stunning. He was tan and trim. His blond-white hair was slicked back. His blue eyes lit up when he saw me. They traveled over me from head to toe, taking in every sequin, bead, and curve along the way. His eyes sparkled and he gave me a big appreciative grin.

"You're beautiful," he said. "You're going to waste with no man in your life."

"You sound like Gloria," I marveled.

He whispered it again as he took my arm and we walked into the Plaza ballroom together. I knew how proud he was to have me with him. I could feel him standing taller, straighter. I could see it in the eyes of other people, how good we looked together. And I knew he saw it, too.

"Jesus, you look great. What a waste," he kept repeating that night.

At least once, I answered, "Find someone for me, big brother. It's all up to you."

We'd had a couple of drinks by then, in addition to the champagne we'd had in the limo. I knew that I was feeling the buzz. And when he said, "Baby, I'll find you one. Right away, sweetheart," he looked at me the way he had on the boat and the same electricity passed between us.

The ballroom was filled with dazzling people, conversation, and music. At one end, tables for black jack, craps, and roulette had been set up as part of the fund-raising effort. At the other there was a band, a dance floor surrounded by dining tables, and a splendid buffet. We moved through the room together. We gambled awhile. When I leaned over to toss the dice, I looked over my shoulder to wink at Chalky for luck. He was looking around, looking like he would kill anybody he caught staring at my beaded behind. When he saw me watching him, he shrugged and grinned. "I'm not the only one who thinks you look great tonight."

Then I asked him to dance with me.

"Gee, Sandy," he began.

"Yeah, I know." I laughed. "You're going to tell me that tough guys don't dance. Tough guys don't go down on a broad. Tough guys don't do this. Tough guys don't do that—"

He studied me for a second with those evil twinkling eyes. "Come on," he said and grabbed my hand and walked me out to the dance floor.

It was more like swaying than dancing. It was more like grinding than swaying. "Where'd you hear that?" Chalky breathed into my neck.

"Where do you think?" I said.

He laughed. "Yeah, well it's true. Most of it anyway," he said. I reared back to look at him and what a sexy, mischievous grin he had on his face.

"Oh, yeah? Which part isn't true?"

"Maybe someday you'll find out," he said.

One dance. Then, while he went to get us some food, I sat at a table where I'd found some couples I'd known when I was married to Bernie.

Willie Rosen, who owned Gatsby's, was there. By that time, everyone was a little loaded and loose. When Chalky came back to the table, Willie started in on us. "You know the two of you make a gorgeous couple. Look at you, Sandy. You're single. He's single. The two of you look like you love each other, or like each other, or whatever. Why don't you give it a try."

And just as I was wondering: Does Willie Rosen know Gloria? Chalky suddenly said, "Well, I would . . . I think about it with her, but . . . She was with my best friend, almost my brother. It isn't right."

"What are you talking about, it isn't right?" said Willie. "The man is dead three years. You've *shtupped* everything that moves and you're still alone. Those broads you're engaged to, what are they, morons? Feh,"

Willie said, disgusted. "The two of you really ought to try it. You look like a winning combination."

Go for it, I could hear Gloria urge.

"Remember, Chalky," I said. "You promised you'd find me a guy. You didn't say which guy—but you promised."

He started to laugh. He looked at me with those glinting blue eyes like, "I'll get you for that." And all the while, Willie went on and on about how right we were for one another.

Well, by this time, I was more than a little tilted. I excused myself to go to the ladies' room, but all the way there my booze-fogged brain was ticking: Go for it, go for it, go for it. So Chalky had thought of me as more than a friend. Hmmm. So he thought I was beautiful and going to waste without a man. So suddenly he couldn't take his evil blue eyes off me. And he looked so handsome in a tuxedo. We looked so good together. We felt so good together. Dancing with him, standing still and swaying. Maybe, I thought. What the hell, I thought. Go for it.

And I did.

Instead of going to the ladies' room, I veered to the right and careened up the stairs and out to the waiting limo. I gave Chalky's driver a twenty-dollar bill and dismissed him. "We don't need the car. We're spending the night at the Plaza," I said.

Then I rushed back inside and rented a suite for the evening. When I returned to the ballroom, Chalky was talking to some men. I waited and when we were alone at the bar for a few minutes, I dangled the room key in front of him. "I had this terrific idea," I said. "I rented us a suite upstairs."

"You did what?"

"Well, this party's going to go on and on. I'm having a fabulous time. Why should I go home exhausted when we can go right upstairs and get undressed and sleep here? And in the morning we can have a nice breakfast and go on about our business. It's Sunday," I continued breathlessly. "And unless you have other plans. I mean, I think it's a great way to end the evening. And anyway, I told the limo driver to go home."

He was staring at me as though he was waiting for the English subtitles to appear.

"I thought it was a terrific idea," I repeated, less enthusiastically.

"Okay," he said finally. "Why not?"

Well, about two or three in the morning, we said our goodnights. Chalky told some people what I had done and everyone thought it was a great idea, ending the evening in luxury, spending the night at the Plaza. What fun, everyone said, what a clever girl, what a lucky man, what a stunning couple. On our way out of the ballroom, I picked up two clean glasses and Chalky pulled a fresh bottle of champagne out of an ice bucket, and I led him through the lobby, very gaily, like something out of a Hollywood movie—a romantic farce . . . which is just about what the evening boiled down to.

In the suite, he took off his jacket dramatically. I kicked off my shoes. I turned on the radio. He poured the champagne. We got comfy on the sofa. We drank. We laughed. We started necking. We started rolling around on the couch. We rolled off onto the floor. I landed on top of him. I smothered his face with kisses. "You are so delicious," I said, "I'm going to eat you up all over." "Do it, baby. Oh, do it," he said. I kissed his face, his neck. "Yes, baby, yes," Chalky rasped. That was all she wrote. I passed out cold on top of him.

Next morning, I woke up naked in bed. I walked into the other room. Chalky came out of the shower wrapped in towels. I saw the pillow and blanket on the sofa. "You undressed me?" I said.

"You think I never saw a woman's body before?"

"I'm sorry I passed out."

"I thought you'd dropped dead."

"It was a stupid idea," I said.

"Best time I ever had. I never had so much fun with anyone."

I went into the shower and came out wrapped in towels. We ordered breakfast.

"You're not mad at me?"

"No," he said. "But everything's different now."

"What's different?"

"You. Me. I don't know. I'm confused."

That was November.

In December he left town. He was taking a couple weeks off—spending Christmas with one of his fiancées and New Year's week with the other. "You're a very busy man," I said.

"I'm a very confused man," he countered. "Be a good girl and play a dead hand, as they say in the game."

"What does that mean?" I asked. But I knew. Be quiet. Just sit there. Wait.

CHAPTER EIGHTEEN

Courting Trouble

They say be careful what you wish for, you might get it.

From the time we tussled on the floor of the Plaza suite, from the morning I woke to find that Chalky—like Bernie our first night together—hadn't laid a glove on me, from the breakfast when he said things had changed between us, I started wishing Chalky Lefkowitz would fall for me.

It seemed inevitable that I'd wind up with someone connected. Some girls had the Midas touch; I had the Mob touch. Every guy I got involved with turned out to be a player. Well then, why not Chalky, I started thinking.

Gloria, who claimed to know everything about straight guys, had probably been right about legit types being put off by my past. And there was Jeffrey to consider—he needed a father. But who would love him the way Bernie had? And who would love him without judging his real father, without looking down on who Bernie had been, what he'd done? Where was I going to find a guy like that?

A guy who loved and respected Bernie. A guy who adored Jeffrey. A guy who knew everything about my past that I'd tried to hide from other men . . . and still thought of me as an attractive, bright, successful woman—going to waste without a man.

New Year's Eve at one in the morning Chalky called from Florida to wish Jeffrey and me a healthy and happy New Year. "I'll be back soon," he said. "I can't wait to see you."

"You must be exhausted running from fiancée to fiancée," I teased. "How was Miss Christmas?"

"It's over. I told her she could keep the ring. I'll call you as soon as I get home."

The week he got back, we went to dinner with a crowd of people. He stared at my legs all evening. "What's with you?" one of his friends said. "You haven't taken your eyes off her legs."

"I don't know," Chalky said. "I just never noticed what dynamite legs she has. When I look at them it makes me feel good.'' Before the evening was over, I had a new nickname. Everyone was calling me "Legs.''

That's how it went. Little by little, Chalky began noticing things he liked about me that he hadn't seen the day or week or month before.

And little by little I became aware of how attractive he was; how the tan made up for the lack of hair; how the blue eyes always sparkled, and how sometimes they looked mischievous and sexy, sometimes evil. The impeccable conservative suits I'd teased him about, the ones I'd thought made him look always ready for a wedding or a funeral, began to seem more elegant and distinguished than stodgy or formal. And I began to notice that when we ran into old friends of Bernie's, connected guys, they treated Chalky with respect. Not the affection they'd shown toward Bernie, but respect, equality, sometimes even fear.

And little by little, the idea of the *shiddach,* the romantic match everyone was promoting, shifted from preposterous to possible.

"Be a good girl, Legs," he'd say.

And I'd try to be. I'd find myself waiting patiently at the bar while he talked business. I'd cross my long legs and stir my drink and tune out when certain names were dropped. When we were out to dinner, I stopped putting my two cents into every conversation—particularly when the Italians were at the table. Chalky mingled with the heavy hitters differently than Bernie had. Bernie kidded and kibitzed with them. Chalky watched and waited. Bernie with his easy wit and laughter made them smile. Chalky with his thin smile and dangerous, sparkling eyes made them listen.

Although we'd start out as pals and partners at the beginning of the evening, little by little, I'd find myself shifted off to the side. Bernie had shown me off, gotten a kick out of my big mouth, asked my opinion, laughed at my mistakes. Chalky and the Italians preferred me quiet and smiling.

"Be a good girl," he'd say. And I'd light up a Parliament and watch him make his way across the room to the tables against the wall where the guys in silk suits were sawing through sirloin. And, little by little, I'd find myself sitting in smiling silence, mindlessly tapping the bar or table top with my solid gold cigarette lighter.

Gloria phoned me. "I've got a new fella," she said. "He's a diplomat from Ghana. Do you know anything about Ghana? It's an incredibly poor country. They need appliances, clothes, cars, things we have here and never think twice about. They don't have those things but, honey, they are rolling in gold.''

As they say, it was déjà vu all over again.

Believe it or not, Gloria had in mind almost the exact same deal that had gotten Red, Bernie, and me a military escort out of Africa. I tried to talk her out of it. I told her what had happened to us. But Gloria was a hard-headed woman. When it came to business, in a lot of ways she was tougher than Bernie had been. She'd learned early in life to never let her heart get in the way of her head.

"We can do this all very legitimately. But I've got to get the merchandise. I need everything from washing machines to tanks, guns and ammunition. Chalky's got connections, hasn't he?" she said. "You and he can be partners on your end. Ask him."

So Chalky and I had lunch at Tavern on the Green one Sunday afternoon to discuss the possibilities. He was very interested. "This could turn out to be a real score," he said. "It could be set up very legitimately. It can be done on the up-and-up."

I remember staring at him through lunch. Oh, I was talking like a big shot. Laying out the plan. Batting around numbers. Laughing like I had the world by the tail. But another part of my mind was watching Chalky and thinking, I'll be damned, this is it—I've fallen for the guy. Another outlaw old enough to be my father. Another nice Jewish boy who's made the trip from Delancey Street to Dannemora. Another wise guy. And this one's in it even deeper than Bernie was. God help me, I remember thinking, I'm in love with Chalky Lefkowitz.

Instead of making me feel excited, elated, or optimistic, the thought sent a chill through me. The unhealed ache in my gut, the one I'd first felt after my father left, the one that was my constant companion through the days of sitting *shivah* for Bernie and for months after . . . I felt it again. A trembling fear, an aching emptiness. Then it passed.

What did I know about love? What did I know about the men I'd trusted, depended on, and cared most about in my life? That they'd left me. It was unbelievable. Almost as soon as I realized that I was in love with Chalky, I began to dread losing him. I felt it in my gut, in my heart—though I didn't understand it that day or for many years to come.

Chalky was demanding, careful, mistrustful, cold. He was an emotional mine field. I never knew whether or not I was doing the right thing around him. And I'd never really cared before. But, once I fell in love with him, it began to matter more and more.

We became partners. My job was to check out prices on TVs, washers and dryers, irons and toasters. I was in charge of appliances. Chalky was researching the heavier hardware. Gloria was pulling the legal end together. And, in a matter of months, contracts had been signed and we were actually doing a little business.

As part of the terms of his parole, Chalky was living with his mother in a fifth-floor walkup on First Street. And he was on the books as an employee of his sister's business in the Garment Center. Chalky's mother, who'd been Bernie's mother's best friend, was an absolute angel, the living image of the good-hearted *Yiddishe Momme* the out-of-towners wept over at Molly's; the kind of Jewish mother whose son could do no wrong. She had carried home-made chicken soup for him to Sing Sing and Dannemora and shlepped to Trenton State every weekend for twelve years with shopping bags full of delicacies from the old neighborhood—and she'd never lost faith in him.

We became friends. Because Chalky and I were together so much, I got to know his family, and Jeffrey and I would sometimes go down to the Essex Street Market where Sarah had a fish stand. The woman had worked her entire life. Her son tipped doormen more in one shot than she probably earned in a week, but Sarah was the original stand-up broad. She knew about me from Bernie's mother and, from the beginning, she was as sweet to Jeffrey and me as if we were her own. She was rooting for me to win out over Chalky's other girls.

And, for better or worse, it looked like I was.

Chalky and I had gone into business together in February. In early April, Red and I went to see about getting the *Pride of Rahemia* out of dry dock and ready for the coming season. We left the boat yard kind of depressed. It was like a visit to the hospital and the doctor had diagnosed *Rahemia* as weather-beaten and in need of a lot of repairs. About $9,000 worth.

"What do you think?" I asked Red on the drive home. "It's a lot of money. And I've been spending like crazy this year—I've lent to friends, I'm helping out my mother and sister, I've got Nora a couple of times a week and household expenses, and I've gone a little crazy over clothes, too. Nine grand. And that's just to get her back into the water."

"You know, I'm getting old and tired," Hot Dog said. "It's up to you, partner. You're the one who uses it most of the time. It's for you and the Jab and for Tillie. What do you want to do?"

Well, we went back and forth on it and, very reluctantly, we decided to sell her. That day, I talked to Red about my changing relationship with Chalky. He was happy for me. Like everyone else I knew, he hoped I'd marry the guy.

"You never can tell," I teased. "Only one more fiancée to go."

A week later, an offer came in for *Rahemia* and after talking it over with me, Red, in whose name the boat had been registered, sold her. I had dinner with Chalky that night.

"What's the matter with you?" he asked, stopping in the middle of a sentence.

"I sold the boat today," I began. "We didn't get much for it and I'm feeling kind of blue because I really—"

He looked as though I'd slapped him across the face. "You did what?" he said very slowly.

"I sold my boat."

"Are you crazy? Without saying a word to me? How could you do that?" he demanded angrily.

"What are you talking about, Chalky? It was my boat. My money—"

"You know, you've got a really big mouth," he growled.

"Chalky," I said, angry myself now. "It was mine. Don't tell me what to do with my possessions. I don't like it."

"Who do you think you're talking to like that? Who do you think you are to open up a mouth like that to me?"

Like what, I wanted to demand? We're friends. We're equals. We're business partners. You don't talk to your friend and partner that way. You talk to some bimbo you have no respect for at all, I thought. You talk that way to some brainless girlfriend, some beaten-down wife. But I said: "Who died and left you boss?"

"Bernie," Chalky answered. It was the first time he said it. It became his classic answer.

"Well, Bernie never told me that." I said.

It was our first fight. He was appalled that I'd talk back to him. I was confused and upset that he felt I owed him explanations about my personal affairs. But my matchmaking girlfriends took it as a good omen.

"I told you he was crazy about you," Lila said, "I mean, look, he's already acting like what's yours is his."

"I know," I said. "And I don't like it."

Two weeks later, at the end of April, a phone call from Gloria woke me up. "Well, baby," she said, "you got some fresh bread in your pocket, don't you?"

I said, "What are you talking about?"

"Didn't Chalky give you money last night?"

I actually laughed. "Chalky never gives me money for anything. Remember that fund-raiser? Gloria, it cost me a fortune. Fourteen hundred for the dress, another two bills for the Plaza suite. He's an expensive guy to go out with—"

"Forget that. Sandy, you mean he didn't give you anything?"

"What are you talking about? You're starting to make me crazy. I thought you meant maybe he gave me some money to buy myself something—"

"Okay. I've got to tell you this. Yesterday afternoon Chalky was over at my place. You know we shipped a load of tools over to Ghana and we made a little profit. Chalky and I split seventeen thousand dollars. And you're going to get paid on his end because you and he are partners. So, let me see, half of seventeen is eight five. So he's got to give you over four grand. He had the money on him yesterday. I knew you two were having dinner, so I thought—"

"Gloria," I said through clenched teeth. "Look, it's early in the morning and you woke me up. I'm confused. Run that by me again."

She did.

"Gloria, I had dinner with the man last night and he never mentioned a single word about the money."

"Well, then," said Gloria, whose clients and friends were among the bluest of blue bloods, "baby, you'd better straighten that cocksucker out."

I hung up the phone with a sick feeling. I paced and smoked and cursed Chalky. I phoned my mother. I blew my top. "Whatever you're going to do," said Tillie, "you'd better do it very quietly. Go see him today. Very quietly. Don't do it over the phone. Do it in person. You hear me, Sandy— do it quietly."

"You're right," I said. And I pulled myself and my battle plan together. I made a production out of getting dressed. I must have changed about a hundred times. I took time with my makeup. My mother always said, when you're meeting an opponent, no matter who it is, look gorgeous. Look your best. And I did.

I went up to Chalky's sister's place in the Garment Center. I walked into his office and he was so surprised and happy to see my beautiful, smiling face that he made a big fuss over me. There were some men in his office when I arrived, so I walked around and chatted with a few people and waited until we were quietly alone. And then I opened fire:

"Did I buy dinner last night, Chalky? Was that my share of the profits you paid the check with, partner? There's got to be a little change left out of *my* four thousand two hundred and fifty dollars—or did you tip big? Goddamn it, Chalky, where's my money?! Why didn't you give me my end?"

He leaned back in his executive leather swivel chair. "You'll get it. You'll get it," he said, grinning.

"It's not funny! Where's my share?!" I hollered.

He let me rant and rave for a while. Then he said, with that little twinkling smile, "Are you finished?"

I was. I'd absolutely exhausted myself. I fell back onto a chair. I just *plotzed*.

"Do you need money?" he asked.

"Yes," I said.

"Naw, you're worth a fortune."

Suddenly everything had switched around. It wasn't about him *owing* me money, now it was about whether I *needed* it. "Don't tell me what I'm worth. You don't know what I'm worth. But it's not a fortune, Chalky," I said. "And I want my piece. I brought you into this deal. It was me. Now, give me my share of the profits and, I'll tell you what, you do whatever you want from now on. I'm out of this partnership. I don't want to have to fight with you."

"There goes that big mouth again," he said. He was grinning. The evil blues were twinkling. "What's right is right," he said. "I'll tell you what—I'll marry you instead."

It caught me totally off guard. I'd come to do battle. I'd been angry and frustrated. I'd felt cheated and misused. Suddenly, I didn't know what I felt.

"How can you marry me?" I asked. "You're engaged."

"Not anymore," he said. "I broke off with the other one. I'm woman-less. It's you and me against the world."

He took a small box out of the drawer and slid it across the desk top at me. "I was going to give you this tonight but, here, take it now."

I opened the box and saw the most gorgeous pair of diamond earrings I'd ever seen in my life.

I was speechless—thank God. Because, right that minute, if I'd opened my mouth, I think I would have said, "Did the diamonds run you forty-two-fifty, or do I get change back from my engagement present?"

"You like them?" he asked, proud and grinning.

"Chalky, they're incredible," I said.

Four months later, on August 12, 1969, we were married in the little *shul* on Rivington Street where Chalky had been Bar mitzvahed. He'd teased me into paying for the license. It was only about five dollars—the costliest bargain of my life.

1969. The whole world was changing. There were riots everywhere. Students against universities. Blacks against whites. Hard-hat construction workers against long-haired hippies. Women against traditional values.

Some women. Not me.

"I'm an old-fashioned guy with old-fashioned ideas," Chalky kept telling me during our courtship. "I want a normal life."

It was music to my ears. Normal. Every time he said it, I could see roses growing around the doorman's desk at East Seventy-eighth Street, a white picket fence bordering the circular driveway.

"Whatever business you've got going, whatever you're doing, Sandy, I want it stopped," he announced a couple of months before we were married.

"You mean with Red, and the bar, everything?" I asked.

"Everything," he said. "You're going to be a housewife. You've got a house to take care of, and a child. I'll take care of business and you'll stop running around and you'll be normal."

We were having dinner alone at Oscar's, a seafood place on Third Avenue. Chalky had put away a couple of drinks at the bar and a glass or two of wine. And suddenly, he had a bad edge on.

"Do you know exactly what I do for living?" he asked.

"Exactly? No. I know you're not kosher, Chalky. You're not straight, but I really don't know what you do."

"And you never will," he said triumphantly. "You might hear stories about me, you might hear conversations. But as long as you're with me, you will never know exactly what I do for a living."

He said it very slowly. I'd begun to notice that whenever Chalky wanted to make a point, he spoke slowly and softly so that you had to bend toward him to hear. You had to bow to him.

"You can think what you want, Sandy, that's your problem," he continued in that slow, deliberate way. "You'll never be involved in my business. After we're married, all I want you to do is be my wife, take care of my home, take care of your son who'll become our son, and that's it. Stay home and be a good girl."

It was the standard rap—familiar to every mob mate. Stay out of my business. I'm only doing this for your own good. It's better if you don't know what's up.

"Okay," I said cheerfully. I'd heard the same little speech from Bernie, but then he'd kept me close to him and his business. He'd get excited about some venture or scheme, and I'd be part of it, however cockeyed some of them turned out to be—the House of Yenom, the African adventure, banking bonds at the Vatican.

But something told me Chalky meant it. He wouldn't bend the way Bernie had. He'd kept me at a distance from his business associates throughout our relationship; more since we'd become engaged than when we'd been just friends. He seemed to be dead serious about wanting me to be a typical TV wife and mother. Nothing more.

About a week after the you'll-never-be-involved-in-my-business chat, the two of us went to a gala at Gatsby's. The occasion was Ruby Stein's "going away" party. Ruby, who put syndicate money to work at outrageous interest by lending it to lesser loansharks, Ruby, the shylock's shylock and sometime employer of Brooklyn's own head-bashing, debt-collecting Gallo gang, Charles Ruby Stein of the Copa and the eye tic, had been busted and was going away to Danbury to do short time.

But before he went, his friends and colleagues were throwing him an all-star send-off. Gatsby's was crowded with the famous and infamous that night. I don't remember exactly who was in or out at that particular moment in time—in or out of jail, in or out of power—but the joint was jumping with Profacis and Colombos, Gambinos and Luccheses. And, true to his words, Chalky parked me at the bar while he joined a couple of other family men at a table across the room.

I was standing alone at the end of the bar. An elderly gray-haired man with a fat nose, fat knuckles, and a big cigar hanging out of his mouth was standing next to me talking to another man. Suddenly, the guy took the cigar out of his mouth and spit on the floor.

"Ugh! That's disgusting," I said. "Don't you have any manners? I'll have the bartender get you a spittoon," I said to him.

He looked at me through narrowed eyes. "Who are you, girlie? Who're you here with?"

I said, "Number one, I'm not your girlie—"

"Oh, yeah. Now I recognize you!" he said. "I remember you from Bernie. Don't you recognize me? I'm Tony Salerno."

Oh, great, I thought. Fat Tony Salerno was a big boss, a don, head of one of the New York families. A great sense of humor was not one of the things he was famous for. "You know," he said, shaking the cigar in my face, "no one else would ever say that to me."

"Well, I'm sorry, but even if I knew who you were I would have said that's disgusting," I told Fat Tony, who is now doing about a hundred years in prison.

"You know something, sweetheart," he said, dribbling tobacco juice through a sudden grin. "You're okay. You've got moxie. Too bad you weren't born a man. I'd like to have you on my side."

He left and I looked across the room at the table full of dark-suited, serious men sitting with Chalky. He was deep in discussion. I thought, thank God he didn't see me with Fat Tony; thank God he won't ask me what we were talking about. He'd have been mortified, I knew. He'd have read me the riot act for not being a good girl, for shooting off my big mouth. And then I thought, if only Bernie were alive; he'd have laughed his head off at the exchange.

There were a lot of differences between Bernie and Chalky. Bernie was hot; Chalky was cold. Bernie wanted to do what was good; Chalky wanted to do what was right. Bernie took risks; Chalky took care. Bernie thought the world of me. Chalky cared about what the world thought of me.

Never mind that he was forty-eight years old and had never been married. Never mind that he'd spent more than a decade locked away from real life. Chalky had a lot of ideas about what the perfect family should look like, sound like, act like. And I bought it. When we were courting, I loved listening to him paint the picture of our lives together, our little family. I loved it. I wanted to believe it. And in some areas, he definitely had me convinced.

"I'm not going to push you about sex," he said the day after we became engaged. "You know, I spent twelve years in prison and I did a lot of reading. I know all about the anatomy of a woman's body. And how a woman should be made love to." We were having a romantic little dinner at Les Champs. Chalky was cutting his roast chicken into neat, bite-sized pieces. Everything about him was neat, clean, precise, thought-out. Even the discussion of sex.

"So if there's anything you want me to do, just ask for it," he said. "Whatever you want, whatever you like sexually or you don't like, don't be ashamed to tell me. Sex is very important between people."

The man was as good as his word. Twelve years of reading had paid off. Big time. When it came to sex, Chalky knew every trick in the book—literally. The guy could've done testimonials for literacy on the rewards of reading.

His relationship with Jeffrey was also a convincer. When he'd stay at my apartment before we were married, he always made sure that Jeffrey would find him on the couch in the morning and not in my bed. I'd wake some days to find them coloring together on the floor of the baby's room. And Chalky would say to Jeffrey, "Would you mind if I married your mommy?" And Jeffrey, who'd been calling him Uncle Chalky forever, would always say, "No." Chalky would say, "Would you want me to be your daddy?" And Jeffrey would always say, "Yes." And, after a while, Chalky started saying, "Why don't you practice calling me daddy," and Jeffrey did. And I'd think, it's going to work out; we're going to be a real family.

CHAPTER NINETEEN

Sadie, Sadie

A couple of Chalky's friends threw us a wedding reception. Because Willie Rosen was one of them, the party was held at Gatsby's. Because Tom Sullivan was another, the Irish mob was well represented. Between family, friends, and business associates, more than a hundred people showed up. Among the associates, the Italians were in the majority. Again, I noticed how, even at our wedding reception, Chalky chose the company of the heavy hitters over family and friends, who didn't have strong mob connections. And, although he drank and smiled, there was a quiet seriousness to everything he did.

I was wearing a long-sleeved, high-necked, A-line mini-dress of beige and gold brocaded lace with two big patch pockets—very 1969. And very convenient, as it turned out, because while Chalky romanced the *machers,* I wandered through the crowd and men would stop me and put envelopes into those pockets and say, "Here's a present. Spend it nicely, honey, and give me a kiss."

When we got home to my apartment that night, we emptied the envelopes. The gifts came to nearly $20,000.

"How do you like this," Chalky said, pleased. "Look at the respect these people have for me. And everyone did it the right way. No one gave me any envelopes. They gave it to the bride."

Then he really surprised me. "You want to redo the house, so do it," he said, grandly handing me the cash. "Buy whatever you need for the place."

"I can do whatever I want?" I was looking forward to it. The apartment still reflected Bernie's early-Liberace taste. I wanted the place to look Hollywood sleek and sharp.

"Whatever you want," Chalky said, "but keep a record of how much everything costs. Keep receipts. When it comes to money, I like to know where it's going and what it's going for."

So I hired a decorator and I bought new linens and dishes and a vacuum cleaner. And, because Chalky never gave me any household expense money, I started buying food and paying other bills out of that "pocket money," and by and by it was gone. At Chalky's request, I'd given up my other businesses and there was no extra bread coming in. So I started using the money Bernie had left me. And one day, I said to Gloria, "He's been living with me for a couple of months and he hasn't asked if I need money, for groceries, for a cleaning girl, for whatever. He's seen the receipts. He knows there's nothing left of the wedding money—"

"Well, you did marry a bachelor," she said. "Maybe you just have to talk to him. You know, like say, 'You're a married man now, this is your responsibility.' "

I told Margo, "I don't know what to do. He just comes and goes and he doesn't ask me if I need anything for the house. I think he's cheap."

"Oh, he's wonderful," she said. "Why don't you sit down and tell him and I'm sure he'd give you the world."

Now, Chalky had no casual friends, no civilians. Everyone he socialized with had either done time or was likely to. The people he did business with were the only ones he trusted. And they were wise guys.

He didn't like my friends. "I know you love these people," he'd say about Warren and Margo, Judy, Leona, even Gloria once their business together had been concluded. "They're your people," he'd say. "You can see them alone, but I don't want to have anything to do with them. They're not my cup of tea." He didn't trust anyone who wasn't part of the mob.

But this was in the early days when Chalky would agree to go to dinner with Margo and Warren; when Chalky and Warren were briefly nuzzling up to one another, trying to find out what business deals they could cook up. It was a short-lived friendship. But while it lasted, Chalky played the big shot and always picked up the check, hundreds of dollars' worth of dinner tabs, while Margo and Warren just sat there or conveniently looked away. Of course, Margo thought he was wonderful.

"Let a few weeks pass," she suggested.

"Give him a little time," Gloria said. "Then sit him down and tell him the facts of life. Some men have to be taught. They can be great boyfriends, lay gifts on you and everything, but a husband is a whole different thing."

It sounded like good advice. All right, I said to myself. I'll give the man time to settle in. After all, he's never been married. And he spent so many years in jail, it may take awhile for him to figure out how to behave like a husband.

So I waited. And I watched. I saw him fling fifties at doormen and cocktail waitresses. Every time we went to his sister's for Sunday dinner, all the nieces and nephews lined up and they each got $100 apiece from him. Whenever they needed something, there was Uncle Chalky with ready cash. I gave it a little time. Then I started in.

"Chalky, it's been a couple of months now and I've been paying the bills out of my own money—" I'd begin.

"You mean the money Bernie left you," he'd correct me.

"They're *our* household bills, Chalky. Bernie has nothing to do with this."

"Leave me alone," he'd say. "Stop nagging."

Tell me to stop nagging? Tell a fish to breathe through its mouth. Chalky got to play the big shot and I got to pay the bills? So I kept "nagging." But I did try to be tactful. To be nice. To be a good girl.

Finally, one day he said, "Okay. What are the monthly bills here? What's the rent? How much is the phone?"

And, good girl that I was, I shaved the rates. I told him less on each item, thinking he wouldn't be as mad if our expenses weren't as much. I still have a few bucks put away. I figured I'd make up the difference. So we agreed on a figure he'd give me weekly to pay for everything. I think it was $300. I know it wasn't enough. And Fridays became my pay days. That's what Chalky called the household money—my pay.

Now, Chalky was a clothes horse. The way Norman Bates was a devoted son. When it came to his wardrobe, he was incredibly fastidious. There was a very big walk-in closet in our bedroom. And that closet, which became his, was set up with extreme care. Shirts were hung by color, sleeve length, style, each two inches from the next—*exactly* two inches. Chalky used a tape measure to make sure. Each of his suits, too, about twenty of them, hung exactly two inches apart. There was a chart on the closet wall indicating which shirts, ties, and shoes went with each suit. He had hundreds of ties. And they also were perfectly placed. Suits, pants, shoes, ties, all color-coordinated, all two inches apart, all lined up like little soldiers. The Lefkowitz Collection, I used to call it.

And in that closet was a little bench that Chalky used when he put on his shoes and socks. Come Friday morning, he'd be sitting in the closet on his bench. "Sandy, come here," he'd say. And he'd count out $300 in the closet. In the dark. He paid me off in a dark closet so that I couldn't see his bankroll!

Three hundred dollars. I think the rent at that time was four hundred. And I'd squirrel the cash away in little envelopes, like a miser. I'd put so much in the rent envelope and so much in the food envelope and so much toward the phone. I was a maniac about it. I couldn't believe what I was doing. But I did it. And he sent me flowers.

For the first couple of months of our marriage, he sent flowers twice a week. Not just bunches of roses or pretty bouquets. No, these were big floral arrangements—the kind people would send to a wake. My girlfriends would say, "Oh, look how thoughtful he is. Oh, Sandy, he really loves you. He's so romantic." It turned out that the guy who owned the flower shop owed Chalky money and was paying him off in funeral arrangements.

Mr. Wonderful.

Six, seven, eight hundred on a custom suit, four hundred dollars for shoes. Never went out wearing less than a couple of grand on his well-scrubbed back. And I remember one day I said, "The sheets are torn, they have holes in them. I want to buy some new ones."

And Chalky said, "Why? No one sees them."

"Yeah, but we sleep on them."

"Aah," he said, "what's the difference?"

"Look, I'll go down to Grand Street, to the Lower East Side. I won't spend a lot, okay?"

He wouldn't give me the money. Instead, he shlepped all the way downtown with me to make sure we got the cheapest sheets in the discount store.

I didn't say anything. It wouldn't have mattered. Chalky had to have the last word in every discussion. "Sandy, when I'm wrong, I'm right," he used to say, "and when I'm right, I'm very right. You can't argue with me about that."

He'd say it into the mirror. "When you're wrong, you're right. And when you're right, you're very right. No argument. That's it."

Being right—even when he was wrong—was very important to Chalky. He was new to the husband game. He wanted to do it right. And in the first year of our marriage, right meant making Jeffrey his legal son.

I was thrilled when Chalky said he wanted to adopt Jeffrey. It was a warm, loving, beautiful gesture. And Jeffrey, who at four and a half years old, had never known a real father, was all for it. He was already calling Chalky daddy, and it was clear to everyone that Chalky was crazy about the kid. Why wouldn't he be? Jeffrey was adorable, smart, polite, good-natured.

There was a minor hitch. After examining Chalky's arrest record, the surrogate court law clerk, who made recommendations in adoption proceedings, refused to even put the case before the deciding judge.

"Don't worry," Chalky said, on the way home from court. "We'll get around this shmuck." He chatted with some friends and, a few bucks and a couple of days later, he phoned and said, "Okay, the adoption is in the bag."

"What happened?" I asked.

"I made a donation to the Democratic Party for five thousand dollars and the adoption is going to go through. How much did it cost you to give birth?" he asked.

"I don't know, not a lot. Much less than five thousand dollars."

"Well, just remember, it's costing me more to adopt Jeffrey than it cost Bernie to pay for his being born," said the proud papa-to-be.

Less than a week later, our attorney got a call from the judge's clerk. We went down to surrogate court—Jeffrey, Chalky and me, all dressed up like citizens—and were ushered into the judge's chambers. I'd never seen such a magnificent office in my life. The man sat at a desk as big as my mother's apartment. As we walked through the door he said, "Hi, Chalky, I had dinner the other night at Gatsby's with Tommy Ryan and a couple of your other pals."

Tommy Ryan, whose real name was Tommy Eboli, was a member of the Genovese mob; a major member. I'd met him back in the Bernie days with Ruby Stein and Jiggs Forlano. He was supposed to be Vito Genovese's right-hand man. Apparently, he was the judge's friend, too.

"Yeah, I heard," Chalky said. "I know all about it."

"Come here, young man," the judge called to Jeffrey. "I know you like chocolates. Your daddy told me you like chocolates." The judge pulled a bag of Hershey Kisses out of a drawer and called Jeffrey over. "Now, let me ask you something Jeffrey. Do you want Chalky to become your real father?"

Jeffrey looked over at Chalky. He was crazy about him. "He is my real father," he said. "My other daddy died when I was born."

The judge winked at Chalky. "Congratulations, daddy," he said.

We drove to First Street, to Chalky's mother's apartment, to celebrate. Sarah was thrilled. "My new little Lefkowitz," she kept saying, pinching Jeffrey's cheeks, smoothing down his hair. She had a huge, delicious, Jewish lunch waiting—a goulash stew and chicken, and Jeffrey's favorite chicken soup with homemade noodles and matzo balls. She'd even baked a cake which she served with one candle on it, for Jeffrey to blow out for good luck. And she gave him a five-hundred-dollar bond. "For my new little

Lefkowitz grandson, who will carry on the name one day, *mine einekle,* my gorgeous grandchild.'' And every time Jeffrey called her *bubbie,* grandma, her eyes misted. And so did mine.

I looked around the table. It was just the four of us. And Chalky looked so comfortable and happy. Sarah was glowing, *kvelling.* She couldn't stop touching Jeffrey's cheeks, his forehead, running her work-worn hand through his hair. We were all right, I thought. We were a family.

In moments like this, I told myself it'll work out. I have what I wanted. I'm really Sadie-Sadie now.

So what if Chalky didn't kid around with me the way Bernie had or hang around the house to kibitz or invite me to meet him somewhere for a drink or dinner just for the hell of it. So what that he left at eleven each morning and rarely returned before three or four A.M. and that he attended more and more gatherings alone because there would be business done at those places and I was his wife, not his partner. So what that when his friend Tom Sullivan finally went to trial on the armed-robbery charge that had been hanging over his head for months, Chalky had to be there for him, in the courtroom day after day, lending emotional support to Tom's wife but getting more irritable, more irrational at home.

Chalky was very attached to Tom, almost like a Siamese twin, and as the trial began to go badly for Tom, Chalky got crazier and crazier. He'd begun waking me up at two or three in the morning. ''Make me blueberry pancakes,'' I'd hear, struggling out of sleep, knowing that Jeffrey would be up bright and early and that I'd have to make breakfast for him in just a few hours. Or Chalky would show up drunk in the middle of the night after being away from home for a day or two and he'd demand sex. Or bacon and scrambled eggs. Or an explanation for why there was a wrinkle in the left sleeve of his favorite blue shirt. He'd ring the doorbell at four A.M. until I woke and let him in. ''Where's your key?'' I'd ask. ''What do you care?'' he'd snarl. ''I didn't feel like using it.''

When Bernie had come home late, or sometimes if he stayed out all night, I used to toss and turn and worry about him. When Chalky went out my only worry was he'd surprise me by coming home early. At first I'd resented being left alone so much of the time. But after a while, I came to cherish my nights without him. When the doorbell rang, I never knew who'd be waiting for me—the lover or the beast.

Rosh Hashona was early that fall. It fell on a Friday. Chalky was going to be home for the holiday dinner and I was very eager to please him. We'd been married for a little more than a year. Things had gone rapidly downhill after Tom Sullivan was convicted and sentenced to eight years in Atlanta. Not only was Chalky furious over what had happened to his best friend, but he'd taken over Tom's business and was stretched pretty thin, working all the time now. At what, believe me, I didn't ask. He was home less and less. And he was never home for dinner on a Friday. So this dinner, this Jewish holiday, was really a special occasion, one of the rare chances for all of us to be together again, family style.

I shopped and cleaned and cooked for days. I roasted a beautiful chicken. I set the table with crystal and candles. Jeffrey was spotless and all dressed up in a handsome new suit. I had my hair and nails done. Chalky brought home flowers—a beautiful bouquet, not a funeral floral arrangement. I think I was even wearing a little TV Mom-type apron when I brought the food to the table. Everything was just the way I thought Chalky would like it. Everything was right.

Right.

"This chicken is delicious," he said. "It's a kosher chicken, isn't it?"

"No," I said. "There are no kosher butchers around here."

"What the hell are you talking about?" He threw his knife and fork into his plate. "You're telling me this chicken isn't kosher? You can't get a kosher chicken for Rosh Hashona? My mother would walk twenty miles for a kosher chicken! Whatever she had to do, wherever she'd have to go!"

"Chalky, you eat bacon," I reminded him. "When did you become kosher?"

He shoved his plate across the table, knocking over a candlestick. "Don't you open that big mouth to me! On the holidays! How often do I come home? How often do you cook for me, you dumb bitch?!"

Jeffrey's eyes widened with fear.

Chalky stood up suddenly. "Don't you start with me, you pig, you miserable bitch!" He tore at the tablecloth. Dishes and food went flying. Before everything fell to the floor, he jumped up and upended the dining room table and dumped whatever remained.

Jeffrey screamed and ran for cover.

"Stop it!" I yelled. "What's the matter with you? You're scaring the baby! Stop it!"

But Chalky was already at the bar. He began hurling glasses across the room. He threw them at the mirror above the couch. "Couches, you'll have!" he bellowed, as the glass tore into the upholstery. "Glasses, you'll have!"

He was throwing things and smashing things. He grabbed the cartons of cigarettes that were in the bar and began ripping them up and throwing them around the room. Then he found a handful of matchbooks. He lit them one, two at a time, the whole books, and began flinging them at the drapes, the sofa, and chairs. The place was a disaster. Jeffrey, the son Chalky adored, was quaking and crying in my arms.

"You bitch, you cunt, you filthy pig," Chalky yelled.

"Why, because I tried to make dinner for you? Because I wanted a normal family dinner? A family like you promised. You're never here. You're never home! You wanted a housewife. I'm a housewife. Not *your* wife. I'm married to this *house*. This house that you're trying to destroy!''

While Chalky ranted, raved, and threw flaming matchbooks, I grabbed Jeffrey and ran. We spent that night upstairs in my girlfriend's apartment. I was afraid to go home. The next morning I took Jeffrey to the park. And, all afternoon, I tried to figure out what had happened.

Sitting on a bench facing the East River, after running out of "knock-knock" jokes to tell Jeffrey, I reminded myself that Bernie'd had a temper, too. He'd thrown and broken things and cursed and threatened me. But we'd always gone toe-to-toe. We'd taken turns. And when the smoke cleared, we'd have a good laugh over it. Chalky's tantrums were a one-way deal. He got to scream and holler. Then he'd ice you for making him lose his cool.

Also, with Bernie, there'd been no child around. He'd never have let loose like that in front of his son—or any kid, for that matter. But Chalky, who'd read so many books and had so many ideas about how a family should be, had begun to say and do things in front of Jeffrey that you didn't need a Ph.D. in child psychology to know were frightening and harmful.

Not that Chalky didn't love Jeffrey. He did. He wanted to be the perfect dad. He wanted me to be the perfect wife and mother. And, with Jeffrey, really, he had close to the perfect child. But Chalky was trying to live in two different worlds—a normal one at home; a mob life in the world—and it seemed inevitable that the one he'd lived most would win out over the picket-fence fantasy Jeffrey and I were supposed to deliver.

After the jokes and swing rides in the little playground behind our house, we walked to Central Park, to the Alice in Wonderland statue. On the way, I thought of Bernie's generosity and Chalky's cheapness—of spirit as well as cold cash.

Bernie treasured his friends—whether they were up or down on their luck, in or out of prison, straight or crooked, new or old. Chalky's loyalty was reserved for certain people—for the high-echelon mobsters who were his only friends. I couldn't imagine him going to the Dio brothers to plead for an ex-girlfriend, the way I'd seen Bernie do. Women were nothing to Chalky. He had no sense of loyalty or fairness with them. He'd cheated on his fiancées, played them off against one another and me. He demanded loyalty in a wife, but never trusted me. He always required proof. Receipts! And he definitely cared more about what his friends thought of me than what I thought of them.

Chalky was one of the people Bernie had never allowed anyone to say a word against. "He's done hard time. Twelve years locked away will change a guy. But Chalky's solid. He'll be there for you if you need anything," he used to tell me.

And now, walking through the park, knowing it was not just the chill

September air making my son shiver, I remembered an incident I'd worked very hard to forget, to tell myself hadn't really meant anything. It had happened about a month before Chalky and I were married.

Downtown, one night, we ran into a man named Black Sal, a well-connected old wise guy with white hair and thick black eyebrows. He sat down with us and Chalky proudly introduced me. "Sal, this is my future wife. You knew her late husband, Bernie Barton."

The old guy had really been putting away the vino when Chalky excused himself to make a telephone call. It was a little awkward, sitting there with this slightly soused stranger. To make conversation, I said, "So you knew Bernie."

"Yeah, I knew him," he said, squinting at me through his cigar smoke. "Never liked him, your husband, your late husband. He was a junkie, Bernie Barton. He fucked around with cocaine. I heard he sold it, too. That's why he died. That's what killed him."

I was stunned. "How dare you?" I gasped. "Who the hell do you think you are to talk to me that way? To talk about my dead husband? You didn't know Bernie. Not really, or I would've met you before. Who the fuck do you think you are?"

He reared back. "Your future husband knows who I am," he answered, furious. "And when I tell him the kind of mouth you got on you— What's wrong with him that he can't control you, he lets you talk this way?"

Chalky returned right then with a smile on his face. I watched it fade as Black Sal complained to him about me. I saw his eyes narrow into glinting blue knives. It was me he was glaring at, not the man who'd insulted me and his dead best friend.

"Chalky, you should have heard what he said about Bernie," I said. "He doesn't even know me and he tells me these disgusting lies. He's bad-mouthing one of your dearest friends, who you say you love as a brother, my late husband, my son's father—I have no right to defend him?"

Chalky was staring at me coldly.

"Who is this man that you have to pay so much homage to, that you make me feel like nothing, like I have no respect and no rights? Why are you putting the importance of this stranger above me?"

"I'm very sorry, Sal," Chalky said. "Let me buy you a drink."

I stalked out of the restaurant and refused to see him. And he called five times a day, every day, for a week. And he must have sent fifty different bouquets and flower arrangements to pacify me—all of them, I learned later, came from the florist who owed him money. And, finally, by the end of the week, he'd convinced me that I'd misunderstood everything. That Bernie had, indeed, been his best friend and that, of course, he'd never tolerate anyone talking against him.

Toward evening, that High Holy Day, in the darkness of a movie theater on Third Avenue, with Jeffrey exhausted and dozing in the seat next to me,

I realized the differences in my marriages were not just between Chalky and Bernie. *I* was different now. With Bernie, I'd been a child. He'd taught me everything—from what to wear to how to think. And I'd been grateful for it.

After Bernie's death I'd been on my own. And once the unbearable pain of loss had let up, I'd made a pretty good life for myself. I'd had money, friends, and freedom. I'd made some dumb choices when it came to men. But, basically, I'd been on my way to being the kind of woman Bernie would have wanted me to be, and more importantly, the kind of person I wanted to be, and *most* importantly, the kind of mother Jeffrey needed me to be.

Now, suddenly, it seemed as though everything Bernie had loved and nurtured in me—my outspoken honesty, my curiosity and eagerness to learn new things, my sense of humor, my ability to stand up for myself—Chalky hated and was trying to destroy.

It was dark out when we left the movie theatre. With Jeffrey half asleep in my arms, I went home. Only it wasn't our home anymore, Jeffrey's and mine. It wasn't a safe place. The streets had seemed safer.

The apartment was in shambles. Chalky was sitting out on the terrace. He didn't say a word to either of us. I put Jeffrey to bed and then I went to the door of the terrace.

"I want out," I said in a voice so calm I hardly recognized it as my own. "I don't want Jeffrey growing up in a house like this. I don't want to be treated this way anymore—"

He didn't even turn his head. "You're not going anywhere. My ego couldn't take it, Sandy," he said. "You're not leaving. I won't let you. Jeffrey is my son. You're not taking him anywhere. Nobody's leaving. Nobody ever leaves me. When it's time, I'll do the leaving."

"You're wrong, Chalky," I said. "I'm walking."

He glanced at me over his shoulder. His eyes were ice. His thin lips were tight, twisted in a sick smile. "You can't walk without legs," he said.

At least I had Red.

When things were bleak at home, when Chalky drove me crazy, I'd sneak up to Harlem and hang out with Hot Dog. Walking around uptown with that sweet, caramel-colored man, with his skinny little mustache and quick Cab Calloway grin, always restored me, reminded me of the old days when I felt respected and secure.

We didn't talk about Chalky. We'd just shmooze and gossip and have a few laughs. But a couple of months after the Rosh Hashona chicken-hurling, I decided to tell Red what was going on at home. I knew Chalky hadn't been kidding when he said he'd never let me leave him. For the time being, I was trying to make the best of a bad situation. I was trying to get along with Chalky for Jeffrey's sake and my own. Trying to act as though that horrible holiday dinner had never happened. But nothing I did seemed to please him. Or comfort me.

Chalky wanted us to get back to a normal life.

His idea of normal—starring me as the silent, smiling housewife buying kosher chickens, ironing underwear, and toasting bagels at three A.M.—was making a wreck of me. I had to do something. I decided to drive uptown and talk to Red about it. He loved Jeffrey and me. He knew us. He knew me as I used to be—a fun-loving, big-mouthed, happy human being, not the nervous rag I was turning into. I thought I'd ask his advice.

It was a warm day in November. Red bought us both ice-cream cones. I was working up to telling him what was on my mind. We'd wandered over to Spanish Harlem. As usual, with the Dog at my side, I was laughing, my steps were springier, my heart was lighter. He saw a couple of men he knew and walked over to talk to them. I waited, leaning up against a car eating my ice cream. Suddenly, his ice-cream cone splattered onto the sidewalk. He turned, reached out to me, and fell.

Hot Dog Red had a massive heart attack. He died in my arms.

It was like the door to a garden had slammed shut in my face. Nothing but darkness left. My best friend was gone. My heart. My last link to a world where I was strong and everything was possible.

CHAPTER TWENTY

The Long Goodbye

Normal. Once it had been my favorite word, my girlish fantasy, my best hope. With Chalky it had become hazardous to my health.

What did a man who'd spent maybe twenty years of his forty-eight behind bars know about normal? But normal was what he wanted his home life to be. Okay. So what's more normal than a wife doing laundry?

"Lint!" he raved. "You got lint on my socks! You put my socks in the washing machine?! Never. You'll never do that again. You'll wash them by hand from now on!"

"When you were in jail all those years you didn't care if your socks were linty," I reminded him. But this was no ordinary human being I was trying to reason with. This was Chalky Lefkowitz, who used a tape measure to make sure his closet looked good, and who, if someone touched him on the arm, would pull away and say threateningly, "Don't touch my clothes." This was also a man who'd thrown a hair brush at me, causing a welt the size of an egg on my leg, because he'd found a wrinkle in a suit I'd packed for him.

So I washed the socks by hand. And I did a very good job of it for a couple of weeks. And, of course, I continued doing the rest of the laundry like a good girl. Each morning, in the darkened room where Chalky was sleeping, I'd pick up the shirt he'd worn the night before and put it into the hamper in the bathroom.

One morning, shortly after our third anniversary, a balled-up shirt I was carrying fell onto the bathroom floor and I saw it in bright light. It was covered with makeup. Not just a little pink smudge on the collar. Big-time makeup—green eyeshadow and brown highlighter and streaks of black and smears of red. The shirtfront looked like a Max Factor test swatch.

I was wild with rage. I was nauseated with hurt and upset. I had to take Jeffrey to school. I hurled the shirt at Chalky's sleeping head. He sat up. "You miserable creep!" I said and left the apartment.

When I came back, he was at the bathroom sink, stark naked, trying to scrub the stains out of the shirt with a wet washcloth.

"Don't bother," I said. "It won't work."

"I'm at a restaurant," he said. "People come in. Women kiss me on the neck. What's wrong with you?"

I went nuts. I was foaming at the mouth like a dog. I cried, I screamed, I broke things.

"Sandy, what's the matter with you? This means nothing. It's dumb. Let's not even talk about it. Listen to me, honey," Chalky urged. "Let's spend the day together."

Honey? What have we here, I wondered.

He took me to Lutèce for lunch and ordered champagne. He took me to Gucci and bought me a pocketbook. And one for my mother and one for my sister. We walked through Central Park and he bought me a balloon. It was honey, baby, sweetie all day long. And then I got it.

"You're in trouble," I said. We were sitting on a bench near the zoo. "You've got problems, right? You're under investigation, aren't you?"

"Yes," he said. "If things don't get better fast, I've to leave town for a while. I might be subpoenaed. I might be summonsed. They might even be working on an indictment."

I handed him the balloon and lit up a cigarette. "And you're afraid if you're arrested, they might want to put me on the witness stand?"

He didn't have to answer.

"Don't worry," I said. "I wouldn't do that. I'm not made that way. Anyway, don't you know the law? A wife can't testify against a husband."

"You know something," said Mr. Generosity, blue eyes atwinkle.

"You're a smart woman. You're a lunatic, a crazy lady, but once you get it out of your system, you're okay."

Well, I hadn't really gotten it out of my system. And how smart I was I couldn't say, but smart enough to know that I couldn't go head to head with Chalky. He was cheating on me. He was seeing someone else. He probably had a mistress. He probably had a mistress *and* he was seeing someone else. It was killing me. And little by little, as I scrubbed his little silk socks, I knew I had to do something.

I couldn't leave. The couple of times I'd threatened to, he'd pin me with those cold blue eyes, he'd say in that slow, scary voice, "I told you, Sandy. Nobody leaves me. I do the leaving." Or, again, "You can't walk without legs." That was his favorite.

Don't get mad, get even, Bernie used to tell me. Standing in the kitchen, hand-rinsing Chalky's expensive socks, it was like Bernie was right there at my elbow, whispering in my ear. The step I took that morning was a tiny, baby step, but it was in the direction of freedom.

I starched his socks.

Chalky had fabulous feet. No corns or calluses. Soft, perfect, pampered feet that he treated to only the best socks and softest leather.

Within the week, he was home scratching and complaining bitterly. "My feet are killing me," he said. "They're burning. They itch. I'm getting big red blotches all over them. They're killing me!"

It was the best I could do at the time.

That and begin to hope an indictment did come down for him.

Chalky was never home on Fridays. Never. He spent every Friday night with his girlfriend. He'd say he was playing cards. He'd even come home with a bag full of money on Saturday and make me count it for him. But toward the end, I knew he was seeing his mistress. Every Friday night. What a lucky girl.

Sunday he was all mine. It was another one of those great ideas he had about what normal people do. Sunday was family day. So he'd hang around the house with the football game on like Mr. America. Never mind that the man couldn't tell you the name of a team, let alone a player. He just liked the idea of it—lying around in pajamas on Sunday, with what was left of his hair sticking up every which way, rolling up the couch pillows and watching the game. And, every two minutes, he'd call out orders for something else he needed to eat or drink or wanted me to do. Then, in the late afternoon, he'd cook his famous jailhouse spaghetti sauce.

My girlfriends used to kid me about what a great diet it was—I could eat as much sauce as I wanted, because spending one Sunday with that man I'd lose seven pounds from aggravation.

On the advice of one of the mafia wives I knew, I started putting Valium in his coffee. It really worked, too. He was much quieter on Sundays after that. Very mellow.

That third year we were married, I became close to the wives of two of Chalky's pals. One was an Irish girl named Terry, who was married to this big, fat mob slob, who was a very rough guy but good to her financially. The other was Crazy Tina, who was married to Frankie, the nut case. Frankie was who they meant when they said he'll kill you first and ask questions later.

I met Terry and Tina at a wedding. We were at the same table and during a lull in the conversation about kids and lipstick, I noticed that Terry was tapping her fingernails on the table and Tina was tapping her cigarette lighter and the three of us were smoking like crazy.

I said to Tina, "Oh, you have the same habit I do." And she said, "Married to men like this, you develop lots of habits. I'm surprised we're not all junkies here."

We had a lot in common. Before I knew for sure that Chalky had a girlfriend, I knew that Tina knew her husband had one. In fact, Tina had threatened the girl once. But the girl had passed out and then Tina felt sorry for her. Terry's husband had a girlfriend of long standing whom he'd put into business.

The three of us exchanged phone numbers. Terry and Tina lived in Brooklyn but we were constantly in touch by phone—often at two or three in the morning, keeping each other company while our husbands were out. And we'd see each other at funerals. Funerals were a big deal for the wives. I mean, it was one of the sacred social events where the guys couldn't bring their girlfriends.

I remember Tina called me one day, all excited, and said, "What are you wearing tonight?" I didn't know what she was talking about. She said, "We're going out. Chalky'll probably call you soon. Didn't you hear, Little Georgie died. It's going to be the biggest event ever."

We got dressed to kill for the funerals and wakes. I remember once ruining a gorgeous pair of high heels walking to a funeral in the snow in Williamsburg, Brooklyn. You never parked your car near the funeral parlor. Nine times out of ten the FBI was there taking pictures and checking license plates. So everyone but the immediate family parked miles away and wore sunglasses, even if it was nighttime, so that they couldn't be identified in the photographs.

Chalky was a maniac about security. He was sure the FBI had our phones tapped, our car wired, agents following him, following me. I thought he was flattering himself. He'd yell at me for saying things on the phone like, "Chalky's going out tonight," or, "He's going to work in five minutes." And I'd remind him that he'd threatened to break someone's legs or have their mother shot on the same phone a couple of hours earlier when he'd come in drunk and spoiling for a fight.

He was always on the lookout for places the FBI wouldn't bug. When I was in the hospital to have a tumor removed from my ear, he showed up with flowers, candy, and four other guys. Everyone said hello, how you doing, Sandy? Then Chalky asked me to take a walk down the hall with him. I shlepped along in my bandages and bedroom slippers and sat down in a little plastic chair near the nursing station. "Wait here. I'll come and get you in a little while," he said. And he and his friends locked themselves into my private room and had a little meeting.

Nurses and orderlies were banging on the door. They were angry at me, telling me I wasn't supposed to be out in the hall. I wasn't supposed to be sitting up, I had to get back into bed right that minute. Fat chance. There was an Appalachian mafia conference going on at Doctors Hospital and no one was going to get those guys to budge.

When the meeting was over, they filed out. Each one, sweet as could be, kissed me on the cheek. "Get well soon, sweetheart." "Get into bed." "Take care of yourself, honey," they urged me.

At his mother's funeral, Chalky took over the funeral director's office and held a meeting there. He had me go outside into the street to check and see if the FBI was taking down license plate numbers. At his own mother's funeral!

Then, one day, he phoned me and said, "I'm having a meeting in the house. I don't care where you and Jeffrey go, but be out of there by six and don't come back for at least three hours." It was no big deal. It had happened before. But then he added, almost as an afterthought, "And, Sandy, before you go, make a meat loaf. Enough for seven guys. Get the best steaks you can find and have them ground up. I want you to make it like my mother taught you, with the egg slices in the center. And also, make a salad and some garlic bread and just leave it on the table."

"Steaks?" I said. "You want me to make meat loaf for you and your friends out of the best steaks I can find?"

Less than a week before, Chalky had come home drunk in the middle of the night, gone rummaging for ice cream in the fridge, and pitched a fit because he'd found two lamb chops wrapped in butcher paper in the freezer. Chalky decided they were too expensive. So he woke me up, at four A.M., by throwing the frozen lamb chops at me. "This is how you spend my money?!" he'd demanded.

"They're for Jeffrey," I had tried to explain.

"A kid doesn't need eight dollars' worth of lamb chops!"

Now he said, "Yeah, get steak. You make a good meat loaf. Make it out of steak. At least let me be able to show you off."

I hung up fuming.

Chalky ranted about money all the time. His son's lamb chops were too expensive. The phone bill was too high. The cleaning woman cost too much. But nothing was too good for his pals.

I paced the kitchen for a couple of minutes, unconsciously rubbing my arm where the bruise from the frozen lamb chops was beginning to turn from blue to yellow. Twice, I picked up the phone to call the butcher. Then I got a better idea.

I hurried downstairs to the supermarket and bought salad greens and bread. And then I bought two pounds of the cheapest chopped meat I could find. And then I bought six cans of dog food. Alpo.

A can at a time, I spooned the dark, almost purple, mystery meat into the bowl of cheap ground beef and blended and shaped the mixture with a vengeance. It smelled awful, like organ meat, like dead horse flesh. It smelled like what it was—dog food! While it was cooking, the whole house stunk. I had to open every window in the place and turn on the kitchen and bathroom fans. Finally, I sprayed everything with Lysol deodorant spray—even the meat loaf. But in the end it was gorgeous. Egg slices and all.

I didn't dare come home that night, until I looked up from the street and saw that the apartment was dark. Of course the dirty dishes were still there on the pretty dining table I'd set. And there was a little bit of food left— some salad, some pickles, but only a nibble of the meatloaf.

The dirty dogs, they loved it.

I called my mother, my sister, Terry, and Tina. We howled. But it was pathetic really. This was what I was reduced to. Childish pranks. Starching socks, putting Valium in his coffee, feeding him Alpo. It wasn't exactly the French Resistance.

A word about the FBI. Chalky was right. They were after him. They had our phones tapped. They had guys assigned to me. They had guys in the Garment Center watching him. He'd tip the doorman fifty bucks a shot and it paid off. They'd ring up and say, "Sandy, there are some guys asking around about your husband." Or "Sandy, the FBI is here. They're looking for Chalky. Is he around? Is he home?"

Of course, I'd say, "No, there's no one here." And the doormen would tell the FBI that they'd seen us go out or that they'd just tried to call and there was no one home. Sometimes the doormen would ring up and say, "There's a strange car circling the building. Tell your husband." Sometimes I think they enjoyed getting caught up in the excitement, the games, the racket club life.

Why not? You met a very interesting class of people in the life. Like Roy Cohn, the lawyer, whose name was in the papers every other day. You couldn't read a gossip column in the seventies without finding out he'd been at this society party or that new disco with Steve Rubell, with Liza, with Halston, with Bianca. So I was impressed when Chalky said he had a little problem with the Feds (and none of my fucking business *what* little problem) and that he was going to hire Roy Cohn to see if he could squash it. I don't know why, but he wanted me to get dressed up and go with him to Cohn's place in the East Fifties.

I've seen some gorgeous houses in my day, but Roy Cohn's three-story townhouse was to die for. Antiques, sculptures, paintings. He showed me around. He was shorter than Chalky, shorter than me, and gracious and gay. In his bedroom, he had an oversized king-size bed with a leopard throw on it and a bathroom you could've lived in. Everything sparkled. It was mirrored and had a hot tub and a separate sunken bathtub and a stall shower *and* a refrigerator.

We all sat down together in Roy's study. While Chalky explained whatever the problem was, I made sure to occupy myself looking around at the knickknacks and clocks from France and other elegant little furnishings. Finally, the meeting was over. Cohn stood up and told Chalky not to worry, he had the deal clinched. "You'll never have a problem," he said.

Chalky said, "Okay, Roy, what do I have to give you for this?" And he started reaching in his pocket for the dough.

Cohn looked up at him, looked him square in the eye. And in this very throaty, very quiet voice, he said, "Chalky, take an attaché case and just fill it up with hundred dollar bills until you can't close it anymore. That's my fee."

Chalky said, "You're kidding."

Roy said, "No, Chalky, I'm not."

Chalky paid up.

Months later, Jeffrey's second-grade teacher called me aside when I went to pick him up from school. She said the principal wanted to see me. It seems two men representing themselves as FBI agents had come into the school and they wanted to know how much it cost a year to go there. They said they were interested in Jeffrey Lefkowitz—and how much tuition his parents had paid for the year. The principal was shocked. She said it was free, hadn't they seen the sign outside that said public school? It was a big sign. P.S.—that meant Public School, she'd had to tell them. She said they were embarrassed. Shmucks.

Okay. A little time passed. All of a sudden I start getting credit-card offers from every department store in New York. Bergdorf's and Macy's want me to have their cards. Lord & Taylor sends me an application with a lovely letter offering me the world. Finally, I get one from Saks Fifth Avenue saying they've recently checked their records and found that I don't have a charge account with them and they think I ought to. So I called the number on the application and I asked the woman how they got my name.

She said the Treasury Department had been there a week ago looking at their records. They'd said my husband was very wealthy. So Saks wanted me to have a line of credit with them.

One day I got a tip from a friend who worked in the post office. "Mrs. L., there's something you should know. We just got orders down at the post office to hold and X-ray all mail addressed to you before delivering it."

"Thank you very much." I said. As if a wise guy was going to send checks to Chalky or drop him a line about the nice little heist that went off last week or the union pension fund they skimmed.

Next they sent for us to come down to the Income Tax Bureau and discuss the cost of Jeffrey's day camp and where the money to pay for it had come from. They sat us in a room, which had a bulletin board at the front of it. And on the board were all these mug shots of tax evaders with little "Apprehended" stickers over their faces and the time and fines they were doing for their crimes. If the day camp cost a big $500, it was a lot. We answered their questions. They looked angry. They looked sad. They looked like the shmucks they were. And we left.

In the fourth year of my marriage to Chalky, the FBI gave me a boyfriend. He was an agent named Richard—not Richie, he'd correct me, not Richela. "Mrs. Lefkowitz, my name is Rich-hard," he'd say, exasperation creeping into his hard-working, just-the-facts-ma'am voice. Poor Richard. Sweet Richard. Every night between seven and seven-fifteen, he'd phone the house and say, "This is Richard Stanley of the OC Task Force." The Organized Crime Task Force. "Is Chalky there, Mrs. Lefkowitz?"

"Richie, he's not here. You know he's never here in the evening, Richela. So what are we going to talk about tonight?"

Sometimes it was Bernie Richard wanted to talk about. He knew all about Bernie. He knew about Jeffrey. He'd followed my life like a soap opera fan. He'd listened in on it, replaying the taped triumphs and tragedies with a fan's determination not to miss a single thrilling moment.

"You know, Bernie wasn't bad. He was a nice guy, really," he'd say, "compared to Chalky. Why do you stay with Chalky, Sandy?" We'd moved on to such familiarities. After all, he was the most faithful, most dependable man in my life. He'd earned the right to call me Sandy. To call my husband Chalky.

If he failed to phone for a night or two, I missed him. I'd say, "Richard, what happened to you?"

He had a cold. I told him what to take for it. Chicken soup, of course. Jewish penicillin, I told him.

He tore a ligament in his leg. I said, "You've got to keep your foot above your heart otherwise you'll get a bloodclot, Richela." He said his doctor had told him the same thing.

He'd call when I was busy. I'd say, "The baby's in the bathtub. I can't talk to you now." And he'd say, "Oh, I'm sorry. Go ahead, take care of him. How long do you think it'll take? I'll call you back."

One afternoon, I spotted a couple of guys following me. One of them was wearing a leather trenchcoat and gum-soled shoes. He was a tall, thin WASP, squeaky-clean looking even in black leather. I bumped into him and his partner as I was coming out of Gristede.

"Richard?" I said.

He blushed.

"Well, as long as you're going my way," I said, and I gave each of them a bag of groceries to carry. "You look like I thought you would," I said to Richard.

"Really?"

"A *goy*," I said, walking between them. "You know what a *goy* is?"

"Someone who's not Jewish," his friend, who looked Italian, said.

"That's it. So Richie, how's your foot? Did you do what I said?"

They walked along with me to the cleaners, to the pizza parlor. They walked me home.

On the phone that night, it was business as usual.

"What are you doing with a guy like him? You deserve better," he'd say. "When are you going to leave him?"

I didn't say, "Nobody leaves Chalky. Chalky has to do the leaving." I didn't say, "I can't walk out on him without legs."

And I didn't tell him the story of the last time Chalky had gone on the lam to avoid a subpoena. A man had come to my house in the middle of the night with a list of clothing to be packed. There was trouble brewing, he'd said, and Chalky had to get out of town for a little while.

What a list it was. Everything itemized, everything coordinated. Shirts, shoes, socks, and ties. The Lefkowitz traveling collection. And at the bottom of the list was a little note in the master's own neat scrawl, "Please pack everything nicely and fold things so they don't wrinkle."

Maybe I'd seen too many old gangster movies, but since when did a guy go on the lam with color-coordinated outfits?

I didn't see Chalky or hear a word from him for six weeks. My friends were commenting on how relaxed I looked, how happy I seemed. It must've gotten back to him that I was feeling fine. Next thing I knew, his friend showed up again and told me Chalky was in Florida and that he wanted me and Jeffrey to come down and join him. "It'll be like a second honeymoon," the guy said.

I didn't tell him I wished I'd passed on the first one.

"I don't want to go," I said. "I don't want to take Jeffrey out of school."

Next morning, two bruisers, two huge, young Italian *bulvons,* showed up at my door. They were enforcers, probably hit men. But they were very polite. Very uncomfortable. "Sorry," they said, "but we're here to help you pack and put you on the plane." Which is exactly what they did. At least they had the decency to be embarrassed about it.

For me, it proved again that there was no escaping Chalky. Not when all he had to do was make a telephone call and have me delivered to him like Chinese Take Out.

I never explained to Richard why leaving Chalky was not an option. But I did, occasionally, break down and cry with frustration. And sometimes, I'd say, "Do me a favor, Richie. Put him in jail already." Especially after they started telling me about Chalky's girlfriend.

It was during our last year together. "He has a mistress, you know," Richard said one night.

"Really? Great," I answered glibly. "It'll take the pressure off me."

"She lives in Queens," he said another time.

"Sure, you think he'd pay Manhattan rents for her?"

They didn't let up. And I didn't let on. But it got to me. And they must've sensed it. "He was at his girlfriend's again," Richard would say. "Yesterday. Three o'clock. We followed him to her house."

He had a mistress. He saw her regularly. The FBI knew about her before I did. Probably all my girlfriends had known about her, too. It got to me. It made me one of them. The final, full transition from picket-fence promises to racket club wife.

I started confronting Chalky with it. "You've got a girlfriend," I'd say, slamming down his morning orange juice.

"What's the matter with you? You're crazy," he'd answer. "When have I got time for a girlfriend?"

"How about Friday nights when you're never home. How about holidays when you send Jeffrey and me to the Catskills, while you're in town for business? How about every night when you stay out till two or three or don't come home at all?"

"You know where I am. I tell you. I'm busy. I've got people to see. I go to dinner, to restaurants. You know that. You see the matchbooks."

See them? They were driving me crazy. Late at night, he'd wake me up, reeling drunk. He'd throw a matchbook from a fancy restaurant at my head. "You see, if you were a good girl, you could've been with me at this fancy place tonight." If you didn't have such a big mouth. If you treated me nice. If you fixed my collar button like I told you. If you were a good girl.

For years, I'd tolerated this insanity. For years, I'd turned myself inside out trying to be a good girl and never quite making the grade. I was worn out. I rarely got a decent night's sleep because he'd wake me at all hours. Either he'd ring the doorbell till I woke up and let him in or he'd crash into the bedroom and turn on the bright light next to where I was sleeping. And, on top of it, he was throwing these matchbooks in my face, literally.

Matchbooks from romantic, elegant restaurants where I now knew he'd been with his girlfriend.

Well, one night, after my FBI boyfriend Richard had given me an earful on the girlfriend, Chalky shook me awake and tossed a matchbook at me. He was bobbing and weaving and reeking of booze. He leaned over me, slamming his hand on the night table. "*You* could have been with me tonight," he was saying, "but no. If only you'd be a good girl and control that mouth, I'd give you whatever you want. But you've got a *big Jewish mouth—*"

I shook every time his angry hand slammed down, going flat, fingers spread out. I was scared, but I was also angry. I'd had it. I noticed the Christmas gift from one of the mob wives on the nightstand. It was a magnificent jewel-encrusted letter opener worth a couple of thousand dollars, standing in its own holder at arm's length from me.

"You don't know how to do anything right!" he yelled.

"Shut up and let me sleep," I screamed, amazing myself.

"You dumb bitch," he said. "You don't know how to be a wife."

"Shut up!" I screamed.

In one clean sweep, I pulled the letter opener out of its holder, grabbed his wrist, and stabbed his hand. I got him through the little fold of flesh between his thumb and forefinger. Blood shot out like Old Faithful. You'd never guess there could be a geyser of blood like that out of such a skinny slab of skin. When I saw what I'd done, I rolled out of his reach as fast as I could. He pulled the letter opener out of his hand and ran into the bathroom.

There was blood everywhere, on the headboard and the walls. I cowered on the floor behind the bed, then crept out and ran and hid in the kitchen.

I grabbed a knife and waited, quaking with fear. I figured he'd come in any second and try to murder me. When he didn't show up, I got scared. Oh, my God, I really killed him, I thought. There was enough blood around to convince anyone that it was possible. I tiptoed carefully back into the bedroom. The bathroom door was locked. "Chalky," I whispered. "Are you okay?"

I put my ear to the door. And I heard a very weird sound. Click, pop, click, pop, click, pop. I had no idea what it was but something was alive and moving in there, so I sat down on the bed and waited.

The door flew open and he charged out like a mad animal. This is it, I said to myself. He's alive and I'm going to be dead in one second. My son won't have a mother. Or he'll disfigure me.

There was blood all over him, all over his fancy suit and shirt and pants; all over the towel he had wrapped between his fingers. And all over the Polaroid camera he was brandishing in his other hand.

"Okay, you've had it!" he said to me. "This is it. I'm through. I'm leaving you. We're getting a divorce. I'm calling my lawyer and I'm taking you to court. And when the judge sees these pictures—'' He threw a handful of Polaroid snapshots at me, color pictures of his bleeding hand! ''It will be on record that you stabbed me! And it will be on record because I'm going to go to the hospital now. They'll give me a divorce instantly. And you won't get a penny!''

I became hysterical laughing.

He'd lost a lot of blood. He was turning very white.

''Come on,'' I said, ''I'll take you over to Lenox Hill. I'll get a neighbor to stay with Jeffrey and then we'll go over to the hospital.''

While I waited for the doctors to sew him up, I couldn't stop laughing. I kept thinking, an Italian would have grabbed a gun. Only a Jewish mobster would reach for a Polaroid to prove his case in divorce court.

He didn't divorce me. That would have been too easy. But the knifing had made him nervous. He stayed away more often, but when he was home he gave me, if not respect, at least respectable distance.

Coincidentally, the FBI started giving me distance, too. Richard's calls tapered off to once or twice a week. Then in the early summer of 1974, the calls stopped altogether.

And Chalky started treating me differently. It was almost as if he were courting me again. We went out to dinner a couple of times a week. He'd send flowers once in a while. Sex, which had always been good, got better toward the end of summer as we approached our fifth wedding anniversary.

''Something's going on,'' I told Tina. ''Chalky's acting too nice.''

''You probably should have knifed him years ago,'' she said.

I told my mother. ''I have a premonition, a feeling. He's getting me ready for something.''

''For what?'' she'd ask.

''He's leaving,'' I said.

Of course, everyone thought I was nuts. I even thought so. But the feeling that Chalky was saying a long goodbye haunted me.

In late August, when Jeffrey came home from camp, Chalky announced that we were all going up to the Raleigh Hotel in the Catskills for a little vacation. He invited my mother along, too. Tillie had been diagnosed with cancer by then, but she'd just finished a series of cobalt treatments and seemed in good shape and terrific spirits. I was grateful that Chalky had asked her to join us. I started looking forward to a week in the country with the whole family.

My friend Crazy Tina called a couple of days before we were to leave. ''I hear you're baby-sitting the Jaw's wife. You'll like her, Sandy. She's a sweet woman, very quiet though.''

Giorgio the Jaw was a major player from Mulberry Street. His brother was a priest. It was a good thing, too. From what I knew of the Jaw's reputation, he'd need a close relative to intercede with God to get him into heaven. When it came to family matters—marriage *and* mafia—the Jaw made Chalky look like a liberal.

"What are you talking about?" I asked Tina. "I don't even know the woman."

"Hey, I didn't know her two summers ago when Frankie made me baby-sit her. Terry's done it, too. All the wives do it. They take turns. It's no big deal. Only you'll be pulling your hair out from boredom."

Sure enough, the day after we arrived at the Raleigh Hotel, he said, "There are some friends here I want you to meet." We went down to the dining room and at our table was a woman in her thirties, very quiet, very sweet. And three children, ranging in age from four to eleven. The kids were wild animals, *vilda khaye* running all over the place, whining, arguing, shoving each other. But the woman sat placid as a plaster Virgin. In fact, her name was Mary. Mary, wife of the Jaw.

That afternoon, I was given my assignment. Stay with her. Keep her company. Don't leave her alone. "This is important to me, Sandy," Chalky said, giving me the old familiar, cold-eyed squint to make sure I got the message. "I've got some business with Giorgio. I've got to leave for a couple of days."

Three days. Tillie and I made small talk with Mrs. Jaw. We sat side by side at the pool. We sat side by side at dinner. We went for a little walk side by side. And then, at about seven or eight in the evening, Mary would take the kids up to bed and lock herself in the room for the night. And, for three days, Tillie and I would put Jeffrey to bed and lock ourselves in our adjoining room. And we stayed like that, side by side.

By the fourth night, my mother and I were bored to death. We'd already watched television and played cards for hours, and it was only ten o'clock. Tillie said, "Come on, let's sneak down to the bar."

Like children.

We did. We were sitting there, at the bar in the lobby, chatting with a couple of other guests, when my mother laid an icy, air-conditioned hand on my arm and said, "Don't turn around. Chalky and another guy are coming toward you. And from the look of him, I think it's the Jaw."

It was. And Chalky went nuts. "What are you doing downstairs here? Where's Mary? I told you not to leave her alone." He was wild, ranting and screaming. "I go away and I gotta come back to find the two of you holding up the bar!"

"Yeah, with a Coca-Cola in front of me, and ginger ale for my mother," I pointed out.

The Jaw turned on his heels and went upstairs to check on his wife and kids.

"You're an embarrassment!" Chalky yelled at me in our room that night. "You disgraced me. I can't depend on you for anything! I've got things on my mind. Important things. I don't have time for you to fuck up now. I'm in trouble! There's an indictment coming down! They're looking to arrest me!''

An indictment? An arrest?

I knew it. I'd known something big was breaking. Ah, Richard, my telephone hero, I thought. He'd heard me all those times I'd begged him to put Chalky away. He and the other agents who'd planted bugs and harvested hundreds of hours of tape, who'd phoned and followed us in conspicuously unmarked cars and checked our credit-card status with Saks and our license plate numbers at cemeteries and tried to look casual at the supermarket in black leather coats—hooray for the whole hardworking lot of them. They'd finally found what they'd been looking for. Freedom was at hand.

Within a month of the failed babysitting gig, Chalky announced he was leaving. He'd spent weeks checking the closets and asking for things. "Have you seen that old key chain of Mama's I used to have? I kept it after she died. Find it for me and put it in my jewelry box." Or "Where are the ruby cufflinks?" Or "Get everything back from the cleaners. I need the gray double-breasted you brought in last week and the two pink shirts. Put them in the closet. Neatly."

He came home with an attaché case one night. "What's that?" I asked. "Nothing," he said. "For papers, for business, for the lawyers." Those blue eyes sparkled nervously. He put the attaché case, which had a combination lock on it, into his clothes closet. Neatly.

It's for money, I thought. He's taking his money with him.

That got me nervous. I didn't have much left of my own cash. And knowing Dr. Generosity's record on these matters, I could see trouble coming.

Finally, in the middle of September, he came home one afternoon and said, "Come into the bedroom. We've got to talk."

I did. I sat down on our bed. Chalky was pacing back and forth in front of me. He didn't look at me when he began speaking. "I'm leaving tomorrow," he said, catching a glimpse of himself in the mirror. "I'm going away—for a month, a year, forever. I don't know." He was pacing, brushing something off his shoulder, straightening the crease in his trouser leg. "I don't want this life and I don't want to go to jail. I feel trapped. And I want out. There are things happening. You don't know the half of what's going down."

"Tomorrow?" I'd watched him getting ready. I'd known this was coming. I thought I'd feel relieved, triumphant. Instead, his words hit me like an icy fist in the gut.

"I have to straighten my head out," Chalky said. He hadn't heard me. He hadn't looked at me yet. Which was okay with me because, much to my surprise, I felt tears coming. Old feelings, old fears. I felt again the aching hole in the heart I'd first felt when my father left. The sadness and dread of waking up without Bernie. At the moment I should have jumped for joy, the moment I'd been waiting and praying for, I felt sick and scared.

Next thing I knew, Chalky was dragging suitcases out of the closet. "Help me. Come here. Help me pack."

I took a Valium and we packed his things together. We must have filled eleven suitcases. I was very quiet. We packed quietly. Then he said, "Okay, now I'm going to leave you enough money to live on for a year." And he sat down at the dining room table and started figuring it out to the penny.

"What happens if the price of milk goes up?" I asked, trying to make a joke of it.

"Don't be funny, don't be cute," he said. "You're lucky to get this. Just be a good girl. For all I know I'll be back in a month. This is just in case."

He made love to me that night. He kissed Jeffrey goodbye when he went off to school the next morning. Then he went out to make a phone call. And I walked into the bedroom and took a look at the suitcases lying open on the floor, the neatly packed garment bags draped over the bed, the locked attaché case sitting on top of the dresser.

Old habits die hard. I strolled over to the dresser. I started fiddling with the leather case. It was full, nothing rattled inside, and it was fairly heavy. The latch was a combo lock. Hmmm, I wondered, what combination would Chalky choose? And I started trying some out. And the more involved I became in trying to break the combo, the more the icy knot in my gut loosened and the warmer and happier I felt.

151 First Street, I thought. Chalky's mother's address, the house he grew up in. I spun the dials. Click. Click. Click. The latch popped. I opened the leather attaché case carefully. It was filled to the brim with cash. Rubber-banded packets of big bills, thick as bricks. It was an awful lot of money. Chalky wouldn't have to worry about the price of milk for quite a while.

I lost it.

I burst into tears. The sight of all that cash, the realization that Chalky had been rich all the time he was crying poor to me, tore me up. He'd lied about money, picked fights with me about it—for nothing! For no god-damned reason, he'd made my life hell and Jeffrey's less than it should have been.

I was standing at the dresser, staring at the attaché case full of money, bawling my eyes out. And then I got mad. Really mad. Anger roared through me. I didn't shake my fist the way Scarlett O'Hara did when she swore, "God as my witness, I'll never go hungry again," but that was how I felt. Abandoned, betrayed, desperate, angry! I can't remember ever feeling as high or low at the same time.

Before I knew what I was doing, I ran into the kitchen and grabbed a pair of scissors. I had no idea what the hell I was going to use them for until I got back to the bedroom. I remember thinking, "What? Are you going to cut up the money? Are you insane?!"

Then I answered myself aloud. "Yes!" I yelled, because I *was* insane at that moment. I was having an insane little dialogue with myself. "Me?" it went. "I'm crazy? Why? Am I the one whose life is over if there's a wrinkle in my suit or a shirt button missing?" And as I was saying these things, I was already standing beside the bed, in front of Chalky's unzippered garment bag, reaching behind the carefully laid out $500 sportcoat to the new $1500 single-breasted navy blue suit lying under it. Half-blinded by tears, I made one long cut in the sleeve, from wrist to elbow. Then I picked carefully through the suitcases, snipping a couple of buttons off a shirt here, a little piece of a cuff there. I cut through the fly of a pair of white linen pants. And, finally, I sliced the looped fringe off a gorgeous pair of shoes Chalky had recently brought home.

Then I neatly closed the garment bag and suitcases, and ambled over to the attaché case on the dresser. Because Jeffrey needed a mother, preferably one still breathing who could walk without crutches and hadn't had her face rearranged by fists-for-hire, I didn't give in fully to the insanity and rage for revenge I was feeling. I reached into the case and peeled off exactly four thousand two hundred and fifty dollars. The precise amount of money Chalky had swindled me out of the day he decided to marry me.

There was no doubt in my mind that he'd count the money once he got where he was going. I wanted him to. I wanted him to wonder and remember. Truth be told, I wanted to make a much bigger dent in Chalky's nest egg than that, but I pulled back my hand as if it had touched fire, and snapped the lid shut.

Case closed.

It was over. It felt over. The anger started to subside. The hole in the gut didn't feel quite as empty. I turned my back on the luggage filled with all that was precious to Chalky and left the bedroom. I could hardly wait for him to come back for the goddamned suitcases and money. I wanted it out of my house, out of my life, and Chalky Lefkowitz with it.

I lit a cigarette and went out to the terrace to wait. By the time Chalky returned with the two guys who were going to help him carry his bags down to the garage, to the limo that was taking him to the airport, I was practically a new woman.

He took one look at my face and said, "What's the matter with you? What're you smiling about?"

"I'm being brave," I said. "I'm just trying to be a good girl, like you told me."

I called Tillie about ten minutes after Chalky's limo pulled out of the garage. She was at my house with her little overnight bag in less than an hour. Crazy Tina showed up at my apartment about five minutes later. "Frankie sent me over," she said apologetically. "I'm supposed to baby-sit you for a couple of days."

"He must've told Frankie he was leaving before he told me," I said. "I'm glad to see you, but why do they think I need a sitter?"

"They must've thought you'd be so broken up about his leaving you might try something." She paused. "You don't look broken up," she said.

"Is it too early for champagne?" I asked.

The Strike Force agents showed up three weeks later at six-thirty in the morning. There were four of them, all pounding on the door and ringing the bell at the same time. "We're here to arrest Chalky Lefkowitz!" one of them shouted like a nervous wreck the minute I opened the door. Big boys, they were. There was one from the OC Task Force. Another one was from Treasury and there were two huge marshalls who looked like the lard-assed Southern sheriffs who gave guys like Cool Hand Luke a hard time.

One of the marshalls handed me a search warrant rolled up like a sacred scroll. On it was listed the indictments against Chalky—*twenty* of them. Shylocking, racketeering, income tax evasion. It was like a Torah of shame. I didn't even finish reading it. I was still married to the man, and the people who'd prepared this little scroll obviously knew him a whole lot better than I did.

"He's not here," I said. "You guys know Chalky's not here. You know everything, right?"

Tillie came in from the bedroom. She looked pale and fragile in her long nightgown. But she was a rock. *"Shah!"* she commanded. "Be quiet. What's wrong with you people? What do you want from my daughter's life? And my grandson. You'll wake my grandson."

"We've got to look around," the Treasury guy said. "We showed you the warrant. Okay." He gave the marshalls a high sign and they pulled out guns.

I said, "Are you insane? What are you going to do, shoot me?"

"Lady," one of the marshalls said, "this is a violent man. We know this man's background. If he's in the house, he's going to come out shoot-ing."

I told them again that Chalky wasn't there, but they went from room to room, poking under beds, pointing their guns at the closet doors. Against my mother's protests and mine, they woke Jeffrey up and looked under his bed. He began to shake at the sight of the guns. He was crying. It was pandemonium. Finally, they left.

A month later, Chalky sent word through a lawyer friend that I should begin divorce proceedings against him. He didn't say anything about the missing money, nothing about his wardrobe. He just couldn't come back.

He'd beaten the indictment by a couple of weeks, but things were really hot now. It looked like the Feds wanted him badly enough to wait him out. If he returned, he'd be a cooked goose. So he was graciously cutting me loose. Go have a life, was the message from generous Chalky Lefkowitz. And anyway, he didn't want to be married to me anymore.

He'd left me. He'd walked. His ego was intact. And I still had my legs. And my life.

EPILOGUE
NEW YORK CITY
JUNE 1989

Almost from the day Chalky left, I'd been working in the Garment Center. I'd done all right supporting myself and Jeffrey. But I was always looking to trade up. And the doormen in our building knew that.

One of them said to me, "You know Briskin, from the twelfth floor? He's a big manufacturer of sports wear. You should talk to him."

I filed the information.

Then came the big day, Jeffrey's graduation. In my new linen dress and high-heeled summer shoes, I stepped onto the elevator. I'd put my makeup on carefully, but the real glow lighting my face was coming from joy, not cosmetics.

We'd made it, the Jab and me. There weren't too many people we'd known in the old days who would've put money on how well we'd do out on our own. I'd been earning a living like a regular working stiff for almost fifteen years. I had a son graduating from college. I felt great. I looked great. And as I stepped onto the elevator I could tell that Mr. Briskin from the twelfth floor thought so, too.

"Hi," I said. "Your name is Briskin, isn't it? I'm Sandy Lefkowitz. The name used to be Barton. The doorman said that I should—"

Briskin nodded. "I know both your names," he said, starting to grin. "You still look good."

A lot of years and guys had come and gone. "Uh, did we ever . . . ?" I asked nervously. He didn't look familiar, but who knew.

"You were my first case out of the academy," he said. "I'm in *shmattes* now, the rag business. But I used to be with the FBI. In fact, I used to listen in on your phone conversations. When your first husband was sick . . . What was his name? Bennie?"

"Bernie," I said, stunned. "You were an FBI agent?"

"With the Organized Crime Task Force. That's right," he said, "his name was Bernie. Bernie Barton. What a character. We used to follow you to the hospital every day. I used to. It was my first assignment. God, you look terrific."

"Thanks. I feel terrific today," I said.

"How's your kid? You had just had a baby, right? A little boy?"

"Jeffrey. That's why I'm all dressed up," I said. "I'm on my way to his graduation. From John Jay College of Criminal Justice."

"You're kidding," Briskin said. "Bernie Barton's son is going into law enforcement? Well, well. Imagine that. *Mazel-tov!*"